C000181162

Politics in Dark Times
Encounters with Hannah Arent

This outstanding collection of essays explores Hannah Arendt's thought against the background of world-political events unfolding since September 11, 2001. It engages in a contentious dialogue with one of the greatest political thinkers of the past century, with the conviction that she remains contemporary. Themes such as moral and political equality, action, natality, judgment, and freedom are reevaluated with fresh insight by a group of thinkers who are themselves well known for their original contributions to political thought. Other essays focus on novel and little-discussed themes in the literature by highlighting Arendt's views on sovereignty, international law and genocide, nuclear weapons and revolutions, imperialism and Eurocentrism, as well as her contrasting images of Europe and America. Each essay displays not only superb Arendt scholarship but also stylistic flair and analytical tenacity.

Seyla Benhabib is the Eugene Meyer Professor of Political Science and Philosophy at Yale University. She is the author of *Critique, Norm and Utopia: A Study of the Normative Foundations of Critical Theory* (1986); *Situating the Self: Gender, Community and Postmodernism in Contemporary Ethics* (2002); *Feminist Contentions: A Philosophical Exchange* (coauthored with Judith Butler, Drucilla Cornell, and Nancy Fraser, 1996); *The Reluctant Modernism of Hannah Arendt* (1996); *The Claims of Culture: Equality and Diversity in the Global Era* (2002); *The Rights of Others: Aliens, Citizens and Residents* (2004); and *Another Cosmopolitanism: Hospitality, Sovereignty and Democratic Iterations* (2006). She has edited and coedited seven volumes, most recently with Judith Resnik, *Mobility and Immobility: Gender, Borders and Citizenship* (2009). Her work has been translated into fourteen languages, and she was the recipient of the 2009 Ernst Bloch Prize for her contributions to cultural dialogues in a global civilization.

Politics in Dark Times

Encounters with Hannah Arendt

Edited by

SEYLA BENHABIB
Yale University

With the assistance of

ROY T. TSAO

PETER J. VEROVŠEK
Yale University

CAMBRIDGE
UNIVERSITY PRESS

CAMBRIDGE UNIVERSITY PRESS
Cambridge, New York, Melbourne, Madrid, Cape Town,
Singapore, São Paulo, Delhi, Mexico City

Cambridge University Press
32 Avenue of the Americas, New York, NY 10013-2473, USA

www.cambridge.org
Information on this title: www.cambridge.org/9780521127226

First published 2010
Reprinted 2011 (twice), 2012

A catalog record for this publication is available from the British Library.

Library of Congress Cataloging in Publication Data

Politics in dark times : encounters with Hannah Arendt / edited by Seyla Benhabib.
   p. cm.
Includes bibliographical references and index.
ISBN 978-0-521-76370-7 (hardback) – ISBN 978-0-521-12722-6 (paperback)
1. Arendt, Hannah, 1906–1975. 2. Political science – Philosophy. I. Benhabib, Seyla.
II. Title.
JC251.A74P66 2010
320.5092–dc22   2010024375

ISBN 978-0-521-76370-7 Hardback
ISBN 978-0-521-12722-6 Paperback

Contents

Notes on Contributors   *page* vii

   Introduction   1
   Seyla Benhabib

PART I. FREEDOM, EQUALITY, AND RESPONSIBILITY

  1 Arendt on the Foundations of Equality   17
    Jeremy Waldron

  2 Arendt's Augustine   39
    Roy T. Tsao

  3 The Rule of the People: Arendt, *Archê*, and Democracy   58
    Patchen Markell

  4 Genealogies of Catastrophe: Arendt on the Logic and Legacy
    of Imperialism   83
    Karuna Mantena

  5 On Race and Culture: Hannah Arendt and Her Contemporaries   113
    Richard H. King

PART II. SOVEREIGNTY, THE NATION-STATE, AND THE RULE OF LAW

  6 Banishing the Sovereign? Internal and External Sovereignty
    in Arendt   137
    Andrew Arato and Jean L. Cohen

  7 The Decline of Order: Hannah Arendt and the Paradoxes of
    the Nation-State   172
    Christian Volk

  8 The Eichmann Trial and the Legacy of Jurisdiction   198
    Leora Bilsky

9 International Law and Human Plurality in the Shadow of
   Totalitarianism: Hannah Arendt and Raphael Lemkin   219
   Seyla Benhabib

PART III. POLITICS IN DARK TIMES

10 In Search of a Miracle: Hannah Arendt and the Atomic Bomb   247
    Jonathan Schell

11 Hannah Arendt between Europe and America: Optimism in
    Dark Times   259
    Benjamin R. Barber

12 Keeping the Republic: Reading Arendt's *On Revolution* after
    the Fall of the Berlin Wall   277
    Dick Howard

PART IV. JUDGING EVIL

13 Are Arendt's Reflections on Evil Still Relevant?   293
    Richard J. Bernstein

14 Banality Reconsidered   305
    Susan Neiman

15 The Elusiveness of Arendtian Judgment   316
    Bryan Garsten

16 Existential Values in Arendt's Treatment of Evil and Morality   342
    George Kateb

Index   375

Notes on Contributors

Andrew Arato is Dorothy H. Hirshon Professor in Political and Social Theory at the New School for Social Research. He is the author of *Constitution Making under Occupation: The Politics of Imposed Revolution in Iraq* (2009); *Civil Society, Constitution and Legitimacy* (2000); and *From Neo-Marxism to Democratic Theory* (1993) and coauthor of *Civil Society and Political Theory* (1992). He is currently working on a book on constituent authority and an essay volume on dictatorship and modern politics.

Benjamin R. Barber is a Distinguished Senior Fellow at Demos in New York and Walt Whitman Professor Emeritus at Rutgers University. His seventeen books include the classic *Strong Democracy* (1984), issued in a new twentieth-anniversary edition in 2004; the international best-seller *Jihad vs. McWorld*, now in thirty languages (1995); and, most recently, *Consumed: How Markets Corrupt Children, Infantilize Adults and Swallow Citizens Whole* (2008). He is president and founder of CivWorld, the nongovernmental organization (NGO) that since 2003 has convened the annual Interdependence Day Forum and Celebration in a global city on September 12.

Seyla Benhabib is Eugene Meyer Professor of Political Science and Philosophy at Yale University. Some of her books include *The Reluctant Modernism of Hannah Arendt* (1996; reissued in 2003); *The Rights of Others: Aliens, Citizens and Residents* (2004; winner of the Ralph Bunche Award of the American Political Science Association); *Another Cosmopolitanism*, with responses by Jeremy Waldron, Bonnie Honig, and Will Kymlicka, based on her Berkeley Tanner Lectures and edited by Robert Post (2006); and most recently *Mobility and Immobility: Gender, Borders and Citizenship* (2009), edited with Judith Resnik.

Richard J. Bernstein is Vera List Professor of Philosophy at the New School for Social Research. His books include *Hannah Arendt and the Jewish Question*

(1996); *Freud and the Legacy of Moses* (1998); *Radical Evil: A Philosophical Interrogation* (2002); and *The Abuse of Evil: The Corruption of Politics and Religion since 9/11* (2005). His most recent book is *The Pragmatic Turn* (2010).

Leora Bilsky is Professor of Law at Tel-Aviv University and the author of *Transformative Justice: Israeli Identity on Trial* (2004).

Jean L. Cohen is Professor of Political Theory at Columbia University. She is the author of *Class and Civil Society: The Limits of Marxian Critical Theory* (1982); *Civil Society and Political Theory* (1992) with Andrew Arato; and *Rethinking Intimacy: A New Legal Paradigm* (2002). She is completing a book for Cambridge University Press on legality and legitimacy in the epoch of globalization.

Bryan Garsten is Professor of Political Science at Yale University and author of *Saving Persuasion: A Defense of Rhetoric and Judgment* (2006). He has also written articles on themes related to representative government in the thought of Hobbes, Rousseau, Tocqueville, and Benjamin Constant.

Dick Howard is Distinguished Professor of Philosophy at the State University of New York at Stony Brook. He is the author of fourteen books, most recently *The Specter of Democracy* (2002); *La naissance de la pensée politique américaine* (2005); and *La démocratie à l'épreuve: Chroniques américaines* (2006). *The Primacy of the Political: A History of Political Thought from the Greeks to the American and French Revolutions* was published in 2010.

George Kateb is William Nelson Cromwell Professor of Politics Emeritus at Princeton University. His books include *Hannah Arendt: Politics, Conscience, Evil* (1984); *The Inner Ocean: Individualism and Democratic Culture* (1992); *Emerson and Self-Reliance* (1994, 2002); *John Stuart Mill, On Liberty*, coedited with David Bromwich (2003); and *Patriotism and Other Mistakes* (2006).

Richard H. King is Professor Emeritus of American Intellectual History at the University of Nottingham, UK. He is the author of *Race, Culture and the Intellectuals, 1940–1970* (2004), and coeditor of *Hannah Arendt and the Uses of History: Imperialism, Nation, Race and Genocide* (2007). He is currently at work on *The American Arendt*, which will focus on Arendt's impact on American thought and the impact of her experience in America on her own thought.

Karuna Mantena is Assistant Professor of Political Science at Yale University. She has researched and written on empire and imperialism in modern political thought and, especially, on nineteenth-century British imperial ideology. She is the author of *Alibis of Empire: Henry Maine and the Ends of Liberal Imperialism* (2010).

Patchen Markell is Associate Professor of Political Science at the University of Chicago and the author of *Bound by Recognition* (2003). He is currently writing a book-length study of Hannah Arendt's *The Human Condition* and is pursuing a longer-term project on conceptions of power, agency, and rule in democratic theory.

Susan Neiman is Director of the Einstein Forum in Berlin, Germany. Her most recent books are *Evil in Modern Thought* (2004), which has been translated into nine languages, and *Moral Clarity: A Guide to Grown-Up Idealists* (2008), a *New York Times* Notable Book.

Jonathan Schell is the author of *The Fate of the Earth* (1982) and *The Unconquerable World: Power, Nonviolence, and the Will of the People* (2004), among other books. His most recent book is *The Seventh Decade: The New Shape of Nuclear Danger* (2008). He is a Peace Fellow at the Nation Institute and a lecturer in international studies and ethics, politics, and economics at Yale University.

Roy T. Tsao has taught political theory at Yale, Georgetown, and Brown universities. He has published numerous articles on aspects of Arendt's thought.

Peter J. Verovšek is a Ph.D. candidate in political science at Yale University. Before coming to Yale, he spent a year on a Fulbright Grant researching how memories of World War II continue to affect politics within the former Yugoslavia and in the relations of its successor states with Italy. His dissertation examines the connection between memory and political community through the development of the European Union.

Christian Volk received his doctoral degree from Aachen University (Germany) in 2009. He is the author of *Die Ordnung der Freiheit. Recht und Politik im Denken Hannah Arendts* (2010). He currently holds a postdoctoral position at the Humboldt-University in Berlin and is working on his *Habilitationsprojekt* "The Paradigm of Post-Sovereignty: Law and Democracy in a Global Order."

Jeremy Waldron is University Professor at New York University School of Law. He is the author of *Law and Disagreement* (1999) and *God, Locke and Equality* (2002) among other books. He is the author of "Arendt's Constitutional Politics" in Dana Villa (ed.), *The Cambridge Companion to Hannah Arendt* (2001) and "What Would Hannah Say?" in *The New York Review of Books*, March 15, 2007.

Introduction

Seyla Benhabib

Few if any political thinkers of the twentieth century have attracted public attention and scholarly discussion as wide-ranging as has Hannah Arendt. Her theoretical reflections on the human condition have attained classic status in political philosophy, while her writings on the political crises of her time are a continuing source of intellectual inspiration and provocation.

A former student of Martin Heidegger and Karl Jaspers and a comrade in exile from Nazi Germany with Walter Benjamin, Arendt first came to public prominence ten years after her emigration to the United States, with the publication of *The Origins of Totalitarianism* (1951). That celebrated work's highly original analyses of antisemitism, imperialism, and totalitarianism immediately established her as a leading commentator on the political upheavals and catastrophes of the era. With that book, she not only offered a uniquely clear-sighted, broad account of twentieth-century totalitarian politics and their antecedents; she also provided an exceptionally subtle and penetrating analysis of the modern mentalities that gave succor to those politics. Within those same pages, she also made a landmark contribution to the discourse of international human rights, with a strong critique of the misuse of the institution of citizenship in the modern nation-state. She followed that achievement with even more far-reaching analyses of the exhausted traditions and neglected resources of Western political thought, culminating in her books *The Human Condition* (1958) and *On Revolution* (1963). Her fearlessness in exploring the nature of political evil and personal responsibility found further expression in *Eichmann in Jerusalem* (1963), the source of her famous, much-misunderstood phrase, "the banality of evil." All of these books – along with the numerous other volumes, essays, and lectures that constitute the corpus of Arendt's work – were the focus of extensive critical notice and often controversy in her lifetime, and in more recent years they have gained an ever-widening circle of attentive readers, both within and outside the academy.[1] With the passage of time, her stature as a major thinker of the twentieth century has received ample confirmation.

In the fall of 2006, the centenary of Hannah Arendt's birth was celebrated with conferences from New York to Istanbul, from Paris to Lima, from Berlin to Sofia and beyond. These not only marked her worldwide recognition and reputation,[2] they also revealed an urgent need, an intellectual hunger, "to think with Arendt, against Arendt."[3] This need was increased by the global struggles that ensued after the September 11, 2001, attacks on the World Trade Center and the Pentagon, and the subsequent American-led wars in Afghanistan and Iraq. Many have presented the conflict between the resurgent forces of an Islamist Jihadi movement, spearheaded by al-Qaeda, against the 'West,' as a confrontation between liberal democracies and the new face of totalitarianism in the twenty-first century. In this context, Arendt's epochal analysis of Nazi and Stalinist totalitarianism has often been invoked as a source of analytical insight about current problems and also to support entrenched ideological positions, with which Arendt most likely would not have agreed.[4]

The month of October 2006 was a particularly dark one for the American republic in Arendtian terms: With congressional midterm elections only a month away, it appeared to many that nothing less than the future of constitutional government in the United States was at stake. Guantanamo and Abu Ghraib were only the most infamous of the sites of illegality where the U.S. Constitution was hemorrhaging in the hands of those who claimed that executive power, beyond the rule of domestic and international law, would determine the status of enemy combatants. Evidence was mounting daily that

---

[1] See Samantha Power, "Introduction," *The Origins of Totalitarianism* (New York: Schocken, 2004), pp. ix–xxiv.

[2] See the two volumes published by *Social Research* documenting these conferences: *Hannah Arendt's Centenary: Political and Philosophical Perspectives*, Part I, edited by Arienne Mack and Jerome Kohn, 74, 3 (Fall 2007); *Hannah Arendt's Centenary: Political and Philosophical Perspectives*, Part II, edited by Arienne Mack and Jerome Kohn, 74, 4 (Winter 2007).

[3] I introduced this phrase in Seyla Benhabib, "Preface to the New Edition," *The Reluctant Modernism of Hannah Arendt* (new edition, New York: Rowman and Littlefield, 2003; first published by Thousand Oaks, CA: Sage, 1996), pp. xix–xx.

[4] In the fall of 2001, shortly after the September 11 attacks on the World Trade Center, a conference was held at the New School for Social Research that had been originally planned to mark the fiftieth anniversary of the publication of *The Origins of Totalitarianism*. Impassioned participants debated whether the al-Qaeda movement and Islamic Jihadism could be considered "totalitarian" in the way spelled out by Hannah Arendt. Cf. *The Origins of Totalitarianism. Fifty Years Later*, *Social Research*, edited by Arienne Mack and Jerome Kohn, 69, 2 (Summer 2002).

   The thesis of "Islamo-fascism" has been put forward by Paul Berman, who has called for an "anti-totalitarian war." Paul Berman, *Terror and Liberalism* (New York: W.W. Norton, 2003); Cf. also Christopher Hitchens, *A Long-Short War: The Postponed Liberation of Iraq* (London: Penguin, 2003); and Thomas Cushman, Simon Cottee, and Christopher Hitchens, *Christopher Hitchens and His Critics: Terror, Iraq and the Left* (New York and London: New York University Press, 2008).

   Cf. Chapter 11 in this book, by Benjamin Barber, who radically disagrees with these views of Islam.

Human Rights in the Twentieth Century

Has there always been an inalienable "right to have rights" as part of the human condition, as Hannah Arendt famously argued? The contributions to this volume examine how human rights came to define the bounds of universal morality in the course of the political crises and conflicts of the twentieth century. Although human rights are often viewed as a self-evident outcome of this history, the essays collected here make clear that human rights are a relatively recent invention that emerged in contingent and contradictory ways. Focusing on specific instances of their assertion or violation during the past century, this volume analyzes the place of human rights in various arenas of global politics, providing an alternative framework for understanding the political and legal dilemmas that these conflicts presented. In doing so, this volume captures the state of the art in a field that historians have only recently begun to explore.

Stefan-Ludwig Hoffmann is Research Director at the Center for Research in Contemporary History, Potsdam, Germany, and has been a visiting scholar at the University of California, Berkeley, and Stanford University. He is the author of the prizewinning *The Politics of Sociability: Freemasonry and German Civil Society 1840–1918* (2007). Currently, he is preparing a short history of human rights and a book on Berlin in the wake of the Second World War.

Human Rights in History

Edited by

Stefan-Ludwig Hoffmann, *Zentrum für Zeithistorische Forschung*
Samuel Moyn, *Columbia University*

This series showcases new scholarship exploring the backgrounds of human rights today. With an open-ended chronology and international perspective, the series seeks works attentive to the surprises and contingencies in the historical origins and legacies of human rights ideals and interventions. Books in the series will focus not only on the intellectual antecedents and foundations of human rights, but also on the incorporation of the concept by movements, nation-states, international governance, and transnational law.

Human Rights in the Twentieth Century

Edited by

Stefan-Ludwig Hoffmann

CAMBRIDGE
UNIVERSITY PRESS

32 Avenue of the Americas, New York NY 10013-2473, USA

Cambridge University Press is part of the University of Cambridge.

It furthers the University's mission by disseminating knowledge in the pursuit of education, learning and research at the highest international levels of excellence.

www.cambridge.org
Information on this title: www.cambridge.org/9780521142571

First published 2011

A catalogue record for this publication is available from the British Library

Library of Congress Cataloguing in Publication data
Human rights in the twentieth century / [edited by] Stefan-Ludwig Hoffmann.
   p.   cm.
ISBN 978-0-521-19426-6 (hardback) – ISBN 978-0-521-14257-1 (pbk.)
1. Human rights.   2. Human rights – Cross-cultural studies.   I. Hoffmann,
Stefan-Ludwig.
JC571.H76962   2010
323.09′04–dc22   2010031355

ISBN 978-0-521-19426-6 Hardback
ISBN 978-0-521-14257-1 Paperback

Contents

Notes on Contributors   *page* ix

Acknowledgments   xiii

Introduction: Genealogies of Human Rights   1
Stefan-Ludwig Hoffmann

PART I THE EMERGENCE OF HUMAN RIGHTS REGIMES

1   The End of Civilization and the Rise of Human Rights:
     The Mid-Twentieth-Century Disjuncture   29
     Mark Mazower

2   The "Human Rights Revolution" at Work: Displaced
     Persons in Postwar Europe   45
     G. Daniel Cohen

3   'Legal Diplomacy' – Law, Politics and the Genesis
     of Postwar European Human Rights   62
     Mikael Rask Madsen

PART II POSTWAR UNIVERSALISM AND LEGAL THEORY

4   Personalism, Community, and the Origins of Human Rights   85
     Samuel Moyn

5   René Cassin: *Les droits de l'homme* and the Universality
     of Human Rights, 1945–1966   107
     Glenda Sluga

6   Rudolf Laun and the Human Rights of Germans in
     Occupied and Early West Germany   125
     Lora Wildenthal

PART III HUMAN RIGHTS, STATE SOCIALISM, AND DISSENT

7   Embracing and Contesting: The Soviet Union and the
     Universal Declaration of Human Rights, 1948–1958   147
     Jennifer Amos

8   Soviet Rights-Talk in the Post-Stalin Era   166
     Benjamin Nathans

9   Charter 77 and the Roma: Human Rights and Dissent
     in Socialist Czechoslovakia   191
     Celia Donert

PART IV GENOCIDE, HUMANITARIANISM, AND THE
LIMITS OF LAW

10   Toward World Law? Human Rights and the Failure
     of the Legalist Paradigm of War   215
     Devin O. Pendas

11   "Source of Embarrassment": Human Rights, State of
     Emergency, and the Wars of Decolonization   237
     Fabian Klose

12   The United Nations, Humanitarianism, and Human Rights:
     War Crimes/Genocide Trials for Pakistani Soldiers
     in Bangladesh, 1971–1974   258
     A. Dirk Moses

PART V HUMAN RIGHTS, SOVEREIGNTY, AND THE
GLOBAL CONDITION

13   African Nationalists and Human Rights, 1940s–1970s   283
     Andreas Eckert

14   The International Labour Organization and the Globalization
     of Human Rights, 1944–1970   301
     Daniel Roger Maul

15   "Under a Magnifying Glass": The International Human Rights
     Campaign against Chile in the Seventies   321
     Jan Eckel

Index   343

Notes on Contributors

Jennifer Amos, PhD Candidate History, University of Chicago. She is preparing a dissertation on Soviet conceptions of human rights.

G. Daniel Cohen, Associate Professor in the Department of History, Rice University, Houston. He is the author of *Europe's Displaced Persons: Refugees in the Postwar Order* (Oxford, forthcoming) and of several articles on refugees and human rights after World War II.

Celia Donert, Post-doc at the Zentrum für Zeithistorische Forschung Potsdam. She is currently working on the Gerda Henkel Stiftung–funded research project *The Human Rights of Women in Postwar Europe* and revising her dissertation for publication as *The Rights of the Roma: Citizens of Gypsy Origin in Socialist Czechoslovakia*.

Jan Eckel, Assistant Professor in the Department of History, Albert-Ludwigs-Universität Freiburg. Major publications include *Hans Rothfels. Eine intellektuelle Biographie im 20. Jahrhundert* (Göttingen, 2005); *Geist der Zeit: Deutsche Geisteswissenschaften seit 1870* (Göttingen, 2008); "Utopie der Moral, Kalkül der Macht. Menschenrechte in der globalen Politik seit 1945," *Archiv für Sozialgeschichte* 49 (2009), 437–84; and (as co-editor) *Neue Zugänge zur Geschichte der Geschichtswissenschaft* (Göttingen, 2007). He is currently preparing a book on the history of international human rights politics, 1945–1995.

Andreas Eckert, Professor of African History, Humboldt-Universität zu Berlin, and Director of the Internationales Geisteswissenschaftliches Kolleg (IGK) "Work and Human Lifecycle in Global History." Major publications include *Grundbesitz, Landkonflikte und kolonialer Wandel. Douala 1880–1960* (Stuttgart, 1999); *Herrschen und Verwalten. Afrikanische Bürokraten, staatliche Ordnung und Politik in Tansania, 1920–1970* (Munich, 2007); and (as co-editor) *Globalgeschichte. Theorien, Themen, Ansätze* (Frankfurt, 2007); *Vom Imperialismus zum Empire – Nicht-westliche Perspektiven auf* *die Globalisierung* (Frankfurt, 2008); and *Journal of African History* (since 2005). Currently he is preparing a history of Africa since 1850.

Stefan-Ludwig Hoffmann, Research Director at the Zentrum für Zeithistorische Forschung Potsdam. Major publications include *Civil Society, 1750–1914* (Basingstoke and New York, 2006); *The Politics of Sociability: Freemasonry and German Civil Society, 1840–1918* (Ann Arbor, 2007); *Geschichte der Menschenrechte* (Munich, forthcoming); and (as co-editor) *Demokratie im Schatten der Gewalt: Geschichten des Privaten im deutschen Nachkrieg* (Göttingen, 2010). He is currently completing a book on Berlin under Allied occupation.

Fabian Klose, Lecturer in the Department of History, Ludwig-Maximilians-Universität Munich. His dissertation has been published as *Menschenrechte im Schatten kolonialer Gewalt. Die Dekolonisierungskriege in Kenia und Algerien 1945–1962* (Munich, 2009). He is currently working on a history of humanitarian interventions in the nineteenth century.

Mikael Rask Madsen, Professor of European Law and Integration and Director of the Centre for Studies in Legal Culture (CRS), Faculty of Law, University of Copenhagen. Major publications include *La genèse de l'Europe des droits de l'homme: Enjeux juridiques et stratégies d'Etat (1945–1970)* (Strasbourg, forthcoming) and (as co-editor) *Paradoxes of European Legal Integration* (London, 2008). He is currently completing a large research project on the rise and transformation of human rights in Europe since World War II.

Daniel Roger Maul, Researcher in the Department of History, Justus-Liebig-Universität Gießen. Major publications include *Menschenrechte, Entwicklung und Dekolonisation – Die Internationale Arbeitsorganisation (IAO) 1940–1970* (Essen, 2007; in trans. London, 2011). He is currently working on a history of international relief in the twentieth century.

Mark Mazower is Professor of History and Program Director of the Center for International History at Columbia University, New York. Major publications include *Greece and the Inter-War Economic Crisis* (Oxford, 1991); *Inside Hitler's Greece: The Experience of Occupation, 1941–1944* (New Haven, 1993); *Dark Continent: Europe's Twentieth Century* (New York, 1998); *Salonica, City of Ghosts: Christians, Muslims and Jews, 1430–1950* (New York, 2004); *Hitler's Empire: Nazi Rule in Occupied Europe* (London, 2008); *No Enchanted Palace: The End of Empire and the Ideological Origins of the United Nations* (Princeton, 2009); and (as editor) *The Policing of Politics in Historical Perspective* (London, 1997); *After the War Was Over: Reconstructing the State, Family and the Law in Greece, 1943–1960* (Princeton, 2000); and *Networks of Power in Modern Greece* (London, 2008). He is currently working on a history of ideas and institutions of international governance since 1815.

A. Dirk Moses, Associate Professor in the Department of History, University of Sydney, and Professor of Global and Colonial History at the European University Institute, Florence. Major publications include *German Intellectuals and the Nazi Past* (New York, 2007); and (as editor) *Genocide and Settler Society: Frontier Violence and Stolen Aboriginal Children in Australian History* (New York, 2004); *Colonialism and Genocide* (London, 2007, with Dan Stone); *Empire, Colony, Genocide: Conquest, Occupation and Subaltern Resistance in World History* (New York, 2008); and *The Oxford Handbook of Genocide* (Oxford, 2010, with Donald Bloxham). He is preparing two books, *Genocide and the Terror of History* and *The Diplomacy of Genocide*.

Samuel Moyn, Professor of History at Columbia University, New York. Major publications include *Origins of the Other: Emmanuel Levinas between Revelation and Ethics* (Ithaca, 2005); *A Holocaust Controversy: The Treblinka Affair in Postwar France* (Waltham, Mass., 2005); *The Last Utopia: Human Rights in History* (Cambridge, Mass., 2010); and (as ed. with intro.) Pierre Rosanvallon, *Democracy Past and Future* (New York, 2006). He is currently in the process of writing a book, *A New Theory of Politics: Claude Lefort and Company in Contemporary France*.

Benjamin Nathans, Ronald S. Lauder Endowed Term Associate Professor of History, University of Pennsylvania. Major publications include *Beyond the Pale: The Jewish Encounter with Late Imperial Russia* (Berkeley, 2002); and (as co-editor) *Culture Front: Representing Jews in Eastern Europe* (Philadelphia, 2008). He is currently preparing a book on human rights, legal thought, and dissent in the Soviet Union after Stalin, under contract with Princeton University Press.

Devin O. Pendas, Associate Professor of History, Boston College. Major publications include *The Frankfurt Auschwitz Trial, 1963–1965: Genocide, History and the Limits of the Law* (Cambridge, 2006). He is currently preparing a book on *Law and Democracy: Transitional Justice in German Courts, 1945–1955* (under contract with Cambridge University Press).

Glenda Sluga, Professor of International History, Department of History, University of Sydney. Major publications include *The Problem of Trieste and the Italo-Yugoslav Border: Difference, Identity and Sovereignty in Twentieth-Century Europe* (Albany, 2001); *The Nation, Psychology, and International Politics, 1870–1919* (Basingstoke, Palgrave Transnational History series, 2006); and (as co-author), *Gendering European History* (Leicester, 2000). She is currently working on two Australian Research Council–funded projects: a study of the twentieth century as the great age of internationalism, and a book and Web site on women, nationalism, and cosmopolitanism at the Congress of Vienna.

Lora Wildenthal, Associate Professor of History, Rice University, Houston. Major publications include *German Women for Empire, 1884–1945* (Durham, 2001) and (as co-editor) *Germany's Colonial Pasts* (Lincoln, Neb., 2005). Currently she is preparing a study on the politics of human rights activism in West Germany.

Acknowledgments

The essays in this volume were initially presented at a conference held in Berlin in June 2008 entitled "Human Rights in the Twentieth Century: Concepts and Conflicts." I had discussed the idea for such a conference two years earlier with Mark Mazower in Cambridge, Mass., and with Dieter Gosewinkel in Berlin, while I spent a research year away from teaching, thanks to a generous grant by the Fritz Thyssen Foundation. The conference and then this volume were made possible by the financial support from the Fritz Thyssen Foundation, the Social Sciences Research Center Berlin, and the Center for Research in Contemporary History Potsdam. The Potsdam Center also provided logistical support and, more generally, a research environment conducive to the project.

I would also like to express my appreciation to Eric Crahan at Cambridge University Press for taking on this volume and for working so assiduously to see to its timely publication. Finally, I thank Tom Lampert for helping me with the translation, and Małgorzata Mazurek, Celia Donert, Willibald Steinmetz, Kathleen Canning, and Samuel Moyn for a careful reading of the introduction.

Introduction

Genealogies of Human Rights

Stefan-Ludwig Hoffmann

> *How can we adjudge to summary and shameful death a fellow creature inno-*
> *cent before God, and whom we feel to be so? – Does that state it aright? You*
> *sign sad assent. Well, I too feel that, the full force of that. It is Nature. But do*
> *these buttons that we wear attest that our allegiance is to Nature? No, to the*
> *King. Though the ocean, which is inviolate Nature primeval, though this be the*
> *element where we move and have our being as sailors, yet as the King's officers*
> *lies our duty in a sphere correspondingly natural? So little is that true, that in*
> *receiving our commissions we in the most important regards ceased to be nat-*
> *ural free agents.*
>
> Herman Melville, Billy Budd

Who would not agree today with Hannah Arendt's famous dictum that there is
and always has been an inalienable "right to have rights" as part of the human
condition? Human rights are the *doxa* of our time, belonging among those
convictions of our society that are tacitly presumed to be self-evident truths
and that define the space of the conceivable and utterable. Anyone who voices
doubt about human rights apparently moves beyond the accepted bounds of
universal morality in a time of humanitarian and military interventions. The
only issue still contested today is how human rights might be implemented
on a global scale and how to reconcile, for example, sovereignty and human
rights. Whether human rights in themselves represent a meaningful legal or
moral category for political action in the first place appears to be beyond
question. The contributions to this volume seek to explain how human rights
attained this self-evidence during the political crises and conflicts of the twentieth century.

Implicit in this objective is the hypothesis that concepts of human rights
changed in fundamental ways between the eighteenth and twentieth centuries. Like all legal norms, human rights are historical. Initially formulated in
the revolutions of the late eighteenth century, they almost disappeared from
political and legal discourse in the nineteenth century, while other concepts
such as "civilization," "nation," "race," and "class" gained dominance. Only

in the second half of the twentieth century did human rights develop into a political and legal vocabulary for confronting abuses of disciplinary state power (of "governmentality" in the Foucauldian sense)[1] – a claim foreign to revolutionaries of the eighteenth century, who believed that the nation-state would guarantee civil and human rights and who simply assumed that those parts of the world not yet organized as nation-states were extra-legal territories. One of the paradoxical results of the catastrophic experiences of the two world wars and the subsequent wars of decolonization was that the notions of global unity and the equality of rights became objects of international politics. Our argument is that human rights achieved the status of *doxa* once they had provided a language for political claim making and counter-claims – liberal-democratic, but also socialist and postcolonial. It was not until the last two decades of the twentieth century that human rights developed into the "lingua franca of global moral thought."[2] Only at this time were they invoked to legitimate humanitarian and military interventions, thereby serving as a hegemonic technique of international politics that presented particular interests as universal.[3]

"Contemporary history begins," as British historian Geoffrey Barraclough has famously stated, "when the problems which are actual in the world today first take visible shape; it begins with the changes which enable, or rather compel, us to say we have moved into a new era."[4] As a legal norm and moral-political *doxa*, human rights – conceived as inalienable rights accorded to every human being – are a fundamentally new phenomenon indicative of the beginning of a new era, indeed, so recent that historians have only just begun to write their history. The authoritative studies on human rights in international law and politics have not been written by historians.[5] A rapidly expanding literature on human rights has emerged (in the West) since the 1990s, particularly in the disciplines of political science, philosophy, and law. Although scholars from these disciplines do occasionally argue historically,

---

[1] Michel Foucault, "Face aux gouvernements, les droits de l'homme [1984]," In *Dits et écrits*, vol. 4: 1980–1988 (Paris, 1994), 707–708.

[2] Michael Ignatieff, *Human Rights as Politics and Idolatry* (Princeton, 2001), 53.

[3] Martti Koskenniemi, "International Law and Hegemony. A Reconfiguration," *Cambridge Review of International Affairs*, 17:2 (2004), 197–218; Tony Evans, *The Politics of Human Rights. A Global Perspective* (London, 2005).

[4] Geoffrey Barraclough, *An Introduction to Contemporary History* (London, 1964), 12.

[5] A. W. Brian Simpson, *Human Rights and the End of Empire: Britain and the Genesis of the European Convention* (Oxford, 2001); Martti Koskenniemi, *The Gentle Civilizer of Nations: The Rise and Fall of International Law, 1870–1960* (Cambridge, 2002); Antony Anghie, *Imperialism, Sovereignty and the Making of International Law* (Cambridge, 2005); Johannes Morsink, *The Universal Declaration of Human Rights: Origins, Drafting and Intent* (Philadelphia, 1999); Mary Ann Glendon, *A World Made New: Eleanor Roosevelt and the Universal Declaration of Human Rights* (New York, 2001); William A. Schabas, *Genocide in International Law* (Cambridge, 2000); Daniel Thomas, *The Helsinki Effect: International Norms, Human Rights and the Demise of Communism* (Princeton, 2001); Roger Normand and Sarah Zaidi, *Human Rights at the UN: The Political History of Universal Justice* (Bloomington, Ind., 2008).

their primary objective has been to provide a normative and legal grounding
for human rights in the present or to discuss the limits of humanitarian law.
In contrast, recent master narratives of nineteenth- and twentieth-century history have tended to mention the issue of human rights only in passing (for
example, C. A. Bayly's *Birth of the Modern World* or Tony Judt's *Postwar*),
although there have been notable exceptions (such as Mark Mazower's *Dark
Continent*). The standard *Cambridge History of Political Thought* has no
separate entry for human rights, while the article on human rights in the
German conceptual-historical lexicon *Geschichtliche Grundbegriffe* does not
move beyond the early nineteenth century. In short, there is an abundant literature on how to make human rights work, but less on the actual workings
of human rights in the past.

   This situation is beginning to change, as is demonstrated by Lynn Hunt's
recent study *Inventing Human Rights*. However, Hunt's important account
also makes clear how much this historical field is still in the making, particularly in regard to the question of presumed continuities in the history of
human rights after 1800.[6] Recent histories of human rights, in most cases
written by Anglophone scholars, have tended to provide a triumphalist and
presentist account ("the rise and rise of human rights"),[7] thereby distorting
past figures and institutions such as the anti-slavery movement, which did not
employ rights-talk and had rather different objectives and accomplishments.
In contrast, our contention in the present volume is that human rights in their
specific contemporary connotations are a relatively recent invention.

   By focusing on the actual workings of human rights in the twentieth century, we hope to provide a more nuanced account of the emergence of human
rights in global politics and to establish an alternative framework for analyzing the political and legal quandaries of that history. Most of the contributors
are currently preparing or completing major studies on the history of human
rights politics in the past century, with a particular emphasis on Europe in a
global context. These studies focus on reconstructing cases of human rights
"in action," rather than engaging in normative theorizing about human rights.
In doing so, we seek to move beyond the false dichotomy in contemporary
human rights scholarship between moral advocacy, on the one hand, and
charges of political hypocrisy, on the other.

---

[6] Lynn Hunt, *Inventing Human Rights: A History* (New York, 2007); similarly teleological are Paul Gordon Lauren, *The Evolution of International Human Rights: Visions Seen*
   (Philadelphia, 1998); Micheline R. Ishay, *The History of Human Rights: From Ancient Times
   to the Globalization Era* (Berkeley, 2004). For critical accounts of this narrative see Kenneth
   Cmiel, "The Recent History of Human Rights," *American Historical Review* 109:1 (2004),
   117–135; Reza Afshari, "On Historiography of Human Rights Reflections on Paul Gordon
   Lauren's *The Evolution of International Human Rights: Visions Seen*," *Human Rights
   Quarterly*, 29 (2007), 1–67; Samuel Moyn, "On the Genealogy of Morals," *The Nation*,
   March 16, 2007; and, more generally, Moyn, *The Last Utopia: Human Rights in History*
   (Cambridge, Mass., 2010).
[7] See the critique by Kirstin Sellars, *The Rise and Rise of Human Rights* (Stroud, 2002).

In contrast to the prevailing conception of a natural evolution of human rights, our aim is to understand human rights as a historically contingent object of politics that gained salience internationally since the 1940s – and globally since the 1970s – as a means of staking political claims and counterclaims. Only in the crises and conflicts of the second half of the twentieth century did a conceptual version of human rights emerge that corresponds to the current moral universalism. Thus in order to write a genealogy of human rights, this conceptual transformation – elicited by and formative of social and political events, movements, and structural changes – must be traced diachronically and transnationally. We seek to determine more precisely how historical conflicts about the universality of human rights were incorporated into their different meanings, and thus how the genesis and substance of legal norms were historically intertwined. Can we conceive of a genealogy of human rights that narrates their history not teleologically as the rise and rise of moral sensibilities, but rather as the unpredictable results of political contestations?

The Chimera of Origins

Problems emerge at the start with the question of origins. Where should a history of human rights begin? With Roman law perhaps, where the concept *ius humanum* can indeed be historically documented, albeit not in the sense of subjective, natural rights for all humanity, but rather as rights created by humans and consequently subordinate to divine right?[8] Or with Calvinism, in particular with Calvin's idea of the freedom of conscience and the covenant, as John Witte suggests?[9] Can we agree with Wolfgang Schmale that legal conflicts in French Burgundy and German Electoral Saxony in the sixteenth and seventeenth centuries were the precursors of the human rights declarations of the late eighteenth century? Is a basic human need articulated in these conflicts, one that exists independently of whether the concept of "human rights" was employed by contemporaries?[10] Or would the incorporation of all historical struggles for concrete rights and privileges – which were not intended to be universal, but rather were strictly tied to specific groups – amount to rewriting the entire legal history as a history of human rights?

Even the most familiar account of the origins of human rights – that they emerged in eighteenth-century Europe – is historically contested. More than a hundred years ago, Georg Jellinek sought to tear human rights away from the French archenemy, in particular from Jean-Jacques Rousseau, and to antedate them to the German Reformation and the English legal tradition.

---

[8] See, for example, Paul Veyne, "Humanitas: Romans and Non-Romans," in Andrea Giardina (ed.), *The Romans* (Chicago, 1993), 342–369; in contrast to Richard A. Baumann, *Human Rights in Ancient Rome* (London, 2000).

[9] John Witte, Jr., *The Reformation of Rights: Law, Religion and Human Rights in Early Modern Calvinism* (Cambridge, 2007).

[10] Wolfgang Schmale, *Archäologie der Grund- und Menschenrechte in der Frühen Neuzeit. Ein deutsch-französisches Paradigma* (Munich, 1997), 445.

This "Germanic" tradition, according to Jellinek, gave rise to the Virginia Declaration of Rights (1776), which in turn provided a superior template for the Déclaration des Droits de l'Homme et du Citoyen of 1789. The emphatic rejection of this position from beyond the Rhine was hardly surprising. This controversy has continued in its basic form but with more nuanced arguments. In fact, contemporary historiography has affirmed many of Jellinek's positions as well as those of his French critic Émile Boutmy, even if no scholarly consensus has emerged as a result.[11]

A different version of this genealogy can be found in the aforementioned synthesis *Inventing Human Rights: A History* by Lynn Hunt, an eminent scholar of French cultural history, in particular of the early modern period. In order to elucidate the problems of a triumphalist history of human rights, it is worthwhile to review her argument in brief. Hunt, too, believes that human rights were an invention of the Enlightenment, but offers an unconventional explanation for this. Human rights gained currency in the eighteenth century, she argues, because they were based on new experiences and social practices, on a new emotional regime, with imagined empathy at its heart.[12]

It is no coincidence, according to Hunt, that the three novels of this century that impressively invoked a new sentimental subjectivity – Richardson's *Pamela* (1740) and *Clarissa* (1747–1748) as well as Rousseau's *Julie* (1761) – directly preceded in temporal terms a conceptual version of human rights. Male and, in particular, female readers of these epistolary novels adopted a feeling of equality beyond traditional social boundaries. Epistolary novels tied readers' emotional life to the suffering of others and in this way promoted a moralization of politics. A similar thesis about the politics of eighteenth-century moral and social practices can be found decades earlier in Reinhart Koselleck's *Critique and Crisis*, although the latter was more skeptical toward the Enlightenment.[13]

11 See, for example, Keith Michael Baker, "The Idea of a Declaration of Rights," in Gary Kates (ed.), *The French Revolution: Recent Debates and New Controversies* (London, 1998), 91–140; Marcel Gauchet, *La Révolution des droits de l'homme* (Paris, 1989); Knud Haakonssen and Michael J. Lacey (eds.), *A Culture of Rights* (New York, 1991); Michael P. Zuckert, *Natural Rights and the New Republicanism* (Princeton, 1994); Knud Haakonssen, *Natural Law and Moral Philosophy: From Grotius to the Scottish Enlightenment* (Cambridge, 1996); Pauline Maier, *American Scripture: Making the Declaration of Independence* (New York, 1997). On Jellinek see Duncan Kelly, "Revisiting the Rights of Man. Georg Jellinek on Rights and the State," *Law and History Review*, 22:3 (2004), 493–530.
12 Hunt, *Inventing Human Rights*, 32. The two classic accounts of the emergence of "humanitarian sensibility" are Thomas L. Haskell, "Capitalism and the Origins of Humanitarian Sensibility," *American Historical Review*, 90 (1985), 339–361, 547–566; Thomas Laqueur, "Bodies, Details, and the Humanitarian Narrative," in Lynn Hunt (ed.), *The New Cultural History* (Berkeley, 1989), 176–204. See also Samuel Moyn, "Empathy in History, Empathizing with Humanity," *History and Theory*, 45 (2006), 397–415.
13 Reinhart Koselleck, *Critique and Crisis: Enlightenment and the Pathogenesis of Modern Society* (Cambridge, Mass., 1988). On the post-Enlightenment politics of these moral and social practices see, for example, Stefan-Ludwig Hoffmann, *Politics of Sociability: Freemasonry and German Civil Society 1840–1918*, trans. Tom Lampert (Ann Arbor, Mich., 2007).

This emotional regime becomes even more apparent in the moral campaigns for the abolition of torture beginning in the 1760s. In particular the famous Calas affair connected the new emphasis on physical autonomy to this moral sensibility and empathy.[14] Torture could become a scandal in this case only because it was perceived as outdated. It was no longer regarded as a necessary means for publicly reconstructing the body politic. The audience now viewed only the pain and the suffering of individuals. Just six weeks after the Declaration of the Rights of Man and of the Citizen in 1789, the National Assembly abolished torture. The declarations of 1776 and 1789 thus transformed into rights the antecedent evolution of new emotional regimes. Reading accounts of torture or epistolary novels had physical effects that translated into "brain changes" and "came back out" as new concepts of human rights – this is how Hunt summarizes her argument.[15]

Hunt omits the issue at the heart of the Jellinek controversy, whether the revolution of 1776 was perhaps more successful (in the sense of political legitimacy) than that of 1789 because it tied a specific existing tradition (the Bill of Rights of 1688–1689, which defined the rights of Englishmen) to the universal-revolutionary conception of rights.[16] The radical, cascade-like logic of human rights is, for Hunt, much more important. In the French Revolution, one social group after another demanded its rights and received them as well: first the Protestants, then in 1791 the Jews, and following the suppression of the Saint-Domingue rebellion the free blacks. Slavery was abolished in the French colonies in 1794 (but reintroduced by Napoleon several years later). Women remained the only group that was denied legal equality in the French Revolution. But the demand for human rights, once raised, could not be denied forever, even to women. Hunt insists that however restrictive the declarations of 1776 and 1789 may have been in practice, in the long term they opened up a political space in which new rights could be asserted: "The promise of those rights can be denied, suppressed, or just remain unfulfilled, but it does not die."[17] In the end, Hunt argues, human rights will be implemented because they accord with an emotional regime that, once in the world, will ensure through the force of its own logic the establishment of rights and justice, somehow, somewhere.

Rights, Nations, and Empires since 1800

The concept of the "rights of man" (*droits de l'homme, Menschenrechte*), however, essentially vanished from European politics in the epoch between the

<hr/>

[14] Voltaire intervened for Jean Calas, who had allegedly driven his son to suicide because the latter wanted to convert to Catholicism. The son was buried as a Catholic martyr, while the father was killed by having his bones broken with an iron rod and his limbs pulled apart on a wheel, before finally being burned at the stake.
[15] Hunt, *Inventing Human Rights*, 33.
[16] See Michael Zuckert, "Natural Rights in the American Revolution: The American Amalgam," in Jeffrey N. Wasserstrom et al. (eds.), *Human Rights and Revolutions* (Lanham, Md., 2000), 59–76.
[17] Hunt, *Inventing Human Rights*, 175.

eighteenth-century revolutions and the world wars of the twentieth century, or was replaced (again) by (civil) liberties. Rights that were supposed to hold for all humankind were as rare in international law as they were in the constitutions of the era. Nor did the notion of human rights have great currency in nineteenth- and early-twentieth-century political thought. Tocqueville, Marx, and Weber all mentioned human rights only in passing and with palpable contempt.[18] In contrast to prevailing conceptions of a seamless evolution of human rights, it is therefore necessary to explicate more clearly their historical reconfigurations and ruptures between 1800 and 1945.

Let us briefly examine this issue in terms of the following four points: (1) Colonialism, international law, and humanitarianism were not mutually exclusive in the nineteenth century. Rather, those countries with liberal or republican legal traditions such as Great Britain and France engaged in particularly expansive colonialism. The movement to abolish slavery perhaps had less to do with a new enlightened sensibility for the "rights of man" than with the colonial "civilizing mission." (2) The struggle for *civil* and *social* rights, rather than human rights, was central for constitutions and politics in nineteenth-century Europe; and those who claimed such rights had no difficulty in withholding them from others. (3) Beginning in the 1860s international law did seek to delimit and "humanize" wars between states, but excluded the non-European world from this effort. (4) The homogeneous nation-state also served as the regulative idea guiding efforts to protect minorities both before and after the First World War. Genocide and expulsion were not impeded by such efforts, but instead became instruments of state population politics that aimed at an "ethnic cleansing" of the body politic.

1. *Slavery, Humanitarianism, and Empire.* The movement to abolish slavery began in England in 1787 with the Society for the Abolition of Slave Trade founded by the Quakers. Twenty years later parliament passed a related law. In 1833 all slaves in the colonies of the empire were freed – the abolitionists had collected more than one million signatures for a petition to parliament. France followed this example only in the course of the Revolution of 1848. American plantation owners in the southern states were forced to free their slaves after the end of the American Civil War in 1865. Serfdom had already been abolished in Russia in 1861. By the end of the century slavery was also completely abolished in Central and South America. Can one conceive of a more apt example of the rise and rise of human rights?

As Tocqueville had already noted in 1843, it was not the French radical tradition of human rights that had engendered the moral campaigns to abolish slavery.[19] British abolitionists wanted to elevate the "humanity" of slaves to make them Christians. The success of the movement had less to do

[18] See also Jeremy Waldon (ed.), *'Nonsense Upon Stilts': Bentham, Burke, and Marx on the Rights of Man* (London, 1987), who shows that this disdain for human rights was popular among nineteenth-century liberals, conservatives, and socialists alike.

[19] Alexis de Tocqueville, "The Emancipation of Slaves (1843)," in Tocqueville, *Writings on Empire and Slavery*, ed. and trans. Jennifer Pitts (Baltimore, 2001), 199–226, here 209. The

with a new humanitarian sensibility for the "rights of man" than with this new evangelicalism and the political crisis of the British Empire following military defeats overseas and the loss of the American colonies (1783).[20] In search of a moral legitimacy for the Empire, slavery and the slave trade were declared symbols of a colonial past. The reinvention of a specifically British, Protestant-colored idea of freedom provided the justification for an imperial "civilizing mission" that not only aimed to free slaves and subjects in British colonies, but was also supposed to establish Britain's moral primacy vis-à-vis other European powers. Later, in the era of colonial acquisition, the condemnation of slavery was also a motif and pretext for "humanitarian" interventions by European colonial powers.[21] French republicanism, for example, saw in the idea of its own *mission civilisatrice* the justification for "freeing" Africans from "feudal" conditions under indigenous rulers.[22] The abolition of slavery was thus followed by a new European expansionism, justified on humanitarian grounds, parallel and in contrast with the democratization of nineteenth-century European civil societies. As Max Weber noted in 1906, imperial expansion constituted the historical condition for the emergence of civil liberties in Europe.[23]

2. *Constitutionalism and Citizenship.* In the long nineteenth century, European constitutions avoided references to natural rights or human rights, irrespective of whether they were republics, empires, and/or constitutional monarchies. Human rights were no longer mentioned in the French Constitution

---

example of Tocqueville can also be used to show how political liberalism of the nineteenth century could connect the moral condemnation of slavery to the justification of imperial expansion, in this case the French colonization of Algeria. See Jennifer Pitts, *A Turn to Empire. The Rise of Imperial Liberalism in Britain and France* (Princeton, 2006), 204–239.

[20] Christopher Leslie Brown, *Moral Capital. Foundations of British Abolitionism* (Chapel Hill, N.C., 2006). Adam Hochschild, who in his introduction declares the abolitionists to be "towering figures in the history of human rights," later contradicts himself when he writes about the sentiments of the abolitionists toward the slaves: "The African may have been 'a man and a brother,' but he was definitely a younger and grateful brother, a kneeling one, not a rebellious one. At a time when members of the British upper class did not kneel even for prayer in church, the image of the pleading slave victim reflected a crusade, whose leaders saw themselves as uplifting the downtrodden, not fighting for equal rights for all. ... The upper-class Britons comprising that body might be moved by pity, but certainly not by a passion for equality." Hochschild, *Bury the Chains: Prophets and Rebels in the Fight to Free an Empire's Slaves* (New York, 2005), 4, 133–134.

[21] See Kevin Grant, *A Civilized Savagery: Britain and the New Slaveries in Africa, 1884–1926* (New York, 2005); Grant, "Human Rights and Sovereign Abolitions of Slavery, c. 1885–1956," in Grant et al. (eds.), *Beyond Sovereignty: Britain, Empire, and Transnationalism, c. 1880–1950* (Basingstoke, 2007), 80–102.

[22] Alice L. Conklin, "Colonialism and Human Rights: A Contradiction in Terms? The Case of France and West Africa, 1895–1914," *American Historical Review*, 103:2 (1998), 419–442; Conklin, *A Mission to Civilize: The Republican Idea of Empire in France and West Africa, 1895–1930* (Stanford, Calif., 1997).

[23] Max Weber, "Zur Lage der bürgerlichen Demokratie in Rußland," in *Zur Russischen Revolution von 1905: Schriften und Reden 1905–1912*, ed. Wolfgang J. Mommsen and Dittmar Dahlmann (Tübingen, 1996), 100.

of 1799 (and resurfaced only in 1946.) This was true as well for the United States, where the Bill of Rights sank into insignificance after 1800 (and was not ratified by the states of Massachusetts, Georgia, and Connecticut until 1939!).[24] Only the constitutions of the individual states were important for legal practice at the time. This situation did not change with the Fourteenth Amendment of 1868, which granted civil rights to everyone born in the United States, including black slaves. (Lincoln himself long favored the plan to deport the freed slaves to Africa.)[25] The legal situation in the respective states, rather than the Bill of Rights, continued to be decisive for the rights of individuals. Only after the Second World War did the Supreme Court breathe new life into the Bill of Rights.

The draft constitution of St. Paul's Church in Frankfurt am Main in 1848 did include a catalog of "basic rights" (*Grundrechte*), as human rights were now called in German in order to provide distance from the radicalism of the French revolution. As with other constitutions of the era, however, these were civil rights tied to citizenship (*Grundrechte des deutschen Volkes*) and not universal rights. After the failed revolution, the state emerged as the guarantor of rights, which were regulated by laws. Legal positivism rather than natural law became the prevailing doctrine for granting rights, and not only in Germany. The issue of human rights played no role at all in the constitutional conflicts of the 1860s. It was absent from the Constitution of the German Empire of 1871 not because the empire was particularly authoritarian, but because no party attributed any significance to a declaration of basic rights. Not until the Weimar Constitution of 1919 was a detailed catalog of basic rights and duties included.

In the nineteenth century, lines of political conflict within European civil societies were instead defined by the demand for social or political rights. While early socialists did invoke the declarations of 1789 or 1793, the revolutions and civil wars in France of 1830, 1848, and 1871 emphasized collective rights (for example, of workers) or the *droits des citoyens*. Reference to the *droits de l'homme* reappeared only in the constitution of the Fourth Republic of 1946.[26] A just society, according to the socialist utopia, would arise only by transcending capitalism and "bourgeois" rule of law. The European Left emphasized not freedom *from* the state, but rather freedom *in* and *through* the state, over which they thus sought to gain control. Human rights were

---

[24] Orlando Patterson, "Freedom, Slavery, and the Modern Construction of Rights," in Olwen Hufton (ed.), *Historical Change and Human Rights: The Oxford Amnesty Lectures 1994* (New York, 1995), 132–178, here 164.

[25] See, for example, his "Speech in Springfield, Illinois, June 2, 1857," in Henry Louis Gates Jr. and Donald Yakovone (eds.), *Lincoln on Race and Slavery* (Princeton, 2009), 92–102.

[26] Tony R. Judt, "Rights in France: Reflections on the Etiolation of a Political Language," *Tocqueville Review*, 14 (1993), 67–108. William H. Sewell has shown that French workers rarely employed the language of rights in the 1840s, instead formulating their claims in the corporate language of the ancien régime. Sewell, *Work and Revolution in France* (Cambridge, 1980).

therefore closely tied to the concept of the sovereignty of the people.[27] This presumed that only citizens incurred rights, not humanity in general, or, for instance, subjects in the colonies.[28] The same was true of the women's movement, which was organized internationally but aimed above all at political and social rights within nation-states, for instance, women's suffrage (paradoxically this aim was often justified by reference to the special place of women in society).[29] Only during the Dreyfus affair and the founding of the Ligue pour la Défense des Droits de l'Homme at the end of the century did socialists and republicans discover the value of individual rights vis-à-vis the state, a development that was curtailed with the explosion of nationalism during the First World War.[30]

3. *The Meanings of International Law.* For Europeans, the nineteenth-century world was divided: On the one hand were the "civilized" (Christian) states, in which fierce conflicts for political participation took place, but whose legal principles (the right to property, security, religious freedom) were increasingly regulated through constitutions and laws, and in which an ever greater legal equality emerged, and on the other hand the remaining territories and "uncivilized" (non-Christian) peoples outside Europe, whose legal status remained weakly defined. The most important function of the liberal international law that emerged in the 1860s lay in regulating conflicts among European powers in the absence of a world sovereign. Only when a people had become "civilized" to the degree that it possessed its own state was it accorded rights. "[B]arbarians," as John Stuart Mill wrote in 1859, "have no rights as a nation, except a right to such treatment as may, at the earliest possible period, fit them for becoming one."[31] The international standard of civilization did follow its own logic of imperial integration, which Martti Koskenniemi describes as "exclusion in terms of a cultural argument about the otherness of the non-European that made it impossible to extend European rights to the native, inclusion in terms of the native's similarity with the European, the native's otherness having been erased by a universal humanitarianism under which international lawyers sought to replace native institutions by European

---

[27] Alexander J. Schwitanski, *Die Freiheit des Volksstaats. Die Entwicklung der Grund- und Menschenrechte und die deutsche Sozialdemokratie bis zum Ende der Weimarer Republik* (Essen, 2008), 454–455.

[28] Alice Bullard, "Paris 1871/New Caledonia 1878: Human Rights and the Managerial State," in Jeffrey N. Wasserstrom et al. (eds.), *Human Rights and Revolutions* (Lanham, Md., 2000), 79–97.

[29] See Leila J. Rupp, *Worlds of Women: The Making of an International Women's Movement* (Princeton, 1997).

[30] Emmanuel Naquet, "Entre justice et patrie. La ligue des droits de l'homme et la grande guerre," *Movement social*, 183 (1998), 93–109; William Irvine, *Between Justice and Politics: The Ligue des droits de l'homme, 1898–1945* (Stanford, Calif., 2007).

[31] John Stuart Mill, "A Few Words on Non-Intervention," [1859] in *The Collected Works of John Stuart Mill*, ed. John M. Robson, vol. 21: *Essays on Equality, Law, and Education* (Toronto, 1984). http://oll.libertyfund.org/title/255/21666.

sovereignty."[32] Thus in contrast to the constitutions of the era, natural rights arguments did still play a role in international law in a "civilizing" sense; however, they ultimately served European imperialism in that sovereignty was tied to a (European) standard of civilization. In the nineteenth century, international law continued to regard all territories of the world not controlled by sovereign states as *terra nullius* and thus as free to be occupied.[33]

The attempts to "humanize" warfare also focused exclusively on conflicts among or within "civilized" states, and not, for example, on the suppression of revolts in the colonies, which assumed genocidal traits at the end of the century.[34] The wars of the 1860s in Europe and the American Civil War had become increasingly brutal through the mechanization and democratization of killing. Compulsory military service allowed for larger armies and thus deployments with significantly higher casualties among soldiers. At the same time, media reports in the age of an expanding public sphere made the killing more immediate. During the American Civil War, Prussian émigré and political philosopher Franz (Francis) Lieber was commissioned to draw up guidelines for dealing with the rebels. The Lieber Code, issued by Abraham Lincoln to the northern states in 1863, regulated the treatment of deserters and prisoners, regular troops, and partisans for the first time in the history of modern warfare. The report by Swiss entrepreneur Henri Dunant about the bloody Battle of Solferino in June 1859 between the Austrian army and troops of Piedmont-Sardinia and France led to the founding of the Red Cross in 1863 and a year later to the Geneva Convention, which the majority of European states and the United States adopted by the end of the century.[35] Its provisions were expanded and elaborated at the Hague Peace Conferences of 1899 and 1907 encompassing, for instance, the protection of the civilian population during foreign occupation. This new humanitarian international law was only selectively observed in the two world wars of the twentieth century. The

---

[32] Koskenniemi, *Civilizer of Nations*, 130. For a different account see Anthony Pagden, "Human Rights, Natural Rights, and Europe's Imperial Legacy," *Political Theory*, 31:2 (2003), 171–199.

[33] Jörg Fisch, *Die europäische Expansion und das Völkerrecht* (Stuttgart, 1984), 490; Fisch, "Internationalizing Civilization by Dissolving International Society: The Status of Non-European Territories in Nineteenth Century European Law," in Martin H. Geyer and Johannes Paulmann (eds.), *The Mechanics of Internationalism: Culture, Society, and Politics from the 1840s to the First World War* (Oxford, 2001), 235–257; Fisch, "Africa as terra nullius: The Berlin Conference and International Law," in Stig Förster et al. (eds.), *Bismarck, Europe, and Africa: The Berlin Conference and the Onset of Partition* (London, 1988), 437–476; Fisch, *Das Selbstbestimmungsrecht der Völker oder die Domestizierung einer Illusion. Eine Geschichte* (Munich, forthcoming); Anghie, *Imperialism*.

[34] Isabel V. Hull, *Absolute Destruction: Military Culture and the Practices of War in Imperial Germany* (Ithaca, N.Y., 2005).

[35] Michael Ignatieff, *The Warrior's Honor: Ethnic War and the Modern Conscience* (London, 1998); Caroline Moorehead, *Dunant's Dream: War, Switzerland, and the History of the Red Cross* (New York, 1998); John F. Hutchinson, *Champions of Charity: War and the Rise of the Red Cross* (Boulder, 1996).

juridification of war around 1900 thus stands in awkward tension with the lawlessness of warfare in the twentieth century, in particular the systematic killings of enemy civilians.

4. *Nation States, Minorities, and Genocide.* The crisis of the multiethnic Ottoman, Habsburg, and Romanov Empires beginning in the late nineteenth century made nationalism appear to be the most likely path to political rights and state sovereignty. This was true for Turkey and the new nation-states of the Balkans before the First World War, as well as for those nation-states in Central and Eastern Europe that were established after 1918 and in the Middle East, Asia, and Africa after 1945. In all of these cases, the creation of sovereign nation-states led to problems with the treatment of ethnic minorities and consequently to a new politics of genocide and population transfer. The collapse of the empires and the global expansion of the nation-state thus fundamentally altered international politics, from the traditional diplomacy of the great powers all the way to population policies or "bio-politics."[36]

The right to national self-determination propagated first by Lenin and later by Woodrow Wilson at the end of the First World War solved old conflicts while engendering new ones. "Versailles had given sixty million people a state of their own, but it turned another twenty-five million into minorities."[37] Furthermore, after the First World War a completely new group of refugees emerged, stateless people, who as "foreign elements" or "the class enemy" had been stripped of their citizenship by one nation and forced to emigrate, but were unable to officially immigrate to the receiving nation (and apply for political asylum). This was particularly acute for Armenians and the millions of political refugees from the Russian Civil War (1917–1920) and beginning in 1933 a matter of life and death for German Jews. It was only with the dissolution of older multiethnic empires and the reordering of the world into egoistic nation-states that ethnic homogenization and genocide emerged as political imperatives for bio-politics.

National Socialism inverted nineteenth-century imperialism, as Afro-Martinican Francophone author Aimé Césaire wrote after the war, in that it treated Europeans like Africans – without rights and without states that could guarantee these rights.[38] Slavery also returned to Europe in the guise of forced labor. The nation-states of Central and Eastern Europe created in 1918–1919 were either completely annexed by Nazi Germany or turned into colonial protectorates. The *Generalplan Ost* (General Plan East) included no sovereign state or civil rights for the occupied territories and the peoples of the Soviet Union. In contrast to nineteenth-century imperialism, the Nazi empire did not attempt to legitimate itself through an ostensible "civilizing" of the colonized.

---

[36] Eric D. Weitz, "From the Vienna to the Paris System: International Politics and the Entangled Histories of Human Rights, Forced Deportations, and Civilizing Missions," *American Historical Review*, 113:5 (2008), 1313–1343.

[37] Mark Mazower, *Dark Continent: Europe's Twentieth Century* (London, 1998), 42.

[38] Aimé Césaire, *Discourse on Colonialism* [1950]. Translated by Robin D. G. Kelley (New York, 2000), 36.

Exploitation and extermination were no longer the implicit consequences, but rather the declared objective of the subjugation.

The League of Nations created in Versailles in 1919 failed to resolve the issue of minority rights despite its other accomplishments.[39] The League was supposed to monitor the observation of minority rights in the new states of Central and Eastern Europe; the democracies of the West (including defeated Germany) were excluded from this because they were regarded as sufficiently "civilized" to ensure these rights themselves – irrespective of protests, for instance, by Poland. The exclusive standard of civilization thus did not disappear from international law during the First World War, but instead became the sole measuring stick for sovereignty, applied now also to the "immature" states of Central and Eastern Europe. A proposal by Japan to include the equality of all races in the articles of the League of Nations was rejected by the Western victorious powers, as were all attempts to extend the right to national self-determination to the colonies. Thus even the former German colonies in Africa and the Ottoman territories in the Middle East did not become independent states but mandate territories (similar to colonial protectorates) that were now directly administered by the victorious powers. After 1918–1919, the elites of the colonial world abandoned the idea of liberal reform within the British and French empires and embraced other ideologies, for instance, communism (China). The anti-colonial nationalism of the "Third World" emerged at the end of the First World War from the disappointed expectations about a new and just international order.[40]

Competing Universalisms since 1945

One of the results of the two world wars was not only the end of the Nazi racial empire in Europe, but the beginning of the disintegration of the colonial empires, in particular those of the victorious powers Great Britain and France. Only with the Universal Declaration of Human Rights of 1948 and the decolonization of the world did human rights become universal in the sense that they were not supposed to apply exclusively to Europeans. As *Mark Mazower* demonstrates in his contribution to this volume, in this process "human rights" (and later "development") replaced the concept of civilization

---

[39] See, for example, Susan Pedersen, "Back to the League of Nations," *American Historical Review*, 112:4 (2007), 1091–1117; Carole Fink, "Minority Rights as an International Question," *Contemporary European History*, 9 (2003), 385–400; Fink, *Defending the Rights of Others: The Great Powers, the Jews, and International Minority Protection, 1878–1938* (Cambridge, 2004); Donald Bloxham, *The Great Game of Genocide. Imperialism, Nationalism, and the Destruction of the Ottoman Armenians* (Oxford, 2005); Michael Marrus, *The Unwanted: European Refugees in the Twentieth Century* (Oxford, 1985). See also the classic critique of the interwar minority system by Hannah Arendt, *The Origins of Totalitarianism* [1951] (London, 1976), 267–303; on human rights and "bio-politics": Giorgio Agamben, *Homo Sacer: Sovereign Power and Bare Life* (Stanford, Calif., 1998), 126–135.

[40] See Erez Manela, *The Wilsonian Moment: Self-Determination and the International Origins of Anticolonial Nationalism* (Oxford, 2007).

(and of "civilizing missions") in international law and politics. In many ways, human rights acquired universality only after the demise of European international law and its exclusive standard of civilization.

This emergence of human rights during the midcentury crisis as a normative concept that claimed authority even beyond state boundaries stood (and continues to stand today) in tension with the principle of sovereignty. Like human rights, the global expansion of the nation-state as a model of political order is also a result of the cataclysmic history of the first half of the twentieth century and the implosion of the colonial empires. The new international order was thus constructed around two often mutually exclusive principles: individual human rights, which could also be asserted vis-à-vis one's own state; and the principle of state sovereignty, which – as new states from Israel to India and Pakistan were convinced – rendered the state solely capable of guaranteeing rights.

The new intergovernmental organizations, declarations, and conventions, like international politics since 1945 in general, have thus been based on the principle of state sovereignty and have at the same time employed moral imperatives such as human rights that point beyond the nation-state. The second half of the twentieth century was defined by the global expansion of the nation-state *and* the increasing erosion of state sovereignty through (among other things) transnational legal norms such as human rights. Ideas about the equal sovereignty of states and of individuals emerged in tandem and in political tension with one another. This paradoxical constellation helps to explain the trajectories of human rights in the second half of the century, in particular the difficulties involved in their political implementation. Once again we can identify four sets of problems: (1) Cold War contestations and (2) decolonization, both primarily from the late 1940s to the early 1960s; (3) the global campaign against pariah states such as Chile and South Africa and the new humanitarianism; and (4) the demise of communism and the emergence of dissidence in Eastern Europe, both in the 1970s and 1980s.

1. *Cold War Contestations.* Human rights returned to the international arena during the Second World War as a unifying moral imperative for the states allied against Nazi Germany. Indeed, the war experience played a pivotal role for the international constitutionalism of the late 1940s. However, the "strange triumph of human rights" in the 1940s was based as well on the geopolitical interests of the Allies. The (nonbinding) Universal Declaration of Human Rights of 1948 contained a strategic dimension in the sense that it pushed the rights of individuals to the fore for the first time in international law while simultaneously ignoring the rights of minorities, lending the Allies a free hand for postwar population transfers, not least the expulsion of millions of Germans from East-Central Europe.[41] In their contributions to this volume,

---

[41] Mark Mazower, "The Strange Triumph of Human Rights, 1933–1950," *Historical Journal*, 47 (2004), 379–398; Mazower, "'An International Civilisation?' Empire, Internationalism,

Dan Cohen examines the refugee crisis as an example for the postwar human rights revolution while *Lora Wildenthal* discusses the German case: The fact that postwar Germans were not included in the emerging international human rights regime confounded precisely those Germans who had not been Nazis, whereas Carl Schmitt, for instance, merely regarded his own views as confirmed by this.[42]

The consensus among the Allies quickly disintegrated as their interests diverged. During the Cold War the communist bloc and the decolonization movements insisted that a condemnation of racism and a guarantee of collective and social rights were essential dimensions of human rights, while the liberal democracies in the West emphasized individual and political rights, such as the right to free expression, that were already guaranteed in their constitutions. The substance of human rights, in other words, was historically contingent and politically contested. Again, this is a history marked more by ruptures than continuities. In the early 1950s, the United States and the Soviet Union partially withdrew from attempts to establish an international human rights regime – the United States was still a racially segregated society at this time, and the post-Stalinist Soviet Union had only then begun to eliminate forced labor.[43] Within the scope of the European Convention on Human Rights (1950), the post-Fascist democracies of Italy, France, Austria, and Germany were prepared to cede sovereignty rights, in part out of fear of a return of political extremism within their own societies.[44] This ceding of sovereignty rights by Western European nations would have been inconceivable without the constellation of the Cold War (and the demise of the colonial empires, an issue that will be addressed below). As *Mikael Rask Madsen* shows in his contribution, the new institutions of the European Court of Human Rights and the European Commission on Human Rights were not particularly significant for jurisprudence in the first two decades of their existence (the court issued few judgments until the 1970s), but they did serve as instruments for the political unification of the western half of the continent

and the Crisis of the Mid-20th Century," *International Affairs*, 82 (2006), 553–566. For a more sanguine view see Elizabeth Borgwardt, *A New Deal for the World: America's Vision for Human Rights* (Cambridge, Mass., 2005).

[42] See also Paul Betts, "Germany, International Justice and the 20th Century," *History and Memory*, 17 (2005), 45–86. Schmitt wrote the following in a diary entry of December 6, 1949, expressing the prevailing sentiment among postwar Germans: "There are crimes against and for humanity. The crimes against humanity are committed by Germans. The crimes for humanity are committed on Germans." Schmitt, *Glossarium: Aufzeichnungen der Jahre 1947–1951* (Berlin, 1991), 282.

[43] Carol Anderson, *Eyes off the Prize: The United Nations and the African American Struggle for Human Rights, 1944–55* (Cambridge, Mass., 2003); Mark Bradley, "The Ambiguities of Sovereignty: The United States and the Global Rights Cases of the 1940s and 1950s," in Douglas Howland and Luise White (eds.), *Art of the State: Sovereignty Past and Present* (Bloomington, Ind., 2009), 124–147.

[44] Andrew Moravcsik, "The Origins of Human Rights Regimes: Democratic Delegation in Postwar Europe," *International Organisation*, 54 (2000), 217–252.

under conservative auspices in response to the challenge of communism. In the postwar era, anticommunism was more important for the emergence of a European human rights regime than the Holocaust.[45] As *Samuel Moyn*'s essay contends, within the liberal democracies of Western Europe after 1945 it was especially the Christian-Democratic parties that adopted the cause of human rights. Political Catholicism, which in the interwar period had still demonized the French Revolution, now discovered in human rights and the sacred concept of the person an effective strategy to conceal its own entanglement with the radical right and to infuse a religious dimension into the anti-totalitarian consensus of the West.

2. *Decolonization and the Internationalization of Rights.* After 1945 the new United Nations institutions resembled the League of Nations of the interwar era in many ways, and it appeared initially as if the liberal internationalism that still worked in an imperial framework and had been animated by the legal traditions of the British Empire would continue after the war.[46] South African President Jan Smuts, the representative of a Commonwealth state based on racial segregation, composed the preamble to the United Nations Charter in 1945. It is hardly surprising that a condemnation of racism was absent from this document. In contrast to the interwar period, however, representatives of the colonies were no longer willing to be put off. Smuts became the object of attacks within the new international arena in 1946, in particular from Nehru and other Indian politicians, who now demanded recognition of the rights of the Indian minority in South Africa. This became something of a precedent for the aforementioned dilemma: to demand universal rights and nonetheless to respect sovereignty rights. Until the end of apartheid, South Africa remained a kind of pariah state within the international community, but was never subject to any direct military intervention.

With the Cold War division into East and West and the wars of decolonization, human rights became a disputed domain in international politics in the 1950s. One of the many ironies of this process was the "boomerang effect" of the internationalization of human rights: The demise of French and British imperial power coincided with the internationalization of the greatest accomplishments of their political and democratic cultures, that is, human rights. As *Glenda Sluga*'s contribution shows, questions of racial and sexual equality constituted the central focus for the human rights rhetoric of the postcolonial and communist states.[47] At the time, liberal-democratic, socialist, and

---

[45] Marco Duranti, "Conservatism, Christian Democracy and the European Human Rights Project, 1945–50," PhD diss., Yale University, 2009.

[46] See Saul Dubow, "Smuts, the United Nations and the Rhetoric of Race and Rights," *Journal of Contemporary History*, 43 (2008), 45–74; Mark Mazower, *No Enchanted Palace: The End of Empire and the Ideological Origins of the United Nations* (Princeton, 2009).

[47] See also Sunil Amrith/Glenda Sluga, "New Histories of the United Nations," *Journal of World History*, 19 (2008), 251–274. In the 1950s and 1960s it was primarily representatives of the postcolonial world who put women's rights on the UN agenda. See Roland Burke, *Decolonization and the Evolution of International Human Rights* (Philadelphia, 2010), 121–129.

postcolonial human rights norms competed in the international arena, and yet each claimed for itself moral universalism. Consequently the prevailing models for the history of human rights are hardly convincing. In 1949, at the height of the Labour government's reform policies, British sociologist T. H. Marshall proposed as a model for the historical development of citizenship a succession of civil, then political, and then social rights, which Italian philosopher Noberto Bobbio, for instance, subsequently adopted and applied to human rights. Karel Vasak, a legal expert from Czechoslovakia who had fled to France in 1968, developed a similar model containing three generations of rights: first civil and political rights, followed by social and cultural rights, and finally in the twentieth century solidarity rights, such as the right to peace, development, and a healthy environment.[48] These different rights claims did not in fact follow one another as subsequent generations, but rather competed historically. Women's suffrage was adopted in the European democracies only after the Great War, in France not until 1944 and in Switzerland not until 1971. The right to work had already appeared in Article 21 of the Declaration of Human Rights in the French Constitution of 1793 and was thus not an invention of the nineteenth or twentieth century. The United States did sign the International Covenant on Economic, Social, and Cultural Rights (1966) in 1977 at the beginning of the Carter administration, but is one of the few countries in the world that has not ratified it even today, although during the Second World War social rights were a firm part of the Roosevelt administration's postwar agenda.[49]

As British international legal expert A. W. Brian Simpson has argued, the decline of the colonial empires after 1945 can hardly be explained without the moral and political pressure of human rights. This is particularly clear in the revolts and wars in the 1950s against Great Britain and France, both of which had been weakened by the Second World War; these two colonial powers participated in the establishment of a European human rights regime and yet were compelled at the same time to declare states of emergency in their own colonies, for instance, Kenya and Algeria, in order to suppress independence movements, as *Fabian Klose* makes clear in his contribution to this volume.[50]

[48] T. H. Marshall, "Citizenship and Social Class," in *Citizenship and Social Class and Other Essays* (Cambridge, 1950), 1–85; Norberto Bobbio, "Human Rights Now and in the Future [1968]," in *The Age of Rights* (London, 1996); Karel Vasak, "Pour une Troisième Generation des Droits de l'homme," in C. Swinarski (ed.), *Essays on International Humanitarian Law and Red Cross Principles in Honour of Jean Pictet* (The Hague, l984), 837–845.

[49] Martin H. Geyer, "Social Rights and Citizenship during World War II," in Manfred Berg and Martin H. Geyer (eds.), *Two Cultures of Rights: Germany and the United States* (Cambridge, 2002), 143–166.

[50] See also Simpson, *Human Rights;* Kenneth Cmiel, "Human Rights, Freedom of Information, and the Origins of Third World Solidarity," in Mark Bradley and Patrice Petro (eds.), *Truth Claims: Representation and Human Rights* (New Brunswick, N.J., 2002), 107–130; Mikael Rask Madsen, "France, the United Kingdom and the 'Boomerang' of the Internationalisation of Human Rights (1945–2000)," in Simon Halliday and Patrick Smith (eds.), *Human Rights Brought Home. Socio-Legal Perspectives on Human Rights in the National Context* (Oxford,

The fact that Great Britain initially insisted on excluding the subjects of its colonies from the European Convention on Human Rights and that France did not ratify the convention (until 1974) could hardly still be justified in terms of "a civilizing mission."

As a result of decolonization, the institutions that liberal internationalism had created in the mid-1940s were now "globalized." The new independent states of Africa and Asia increasingly gained in influence; since the early 1960s the countries of the "Third World" constituted a majority in purely numerical terms within the institutions of the United Nations. Cold War rivalries and the emergence of "Third World" sovereign states fostered a fundamental change in the constitution of international society, previously dominated by European colonial empires. Now postcolonial states could assert their own perspective on human rights within international organizations. In 1960 the post-colonial states (on the initiative of the Soviet Union and without votes from the West) were able to attain recognition of the right to national self-determination as Article 1 of the Declaration on the Granting of Independence to Colonial Countries and Peoples – and thereby as one of the UN Human Rights Norms.[51] At the first International Human Rights Conference of the United Nations in Teheran in 1968, twenty years after the Universal Declaration, the states of the "Third World" – many of them now autocratic dictatorships such as the regime of Reza Shah Pahlavi in Iran – formulated a rejection of individual rights and a (renewed) turn within the international community to social and collective rights. The socialist states and the new states of the postcolonial world frequently formed an anti-colonial bloc against the West within international organizations (UNO, UNESCO, ILO), although this invocation of human rights had no consequences for jurisprudence within their own societies.[52]

As *Andreas Eckert* argues in this volume, African political leaders invoked human rights in the 1950s primarily to expose the hypocrisy of the West. For anti-colonialist intellectuals such as Julius Nyerere, Frantz Fanon, or Léopold Senghor, the language of nationalism and revolutionary violence was more significant than that of human rights. Whenever it appeared that the invocation of human rights might threaten the sovereign rights of recently independent nation-states, the former were summarily rejected, as *Daniel Roger*

2004), 57–86; Charles O. H. Parkinson, *Bills of Rights and Decolonization: The Emergence of Domestic Human Rights Instruments in Britain's Overseas Territories* (Oxford, 2007); Bonny Ibhawoh, *Imperialism and Human Rights: Colonial Discourses of Rights and Liberties in African History* (New York, 2007); Burke, *Decolonization.*

51 See Burke, *Decolonization*, ch. 4.

52 See, for example, the ILO debates on forced labor between 1947 and 1960: Sandrine Kott, "Arbeit – ein transnationales Objekt? Die Frage der Zwangsarbeit im 'Jahrzehnt der Menschenrechte,'" in Christina Benninghaus et al. (eds.), *Unterwegs in Europa. Beiträge zu einer vergleichenden Sozial- und Kulturgeschichte* (Frankfurt, 2008), 301–321; Daniel Roger Maul, *Menschenrechte, Sozialpolitik und Dekolonisation. Die Internationale Arbeitsorganisation (IAO) 1940–1970* (Essen, 2007).

Maul's article here suggests. This, of course, was no different in the case of the superpowers, the United States and the Soviet Union. Thus from the perspective of the postcolonial world, human rights have constituted both: a moral and political means of applying pressure upon the former colonial powers in the international arena, while at the same time representing a dangerous, modernized version of the nineteenth-century "standard of civilization" that further fostered the social and economic gap between the imperial metropolis and the periphery (or North and South, as it was termed by this time).

Human rights thus became a language of international politics, although still without significant consequences for national governance. International legal experts such as Paul Kahn have even argued that one reason for the rapid juridification of the world (in different regional and international human rights regimes) was the fact that this emerging global law proved unenforcable. Torture, for instance, became a common practice in the dictatorships of Latin America at precisely the same time it was officially prohibited by the International Covenant on Civil and Political Rights (1966, in force since 1976).[53]

3. *Global Hegemony and the New Humanitarianism.* The situation changed in the early 1970s, at the moment when human rights left the restricted space of international diplomacy and became a global concept for non-state actors such as Amnesty International and Médecins Sans Frontiéres, which began to demand the enforcement of human rights beyond national borders.[54] Nongovernmental organizations (NGOs) dedicated to humanitarian issues have existed since the late eighteenth century. For example, the British Defence and Aid Fund, which assisted people persecuted by apartheid laws in South Africa, developed from the Treason Trial Defence Fund out of Christian Action, which had been established in the period after the Second World War and which in turn had its origins in the British Anti-Slavery Society.[55] Now, however, a variety of new organizations emerged that regarded the "global

---

53 Paul W. Kahn, *Sacred Violence: Torture, Terror, and Sovereignty* (Ann Arbor, Mich., 2008), 57–58.

54 See Akira Iriye, *Global Community: The Role of International Organizations in the Making of the Contemporary World* (Berkeley, 2002); Ann Marie Clark, *Diplomacy of Conscience: Amnesty International and Changing Human Rights Norms* (Princeton, 2001); Kenneth Cmiel, "The Emergence of Human Rights Politics in the United States," *Journal of American History*, 86 (1999), 1231–1250; Tom Buchanan, "'The truth will set you free': The Making of Amnesty International," *Journal of Contemporary History*, 37 (2002), 575–597; Buchanan, "Amnesty International in Crisis, 1966–7," *Twentieth Century British History*, 15 (2004), 267–289; David Kennedy, *The Dark Sides of Virtue. Reassessing International Humanitarianism* (Princeton, 2005); Dominique Clement, *Canada's Rights Revolution. Social Movement and Social Change 1937–1982* (Vancouver, 2008); Jean Quataert, *Advocating Dignity: Human Rights Mobilizations and Global Politics* (Philadelphia, 2009); Matthew Hilton, *Prosperity for All: Consumer Activism in the Era of Globalization* (Ithaca, N.Y., 2009).

55 Hakan Thörn, *Anti-Apartheid and the Emergence of a Global Civil Society* (Basingstoke, 2006), 6–7.

community" rather than national governments as the source of authority and the audience for their campaigns. This began with the Biafra crisis in the late 1960s, which triggered a wave of new humanitarian aid organizations in the West.

Certainly one factor in this development was the political disillusionment of the radical Left in Western Europe after 1968, as well as what it regarded as the toothless internationalism of the UN human rights regime. Historians speak of a second globalization beginning in the early 1970s, which, for example, also gave rise to a new global media public and a sense, at least in affluent Western societies, to share global concerns. The images of suffering children in Biafra evoked among Western viewers the feeling they had to act immediately in order to end humanitarian emergencies in postcolonial crisis states – a politically double-edged form of empathy that bore similarities to the imperial humanitarianism of the early nineteenth century. Entirely new forms of media resonance have also been part of this constellation, for instance, the worldwide broadcasts of pop concerts, beginning with the *Concert for Bangladesh* in New York organized by Ravi Shankar and George Harrison (for refugees of the civil war), including Bob Geldorf's *Live Aid* concerts for Africa in 1984 and 1985, and the *Tribute to Nelson Mandela* in London's Wembley Stadium in 1988, which was watched by more than 60 million people on television. Human rights became popular in the 1970s. They left the conference room of international organizations and became an issue for humanitarian engagement by individual groups, which used transnational organizational networks and media to mobilize a global audience. Only now did it appear that "the narrower or wider community of the peoples of the earth has developed so far that a violation of rights in one place is felt throughout the world," as Kant had claimed in his foundations of a cosmopolitan law two hundred years earlier.[56]

In the campaigns against individual states (for example, Chile and South Africa, but also the Soviet Union in the course of the Helsinki process), it became clear that both national and transnational actors could invoke human rights as moral and political leverage against individual states and their governments. Still, as *Jan Eckel* suggests in this volume for Chile, the global moral campaigns exerted pressure only on those states that wanted to be regarded internationally as democracies. The contributions by *Devin O. Pendas* and *A. Dirk Moses* point to the failure of the "legalist paradigm of war," according to which individual and state violations of human rights were to be prosecuted internationally after 1945. This paradigm failed because of the principle of nonintervention into the domestic affairs of sovereign states, even when governed by brutal dictatorships. Indeed, the capacity of international law and politics to enforce the observation of rights was

---

[56] Immanuel Kant, *Perpetual Peace* [1795], ed. H. S. Reiss, trans. H. B. Nisbet (Cambridge, 1991), 23.

actually weakened. The fact that the prosecution of genocide became a *jus cogens* of international law since 1945 has reduced neither state violence against ethnic minorities nor genocidal wars. Thus, for example, the frequent invocation of the genocide convention of 1948 in the civil wars of the 1960s and 1970s (Biafra, Bangladesh, or Cambodia) never prompted UN military intervention. NGOs in the West did not undertake moral campaigns against the crimes committed in these states, which by far surpassed those in Chile or South Africa, because moral and political pressure could be exercised solely upon those regimes that sought membership in the "global community."

Western NGOs engaged in their work without state commission or democratic legitimation. The appeal of the humanitarian engagement of many NGOs lay precisely in their renunciation of traditional politics. These organizations testify less to the existence of a "global civil society" than to a growing concern within the West in the late 1960s and early 1970s for the social and economic consequences of decolonization in the global south.[57] The debate about human rights politics now also resonated among governments and parliaments of Western states. Post-imperial states such as Canada and the Netherlands were especially active in human rights politics. Particularly significant was the Carter administration's abandonment in 1975–1976 of the Realpolitik of the Nixon-Kissinger era, internationally disavowed after the Vietnam War, as well as its rediscovery of human rights. Human rights not only continued to serve as an argument in the Cold War against the Soviet Union, but now figured as a moral imperative for the new political and economic hegemony of the United States in an era of the global integration of markets and spaces. Like the British Empire at the beginning of the nineteenth century, the United States searched for new legitimacy in the world after its moral defeat in a war against insurgents. In addition to institutions such as the World Bank and the International Monetary Fund, which secured the leading economic position and interests of the United States, human rights became a central argument for the United States' claims to political hegemony in the world.[58] This led to a reconfiguration of global politics that moved beyond the framework of the Cold War and ultimately paved the way for the preoccupation with human rights and humanitarian interventions since the 1990s, when the United States became the global hegemon. Western

---

[57] See Giuliano Garavini, "The Colonies Strike Back: The Impact of the Third World on Western Europe, 1968–1975," *Contemporary European History*, 16:3 (2007), 299–319.

[58] See, for example, Charles Bright and Michael Geyer, "Where in the World Is America? The History of the United States in the Global Age," in Thomas Bender (ed.), *Rethinking American History in a Global Age* (Berkeley, 2002), 63–99; Bright and Geyer, *The Global Condition in the Long Twentieth Century* (Berkeley, forthcoming), and more specifically Daniel Jonathan Sargent, "From Internationalism to Globalism. The United States and the Transformation of International Politics in the 1970s," PhD diss., Harvard University, 2008; Sarah Snyder, *Human Rights Activism and the End of the Cold War: A Transnational History of the Helsinki Network* (New York, forthcoming).

claims to political hegemony and the new humanitarianism have thus gone hand in hand, although human rights activists in NGOs have rarely recognized this connection.[59]

4. *The Demise of Communism.* Beginning in the late 1940s the Soviet Union sought to promote their version of human rights within international politics, as *Jennifer Amos* demonstrates in her contribution. The Soviet Union took part in the Universal Declaration of Human Rights, the Genocide Convention, as well as the war crime tribunals in Nuremburg and Tokyo – a fact that was played down in the liberal democracies of the West during the Cold War and that has been forgotten since the end of Soviet-style socialism.[60] Precisely because human rights long served as a diplomatic code (or propaganda ploy) within the international arena, socialist countries had no difficulties with participating in the UN human rights conventions and the Helsinki process in the 1960s and 1970s. This participation was motivated by hopes of international recognition of the socialist world and by trust – as it turned out, an outmoded trust – in the fact that the language of human rights would remain in the international arena ("covenants without the sword are but words," as Hobbes wrote in *Leviathan*).[61]

Moreover, human rights could develop such a dynamic within the Eastern bloc only because of the Socialist rights talk that the domestic opposition was able to invoke.[62] There was no rule of law under Communist regimes, but there were laws and the promise of rights that the opposition could exploit. It is no coincidence that the only effective mass opposition movement in the Eastern bloc was Poland's Solidarity, founded in 1980, a free trade union that demanded civil and social rights for workers.[63] "Socialist

---

59 Yves Dezalay and Bryant Garth, "Droits de l'homme et Philanthropie Hégémonique," *Actes de la recherche en sciences sociales*, 121 (1998), 23–41.

60 Francine Hirsch, "The Soviets at Nuremberg: International Law, Propaganda, and the Making of the Postwar Order," *American Historical Review*, 113:3 (2008), 701–730, here 710. See also, for example, Catriona Kelly, "Defending Children's Rights, 'In Defense of Peace': Children and Soviet Cultural Diplomacy," *Kritika* 9 (2008), 711–746, esp. 735–743.

61 Thomas Hobbes, *Leviathan: The Matter, Form and Power of a Commonwealth Ecclesiastical and Civil* [1651] (Oxford, 1929), p. 2, ch. 17, 128.

62 The *Great Soviet Encyclopedia*, for example, first included an article on the Universal Declaration of Human Rights in its third edition (in the second edition of 1952 there was only on entry on the declaration of 1789, which emphasized its bourgeois "class basis"). The article in the third edition was quite positive, albeit with one restriction: "The declared rights and freedoms may be claimed by every human being, without distinction of race, skin color, sex, language, religion, political or other convictions, national or social origin, or property, birth, or other circumstances. The Soviet Union recognizes the Declaration of Human Rights as a progressive document, but refrained from voting for its passage because it contained no references to concrete measures to implement the declared rights and freedoms." "Deklaracija prav čeloveka OON Vseobščaja," in *Bol'šaja Sovetskaja Ènciklopedija*, 3rd ed., vol. 8 (Moscow, 1972), 47. See also "Pakty o pravah čeloveka," ibid., vol. 19 (Moscow, 1975), 93.

63 Stephen Kotkin, with a contribution by Jan T. Gross, *Uncivil Society. 1989 and the Implosion of the Communist Establishment* (New York, 2009), 9.

legality" gained salience as a legal practice beginning in the early 1970s, when socialist states could no longer rely on terror and utopian promise alone. Human rights were thus not simply an invention of a small group of dissident intellectuals, as is usually assumed today. Rather, dissidents often merely took at face value (and much to the distress of authorities) the constitutions of state socialism or the international declarations and conventions signed by socialist countries, as the essays by *Celia Donert* and *Benjamin Nathans* argue.[64]

Eastern European critics of state socialism such as Aleksandr Solzhenitsyn were long regarded in the West as antiquated representatives of Cold War anti-totalitarianism. This changed with the general disillusionment of the political Left after 1968, in particular in France. Put simply, in the 1970s the dissident replaced the revolutionary as the political paragon.[65] The figure of the "dissident" became an object of projection for the Western European Left, but also for conservatives and liberals: Each claimed the dissident and thus the language of human rights for their own political objectives. This distorted image of dissident intellectuals omitted (and continues to omit) many significant dimensions. György Konrád's *Antipolitics* of the 1980s, for example, was still skeptical about the selectivity of the moral rhetoric in both East and West and was thus aware of the competing universalisms of a liberal and a socialist human rights discourse.[66] In general, for East-Central European dissidents, human rights always remained tied to a return to national history.[67] For this reason, they never embraced the idea of a postnational "global civil society" propagated by left-liberal intellectuals of the West who in the 1990s retrospectively invoked dissidents and human rights.[68]

Only in the last twenty years, in our current era of terror, humanitarian emergencies, and "global governance," have human rights become a *doxa* (or secular religion, as Michael Ignatieff noted early on).[69] Nineteenth-century

---

[64] See also Robert Horvath, *The Legacy of Soviet Dissent: Dissidents, Democratisation and Radical Nationalism in Russia* (London, 2005), ch. 3: "The Rights-Defenders"; Benjamin Nathans, "The Dictatorship of Reason: Aleksandr Vol'pin and the Idea of Rights under 'Developed Socialism,'" *Slavic Review*, 66:4 (2007), 630–663; Peter Bugge, "Normalization and the Limits of Law: The Case of the Czech Jazz Section," *East European Politics and Society*, 22 (2008), 282–318.

[65] Robert Horvath, "'The Solzhenitsyn Effect': East European Dissidents and the Demise of Revolutionary Privilege," *Human Rights Quarterly*, 29:4 (2007), 879–907; Kristin Ross, "Ethics and the Rearmament of Imperialism: The French Case," in Jeffrey Wasserstrom et al. (eds.), *Human Rights and Revolutions*, 2nd ed. (Lanham, Md., 2007), 155–167.

[66] Gyorgy Konrád, *Antipolitics: An Essay* (New York, 1984).

[67] Michal Kopeček, "Citizenship and Identity in the Post-Totalitarian Era: Czech Dissidence in Search of the Nation and its Future," *Transit Online*. http://www.iwm.at/.

[68] Jürgen Habermas, *The Postnational Constellation: Political Essays* [1998], trans. Max Pensky (Cambridge, 2001); John Keane, *Global Civil Society* (Cambridge, 2003).

[69] Ignatieff, *Human Rights*, 53

political models of empires and clashes of civilizations returned as did humanitarian interventions.[70] Human rights were now frequently grounded or rejected in cultural rather than political terms, for instance, in the debate over *Asian values* in the early 1990s.[71] Cultural relativism, which colonial empires had invoked after 1945 in order to oppose the implementation of human rights in their colonies, was now taken up by postcolonial states against the hegemonic human rights claims of the West. Postcolonial legal scholars too regarded human rights now merely as an imperialist strategy of the West masked as universalism.[72] Conversely, attempts to locate human rights in the cultures of the world (for instance, in an African or Confucian human rights tradition) tended to obscure the fact that there had been political contestations between and among Western, socialist, and postcolonial human rights claims, through which human rights had become universalized in the first place. Those solidarity rights that were recognized by the UN over the past thirty years (in almost every case opposed by the United States), for instance, the "right to development" outlined in the early 1970s by Senegalese international legal expert Kéba M'Baye and adopted in a UN declaration in 1986, have scarcely counted in the West as valid human rights norms.[73] Attempts by the UN to tie human rights regimes to development policies in order to respond to the social and economic consequences of globalization (for instance, at the Vienna Conference of 1993) have had little impact. Instead the global discrepancy between rich and poor has increased dramatically over the past decades, while visual representations of the "Third World" have shifted from developing nations to suffering individuals, victims of natural or manmade disasters without political agency in the international arena.

Contestations between different human rights norms continues to exist (the Chinese government, for example, has invoked solidarity rights since the 1990s, opposing them to the individual rights demanded by the West).[74] Nevertheless, the Western perspective on human rights and humanitarianism has gained hegemony on a global scale. Only now have enlightened experts

---

[70] Samuel P. Huntington, "The Clash of Civilizations?" *Foreign Affairs*, 72:3 (1993), 22–49; Huntington, *The Clash of Civilizations and the Remaking of World Order* (New York, 1996).

[71] On the rise of cultural relativism as an argument against human rights in the 1980s see Burke, *Decolonization*, ch. 5. On the Asian values debate see Joanne R. Bauer and Daniel A. Bell (eds.), *The East Asian Challenge for Human Rights* (Cambridge, 1999).

[72] See, for example, Makau Mutua, *Human Rights: A Political and Cultural Critique* (Philadelphia, 2002); Anghie, *Imperialism*, chs. 5, 6.

[73] For an eloquent defense of solidarity rights see Upendra Baxi, "The Development of the Right to Development," in Janus Symonides (ed.), *Human Rights: New Dimensions and Challenges* (Dartmouth, 1998), 99–116; Baxi, "Voices of Suffering, Fragmented Universality, and the Future of Human Rights," in Burns H. Weston and Stephen P. Marks (eds.), *The Future of International Human Rights* (Ardsley, N.Y., 1999), 101–156.

[74] Jeremy T. Paltiel, "Confucianism Contested: Human Rights and the Chinese Tradition in Contemporary Political Discourse," in Wm. Theodore de Bary and T Weiming (eds.), *Confucianism and Human Rights* (New York, 1998), 270–296; Stephen C. Angle, *Human*

and managers of the global – Western specialists in international law, social scientists, and NGOs – discovered human rights as their cause. And only now has this cosmopolitan elite begun to invent a history of human rights that extends back into antiquity and is supposed to demonstrate the evolution of universal morality.

Human Rights as History

The *doxa* of a society, those convictions that are tacitly accepted as naturally given, can be recognized as such only in the moment that they lose their self-evidence, that is, when they become historical. Does approaching human rights as history implicitly call into question the universality of those rights? For how can human rights be universal if they are – as the contributors of this volume argue – the product of a global history of violence and conflict? If we understand this history as one of "hegemonic contestations" (Martti Koskenniemi) that possesses no telos and could also have occurred entirely differently, as it becomes clear that there was not one but several competing universalisms, each able to invoke human rights? Moreover, this contends that the emergence of global law in the twentieth century went hand in hand with the fragmentation of the means for its enforcement. Should we thus agree with critics from Edmund Burke to Hannah Arendt who preferred the rights of citizens to human rights because only the state, and not "humanity," represented a historically viable political entity that could guarantee concrete rights? Does the invocation of absolute morality (or moral emergencies) in politics ultimately lead to violence, as Arendt holds in her reading of the predicament of Captain Vere (of the ship *Rights of Man*), in Melville's *Billy Budd*, since politics is about conflict and compromise and not about good and evil?[75] And yet it was Arendt who insisted, as quoted at the beginning of this introduction, that human beings have the right to have rights. According to Arendt, however, this right should be derived not from the teleologically loaded laws of "history" or "nature," but rather from concrete, contradictory human experiences and the unpredictable histories resulting from them.[76] Or as Edmund Burke wrote in a letter to a correspondent in Paris in November 1789: "You have theories enough concerning the rights of man; it may not be amiss to add a small degree of attention to their nature and disposition. It is with men in the concrete; it is with the common human life, and human actions, that you are to be concerned."[77]

Rights and Chinese Thought: A Cross-Cultural Analysis (Cambridge, 2002), 239–249; Mireille Delmas-Marty and Pierre-Étienne Will (eds.), *La Chine et la démocratie* (Paris, 2007).

[75] Hannah Arendt, *On Revolution* (New York, 1963), 74–83.

[76] See Stefan-Ludwig Hoffmann, "Koselleck, Arendt, and the Anthropology of Historical Experience," *History and Theory*, 49 (May 2010), 212–236.

[77] Letter to Charles-Jean-François Depont, in Edmund Burke, *Further Reflections on the Revolution in France*, ed. Daniel E. Ritchie (Indianapolis, 1992), 13.

In this respect, writing the history of human rights has only just begun. Human rights as a history of political contestations, as proposed in this volume, does not have to diminish our moral convictions about such rights.[78] On the contrary, by gaining an insight into the historical contingency of our normative concepts, their emergence from concrete experiences of violence and conflict, we may comprehend better why the politics of human rights continues to fail in our time.

---

[78] Similarly Thomas L. Haskell, "The Curious Persistence of Rights Talk in the 'Age of Interpretation,'" *Journal of American History*, 74:3 (1987), 984–1012, here 985–86, as well as Hans Joas, "The Emergence of Universalism: An Affirmative Genealogy," in Peter Hedström and Björn Wittrock (eds.), *Frontiers of Sociology* (Leiden, 2009), 15–24.

PART I

THE EMERGENCE OF HUMAN RIGHTS REGIMES

I

The End of Civilization and the Rise of Human Rights

The Mid-Twentieth-Century Disjuncture*

Mark Mazower

The recent upsurge of interest in the history of human rights must surely be seen as one of the more productive intellectual consequences of the ending of the Cold War. The early 1990s spawned hopes for the emergence of a new world order in which the United Nations would be able to regain some of the lustre it had lost while sidelined over the preceding decades, and the sense of the start of a new historical epoch directed scholarly attention back toward the start of the previous one, in 1945. The increasingly grim spiral of events thereafter if anything confirmed the importance of historicizing the human rights phenomenon: The war in the former Yugoslavia and genocide in Rwanda put in question the robustness of the human rights regime that had been established after the Second World War, while the advent of a unilateralist American administration with a thinly veiled contempt for the UN has inspired several American historians to write accounts of the internationalism of earlier administrations in an effort to remind people of the alternatives.

The year 1945 was not a Year Zero for internationalists: The roots of the UN were much more firmly embedded in the past than its founders felt it was expedient to admit. Nevertheless, in at least one crucial respect, 1945 did represent a break with the past. It is commonplace to regard that year as the 'end of the European era', meaning the end of an era in which the European Powers effectively dominated world politics; but this collapse of European power carried with it something rather less discussed – the parallel erosion of Europe's normative dominance of international affairs. Between 1815 and the war, a system of states had grown up that was based on the primacy of European power and values, and the rationalization of their imperial expansion in terms of the spreading of civilization and its accompanying rights. The First World War had dented confidence in the idea of Civilization (with a capital C), but it was, above all, the rise of Nazism that spelled its doom. The rise of a new order after 1945 was based on new, or at least, substantially adapted principles, and,

---

* An earlier and shorter version of this essay was published in *International Affairs*, 82:3 (2006), 553–566.

for perhaps the first time, the question of rights was detached from the notion of civilization. This essay explores the rise and fall of the concept of civilization as an ordering principle for international politics, a concept bound up with the idea of freedom, humanity and rights, and one whose demise could not but affect the projection and political significance of those values as well.

It is not only in our own day that the 1815 Congress of Vienna has been recognized as the inauguration, not merely of the post-Napoleonic settlement, but more generally, of a new era in international governance. After both the First and Second World Wars, we find writers turning their attention back to 1815. But one of the most striking interpretations of the Congress's achievement was one of the earliest, and least known. I refer to a study (really an exercise in special pleading) that appeared in the same year as the Congress itself, a study that was penned by that extraordinary political chameleon the Abbe de Pradt. In his time, de Pradt had been a royalist, a counter-revolutionary and a confidant of Napoleon. But he was also friendly with Benjamin Constant – the two men frequented the salon of Madame de Staël at the restoration – and it is Constant's spirit that permeates Pradt's book.

In it, he disavows the defeated Emperor: Napoleon, he writes, has covered Europe with 'wrecks and monuments'. The task of the victors was to eradicate 'the military spirit' and to return Europe to 'its civil state'. He went on to say that this required them to recognize the 'rise of a new power called opinion' and what this power carried with it – civilization. It was civilization, he wrote, that 'divinity', that had emerged through commerce and communication over the previous century, delegitimizing despots, prompting belief in the idea of humanity, and bringing war into disrepute. 'Nationality, truth, publicity – behold the three flags under which the world for the future is to march.... The people have acquired a knowledge of their rights and dignity'. Europe had been military; now it would become commercial and constitutional. A colonial order would carry civilization and spread European tastes around the world; the process had already worked in Russia and North America, and had been started in Egypt. It should be applied to the Ottoman empire as well, through a 'moral not a territorial conquest'.[1]

The term 'civilization' itself had emerged in both Britain and France several decades earlier, around the middle of the eighteenth century. It connoted both the process by which humanity emerged from barbarity, and by extension the condition of a civilized society, and in particular, the sense of 'a certain security of the person and property'. What is striking about the word's development after Napoleon's defeat is its increasingly programmatic political coloration. Civilization now conveyed – as in de Pradt's account – a liberal program for Europe based on cooperation rather than conquest. Guizot's *History of Civilization in Modern Europe* defines civilization as 'the history of the progress of the human race toward realizing the idea of humanity', and

[1] Abbe de Pradt, *The Congress of Vienna* (Philadelphia, 1816), 32–42, 202–215.

highlights the key themes for the future – the 'expansion of mind', the full and rational enjoyment of the human faculties, and the spread of rights. Guizot acknowledged that there had been other civilizations – in Egypt and India – in the past. But European civilization was superior because it combined cultural community with an acceptance of political diversity. J. S. Mill, perhaps influenced by de Tocqueville, offered a gloomier assessment in his 1836 essay: It is true, he asserted, that the 'present era is the era of civilization in the narrow sense' (i.e., as the converse of barbarism), and that the elements of civilized life existed in modern Europe (and especially in Great Britain) 'in a more eminent degree and in a state of more rapid progression, than at any other place or time'. But Mill was not completely positive about this; civilization – he noted, striking a Tocquevillean note – meant that individuals mattered less, and masses more. It bred materialism and avarice, and popular literature that pandered to base sentiments rather than improving them.[2]

These uncertainties did not vanish, and they were to reappear with a vengeance as we shall see (often inspired by the same force that had given de Tocqueville pause – the rise of the United States); but for the rest of the nineteenth century, it was the relatively sunny version that came to dominate thinking about international affairs. For Guizot, civilization had been what united the states of Europe. But what about Europe's relations with the rest of the world? Here de Pradt's formulation foreshadowed the tropes of the civilizing mission that emerged with the age of imperialism. If civilization was located in Europe, then Europe's overseas expansion required deciding how far civilization was for export.

One fertile intellectual elaboration of this belief emerged – as we have learned from the work of Martti Koskenniemi and Antony Anghie – through the new discipline of international law.[3] A rationalization of the values of the Concert of Europe, international law was designed as a moral-procedural aid to the preservation of order among sovereign states, and its principles were explicitly stated as applying only to civilized states much as Mill saw his principles of liberty as applying solely to members of 'a civilized community'. In 1845 the influential American international lawyer Henry Wheaton had actually talked in terms of the 'international Law of Christianity' versus 'the law used by Mohammedan Powers'; but within twenty or thirty years, such pluralism had all but vanished. According to the late-nineteenth-century legal commentator W. E. Hall, international law 'is a product of the special civilization of modern Europe and forms a highly artificial system of which the principles cannot be supposed to be understood or recognized by countries

[2] F. Guizot, *History of Civilization in Europe* (Penguin, 1997), 15–31; J. S. Mill, 'Essay on Civilization' (1836); and M. Levin, *Mill on Civilization and Barbarism* (London, 2004). The classic study is E. Benveniste, 'Civilization. Contribution a l'histoire du mot', in his *Problemes de linguistique generale*, 2 vols. (Paris, 1971).

[3] M. Koskenniemi, *Gentle Civiliser of Nations: The Rise and Fall of International Law, 1870–1960* (Cambridge, 2002); A. Anghie, *Imperialism, Sovereignty and the Making of International Law* (Cambridge, 2004).

differently civilized.... Such states only can be presumed to be subject to it as are inheritors of that civilization'.[4]

Thus conceived, international law defined the problem of global community in terms of the nature of the relationship between a civilized Christendom and the noncivilized but potentially civilizable non-European world. States could join the magic circle through the doctrine of international recognition, which took place when 'a state is brought by increasing civilization within the realm of law'.[5] In the 1880s James Lorimer suggested there were three categories of humanity – civilized, barbaric and savage – and thus three corresponding grades of recognition (plenary political; partial political; natural, or mere human). Most Victorian commentators believed that barbaric states might be admitted gradually or in part. Westlake proposed, for instance that 'Our international society exercises the right of admitting outside states to parts of its international law without necessarily admitting them to the whole of it'. Others disagreed: Entry 'into the circle of law-governed countries' was a formal matter, and 'full recognition' all but impossible.[6]

The case of the Ottoman empire exemplified this ambivalent process. European states had been making treaties with the sultans since the sixteenth century. But following the Crimean War the empire was declared as lying within the 'Public Law of Europe' (a term which some commentators then and now saw as the moment when international law ceased to apply only to Christian states but which in my opinion is better viewed as a warning to Russia to uphold the principles of collective consultation henceforth rather than trying to dictate unilaterally to the Turks). In fact, despite its internal reforms, the empire was never regarded in Europe as being fully civilized, the capitulations remained in force, and throughout the nineteenth century the chief justification of the other powers for supporting first autonomy and then independence for new Christian Balkan states was that removing them from Ottoman rule was the best means of civilizing them and securing property rights and freedom of worship.

In fact, the spread of rights could be tied directly to a willingness to override the formal sovereignty of non-European powers, and law became a mechanism for justifying differential policies toward the sovereignty of different types of states. After the Franco-Prussian War, international lawyers devised

---

[4] H. McKinnon Wood, 'The Treaty of Paris and Turkey's Status in International Law', *American Journal of International Law*, 37:2 (April 1943), 262–274; Hall quoted by Wight, 'The Origins of Our States-System: Geographical Limits', in his *Systems of States*, ed. Hedley Bull (Leicester, 1977), 115–116. See also Lydia Liu, "The Desire for the Sovereign and the Logic of Reciprocity in the Family of Nations," *Diacritics*, 29:4 (1999), 150–177.

[5] W. E. Hall, *A Treatise on International Law* (1884) cited by A. Anghie, 'Finding the Peripheries: Sovereignty and Colonialism in Nineteenth-Century International Law', *Harvard International Law Journal*, 40:1 (1999), 1–80.

[6] Lorimer in G. Gong, *The Standard of 'Civilization' in International Society* (Oxford, 1984), 49; Westlake in Anghie, 'Finding the Peripheries'; Hall in Wight, 'The Origins of Our States-System', 115–116.

the notion of belligerent occupation – a state of affairs in which a military occupant interfered as little as was compatible with military necessity in the internal affairs of the occupied country. This was so as not to prejudice the rights of the former ruler of that territory, who was regarded as remaining sovereign until a peace settlement might conclude otherwise. But belligerent occupation was a compact solely between so-called civilized states not to unilaterally challenge each other's legitimate right to rule. In the case of Ottoman territory, for instance, the powers felt no such inhibitions: The Russians in Bulgaria in 1877, the Habsburgs in Bosnia the following year, and the British in Egypt in 1882 all demonstrated through their extensive rearrangement of provincial administrations that, although they would allow the Ottoman sultan to retain a fig leaf of formal sovereignty, in fact the new theory of belligerent occupation did not apply in his lands. Thirty years later, the Austrians (in 1908) and the British (in 1914) went further: On both occasions they unilaterally declared Ottoman sovereignty over the territories they were occupying at an end, suggesting that whatever had or had not been agreed at Paris in 1856, by the early twentieth century, the Ottoman Empire was regarded once again as lying outside the circle of civilization. (The fact that it was a Muslim power was certainly not irrelevant to this. In 1915, when the French and Russians prepared a diplomatic protest at the mass murder of Ottoman Armenians, their initial draft condemned the massacres as 'crimes against Christendom'. Only when the British mentioned that they were worried over the possible impact of such a formulation on Indian Muslim opinion was the wording changed to 'crimes against humanity'.)

If the Ottoman empire was, as it were, semicivilized, then sub-Saharan Africa – site of the main European land grab in the late nineteenth century – was savage. European and American lawyers extended the notion of the protectorate – originally employed for new European states such as Greece – to the new colonial situation, ostensibly as a way of shielding vulnerable non-European states from the depredations of other European powers, but really to avoid complications among the powers which might trigger further conflict. In Africa itself, the spread of civilization was a useful liberal justification for expansion, and appeared prominently in France in particular, where the colonial lobby was fighting hard after 1871 to find a reason to deploy the resources of the Third Republic overseas after the country's humiliation in the Franco-Prussian War. Geographers, economists and administrators all stressed France's obligation to 'contribute to this work of civilization': Such a contribution was now seen as a mark of national greatness.[7] Yet in the increasingly racialized worldview of late-nineteenth-century European imperialism, it was above all in Africa that the civilizing mission was put in question as

[7] The French debate may be followed in A. Conklin, *A Mission to Civilize: The Republican Idea of Empire in France and West Africa, 1895–1930* (Stanford, 1997), quote from p. 12; and J. P. Daughton, *The Civilizing Mission: Missionaries, Colonialists and French Identity, 1880–1914* (Berkeley, 2002).

colonial experts cast doubt on Africans' readiness to take advantage of what was being offered them. From such a perspective, protectorates might be a way of slowing down social transformation – in the interests of 'native customs' – as much as they were of introducing it. 'Much interest attaches to legislation for protectorates, in which the touch of civilization is cautiously applied to matters barbaric', wrote a commentator in the *Journal of the Society of Comparative Legislation* in 1899. Yet the concept of civilization remained vital. The treaty that followed the Berlin Colonial Conference of 1884–1985, which marked the attempt to diplomatically manage the scramble for Africa, talked of the need 'to initiate the indigenous populations into the advantages of civilization'. The Congo Free State was one disastrous outcome.[8]

In this way, Victorian international law divided the world according to its standard of civilization. Inside Europe – and in other areas of the world colonized by Europeans – there was the sphere of civilized life: This meant – roughly – property rights; the rule of law on the basis (usually) of codes or constitutions; effective administration of its territory by a state; warfare conducted by a regular army; and freedom of conscience. The fundamental task of international law in this zone was to resolve conflicts between sovereign states in the absence of an overarching sovereign. Outside this sphere, the task was to define to terms upon which sovereignty – full or partial – might be bestowed. It was in the non-European world that the enormity of the task required in acquiring sovereignty could thus best be grasped. There, too, the potential costs – in terms of legalized violence – of failing to attain the standard of civilization were most evident.

Until well after the First World War, in fact, it was axiomatic that 'international law is a product of the special civilization of modern Europe itself'. Siam was admitted to the Hague conferences as a mark of respect; but in China, where the Boxer Rebellion was put down with enormous violence – on the grounds that it was 'an outrage against the comity of nations' – the unequal treaties remained in force. It was only the Japanese who seriously challenged the nineteenth-century identification of civilization with Christendom. Having adhered to several international conventions, and revised their civil and criminal codes, they managed to negotiate the repeal of the unequal treaties from 1894 onwards, as well as to win back control over their tariffs, and their victory over Russia in 1905 simply confirmed their status as a major power. Not surprisingly, the Young Turks – desperate to repeal the humiliating capitulations – could not hear enough of the Japanese success.

The Japanese achievement confirmed that the standard of civilization being offered by the powers was capable of being met by non-Christian, non-European states. But the Japanese achievement was also unique and precarious. After the ending of the Russo-Japanese War, the Second Hague Conference of 1907 talked of 'the interests of humanity, and the *ever progressive* needs of civilization'. But could civilization (with a capital C) really ever be universalized?

---

[8] A. Gray, 'West Africa', *Journal of the Society of Comparative Legislation* (1899), 129.

Doubts were growing. German and Italian jurists essentially ruled out any non-European power receiving *full* recognition; the prominent Russian jurist de Martens was equally emphatic. As for the empire builders, in Africa, in particular, as well as in the Pacific, many liberals and Gladstonians came to terms with imperialism at century's end – as Saul Dubow has recently reminded us – because they thought in terms of a kind of an imperial cosmopolitanism or commonwealth, in which individual peoples might preserve their own distinctive cultures. Where necessary, of course, civilized powers had to rule others to ensure this.[9]

Although it inherited many of these ways of imagining the relationship between empire and sovereignty, the League of Nations, established at Versailles after the First World War, adapted and transformed the idea of international civilization. A permanent international organization whose members included Abyssinia, Siam, Iran and Turkey was already something with a very different global reach from the old European conference. That was chiefly thanks to the Americans, not the British, whose schemes for a beefed-up version of the old Concert of Europe were shot down by the heavier firepower of messianic Wilsonian liberalism; Whitehall's idea for an international organization run by a small group of select powers lost out to his vision of 'a *general* association of nations'.

Sovereignty was henceforth explicitly shaped by the doctrine of national self-determination in its most anti-autocratic and optimistic guise so that the task for the civilized nations became that of guiding the less, or uncivilized, into the way of *national* self-realization. 'Imperialism' was suddenly once more a term of rebuke, and trusteeship and mandates became – in the minds at least of some idealistic or self-deluded British civil servants – something entirely different from prewar empire building.[10]

On the other hand, the new Society of Nations in Geneva still depended on the same civilizational hierarchies that had underpinned so much pre-1914 liberal thought: The peace settlement made this *crystal* clear. (Curzon was more honest than his colleagues when he remarked that the British were supporting the doctrine of self-determination because they believed they would benefit more from it than anyone else.) In eastern Europe, the victors at Versailles bestowed sovereignty upon the so-called New States, but insisted upon instituting League oversight of their protection of the rights of their national minorities. Should the new minorities rights regime be imposed on established defeated states such as Germany? That was not deemed necessary, still less to universalize it to apply to Britain, France or the United States.

---

[9] S. Dubow, 'The New Age of Imperialism?' Professorial lecture, Sussex, 19 Oct. 2004; see also R. Koebner and H. Dan Schmidt, *Imperialism: The Story and Significance of a Political Word, 1840–1960* (Cambridge, 1965).

[10] A. Zimmern, *The League of Nations and the Rule of Law, 1918–1935* (1936); James C. Hales, 'The Reform and Extension of the Mandate System', *Transactions of the Grotius Society* (1940), 153–210; W. Roger Louis, 'Great Britain and the African Peace Settlement of 1919', *American Historical Review*, 71:3 (1966), 875–892, here 875.

Minority rights were, in other words, a badge of the new states' secondary and relatively uncivilized status, their need for tutelage in the exercise of their own sovereignty. This was bad enough for East European politicians, but it was considerably less humiliating than the fate assigned to those outside Europe. In Egypt, which was not, of course, a mandate, the British imprisoned the leading Egyptian nationalists and made it clear that Wilson's new dawn did not apply to them. Not surprisingly, what one historian calls 'the Wilsonian moment' was greeted with demonstrations and protests from North Africa to China. Even Japanese diplomats felt rebuffed when their proposed racial equality clause was summarily dismissed by the British and the Americans.[11]

The other former Ottoman lands were brought within the new mandate system whose tripartite system classified non-European societies on the basis of their likely proximity to 'existence as independent nations'. The Arab provinces of the Middle East became Class A mandates – to the fury of their inhabitants, whereas former German colonial possessions in central Africa and elsewhere were placed in the B and C classes, to be administered as 'a sacred trust for civilization' until such time as, in the long-distance future, they might be fit to govern themselves. Smuts, a powerful influence on the mandate system as a whole, and keen to see the dominions allowed to acquire colonial possessions themselves, thought the time was never: The B and C class colonies were 'inhabited by barbarians, who not only cannot possibly govern themselves but to whom it would be impracticable to apply any ideas of political self-determination in the European sense'.[12]

All of this was, for British liberal imperialists, at least, still entirely in harmony with the idea of spreading civilization around the world. They hailed victory over the Germans in 1918 as confirmation of the fundamental harmony between empire – at least in its British incarnation – and the spread of civilized values. The Round Table group offered Britain as a moral example for the world and saw empire as a way of defending the weak against the unscrupulous. It was, essentially, an exercise in altruism. In his 1919 *The Expansion of Europe*, the 'forgotten giant' of interwar British liberalism, Ramsay Muir, described the empire as the 'supreme expression of the very spirit of Liberalism' and thought the British victory would allow 'the victory of Western civilization', by allowing that 'extension of the influence of European civilization over the whole world' that had been such a feature of the previous centuries. People wrongly dismissed this process, he went on, as 'imperialism' – a term suggesting 'brute force, regardless of the rights of conquered peoples'. In fact, it was all for the best: 'the civilization of Europe has been made into the civilization of the world'. The philosopher Alfred Whitehead was similarly optimistic. In his 1933

[11] E. Manela, 'The Wilsonian Moment and the Rise of Anticolonial Nationalism: The Case of Egypt', *Diplomacy and Statecraft*, 12:4 (2001), 99–122; N. Shimazu, *Japan, Race and Equality: The Racial Equality Proposal of 1919* (London, 1998).
[12] A. W. Brian Simpson, *Human Rights and the End of Empire: Britain and the Genesis of the European Convention* (Oxford, 2001), 146.

The Adventure of Ideas he depicted the rise of the West in terms of the spread of rights and the idea of freedom: 'The growth of the idea of the essential rights of human beings, arising from their sheer humanity affords a striking example in the history of ideas. Its formulation and its effective diffusion can be reckoned as a triumph – a chequered triumph – of the later phase of civilization'.[13]

Such confidence did not last long beyond Hitler's triumph. But even before then others, less wedded to empire, were driven to doubt. Some followed Freud's diagnosis: Civilization was a fragile crust barely covering harsher instincts shared by Europeans and non-Europeans alike. For others, the Bolshevik Revolution and the rise of socialism not only threatened bourgeois values, but could also be seen in racialized guise as the spearhead of an Asiatic threat to Europe. Meanwhile, Europe itself was tearing itself apart through political polarization, as the constitutional regimes established across the continent after 1919 gave way to varieties of right-wing authoritarianism. The crisis of democracy in Europe made liberals conscious that their own values and hierarchies of rights required extensive revaluation – replacing the old bourgeois stress on protection under the law with a new recognition of the lower classes' social and economic needs – if they were to compete in the modern world against the temptations of Left and Right. To be civilized, in the old liberal sense, was not necessarily to be modern – quite the contrary: It was to prioritize a set of civil liberties which many Marxist and fascist political theorists dismissed as antiquated and self-serving.

Fears of biological decline, intensified by the bloodletting of the war, also merged with vitalist conceptions of history to reinforce fears about Europe's waning position in the world. Spengler's gloomy survey confirmed the idea that its civilization faced inevitable organic decline. Race popularizers such as Lothrop Stoddard warned of the white man's peril in the face of the teeming hordes of the coloured races and saw civilization as leading to a 'growing underclass of individuals who cannot keep up'. Common to both was a deep anxiety about cultural and social mixing and a sense of foreboding as power shifted toward what the classicist and League activist Gilbert Murray called 'the politically immature peoples of the world'. Like his friend Jan Smuts, Murray was deeply worried that 'the domination of the white races was shaken'. Who else had the power or the essential fairness of mind to distribute the world's territories fairly, to apportion the Middle East between Turks and Armenians, Jew and Arabs, so that each would have a national home where they might flourish and play their part in the 'ultimate solidarity among the peoples of the world'. Paternalism and the language of humanity fused here so deeply as to be inextricable.[14]

[13] R. Muir, *The Expansion of Europe* (London, 1919), xi, 2; see also R. Grayson, *Liberals, International Relations and Appeasement: The Liberal Party 1919–1939* (London, 2001); Whitehead cited in C. Wilcox, *Robert Redfield and the Development of American Anthropology* (Lexington, Ky., 2004), 125–126.
[14] J. Morefield, *Covenants without Swords: Idealist Liberalism and the Spirit of Empire* (Princeton, 2005), 106–108.

Rather different in spirit was the Spengler-inspired work of Gilbert Murray's son-in-law, Arnold Toynbee. Toynbee too wanted to think through the implications of the war, but he sought to make Europeans realize that their civilization was merely one among many and to accept the loss of their central place in the world. Having imbibed ancient Greek at school, he saw the tragic cycle of Hellenic civilization as foreshadowing the fate of *all* future civilizations. 'I am conscious of having a certain "down" on Western civilization', Toynbee wrote to his father-in-law in 1930, attributing it 'partly to the effect of the War, which for anyone of my age, is bound to seem the chief expression of Western civilization, so far, in one's own lifetime, and partly it is the effect of a classical education'. But unlike Spengler, Toynbee did not see civilizations as closed – he did not share Spengler's Herderian conception of cultural unity – and he increasingly detected spiritual progress and meaning amid the collapse of defunct and exhausted civilizations.[15]

A not dissimilar discourse of civilizational relativity was also emerging from outside Europe at this time. The war had accentuated long-standing criticisms by Muslim, Chinese and Japanese intellectuals of the pretensions of Western claims to civilizational supremacy and in the immediate aftermath of the 'Wilsonian moment' many talked about Asia as an alternative civilizational force, one which – unlike the Europeans – would naturally fight for the 'rights of nations' around the globe. Tagore, for one, described the European conflict as suicidal, the product of excessive competitiveness and a love of violence fed by an addiction to industry and science.[16]

But as the 1920s went on, such talk subsided, and in any case, most European liberals were sublimely indifferent to extra-European critiques of this kind. They were, in this sense, Hegelians, uninterested in what one interwar historian termed 'all that human misery which prevails in the vast spaces of Asia, Africa and South America, where thousands of millions of men and women have lived, worked and died, leaving no memorial, contributing nothing to the future'[17]. What did give these latter-day Victorians pause for reflection was not Indian or Japanese criticism, nor even the rise of the USSR (hailed by the Webbs as a 'new civilization'), but the Nazi seizure of power in 1933. It was this that really worried the British historian H. A. L. Fisher as he completed his best-selling history of Europe. Sounding like some latter-day de Pradt, he insisted Britain should not withdraw from the Continent if it wished peace to be preserved. Yet it was as though the era that de Pradt had heralded more than a century earlier was drawing to a close. Fisher saw unavoidable threats to peace and liberty in modern science, which allowed new despotisms to tyrannize the masses – 'the spiritual servitude of the totalitarian state' – and permitted the destruction of entire cities by aerial bombing. His concluding plea that Europeans remember they were 'trustees for the civilization of the world'

[15] W. McNeill, *Arnold Toynbee: A Life* (Oxford, 1989), 161.
[16] Cemil Aydin, *The Politics of Anti-Westernism in Asia: Visions of World Order in Pan-Islamic and Pan-Asian Thought* (New York, 2007), 114.
[17] H.A.L. Fisher, *A History of Europe* (London, 1935), 3 vols. vol. 3, 1219.

sounds half-hearted and unconvinced. He was keenly aware that the peoples of the Continent had already once allowed their divisions to lead to conflict and that this had had a dramatic impact on the 'place of Europe in the world' and destroyed its 'moral unity'. Now, he wrote in 1935, it faced a choice: a new war which would lay 'civilization in ruins', or work toward a permanent organization of the peace, a new period of plenty and well-being.

The latter meant continuing to have confidence in the experiment of the League of Nations. But the expansion of the League had itself made it less acceptable to use the old Eurocentric language. In 1929, for instance, Sir John Fischer Williams confessed that 'the concept of "civilized society" as a community of nations or States distinct from the rest of the world no longer corresponds with the main facts of contemporary life'. According to a French jurist in 1930, 'The family of nations is the totality of states [civilized and uncivilized] and other subjects of international public law'. Writing in *The Listener*, Prof. H. A. Smith of London University drew attention to some of the consequences; the age of what we would call humanitarian interventionism was over: 'In practice, we no longer insist that States shall conform to any common standards of justice, religious toleration and internal government. Whatever atrocities may be committed in foreign countries, we now say that they are no concern of ours.... This means in effect that we have now abandoned the old distinction between civilized and uncivilized States'.[18]

Nazism's rise was particularly worrying because the Germans were among the most highly 'civilized' peoples of Europe, so civilized indeed that they had not been made subject to the minorities rights treaties at Versailles. The implications, therefore, of their rejection of the premises of international law were acute; the very foundations of the old system were being thrown into question from within Europe itself. 'European civilization has shaped modern International Law', noted a London University professor in 1938. 'But is European civilization still what it was, and if not, how do the changes affect international law?'[19] 'International law is seriously discredited and on the defensive', commented another. Cordell Hull, the U.S. Secretary of State warned, in an address of June 1938, of a world 'growing internationally more and more disordered and chaotic'. One of his assistants, Francis Sayre, followed a few days later: 'The supreme question which we and all the world face today is whether or not we are to live henceforth in a world of law or a world of international anarchy'.[20]

Of course, for many German jurists, this was a false dichotomy, or better, false consciousness. The world had always been shaped on the basis of power, and the language of international civilization and humanity had merely

---

[18] G. Schwarzenberger, 'The Rule of Law and the Disintegration of International Society', *Transactions of the Grotius Society*, 22 (1937), 66.

[19] Gong, *Standard of 'Civilization'*, 84–85; W. Friedmann, 'The Disintegration of European Civilization and the Future of International Law', *Modern Law Review* 194:2 (Dec. 1938), 194–214.

[20] Gong, *Standard of 'Civilization'*, 57; Schwarzenberger, 'The Rule of Law', 66.

masked the claim to power of the victors at Versailles. For Carl Schmitt, a state could try to identify itself with humanity 'in the same way as one can misuse peace, justice, progress and civilization in order to claim these as one's own and to deny the same to the enemy'. It was not just the Nazis' indifference to the premises of interwar liberal jurisprudence that was so fatal to the continued faith in the power of international law; it was the way they subverted the traditional division of the world between (civilized) Europe and (non-civilized) Rest. This was clear from the spring of 1939. By creating a protectorate out of much of prewar Czechoslovakia, they brought a colonial constitutional institution to Europe itself, and made it clear that they would treat their racial inferiors as colonial subjects. Churchill and others pretended that what was happening in Europe had no obvious relevance to the fate of the empires; but others knew better. Europeans, wrote Aime Cesaire, were learning what it was like to be treated as colonial subjects. Suddenly they were discovering the value of human rights. But could they seriously maintain the old dichotomy between the defence of rights at home and the deprivation of rights abroad?[21]

The short answer was: They could try. After the war, the United Nations committed itself to fighting for human rights, but it made no formal commitment to forcing imperial powers to disgorge their colonies. Empire, as Fred Cooper and Jane Burbank argue, was not doomed in 1945, or at least it did not seem so – and the new UN was certainly not initially an anti-imperial body. On the contrary, at San Francisco, the U.S. delegate Harold Stassen stated that it would be better for colonial peoples not to force issue of freedom: Better think about interdependence than independence. African and Asian journalists and commentators were deeply dismayed at the conservatism of what emerged. As they understood, the founders of the UN were trying their hardest to keep the Victorian civilizational dichotomy intact.

But by this point it had largely lost credibility. Few talked any longer as though there was a single civilization, let alone a single standard. International law, which had elaborated this, was in disarray; one of the conditions for the new international organization to work was its much weaker legal regime compared with its predecessor; far fewer legal shackles bound the Great Powers in particular in 1945 than had done so in 1919. It was the very opposite of what a latter-day Victorian such as international lawyer Hersch Lauterpacht had predicted or wanted; in his 1943 paper on the rights of man, he had argued that recognition of the fundamental rights of man had become a general constitutional principle of the law of 'civilized states'. But this was perhaps to mistake the wish for the deed, for the enforceable rights regime that he had called for never came into existence. He and others (such as Quincy Wright) had hoped to see new the new international organization defending rights against tyrannical national states. Instead what they got was a body committed even more than its

[21] Schmitt in Koskenniemi, *Gentle Civiliser of Nations*, 433.

predecessor to the sanctity of state sovereignty – and this was not compatible with the sort of civilizational intervention that had been routine before 1914. The 1948 Declaration on Human Rights, as Lauterpacht despondently noted, was little more than decoration – a substitute for a real legally binding commitment and a retreat from the minority rights regime of the interwar era.[22]

Some commentators, such as Ian Brownlie, have recognized that the collapse of the standard of civilization created a normative vacuum at the UN – for states were no longer united by virtue of regarding one another as 'civilized' members of the same moral community. On the contrary, the term in its original usage was denounced as insulting, and UN General Assembly resolutions specified that claims about the level of civilizational backwardness could not be allowed to delay grants of independence. Brownlie argues that by the mid-1960s at the latest, respect for human rights had come to serve as a successor norm for the international community. Indeed, one participant in the drafting of the Universal Declaration itself had segued neatly from one norm to the other, arguing that 'civilized states' were to be equated with respect for 'fundamental human rights'.[23]

But this was to move too fast, for the concept of civilization itself was being transformed under the pressure of the Cold War; it was being used in a newly partial way, and increasingly relativized. Even before the war, as faith in the League of Nations and the rule of international law had waned, liberals using the language of civilization had cast it in increasingly spiritual terms. They had talked about the development of an 'international mind' as an emanation of the Spirit beyond the state. Such talk became part of the West's reinvention of itself during the Cold War. In the crucial months of 1947 and 1948 that lay between the Truman Doctrine and the Treaty of Brussels, the idea that the United States and Western Europe were joined in some kind of a 'spiritual union' crept into speeches on either side of the Atlantic. Truman praised American 'faith' in the face of godless Bolshevism. In London Ernest Bevin talked up Britain as the bastion of Western civilization. Following the collapse of the London conference of foreign ministers at the end of 1947, he told George Marshall that 'he now felt that the spiritual consolidation of western civilization was possible' and suggested a kind of 'spiritual federation of the West'.[24]

The Oxford historian Ernest Woodward echoed such thoughts in the lectures he gave at this juncture on 'the heritage of Western civilization'. A western tradition, he reminded his audiences, had emerged relatively recently – perhaps only with what people just at this time starting to call the 'scientific revolution'. But it was a religious tradition as well as a technological one, and it had to be defended against totalitarian materialism. America would have

---

[22] Ibid., 391–395.
[23] Cited in Gong, *Standard of Civilization*, 90–91.
[24] Dianne Kirby, 'Divinely Sanctioned: The Anglo-American Cold War Alliance and the Defence of Western Civilization and Christianity', *Journal of Contemporary History*, 35:3 (July 2000), 385–412.

to save Europe; for this was in its own interest and for the sake of the 'good life' of the entire world.[25]

In this way, *Western* civilization – a term which asserted America's role as heir to a fading Europe – became part of a beleaguered liberal tradition's struggle against totalitarianism. American intellectuals were especially prone, naturally, to such a view, especially as they tended to worry about what one might call a spirituality deficit in a culture increasingly defined for its technological and especially industrial character. The United States could preserve European values and save its soul in the process. In 1941, perhaps the most prominent exponent of this view, the Chicago professor John Neff, founded the Committee on the Study of Civilization (note the singular). He had long been arguing that the United States had to save civilization as it collapsed in Europe, and that American universities in particular needed to act as agents of spiritual transformation, preaching truth and the universal values embodied in the Western canon. (Neff was persuaded to change the title to the more neutral Committee on Social Thought, in which form it survives to this day at the University of Chicago.)

But others found this kind of moral absolutism anachronistic and parochial. The dominant paradigm in American international relations thought in the 1950s moved in an entirely different direction, toward the kind of Schmittian-inflected cult of the national interest, of realism, propounded by Hans Morgenthau, Henry Kissinger and others. In realist thought there was little or no space for civilizational aspirations and the moral certainty that accompanied them. And even those who did take the idea of civilization seriously saw the postwar globalization of the idea of humanity – the extension of the idea of the Family of Man into the colonial Third World – as something which necessitated a much greater modesty about the pretensions of Western or European civilization itself.

Toynbee, for one, agreed that the world could not afford for European civilization to be 'snuffed out'; but he was increasingly alarmed by the messianism he detected among the American enthusiasts for western civilization. 'I suppose it is the first phase of a coming American world empire', he grumbled to Gilbert Murray at the time of the Truman Doctrine, which had been talked up in *Time* magazine – in an article on Toynbee – as 'a crisis in Western civilization itself'. Soon he was worrying about American belligerence, a much greater threat in his view than the Russians. By the time of his controversial 1952 Reith Lectures, Toynbee was portraying Russia as one among the many victims of western aggression and arguing that 'Western imperialism, not Russian communism, is Enemy no.1 for the majority of the human race'. Humanity had to place its faith, not in the United Nations – which he saw as a political association that would probably not outlast the breakup of the wartime alliance – but in the idea that 'a unified world gradually works its

[25] E. L.Woodward, 'The Heritage of Western Civilisation', *International Affairs*, 25:2 (April 1949), 140–145.

way towards an equilibrium between its diverse component cultures'. This was a task that fell to academics who had to help people escape the 'prison walls of the local and short-lived histories of our own countries and our own cultures' and accustom them to 'taking a synoptic view of history as a whole'. Only in this way could one harness the 'unprecedented degree of humanitarian feeling' that had arisen, the 'recognition of the human rights of people of all classes, nations and races'. After all, Western civilization might have unified the world; but in this world, the eighteen non-Western civilizations that Toynbee had identified (four living, fourteen extinct) 'will assuredly reassert their influence'.[26]

It was Neff's Chicago colleague, the anthropologist Robert Redfield, who took up Toynbee's challenge and tried to put the study of world civilizations on a scientific basis. Redfield had come to see that 'folk cultures' were themselves worthy of study in the way they interacted with the forces of social and technical change to produce what he called 'new moral orders'. Civilizational development did not lead to a single set of values – as Neff asserted – nor to disbelief, psychic disequilibrium and confusion, as the Freudians believed. Rather, civilizations were multiple – formed out of the interaction of Western technology and moral belief systems. As an alternative to Neff's Committee on Social Thought, Redfield founded a Comparative Civilizations project. Its purpose, or so he told his backers, was to 'move towards a better understanding of that humanity which is widespread or universal, and on which a world community must rest'. Neff's approach to civilization focused on European high culture; Redfield's blurred the distinction between culture (from the bottom up, best studied in the village) and (urban) civilization, and redirected attention away from Europe, toward India, China and the Middle East in particular.[27] Inside the universities, this sort of approach fed into the development of area studies and courses on 'non-Western civilizations', while the moral certainties that had underpinned the old Victorian standard of civilization were now decried as unscientific idealism by a new generation of social scientists. Civilization met social science and dissolved increasingly into the more comfortable language of culture.[28]

After 1945, therefore, claims to civilization were made in a very different, and much less propitious, context for interventionist policies than had been the case. The old standard of civilization had made being civilized the precondition for recognizing states as independent; now, during the Cold War, independence was granted in the context of a struggle between rival claimants to European civilizational superiority (the United States and the USSR).

[26] McNeill, *Arnold Toynbee*, 218–225; Toynbee, *Civilisation on Trial: Essays* (New York, 1948), 158.
[27] Wilcox, *Robert Redfield and the Development of American Anthropology*, 139–140.
[28] As it did in the 2001 UN International Conference on the Dialogue of Civilizations, which equated the concept of civilization with that of culture.

Civilization – increasingly parsed in less morally loaded terms as the condition of being modern – was something to be attained with the help of technical and social scientific expertise *after independence* by a means of state policy and external assistance. But what did civilization in the new Cold War sense actually mean? Rationality, the defence of property rights, to be sure; and liberty? Initially yes, but as modernization theorists came to entertain doubts about the capacity of Third World countries to modernize under democratic leadership, the spread of liberty came to be equated with defence of property rights against communism and the leadership of army generals and dictators.

In this postwar world, law and claims of ethical superiority no longer offered justifications for intervention, least of all to defend rights. As the number of sovereign states mushroomed, pressure on states to expand the realm of rights depended more than ever on public opinion – domestic and foreign, sometimes swept up into the official policy of states, at others expressed through newly powerful NGOs such as Amnesty International. As international organizations such as the UN backtracked from earlier more interventionist regimes where sovereignty was concerned, it was NGOs that acted as chief defenders of individuals and collective groups against their own states, but this was a much weaker kind of defence.

In short, the collapse of the old civilizational certainties both fostered a more global sense of international community and simultaneously weakened the system's capacity to force through observation of rights of various kinds. A combination of NGOs and rhetorical exhortation made little headway against the spread of sovereign states in the former colonial world. The European Convention showed that states *could* derogate powers to a genuinely enforceable rights regime, but this regional arrangement was the exception, not the rule. Perhaps this brief sketch helps explain why, in the 1990s, with the re-emergence of genocide as an international problem, frustration with the UN's inability to respond adequately fed calls for a new basis for intervention, new criticisms of the doctrine of sovereign sanctity, and calls for some kind of return to an idealized version of nineteenth-century liberal imperial crusades. Currently one reads about demands to replace – or supplement (but doesn't it come to the same thing?) – the UN with a 'league of democracies' that can act when state leaders sacrifice their right to rule by failing to respond to humanitarian crises. Here too the sovereignty criterion is under challenge. But that is not so surprising as the way proponents of such arrangements unproblematically return to the language of civilizational superiority in the name of defending rights. It is hard, I think, if the kind of conceptual trajectory I have outlined here has any validity, to avoid seeing such moves, for all their self-proclaimed practicality, as exercises in nostalgia for a world centred on Europe and 'European values' (whatever those may be thought to be) at the very moment when the world is moving in a different direction.

2

The "Human Rights Revolution" at Work

Displaced Persons in Postwar Europe

G. Daniel Cohen

"When this ghastly war ends," gloomily predicted Franklin D. Roosevelt in October 1939, "there may be not one million but ten million or twenty million men, women and children belonging to many races ... who will enter into the wide picture – the problem of the human refugee."[1] Six and a half years later, Eleanor Roosevelt confirmed the forecast of her then deceased husband. "A new type of political refugee is appearing," she wrote in February 1946, "people who have been against the present governments and if they stay at home or go home will probably be killed."[2] To be sure, these statements could have adequately described earlier instances of forced displacement, none the least the refugee exodus from the Reich of the late 1930s. But although continental Europe had been awash with stateless and exiled people from the end of the First World War to the advent of Nazism, the presidential couple envisioned "the problem of the human refugee" as an impending postwar crisis more than the continuation of an older phenomenon. Two decades of isolationism and restrictive immigration quotas may have blinded American eyes to the magnitude of European displacement prior to 1939. The prospect of renewed American engagement with the world, however, revived strong interest for "Europe on the move." Observing this phenomenon at both ends of the conflict, Franklin and Eleanor Roosevelt were undoubtedly right: the scale of the European refugee problem at the end of the Second World War went beyond anything seen before.

Writing on the eve of Victory in Europe, Hannah Arendt similarly reflected upon the impending refugee crisis. "It would be a good thing," she observed in April 1945, "if it were generally admitted that the end of the war in Europe will not automatically return thirty to forty million exiles to their homes." And then the former refugee from Nazi Germany divulged one of the greatest challenges the authorities would face:"[A] very large proportion," she warned, "will

[1] *The New York Times*, October 18, 1939.
[2] Quoted by Mary Ann Langdon, *A World Made New. Eleanor Roosevelt and the Universal Declaration of Human Rights* (New York, 2001), 29.

45

regard repatriation as deportation and will insist on retaining their statelessness." Arendt had evidently in mind the yet unquantified Jewish survivors
of the Final Solution but also referred to other types of anti-Soviet Eastern
European displaced persons (DPs). Altogether, she presciently pointed out,
"the largest group of potentially stateless people is to be found in Germany
itself."[3] Contrary to the military and humanitarian focus on population management, Arendt believed that the "DP problem" was first and foremost political in nature. From 1946 to the end of the decade, the vocal and conspicuous
"last million" of Europe's DPs – a multinational group of Jewish and non-
Jewish asylum seekers unwilling or unable to go home – amply corroborated
her predictions.

Indeed, the "DP story" comprised two distinct chronological sequences,
one logistical and one more markedly political. It is generally assumed that
at the end of the war there were approximately eight million civilians in
Germany who qualified as "displaced persons" under the United Nations
Relief and Rehabilitation Administration (UNRRA, 1943–1947) and Allied
military directives: foreign workers, slave laborers, prisoners of war, and liberated concentration camp inmates formed the bulk of this predominantly
Eastern European population. Between the spring and the fall of 1945, six to
seven million DPs were returned to their countries of origins – forcibly and
often tragically in the case of Soviet nationals. Yet in September 1945, 1.2 million refugees still remained in Western Allied hands. As it became increasingly
clear to humanitarian personnel and Allied military commanders at the start
of 1946, return rates significantly dwindled among the remaining DPs. Their
refusal to go home, routinely analyzed by various surveys, was motivated by
political, economic, or psychological factors. Combined with fresh arrivals
from beyond the "iron curtain," the diminishing appeal of repatriation facilitated the long-term presence of one million DPs in occupied Germany (small
numbers of refugees also lived in the DP camps of Austria and Italy). Brought
to Germany by the Nazis as foreign workers and slave laborers, 400,000
Poles and Polish-Ukrainians amounted in March 1946 to nearly 50 percent
of the DP population (Polish-Ukrainians were later independently classified
as "Ukrainians"). From 150,000 to 200,000 Estonians, Lithuanians, and
Latvians formed a sizeable Baltic group, including former Wehrmacht con-
scripts and volunteers, migrant workers, and slave laborers as well as civilians
who fled the advance of the Red Army. In early 1946, Holocaust survivors
represented less than 10 percent of the overall DP population. But to the small
group of Jews liberated by the Allies in the spring of 1945 was gradually added
a substantial number of postwar Jewish "infiltrees," predominantly of Polish
origin: At the peak period of 1947–1948, approximately 200,000 Jewish refugees lived in the American occupation zone of Germany. Alongside these main
groups whose size constantly evolved because of repatriation, emigration,

---

[3] Hannah Arendt, "The Stateless People," *Contemporary Jewish Record*, 8 (April 1945),
    137–153.

and the entrance of newcomers, small numbers of anticommunist Yugoslavs, Slovaks, Hungarians, and other Eastern European nationals completed the demographic makeup of the "last million."[4]

Like many contemporary statistics documenting the DP world, this figure, if never far from the reality, was not always accurate. The International Refugee Organization (1946–1952), the agency created by the United Nations to care for the ever-fluctuating "last million," generally added prewar refugees and other European stateless persons situated outside of Germany in order to round up this tally. But without much empirical distortion, the IRO could safely advertise the DPs to the world as the "last million" of refugees from the Second World War desperately searching for asylum countries. Emblematic of the longer political sequence of postwar displacement, this expression essentially pertained to Holocaust survivors and non-Jewish anticommunist refugees, the two distinct components of a DP camp system that stretched from northern Germany to Sicily.

The history of postwar refugees has been thoroughly documented by the official historians of the humanitarian agencies in charge of the DPs. More recently, scholars have delved into the records of these organizations to cast new light on the DP experience in postwar Germany and Austria, whether by focusing on particular nationalities or by offering a more comprehensive view.[5] Recent or more dated, most accounts predominantly concentrate on the humanitarian aspect of "relief and rehabilitation." Undeniably, the difficult delivery of food rations, health care, or housing accommodations amid the material devastation of postwar Germany remained a daunting challenge for the charity organizations and international agencies entrusted with this mission. "Surely in recorded history," observed the head of UNRRA "Displaced Persons" division in 1947, "there has been no group of unwilling migrants that has posed such complex problems."[6] But whereas the DP episode provided the arena for the largest humanitarian intervention in the immediate postwar years, it also informed the rise of the human rights movement characteristic of the 1940s. "Today," Hannah Arendt observed in 1949, "the whole question of the Rights of Man has taken a new life and pertinence." This new concern was partly due to the interwar "emergence of an entirely new category of human beings ... who do not possess citizenship" but also to the "new millions of displaced persons" added by "the events of the forties." The DPs, argued Arendt, propelled human rights to the center of postwar international politics: "[T]he problem of statelessness on so large a scale had the effect of confronting the nations of the world with an inescapable and perplexing question: whether or not there really exist such 'human rights'

[4] George Woodbridge, *UNRRA. The History of the United Nations Relief and Rehabilitation Administration*, vol. 3 (New York, 1950), 423.
[5] The most thorough overview to date is Mark Wyman, *DPs: Europe's Displaced Persons 1945–1951*, 2nd ed. (Ithaca, N.Y., 1998).
[6] Fred Hoehler, "Displaced Persons," in George B. Huszar (ed.), *Persistent International Issues* (New York, 1947), 10.

independent of all specific political status and deriving solely from the fact of being human?"[7] For contemporary international jurists, the "DP question" – namely, the fact that nearly a million people refused, for various reasons, to abide by the directives of their national government – reflected one of the main features of the postwar human rights agenda: the curtailment of state sovereignty in favor of the rights of individuals. "Behind the affairs of people deported and exiled from their homes," wrote a legal scholar in 1948, "there is the chief question of the relation of the individuals towards the international community."[8]

Although seldom used by the activists and political actors of the 1940s, the expression "human rights revolution" is commonly employed today to describe the advent of the human rights era in the aftermath of the Second World War. According to this widely held view, it was during this pivotal decade that a handful of dedicated "visionaries," not all of them of Western origin, mounted a successful assault against the old concept of state sovereignty: Following the "gathering storm" of the interwar years and the ideological "crusade" of the wartime period, the "revolution" launched in 1945 challenged the "Leviathan-state" to curtail some of its traditional prerogatives in favor of the rights of individual citizens.[9] In this evolutionary narrative, the predominantly "juridical revolution" of the postwar years allegedly laid the groundwork for subsequent "advocacy" and "enforcement" phases in the last decades of the twentieth century.[10] The idealist celebration of human rights as the "idea of our time," particularly prevalent in the West since the end of the Cold War, hinges therefore on a revolutionary reading of the 1940s: Against overwhelming odds and despite many contradictions (such as the persistence of racial segregation in the United States and of European rule in the colonial world), human rights became at that time a matter of international responsibility by challenging the nation-state's monopoly on the conduct of international affairs.

Realist-minded writers have recently cautioned against idealization and morality tales. The emergence of international human rights, they maintain, was not the sole product of tenacious visionaries bent on creating "fire-walls against barbarism"; nor was it only spurred, as idealists contend, by a "war-weary generation's reflection on European nihilism and its consequences."[11] The historian and legal scholar A. W. Brian Simpson, for instance, argued in a detailed study that the meteoric rise of human rights after 1945 primarily resulted from "complicated interrelationships between individuals and institutions, and governments, with their varied ideological commitments

---

[7] Hannah Arendt, "'The Rights of Man'. What Are They?" *Modern Review*, 3 (1949), 24–37.
[8] Eduard Reut-Nicolussi, "Displaced Persons and International Law," in *Recueil de Cours*. Institut de droit international (Paris, 1948), 64.
[9] Paul Gordon Lauren, *The Evolution of International Human Rights* (Philadelphia, 1998), 130–205.
[10] Michael Ignatieff, *Human Rights as Politics and Idolatry* (Princeton, 2001), 5.
[11] Ibid., 4.

and perceptions of reality, history and self interest."[12] For Mark Mazower, pragmatic calculations chiefly accounted for the widespread preoccupation with human rights during and after the Second World War. Rather than a smiling revolution in moral standards, the dawn of the human rights age was a "strange triumph" largely made possible by the desire of the Great Powers and many small nations alike to finish off the moribund interwar system of minority rights in favor of more expedient individual rights, abstract enough to be safely embraced. Thus staunch advocates of mass expulsions of ethnic minorities, such as the Czechoslovak leader Edvard Beneš, could at the same time ardently champion "a Charter of Human Rights throughout the world" for the postwar era. Seen in this light, the ideology of human rights paradoxically reinforced – as much as it sought to restrict – the supremacy of state interest.[13]

Nonetheless, one common feature unites these diverging lines of interpretation: Whether critical or apologetic, assessments of the "revolution" primarily focus on the motivations of the drafters rather than on the actual enforcers of human rights. This imbalance is easily justifiable: As pointed out by most international jurists in the 1940s and 1950s, the international proclamation of human rights, resounding as it may have been, was noticeably devoid of enforcement mechanisms. As the renowned international lawyer Hersch Lauterpacht pointed out in 1947, the cautious refusal of the United Nations Commission of Human Rights to recognize the right of individual citizens to petition the world organization against abusing states significantly weakened the challenge against national sovereignty.[14] The French jurist René Cassin, and with him a substantial number of legal commentators, opposed this pessimism: "From one side of the world to the other and from the bottom to the top of the social ladder, workers on strike, victims of racial and religious discrimination, persecuted intellectuals ... all invoke with great hope this Universal Declaration." Yet Cassin readily admitted that this landmark document, as its preamble stated, set only "a common standard of achievement for all people and all nations" to be attained in the future. For the time being, he recognized, the Declaration – including its important provisions regarding refugees and political asylum – served only as "a magnet and a goal for the aspirations of mankind."[15] Despite the efforts deployed by the United Nations to underscore the impact of the Universal Declaration and encourage the worldwide celebration of a newly created "Human Rights Day" (1949), the "revolution" of the 1940s was overwhelmingly perceived by its advocates

---

[12] A. W. Brian Simpson, *Human Rights and the End of Empire. Britain and the Genesis of the European Convention* (New York, 2001), vii.

[13] Mark Mazower, "The Strange Triumph of Human Rights, 1933–1950," *Historical Journal*, 47 (2004), 379–398.

[14] Herch Lauterpacht, *International Law and Human Rights* (London, 1950), 397.

[15] René Cassin, "La déclaration universelle et la mise en oeuvre des droits de l'homme," in *Académie de droit international. Receuil de cours*, vol. 2 (The Hague, 1951), 239–267.

and critics alike as being more declarative than legislative, more suggestive than binding.[16]

The limited number of nongovernmental organizations (NGOs) specifically concerned at the time with international human rights further prevented the "revolution" from being fully put into force. As opposed to the thousands of human rights NGOs operating in the world today, only a handful of such organizations were in existence in the mid-1940s. The most prominent among them, the New York–based International League for the Rights of Man and the Paris-based Fédération Internationale des Droits de l'Homme, epitomized the historical and geographical continuity uniting the "human rights revolution" of the 1940s with the "Atlantic revolutions" of the late eighteenth century. But like the more numerous (and predominantly American) civic, religious, labor, educational, or women's organizations enlisted by the United Nations to participate in the drafting of human rights, their role remained essentially consultative. Indeed, as a study by William Korey indicates, the first postwar NGOs saw standard setting as their main priority: namely, "the establishment of international norms by which the conduct of states can be measured or judged."[17] As such, early NGOs may well have "revolutionized the language of international relations, which statesmen of an earlier era and even some of the recent period would have found strange and unacceptable."[18] But until the later appearance of more militant watchdogs committed to fact -finding and implementation – such as Amnesty International after its creation in 1961 – the "enforcement revolution," facilitated by the détente era and the unraveling of the Cold War, still remained a fairly distant prospect.

The history of DPs in postwar Europe, however, complicates this established chronology. As the following essay argues, the DP experience immediately put to test the language of human rights hammered out in the 1940s. Deemed by the Big Powers "the most important show on earth" despite the fact that from China to India/Pakistan and the Middle East mass displacement spanned a large part of the globe between 1945 and 1949, Europe's DPs provided the first concrete field of experimentation for postwar human rights principles. The international agencies in charge, alongside Allied military authorities, of the governance of European refugees in occupied Germany and Austria – including, during the peak period of 1947–1948, approximately 250,000 Jewish refugees and Holocaust survivors – enforced some of the most important rights forged and adopted by the United Nations. The right of everyone "to leave any country" (Article 13 of the 1948 Universal Declaration), "to seek and enjoy in other countries asylum from persecution"(Article 14), and "to a nationality"(Article 15) all directly pertained to the ongoing DP crisis;

[16] United Nations, Department of Social Affairs, *The Impact of the Universal Declaration* (New York, 1951).
[17] William Korey, *NGOs and the Universal Declaration of Human Rights* (New York, 1998), 3.
[18] Ibid.

and so did newly proclaimed guarantees against arbitrary deprivation of citizenship and state interference with freedom of movement, opinion, and faith. Displacement, in short, prominently loomed in the background of human rights activism; it also served as an important testing ground for the new principles set forth in the international arena.

To make sense of the relationship between the "revolution" and this laboratory phase of modern political asylum, I will examine how some of the main human rights principles discussed throughout the decade were implemented, or at times bypassed, in the Western management of forced displacement. The governance of DPs served as an immediate echo chamber for the language of human rights in the 1940s. The affirmation of a new relationship between individuals and states, the universal scope of individual rights, and the lingering question of protection of minorities not only were issues debated by visionaries, drafters, and international delegates in lengthy deliberations, but also directly pertained to the lives of postwar European refugees.

Individuals versus Nation-States

The Second World War seriously challenged the idea that the normal place for citizens is within the territory of their state. The rough estimate of seven to eleven million DPs found by the Western Allies in the course of their push to Berlin was a vivid illustration of this new possibility. Postwar Germany, one historian observed, unexpectedly became the "unlikely host to hundreds of thousands of its former victims," including Jews, concentration camps inmates, and forced laborers, mostly regrouped in the American and British occupation zones.[19] The nation-state order, however, was promptly reasserted: Most DPs voluntarily returned home in the summer and fall of 1945. For Soviet nationals, unfortunate "pawns of Yalta," return was compulsory.[20] Under UNRRA, an agency curbed to allied military control, the overall policy was to repatriate all (non-Jewish) DPs to their country of origin as a means to swiftly eliminate the disrupting effects of the Second World War. Repatriation was supposed to be voluntary, but because of Grand Alliance considerations, Soviet nationals (most of them liberated POWs) were initially targeted for forcible return "home," where they more often than not faced execution, deportation, or retribution.[21] The recognition of the individual's rights against the omnipotence of the state –one of the key human rights principles of the postwar era – was therefore blatantly violated by Western powers despite the multiple references to human rights contained in the Charter of the United Nations adopted at

---

[19] Atina Grossmann, "Victims, Villains, and Survivors: Gendered Perceptions and Self-Perceptions of Jewish Displaced Persons in Occupied Post-War Germany," *Journal of the History of Sexuality*, 11 (2002), 291–318.

[20] Mark R. Elliott, *Pawns of Yalta. Soviet Refugees and America's Role in Their Repatriation* (Urbana, Ill., 1982).

[21] Pavel Polian, *Deportiert nach Hause. Sowjetische Kriegsgefangene im "Dritten Reich" und ihre Repatriierung* (Munich, 2001).

the San Francisco Conference in June 1945. At the end of the Second World War, Allied repatriation policies still reflected the enduring supremacy of state sovereignty in the emerging postwar order.

However, the policy of forcible return eventually subsided with the rise of Cold War tensions. In February 1946, a UN resolution stipulated that DPs who expressed "valid objections" to returning to Soviet bloc countries should not be compelled to do so: Repatriation was from then on a free offer to all DPs. Even if claimed by their countries of origin –for punishment and/or reconstruction purposes – DPs found in the network of UNRRA camps in Germany a protective environment. The pace of voluntary repatriation dramatically dwindled in 1946, when it became clear that most of the remaining DPs refused to go home. As one of the first historians of DPs pointed out, it then "dawned upon Allied authorities that repatriation would no longer be acceptable for this group."[22] In December 1946, the International Refugee Organization (IRO) was created by the United Nations (without the support of the Soviet bloc) to find resettlement solutions for the DPs. Free from military control, the IRO was a modern-type agency imbued with internationalist spirit. In Germany, the IRO became in charge of nearly a million refugees composed of Poles, Jews, Ukrainians, and nationals of the Baltic states who refused or were simply unable to return "home." Many factors accounted for this refusal: for Jewish Holocaust survivors, the resurgence of anti-Semitism in Poland and a desire to "divorce Europe"; for Baltic and Ukrainian DPs, the fear of Soviet retribution and strong nationalism; for Poles, anti-communism as well as straightforward economic motives; and for all, the continuation of a century-old East–West migration trend.

Placed under the Western guardianship of the IRO after 1947, the "last million" of the DPs experienced the advent of a new and more balanced relationship between individuals and states: With repatriation no longer an option, the DPs were indeed free to opt (if accepted by a host country) for citizenship elsewhere, Israel or the New World in most cases. As such, they became the first group to concretely and simultaneously realize a possibility inscribed in Article 15 of the UN Declaration: "No one shall be denied the right to change his nationality." The recognition of the right to secede from a state ("the right to leave a country" in the Declaration) reflected the increasing Western awareness of the repressive nature of Soviet communism and of the desire of Holocaust survivors to leave Europe behind. But if postwar European refugees became subjects of international law, it is also because of a groundbreaking shift in internationalist politics: the collapse of minority rights into individual rights, one of the main staples of the "human rights revolution."

A predominant view in the scholarship of human rights history is that this shift occurred in the early 1940s, when Great Powers politicians and

---

[22] Wolfgang Jacobmeyer, "The Displaced Persons Problem: Repatriation and Resettlement," in Johannes-Dieter Steinert and Inge Weber-Newth (eds.), *European Immigrants in Britain 1933–1950* (Munich, 2003), 137–149.

"visionaries" alike seized upon the war to devise a different future by shy-ing away from the League of Nation's failed system of minority protection.[23] Alongside philosophical idealism and a desire to demarcate the West from totalitarian tyranny, political pragmatism loomed large behind the wartime acceptance to let the interwar minority treaties die an unlamented death. Some wartime proponents of individual human rights, such as the Czech leader Eduard Beneš, were at the same time planning the eviction of ethnic minorities (in this case, ethnic German) after the defeat of Nazism. "Behind the smoke-screen of the rights of the individuals," caustically writes Mark Mazower, "the corpse of the League's minorities policy could be safely buried."[24]

It is significant, however, that former political refugees stood among the most idealistic supporters of individual rights. To be sure, not all refugee law-yers, scholars, or activists were enthusiastic about the individualization of human rights. Raphael Lemkin's intense preoccupation with genocide (which the Polish refugee lawyer framed as the murder of a *group*, not of a mere aggregate of *individuals*) was very much at odds, politically and culturally, with the individualist overtones of postwar human rights discourse.[25] But although Lemkin, the solitary crusader, sought to salvage part of the heri-tage of interwar minority protection in his plans for a Genocide Convention, others celebrated the Kantian promises of postwar individual rights. In exile in New Zealand during the war, the Austrian-born philosopher Karl Popper envisioned an "open society" in which "human individuals and not states or nations must be the ultimate concern not only of international organiza-tion, but of all politics, international as well as national and parochial."[26] For the lesser known jurist Eduard Reut-Nicolossi, who fled Italian fascism in the 1930s, what broke down after the Second World War was no less than "Hegel's apotheosis, the State is God on earth."[27] The distinguished interna-tional lawyer Hersch Lauterpacht, the drafter of an influential "International Bill of the Rights of Man" in 1945, triumphantly hailed the dawn of a new era. "The individual," Lauterpacht declared in 1950, "has now acquired a status and a stature which have transformed him from an object of interna-tional compassion into a subject of international right. The time is now ripe for assessing the significance of these changes ... in the functioning of inter-national society."[28]

One of these most immediate changes pertained to the governance of forced displacement in occupied Germany: The turn to individual rights concretely meant the abandonment of the League of Nation's collective recognition of

[23] Carole Fink, *Defending the Rights of Others. The Great Powers, the Jews and International Minority Protection, 1878–1938* (Cambridge, Mass., 2004), 357–358.
[24] Mazower, "The Strange Triumph of Human Rights," 389.
[25] John Cooper, *Raphael Lemkin and the Struggle for the Genocide Convention* (New York, 2008).
[26] Karl Popper, *The Open Society and Its Enemies* (Princeton, 1950), 576.
[27] Reut-Nicolussi, "Displaced Persons and International Law," 65.
[28] Lauterpacht, *International Law and Human Rights*, 4.

refugees in favor of individual eligibility. The first international charter on the
protection of refugees, the 1933 Geneva Convention, defined refugees according to the principle of national and ethnic origin: "any person who does not
enjoy the protection of the Government of the USSR or the Turkish Republic."
White Russians and Armenians, the largest refugee groups of the post–World
War I era, were the main clients of the Nansen humanitarian system. Under
the auspices of the League of Nations (and in the interwar context of minority
rights), it was theoretically enough to be a member of a designated group of
displaced and stateless persons in order to have access to asylum protection
("Nansen passports") and certain basic rights guaranteed by international convention.[29] After 1945, and especially so under the IRO (1947–1952), DPs were
screened on an individual basis: The hundreds of personal files left in the IRO
archives amply document the fascinating hearings and interviews conducted
by "eligibility officers" in the DP camps.[30] Only Holocaust survivors, deemed
ideal types of victims until communist dissidents supplanted them as the Cold
War unfolded, entirely bypassed the individual screening process.[31] It has been
recently proposed that "ideas of Germany as modernity's consummate 'rogue
state' have deeply colored twentieth-century views of international justice."[32]
Less noticed, however, is the role played by occupied Germany as a field of
experimentation in the individualization of international law. The Nuremberg
Trial and the subsequent war crimes trials (1945–1949), with their emphasis
of individual accountability over *raison d'état* (and their search for individual guilt amid the trumpeting of German "collective guilt"), were one aspect
of this process. Human rights legacies of Nuremberg, convincingly argues
Elizabeth Borgwardt, "included legitimating the idea of individual responsibility against crimes against international law."[33] The administration of refugees in occupied Germany illustrates another aspect of this individualization
process: More than any other groups in the 1940s, the DPs epitomized the
transition from *collective* to *individual* human rights.

Mirroring the individual turn of the "human rights revolution," the abandonment of the League's policy of group acceptance in favor of individual
selection was also triggered by more political motivations. "Who is a genuine,
bona fide refugee?" asked lengthy IRO "eligibility guidelines" designed to help
screeners identify authentic victims among the masses of DPs. Being a Pole, a

[29] Claudena Skran, *Refugees in Interwar Europe: The Emergence of a Regime* (New York,
1995).

[30] G. Daniel Cohen, "Naissance d'une nation: les personnes déplacées de l'après-guerre 1945–
1951," *Genèses*, 38 (2000), 56–78.

[31] "Things began to run smoothly," recalled the director of a Jewish refugee camp, "because
an order was issued from above that every Jew for the very reason that he is a Jew is eligible
for UNRRA assistance." See Malcolm Proudfoot, *European Refugees 1939–52. A Study in
Forced Population Movements* (Evanston, Ill., 1956), 350.

[32] Paul Betts, "Germany, International Justice, and the Twentieth Century," *History and
Memory*, 17 (2005), 45–86.

[33] Elizabeth Borgwardt, *A New Deal for the World. America's Vision for Human Rights*
(Cambridge, Mass., 2005), 242.

Ukrainian, or a citizen of one of the Baltic states was not technically enough to receive DP status. What mattered for the IRO and even more so today was the production by refugees of a persuasive narrative of political persecution, decipherable according to contextual human rights standards. In the postwar years, "anti-fascism" and later "anti-communism" were the political norms that came to define political refugees in the eyes of the West.[34] The careful evaluation of individual refugee tales (a radical novelty in asylum policies) stemmed from both an inclusive and exclusive idea of rights. As persecuted people (or risking persecution if returned to their home country), the DPs were for all intents and purposes protected as refugees even if most of them were not technically "stateless" (many still carried identification documents from their country of origin). The primacy of persecution over statelessness as a key identifier of modern refugees had already been asserted by international-ist advocates in the 1930s: "[O]ther features of the existence of the refugee, such as the absence of national status, may be incidental but are not essential to his quality as refugee."[35] This legal position was translated into a rigor-ous eligibility system after 1945. In the DP camps, the veracity of persecution claims was thoroughly reviewed by military officers and international civil servants trained to identify, among other potential intruders, former "collabo-rators," "Quislings," and "auxiliaries" of the Nazi order. As such, the shift from collective to individual rights – so crucial for the shaping of contempo-rary political asylum – also reflected the broader context of denazification and retribution across the European continent.

Universalism for the Happy Few?

One of the main features of the "human rights revolution" was its strong universalist outlook. From Franklin D. Roosevelt's "supremacy of human rights everywhere" (1941) to the 1948 Universal Declaration of Human rights proclaimed "as a common standard of achievement for all peoples and all nations," universalist rhetoric colored the human rights talk of the decade. That this resuscitation of eighteenth-century natural rights was performed while Southern segregation and European colonialism were still solidly entrenched has been pointed out countless times, not the least by partici-pants in the Civil Rights and anti-colonial movements. The contradictions of human rights universalism, however, were also reflected in the world of European mass displacement. The answer to the fundamental question "Who is a Refugee?" was grounded in the specific context of postwar Europe; yet it was ultimately couched in strong universal language in the 1951 Geneva Convention, a bill of rights for political refugees that crystallized in inter-national law the main legacies of the DP experience. In this document, still

[34] Kim Solomon, *Refugees in the Cold War: Towards a New International Refugee Regime in the Early Postwar Era* (Lund, Sweden, 1991).
[35] Sir John Hope Simpson, *The Refugee Problem: Report of a Survey*, (London, 1939), 4.

governing the attribution of refugee status today, a refugee is broadly defined
as "any person ... outside his country of origin" with a "well-founded fear
of persecution." In 1951, however, the universal language of the Geneva
Convention was strongly curtailed by historical and geographical limitations
inherited from the DP years: In order to seek a compromise and prompt ratification, delegates at Geneva decided that only "events occurring in Europe
before 1 January 1951" should be considered for the future recognition of
political refugees.[36] A few years after the Second World War and in the midst
of the Cold War, the shadow of Hitler and Stalin significantly weighed upon
"universal" perceptions of political persecution.

The universal impulse of international human rights was also cut short by
the rigorous selection of DPs. A French international jurist compared this policy to "picking and choosing." The West, argued Roger Nathan-Chapotot in
1949, was now "fishing chosen individuals among masses of refugees and displaced persons. This fishnet bears the name Allies-United Nations."[37] In postwar Europe, international humanitarianism did not encompass all the DPs
and refugees who viewed themselves as such. The policy of UNRRA and the
IRO, for instance, was to not include ethnic Germans expelled from Eastern
Europe, even the very few who sought DP status instead of reintegration in
West Germany: Refugees with German-sounding family names were particularly scrutinized in the interview process. Similarly, applicants suspected
of collaboration with Nazi Germany were prevented admission into the DP
community. Ukrainians and Baltic states' nationals were especially targeted,
despite their arguing, and at times proving, that their occasional enrollment in
the Wehrmacht was coerced. This "atmosphere of perpetual screening" elicited bitterness and resentment. "Such screenings," lamented American advocates of Ukrainian refugees, "bring real terror to displaced persons."[38] Other
observers of refugee hearings in the camps noted that "each and every question sets a trap."[39] Clearly, the selection of DPs reproduced the norms of the
victors' justice: "How many DPs," worried an IRO official, "sought a shelter
in our camps, merely to hide and escape retribution at home?"[40]

The idea that refugees could now be divided between "true" and "false"
– a dichotomy that would have made little sense for interwar humanitarians

---

[36] United Nations Convention Relating to the Status of Refugees, 28 July 1951. The wording "in
Europe or elsewhere" was offered as an option to the signatories, but was eventually rejected
by the overwhelming majority of contracting states. The temporal and geographical limitations were eventually lifted from the Convention in 1967.

[37] Roger Nathan-Chapotot, *Les Nations-Unies et les réfugiés. Le maintien de la paix et le con-
flit des qualifications entre l'Ouest et l'Est* (Paris, 1949).

[38] Walter Dushnyck and William J. Gibbons, *Refugees Are People. The Plight of Europe's
Displaced Persons* (New York, 1947).

[39] Léon Richard, "Le problème peut-il être résolu?" in *Chemins du Monde. Personnes Déplacées*
(Paris, 1948), 338.

[40] René Ristelhueber, *Au secours des réfugiés. L'oeuvre de l'Organisation Internationale des
Réfugiés* (Paris, 1951), 141.

clinging to the collective approach – was reinforced with the arrival in Germany of the first anticommunist dissidents following the 1948 Prague coup. Here the potential intruders were the "economic adventurers" seeking to emigrate to the West (preferably North America) under the disguise of political dissidence. The IRO swiftly adapted its methods to this new reality: "If a refugee comes from Eastern Europe, he is required to prove that the abandonment of his country of origin was forced upon him by the fear of racial, religious or political persecution." Political refugees, in short, were not ordinary migrants. One important feature of contemporary political asylum was being created in the DP camps of occupied Germany: the obligation for asylum seekers to bear the burden of proof in their claim of political persecution. Opposition to a regime had to be evidenced by religious or political persecution, or "by proven membership to a political party ... known to be the subject of persecution."[41] In the IRO archives, many personal cases illustrate the process through which "true" political and "false" economic refugees were sorted out. A young Czech waiter, for example, said that he escaped to Germany "because his father, during a birthday celebration, expressed anticommunist sentiments and was denounced. Two days later, he was informed that the police had sought him and fled to Germany." His story was not considered convincing, primarily because he made the unfortunate mistake to admit "that his salary of 600 Kcs was insufficient for his needs."[42]

These practices of exclusion, justified by a pervasive worry to provide DP status to "bona fide applicants" only, should not be overstated. Refugees turned down by the IRO – less than 20 percent overall – were not forcibly returned to their countries but simply left to fend for themselves or handed over to West German welfare organizations. In the case of anti-communist dissidents, the qualms of UN agencies and NGOs about "false refugees" soon became irrelevant when the United States tailored its immigration policies to receive a large number of "escapees" from the Soviet bloc. If anything, the exclusion of certain categories of refugees was a reminder that in the modern era, political asylum is not a guaranteed human right, but merely "a right to have rights" (to use Hannah Arendt's famous formulation). The Universal Declaration framed only "the right to seek and to enjoy in other countries asylum from persecution" (art. 14), not the right to be automatically granted asylum. By considering the claims of all applicants to DP status and ensuring due process (including the possibility for DPs to appeal negative decisions), the international civil servants in charge of the postwar refugee question in Europe were faithful to this agenda. In one area, however, the management of displacement did go beyond the scope of contemporary human rights standards: the tacit recognition of self-determination as a human right for Jewish victims of genocide.

---

[41] National Archives (Paris), IRO Records (Paris, Archives Nationales), AJ43/141.
[42] Ibid., Case 15 723.

Genocide and Self-Determination

"The notion of self-determination," wrote Ken Cmiel in an important review article, "was also part of the mid-century human rights debates. The trouble was, Westerners did not agree that this was a fundamental human right."[43] Western liberal thought, once mesmerized by the pacifying promise of self-determination, was now looking askance at "Wilson's reactionary principle ... inapplicable on this earth."[44] The dwindling appeal of Wilsonian idealism was also felt at the level of international politics. Although in 1945, "self-determination" was briefly mentioned in the first article of the UN Charter, the Allies had clearly "lost their enthusiasm for it as anything approaching a panacea."[45] Despite the mobilization of Asian and African anti-colonial activists, Latin American nations and Soviet-bloc countries, the Universal Declaration also fell short of equating self-determination to a right. As an analyst of the deliberations observed, "the colonial peoples were put in the Declaration in more than one place, although not in as clear a manner as their defenders wished."[46] Besides the uneasiness felt by representatives of European colonial powers regarding self-determination, the notion was also problematic because it referred to the entitlement of groups and not individuals, the new backbone of post-1945 human rights. Unsurprisingly, therefore, "self-determination of peoples remained off the radar screen of Western NGOs," even after two UN covenants declared it a right in 1966.[47]

The place of Holocaust survivors in the postwar refugee system complicates this view. The approximately 20,000 Jewish concentration camp inmates found in Germany and Austria by the Western Allies in the spring of 1945 (later joined by nearly 200,000 Jewish refugees, predominantly Polish, who had survived the war in the USSR) did not initially elicit overwhelming compassion. U.S. Army General George Patton, for instance, let it be known that the "Jewish type of DP is, in the majority of cases, a sub-human species," "lower than animals."[48] Yet from being handled by American authorities "just like Nazis treated Jews, except that we do not exterminate them" (to quote the scathing report written by Truman's envoy Earl Harrison in the summer of 1945), Jews evolved into a protected refugee population accommodated in specific Jewish camps. The separation of DPs by nationality or ethnic groups rapidly became a main feature of the refugee universe: Touring Germany, the American journalist Janet Flanner reported in 1948 that "in order to maintain peace and cut down the number of fist fights, the IRO tries to arrange

[43] Kenneth Cmiel, "The Recent History of Human Rights," *American Historical Review*, 109 (2004), 117–136.
[44] Popper, *The Open Society and Its Enemies*, 662.
[45] Rupert Emerson, *The Right to Self-Assertion of Asian and African Peoples* (Cambridge, Mass., 1964), 296.
[46] Johannes Morsink, *The Universal Declaration of Human Rights. Origins, Drafting and Intent* (Philadelphia, 1999), 97.
[47] Cmiel, "The Recent History of Human Rights," 128.
[48] Cited in Roger Daniels, *Guarding the Golden Door. American Immigration Policy and Immigrants since 1882* (New York, 2004), 99.

matters so that each camp houses only one religion or nationality."[49] In the case of Holocaust survivors, however, the creation of separate Jewish camps had a broader significance. It indicated that the remaining Eastern European Jews were not displaced citizens of their country of origin (Poland in most cases), but an acknowledged national entity. Jewish DPs, in short, amounted to a group anomaly in a new human rights regime increasingly geared toward individuals. They remained, even after 1945, an interwar national "minority." A prominent Zionist international lawyer from the Hebrew University in Jerusalem could therefore argue, not incidentally in 1948, that since the end of the First World War, "the Jewish question was raised to the level of a question involving a nation as a whole, an entity entitled to separate national existence and to the organization of its life within the framework of the State."[50] The myriad of Jewish DP camps in the American and British occupation zones, with their vibrant Zionist politics, further reinforced the nationalization of Holocaust survivors.[51] They also reflected the territorialization of Jewish history: As the historian Dan Diner pointed out in relation to Jewish DP camps in Bavaria, "it is arguable that the immediate founding of the State of Israel had its beginnings in southern Germany."[52]

At a time where Western Jewish organizations believed, in the wake of the Second World War, that "being singled out as a minority was itself inviting trouble"[53] and preferred the framework of individual rights, the governance of DPs, just like the Zionist movement, viewed Holocaust survivors as a distinct national group. Jewish demands for self-determination coincided with the declared goal of the IRO: "Jewish refugees," stated its director Donald Kingsley, were "one of the principal group for whose resettlement the Organization was established."[54] With the door of the United States closed until the passing by Congress of the first (and restrictive) DP Act in 1948, and with the scant interest in Jewish refugees shown by other potential host countries, the main resettlement destination was Palestine before May 1948, the State of Israel afterwards. Following the Partition Plan of November 1947, the IRO granted governmental status to the Jewish Agency for Palestine officially mandated to carry out "resettlement." Later, the organization signed an official agreement with the State of Israel formalizing their full collaboration in emigration matters.[55]

[49] Janet Flanner, "Letter from Aschaffenburg," *The New Yorker*, 30 October 1948.
[50] Nathan Feinberg, "The Recognition of the Jewish People in International Law," *Jewish Yearbook of International Law* (1948), 1–26.
[51] Zeev Mankowitz, *Life between Memory and Hope. The Survivors of the Holocaust in Occupied Germany* (Cambridge, Mass., 2002).
[52] Dan Diner, "Elemente des Subjektwerdung: Jüdische DPs in historischem Kontext," *Jahrbuch zur Geschichte und Wirkung des Holocaust* (1997), 229–248.
[53] Mazower, "The Strange Triumph of Human Rights," 388.
[54] United Nations, Department of Public Information, "*Statement of J. Donald Kingsley, Director-General of IRO, before the Third Committee of the General Assembly,*" 10 November 1949 (in IRO Records, 43AJ-166).
[55] Louise Holborn, *The International Refugee Organization. A Specialized Agency of the United Nations* (London, 1956), 677–679.

Although directly involved with the mass emigration of Jewish DPs to Israel (between 120,000 and 180,000), the IRO refrained from taking a straightforward political stance in favor of Jewish self-determination. Financially sponsored by both pro- and anti-Zionist contributors (the United States and the United Kingdom), its official line had to reconcile conflicting positions following the outbreak of the Arab-Israeli war of 1948. Whereas the American delegate to the IRO maintained that former Jewish DPs in Israel worked only "in cooperatives and in areas where the Arabs have not lived," the British representative argued that IRO-sponsored emigration of Jewish survivors was far from neutral: "Who could say that none of those actual persons helped in that way would not occupy a refugee's house or land or join a strategic colony?"[56] Compromise was eventually reached, because most national delegations at the IRO – such as the French – harbored sympathy for Jewish survivors without overlooking the material plight of displaced Palestinians. The IRO was to assist the humanitarian resettlement of Jews in Israel, but did not want "to become a contributor to the intensification of the Arab refugee problem, or to the preemption of the return of the Arabs to their home." It therefore legitimized migration to Israel on technical "resettlement" grounds: The proven absorption and assimilation capacities of the new country provided sufficient guarantees for what the agency called "firm-reestablishment." Jewish proponents of self-determination did not think otherwise: Nationhood, unanimously claimed the political leaders of the "Surviving Remnant," was indeed the most desirable humanitarian shelter.

Conclusion

The "Human Rights Revolution" of the 1940s was for the most part non-binding. The limited declarative status of the 1948 Universal Declaration, in particular, was quickly underlined even by some of the most internationalist-minded lawyers of the time.[57] This helps partially explain why human rights gained astonishing prominence in the postwar international arena: They did not fundamentally challenge the nation-state order. The main achievement of the decade was the shaping of a promising vision for the future more than the creation of effective enforcement mechanisms.

Yet Europe's DPs already stood among the first beneficiaries of new international protections. Indeed, the governance of "Europe on the Move" by humanitarian agencies put into practice a wide array of human rights norms enunciated or declared under the aegis of the United Nations.This comes, after all, hardly as a surprise. The American, British, and French enforcers of human rights in DP camps were kin to the Western instigators of the "revolution" (even if Third World actors played a role in the drafting of the Universal

---

[56] IRO Records, 43AJ-687.

[57] Lauterpacht, *International Law and Human Rights*, 419; Paul Guggenheim, *Traité de droit international public*, vol. 1 (Geneva, 1953), 303.

Declaration). The displaced persons were also part of this extended family, as European victims of events directly related to the emergence of "the idea of our time": the Second World War, the Holocaust, and the Cold War. As the scope and language of the 1951 Geneva Convention for Refugees clearly demonstrated, the first human rights regime reflected the historical experiences of wartime and postwar Europe. From 1945 to the early 1950s, the problem posed by non-German displaced persons and soon after, anticommunist "escapees", strongly impinged upon the formulation and enforcement of international protections. For Hannah Arendt, stateless refugees tragically symbolized the end of the "Rights of Man"; yet paradoxically, the postwar refugee question stood at the core of the frustrating, at times hypocritical yet path-breaking "human rights revolution."

3

'Legal Diplomacy' – Law, Politics and the Genesis of Postwar European Human Rights

Mikael Rask Madsen

It is somewhat of a paradox that Europe was to become the avant-garde of the international protection of human rights following World War II. No continent had been more severely impacted by the hostilities and atrocities of World War II – and no continent was more to blame for the break out of the conflict. Yet, with the radical reconfiguration of Europe following the war – prompted particularly by the breakdown of empire and the rise of European integration in the context of Cold War politics – Europe was to become the bridgehead of the international protection of human rights. The postwar legal and institutional setup dedicated to the protection of human rights in Europe, today, stands out as one of the most far-reaching and successful attempts at an international human rights protection regime. It has even become the de facto model for developing human rights elsewhere.[1] The original objective was, however, more specific and concerned with saving Europe from its own political and legal ills. It is clear from the debates and negotiations leading to the European Convention for the Protection of Human Rights and Fundamental Freedoms (ECHR) that many regarded the Convention as part of a broader European integration project in which human rights was to be a source of legitimacy and politico-moral commitment.[2] Despite these high ambitions in respect to European integration, the actual reality of the initial development of the ECHR is perhaps better described as the laying down of the cornerstones of what became eventually the much celebrated European human rights system. Certainly, as we now know, the two 'Europes' constructed during

---

[1] See, for example, Andrew Moravcsik, 'The Origins of Human Rights Regimes: Democratic Delegation in Postwar Europe', *International Organization*, 54 (2000), 217–252, and Lawrence Helfer and Anne-Marie Slaughter, 'Toward a Theory of Effective Supranational Adjudication', *Yale Law Journal*, 107:2 (1997), 271–391.

[2] See, for example, Consultative Assembly, *Official Report* of 7 September 1949, p. 127, and *Documents of the Assembly* (1949), Document 77, paras. 4–5.

the postwar period – 'Europe of the Market' and 'Europe of Human Rights' – have only recently integrated.[3]

It is the general argument of this article that the historical genesis of the European human rights regime was much less straightforward and politically self-evident than most commentators assume today. With the objective of contributing to the historiography of international human rights, the article examines how a continuous and subtle interplay of law and politics structured early European human rights law, and how this was to have decisive effects on both its institutional and legal development. During the period in focus, from the mid-1940s to late 1960s, European human rights law was, to a large extent, marked by the fact that law and politics were not yet differentiated social spheres as in national legal and political systems. This is not to say that early European human rights law was simply a 'politicised law' or a 'legalised politics', but that the boundaries between these two social fields were blurred. Drawing on the work of Pierre Bourdieu, the subject area can be described as an emerging 'field' – that is, a legal field in the course of being constructed and, therefore, mainly relying on preexisting international and national practices.[4] The European Court was, in other words, constructed at the 'crossroads' of other preexisting fields, ranging from national law on related matters to national politics and diplomacy. It is against this background that the article argues that European human rights law originally emerged as a form of 'legal diplomacy'. In contrast to what has been labelled 'judicial diplomacy'[5] by 'legal diplomacy', the article seeks, more generally, to understand how the development of European human rights, at its early stage, was as much a political process as a legal one. To more concretely analyse this legal diplomacy, the article emphasises the key agents of these developments, the 'legal entrepreneurs' who managed to perfection the subtle game of law and diplomacy, defining the playing field of postwar European human rights.[6]

---

[3] See, for example, Mireille Delmas-Marty, *Le relatif et l'universel. Les forces imaginantes du droit* (Paris, 2004).

[4] This notion of 'emerging fields' draws on an interpretation of the work of Pierre Bourdieu. See further in Mikael Rask Madsen, 'Transnational Fields: Elements of a Reflexive Sociology of the Internationalisation of Law', *Retfærd*, 3:114 (2006), 23–41.

[5] See, for example, Karen Alter, *Establishing the Supremacy of European Law: The Making of an International Rule of Law in Europe* (Oxford, 2001), and J. H. H. Weiler, 'A Quiet Revolution: The European Court of Justice and Its Interlocutors', *Comparative Political Studies*, 26:4 (1994), 510–534. See also the account in Laurent Scheeck, 'Competition, Conflict and Cooperation between European Courts and the Diplomacy of Supranational Judicial Networks', GARNET Working Paper 23/07 (2007).

[6] The notion of 'legal entrepreneurs' has been explored previously. See, for example, Antonin Cohen and Mikael Rask Madsen, 'Cold War Law: Legal Entrepreneurs and the Emergence of a European Legal Field (1945–1965)', in Volkmar Gessner and David Nelken (eds.), *European Ways of Law: Towards a European Sociology of Law*, (Oxford, 2007), 175–202, and Yves Dezalay, 'Les courtiers de l'international : Héritiers cosmopolites, mercenaires de l'impérialisme et missionnaires de l'universel', *Actes de la recherche en sciences sociales*, 151–152 (2004), 5–34.

Make Law, Not War

The origins of the idea of establishing, during the postwar period, some kind of supranational protection of human rights are disputed in the literature.[7] In fact, the very changes implied by the postwar innovations in terms of the internationalisation of human rights are contested.[8] A central issue for this literature is the historical continuity, or possible discontinuity, of many of the issues directly related to postwar human rights – the individual subject, international collective guarantee etc. However, it tends generally to downplay what might very well be the most essential transformations implied by the postwar processes. Building on a larger inquiry into the rise of international human rights after World War II,[9] this article argues that, during the postwar period, some of the main innovations in terms of human rights were on the legal-institutional level.[10] The postwar investments in international human rights created not only new international norms but also a set of new international venues for human rights activism. The latter were to transform the very idea of how to protect human rights and, thereby, eventually the very notion of human rights. This is, of course, not to claim a certain built-in automatism in the rise of the contemporary legal-institutional framework of international human rights, but rather to point to the clear differences between the interwar period and the postwar period in terms of the structure of opportunities for pursuing international human rights. In the long run, the actual effects of postwar international human rights and corresponding institutional setup were to be determined by the interplay of the new institutions and norms and their changing geopolitical contexts.

Generally, the European experience of the international institutionalisation of human rights was to be considerably different from other attempts made

---

[7] See, for example, Jan Herman Burgers, 'The Road to San Francisco: The Revival of the Human Rights Idea in the Twentieth Century', *Human Rights Quarterly*, 14 (1992), 447–477; Paul Gordon Lauren, *The Evolution of International Human Rights: Visions Seen* (Philadelphia, 2003); Johannes Morsink, *The Universal Declaration of Human Rights: Origins, Drafting, and Intent* (Philadelphia, 1999); Elizabeth Borgwardt, *A New Deal for the World: America's Vision for Human Rights* (Cambridge, 2005); Lynn Hunt, *Inventing Human Rights: A History* (New York, 2007); and Samuel Moyn, 'On the Genealogy of Morals', *The Nation*, 16 April 2007.

[8] See, however, Mark Mazower, 'The Strange Triumph of Human Rights, 1933–1950', *Historical Journal*, 47:2 (2004), 379–398, and A. W. Brian Simpson, *Human Rights and the End of Empire: Britain and the Genesis of the European Convention* (Oxford, 2004).

[9] See Mikael Rask Madsen, *L'Emergence d'un champ des droits de l'homme dans les pays européens: enjeux professionnels et stratégies d'Etat au carrefour du droit et de la politique (France, Grande-Bretagne et pays scandinaves, 1945–2000)*, Ph.D. diss., Sociology, L'École des hautes études en sciences sociales, Paris, 2005.

[10] This is also, albeit in different ways, argued in Norberto Bobbio, *The Age of Rights* (Cambridge, 1995), and Louis Henkin, *The Age of Rights* (New York, 1990). See also Costas Douzinas, *The End of Human Rights: Critical Legal Thought at the Turn of the Century* (Oxford, 2000).

during the same period. As argued elsewhere,[11] the comparative success of the European human rights regime was due to both the timing of the ECHR and the ways in which the Convention was perceived among a politically well-connected elite of legal entrepreneurs. The drafting of UN human rights had been carried forward by the general momentum related to the founding of the UN and the universalist ideology of some of the chief negotiators, but it had been limited by the lack of commitment to enforce such universal standards. The ECHR was drafted in a surprisingly different context. In Europe, the atrocities of World War II, as well as the breakdown of the protection of fundamental rights by the legal systems in occupied countries, were present in the memory of the key advocates of the Convention. In many cases, these actors had been active in the resistance struggle or members of the Allied forces during the war. Moreover, fear of the breaking out of new hostilities along the emerging East-West divide gave the whole undertaking a different political urgency of which the advocates of the Convention were not afraid to remind the involved politicians. Their message was clear: If one was, through the use of international law, to seriously hinder the rise of new totalitarian regimes, the European system could not imitate the well-meaning but toothless legal arrangements at the UN level.[12] Real law and effective legal institutions were the necessary conditions for achieving this goal.

Being, thus, an upshot of the emerging Cold War context, the European human rights system was to go further – legally and institutionally – than the other human rights systems created at the same time.[13] Of most significance was the fact that the European system introduced a human rights court. Moreover, the European Convention was not simply an international agreement in the conventional manner, where states could bring legal actions against each other for breach of a mutually agreed Convention; it also allowed for individuals to bring actions against their own governments at the level of a supranational institution. However, although these international legal innovations have now become practically synonymous with European human rights law, it should be underlined that they were very far from a *fait accompli* at the stage of negotiating the Convention. If the right to individual petition has become the landmark of contemporary European human rights, it is interesting to note that in the original Convention of 1950, the right of individual petition before the Court was made optional. Perhaps even more striking is the fact that the jurisdiction of the Court was made optional. In other words, the contracting states could choose to accept only the jurisdiction of

---

[11] See, for example, Mikael Rask Madsen, ' La Cour qui venait du froid. Les droits de l'homme dans la genèse de l'Europe d'après guerre', *Critique Internationale*, 26 (2005), 133–146, and 'From Cold War Instrument to Supreme European Court: The European Court of Human Rights at the Crossroads of International and National Law and Politics', *Law and Social Inquiry*, 32:1 (2007), 137–159.

[12] See, for example, *Preparatory Work on Article 1 of the European Convention of Human Rights* (Strasbourg, 31 March, 1977), 17.

[13] These include the Inter-American human rights system and the UN human rights system.

an intermediate institution, the European Commission of Human Rights, yet the right to individual petition before the Commission was, in fact, also made optional. Further weakening the basic framework of the system, the recommendations of the Commission were not in themselves legally binding and had to be accepted by a Committee of Ministers to gain effect; they were, thus, in principle, under the control of an inter-state political body rather than an independent legal body. The Commission could, however, also choose to bring the case before the Court, granted that the state in question had accepted the jurisdiction of the Court and that the case could not be settled by conciliation. Individuals had no option of bringing a case before the Court, whilst states could choose to bring a case before the Court.[14]

As it appears from this overview of the main institutional features of the original ECHR system, at the time of negotiating the Convention, there was little political will to set up entirely independent legal institutions. The original institutional framework might indeed be described as somewhat opaque. The legal diplomacy, which this article claims was at the heart of the early production of European human rights law, was, in fact, installed as a basic premise in the institutional order laid out in the ECHR. From the historical sources available, it is clear that establishing a European human rights system was anything but a straightforward process.[15] At the Congress of Europe in 1948, a number of problems, which were to hamper the subsequent negotiations, were already apparent. One of them being the most fundamental, namely, the question of the desirability of such a document in light of the existence of the Universal Declaration of Human Rights, adopted just a year earlier. Although this issue was eventually overcome, particularly due to the intervention of Winston Churchill,[16] the next question to arise was whether to pursue simply a Declaration of human rights – in the style of the Universal Declaration of Human Rights – or to attempt a more ambitious project in the form of a legally binding European Bill of Rights.[17] It was a problem which had already been prophetically anticipated in 1945 by the Cambridge Professor of International Law, Hersch Lauterpach:

Should it be decided to reduce any international bill of human rights to a mere statement of political or moral principle, then, indeed, it would be most likely to secure easy acceptance; any possible difficulty in agreeing upon its terms will be merged in the innocuous nature of its ineffectual purpose. But if the second World War ought to end, then a declaration thus emaciated would come dangerously near to a corruption

---

[14] The Committee of Ministers also oversaw that the decisions of the Court were effectuated by the member states.

[15] I refer to the minutes of the Congress of Europe in The Hague in 1948, the work of the main expert group (the Committee on Legal and Administrative Questions, which drafted a preliminary document the 'Teitgen Rapport' of September 1949), the senior officials reworking this draft in 1950 and the final sessions of the ministers in 1950.

[16] J. G. Merrils and A. H. Robertson, *Human Rights in Europe: A Study of the European Convention on Human Rights* (Manchester, 2001), 7.

[17] Many of these issues arose again during the formal negotiation of the ECHR. This is recorded in the *travaux préparatoires* of the ECHR.

of language. By creating an unwarranted impression of progress it would, in the minds of many, constitute an event which is essentially retrogressive. For it would purport to solve the crucial problem of law and politics in their widest sense by dint of a grandiloquent incantation whose futility would betray a lack both of faith and of candour.[18]

This critique resonated well with a widespread sentiment among many of the main advocates of the ECHR. These 'lawyers-statesmen' had almost all experienced the horrors of World War II, and most had developed an ardent dislike of totalitarianism in any form. For them, as for Lauterpacht, a strong legal document – and well-timed political statement – was fundamental. These actors especially made a case against the kind of hypocrisy already observed in the UN, where countries with scant respect for human rights had signed the UDHR with little intention of turning its high prose into effective legal solutions. In Europe, membership of the Council of Europe was, therefore, made conditional upon the respect of human rights and democracy. And the European Convention was precisely to become the benchmark for determining what was to be considered democracy and human rights in Europe.

Having established this founding principle, which obviously implied that the Council of Europe and the ECHR became components of the new ideological divide of Europe, the next question concerned which rights to protect and how to protect them. There was surprisingly little consensus on the rights to protect and the extent to which these rights should be defined in detail. Reflecting the geopolitical context, the debates on the scope of rights, unsurprisingly, saw the tide turn in favour of political and civil rights, while social and economic rights were left for later amendments. The list of rights included in the original Convention was limited, but it was more than sufficient for stating the fundamentals of a democratic society in a world marked by growing Cold War tension. Pierre-Henri Teitgen noted in 1949, when presenting the so-called Teitgen Report: 'The Committee on Legal and Administrative Questions... considered that, for the moment, it is preferable to limit the collective guarantee to those rights and essential freedoms which are practised after long usage and experience in all the democratic countries. While they are the first triumph of democratic regimes, they are also the necessary condition under which they operate'.[19]

The actual list of rights included in the Convention might come across as somewhat restricted and not very innovative.[20] It is certainly no exaggeration to claim that the real innovation of the Convention was on the institutional level. Not only was the idea of a European court, in particular, highly innovative, but it was also to have effects which went far beyond the Cold War political manoeuvrings which were intrinsic to the setting up of the Council of Europe. It should, however, be pointed out that among the member states

[18] Hersch Lauterpacht, *An International Bill of Rights of Man* (New York, 1945), 9.
[19] This statement can be found in the Consultative Assembly, *Official Report* of 7 September 1949, p. 127.
[20] For details, see Merrils and Robertson, *Human Rights in Europe*, 8–15.

no one could have predicted that such an institution would eventually drive toward a dynamic and expansive interpretations of the Convention, with the consequence of considerably altering the very notion of human rights in Europe and, thereby, also the substance and procedures of the protection of human rights in national legal systems. As argued elsewhere, there was a clear element of export trade in the whole exercise of writing the ECHR.[21] This had the effect of somewhat blinding the negotiators toward the potential national ramifications of such a document. They generally assumed that their home countries were in compliance with the Convention, as it was assumed to be based upon existing practices. Their greatest fear was that such a supranational system of law would be abused by subversive agitators with friendly views of the Soviet Union, or the struggle for independence in the colonies;[22] that is, they feared that these rather straightforward politics of containment, in the guise of human rights, were to backfire.

From Great Idea to 'Convention à la Carte'

A key question related to the broader process of drafting the European Convention is where did the idea of establishing a supranational human rights system come from, and which political and legal milieus advocated what was a radical reform of European inter- and intra-state legal affairs. As suggested by A. W. Brian Simpson, the international legal academic Hersch Lauterpacht was clearly very central to the promotion of genuine legal instruments and institutions in the area of human rights in the aftermath of World War II. He shrewdly used the International Law Society to ensure both the diffusion of his ideas among relevant national and international actors and the legitimacy of an organisation counting some 250 leading international lawyers.[23] At the UN, Lauterpacht had also been a central player, but in a somewhat indirect way. Regardless of his status as a pioneer in the subject area of international human rights law,[24] he had not been appointed an official representative of the United Kingdom. This was due to the Foreign Office's considering him a 'disastrous' candidate: He was not 'sound enough', that is, he was considered too idealistically and personally involved to perform the kind of pragmatic diplomacy favoured by the Foreign Office. Perhaps even more critically, the

[21] See Mikael Rask Madsen, 'France, the UK and the "Boomerang" of the Internationalisation of Human Rights (1945–2000)', in S. Halliday and P. Schmidt (eds.), *Human Rights Brought Home: Socio-Legal Studies of Human Rights in the National Context*, (Oxford, 2004), 57–86.
[22] This is particularly clear in respect to the 'imperial societies'. On the United Kingdom, see Geoffrey Marston, 'The United Kingdom's Part in the Preparation of the European Convention on Human Rights, 1950', *International and Comparative Law Quarterly*, 42:4 (1993), 796–826, 825.
[23] A. W. Brian Simpson, 'Hersch Lauterpacht and the Genesis of the Age of Human Rights', *Law Quarterly Review* (2004), 49–80.
[24] He had notably published a shorter, well-timed book on the subject, Lauterpacht, *An International Bill of Rights of Man*.

Foreign Office head legal advisor did not find him 'English enough' because of his Jewish ancestry.[25] Nevertheless, the drafts supplied by the Foreign Office during the negotiation of the Universal Declaration were clearly marked by Lauterpacht's thinking.[26]

On the European level, Lauterpacht's involvement was also indirect; his only direct involvement in the negotiation and drafting of the ECHR was as an inactive member of the Juridical Committee – the Draupier Commission – which had been set up at The Hague in 1948 to produce a draft European Charter. Moreover, Lauterpacht was not involved in drafting the Teitgen Report, nor was he involved in the many debates under the auspices of the Council of Europe. His role was that of contributing to an idea which is now taken for granted: International and European human rights can be protected only if powerful institutions are created to monitor and enforce such legal documents. However, as already suggested, the text finalised in 1950 was to be marked by some striking compromises as regards the institutional mechanisms. The ECHR had at best a 'reflexive' institutional order, balancing legal autonomy with national sovereignty. It is telling that Lauterpacht turned out, eventually, to be in favour of an intermediary Commission, and even denounced the idea of an exclusive Court as 'neither practicable nor desirable'.[27] The original introduction of the idea of a Court in the draft Charter produced after the Congress of Europe was, in fact, mainly seen as a pragmatic solution fitted to another problem, namely, the aforementioned conflicts over the definition of the rights catalogue.[28] A Court, the argument went, could be charged with carving out a detailed jurisprudence, and, thus, the delicate political problem of definition was, if not solved, then left for later, allowing the negotiations to proceed.[29]

Introducing the idea of a Court in order to solve the problem of defining the rights catalogue, however, only opened up a new conflict concerning the actual desirability of such an institution. It is in this light that Lauterpacht's somewhat surprising statement has to be seen. Even if the solution of a Court, at first glance, seemed to appeal to common law traditions, the British delegation was among the fiercest opponents of having an imprecise document left with an uncertain supranational institution.[30] Furthermore, as a later judge at the European Court writes: 'It was considered unacceptable that the code

25 Simpson, 'Hersch Lauterpacht and the Genesis of the Age of Human Rights'.

26 See Madsen, 'France, the UK and "Boomerang"'.

27 Simpson, 'Hersch Lauterpacht and the Genesis of the Age of Human Rights'. Lauterpacht would probably have been more than happy with the way in which the ECHR system was to subsequently develop. As Simpson notes, the idea of 'practical and effective' were to become absolutely central in the jurisprudence of the EHRC.

28 For details, see, for example, Moravcsik, 'The Origins of Human Rights Regimes'.

29 Simpson, *Human Rights and the End of Empire*.

30 It was ironically the British member of the Teitgen Commission, Sir Maxwell Fyfe, who argued most strongly in favour of a Court, evoking the role played by the U.S. Supreme Court. See Council of Europe, *Collected Edition of the Travaux Préparatoires* (1961), 50.

of common law and statute law which had been built up in the country over many years should be made subject to review by an International Court'.[31] Adding the argument of the paramount role of Parliament in the British political tradition, the almost insurmountable task facing the negotiators was plain to see.[32] The question of establishing a Court was, in practice, met with considerable opposition from a host of countries well into the meetings held in the summer of 1950.[33] This had the effect that the idea of an intermediary body in the form of a Commission was gradually gaining support as a viable alternative. Only a small majority supported the question of individual petition, whilst the ongoing issue of whether to draft clear legal obligations or leave it to the Court to carve out the jurisprudence continued to see very conflicting views.[34] The only real agreement was that a document of this kind was needed in light of the geopolitical climate of the day, yet any consensus on the contents remained far off.

In this context, it becomes apparent why, for example, the Teitgen Committee could play a decisive role. It basically provided the right blend of comprehensive legal solutions and 'diplomatic appeasement', which was much in demand if the project was to succeed at all. Moreover, by occasionally playing their trump cards as hardened World War II freedom fighters, these legal-political experts could unambiguously evoke the imminent dangers of the time – the looming imperialism of the Soviet Union – by a double reference to totalitarianism implying simultaneously the Nazis and the 'Commis'.[35] Besides Pierre-Henri Teitgen, a law professor, postwar French Minister of Justice and well-known member of *la Résistance*, the Committee also counted amongst its members Sir David Maxwell Fyfe, a British barrister and former Prosecutor at the Nuremberg War Crime trials, and Antonio Azara, a former Italian Minister of Justice and first President of the Italian Court of Cassation. It was this all-star cast of legal and political expertise that was to ensure that most of the draft Convention could pass the final political screening before signature.

The learned opinions of even the most well-endowed and respected lawyer-politicians, however, do not necessarily equate with what can be voted for in a plenary meeting of politicians assisted by their senior legal advisors. In uncertain policy areas, the crafting, selection and promotion of the main

---

[31] Sir Vincent Evans, 'The European Court of Human Rights: A Time for Appraisal', in *Human Right for the 21st Century*, ed. Robert Blackburn and James J. Busuttil (London, 1997), 88.

[32] For a detailed analysis of the British position during the drafting, see Marston, 'The United Kingdom's Part in the Preparation of the European Convention on Human Rights, 1950'.

[33] These countries included Britain, Denmark, the Netherlands, Norway, Sweden, Greece and Turkey.

[34] Simpson, *Human Rights and the End of Empire*, 711–712.

[35] In one of the draft reports presented by Teitgen, he bluntly stated that the Convention 'will allow Member States to prevent – before it is too late – any new member who might be threatened by a rebirth of totalitarianism from succumbing to the influence of evil, as has already happened in conditions of general apathy'. The message could hardly be lost in translation. See *Preparatory Work on Article 1 of the European Convention of Human Rights*, Strasbourg, 31 March 1977, 17.

ideas obviously constitute a key stage in the manufacturing of consent. In this respect, there is little doubt that the Teitgen Committee, and its predecessor set up at the Congress of Europe, generally managed to define what this new subject should entail. Yet the idea of European human rights was, in a somewhat paradoxical way, both novel and well known; that is, even though Teitgen & Co. carried out impressive lobbying, the politicians and their senior legal advisors eventually started scrutinising these proposals and redrafting them according to national conceptions of human rights. In the course of the many meetings and negotiations, the 'new' subject area of European human rights was also becoming increasingly familiar to the various national delegations, which meant that they also increasingly started to assume their traditional roles as brokers of national interests. As this became the case, it became equally clear that some compromises were badly needed if the Convention was to be saved.

To make a long and complex story short, the outcome of the decisive meetings in the late summer of 1950 was that a series of optional clauses were introduced in the final text. The acceptance of the Court, individual petition and the application of the Convention in the colonies were all made optional. This was done in a last-ditch manoeuvre to satisfy what continued to be insurmountable differences of the not yet united Europe. As an effect, the great moral-politico framework of the 'Free Europe', which the project of the European Convention had first emerged as in the late 1940s, was at the end of the day turned into more of a 'Convention à la carte'. Human rights, the inalienable rights of European men and women, were being Europeanised only inasmuch as the contracting states allowed for it. Furthermore, as a result of this situation, the negotiation of the idea of European human rights was to continue well beyond the day of signature of the ECHR, 4 November 1950: In 1952, the European Social Charter saw the light of day, and in the course of the following decades a series of other amendments, known as Protocols 2–5, also appeared.[36] The bottom line was that the rise of a legal practice of European human rights was to take place in the context of a continuous political meddling with the idea of European human rights. Law and politics did not, in other words, go separate ways after the drafting, as is the custom, but remained mutually dependent variables in the manufacturing of postwar human rights. As suggested in the following, the institutionalisation and juridification of the Convention was to be considerably influenced by this logic of path dependence.

The Double Challenge of the Strasbourg Institutions

For the Convention to be effective, at least ten member states had to ratify. Britain was the first state to ratify in March 1951, followed by Norway,

[36] On the contents of the protocols, see Merrills and Robertson, *Human Rights in Europe*, 15–17.

Sweden and the Federal Republic of Germany in 1952. The Convention entered into force in 1953 after having received six more ratifications from smaller European countries. In light of the many compromises included in the final text, the decisive point was then, in reality, whether the member states would accept the two central optional clauses: the right to individual petition and the jurisdiction of the Court. For the procedure of individual petition to be effective, the Convention required six acceptances: Sweden was the first country to accept in 1952, and was followed by Ireland and Denmark a year later. In 1955, Iceland, the Federal Republic of Germany and Belgium also accepted the right, and the procedure entered into force in respect to these six countries. However, accepting the compulsory jurisdiction of the Court was a more drawn-out affair. In 1953, Ireland and Denmark were the first to accept the jurisdiction of the Court, followed by the Netherlands in 1954. In 1955, Belgium and the Federal Republic of Germany also took this step and were followed in 1958 by Luxembourg, Austria and Iceland. Having then received the necessary eight acceptances, the Court was competent by September 1958, yet was ready to sit only in January 1959 after the election of the judges had taken place.

What is apparent from this overview of the first countries to accept the system is the striking absence of three out of the four major European powers. Although Germany, for obvious reasons, was eager to be included, neither France, the United Kingdom nor Italy had at this point accepted either of the two key optional clauses – and this, regardless of the fact that British, French and Italian actors – on the government level as well as in the expert commissions – had been the most influential participants in the negotiations. Nevertheless, for some rather peculiar legal reasons, this did not completely sideline the big countries. According to the Convention, any country that was a member state to the Council of Europe had the right to have a judge on the EHRC bench, whilst the ratification of the Convention was a condition for being represented at the Commission. This meant, for example, that France and Britain were represented at the Court – in fact, they held the presidency in turn during the first decade – but only Britain had a Commissioner.[37] In 1966, Britain did eventually accept the jurisdiction of the Court and individual petition for a test period. France, however, ratified the Convention only in 1974, with a safe distance from the war in Algeria, and accepted the right to individual petition when Mitterrand was elected President in 1981. What can be deduced is that the challenge facing the ECHR system in its early years of operation was a double one, concerning issues of both building legitimacy, vis-à-vis the contracting States, and providing justice to the many individuals who sought recourse before the Strasbourg institutions.[38] The absence of the major powers in respect to the most central mechanisms of the Convention

---

[37] France, however, had an observer in the Commission.
[38] Cf. Max Sørensen, 'Les experiences personelles de la Convention. L'experience d'un membre de la Commission', *Revue des droits de l'homme* (1975), 329–342, 330.

was obviously a serious problem in both regards. The functionality and legitimacy of the system depended, at the end of the day, upon individual petition
as well as the development of a reasonable jurisprudence in the eyes of the
member states.[39]

It is in this regard important to note that the early human rights system in
Strasbourg was very far from the professionalised and full-time human rights
machinery of the post–Protocol 11 era, currently working out of a steel-and-
glass palace on the banks of the river Ill.[40] In the 1950s and 1960s, the premises were cramped and the judges worked part-time, remunerated on a daily
basis. In fact, they met only sporadically, and, for a period during the 1960s,
they met about once a year and only because the rules required them to do
so. The same was true of the Commission, although it played a more active
role due to its task as a screening body for the applications received. A brief
survey of the actual applications admitted to the two bodies reveals a picture
of a set of institutions having, at best, a very slow start: In the 1950s, only
five applications were admitted, and only 54 throughout the 1960s. Of these,
only a marginal number actually ended up as judgements. As concerns the
Court, it delivered only ten judgements during its first ten years of operation,
in which only a handful found violations of the Convention.[41] In explaining
this situation, it is generally suggested in legal literature that the Commission
– and not the Court – was the key player during the early period, and that this
was due to the particularities of the ECHR screening procedures leaving the
Commission to have a first say on the applications.[42] This explanation of the
early institutional dynamics, however, overlooks the fact that the omnipres-
ence of the Commission was, in part, also the product of the institutional frictions of the dual system of a Court and a Commission, as well as the political
conditions surrounding these emerging institutions more generally.[43]

It appears from interviews conducted for this research that the Commission,
in fact, worked deliberately to carve out its role.[44] According to one of the first

---

[39] It should be underlined that of the first eight declarations of acceptance of the jurisdiction of
the Court, seven were limited to a time period and, thus, up for renewal. Austria, Denmark,
the Federal Republic of Germany, Iceland and Luxembourg had specified this period to be
three years; Belgium and the Netherlands initially accepted the jurisdiction for five years. See
A. H. Robertson, 'The European Court of Human Rights', *American Journal of Comparative
Law*, 9:1 (1960), 1–28, 18.

[40] Protocol 11 provided a substantial reform of the European human rights system in Strasbourg.
Coming into force in 1998, a new and permanent Court was set up to deal with an ever
increasing case load.

[41] Brice Dickson (ed.), *Human Rights and the European Convention* (London, 1997), 19.

[42] Ibid.

[43] Generally, as noted by a civil servant working for the ECHR system from its inception, the
whole enterprise of European human rights was marked more by 'human rights than human
rights law' (interview, 20 November 2002). According to the same source, the staff, the civil
servants working at the institutions' secretariat, saw themselves more as the 'avocats de la
Convention' than a corps of professional bureaucrats (interview, 20 November 2002).

[44] See also particularly Sørensen, 'Les experiences personelles de la Convention'. See also Sture
Petrén, 'La saisine de la Cour europénne par la Commission europénne des droits de l'homme',

civil servants employed at the ECHR, the Commission did, in fact, 'fermé le robinet', that is, it cut off the flow of cases to the Court for some six years during the 1960s as a consequence of 'une affaire d'amour propre' between the two organs: one in *robes* with the power to issue legally binding decisions and with well-paid judges and, the other, in *civilian attire* theoretically only issuing decisions to be given effect by the Committee of Ministers.[45] According to the same source, as a response the Court spent most of its time revisiting its Statute with the objective of enhancing its powers, by seeking, for example, to obtain consultative prejudicial competence. A number of judges even launched a critique of the Commission in professional journals.[46] Such an understanding of the institutional frictions might be somewhat exaggerated, but the basic point is supported by data on the actual flow of cases. After the Court had been called on in the two cases of *Lawless* and *De Becker* in the late 1950s, there was a period of five years between 1960 and 1965 when the Court did not receive a single case from the Commission.[47] The situation is captured in an unpublished essay by the Danish judge on the Court, Alf Ross, titled *The Unemployed Court*.[48]

Considering the available empirical material, there is little doubt that the centrality of the Commission was much more the product of the Commission's self-initiated strategy of enhancing its power vis-à-vis the Court than simply the inevitable outcome of the provisions of the Convention. The Commission made the most of its powers within the dual structure of the Convention, but it does not appear from the legal provisions that the driver for this positioning was intra-institutional frictions and ultimately concerned the Commission's objective of developing its own jurisprudence before it eventually allowed for cases to go to the Court.[49] This analysis, however, provides only a partial answer as to what came out of this intra-institutional turf war in terms of human rights law. Surprisingly, a closer look at the initial practices of the Commission strongly indicates that quantitatively the main task of the Commission was, in fact, to reject claims of human rights violations. It appears that the most significant contribution of the Commission's early jurisprudence on European human rights concerned the notion of 'manifestly ill-founded' claims, that is, the development of a jurisprudence of what are *not* human rights violations under the ECHR. In plain language, the 'coup' orchestrated by the Commission did not imply great breakthroughs as regards

---

in *Mélanges offerts à Polys Modinos. Problèmes des droits de l'homme et de l'unification europénne* (Paris, 1968), 233–244.

[45] Interview, 20 November 2002.

[46] See also Sørensen, 'Les experiences personelles de la Convention', 330 in this respect.

[47] This has to be seen in light of the fact that the number of applications received was actually relatively high.

[48] Alf Ross, 'En arbejdsløs domstol', unpublished manuscript.

[49] This is also apparent when one reads the description of the early years of the Commission provided by its President, Max Sørensen. See Sørensen, 'Les experiences personelles de la Convention'.

the protection of human rights in Europe, but rather cemented the institution's 'first right to reject', which consequently kept the Court at bay.

The Art of Diplomacy and the Need for Legitimacy

In order to more fully explain the early institutional dynamics of the ECHR, these intra-institutional skirmishes obviously have to be analysed in the context of the external constraints of these emerging institutions. Regardless of what is normally implied by the very term 'institution' and certainly 'institutional analysis', it seems relevant to analyse the ECHR institutions as having been produced at the intersection of external and internal constraints. What, hereby, is suggested is not simply to raise the question of input and output legitimacy of these institutions,[50] but to analyse these dimensions as interdependent – that is, to analyse the correlation between the internal structures of these institutions and their positioning within a larger external structure, that of an emerging field of human rights.[51] The applicability of such an approach in the context of emerging European legal institutions is already suggested by the relative clash between the Commission and Court. However, fully explaining the surprising development of a minimalist notion of European human rights under the auspices of the Commission requires a further examination of the specific diplomatic climate in which the rise of the European human rights system and jurisprudence took place. The minimalist notion of human rights did allow the Commission to control the flow of cases, yet the background to this institutional strategy can only partly be located in the internal constraints of the ECHR institutions. It was equally the product of the political-historical context.

As argued elsewhere, the Strasbourg institutions were, in fact, rather hesitant during the first fifteen to twenty years of operation before initiating the dynamic jurisprudence which was to cement their position from the early 1980s as a quasi 'European Supreme Court'.[52] The reasons for this initial reluctance was mainly that the institutions were vulnerable in respect to the member states and, therefore, had to continuously strike a fine balance between promoting European human rights and convincing the member states of its relevance and reasonableness.[53] It is curious to note that the first major cases – the *Cyprus cases* (the Commission) and the *Lawless case* (the Court) – indeed gave the member states the impression that the ECHR system was not going to take an aggressive stance against the member states in the area of human rights.[54] There is little doubt that this cautious course of action was due to the

---

[50] On this notion, see Fritz W. Scharpf, *Governing in Europe: Effective and Democratic?* (Oxford, 1999).

[51] Such a way of conceptualising institutions obviously draws on Pierre Bourdieu, 'Le champ économique', *Actes de la recherche en sciences sociales*, 119 (1997), 48–66.

[52] Madsen, 'France, the UK and the "Boomerang"'.

[53] See Sørensen, 'Les experiences personelles de la Convention'.

[54] See Simpson, *Human Rights and the End of Empire*.

political climate of the late 1950s and early 1960s. During the period, Cold War–inspired clashes in the area of human rights were at their peak,[55] and, more importantly, the battle over decolonisation was still unfinished, which placed European states in the eye of the hurricane of the broader geopolitical scheme of human rights. Moreover, as suggested above, a very central task of the ECHR institutions consisted, in fact, of seeking to convince the major European powers, which also happened to be geopolitically the most vulnerable in this respect, of accepting the optional clauses.

The case of the United Kingdom is exemplary in this regard. As noted, the United Kingdom accepted the individual petition and the jurisdiction of the Court only in 1966 against the backdrop of a very limited jurisprudence. However, the relevant actors had a 'feeling' that these institutions had already developed a sound understanding of what could – and should – be implied by the notion of European human rights. The Foreign Office legal advisor in charge of reviewing the compatibility of English law in respect to the Convention before accepting the optional clauses recalled the situation in an interview:

We had to review our legal system in the light of whatever jurisprudence had developed, and it was very little at that time.... [T]he jurisprudence of the Court had not been developed at all at that time. Two cases [had] come before the Court. Several thousand complaints have come before the Commission. But, the Commission had taken, I would say, a rather restrictive view on the interpretation of the Convention, not a liberal view, despite the fact the Convention is drafted in quite broad terms. But, the effect of this approach of the Commission was, in fact, to build up the confidence of Governments in the system.... They didn't feel that the system was going mad and that, you know, any applications from any old chap that felt his rights had been violated would be successful before the Commission.[56]

As it appears from this quotation, the predictions of what could be expected in Strasbourg played a significant role in convincing the member states of gradually accepting the full ECHR package.[57] The self-constraining strategy of the Commission manifested in its jurisprudence on 'manifestly ill-founded claims', along with the few and restrained decisions of the Court, had in fact produced the image of a solid and politically reflexive institution, that is, an institution that was willing to listen to the arguments of the member states and not (yet) pursue an idealist, even radical, human rights agenda.

Contributing equally to the image and institutional identity of the ECHR system were the very persons appointed to the Commission and Court and their status in national legal fields. A brief look at the main professional

---

[55] See, for instance, Yves Dezalay and Bryant Garth, 'From the Cold War to Kosovo: The Rise and Renewal of the Field of International Human Rights', *Annual Review of Law and Social Science* (2006), 231–255.

[56] Interview, 25 April 2001.

[57] For a detailed analysis of the political process of the British acceptance of the optional clauses, see Lord Lester, 'UK Acceptance of the Strasbourg Jurisdiction: What Really Went on in Whitehall in 1965', *Public Law* (1998), 237–253.

characteristics of the first judges of the Court provides a picture of a set of actors who, for the most part, were legal academics. Of the first fifteen judges appointed to the Court, nine can be characterised as mainly academics, whereof most specialised in international law.[58] It is, in this regard, also important to note that only a few had a background as national judges.[59] Indeed, contrary to the first judges of the European Court of Justice, who for the most part were appointed because of more specific specialisations in law, economics and the administration of justice,[60] the jurists of the EHRC were a far more homogenous group of elite legal academics.[61] What is certain is that this group of actors could provide, if not expertise on how to run a supranational court, then certainly legal legitimacy in respect to the national legal fields of the member states in which they all held great prestige. Hence, despite acting out of an, by all means, uncertain institutional framework, they held a legal capital which was easily exchangeable to the different legal orders of the member states.

It is, in this regard, also important to note that a number of the jurists appointed were also well situated in respect to national political fields. Many of these jurists had been actively involved in foreign policy issues of a legal nature. For example, the second President of the Court, René Cassin, had a long semi-political career behind him during which he had, among other roles, acted as legal counsel to Charles de Gaulle's Free France Government in London during the war, as well as been appointed to a series of key governmental committees and leading NGOs. Another central actor in this respect was the President of the Commission, the eminent Danish public international law professor Max Sørensen, who had previously not only provided expert consultancy for the Danish Ministry of Foreign Affairs but also been an employee of the same institution. The ECHR experts' familiarity with the political environments had a double importance in respect to building the legitimacy of the institution. On the one hand, the legal experts were

---

[58] Kemal Fikret Arik was professor of private international law and Dean of the Faculty of Political Science at the University of Ankara; Frederik Mari Van Asbeck was professor of international law at the University of Leyden; Giorgio Balladore Pallieri was professor of public international law and Dean of the Law Faculty of the Università Cattolica del Sacro Cuore in Milan; Ake Ernst Vilhelm Holmback had been Rector of the University of Uppsala, and Georges Maridakis, Rector of the University of Athens; Hermann Mosler was professor of international law at the University of Heidelberg; Henri Rollin was professor of international law at the University of Brussels; the Danish legal philosopher and expert on public international law Alf Ross was professor at the University of Copenhagen; and the eminent expert on public international law Alfred Verdross was Dean of the Law Faculty of the University of Vienna.

[59] Einar Arnalds (Civil Court of Reykjavik), René Cassin (Vice President of the French Conseil d'Etat but also a professor of law), Lord McNair (former President of the International Court of Justice, as well as professor of international law), Eugene Rodenbourg (President of the Court of Luxembourg) and Terje Wold (President of the Supreme Court of Norway).

[60] See, for example, Robertson, 'The European Court of Human Rights', 13 n. 40.

[61] An examination of the first Commissioners provides a similar picture of a legal academic elite.

acquainted with foreign policy problems and milieus, and, on the other hand,
the foreign policy milieus did see the Judges and Commissioners as, if not
belonging to exactly same social circles, then being perceptive to diplomacy
and issues of national sovereignty.[62]

In retrospect, it might come across as practically self-evident that the external legitimisation of the ECHR system was paramount during the early years,
and that this issue was partly overcome by the means of appointing a set of
legal actors who had both a perfect command of international law and an
understanding of its diplomatic dimension. It is, in this conjunction, important to emphasise that these emerging practices took place in what might best
be described as a vacuum of legal knowledge on European human rights. For
the same reason, the very few statements and decisions of the ECHR institutions were scrutinised by the assembled foreign ministries of the contracting states, and, perhaps more importantly, the individual actors representing
the ECHR institutions were seen as embodying the ECHR institutions and,
thus, were scrutinised as such.[63] It is an important yet generally overlooked
element in the production of early European human rights that many of the
great jurists of the Strasbourg institutions did very little, in fact, to prompt a
broader systematisation and conceptualisation of the subject in their respective countries.[64] In the words of a former Danish judge at the European Court,
then a young academic: '[Human rights] didn't cause discussions or disserta-
tions of any kind.... Human rights became a word but not a concept, and
no one was really interested'.[65] In more interpretive terms, European human
rights – even in the view of many of the jurists developing the ECHR institutions – was at the time not yet 'real law'[66] and, thus, not to be treated with the
usual caution and discipline which serious legal science demands. As implied
by this analysis, this new European law is perhaps better described as a particular tool of the complex diplomacy of transforming a Europe of opposing
empires into an integrated legal space. As history suggests, it did not remain
so. However, during the first two decades of the life of European human rights

[62] An in-depth analysis of the jurists appointed by the United Kingdom almost suggests that the
strategy was to expatriate a cell of the Foreign Office to Strasbourg in order to have an impact
on the legal and institutional developments. See further in Madsen, *L'Emergence d'un champ
des droits de l'homme dans les pays européens.*
[63] See, for example, the Foreign Office's evaluation of the Commission mission to Cyprus in the
late 1950s. Simpson, *Human Rights and the End of Empire*, 941.
[64] Only a very few universities offered programmes in the 1960s which tackled directly or indi-
rectly the subject of European human rights. Strasbourg was one of the exceptions in this
regard. This was due to both the efforts of the Schuman University and the human rights
research institute created by René Cassin after having received the Nobel Peace Prize in 1969.
[65] Interview, 27 April 1999.
[66] Generally on the international and European levels, human rights was originally considered
as a new subdiscipline of international relations to be treated by public international law – the
law between nations – and thus placed in the hands of diplomats backed up by the *judgements*
of law professors of public international law, albeit these professors' actual investments in
human rights in terms of legal science were only sporadic.

law, this new legal knowledge and savoir faire was, at the end of the day, a very advanced form of diplomacy: a legal diplomacy.

Such an understanding obviously draws on Max Weber's notion of legal rationality and associated forms of domination. The Weberian concepts also provide a tool for understanding the role of a set of key individuals in the making of early European human rights law. Although there is little doubt that much of their credibility was due to their symbolic power as a sort of 'honoratiores of law', more important perhaps is the question of what kind of law and legal rationality was being generated by this 'legal nobility'. Was it – following the scheme of Max Weber – 'formal irrational', 'substantively irrational, 'formally rational' or 'substantively rational?'[67] This study generally suggests that the answer is somewhere between 'formally rational' and 'substantively rational' law, leaning toward the former rather than the latter. This interpretation is partly based upon the fact that the general *corpus juris* on European (and international) human rights was practically nonexistent at the time and, thus, could not serve as a source of legal certainty. As well, the ECHR institutions' initial mode of production clearly favoured a case-by-case approach which allowed for balancing national interests and general objectives of human rights.[68] Their initial operations suggest a very subtle balancing act between pursuing the law of human rights and convincing the member states of both the importance and reasonableness of their practices. The few cases that made their way to the European Commission of Human Rights – and the even fewer that went to the Court – were for the same reasons of crucial importance in respect to building these institutions. As A. W. Brian Simpson has dryly noted, the ones on trial during the early period were, in fact, not the member states but the Court and the Commission.[69] It was not until this initial 'trial period' was over, beginning in the mid-1970s, that these institutions could substantially rationalise the law of European human rights; that is, they could neutralise and even reduce the underlying political compromises which had predetermined both the institutional framework and the normative contents of European human rights.

Conclusion

The history of the postwar European human rights regime stands out from the other international and regional human rights systems developed during the

---

[67] For further introduction to these notions, see, for example, Anthony T. Kronman, *Max Weber* (Stanford, 1983).

[68] Although the famous margin of appreciation doctrine is commonly thought to have been first elaborated in the decision *Handyside vs. UK*, a closer look at the two founding cases of *Cyprus* and *Lawless* clearly suggests that this key balancing principle was already being put into play in the late 1950s. See further in Michael R. Hutchinson, 'The Margin of Appreciation Doctrine in the European Court of Human Rights', *International and Comparative Law Quarterly*, 48:3 (1999), 638–650.

[69] Simpson, *Human Rights and the End of Empire*.

same period. This should, however, not overshadow the fact that European and international human rights are deeply enmeshed in the same twentieth-century history. The European Convention continued a legal-politico project already commenced by the UN of impeding large-scale conflict and the rise of militant ideologies by developing international law. The European version of this postwar strategy of international law-making, however, almost immediately gained a set of different drivers and characteristics. Although both European and UN human rights were drafted against the background of the atrocities of World War II, the main driving force behind the European regime became the fear of Soviet imperialism into Western Europe. Almost from the outset, this Cold War dimension created a political unity among the negotiating states, which gave the whole undertaking of institutionalising and developing human rights law a decisive sense of urgency and necessity. The European human rights project, thereby, came to differ significantly from the UN human rights regime. If the UN Human Rights Commission was to be paralysed by Cold War–inspired confrontations, the European human rights regime was fuelled by Cold War–enthused sentiments. This starting point only later and gradually transformed toward an idea of European human rights as a dynamic area of law. As well, the idea of European human rights as the underpinning politico-moral framework of European integration, which originally had been evoked as part of Cold War strategy of the late 1940s, has only recently been achieved with the post–Cold War transformations of Europe.[70]

When seen in respect to the broader history of postwar international human rights, the case of European human rights both confirms some general trends and supplies a number of important nuances. It, first and foremost, confirms the paramount importance of Cold War politics on the development of human rights. Focusing on the European case provides, however, a much needed correction to the widespread assumption that the development of human rights was brought to a standstill by the Cold War. This analysis argues in contrast that the Cold War was highly decisive to the evolution of European human rights. In fact, the early politics of European human rights necessarily have to be understood in the light of what has been termed the *Cultural Cold War;* that is, European human rights was not only part of the ideological contest of the period, it was also part of its cultural battle. The struggle for European human rights, in other words, constitutes a highly central but much overlooked component of the Cold War at large. This chapter also confirms the importance of decolonisation on the development of human rights. In this analysis, decolonisation has not been explicitly emphasised, but it nevertheless appears as the main explanation of the reluctance of France and the United Kingdom. For these two imperial societies, it was vital to maintain that the postwar universalisation of human rights was not in contradiction to colonial politics. Whereas this was more or less achieved on the UN level, European human rights posed a much more serious threat to imperial sovereignty. It

---

[70] Perhaps most strikingly with the EU's Charter of Fundamental Rights.

has been argued that the European Convention played a direct role in the closing act of the British Empire.[71] Following the analysis suggested here, it is more plausible to argue that for European human rights to develop beyond the initial legal diplomacy analysed in this article, it had to await the end of European empire. More precisely, it was only with the fading of colonial conflicts that the European human rights institutions were in a situation where they had the liberty to sharpen the legal tools of the Convention without substantial protest from the larger member states.

This is further linked to a general claim in the literature that the 1970s saw the real breakthrough of international human rights. As concerns European human rights, many of the central legal notions – 'living instrument', 'practical and effective' etc. – did emerge toward the end of the 1970s. However, European human rights did not simply join the bandwagon of human rights activism of the 1970s and 1980s. The metamorphosis of European human rights during the period was, above all, made possible because of the crucial processes of legitimisation of the previous period. This also explains why European human rights law could develop as rapidly and substantially as it did throughout the 1980s compared to other human rights regimes. For the same reason, most analysis of the European human rights regime understands current European human rights as marked by progressive law, not legal diplomacy. A sharper look at the contemporary practice of perhaps the most central legal principles of the early period, the notion of the (national) 'margin of appreciation', however, reveals a more complex picture. The success of European human rights, it appears, remains dependent on the Strasbourg institution's ability to strike a balance between the national and the European. In the early period, this diplomacy concerned balancing European law and national politics, while today it concerns balancing national and European law. Nevertheless, it is a crucial act of diplomacy performed by jurists.

[71] Simpson, *Human Rights and the End of Empire.*

PART II

POSTWAR UNIVERSALISM AND LEGAL THEORY

4

Personalism, Community, and the Origins of Human Rights

Samuel Moyn

In the summer of 1947, the Institute for International Law reconvened after a ten-year hiatus. For decades the self-appointed tribune of European "civilization" and the legal conscience of humanity, the Institute now hoped to retake its former role. Given its prominence in the rhetoric of the Allied new order during World War II, the new concept of human rights – though international lawyers had not even flirted with it before – stood as the first item on their agenda.[1] The atmosphere was one of bitter disappointment: Whatever the idealism of wartime dreams, the sad but obvious fact was that when it came time to enact a peaceful order – most flagrantly in the Dumbarton Oaks documents, in which human rights did not even figure – a theory of sovereign power politics ruled. As for the United Nations Charter, the great powers had it adorned with the phrase human rights without providing either any definition of its values or any institutional means for their defense.[2] The international lawyers of Europe were, they believed, perhaps the last best hope for making good on what now seemed like broken promises.

"Neither the Charter nor diplomatic wrangling is reassuring," noted Charles de Visscher, Belgian international lawyer and judge (1946–1952) on the International Court of Justice who prepared the Institute's report and proposal on human rights, in his opening remarks. "International organization," he complained indignantly, "looks like a mere bureaucracy with neither

---

[1] On the Institute from its nineteenth-century origins through this period, see most notably Martti Koskenniemi, *The Gentle Civilizer of Nations: The Rise and Fall of International Law* (Cambridge, 2002). One émigré Russian international lawyer had proposed an international bill of human rights in 1929, but was essentially ignored at the time. See André Mandelstam, "La Déclaration des droits internationaux de l'homme, adoptée par l'Institut de droit international," *Revue de droit international*, 5 (1930), 59–78 , and Mandelstam, *Les Droits internationaux de l'homme* (Paris, 1931); for comment, Dzovinar Kévonian, "Exilés politiques et avènement du 'droit humain': la pensée juridique d'André Mandelstam (1869–1949)," *Revue d'histoire de la Shoah*, 177–178 (January–August 2001), 245–273.

[2] Cf. Elizabeth Borgwardt, *A New Deal for the World: America's Vision for Human Rights* (Cambridge, Mass., 2005).

direction nor soul, unable to open to humanity the horizons of a true international community." A new international law, based on human rights and theorized and implemented by the caste of jurists, might, however, provide the "morally-inspired salvation" that the world clearly needed. Now comes a very curious statement: "Since the end of the second world war, a powerful current of ideas has arisen against the nameless abuses that we have witnessed: it is the personalist conception of society and power. The intellectual elites of all of the countries with liberal and democratic traditions are rallying to this conception." According to de Visscher, this "personalist conception" alone could provide the basis of an authentic turn to human rights and guide the response of law to Machiavellian power.[3]

In spite of the recent wave of studies of the origins of human rights after World War II, one would be hard pressed to understand what this leading international lawyer of the time was talking about. In fact, however, personalism was a principal feature of human rights consciouness of the 1940s, especially, though not exclusively, on the European Continent. What was personalism, how was it possible to view it as the key to the turn to human rights, and how thoroughgoing a resonance did it really have in the postwar moment? Forgotten now, the spiritual and often explicitly religious approach to the human person was, this essay suggests, the conceptual means through which Continental Europe initially incorporated human rights – and, indeed, became the homeland of the notion for several decades. Recovering the centrality of personalism, however, should deeply unsettle prevailing opinion about what the concept of human rights implied in its founding era.

This essay surveys a few of its sources, looks at the breadth of its percolation (not least in legal thought), and evaluates the significance of the personalist vehicle for rights in the 1940s. If this episode is missing from the emerging understanding of human rights, it should also drive home a larger lesson about the teleology, tunnel vision, and triumphalism that has so deeply affected current historiography. Universalistic and formalistic languages always have a historically specific and ideologically particular meaning, which it is the mission of historians to seek out. In early postwar Europe, human rights were – contrary to current expectations and desires – most associated with neither a revolutionary nor a republican heritage. For almost nobody were they the essence of post-Holocaust wisdom, not least since the crimes of Nazi evildoers were not yet understood to be primarily ones against the Jewish people. Finally, they were not the inspiration for a new sort of private activism, which had other and later sources.

---

[3] "Les droits fondamentaux de l'homme, base d'une restauration du droit international," *Annuaire de l'Institut de Droit International*, 41 (1947), 1–13 (travaux préparatoires by Charles de Visscher), 142–190 (discussion), 258–260 (declaration), at 153–154. For the text of the declaration in English, see "Fundamental Rights of Man, as the Basis of a Restoration of International Law," *International Law Quarterly*, 2:2 (Summer 1948), 231–232. On de Visscher, see François Rigaux, "An Exemplary Lawyer's Life (1884–1973)," *European Journal of International Law*, 11:4 (2000), 877–886.

Instead, human rights need to be closely linked, in their beginnings, to an epoch-making reinvention of conservatism. This defining event of postwar West European history is familiar from the more general historiography of the period in the form of Christian Democratic hegemony, but is absent so far from human rights history – even though this same Western Europe became the earliest homeland of the concept. In sum, human rights came to the world not just as part of a wartime internationalization of the American New Deal, but also, and just as crucially, as one element of a European reinvention of its humanism as it tried to put self-imposed disaster behind it.[4] The first surprise, perhaps, is that concept of the person not only preexisted the mid-1940s, but had originally served different forces.

"We are neither individualists nor collectivists, we are personalists!" So pro-claimed perhaps the earliest personalist political manifesto, put out by the rightist club Ordre Nouveau (New Order) in 1931.[5] In its 1930s populariza-tion, the person was an anti-liberal conception, and the chief task of tracing its eligibility for its postwar role is to follow the reversal that led it to imply rather than forbid a formalistic conception such as rights – or even a reinvention of international law based on it.

The sources of "the person" – besides the Thomistic rendition of Jacques Maritain, who would become the premier postwar philosopher of human rights – were various. One important reference was the émigré Russian Orthodox philosopher Nicholas Berdyaev, who brought to the West an old Russian tradi-tion of religious personalism.[6] Most decisive, according to the historian John Hellman, may have been the influence of the originally Russian-Jewish con-vert Alexandre Marc, who founded Ordre Nouveau together with the shadowy guru Arnaud Dandieu, an atheist follower of Friedrich Nietzsche considered the secret genius of personalism (though a mere librarian by day). In Germany, the most prominent personalist was Max Scheler, who also exerted influence elsewhere. Not just the cacophony of voices starting in the early 1930s but the essential indeterminacy of the concept made personalism highly ambiguous: the common but deeply contentious cause of Christian and para-Christian intel-lectuals from the far right to the communitarian "left." The thinker who was to forge the most durable version of personalism, Maritain, could generously acknowledge as much: "There are at least a dozen personalist doctrines, which, at times, have nothing more in common than the term 'person'."[7]

---

[4] In his classic 1950 indictment of European "pseudo-humanism," Aimé Césaire could complain that "not one established writer, not one academic, not one crusader for law and religion, not one 'defender of the human person,'" yet opposed colonialism in principle. Césaire, *Discourse on Colonialism*, trans. Joan Pinkham (New York, 1972), 17.

[5] See John Hellman, *The Communitarian Third Way: Alexandre Marc's Ordre Nouveau, 1930–2000* (Montreal, 2002).

[6] On the larger tradition of Russian personalism, see George L. Kline, "Changing Attitudes toward the Individual," in Cyril Black (ed.), *The Transformation of Russian Society* (Cambridge, 1960), 606–625.

[7] Maritain, *The Person and the Common Good*, trans. John J. Fitzgerald (New York, 1947), 13.

Yet the ambiguity of personalism was, in a sense, its genius; it signaled the identity of the opposition clearly, while leaving flexibility about what the alternative program was. (Its ambiguity was also a minimum condition for its eventual extrication from its typically reactionary and always illiberal origins.) Personalism – linked quickly to spiritualism and humanism, and not infrequently to European identity – meant a repudiation of the rival materialisms of liberalism and communism. In the first place, then, personalism was different than individualism, for it championed a figure who was supposed to overcome the destitute atomism of the politics and economics of the nineteenth century. If, however, the person provided a connection to community that individualism ruled out, it also provided the key source of value omitted in, and the political bulwark against, communism. Most boldly, personalists claimed that capitalism and communism, apparently foes, deserved each other, and canceled each other out, in their common materialism.

The spectrum of opinion championing personalism in the inaugural years of the early 1930s ranged from the far right to the farrago of publicists now known as experimental "non-conformists." The so-called Young Right (Jeune Droite), an up-and-coming cohort of young reactionaries, self-proclaimed "defenders of the West," were those originally part of Maritain's reactionary circle when he affiliated with the royalist and anti-Semitic Action Française. But, unlike him, they remained within the fold of the French conservative revolution as Maritain cut his ties with it. "Before the tragic failure of materialist prosperity," one of these figures, Thierry Maulnier, wrote in 1932, "political humanism – the just reckoning of the person, and its possibilities and rights – would seem the sole formula... to furnish the acceptable elements of a reconstruction."[8] A group such as Ordre Nouveau was representative of non-conformism, a set of movements "neither right nor left" or rather both, since many of its members thought what was true in Marxism and communism – their opposition to bourgeois decadence and their hankering for the death of individualism – had to be saved, so as to redirect revolution against the bourgeoisie in a spiritualist and often explicitly Christian direction.[9] These were the early themes of personalism, then. But if the essential meaninglessness of the person was a minimum condition for the fact that it could eventually be extricated from its reactionary and non-conformist origins, one must at least

---

[8] Cited in Nicolas Kessler, *Histoire politique de la Jeune Droite (1929–1942): une révolution conservatrice à la française* (Paris, 2001), 208; cf. 230–233, 242–249 for more reactionary personalism.

[9] On the general scene, the classic is Jean Louis Loubet del Bayle, *Les Non-conformistes des années trente: une tentative de renouvellement de la pensée politique française* (Paris, 1969). The allegation that these circles were basically fascistic is most familiar from the controversial works of Zeev Sternhell: Zeev Sternhell, *Neither Right nor Left: Fascist Ideology in France*, trans. David Maisel (Berkeley, 1986). For the best overview, see Robert O. Paxton, "The Church, the Republic, and the Fascist Temptation," in Richard J. Wolff and Jörg K. Hoensch (eds.), *Catholics, the State, and the European Radical Right, 1919–1945* (Boulder, 1986), 67–91.

also note that, for a time after 1934, communism tried to claim the slogan too. In that year, Nicolai Bukharin helped transform the appeal of communism in the West when he announced that the Soviet Union would make the realization of "the personality" for "the first time... a mass phenomenon and not just... part of the slave-owning upper class in its various historical variants." Such a promise profoundly affected the way ordinary people imagined and constructed themselves; but its ramifications were also legal, as the Stalin Constitution of 1936 – in whose drafting Bukharin played an instrumental role – makes clear.[10]

Without question, however, the man who made the intellectual fortune of personalism was Emmanuel Mounier, due to the terrific impact of his nonconformist journal *Esprit* beginning in the early 1930s. Drastically expanding the purchase of the theme of the person in his early essays, Mounier proposed going back to where modernity started out in the Renaissance and trying again with a genuine humanism that freed Europe of the secular and liberal mistake of individualism. For Mounier, the challenge was to use the person to insist on respect for self-realization that "collectivism" ruled out, while pressing it to imply a community that brought atomized individuals back together. This common idea was one that Mounier developed at length, including in his famous *Manifesto in the Service of Personalism*. Far from implying rights, this central personalism of the 1930s instead sought new forms of post-liberal politics as well as a personalist economy to go with them. "On the altar of this sad world," Mounier wrote in an illustrative passage, "there is but one god, smiling and hideous: the Bourgeois":

He has lost the true sense of being, he moves only among things, and things that are practical and that have been denuded of their mystery. He is a man without love, a Christian without conscience, an unbeliever without passion. He has deflected the universe of virtues from its supposedly senseless course towards the infinite and made it center about a petty system of social and psychological tranquility. For him there is only prosperity, health, common sense, balance, sweetness of life, comfort.... Next in line among bourgeois values are human respect and protection of rights.... Law is for him not an institution for justice, but the defence of the injustices he inflicts. Thence comes his harsh legalism.[11]

Repudiating France's then minuscule Christian Democratic party – in a notorious fracas with Paul Archambault, who considered him dangerous in the extreme – Mounier declared that "the ideology that we are combatting, and which still poisons all democrats, even Christian democrats, is the ideology of 89," whose principles such as individual rights had to be "evaluated in

---

[10] Bukharin cited in Jochen Hellbeck, *Revolution on My Mind: Writing a Diary under Stalin* (Cambridge, Mass., 2006), 31. See also Kline, "Changing Attitudes toward the Individual," 624, on the revival of nineteenth-century Russian personalism in this 1930s moment.

[11] Emmanuel Mounier, *A Personalist Manifesto*, trans. Monks of St. John's Abbey (New York, 1938), 17–18.

the light of our conception of man [and] of the Community that completes
him."[12]

The puzzle is how the person, in spite of all these associations, would be
readied for its intellectual – and harsh legalistic! – role later; and much of the
solution to that puzzle depends on Jacques Maritain, who would, not coincidentally, become the most prominent thinker of any kind across the world
to champion rights in the postwar moment. Personalism survived its original
connotations, as the communitarian third way that it promised between individualism and communism transcended its reactionary (and occasional leftist)
connotations to be linked tightly to Cold War conservatism. Maritain's career
provides the best guide, as a proxy for other trajectories in various places.

Ironically, the Young Right's clearest source for claims about the relevance
of the person was that very mentor who, many years later, would make it the
foundation for human rights: Besides a few stray references, Maritain toyed
with the sociopolitical relevance of "the person" first in his popular Action
Française era book *Three Reformers* (1925). There he argued that the catastrophe of modernity, due to the sensualist heresiarch Martin Luther, the solip-
sist metaphysician René Descartes, and the bourgeois reformer Jean-Jacques
Rousseau, left behind Saint Thomas's person for the new individual. Thus,
not just generally, but in Maritain's own case, the basic claim of the political
importance of "the person" antedated any break with the far right of his day,
rather than driving it. "Are you well-informed about the ideological adventure that two pages of *Three Reformers* [those that originally introduced the
person/individual distinction] have allowed?" Maritain's disciple Yves Simon
could ask him in a letter as late as 1941, when the person still remained chiefly
a reactionary conception, in spite of Maritain's extraordinary labors by then
to make it mean something different.[13]

Yet Maritain had left the personalist revolution to others for a decade,
while he continued his original and enduring interests in metaphysics and
aesthetics. In the mid-1930s, this changed. As much as the negative example of the far right, it was Mounier's para-Catholic and this-worldly combat
for a personalist rupture – whatever that meant – that pushed Maritain to
elaborate his own politics. (Intellectually and organizationally, Maritain had
been instrumental in Mounier's path to *Esprit*, but the obverse of the relationship has not been sufficiently stressed. Maritain opposed Mounier's drifts
into apparent proximity to fascism, but would never have become a political

[12] The texts are most conveniently available in René Rémond, *Les crises du catholicisme en France dans les années trente* (Paris, 1996), appendix.
[13] Maritain, *Trois réformateurs: Luther – Descartes – Rousseau* (Paris, 1925); in English, *Three Reformers: Luther – Descartes – Rousseau* (New York, 1955). Simon to Maritain, September 3, 1941, Yves R. Simon Institute, Mishawaka, Indiana. He continued: "Last winter, our seniors had a debate on the question of whether Thomistic personalism is the true interna-tionalism. As a joke it was proclaimed that all that is idiotic is due to individualism, while all that is beautiful stems from personalism."

thinker without Mounier's example.)[14] It is also clear that, though by then an anti-communist of quite long standing, Maritain was angered by the huge propaganda successes of communism in the West in the mid-1930s in the cultural preparation of Popular Front anti-fascism, as figures such as André Gide and André Malraux responded to Bukharin's new propaganda by insisting that the Soviets might have the true recipe for the achievement of dignified humanity.[15] Yet even in his *Integral Humanism* (1936), in which he spelled out his politics of personalism in most classic form, Maritain endorsed the person without endorsing rights, which was a sign of his proximity to non-conformist and illiberal currents in European thought.

There is no way to fathom Maritain's conversion to rights – and that of the whole Continent – without looking to the larger Catholic Church's conversion to personalism. How this happened was unexpected and dramatic, and due above all to events in the mid-1930s that decided Pius XI to commit the Church to anti-totalitarianism.[16] The move toward the later twentieth-century embrace of rights-talk as the essence of Christian social thought occurred neither at a slow and steady pace nor all at once in a single transformative moment. Famously, the Church had treated the notion of rights with vituperation for the entire modern period. It is not impossible to find allusions to the person and even to rights (though always those of family or labor) before the period of reversal. Yet these usages were "neither comprehensive nor tightly systematic."[17] The same was true of the rhetoric of new Catholic social movements that were of such signal importance to interwar history. The crucial leap, which has not been effectively studied, occurred when Pius XI toward the end of his papacy began to use the terms in a more serious and organizing way.

This remarkable turn against "statolatry" by no means compelled any embrace of rights as an organizing doctrine, but it did involve the assertion

[14] These claims are contentious in the literature, but there is no space to defend them here.

[15] See Sandra Teroni and Wolfgang Klein (eds.), *Pour la défense de la culture: les textes du Congrès international des écrivains, Paris 1935* (Dijon, 2005). Thanks to Anson Rabinbach for sharing his illuminating ongoing work on anti-fascism.

[16] This section summarizes the more detailed analysis in Samuel Moyn, "Jacques Maritain: le origini dei Diritti umani e il pensiero politico cristiano," in Luigi Bonanate and Roberto Papini (eds.), *Dialogo interculturale e diritti umani: la Dichiarazione Universale dei Diritti Umani, Genesi, evoluzione, e problemi odierni (1948–2008)* (Bologna, 2008), 97–124. Existing doctrinal histories of the Church and human rights have sectarian versions of the general flaws of teleology, tunnel vision, and triumphalism in human rights history. For examples, see Philippe de la Chappelle, *La Déclaration universelle des droits de l'homme et le catholicisme*, pref. René Cassin (Paris, 1967); Jozef Punt, *Die Idee der Menschenrechte: Ihre geschichtliche Entwicklung und ihre Rezeption durch die moderne katholische Sozialverkündigung* (Paderborn, 1987); Alexander Saberschinsky, *Die Begründung universeller Menschenrechte* (Paderborn, 2002); and Thomas D. Williams, *Who Is My Neighbor? Personalism and the Foundations of Human Rights*, preface by Mary Ann Glendon (Washington, D.C., 2005).

[17] J. Bryan Hehir, "Religious Activism for Human Rights: A Christian Case Study," in John Witte, Jr., and Johan D. van der Vyver (eds.), *Religious Human Rights in Global Perspective: Religious Perspectives* (The Hague, 1996), 101.

of religious sovereignty over personal conscience; very often, this sovereignty attached to the previously peripheral figure of the person. Interestingly, it was most frequently anti-liberal premises that led to what may seem a liberalizing outcome in this denunciation of the era's dictators (Benito Mussolini sometimes exempted), with the modern and "secularist" separation of state from church often presented as having allowed the menacing totalitarian hypertrophy of the state to occur.[18] In any event, it was at this moment that Pius – who knew Maritain well and esteemed his work – turned emphatically to personalism as the foundation of Church's spiritual alternative to totalitarianism, in 1937–1938. "Man, as a person," Pius declared, "possesses rights that he holds from God and which must remain, with regard to the collectivity, beyond the reach of anything that would tend to deny them, to abolish them, or to neglect them."[19] This phraseology, from the anti-Nazi encyclical of March 1937, *Mit brennender Sorge*, was matched by the anti-communist encyclical of the same month, *Divini redemptoris*, the latter with greater emphasis on the right of property in the context of a more general scheme of the rights of the person against the totalitarian collective.[20]

It was thus in a moment of discovering two extreme political ideologies that, in its view, left no room for Christianity that some insisted on sovereignty over the "human," over which in turn no merely temporal politics can claim full authority. Soon to become Pius XII, Eugenio Pacelli, in the summer of 1937, made clear the centrality of this new figure, decrying "a vast and dangerous conspiracy" threatening unlike any prior occasion "the inviolability of the human person that, in his sovereign wisdom and infinite goodness, the Creator has honored with an incomparable dignity." Further, Pacelli cited the critical line from *Mit brennender Sorge* to make clear that this inviolable dignity gave rise to some set of rights. Of course, personalist rights implied moral community, not the selfish entitlements of the bankrupt nineteenth century. All the same, "if a society adopted the pretense that it could diminish the dignity of the human person in refusing it all or some of the rights that come to it from God, it would miss its goal."[21]

What such changes in papal political theory meant on the ground, in the context of much other doctrine and the inherited weight of tradition, varied widely – especially after Pius XII's election a year later to face the final crisis of the 1930s and the difficult choices of the war.[22] With respect to the

---

[18] Cf. Emilio Gentile, *Politics as Religion*, trans. George Staunton (Princeton, 2006), 92–93, and ch. 4.

[19] Pius XI, Encyclical Letter "Mit brennender Sorge," March 14, 1937, as translated in Georges Passelecq and Bernard Suchecky, *The Hidden Encyclical of Pius XI*, trans. Steven Rendall (New York, 1997), 105.

[20] See Xavier de Montclos, "Le discours de Pie XI sur la défense des droits de la personne humaine," in *Achille Ratti, pape Pie XI* (Rome, 1996).

[21] "Lettre de S. Em. le Cardinal Pacelli," in *La Personne humaine en péril* (Lyon, 1937), 5–8.

[22] For a variety of contemporary commentaries on the novel surge of the human person after 1936 in statements by Pius XI and XII, see *The Foundations of International Order* (proceedings

language of rights as well as in other ways, Pius XII, like any good strategist, left his options open, encouraging some possible lines of future development and tolerating others.[23] In different national contexts, rights-talk had different fates: The new language of the rights of the human person was not just passively received, but was creatively interpreted from place to place and moment to moment. As Paul Hanebrink has shown in the case of Hungarian debates, for example, what was at stake for some churchmen and Christian politicians was only "the rights of (Christian) man," chiefly the defense of the right of conversion against racist essentialism, still in the name of a exclusionary vision of a Christianized nation.[24]

But in America – before Maritain ever turned to rights – a small band of liberal Catholics chose a different direction. In tune with his final thought, Pius XI had written barely two months before his death that "Christian teaching alone gives full meaning to the demands of human rights and liberty because it alone gives worth and dignity to human personality." In a pastoral letter in response to this statement in honor of the golden jubilee of Catholic University, American bishops took the argument a (textually unwarranted) step further: "His Holiness calls us to the defense of our democratic government in a constitution that safeguards the inalienable rights of man."[25] American Catholic liberals opposing Father Charles Coughlin's Jew baiting founded the publication *The Voice for Human Rights* in 1939. Historians who have examined the crucial early war years to trace the remarkable afflatus of the hitherto largely unused (in English) phrase "human rights" have discovered minor percolations but little else until something happened to catapult the term into its immediate postwar career. Completely neglected among these

---

of the Catholic Congress on International Peace, The Hague, 1938) (Oxford, 1938); André Saint-Denis, *Pie XI contre les idoles: bolchévisme, racisme-étatisme* (Paris, 1939); or Lewis Watt, S.J., *Pope Pius XII on World Order* (Oxford, 1940), ch. 5, "The Dignity of the Human Person."

[23] For a general picture of Pius's wartime positions, see Peter C. Kent, "Toward the Reconstitution of Christian Europe: The War Aims of the Papacy, 1938–1945," in David B. Woolner and Richard B. Kurial (eds.), *FDR, the Vatican, and the Roman Catholic Church in America, 1933–1945* (New York, 2003).

[24] Paul A. Hanebrink, *In Defense of Christian Hungary: Religion, Nationalism, and Antisemitism, 1890–1944* (Ithaca, 2006), 170–180.

[25] "Pope Bids Church to Guard Man's Rights," *New York Times*, October 13, 1938; "Pastoral Letter [of the American Catholic Hierarchy] on the Teaching of Democracy," *New York Times*, November 25, 1938. The pope made the anti-totalitarian (and anti-capitalist) context of "human rights" clear once again: "The Catholic is necessarily the champion of true human rights and the defender of true human liberties; it is in the name of God Himself that he cries out against any civic philosophy which would degrade man to the position of a soulless pawn in a sordid game of power and prestige, or would seek to banish him from membership in the human family; it is in the same holy name that he opposes any social philosophy which would regard man as a mere chattel in commercial competition for profit, or would set him at the throat of his fellow in a blind brutish class struggle for existence."

percolations so far highlighted, however, is the comparatively early Catholic articulation of the human rights idea.[26]

Soon European Catholics were repeating the slogan, and Maritain, on an American sojourn when France fell but transmitting his ideas back to the Continent throughout the war, made himself the premier interpreter of human rights among Catholics, and indeed almost singlehandedly reinvented them as a Christian tradition. By itself, personalism could have led Maritain, like so many other others, into the arms of the Vichy government, whose leader, indeed, himself proclaimed that "individualism has nothing in common with respect for the human person" (a respect he promised his regime would restore, along with religious civilization as a whole). Maritain's formulae of the "primacy of the spiritual" and "integral humanism" were even used as sloganeering buzzwords by Vichyite intellectuals and youth.[27] But Maritain, in exile, opposed Vichy uncompromisingly and soon became an inspiration for the Resistance, even if he was ambivalent about Charles de Gaulle as the Free French leader, on the grounds that de Gaulle would not concur with his vision of personalistic democracy. It was most clearly in early 1942 that Maritain transformed into the philosopher of human rights that he had never been before. In *Natural Law and Human Rights*, Maritain took what would be a fateful step for postwar intellectual history as a whole, making the claim that a revival of natural law implies a broad set of pre-political human rights.[28]

What would have been – and still is – curious about this claim, of course, is that whatever their opinions of the origins of modern rights-talk, nearly all histories of the political language concur that the rise of rights in political theory occurred after and because of the destruction of the Thomistic natural law tradition.[29] In either a stroke of a master, or a sleight of hand, or both, Maritain – as if the Thomistic movement had not long and unanimously

[26] See esp. A. W. Brian Simpson, *Human Rights and the End of Empire: Britain and the Genesis of the European Convention* (Oxford, 2001), ch. 4; also Paul Gordon Lauren, *The Evolution of International Human Rights: Visions Seen*, 2nd ed. (Philadelphia, 2003), ch. 5.

[27] Cited in Hellman, *Emmanuel Mounier and the New Catholic Left, 1930–1950* (Toronto, 1981), 168. For personalism – including fulsome invocation of Maritain's formulae – at Vichy, see Hellman's writings: "Maritain, Simon, and Vichy's Elite Schools," in Michael D. Torre (ed.), *Freedom in the Modern World* (Notre Dame, 1989), 165–180; "Communitarians, Non-conformists, and the Search for a 'New Man' in Vichy France," in Sarah Fishman et al. (eds.), *France at War: Vichy and the Historians* (Oxford, 2000), 91–106; and *The Knight-Monks of Vichy France: Uriage, 1940–1945* (Montreal, 1994).

[28] The earliest publications are "The Natural Law and Human Rights" (Windsor, Ontario, 1942), an award acceptance speech dated January 18, 1942, published as a pamphlet, and "Natural Law and Human Rights," *Dublin Review*, 210 (April 1942), 116–124. The book is *Les droits de l'homme et la loi naturelle* (New York, 1942), translated into many languages.

[29] For radically contrasting stories of the origins of rights that nevertheless concur on this point, see Leo Strauss, *Natural Right and History* (Chicago, 1953); Richard Tuck, *Natural Rights Theories: Their Origin and Development* (Cambridge, 1979); and Michel Villey, *Le droit et les droits de l'homme* (Paris, 1983). In Catholicism, see the dissident view of Alasdair MacIntyre, *After Virtue: A Study in Moral Theory* (Notre Dame, 1981).

rejected modern rights – claimed that the one implied the other and, indeed, that only the one plausibly and palatably justified the other. Thanks to Maritain above all, the older view that Christianity's political and social doctrine could not be reformulated in terms of rights was dropped in exchange for the claim that only the Christian vision placing them in the framework of the common good afforded a persuasive theory of rights. By his Christmas message of 1942, the one frequently discussed solely for its insufficient reference to Jewish suffering, Pius too was laying out his postwar vision in terms of the dignity of the person and human rights.[30]

This trajectory cemented the resonance of the dignity of the human person as the communitarian framework for the new rights-talk. By 1942, British Catholic Christopher Dawson (who had imported Maritain in his reactionary phase to Great Britain along with Carl Schmitt in his Catholic phase) was sounding similar themes. "We are standing against an order in which all human rights and the human person itself are immolated on the altar of power to the glory of the New Leviathan," he wrote. Alluding to Franklin D. Roosevelt's "four freedoms," he now explained, in spite of his formerly reactionary politics,

The liberties which we demand and which humanity demands are not the right of the strong to oppress the weak or the right of the ambitious to enrich themselves at other men's expense: but the elementary right which are to the human spirit what air and light are to the body: freedom to worship God, freedom of speech, freedom from want and freedom from fear.

All the same, he clarified that if Christianity now implied some sort of democracy, it could not be a liberal kind:

It must be a social order directed to spiritual ends.... From this point of view the use of the term "Democracy" as the definition of our cause is not completely satisfactory. For Democracy has a restricted political significance which by no means covers the whole field of values that has to be defended, and the confusion of Democracy as a general term for our tradition of social freedom, and its more limited but more accurate political meaning, is apt to produce misunderstanding and disagreement. For the cause that we are defending is far more fundamental than any form of government or any political creed. It is bound up with the whole tradition of Western and Christian culture.... No doubt Democracy as an ideal does stand for these things and is the outcome of this tradition. But in practice modern democratic culture often represents only a debased and secularized version of this ideal and in many respects, as de Tocqueville saw more than a century ago, it prepares the way for the coming of the new mass order which achieves political form in the totalitarian State. What we are defending, in short, is not democracy but humanity.[31]

[30] Pius XII, "The Internal Order of States and People," in Vincent A. Yzermans (ed.), *The Major Addresses of Pope Pius XII*, 2 vols. (St. Paul, 1961). See, e.g., John A. O'Brien, "The Pope's Way to Peace," *International Conciliation*, 44 (October 1944), 647–663 (rights of the human person throughout). In the same papal collection, one may wish to compare the 1958 Christmas message, "The Rights of Man."

[31] Christopher Dawson, *The Judgment of the Nations* (New York, 1942), 185–186.

Dawson's argument made sense in light of prewar conceptions of democracy, which prioritized its formalistic associations as a "bourgeois" electoral and economic phenomenon that both far left and Christian politics were agreed in rejecting in the name of substantive moral community. As the war continued, however, one of Maritain's main purposes was to lay out a new, Christian conception of democracy that transcended these narrow limits, and soon the Pope would agree. Democracy and humanity could coincide.

In the flow of Christian political theory in these years, in fact, the original commitment of the non-individualist person in the non-totalitarian community remained stable, as the overall governing framework into which rights were introduced. In other words, the superimposition of rights on personalism meant as much continuity as change. In an atmosphere in which many Catholics understood the defense of the West to mean all-out war against Bolshevism even at the price of alliance with unholy forces, Maritain's message was primarily directed against the European preference for fascism as the lesser evil. "An obscure process of leniency toward totalitarian forms that lying propaganda tries to picture as the upholders of order," Maritain regretted at the University of Pennsylvania bicentennial in 1940, "has thus invaded parts of the believing groups in many countries."[32] "The error of those Catholics who follow Pétain in France or Franco in Spain," Maritain wrote Charles de Gaulle in 1941, "is to convert Catholic thought, through lack of social and political education, in the direction of old paternalistic conceptions of history rejected in the meantime by the popes and condemned by history."[33]

In the process, Maritain's attitude toward the catastrophe of modernity softened slightly but discernibly (though it never reversed). The ambivalence is well captured in his *Fortune* magazine story of 1942 in which he still castigated modern man for "claim[ing] human rights and dignity – without God, for his ideology grounded human rights and human dignity in a godlike, infinite autonomy of human will," while also now referring to the apparently alternative "concept of, and devotion to, the rights of the human person" as "the most significant political improvement of modern times."[34] His relative move toward an affirmation of a specific kind of state framework within which alone a "new Christian order" could come about forced Maritain to quietly but decisively drop old associations of formal liberties and formal democracy with liberal individualism on its deathbed. He broke largely with visions, such as either Marxism or Mounier's personalism, that treated formal rights and democracy as elements of a hypocritical capitalist

---

[32] William L. Laurence, "Political Theory of Religion Is Hit," *New York Times*, September 17, 1940. Though well informed, Maritain consistently presented France as captured, thus drastically understating the extent and zeal of the collaborationism of some of his countrymen.

[33] Maritain to Charles de Gaulle, November 21, 1941, in *Cahiers Jacques Maritain*, 16–17 (April 1988), 61. By the next year he urged de Gaulle to champion a "renewed democratic ideal" rooted in personalism. Ibid., 68.

[34] Maritain, "Christian Humanism," *Fortune*, April 1942.

sham. Formal or "bourgeois" liberties formerly condemned now had to be resurrected as providing the legal carapace of the Christian state and even the spiritual interstate order. Arguably, however, these innovations were in the service of keeping personalist communitarianism the same in new circumstances.

It is true, though, that this substantive vision now prompted a less critical attitude toward formal guarantees and political structures or might indeed invest them with considerable significance. One could say something similar of Pius XII who, having adopted the rhetoric of the rights of the person, was by the time of his 1944 Christmas message following Maritain by endorsing democracy on condition of differentiating between its Christian communitarian and reprobate secularist version.[35] "Defend These Human Rights!" British Catholic John Eppstein wrote in a 1948 pamphlet, explaining that this meant *la défense de la personne humaine* first discovered by Catholics in the later 1930s. ("This was somewhat different from the familiar enumeration of 'the Rights of Man and the Citizen'," he explained, "since by 'the human person' the Christian opponents of State absolutism meant particularly man as a *spiritual* being.")[36] The work of saving the person from its anti-democratic votaries arguably depended on the deeper commitment to a moral and communitarian ethos, which allowed leaving those old versions behind almost as if they had never been. "To avoid all misunderstanding, I must add," de Visscher, the international lawyer, put it rather charmingly in 1947, "that the personalist conception must be defended against some of those who claim it and who have sometimes compromised it in the very process of advocating for it."[37]

Even Mounier, who remained in France, embraced rights after a fashion – albeit very briefly. After having flirted with identifying the National Revolution as a personalist one – he criticized Maritain for his treasonous defense of American democracy before being shut down by the Vichy regime – Mounier penned a declaration of "the rights of persons and communities."[38] This made an important

---

[35] See Pius XII, "True and False Democracy," in *Major Addresses*. Even in America, the major postwar Catholic thinker, Jesuit and Maritain follower John Courtney Murray, could argue in a 1950 essay that the human rights turn showed that the modern world had finally imbibed Catholicism's message rather than vice versa: "The growing conviction of the old attempts to solve the problem of human liberty and social order in purely secularistic, positivist terms had created a new openness to the world of metaphysical and religious values. [The Christian human rights idea provides] such a basis because it is metaphysical in its foundations, because it is asserted within a religious framework, and because it is realist (not nominalist), societal (not individualist), and integrally human (not rationalist) in its outlook on man and society." Murray, "The Natural Law," in Robert M. MacIver (ed.), *Great Expressions of Human Rights* (New York, 1950), as reprinted in Murray, *We Hold These Truths: Catholic Reflections on the American Proposition* (New York, 1960), 320.

[36] John Eppstein, *Defend these Human Rights! Each Man's Stake in the United Nations – A Catholic View* (New York, 1948), 5.

[37] De Visscher, "Les droits fondamentaux de l'homme," 158.

[38] On Maritain, see Mounier, *Oeuvres*, 4 vols. (Paris, 1961–1963), 4:694; for the declaration, see Mounier, "Faut-il refaire la Déclaration des droits?" ibid., 4:96–104. This document

difference to his followers, many of whom essentially made Maritain's move to reconcile personalism with formal democracy while Mounier notoriously moved from non-conformism to the far left in the postwar era. Mounier had, it is clear, a far more serious impact on Belgium and France, whereas Maritain's message found its most significant hearing in Italy and Latin America.[39] Most important, followers of Mounier in the briefly if meteorically successful postwar Mouvement républicain populaire were able to be more faithful than Mounier was to his brief rights-based revision of personalism.

A good example of a Mounier disciple who played a major role in the postwar European human rights moment – besides Charles de Visscher – was François de Menthon, who headed the French prosecution team at Nuremberg. In his spectacular opening address, now understandably attacked for developing the juristic novelty of "crimes against humanity" while failing to mention which part of humanity actually suffered the crimes, Menthon identified the German acts as "crimes against the spirit," a clear reference to interwar and wartime anti-materialism that contemporaries, unlike Nuremberg's many historians since, would have readily identified as such. "National Socialism," he thundered, "ends in the absorption of the personality of the citizen into that of the state and in the denial of any intrinsic value to the human person." Even his glancing reference at the end of his address to "citizens of the occupied countries categorized as Jews" singled out the damage done to "their personal rights and to their human dignity."[40] No one else, including Robert H. Jackson, used similar language at the time: The originally personalist framing of crimes against humanity, and their deep affront to the rights of the dignified human person, has quite simply been missed.

As for Maritain, he continued to defend a personalistic conception of human rights wherever he went during the years after the war: in his work for UNESCO on the philosophical grounding of human rights, as French Ambassador to the Holy See for a few years (where he decisively influenced later popes who would finally overcome institutional resistance within the Church to a full move to human rights language two decades later), or Princeton University.[41] But though Maritain was certainly the most prominent

was widely read in the framing process of the abortive and then the passed Fourth Republic Declaration of Rights.

[39] See esp. Paolo Pombeni, *Il gruppo dossettiano e la fondazione della democrazia italiana (1938–1948)* (Bologna, 1979), and Olivier Compagnon, *Jacques Maritain et l'Amérique du Sud* (Villeneuve, 2003).

[40] François de Menthon, "Opening Address (January 17, 1946)," in Michael R. Marrus (ed.), *The Nuremberg War Crimes Trial 1945–46: A Documentary History* (Boston, 1997), 89–94; cf. Laurent Ducerf, *François de Menthon: un Catholique au service de la République* (Paris, 2006), ch. 10.

[41] His UNESCO address is *La Voie de la Paix: Discours prononcé à la séance inaugurale de la IIe Conférence internationale de l'Unesco* (Mexico City, 1947), in English in many places such as "Possibilities for Co-operation in a Divided World," in Maritain, *The Range of Reason* (New York, 1952); for his UNESCO rights inquiry, see Maritain (ed.), *Human Rights: Comments and Interpretation* (New York, 1949); see also Maritain, *The Meaning of*

thinker on the postwar scene to defend the new concept, it was political shifts that made its fortune in the Western European polities that would become its early homeland. Still, because Catholicism aspired to be and to some extent was even then a global phenomenon, there should be no surprise in discovering that the personalistic framing of the global human rights "moment" of the era affected the language not simply inside Continental Europe but far beyond it. This included, most obviously, the move to human rights at the level of international organization, essentially rhetorical though it was (as European international lawyers were not wrong to note).

Indeed, the human person became a key figure of thought at the United Nations, thanks to Christians impressed by papal language who injected it into founding documents. In a multiculturalist age, it is tempting to look back at storied figures in the origins of human rights at the United Nations and claim them for the third world and alternative values, when in fact they themselves insisted – before the right audiences at least – that they were making a Christian contribution.[42] Charles Malik, the Lebanese Christian who is responsible for the personalistic language of the Universal Declaration of Human Rights proper, is a case in point. "In Christianity, the individual human person possesses an absolute value," Malik explained in 1951, for instance. "The ultimate ground of all our freedom is the Christian doctrine of the absolute inviolability of the human person."[43] Carlos Romulo, Philippines delegate to the United Nations and a crucial figure in the General Assembly debates over the Universal Declaration, provides another illuminating example, as his lectures on the implicit foundation of new impulses in public international law make plain. "Of all the acts of the United Nations," he argued in the period, "the Universal Declaration of Human Rights has demonstrated most clearly the tendency... to work out a system of international law conforming as closely as possible to natural law.... We may yet find ourselves confronted by the seeming paradox of Christianity emerging as the only practical program for lasting peace and equitable order in our troubled world."[44]

There was, however, very little true international human rights law for decades, and the real story of human rights in the early postwar period, with due allowance for the importance of symbolism, is of its nationalization and regionalization. I do not claim that the resumption of the interwar vogue of declarations of rights in the postwar domestic constitutionalism (at least outside the British sphere until the early 1960s policy change) reflected any

---

Human Rights (Waltham, 1949), and, for his own fullest views, Maritain, *Man and the State* (Chicago, 1951).

[42] Cf. Roland Burke, "'The Compelling Dialogue of Freedom': Human Rights at the Bandung Conference," *Human Rights Quarterly*, 28:4 (November 2006), 947–965.

[43] Charles Malik, "The Prospect for Freedom" (address at honorary rectorial convocation, University of Dubuque, February 19, 1951), unpaginated.

[44] Carlos Romulo, "Natural Law and International Law," *University of Notre Dame Natural Law Institute Proceedings*, 3 (1949), 121, 126.

personalistic consensus.[45] Early steps in European unification and the – also initially quite unimpressive – European human rights regime, however, very much did. As Wolfram Kaiser has now shown, Christian Democracy, hegemonic starting in this era as the Continent restabilized, made personalist communitarianism the fundamental ideology of its work nationally and construction of Europe regionally.[46] "In the inter-war period catholicism had been closely linked to nationalism and the League of Nations had been presented as being a dangerous centre of masonic power," Richard Vinen observes, in a similar vein. "After 1945, this changed. Catholic organizations were enthusiastic proponents of international harmony, within the western bloc at least, and Christian Democrat parties in all European countries were so intimately linked to European integration that some began to feel that Europe was being built under the aegis of the 'catholic international.'"[47]

It is true that personalism, in both Maritain's and Mounier's renditions, could have had left-wing implications, and to some extent did, prompting an evanescent "left Catholicism" that quickly sputtered.[48] This was not, however, because of any dispute about the role of the state in the economy: Though Continental Europeans needed Americans in the 1940s, it was not to learn commitment to an economic New Deal. As de Visscher argued, no one believed that personalism implied a return to "the economic liberalism of the eighteenth or nineteenth centuries."[49] Rather, Christians on the left and right agreed that some management of the economy was necessary, and diverged from there. Very quickly, as it turned out, left versions of personalism were extinguished, and the ideology underwrote a reinvention of conservatism in power. This "re-recasting of bourgeois Europe," as one may call it, occurred under the political hegemony of Christian Democracy, even if one wants to see it as redounding to the benefit of liberal capitalism in the long run.[50] It should

[45] See Boris Mirkine-Guetzévitch, *Les constitutions européennes* (Paris, 1951), ch. 8, and, for British developments, Charles O. H. Parkinson, *Bills of Rights and Decolonization: The Emergence of Domestic Human Rights Instruments in Britain's Overseas Territories* (Oxford, 2007).

[46] Wolfram Kaiser, *Christian Democracy and the Origins of the European Union* (Cambridge, 2007). See also the more affirmative and invested views in Roberto Papini (ed.), *L'apporto del personalismo alla costruzione dell'Europa* (Milan, 1981), and Philippe Chenaux, *De la chrétienté à l'Europe: les Catholiques et l'idée européenne au XXe siècle* (Paris, 2007), esp. ch. 3, "L'influence du personnalisme dans la construction de l'Europe."

[47] Richard Vinen, *Bourgeois Politics in France, 1945–1951* (Cambridge, 1995), 152, footnote omitted.

[48] See Gerd-Rainer Horn and Emmanuel Gerard (eds.), *Left Catholicism: Catholics and Society in Western Europe at the Point of Liberation* (Louvain, 2001), esp. Martin Conway's synthesis, "Left Catholicism in Europe in the 1940s: Elements of an Interpretation," 270–271 and 277–278: "In comparison with the rapid growth of Christian Democracy, the Left Catholic groups must inevitably appear as something of a historical footnote."

[49] De Visscher, "Les droits fondamentaux de l'homme," 158.

[50] The allusion is to Charles Maier's work on Europe after World War I, which has not been comparably repeated for the post–World War II period. As Conway puts it, "perhaps the most durable change in European political life brought about by the war was in fact conservative

not be surprising, therefore, that many of the chief founders of the European project, both in politics generally and in the tradition of European human rights specifically, were avowed personalists (for instance, Robert Schuman, Paul-Henri Spaak, and Pierre-Henri Teitgen).

In its regionalized domain, human rights law gained only slightly more traction than on the global scene: The case of the European Convention of Human Rights (1950) involved – in the early decades when there was no right of petition and little serious activity, not least because of its derogability during colonial emergencies – much more ideological signaling about the values on which Western European identity depended than it did legally enforceable guarantees. The common Christian basis for unity mattered a lot here, only now what that meant was the centrality of the human person. The Convention itself, given signal British participation in its origins, is not an exception to this statement but illustrates how powerfully the revolt against materialism as the essence of Europe resonated in these years. As the Convention's historian Brian Simpson has emphasized, it emerged thanks to Britain's commitment to "spiritual union" of Western Europeans against communism, in Ernest Bevin's own phrase. "In the event Bevin's idea of a spiritual union came to be secularized," Simpson comments with distinct understatement, "but this was not perhaps how it began."[51]

That the incipient Cold War would soon come to be widely understood in terms of the defense of religion and "the West" that the Church's struggle against communism had already been for three decades was no doubt crucial in the larger postwar spiritualist consensus among Western European liberal-conservatives.[52] In this sense, not just British commitment to "spiritual" values in international affairs, which had also antedated the war, could allow new collaborations with Continental religious ideology in the postwar years, of which the Convention is only one example.[53] More generally, there had been important Protestant defenders of third-way personalism all along (perhaps most importantly, Swiss writer Denis de Rougemont, who had been a non-conformist close to both Marc and Mounier before becoming a Europeanist).[54] The larger phenomenon, without which the picture would remain incomplete, is the cross-denominational ratification of human dignity

in nature.... Catholicism in the later 1940s and 1950s ... while presiding politically over the postwar reconstruction of Western Europe, retained within it the intellectual components of a profound critique of liberalist and individualist values which underpinned that same process of reconstruction." Conway, "Left Catholicism in Europe in the 1940s," 277, 281.

[51] See Simpson, *Human Rights and the End of Empire*, esp. 568–570 ("Saving Western Civilization") and 577–579 ("What Was the Spiritual Union?") at 579.

[52] Dianne Kirby, "Divinely Sanctioned: The Anglo-American Cold War Alliance and the Defence of Western Civilization and Christianity, 1945–1948," *Journal of Contemporary History*, 35:3 (2000), 385–412, and Kirby (ed.), *Religion and the Cold War* (New York, 2003).

[53] Jeanne Morefield, *Covenants without Swords: Idealist Liberalism and the Spirit of Empire* (Princeton, 2005).

[54] Bruno Ackermann, *Denis de Rougemont: De la personne à l'Europe* (Lausanne, 2000).

as part of an ecumenical reinvention of Christianity of both Catholic and Protestant varieties. A few notes on the German case – a crucial link in the Catholic international but with decisive Protestant participation – are useful in this regard.

There is no reason to hypothesize the direct impact of the various thinkers in the Francophone orbit on German developments, though the full ramifications of dissident networks across the Rhine in the interwar period are only beginning to be reconstructed.[55] Certainly, the spiritualistic consensus and emphasis on dignitarian personalism – including sometimes human rights – prevalent in the early years after World War II suggest German Christians developed their own versions of the doctrines canvassed so far, based on easily available papal pronouncements. Even if it is true that they had no home-grown Maritain, a cognate spiritualist credo came close to providing the central ideological fulcrum of Christian Democracy in Germany, as Maria Mitchell has shown.[56] And just as in the case of the Universal Declaration on which it drew, the Federal Republic Basic Law's opening affirmation of human dignity has to be read not just retrospectively as a response to the Nazi past but prospectively as an allusion to the kind of moral future that would alone overcome that past. It is a mistake, in other words, to think about the "recivilization" of West Germany in the absence of the religious ideology that provided its justification and explained the specific, nonsecular, moralized form it was supposed to take.[57] Premier historian and Protestant conservative Gerhard Ritter thus spoke for many when, in 1948, he rallied to human rights, declaring that on the concept "depends nothing less than the survival of Western culture.... Despite all that has divided us for centuries,

[55] See Hans-Manfred Bock (ed.), *Entre Locarno et Vichy: les relations culturelles franco-allemandes dans les années 30* (Paris, 1993), and Thomas Keller, *Deutsch-französische Dritte-Weg-Diskurse: personalistische Intellektuellendebatte der Zwischenkriegszeit* (Munich, 2001). See also Heinz Hürten, "Der Einfluß Jacques Maritains auf das politische Denken in Deutschland," *Jahrbuch für christliche Sozialwissenschaften*, 26 (1985), 25–39.

[56] Many German Catholics in the emigration, such as Waldemar Gurian or Heinrich Rommen, did not return. A parallel German story to Maritain's creation of a nonreactionary personalism can be told about Dietrich von Hildebrand, a Scheler disciple who fled Germany to Austria (where he favored "Austro-fascist" corporatism) before fleeing to France, then the United States and taking up Maritain's cause. See, e.g., Hildebrand, "Der Kampf um die Person," *Die christliche Ständestaat*, 6 (January 14, 1934), reprinted in Ernst Wenisch (ed.), *Memoiren und Aufsätze gegen den Nationalsozialismus 1933–1938* (Mainz, 1994), 191–197, and "The World Crisis and the Human Personality," *Thought*, 16:62 (September 1941), 457–472. However, I do not currently have evidence of parallel impact of German personalist political theory on the postwar German scene to match the legal evidence introduced below.

[57] Maria Mitchell, "Materialism and Secularism: CDU Politicians and National Socialism, 1945–49," *Journal of Modern History*, 67:2 (June 1995), 278–308, and Mitchell, "'Antimaterialism' in Early German Christian Democracy," in Thomas Kselman and Joseph A. Buttigieg (eds.), *European Christian Democracy: Historical Legacies and Comparative Perspectives* (Notre Dame, 2003), 199–227; cf. Konrad Jarausch, *After Hitler: Recivilizing Germans, 1945–1995* (New York, 2006).

[there still exists] among the great nations of the one-time Christian West a community of moral-religious convictions which is broad and firm enough to serve as the foundation for a new solid structure of a Christian oriented social ethics." Everything depended on human rights – but only so long (Ritter insisted) as they were treated as a reformulation of those ethics, and were clearly distinguished from "the mechanical principle of equality" of secular culture, which had given rise to atomistic capitalism and totalitarian collectivism alike.[58]

The transformation of the political meaning of Christianity works far better than the continuation of fascism proper to explain the centrality of dignitarian rights not just in postwar politics, but also in postwar law – most famously, of course, postwar German constitutional law.[59] Catholic jurists such as Willi Geiger and Josef Wintrich, although at times quite compromised during the Nazi regime, could come to draw directly on new papal traditions in the postwar years, to give a strongly communitarian view of the Basic Law. As a judge on the Bundesverfassungsgericht, Geiger, for instance, championed the centrality of dignitarian rights in public and private law in the early Federal Republic, which he saw as totally different in basis now that they had been reassigned from being Weimar-era products of the sovereign will to being rooted in the pre-constitutional nature of persons.[60] But others found relatively independent routes to similar conceptions. Protestant Gerhard Leibholz, an émigré in Britain during the war (and Dietrich Bonhoeffer's brother-in-law), early established contact with the crucial intermediary figure between British and resisting German Protestants George Bell, bishop of Chichester.[61] Developing

---

[58] Gerhard Ritter, "Ursprung und Wesen der Menschenrechte," *Historische Zeitschrift*, 169:2 (August 1949), 233, 263, and Andreas Dorpalen, "Historiography as History: The Work of Gerhard Ritter," *Journal of Modern History*, 34:1 (March 1962), 10. See also Ritter, "Die Menschenrechte und das Christentum," *Zeitwende*, 21:1 (July 1949), 1–12, and my "The First Historian of Human Rights," *American Historical Review* 116:1 (February 2011).

[59] Cf. James Q. Whitman, "On Nazi 'Honour' and the New European 'Dignity'," in Christian Joerges and Navraj Singh Ghaleigh (eds.), *The Darker Legacy of European Law: Perceptions of Europe and Perspectives on a European Order in Legal Scholarship during the Era of Fascism and National Socialism* (Cambridge, 2003), 243–266.

[60] See Willi Geiger, *Grundrechte und Rechtsprechung* (Munich, 1959), and "Die Wandlung der Grundrechte," in Max Imboden (ed.), *Gedanke und Gestalt des demokratischen Rechtsstaats* (Vienna, 1965), 9–36. See Gerhard Leibholz et al. (eds.), *Menschenwürde und freiheitliche Rechtsordnung: Festschrift für Willi Geiger zum 65. Geburtstag* (Tübingen, 1974). Also of importance was the Bavarian judge Josef Wintrich, whose personalist formulae the Bundesverfassungsgericht took over; see, for example, *Zur Problematik der Grundrechte* (Cologne, 1957), and Ulrich Becker, *Das "Menschenbild des Grundgesetzes" in der Rechtsprechung des Bundesverfassungsgerichts* (Berlin, 1996). On Geiger under Nazism, see Ingo Müller, *Hitler's Justice: The Courts of the Third Reich*, trans. Deborah Schneider (Cambridge, Mass., 1992), 218.

[61] Bell's postwar writing shows that Anglicans signed, if slightly less frontally, onto anti-totalitarian Christian personalism too. Bell, "The Church in Relation to International Affairs" (address at Chatham House), *International Affairs*, 25:4 (October 1949), 405–414.

Protestant versions of anti-totalitarianism emphasizing spiritual freedom, both worked together with Anglican Alec Vidler and Continental Catholic refugees to argue for a return of natural law based on the person. "Must not theonomic thinking demand that the State ought to abandon the idea of being a self-contained sovereign entity with only rights of its own, and acknowledge that it is a member of a community of nations each and all of which are bound to serve the rights of the human person?" Leibholz asked in 1946. In the postwar era, he returned to Germany, and as a judge on the nation's highest constitutional court, he tirelessly promoted the centrality of the human personality (*Persönlichkeit*) as the foundation stone of democratic order.[62]

The intellectual and cultural sources for such a conservative rapprochement with the rights of man were not individualist in general or Kantian in particular, certainly not in the early going. In a first moment, in fact, the dominant view was to connect the human dignity affirmed at the outset of the Basic Law with naturalistic premises, and indeed "the dominant Catholic natural law teaching possessed in the first postwar years such a powerful radiance amongst constitutional experts that Protestants themselves could not withdraw from it."[63] In a second moment, Catholic personalist and author of the leading commentary on the Basic Law Günter Dürig moved away from natural law to a theory of human dignity, and rights generally, as "objective values" (here Scheler's old critique of Kant's putatively subjectivist proceduralism in the name of material values provided the main inspiration).[64] In both moments, personalist conceptions of dignity purporting to leave behind the

---

As he put it, "Chief among [the idolatries of the day] are the worship of power, the totalitarian State, nationalism, racialism, the craving for riches.... Put against them the great Christian ideas of the sovereignty and fatherhood of God, the solidarity of the human race with all its varieties, the sacredness of the human personality.... [T]he rights of men derive directly from their condition as children of God and not of the State" (407, 409).

[62] Gerhard Leibholz, *Christianity, Politics, and Power* (London, 1943), and "Politics and Natural Law," paper delivered at the conference that led to A. R. Vidler and W. H. Whitehouse (eds.), *Natural Law: A Christian Re-consideration* (London, 1946), 31–36. Both of Leibholz's texts and many others from his émigré years are in Leibholz, *Politics and Law* (Leyden, 1965), citation at 23. On the postwar career, see Manfred Wiegandt, *Norm und Wirklichkeit: Gerhard Leibholz, 1901–1982: Leben, Werk und Richteramt* (Baden-Baden, 1995).

[63] Frieder Günther, *Denken vom Staat her: Die bundesdeutsche Staatsrechtslehre zwischen Dezision und Integration 1949–1970* (Munich, 2004), 192, and, for the larger context of rights, 192–196, 202–204. For the view of a contemporary, see Hans Maier, "Katholische Sozial- und Staatslehre und neuere deutsche Staatslehre," *Archiv des öffentlichen Rechts*, 93:1 (1968), 1–36.

[64] Günter Dürig, "Die Menschenauffassung des Grundgesetzes," *Juristische Rundschau* 7 (1952), 259–263 reprinted in Walter Schmitt Glaeser and Peter Häberle (eds.), *Gesammelte Schriften* (Berlin, 1984). For his classic commentary on the *Grundgesetz*, Art. 1, see Dürig and Theodor Maunz, *Grundgesetz: Kommentar* (Munich, 1958); cf. Ernst-Wolfgang Böckenförde, "Die Menschenwürde *war* unantastbar," *Frankfurter Allgemeine Zeitung*, September 9, 2003.

choice between individual and collective provided the dominant framework and affected many aspects of what human rights meant within the postwar constitutional framework.[65]

It may be true, then, that (as Mark Mazower has argued) there was a conceptual shift from group to individual in diplomatic and legal circles that set the stage for the post–World War II human rights moment. But there was also a shift afoot from the individual to the person, and in terms of its *cultural meaning* at the time; and the embedding of its ideas in postwar European politics, the Universal Declaration is a profoundly communitarian document – precisely a moral repudiation of dangerous individualism, albeit one equally intended to steer equally clear of communism.[66] Indeed, in my view this is the key to placing the document – along with the human rights idea in general – more securely in the ambiance of the war's aftermath, as part of the moral reconstruction of Europe perceived to be necessary to stave off future world crises and conflicts.

One significant irony of this history is that the availability of a now far more familiar paradigm of the moral value of the person – one with roots in Roman law, and embedded in Immanuel Kant's political thought – may easily promote oblivion of the primacy of a very different human person in the years when the Universal Declaration was framed and the concept was embedded in early postwar European law and common sense. Kantians were few and far between in the 1940s. In a later era, communitarianism could come to seem a major challenge to rights-talk, but few in that debate are even aware that rights-talk in immediate postwar Europe did not exclude communitarianism but instead presupposed it.[67]

In short, the original context of the European embrace of human rights – in which they were linked to the conservative defense of human dignity and attached to the figure of the human person – was in Christianity's last golden age on the Continent, which lasted for two decades before the shocking reversal for the fortunes of religion after the mid-1960s. The "death of Christian Europe," as one might call it, forced – along with many other developments – a complete reinvention of the meaning of the human rights embedded in

[65] "A strong personalist and communitarian philosophy pervades this conception of the human person," the leading Anglophone authority on German constitutional jurisprudence confirms. Donald P. Kommers, *The Constitutional Jurisprudence of the Federal Republic of Germany*, new ed. (Raleigh, 1997), 304.

[66] Cf. Mark Mazower, "The Strange Triumph of Human Rights, 1930–1950," *Historical Journal*, 47:2 (June 2004), 379–398.

[67] For graphic evidence of the sheer difficulty of defending individualism in law in the 1940s, see Marcel Waline, *L'individualisme et le droit* (Paris, 1945). But, for an attempt to inject personalism into the hitherto powerful – and still anti-individualist – "institutionalist" movement in legal thought by one of its leaders, cf. J. T. Delos and Bruno de Solages, *Essai sur l'ordre politique national et international* (Paris, 1947), esp. 86–88.

European identity both formally and really since the war.[68] The only serious thread of persistence was, ironically, in Eastern Europe, and especially in Poland, not coincidentally the main exception to Christian collapse. There Maritain, Mounier, and Scheler enjoyed huge discipleships, not least in the personalism of Karol Wojtyla, eventually Pope John Paul II.[69] But by the time of the explosion of human rights in the later 1970s, when the concept gained a currency out of all proportion to any other moment in history, Christian personalism, while not absent, was decidedly peripheral. Human rights had become a secular doctrine of the left; how that happened is another story.

[68] This collapse, which ought to be shocking, remains essentially unexplained, but see Callum Brown, *The Death of Christian Britain: Understanding Secularization, 1800–2000* (New York, 2001), and Mark Edward Ruff, *Wayward Flock: Catholic Youth in Postwar West Germany* (Chapel Hill, 2005).

[69] The literature here is large, but see Karol Wojtyla, "Thomistic Personalism" (1961), "On the Dignity of the Human Person" (1964), and other essays in *Person and Community: Selected Essays (Catholic Thought from Lublin)*, trans. Theresa Sandok (New York, 1993); cf. Avery Cardinal Dulles, "John Paul II and the Mystery of the Human Person," *America*, February 2, 2004, reprinted in Dulles, *Church and Society: The Laurence A. McGinley Lectures, 1988–2007* (New York, 2008), 414–429. Cf. Jens David Ohlin, "Is the Concept of the Person Necessary for Human Rights?" *Columbia Law Review*, 105:1 (January 2005), 209–249.

5

René Cassin

Les droits de l'homme *and the Universality of Human Rights, 1945–1966*

Glenda Sluga

In January 1947 sixty-year-old René Cassin, Vice-President of the French Conseil d'État and official French delegate to the newly created United Nations Human Rights Commission, arrived in New York from Paris. That commission was to define and implement a postwar international regime of rights, beginning with the drafting of a human rights document that might become internationally binding.[1] Cassin's mood was less than propitious. The Atlantic had been rough and delayed him. Added to the bitter cold was the isolated locale of his international adventure; the UN had moved its provisional administrative headquarters to the relatively isolated village setting of Lake Success, in upstate New York. His general dissatisfaction was only exacerbated when he discovered that the commission's chair, Eleanor Roosevelt, wife of the former president, had no Europeans on her team of drafters, an omission he regarded as 'symbolic'. Instead, at her side there stood 'two philosophers, M[onsieur] Chang, Chinese, vice-president, and M[onsieur] Malik, Lebanese, rapporteur'. From Cassin's perspective there was worse in store. French had been demoted to an auxiliary language at the meeting, and he felt his own contribution to the discussions was incapacitated by the simultaneous translation process, which matched the French concept *les droits de l'homme* (literally, 'the rights of man') with the English 'human rights'.

The question of cultural relativism has been long at the heart of the historiography of the international programme of human rights introduced in the aftermath of the Second World War. Overall, historians have tended to characterize the universalism of this programme as a European ambition that stood in sharp contrast to an inevitable position of cultural relativism taken up by contemporary anti-colonialists.[2] Ironically, the story of Cassin's

[1] The original intention was to draft an International Bill of Human Rights, but this was downgraded to a Declaration, which was finally adopted at the end of 1948.

[2] This is a history that is only beginning to be challenged; see, in particular, Roland Burke, 'From Individual Rights to National Development: The First UN International Conference on Human Rights, Tehran 1968', *Journal of World History*, 19:3 (September 2008), 275–296; 'The Compelling Dialogue of Freedom: Human Rights at the 1955 Bandung Conference',

attachment to *les droits de l'homme* and his distress at the marginalization of Europeans and the French language offer evidence against this reductive characterization. Cassin was also the drafter who 'spent the post-adoption years interpreting the Declaration to the larger world, almost always stressing the theme of universality'.[3] In his role as a drafter of the 1948 Universal Declaration of Human Rights, he proposed appointing individuals rather than nation-state delegates to the Human Rights Commission. Although unsuccessful, his efforts helped sustain a vision of an international organization not only represented by individuals but also representing them. Cassin also supported, against the majority, the right of petition over and above the rights of state representation to the UN. Unusually for a man in high national office, he defended the inclusion in the postwar French Constitution of a clause allowing the abrogation of French national sovereignty in the interests of established international principles. His imprint is also obvious in the Universal Declaration's invocation of the equality of all individuals as members of 'the human family'.

The reduction of the postwar history of human rights to the problem of cultural relativism versus universalism ignores the more complicated history of human rights as an idea. One need only think of the term 'human rights' itself, which, according to Kenneth Cmiel, was hardly used before the 1940s.[4] By contrast, Cassin's preferred term, the French *les droits de l'homme*, like its English equivalent 'the rights of man', had well-known and well-worn roots in the late-eighteenth-century Enlightenment tradition. Cassin's usage of *les droits de l'homme* was meant to provide the distinctive stamp of an unchanging European and French political heritage for the universal claims of human rights. But he invoked that phrase in radically shifting political and cultural circumstances: the twentieth-century trajectory of French imperialism, the rise of international institutions (from the League of Nations to the United Nations), and feminist and anti-colonialist negotiations of *les droits de l'homme*. Cassin's own role could change in each of these settings. At times he adopted the stance of the beleaguered European, at others the French patriot defending republican values from the challenges of authoritarianism, chauvinism and anti-colonialism. Cassin took international action not only as a delegate to the UN Human Rights Commission from 1947 to 1971 but also as President of the European Court of Human Rights from 1965 to 1968, and as a member of one of the world's

---

Human Rights Quarterly, 28:4 (November 2006), 947–965; *The Politics of Decolonization and the Evolution of the International Human Rights Project* (Philadelphia, 2010). See also Reza Afshari, 'On the Historiography of Human Rights: Reflections on Paul Gordon Lauren's *The Evolution of International Human Rights: Visions Seen*', *Human Rights Quarterly*, 29:1 (2007), 1–67; and Johannes Morsink, *The Universal Declaration of Human Rights: Origins, Drafting, and Intent* (Philadelphia, 1999).

[3] Morsink, *Universal Declaration of Human Rights*, 29.

[4] Kenneth Cmiel, 'The Recent History of Human Rights', *American Historical Review*, February 2004, http://www.historycooperative.org/journals/ahr/109.1/cmiel.html.

most vulnerable minorities brought to consciousness of his Jewishness by the Holocaust.[5]

This essay draws together the strands of Cassin's conception of human rights in order to illuminate a more complex account of human rights as a 'fluid'[6] idea mobilized in historically specific contexts and amidst competing accounts of its culturally specific pasts.[7] The shifting settings and circumstances of Cassin's long twentieth-century engagement of human rights as *les droits de l'homme* are presented here chronologically, beginning with the period before the Second World War, followed by his postwar role in the drafting of the 1948 Universal Declaration of Human Rights, and concluding with the discussions surrounding the International Conventions on Human Rights adopted in 1966. Across these decades, Cassin's story has much to tell us about the importance of thinking about a twentieth-century history of human rights from the perspective of individuals navigating the cross-currents of social and political change. By emphasising the fluidity of human rights as an idea my aim is to show just how persistently the imperatives of imperial and national sovereignty, and the tensions between them, have shaped and constrained the career of human rights as an international ideal.

Empire and the League of Nations

Even though René Cassin was only one of a significant team responsible for drafting the Universal Declaration of Human Rights, he alone received the Nobel Prize for Peace in 1968 on the basis of 'his contribution to the protection of human worth and the rights of man'.[8] Cassin believed he was deserving of this accolade. His acceptance speech crafted a narrative of a lifetime devoted to the crusade for *les droits de l'homme*. He ranked his interwar international activism and his postwar role on the Human Rights Commission as contiguous with the *longue durée* history of human rights in the tradition of *les droits de l'homme*.[9]

In the period after the First World War (he was a decorated veteran), the young lawyer Cassin energetically devoted himself to the economic and social rights of the thousands of French veterans and war widows whose lives had been ruined by the first total war. Through the 1920s and 1930s he concentrated

---

[5] Cassin was the Commission's Vice-Chair in 1949 and Chair in 1955; in the early stages of the drafting of the Universal Declaration of Human Rights, he was solely responsible for crafting a working version of that document.

[6] See Cmiel, 'The Recent History of Human Rights'.

[7] Most of Cassin's biographers have tended to the celebratory when discussing his part in the history of human rights; see, for example, Marc Agi, *Rene Cassin: Père de la Déclaration universelle des droits de l'homme* (Paris, 1998), and in English, the chapter on Cassin in Jay Winter, *Dreams of Peace and Freedom: Utopian Moments in the Twentieth Century* (New Haven, Conn., 2006).

[8] See the Presentation speech for Cassin's Nobel Peace Prize, 1968, at www.nobel.org.

[9] René Cassin, Nobel Lecture, December 11, 1968, 'The Charter of Human Rights', http://nobelprize.org/nobel_prizes/peace/laureates/1968/cassin-lecture.html.

on the League of Nations as an instrument for improving the circumstances of veterans worldwide. He was also widely regarded as a supporter of efforts to eradicate political and legal discrimination against women.[10] The alliance of women's international organizations working with the League of Nation's Social Questions unit to challenge the panoply of state-based laws that denied married women the right to keep their nationality turned to Cassin to draft a legal resolution to the situation of 'stateless' abandoned, widowed and displaced women. By then, Cassin was also the French national delegate to the League of Nations, as well as a member of the Ligue des droits de l'Homme (League of the Rights of Man), a national organization devoted to universal rights. In 1936, at a conference in Dijon attended by Cassin, the Ligue adopted a 'Declaration of The Rights of Man', demanding that '[t]he international protection of the rights of man must be universally organized and guaranteed so that no State can refuse the exercise of these rights by any human being living in its territory'.[11] The Ligue Declaration's enunciation of the principles of universalism, internationalism and equality resonated a decade later as Cassin exerted his influence over the UN's own Declaration. Of course, the drafters of the 1936 Ligue Declaration were themselves self-consciously echoing a prototype – the 1789 French *Déclaration des droits de l'homme et du citoyen*. But, whereas that late-eighteenth-century document had described 'droits naturels, inaliénables et sacrés', the Ligue's 1936 Declaration marked a more inclusive conception of rights, emphasizing the individual rights of the 'human being' (*être humain*) without distinction of sex, race, nation, religion or opinion. It posited social and economic rights, the right to a job, culture and property, but only insofar as the latter did not impede on 'community interest' (which, it was claimed, could be the case when cartels, trusts and financial consortiums were given free reign). Such rights included the right to life and, in this regard, the special rights of mothers and children, and of the aged and the ill. For all these cases, the Declaration made no reference to national specificity; it was intended to have universal relevance.

Cassin was deeply committed to this interwar conception of the individual as a fundamentally social human being, and to the Ligue's social-democratic objectives. It is also true, as the historian Jay Winter has pointed out, that Cassin's vision of *les droits de l'homme* was as consistently oriented around the individual, not as a member of a social class or nation, 'but as the common denominator of humanity' and as the antithesis of collectively based rights whose potential was to undermine the universality of rights.[12] This emphasis on the individual was in part motivated by the events of the interwar period, specifically the Nazi state's exploitation of the League of Nation's minority

---

[10] See René Cassin, 'L'inégalité entre l'homme et la femme dans la legislation civile', in *Annales de la Faculté de droit d'Aix*, Nouvelle série no. 3, 1919.

[11] Article 1. 'Le complément à la déclaration des droits de l'homme elaboré par la LDH en 1936', 'Ligue des droits de l'homme', http://www.ldh-france.org/docu_textesfonda2.cfm?ifond=62.

[12] Winter, *Dreams of Peace and Freedom*, 6.

legislation as the legitimation for its aggressive foreign policy on behalf of Germans outside Germany. Cassin had also grown frustrated at the inability of the League of Nations to protect individual Jews from the discrimination and abuses enacted by states in which they held national citizenship. In this context, Cassin's preference was for the codification and enforcement of individual rights over the interwar trend toward minority rights and their nationalist and statist rationales.[13] Just as Cassin's experience at the League of Nations, and with the Ligue des droits de l'Homme, helped define his internationalism, the Nazi occupation of France, the establishment of the Vichy regime and his growing awareness of the terrible fate of Jews across Europe (including the disappearance of his own extended family) alerted him to the politically strategic significance of universally-conceived and internationally-sanctioned individual rights. Ironically, this same pragmatism reinforced his view of the crucial international role of the French Republic as the source and defender of those rights.

During the war, while in self-imposed political exile in London,[14] Cassin had volunteered his legal expertise in service to Charles de Gaulle, the leader of the Free France resistance and future French President. De Gaulle rewarded him with the role of Permanent Secretary to the Council of Defense of the Empire. In December 1941, Cassin was sent off on a difficult journey across the French empire, from the 'Near East' of Palestine, Lebanon and Egypt, to Indochina, Chad and the Cameroons, collecting information on the state of support for the French Republic in each of these outposts. With this new responsibility came an acquaintance with the Alliance Israélite Universelle, a secular Jewish organization established in the mid-nineteenth century and devoted to the dissemination of the French language and the republican values of *les droits de l'homme*, particularly in the French colonies. His attention newly focused on the protection of the rights of Jews, as minorities. within the French Republic and its empire, Cassin found affirmation of a tradition of *les droits de l'homme* that was as intrinsic to secular Judaism as it was to the values of the French republic. Despite evidence that de Gaulle and his French Cabinet members were personally inclined to anti-Semitism, Cassin's memoirs announce that these wartime travels had made him more profoundly French. They had given him an insight – not shared by most other Frenchmen – into the many departments, possessions, protectorates and mandates of the French empire, as well as into the universal capacity of *les droits de l'homme*.[15]

[13] For a full discussion of Cassin's position on the League's fascination with minorities, see Greg Burgess, 'The Human Rights Dilemma in Anti-Nazi protest', *CERC Working Paper* 2/2002, University of Melbourne.
[14] Cassin quit Paris in 1940; when he returned, he left on the door of his apartment on the Boulevard Saint-Michel the black seal of the Gestapo that the Nazis had put there when they condemned him to death *in absentia*.
[15] See René Cassin, *Les hommes partis de rien: le réveil de la France abattue 1940–41* (Paris, 1974), 128.

Cassin's commitment to imperial France as the preferred setting for the implementation of universal individual rights in existing French territories is well captured in the advice he offered de Gaulle on the form of a future international organization during the early discussions among the Allies (a grouping known at the time as the 'United Nations') on a postwar order. Cassin took the opportunity to reject the League of Nations model, and what he saw as its overwrought legal investment in national sovereignty. He contrasted its inefficiencies with the international agency exercised by nineteenth-century empires such as Britain and France in the pre-League era. Those empires had been able to take unilateral action to eradicate slavery and, less successfully, to protect Armenians (against Turks), Lebanese Christians (against the Druze) and Jews (against the Tsar's pogroms).[16] Cassin proposed that the new international organization should be legally enabled to intervene in international crises when individual *les droits de l'homme* were at risk, regardless of national sovereignty. He also defended the integrity of the French empire as crucial for the universal destiny of *les droits de l'homme* – to the extent of alerting de Gaulle of the creeping influence of the concept of national self-determination in colonies such as Indochina. From Cassin's perspective, there was no inevitable correspondence between *les droits de l'homme* and national self-determination. In the micro-cosmopolitan spaces of the French empire, Jews such as himself and Muslims, white and black, could seek politico-cultural convergence as French citizens and patriots. The anti-colonial alternative augured ethnic and religious nation-states (in the context of Algeria and Morocco, the assumption was they would be predominantly Muslim) that would reconstitute their Jewish and other non-Muslim citizens as vulnerable minorities.

Cosmopolitanism, Human Rights and the UN

In the period extending roughly from 1945 to 1950, another way of conceptualizing the implementation of universal human rights began to be discussed in the context of the creation of the United Nations, namely, the prospect of a cosmopolitan 'world citizenship' that was distilled from cultural differences and potentially transcended them.[17] Although world citizenship was not an ideal that Cassin ascribed to with any obvious enthusiasm, its ambitions shaped the larger discussion amidst the agencies and committees of the UN and the presentation of human rights as simultaneously individualist and universal. In 1950, Jaime Torres Bodet, the Mexican politician and educationalist and second Director-General of the United Nations Educational, Scientific and

[16] See Paris, Archives de la Ministère des Affaires Étrangères, NUOI: S-1 Dumbarton Oaks, 'Commission pour l'étude des principes d'une organisation internationale', Séance Dossiers Générale.
[17] See G. Sluga, 'The Cosmopolitan History of Julian Huxley and UNESCO', *Journal of World History* 21:3 (2010).

Cultural Organization (UNESCO), described 'world citizenship' as 'engendered by the sense of justice, by that principle in the Universal Declaration of Human Rights which assigns to the individual universal rights of which none can be legally or morally deprived'.[18] To be sure, Bodet's assertion was made against the rising tide of Cold War polarization and anti-colonialist pressures. The period after 1950 signalled the renunciation by the UN and UNESCO of world citizenship and a return to an older particularist agenda of national 'self-determination', claimed anew in the context of emancipatory aspirations for decolonization. Even though the process was gradual, and the universal underpinnings of the new international human rights agenda continued to be defended by the representatives of anti-colonialism well into the period of the Bandung Conference of 1955,[19] by the time the two Covenants on Human Rights – one on Social and Economic Rights, and one on Political and Civil Rights – were adopted by the UN in 1966, world citizenship had been irreparably severed from cosmopolitanism, just as the world citizen had ceded to the rights of 'peoples'. It was in this shifting ideological setting that Cassin, through his ongoing role on the Human Rights Commission, affirmed the importance of a conception of human rights that existed over and above that of the *patrie*, at the same time as he insisted on the historical role of France in inventing, interpreting and implementing *les droits de l'homme*.

As we have seen, when Cassin arrived in New York for the first sessions of the Human Rights Commission in 1947, he was concerned to ensure a prominent role for France and Europe in the formulation of the fundamental principles that could comprise a universal human rights declaration.[20] By this time the terms human rights and *les droits de l'homme* were interchangeably drawn upon in the (mostly) simultaneous French and English discussions. Cassin found too that his non-European colleagues on the Human Rights Commission were keen to identify their own cultures and states in the exposition of that universalism, and in the narrative of the origins of human rights as an idea. Delegates from the newly independent (formerly American colony) Philippines, for example, made good weather of the specific language of world citizenship, describing their nation as the most cosmopolitan state in the world. Indeed, Cassin found his own view of universal rights positioned between a conservative portrait of human nature and humanity put by European delegates in defence of empires, and a relatively radical cosmopolitan vision of the history and significance of human rights proposed by these 'non-European' commissioners. The Philippines' representative on the Human Rights Commission, Carlos Romulo, appealed for 'a rational bill of rights that will take into account all the different cultural patterns there are in the

---

[18] Bodet's published speech, 'Human Rights: The Task before Us', was presented to an audience of the International Federation of University Women.

[19] For more on this history, see Burke, *The Politics of Decolonization*.

[20] The First Session of the commission was held over January and February 1947 and attended by delegates from Chile, China, France, India, Iran, Lebanon, Panama, the Philippines, the Soviet Union, the United Kingdom, the United States, Uruguay and Yugoslavia.

world, especially in respect to popular customs and legal systems'.[21] Romulo gave words also to a common postwar interpretation of how universal human rights might work – it would distil from the variety of different positions an essential body of law relevant to all humans, who belonged to one human family. He was, of course, offering an implicit critique of colonialism along the way, since the hierarchical classification of collective human differences had acted as the justification of European colonialism. Rather than promote human rights in the context of national self-determination, Romulo invoked the potential for indulging 'the vision of World Government which the implementation of the proposed international bill of rights will doubtless require in some degree, and of which, as a matter of fact, it will be the cornerstone'.[22]

In the same session of the Commission on Human Rights, Peng-Chun Chang, the Kuomintang delegate, presented his own history of the cosmopolitan nature of the eighteenth-century world. Chang (who, like Romulo, had passed through North American institutions as well as universities in his own country)[23] argued that a nineteenth-century European 'myopia' had recast the eighteenth century as a period when civilization stood for Europe: 'That was not true in the eighteenth century. All cultured men in the eighteenth century, especially concerning this idea of the conception of man, knew their Chinese thoughts very clearly'. Chang insisted that his point was not a nationalist one on behalf of China, rather that there was an eighteenth-century tradition of cosmopolitanism, which had been lost to the nineteenth century and which the current international experiment in human rights could restore.

Cassin did not let Chang's foray into the history of the eighteenth-century pass without comment. He agreed with the view that before the nineteenth century there was a universalistic trend of thought; but he also believed that it had been reasserted in the twentieth century through the efforts of Europe. The European found himself curiously on the defensive among the non-Europeans of the commission who claimed for themselves a share of the historical ownership of human rights as an idea. Throughout the 1950s and 1960s, as the UN grew more 'cosmopolitan', with its rapidly expanding member states and African and Asian representation, the French jurist grew more insistent on the very point of a *Western*, European, liberal tradition of human rights. By then, the real rift was not between Paris and Peking intellectuals, but the West and East of the Cold War, and a new North–South axis – polarities that were in turn defined by an ideological distinction between individual and collective rights.

---

[21] Romulo served as the President of the Fourth Session of the United Nations General Assembly in 1949–1950 and Chairman of the United Nations Security Council. He later ended up a defender of the Marcos regime, just as Cassin became an apologist for de Gaulle's creeping authoritarianism in the 1950s – until de Gaulle verbally attacked Israel.

[22] Commission on Human Rights, Meeting, February 1, 1947, p. 12, Verbatim Records from Charles Malik archive, and kindly provided by Roland Burke.

[23] Chang earned his doctoral degree from Columbia University, specializing in Chinese studies.

There is no little irony in the fact that in the early UN debates on human rights the representatives of non-European states at times found themselves defending a more cosmopolitan version of the universal qualities of human rights than their European peers. What most of them paid less attention to was the gender stereotypes that had in the past compromised the universalism of the rights of man rhetoric, and threatened to do the same even when contemplated as the rights of humans.

Human Rights and *Les droits des femmes*

At San Francisco in 1945, and then at the London, Paris and New York gatherings that shaped the UN's social and political programme, feminists from the old and new worlds expressed their concern that 'human rights' as much as *les droits de l'homme,* or 'the rights of *man*', implied men, and women by exception only.[24] Feminists were also wary of the inclination to emphasize the espousal of universality as the antithesis of chauvinist cultural or racial hierarchies as the central motivation for this postwar human rights agenda.[25] Nora Stanton Barney, writing in the feminist periodical *Equal Rights* in 1946, echoed the sentiments of numerous feminist lobbyists of the UN organization when she claimed:

We all know only too well, and have heard only too often great speeches on human rights by people who have in mind only the rights of men, and never think of the human rights of women. Even women who have taken to heart mainly discriminations on account of race and color, completely forget discriminations on account of sex. The Commission on Human Rights will probably emphasize these racial discriminations rather than those of women.[26]

Although the UN's Charter stipulated the equality of men and women,[27] some feminists were so concerned about a bias inherent in the concept of human rights that they supported the establishment of a separate human rights commission for women. Others who had grown disillusioned with the segregation of women's issues in the League of Nations were as adamant that the League precedent should not be followed in the new organization. Cassin

---

[24] Marilyn Lake, 'From Self-Determination via Protection to Equality via Non-Discrimination: Defining Women's Rights at the League of Nations and the United Nations', in P. Grimshaw, K. Holmes and M. Lake (eds.), *Women's Rights and Human Rights: International Perspectives* (Basingstoke, 2001), 263.

[25] See, 'Status of Women', *UN Weekly Bulletin*, 1:7 (September 16, 1946), 11.

[26] Nora Stanton Barney, 'The World and The Nation', *Equal Rights*, September–October 1946, 46. Stanton was a pioneering female civil engineer and the author of *World Peace through a Peoples Parliament* (1944). See also my 'National Sovereignty and Female Equality. Gender, Peacemaking, and the New World Orders of 1919 and 1945', in J. Davy, K. Hagemann, and U. Katzel (eds.), *Frieden – Gewalt – Geschlecht: Friedens-und Konfliktforschung als Geschlechterforschung* (Essen, 2005).

[27] See Laura Reanda, 'Human Rights and Women's Rights: The United Nations Approach', *Human Rights Quarterly*, 3:2 (1981), 11–31.

kept a relatively low profile in these discussions, but we know that he was generally in accord with Eleanor Roosevelt, the chair of the Human Rights Commission. Roosevelt opposed the creation of a second women's body on the basis that human signified women as well as men. She did not agree that women required 'identical treatment with men in all cases', but she believed that the rights of men and women could be represented in the one human rights commission.[28] Nevertheless, in 1946 the UN's Third Committee created the Sub-Commission on the Status of Women as part of the Human Rights Commission. The Sub-Commission was quickly promoted to the status of an independent body, the Commission on the Status of Women, with a focus on political rights and civil equality. The rights it promoted were concretely juridical and in many ways borrowed from the League of Nations: equality in marriage, monogamy, nationality, property and guardianship of children, social and economic equality, the prevention of traffic in women and equal opportunity in the domain of education.[29]

As Johannes Morsink has shown in his study of the drafting of the Universal Declaration of Human Rights, those critics who anticipated the neglect of women's rights in the articulation of human rights had a point. Even as the new communist bloc pushed for a conception of nondiscrimination as relevant to sex as well as race, the Economic and Social Committee delimited the scope of the Commission on the Status of Women to a 'very narrow and harmless set of activities around women's concerns'.[30] In terms of the crafting of the declaration, the human rights propositions decided upon reflected historically specific gender norms, particularly in regard to the place of men and women in families[31] – norms which, to be sure, were accepted by the feminist organizations, as well as by Cassin. A week before the General Assembly adopted the Universal Declaration, Andrée Lehmann, the president of the Ligue Française pour le Droit des Femmes – an organization that originated in the mid-nineteenth century well before the Ligue des droits de l'Homme – wrote to Cassin, reminding him of a letter she had sent a month earlier about Article 16 of the Declaration. Lehmann was concerned that the use of 'they' to indicate the sharing of equal rights in the matter of marriage was too ambiguous. She urged the more specific wording 'men and women', including the addition of a clause that gave men and women 'the same rights during the marriage and in respect of its dissolution'.[32] In writing to Cassin, Lehmann was reinforcing the suggestions offered to the Human Rights Commission by

---

[28] Cassin had asked for a copy of Mrs Roosevelt's statement on equality of treatment for women, under which he then wrote 'je suis d'accord'.

[29] Reanda, 'Human Rights and Women's Rights', 18.

[30] Deborah Stienstra, *Women's Movements and International Organizations* (New York, 1994), 84.

[31] Morsink, *The Universal Declaration of Human Rights*, 93, 118. See Articles 23 and 25 of the Declaration, which refer to 'himself and his family'.

[32] Paris, Archives Nationales, Fonds Cassin, AP 382, cote 128, dossier 2: Andrée Lehmann, 2 décembre 1948, à Cassin.

the Status of Women Commission. The final version of Article 16 reflects in part these suggestions, since it unambiguously employs 'men and women'. But, rather than enshrine what was ostensibly a right to divorce, its third clause turned completely in the other direction, affirming that '[t]he family is the natural and fundamental group unit of society and is entitled to protection by society and the State'. This claim was certainly the consequence of the influence of Christian delegates, only some of them European. Yet it also accorded with Cassin's choice of the 'human family' metaphor in the preamble to the Declaration, as well as his theoretical understanding of the family as a primary social setting for the individual, and a corollary conception of the protection of motherhood as a special condition of women's equal rights. It also echoed the interwar welfarist emphases of the Ligue des droits de l'Homme, as well as the postwar agenda of the Commission on the Status of Women. By contrast, feminists such as Cassin's Indian colleague Hansa Mehta (the one other woman on the Human Rights Commission in this period) were not successful in their demands that the interests of children and mothers be separated in order to emphasize women's intrinsic rights as individuals or humans. Instead, in Article 25 of the Declaration the needs of mothers and children were essentially yoked together.

We can interpret the problem of women's status vis-à-vis human rights as another related dimension of the larger controversy surrounding universalism and the question of difference in the postwar debates about the nature of rights. At a practical level, Lehmann's letter reflects the extent to which a variety of nongovernmental organizations (NGOs), including Jewish and feminist organizations, were incorporated into the drafting of the Declaration often thanks to Cassin who sat on endless NGO boards and committees (including the Alliance Israélite Universelle, the World Jewish Congress, and the central committee of the Ligue des droits de l'Homme).[33] It also highlights the difficult position of the Commission on the Status of Women, a body which emerged out of the fear expressed by some feminists that women would be forgotten or submerged in the assumption of universality and then, once it was created, was effectively marginalized by the Human Rights Commission.[34] Even as conventions about gender difference made their way into the Declaration in the form of the special status of women – whether as mothers, wives or workers, or in the family – the question of women's status intruded in the dominant discussions of the relevance of race and cultural difference usually in ways that some feminists had feared.[35] For Belgium's delegate to the Human Rights Commission, the fact of sex difference was the basis for accepting the fact of

---

[33] Fonds Cassin, AP 382, cote 128, dossier 2: Cassin, 30 avril 1948, à Monsieur Parodi, Ambassadeur, Chef de la délégation française, NY.

[34] See John Humphrey, *On the Edge of Greatness: The Diaries of John Humphrey, First Director of the United Nations Division of Human Rights* (Montreal, 1994–2000).

[35] Cassin was also inspired in his relatively radical conception of the rights of asylum and refugees by his League work on the nationality of women, and their unfixed status – that is, since according to many legal codes women had no intrinsic nationality, but rather a nationality

race difference as a fundamental qualification of any universal application of human rights.[36] Chang, for his part, had no problem with *mui jai* – the selling of Chinese girls to wealthy families as domestic laborers – even as British delegates who rejected the universal applicability of human rights in their own colonial territories were depicting this practice as a form of slavery. As we will see, Cassin's postwar identification of *les droits de l'homme* with a specifically French and Judaeo-Christian tradition similarly made the status of women a marker of a society's capacity to value and enact human rights and, concurrently, a basis for denying the universal application of human rights in culturally differentiated communities.

Decolonization and the Right of Peoples to Self-Determination

One of the most important contexts for the postwar discussion of human rights in the international domain occurred after the adoption of the Universal Declaration, in the course of the drafting of the binding Covenants on Human Rights. In his 1968 Nobel Peace Prize lecture Cassin pointed out rather despondently that the drafting of the Covenants had taken eighteen difficult years. Over the course of that journey, the first issue to be favourably dealt with 'was the problem of deciding whether the right of peoples to self-determination, which had previously been considered a principle of political and essentially collective nature, should be inserted in the Covenants intended to implement the rights proclaimed in the Universal Declaration, which was concerned only with the rights exercised separately or communally by the individual'.[37] This shift in priorities, from individual to collective rights, coincided with the disparagement of world citizenship and a renewed emphasis on the nation-state as the most significant form of governance and liberty. As Cassin described in his lecture, 'the solution arrived at can be explained historically by the movement toward decolonization and, more exactly, toward the political emancipation of territorial entities, which was a logical outcome of the victorious libertarian principles fostered in the course of the Second World War'.

Cassin, like many European delegates, was not always this sure of the compatibility of decolonization and *les droits de l'homme*. During the 1950s Covenant debates, which privileged the self-determination of peoples as a principle of human rights, Cassin is to be found opposing the attempt by the Soviet-linked states and Danish and Yugoslav representatives to equate human rights with minority rights, and minority rights with nationality.[38] Although Cassin did not always associate the universal implementation of human rights

status that depended on their domicile, this provided a useful precedent for dealing with refugees, who should be able to get domicile regardless of nationality.

[36] Ronald LeBeau, Meeting 7 of Commission for Human Rights, February 1, 1947, verbatim records.

[37] Cassin, Nobel Prize lecture, December 11, 1968.

[38] Fonds Cassin, AP 382, cote 129, dossier 6: typescripts of Commission des droits de l'homme des Nations Unies, mai 1949, Premier rapport du President Cassin.

with the maintenance of the French empire, he always implied a fundamental ideological antagonism between the self-determination of peoples and the cosmopolitan conception of a state such as France as a society comprising equal individuals.[39] Certainly some delegates to the Human Rights Commission and the Third Committee fought incorporating 'the self-determination of peoples' into a binding international convention on human rights on the basis that it would undermine the status of their empires (the Netherlands, Britain, France). Others fought it because they had a profound sense of the unequal difference of the colonized (Greece, Belgium), while others still fought it as an intrusion on the sovereignty of their own states, which contained movements for secession (India). Cassin's personal objections to the view that the self-determination of peoples is a human right were consistent with his general preference for individual rights over group rights.[40] When the Soviet representative on the Sub-Commission on the Prevention of Discrimination and the Protection of Minorities (it met during the preparation of the 1948 Declaration) urged a text on territorially based minorities, Cassin, the Sub-Commission's Chair, objected that 'there were certain countries where different peoples, Christians, Mohammedans and Jews, had lived side by side for centuries; as in North Africa, for instance, and where such a [territorial] text would be inapplicable'. He added, in acknowledgement of the related colonial question, 'There were some non-self-governing or trust [formerly colonial but not yet independent] territories where, no doubt, a problem of self-government existed, but there was no minorities problem'.[41] This was a point in favour of individual rights and against minority rights with which even Lakshmi Menon, an outspoken Indian feminist (and in 1949–1950 the head of the Commission on the Status of Women secretariat), agreed. Menon argued that in India minority rights were as problematic because they assumed the introduction of new communities, rather than historically constituted communities where difference was the norm. In her home region of Lucknow, she explained, school exams were held in four languages.

What changed after 1948 was Cassin's reasoning. He now argued that if France were required to implement across its empire the intended equality of sexes provision, it would not be able to ratify the covenant at all because not all the constituencies within its political administration would be either willing to accept such a provision owing to their cultural difference or able by virtue of their 'backwardness'. 'Thus, the result obtained would be the opposite of that which was sought'.[42] Hélène Lefaucheux, the former resistance fighter and longstanding French delegate to the Commission on the Status

---

[39] For more on the history of the fate of a minority rights clause in the 1948 Declaration, see Morsink, *The Universal Declaration of Human Rights*, 274.

[40] Commission on Human Rights, Lake Success, Meeting 292, October 25, 1950, Third Committee, Lake Success.

[41] Morsink, *The Universal Declaration of Human Rights*, 272.

[42] Commission on Human Rights, Lake Success, Meeting 129, June 15, 1949, Draft International Covenant on Human Rights (Articles 23, 24, 25).

of Women (its chair for six years) and a close contact of Cassin's, was concerned that women's rights would be taken up by anti-colonial forces in the Islamic territories of France's *outre-mer*.[43] If that happened, she argued, it would put at threat the political relevance of the 'French Union' – the newly fashioned relationship between France and its colonies which both Cassin and Lefaucheux conceived as the manifestation of French respect for its colonials' 'own traditions', and 'the desires of her populations'.[44] It is important to note that both kept to this view even when confronted with allegations of human rights abuses by French forces in Algeria.[45]

Inevitably, arguments that contrasted the 'high degree of civilization' of the contracting parties with the 'ideas of peoples who had not yet reached a high degree of development',[46] and singled out Islamic traditions as particularly backward, did not go unrepudiated by other members of a rapidly expanding UN. The delegates from Syria, Lebanon, Egypt and Iran were among those voicing their scepticism of the sudden colonial respect for cultural difference in non-self-governing territories. They took turns contrasting human rights traditions – the greater rights of women – in Islamic countries that had political freedom (such as Syria, Iraq and Egypt), with human rights conditions in those Islamic territories still dependent on colonial masters (Algeria, Morocco, Tunisia and Libya). Menon was as vocal in her scepticism of the human rights advances in these post-colonial states, but she also described human rights legislation as most required in the non-self-governing territories and in the colonies 'since it was there that violations of human rights were unfortunately most frequent'.[47] Menon, who otherwise shared Cassin's perspective on the threat posed by minority rights to culturally diverse states, charged that

differences in the degree of development of various territories ... was an outworn argument, and India, speaking for all those countries in Asia which had so often been told that they were not ripe for independence, that they would have to be patient and wait for the day when, after a gradual evolution, they would be able to achieve

---

[43] Archives de la Ministère des Affaires Etrangères, NUOI: S-50, Organisation des Nations Unies, 6. Commission de la condition de la femme, 1946–59; Report on Commission de la condition de la femme, Genève, 13 août 1948.

[44] Cassin, like the Belgian delegate, argued that his country had no colonies because 'all the peoples of the French Union had won the right either to sign their own international agreements or to be consulted' and 'the peoples who were directly under French jurisdiction were no longer subjects; they were citizens and were represented in that capacity in the French assemblies'. Meeting 286, Friday, October 27, 1950, Lake Success, 'Draft first international covenant on human rights and measures of implementation'. See also United Nations Archives, New York, S-50 Organisation des Nations Unies, 3–8–6 (1), Lettre à Broustra, 4 janvier 1956.

[45] In the late 1950s Cassin, as Vice-President of the Conseil d'État, authorised the enactment of 'emergency powers' for the French President, for use in the management of anti-colonial opposition in North Africa; Fonds Cassin, AP 382, cote 129, dossier 6.

[46] Mr Soudan, Belgium, Meeting 292, October 25, 1950, Third Committee, Lake Success.

[47] Draft of first international covenant on human rights and measures of implementation, Meeting 294, Thursday, October 26, 1950, Lake Success.

autonomy, wished to state that all peoples, whatever stage of development they had reached, had the right to govern themselves.

Significantly, before Menon arrived at the UN, her argument had been rehearsed at the Status of Women Commission, not by its Indian delegate, but by American and Australian representatives. In 1947 a different Indian representative had suggested a time-frame of ten to twenty years for the introduction of universal suffrage in 'backward', non-self-governing territories. The American lawyer Dorothy Kenyon and the Australian activist Jessie Street both dismissed the idea that any group of people had to be 'prepared' for democracy. With perhaps a clear eye on the implications for women, they encouraged the view that differences were irrelevant, the introduction of rights itself brought new practices and possibilities.[48]

Read back into this broader context of debate across the organs of the UN, Cassin's role on the Human Rights Commission was one of increasing conservatism. We do know, however, that his viewpoint, if not his actions, are difficult to assess in the period after the adoption of the Universal Declaration because he felt forced by his superiors to argue for culturally relative human rights. In April 1952 he complained to the French Foreign Ministry that his instructions prevented him 'from defending the principles of unity, universality and the reciprocity of States, and forced him to protect the interests at the Human Rights Commission of nations such as France that were particularly exposed in their administration of non-self-governing territories'.[49] Little wonder that in his lectures outside the UN system he persisted in reminding his audience of the opportunity that had been lost when it was decided that delegates to the Human Rights Commission should act as the representatives of states, rather than as independent counsels. When he reflected publicly on *la Déclaration universelle des droits de l'homme*, Cassin again and again emphasized that it proclaimed the universal and fundamental rights of individuals no matter where they lived or among which group.[50]

Cassin's perspective shifted not only in relation to his different roles, and audiences, but also the changing rhetorical strategies of his peers, including anti-colonialists. As Roland Burke has described, the same year Cassin accepted his Nobel Prize, he was 'the only Western delegate to come to the defence of the Universal Declaration during the First International Conference on Human Rights held in Tehran'. Tehran marked the consolidation of a significant shift in rhetoric among anti-colonial powers, which now emphasized the need for culturally-distinctive conceptions of human rights to match the conditions of the Third World. In this context, Burke explains, Cassin 'urged the rejection of the emerging post-colonial rights concept, which created one

[48] Sophia Smith Collection, Smith College, Dorothy Kenyon Papers, 1850–1998, Box 53, MS 85, Commission on the Status of Women, First Session, Meeting 6, February 13, 1947.

[49] Fonds Cassin, AP 382, cote 129: Cassin, 17 avril 1952, à M. le Ministère des Affaires Etrangères.

[50] Fonds Cassin, AP 382, cote 128, dossier 2: 'Droits de l'homme'.

set of rights for the 'South', and another for the 'North'. Rights, argued Cassin, 'could not be different for Europeans, Africans, Americans and Asians'.[51]

The simultaneous universalism and Frenchness of *les droits de l'homme* espoused by Cassin, along with his difficult relationship with the process of decolonization, tells a complex story about the transition from individual rights to the rights of 'peoples', from the cosmopolitanism of empires and a new internationalism, and the return, after a brief postwar hiatus, to the political supremacy of state-centrism and cultural nationalism, even in international forums and institutions. That story also includes the fragility of Europe's moral standing at the end of the Second World War, and into the era of decolonization. It is not surprising that as Cassin felt his 'European' voice marginalized in the setting of the UN, he turned his attention to the European Community's own Human Rights Convention (adopted in 1950), and its establishment of a European Court of Human Rights.[52] It could be argued this was partly for idealistic reasons, because, unlike the United Nations, the European Court allowed individual petitioning and had the legal authority to implement human rights, rather than just advise, a contrast Cassin noted in his 1968 Nobel Prize lecture: 'Europe has really offered a good example after the turning point of 1948, and I, a determined universalist, was able to conclude that certain means of implementation are more readily accepted if they are organized among neighboring nations of similar culture. Communities of law and customs are not invented arbitrarily.'[53]

Cassin was obviously delighted at the advances on offer for *les droits de l'homme* in this new European institutional setting. But they were advances that saw him retreat radically from his earlier invocations of the political salience of the human family in favour of the inevitability of national and civilizational differences. The assumptions that informed the preamble to the European Convention on Human Rights, with its description of 'European countries which are like-minded, and have a common heritage of political traditions, ideals, freedom, and the rule of law', situated Cassin comfortably not in the family of man, but of European lawyers.

Conclusion

The history of Cassin's role in the Universal Declaration of Human Rights has much to add to current debates about the cultural relativism of human rights. There is no doubt that Cassin conceived of human rights as emerging out of a French political tradition engrained in the 'true' culture of France – its language, its laws and its literature. At the same time, the relationship

---

[51] Burke, 'From Individual Rights to National Development', p. 293.

[52] From 1959 to 1970 Cassin was a judge on the newly created, and to some extent competing jurisdiction of the European Court of Human Rights in Strasbourg, and from 1965 to 1968 was President of that Court.

[53] Cited in Frederik W. Haberman, ed., *Nobel Lectures, Peace 1951–1970* (Amsterdam, 1972), 173.

between Cassin's views and those represented by 'non-Europeans' involved in the formulation of an international bill of human rights in the second half of the twentieth century – women and men such as Menon, Mehta, Romulo and Chang – also makes clear that we cannot simply dismiss the history of human rights as a parochial story of European ambitions. In the early postwar years it was these non-Europeans who often invoked the importance of a cosmopolitan politics in order to sustain the universality and practicality of the idea of human rights as individual rights, and in order to challenge Cassin's invocation of a European, and ultimately French imperial, version of universal human rights as *les droits de l'homme*. Feminists too had an important part to play in the articulation of a universalist vision of human rights as an alternative to the gender specificity of the rights of man political tradition. Taken together, these strands of the history of human rights remind us of the extent to which the terms human rights, rights of man and *les droits de l'homme*, despite not being the same, have overlapped, and belonged to the world, even as they have implied historically specific traditions, or summoned up culturally specific pasts. Their histories highlight the variety of contexts that influenced the postwar conceptualization of the relative importance of individual and group rights, as well as the similarity in the values and rhetorical strategies of universalists, colonialists and anti-colonialists, of cultural relativists and anti-democrats at different moments, and the important although undermined influence exerted by cosmopolitanism and feminism as complementary ideals.

The changing contexts in which human rights were internationalized, and Cassin's own shifting positions, fundamentally problematize what Reza Afshari has described as the single-cause explanation of human rights. Afshari has in mind specifically the presentation of 'anti-colonial struggle as a human rights movement', its domination of human rights historiography, and its negative impact on 'a new awareness for human rights'.[54] When read back into a history of the fluidity of the meaning and significance of human rights, the connection between human rights, empire and national self-determination no longer seems so obvious or historically inevitable. In theory, empire offered as powerful a context as the nation-state for imagining a conception of rights that transcended cultural or racial hierarchies – hierarchies that in the modern period, it should be remembered, were as liable to be reproduced in national as much as imperial settings. Indeed, in the twentieth century the shibboleth of national sovereignty has posed the greatest obstacle to the international implementation of human rights.

The question remains, as Kenneth Cmiel has reminded us: What if anything is the impact of this international history of the idea of human rights on the actual status of human rights? Cmiel offers that '[i]t is precisely in not treating assertions of "human rights" in hushed, reverential tones that the best

---

[54] Afshari, 'On the Historiography', 52.

possibilities lie'.[55] The story of another of Cassin's transnational adventures reinforces the edifying value of historical demystification.

In January 1954 René Cassin set off on one of his routine voyages away from France, across the Channel to London (his former home-in-exile) for a meeting of the International Institute of Administrative Scientists, only to find himself confronted with the shortcomings of the international human rights project.[56] It was in the middle of the Cold War, and Cassin, on arrival at London's Victoria Station, was subjected to hours of questioning by immigration officials. Their suspicions had been aroused by his diplomatic passport, which described him as France's UN delegate to the Human Rights Commission. In an interview with the press Cassin related that 'Officials seemed puzzled about "human rights", they kept asking what these words meant'. To rewrite the history of human rights as a historically specific idea is not to challenge its relevance; it is to acknowledge the importance of continuing to ask with more precision, what these words have meant, what might they mean, and for whom.

[55] Cmiel, 'The Recent History'.
[56] Fonds Cassin, AP 382, cote 147: Europe 1944–74, I, Angleterre 1944–72, Newspaper cutting, *News Chronicle*, n.d.

6

Rudolf Laun and the Human Rights of Germans in Occupied and Early West Germany

Lora Wildenthal

What are human rights? The technical answer is that they are norms of international law that are formulated in abstract, universally applicable terms. For example, Article 3 of the Universal Declaration of Human Rights reads: "Everyone has the right to life, liberty and security of person." Such a norm contains no reference to any context or circumstances that might justify limiting those rights – and therein lies the power of human rights language. When lawyers or activists attach a particular situation to a human rights norm, they seek to persuade others to see that situation in isolation from its historical context and usual justifications, *as* a violation. Human rights norms are ahistorical and decontextualized, and that is the point of invoking them.

After the Second World War, activists around the world hoped that people would think ever more in terms of human rights norms, and the Allies encouraged that hope. However, the use of the ahistorical language of human rights in occupied and West Germany – the subject of this essay – was difficult and inevitably controversial. In practice, the language of human rights in West Germany highlighted the tension between the Federal Republic's most prized moral claims: to have enshrined timeless, universal human rights, and to have accepted the specific historical responsibility of Nazism. While the former asks listeners to set aside context, the latter depends on a specific context for its significance.

There was and is no single, typical West German "take" on human rights. Rather, West Germans have applied a range of opinions and approaches. However, there have been certain highly typical confrontations among West Germans concerning human rights. One such confrontation emerged already under occupation in the second half of the 1940s, and it still animates human rights debate today in the Federal Republic. On one side stood those who wished to sharpen West Germans' awareness of human rights by emphasizing Germans' violations of others' human rights under Nazism. These "others" were non-Germans and German minorities targeted according to racial, political, or sexual criteria. Informing the West German public about the

Nazi past and critically analyzing postwar Germany in light of that past were to be central to any discussion of human rights. On the other side of the confrontation stood those who attached human rights language to those Germans who, while not targeted under Nazism, had suffered under the Allied occupation. It was possible, but not technically necessary, to include the context of the Nazi past in order to define the norms violated here. As it happened, however, criticism of the Nazi past usually was absent on this side. This lack of a critical approach to the Nazi past provoked the irritation of the former side.[1]

In the immediate postwar period, those Germans who claimed that the Allies had violated their or other Germans' human rights were dominant in this confrontation, and not just on the right.[2] They cited aerial bombardment, arbitrary seizure of property, extended detention for prisoners of war, and the expulsion of ethnic Germans from Poland, Czechoslovakia, and other points in Eastern Europe.[3] During the Allied occupation, organizations representing the expellees were banned; the Allies feared their far-right political potential.[4] After the creation of the Federal Republic in 1949, the Basic Law guaranteed the right of such groups to form, and they quickly grew. German international lawyers worked with these groups, applying their professional skills to defining occupation and expellee issues as human rights violations. The tension between the Federal Republic's two moral claims, to universal human rights and to the historical responsibility for Nazism, emerged most sharply in these claims that the Allies had violated Germans' human rights.

This essay focuses on one actor in this confrontation, the international lawyer Rudolf Laun (1882–1975). Laun, a professor of law and legal philosophy at the University of Hamburg, was the earliest of the German international lawyers to criticize the Allies for violating Germans' human rights. His insistence on applying concepts consistently, in spite of their different political meanings in different contexts, exemplifies the confrontation described above. Yet Laun's case is more than merely illustrative, for his arguments allow us to connect that typical West German confrontation to larger themes in the twentieth-century history of human rights. Laun's case certainly shows us that human rights functioned as a political language, allowing Germans to cast themselves

---

[1] Lora Wildenthal, "Human Rights Activism in Occupied and Early West Germany: The Case of the German League for Human Rights," *Journal of Modern History*, 80:3 (2008), 515–556.

[2] Josef Foschepoth, "German Reaction to Defeat and Occupation," in Robert G. Moeller (ed.), *West Germany under Construction* (Berkeley, 1997), 73–89, and Robert G. Moeller, *War Stories. The Search for a Usable Past in the Federal Republic of Germany* (Berkeley, 2001).

[3] Petitions to the UN Human Rights Commission regarding German POWs detained in the Soviet Union show this use of human rights language. See Paul Gordon Lauren, *The Evolution of International Human Rights. Visions Seen*, 2nd ed. (Philadelphia, 2003), 237 n. 12. The United Nations Archive in Geneva also has petitions regarding expellees.

[4] Pertti Ahonen, *After the Expulsion. West Germany and Eastern Europe 1945–1990* (Oxford, 2003), 25–28.

as victims and to suggest that Germans' own earlier heinous actions had been balanced out. Yet his human rights concepts also had a specifically legal significance. Laun helped to import discussions about self-determination and peace from Habsburg Austria and from the Western European progressive international law movement into the postwar West German international law field. The problems that Laun foregrounded continue to be important and controversial today. Germans' claims against the Allies fed into the larger question of whether individuals and non-state groups (such as ethnic groups) could be subjects of international law with standing in international institutions. The German expellees' claims also raised the question of whether such groups had a right to self-determination, including, by right of indigeneity, a right not to just any homeland, but to a specific and irreplaceable homeland.[5] These discussions are part of the history of those globally resonant concepts. This may not be well known to historians, but it ought to be familiar to West German international lawyers working today on minority and indigenous peoples' rights.[6] Politically, by the end of Laun's career in the late 1950s, the expellee issue had become associated with the right, yet the human rights concepts with which he worked are associated today with the left. Such divergent disciplinary and political histories, with their mutual antagonisms and borrowings, belong in a more comprehensive narrative of human rights in the twentieth century.

Laun's Concepts: The Autonomy of Law, the *conscience publique*, and the Right to National Self-determination

Laun was an important figure in interwar German jurisprudence. An ethnic German from the Bohemian lands of Austria-Hungary, he became involved with pacifism while serving as an officer in the First World War.[7] He was active in attempts to revise the Austrian Constitution's treatment of nationalities both during and immediately after the war. Laun strongly advocated the union of Austria and the Sudetenland region with Germany. When the Entente forbade that and instead placed the Sudetenland inside the new Czechoslovakian state, Laun experienced one of the greatest disappointments of his life. He left Austria for Germany to become professor of public law

---

[5] On these topics, see Christian Tomuschat, *Human Rights. Between Idealism and Realism* (Oxford, 2003), 305–309 (on the individual as a subject of international law); the German contributions in Catherine Brölmann, René Lefeber, and Marjoleine Zieck (eds.), *Peoples and Minorities in International Law* (Dordrecht, 1993) (on ethnic groups); and Christian Tomuschat (ed.), *Modern Law of Self-Determination* (Dordrecht, 1993) (on self-determination).

[6] Georg Dahm, Jost Delbrück, and Rüdiger Wolfrum, *Völkerrecht. Der Staat und andere Völkerrechtssubjekte; Räume unter internationaler Verwaltung*, 2nd, rev. ed., vol. I/2 (Berlin, 2002), 259, 268–269.

[7] Egmont Zechlin, "Die 'Zentralorganisation für einen dauernden Frieden' und die Mittelmächte. Ein Beitrag zur politischen Tätigkeit Rudolf Launs im ersten Weltkrieg," in Forschungsstelle für Völkerrecht und ausländisches öffentliches Recht der Universität Hamburg (ed.), *Festschrift für Rudolf Laun zu seinem achtzigsten Geburtstag* (Göttingen, 1962), 448–515.

and legal philosophy at the newly created University of Hamburg.[8] By the end
of the First World War, Laun had become a Social Democrat (though not a
Marxist), and he joined the SPD in Hamburg.[9] He was a vocal defender of
the Weimar Republic. At the same time, he continued to advocate the union
– through peaceful means – of Austria and the Sudetenland with Germany.[10]
His work in legal philosophy, meanwhile, contributed to debate on administrative discretion, and the relationship between morality and law. These were
vital concepts for the new democracy.[11]

During the Weimar Republic, Laun set out his basic concepts regarding
international law's sources. These were: the notion of the autonomy of law,
that is, that law was a category of human action separate from mere power or
coercion; the notion of a *conscience publique*, or widely held sense of justice;
and the right of national (today one might say ethnic) self-determination. This
last concept was, in his view, an outgrowth of the first two. Laun drew these
concepts from the work of the Belgium-based progressive Institut de droit
international, founded in 1873.[12]

To turn to the first of these concepts: the autonomy of law, a Kantian concept, held that it was impossible to impose genuine law on people without
their participation, such as through autocratic political authority or brute violence.[13] Rather, genuine law was created when people obeyed statutes out of
their own conviction that those statutes were moral. For Laun, a state could
not govern over people, but only through them. That was a significant limitation on state sovereignty. The autonomy of law in effect shifted to ordinary persons the power to define law. The autonomy of law also applied to

[8] Gustaf C. Hernmarck, "Rudolf Laun. Sein Leben und Werk," in Hernmarck (ed.), *Festschrift zu Ehren von Prof. Dr. jur. Rudolf Laun, Rektor der Universität Hamburg, anlässlich der Vollendung seines 65. Lebensjahres am 1. Januar 1947* (Hamburg, 1948), 8–18; Norman Paech and Ulrich Krampe, "Die Rechts- und Staatswissenschaftliche Fakultät," in Eckart Krause et al. (eds.), *Hochschulalltag im "Dritten Reich." Die Hamburger Universität 1933–1945* (Berlin, 1991), 3:867–912; and Rainer Biskup, *Rudolf Laun (1882–1975): Leben und Wirken eines Rechtslehrers in vier Epochen (österreichischer und) deutscher Geschichte.* Rainer Biskup has generously shared that manuscript-in-progress with me.

[9] Biskup, *Rudolf Laun*, 5.

[10] Barbara Vogel, "Der Verein für das Deutschtum im Ausland (VDA) an der Hamburger Universität in der Weimarer Republik," *Zeitgeschichte*, 16:1 (1988), 12–21.

[11] Rudolf Laun, *Das freie Ermessen und seine Grenzen* (Leipzig, 1910), argued for the judicial review of administrative acts. See Biskup, *Rudolf Laun*, esp. 24. Rudolf Laun, *Recht und Sittlichkeit. Antrittsrede, gehalten anlässlich seiner Inauguration zum Rektor der Universität Hamburg am 10. November 1924* (Hamburg, 1925) was his major statement against legal positivism and for the autonomy of law.

[12] Martti Koskenniemi, *The Gentle Civilizer of Nations. The Rise and Fall of International Law 1870–1960* (New York, 2001), 14–16, 41–42, 51, and chapters 1 and 3. Laun's emphasis on national self-determination was not typical of all progressive international lawyers, but some did share it, including Pasquale Mancini, one of the founders of the *Revue de droit international et de législation comparée* and much admired by Laun. See Koskenniemi, *The Gentle Civilizer of Nations*, 14, 63.

[13] Laun, *Recht und Sittlichkeit* (1925), 25.

international law contexts. For example, if a state annexed territory and denied self-administration in a manner that violated inhabitants' nationality rights, that state would be ruling through sheer coercion.[14] Coercion was a fragile form of rule, Laun argued, because if rule were based merely on power, then no one could be certain who would hold power in the future, and the door would be opened to anarchy as various factions vied for power. As this brief summary suggests, Laun was vehemently opposed to legal positivism, the conventional doctrine in nineteenth- and early-twentieth-century Germany (and elsewhere), according to which law consisted of the explicit, positivized acts of sovereign states, rather than deriving from some source outside or above the state such as God or nature. While traditional international law, which confined itself to the willed acts of sovereign states, fit well with legal positivism, the progressive international law movement argued that states had obligations that limited their power to act unilaterally and arbitrarily. For Laun, adherence to legal positivism was tantamount to capitulating to amoral state coercion, and could not be reconciled with democracy.

The second of Laun's central ideas was the *conscience publique*, which he defined as people's views regarding what was just.[15] Like the autonomy of law, the *conscience publique* gave ordinary people the power to define law. It emerged from individual persons' moral reflection, and Laun claimed that it was remarkably consistent among the majority of populations and across state boundaries. He conceded that this form of public opinion could not be observed at moments when people's views were likely to be deformed by propaganda or warfare. Like the founders of the progressive international law movement, Laun argued that the *conscience publique* was a valid source of international law, just like treaties and customary law. The concept of the *conscience publique* allowed progressive international lawyers to locate a source of power beyond the reach of any state. That may sound similar to natural law, but progressive international lawyers in fact wished to distance themselves from natural law doctrine as well. Laun considered the German historical school of law of the early nineteenth century to have invalidated natural law, and held that efforts to revive natural law merely promoted arbitrary legal reasoning.[16] Laun and other progressive international lawyers claimed that the *conscience publique*, unlike natural law, was grounded in sociological reality.

Over the long term, Laun insisted, the *conscience publique* favored democracy and popular sovereignty. Given the chance to express themselves without coercion, most people would prefer democracy over undemocratic forms of state rule. Coercion could never be the ultimate guarantor of state power in a

---

[14] Ibid., 27.
[15] Rudolf Laun, *La Démocratie. Essai sociologique, juridique et de politique morale* (Paris, 1933).
[16] Rudolf Laun, *Der Wandel der Ideen Staat und Volk als Äusserung des Weltgewissens* (Barcelona, 1933), 335–337. See also Koskenniemi, *The Gentle Civilizer of Nations*, 24.

democracy.[17] Violence as a means of settling human affairs was being steadily
displaced by "voluntary obedience and above all autonomous juridical-moral
action."[18] Obviously, there was reason to doubt this trend in the years before
1933. Yet Laun saw Soviet Communism, Italian fascism, and Hitler's seizure of
power as only temporary aberrations. A dictator's rule did not mean that the
population had by and large rejected democracy; if people could speak without
fear, they would still prefer democracy, he argued.[19] He also noted that even
dictators invoked mass support, which revealed that the idea of democracy
retained its power.[20] In his July 1933 afterword to his book-length exposition
of the *conscience publique*, he insisted that "the recent events in Germany do
not authorize us to change the judgment regarding this ancient process of twenty-five centuries that we have set forth in the last chapters of our work."[21]

Laun's third major concept was the right to national self-determination.[22]
Just as the *conscience publique* had come to embrace democracy, so had it
come since the nineteenth century to embrace the value of nationality. Laun
believed that nationality, like the *conscience publique*, was natural, prepoliti-
cal, and perduring: people naturally valued freedom, and if they were free,
they would naturally seek to sustain and express their nationality. It is important to note that Laun rejected the nation-state as a political goal. While I will
use a literal translation of his terms *Nationalität* (nationality) and *nationale
Selbstbestimmung* (national self-determination), the reader must bear in mind
that Laun does not mean here a right or a movement to achieve state power
for a nationality. For Laun, state power and a nationality's power ought not
to be combined, because a nation-state, once established, would simply use
state coercion to oppress the inevitable minorities inside its borders. In fact,
he also rejected the term "minority," because he held that in a multinational,
federal state each group deserved to exercise its cultural rights regardless of
the numerical proportions among groups.

For Laun, the political, amoral state was a threat to the natural, moral
nationality. Nationalities needed international law to protect themselves from
state coercion. Displaying the Austro-Marxist influence on his thinking, Laun
described his ideal political arrangement as a federal, multinational state
that was limited domestically by its constitution as well as internationally by
strong international law controls.[23] Only such a state would reliably enable the

[17] Laun, *La Démocratie*, 78.
[18] Ibid., 214.
[19] Ibid., 209; see also 57.
[20] Ibid., 215–216, 217.
[21] Ibid., 221. Laun had completed the manuscript in 1932, before Hitler became Chancellor, but
    it was not published until mid-1933, in France. Ibid., 5 and 217.
[22] Laun, *Der Wandel der Ideen Staat und Volk*. Like *La Démocratie*, this book was completed
    before the Nazi seizure of power and published, in this case in Spain, afterward.
[23] The Austrian Social Democrat Karl Renner sought to combine individual rights with group
    rights of self-determination in a multinational constitutional state. See Rudolf Springer (Karl
    Renner), *Der Kampf der österreichischen Nationen um den Staat* (Vienna, 1902). Laun had

democratic exercise of cultural rights. True nationality rights, then, required stronger international law: "The more validity that the national idea conquers in the legal sensibility and conscience of the world, and the more the idea of state sovereignty recedes accordingly, the stronger the influence of international on domestic law must be in all areas that are in any way connected with the national question."[24] Moreover, strong international law controls promised to democratize international law, by giving non-state groups a place on the international law stage – a stage that had been dominated for so long by states. Laun thereby separated the right to national self-determination from state sovereignty – an approach quite different from that, for instance, of postcolonial politicians, who have wielded the right of national self-determination as a state's prerogative.

By 1933, then, Laun had laid out his basic concepts of the autonomy of law, the *conscience publique*, democracy, and the right of nationalities to self-determination. Genuine law emerged from people's voluntary obedience based on their moral beliefs, which had come to include nationality and democracy, he argued. Domestic and international law ought to take account of these. For Laun, the clauses in the peace treaties after the First World War that forbade the union of Austria and the Sudetenland with Germany were both illegal and undemocratic – a position with which the Nazis would have agreed.

Laun after 1945: The Individual as a Subject of International Law and the Right to the Homeland

As an active Social Democrat, Laun faced dismissal under the Law for the Restoration of the Professional Civil Service in 1933. However, he managed to keep his professorial post, at a reduced salary, probably due to his activism on behalf of German minorities in interwar East-Central Europe.[25] In 1935 Laun published a new, expanded edition of his main work on the relationship between morality and law.[26] In 1942 he published *Der Satz*

---

already departed from Renner in one important respect by the time of the First World War peace settlement: While Renner and his colleague Otto Bauer advocated the "personality principle" (*Personalitätsprinzip*), which allowed scattered individuals to administer their national affairs collectively, Laun favored a "territorial principle" (*Territorialprinzip*) that granted regional autonomy over a homogeneous enclave of a multinational state. See Rudolf Laun and I. Lange, *Czecho-Slovak Claims on German Territory*, 3rd ed. (The Hague, 1919), 22.

[24] Laun, *Der Wandel der Ideen Staat und Volk*, 326.

[25] He appealed his dismissal on those grounds. See Paech and Krampe, "Die Rechts- und Staatswissenschaftliche Fakultät," 905 n. 5 and 867, and Barbara Vogel, "Anpassung und Widerstand. Das Verhältnis Hamburger Hochschullehrer zum Staat 1919 bis 1945," in *Hochschulalltag im "Dritten Reich*," 22.

[26] Rudolf Laun, *Recht und Sittlichkeit*, 3rd, exp. ed. (Berlin, 1935). It contained the unchanged 1924 text as well as new essays. In the new essays, he reiterated that racial or economic categories could not serve as sources of law, and that only the "autonomous conscience and legal sensibility of individuals" was the source of law. Laun, *Recht und Sittlichkeit* (1935), 98.

vom Grunde. Ein System der Erkenntnistheorie (1942), his most complete
account of the autonomy of law. It implicitly criticized Nazi concepts such
as the *Führerprinzip* and racial hierarchy, stating, for example, that "there
are many religions, many peoples, many states, many languages, but only
one science."[27] In 1945, that anti-Nazi reputation propelled Laun into leading positions at the university: He became dean in May 1945 and once
again rector in 1947. Laun was also pivotal in his field's professional society,
as the re-founder and first postwar Chairman of the German Society for
International Law (Deutsche Gesellschaft für Völkerrecht, DGVR). Before
1933, this group had been the forum of German progressive international
lawyers such as Walther Schücking and Hans Wehberg.[28]

The Allied occupation of Germany shocked and infuriated Laun. He continued to write about nationality rights and democracy after 1945, just as
he had before and during Nazism. Laun pointed out his consistency to his
students with sarcastic pride, telling them that his lectures, "which had their
roots in Imperial Austria, could be given again, essentially unchanged, in the
Austrian Republic, the Weimar Republic, National Socialist Germany and
most recently in the British Military Government's regime of the military leadership principle (*soldatischen Führerprinzips*)."[29] Two aspects of his thinking emerge here. First, he clearly considered the cause of German nationality
politics in East-Central Europe to be unscathed by its horrific mobilization in
dictatorship, world war, and genocide. Second, he perceived a continuum of
German victimhood across 1945: Germans had been victimized by the Paris
peace settlement, Nazi rule, Allied occupation, and as expellees.

Immediately after 1945, Laun applied his basic concepts to Germans *qua*
victims. Referring to the autonomy of law, he argued that Germans' compliance with the Nazi regime was overwhelmingly due to coercion. What the Nazis
imposed was not genuine law, because it had been imposed on the Germans;
they had not embraced it. Using the *conscience publique*, he made a similar
point, arguing that just because many Germans obeyed Nazi precepts did not
mean that they accepted them. On the contrary, he insisted, most Germans had
favored democracy and human rights all along.[30] Laun seemed to reason that if
coercion were present at all, then any inquiry into political will or opinion was
moot. His idea of a *conscience publique* allowed him to avoid considering the
possibility that dictatorship could be genuinely popular (or that that popularity

---

[27] Rudolf Laun, *Der Satz vom Grunde. Ein System der Erkenntnistheorie* (Tübingen, 1942), 18.
On this book, see Paech and Krampe, "Die Rechts- und Staatswissenschaftliche Fakultät,"
898.
[28] On Schücking and Wehberg, see Koskenniemi, *The Gentle Civilizer of Nations*, 215–222.
[29] Rudolf Laun, *Studienbehelf zur Vorlesung über Allgemeine Staatslehre*, 2nd ed. (Hamburg,
1946), 7.
[30] Rudolf Laun, *Die Menschenrechte* (Hamburg, 1948), 16; Laun, *Die Haager Landkriegsordnung. Das Übereinkommen über die Gesetze und Gebräuche des Landkriegs. Textausgabe
mit einer Einführung*, 4th ed. (Wolfenbüttel, 1948), 49, 50, 53. This book first appeared
in 1946.

could be complexly layered). Laun insisted that coercion – now Allied coercion – could not create genuine law. He argued that Germans were victims of numerous human rights violations under Allied occupation, and cited the right of national self-determination to condemn the expulsions of ethnic Germans from Poland, Czechoslovakia, and elsewhere in Eastern Europe.

Indeed, Germans were the unrecognized pioneers in the history of human rights thought for Laun. Religious freedom was the first human right to gain recognition, and "thus human rights first emerged in the first half of the sixteenth century in Germany," demanded by the Anabaptists and Luther.[31] Germans – including a delegate from Austria – had also produced the Weimar Constitution, the "freest constitution in the world."[32] No wonder Laun was popular in those years immediately after the war: He had a clean political past, he imparted clear lessons in law that were explicitly informed by morality, and he reassured Germans that they were valuable people with a distinguished past who were being maltreated. Laun repeatedly likened the Allies to Hitler and the Nazi regime. Both were, for Laun, the pure expression of amoral coercion legitimized by legal positivism, under which Germans had to suffer: "We yield to the new positive law ... as we had to yield to the positive law of the Hitler regime."[33] Everyone ought to be concerned about the treatment of defeated Germany after 1945, Laun insisted, because it was a warning to all who may one day experience defeat themselves.[34] His was not a discussion of human rights that was intended to provoke Germans' critical introspection. For that reason, some in Germany as well as abroad responded angrily to his writings, seeing him as nationalist and – unfairly – as an apologist for Nazism.[35] It is indeed frustrating to read arguments as narrowly cast and self-pitying as Laun's, but Laun was no apologist for Nazism. For that reason, some in Germany as well as abroad responded angrily to his writings, seeing him as nationalist and – unfairly – as an apologist for Nazism.

Laun formulated two new concepts in the post-1945 era: the individual and non-state group as full (or fuller) subjects of international law, and the right to the homeland. They were outgrowths of his work before 1933: The autonomy of law and *conscience publique* had already broached the issue of the individual's voice in international law, and the right to the homeland was a reformulation of the right to national self-determination. As was true of his interwar concepts, these new concepts in his late work were not unique to Laun. Along with many others in the post-1945 era, Laun claimed that an

---

[31] Rudolf Laun, *Das Grundgesetz Westdeutschlands. Ansprache, gehalten im Auftrag der Universität Hamburg an die Studenten der Universität Hamburg am 24. Mai 1949* (Hamburg, 1949), 16.

[32] Ibid., 12 (quote) and 13.

[33] Rudolf Laun, "Gegenwärtiges Völkerrecht," in Laun, *Reden und Aufsätze zum Völkerrecht und Staatsrecht* (Hamburg, 1947), 10.

[34] Laun, *Die Menschenrechte*, 5, 6, 8, 14, 26.

[35] For example, Ernst J. Cohn, "German Legal Science Today," *International and Comparative Law Quarterly*, 2 (April 1953), 191.

"international law of human rights" was gradually displacing an older "international law of the sovereignty of state power."[36] His postwar concepts fit with that development, by limiting state power and augmenting the voice of non-state actors (individual persons, nationalities) in international law. In his international professional context, Laun's distinctiveness lay in applying these concepts to Germans.

According to traditional international law, only states were recognized actors in international law. If an individual were to be recognized as a subject of international law, the international legal order would place states in a very different position. A plaintiff could advance directly to an international forum to have a complaint heard or a case tried, without having first to find a state to represent him or her. The states' monopoly on international law would be broken. The standing of individuals was important not just as an abstract ideal, but as a practical reality for Germans under occupation between 1945 and 1949. The German state had ceased to be effective; in the view of some, it had ceased to exist entirely.[37] The Allies stepped into its place: Neither annexing nor occupying Germany in the traditional sense, they replaced the state. In such a case, traditional international law seemed to afford individual Germans no standing to raise complaints. They seemed to be outside the realm of international law.[38]

Laun's own position was that Germans did have standing under international law to protest violations of human rights by the Allies. First, he argued that international law had recognized individuals as a kind of subject in the Hague Convention of 1907, which outlined the laws of war. The Hague Convention defined a military occupier's obligations to protect individual civilians, thereby protecting the rights of individuals, not governments.[39] For example, it set limits on requisition in order to protect individuals' private property, it banned collective punishment to protect individuals, and civilians were not to be relocated unless it was militarily necessary. It also protected soldiers as individuals, by requiring adequate care for prisoners of war, freedom from forced labor, and their earliest possible release. Second, Laun argued that Germans were not in fact without a state after 1945: If the Allies had eliminated the state, then they must have annexed the territory, giving the population the rights of their own citizens. If the Allies were occupying the

[36] Rudolf Laun, "Zweierlei Völkerrecht," *Jahrbuch für internationales und ausländisches öffentliches Recht*, 2 (1949), 636.
[37] Hans Kelsen, "The International Legal Status of Germany to be Established Immediately upon Termination of the War," *American Journal of International Law*, 38 (October 1944), 689–694, and Kelsen, "The Legal Status of Germany according to the Declaration of Berlin," *American Journal of International Law*, 39 (July 1945), 518–526. Laun's furious response was "Eine Lehre des Hasses," in Laun, *Reden und Aufsätze*, 21–24. On the debate, see Bernhard Diestelkamp, *Rechtsgeschichte als Zeitgeschichte. Beiträge zur Rechtsgeschichte des 20. Jahrhunderts* (Baden-Baden, 2001), 32–49 and references cited there.
[38] Laun, "Zweierlei Völkerrecht," and Josef L. Kunz, "The Status of Occupied Germany under International Law: A Legal Dilemma," *Western Political Quarterly*, 3 (December 1950), 538–565, here 555.
[39] Laun, *Die Haager Landkriegsordnung*, 26–34, 53–55.

state, then the Hague Convention covered Allied actions. Either way, issues such as forced deportation, forced labor, and requisitioning were subject to review. And, importantly for Laun, the Hague Convention mentioned – and thereby positivized – the *conscience publique* as a source of law.[40]

One of the most important tools for enacting individuals' status as subjects of international law was the right of individual petition. Like numerous other human rights advocates in the wake of the Second World War, Laun insisted that the right of individual petition was the only effective way to protect human rights. Yet, as Laun complained, it was already falling victim to the opposition of the great powers by 1950, when the UN's Commission on Human Rights decided that its human rights convention would permit petitions from individuals and NGOs, but that these petitions would not entail a binding hearing before the Commission. This amounted to an empty right of individual petition, as Laun pointed out, and indeed petitions were filed away, unheard, for years.[41] The right of individual petition was also discussed, though initially rejected, during the drafting of the European Convention for the Protection of Human Rights and Fundamental Freedoms (1950). After a few years, the right of petition became part of an optional protocol, so that signatory countries were not obliged to accept it.[42] Here again, we see that Laun's concepts were part and parcel of current thinking in progressive international law. What was unusual, at least outside of Germany, was Laun's expectation that Germans might use them effectively on their own behalf.

Laun's arguments concerning the Hague Convention and occupied Germany appeared mostly in law journals. In more popular versions of his arguments, Laun summarized the issue as a matter of "human rights." *Human Rights* (*Die Menschenrechte*) was the title of a 1948 public lecture for a lay audience, given on the fifteenth anniversary of Hitler's appointment as chancellor.[43] That date, together with his lecture's content, were intended to indicate that Germans were now subject to dictatorship for a second time. Laun explained that human rights were, by their very nature, rights held by individuals against states – their own as well as foreign.[44] As such holders of human rights, Germans could not be legitimately subjected to the "total authority" (*totale Gewalt*) of the Allies that the formula of unconditional surrender implied.[45] Laun's main examples of such total authority were the expulsions of ethnic Germans and

---

[40] Ibid., 22; see also Laun, "Allgemeine Rechtsgrundsätze," 132–133.
[41] Rudolf Laun, "Die Menschenrechte der Heimatvertriebenen," *Der Weg/El Sendero*, 4 (October 1950), 919–920. This was a Nazi-apologetic periodical published in Argentina. The convention referred to here was eventually passed by the United Nations General Assembly as two documents in 1966: the International Covenant on Civil and Political Rights, and the International Covenant on Economic, Social and Cultural Rights.
[42] A. W. Brian Simpson, *Human Rights and the End of Empire. Britain and the Genesis of the European Convention* (Oxford, 2001), 649–753, esp. 707–710.
[43] Laun, *Die Menschenrechte*; see also Laun, "Die Menschenrechte der Heimatvertriebenen."
[44] Laun, *Die Menschenrechte*, 8.
[45] Ibid., 18.

the retention of German POWs. He argued that the Allies ought to be held to their own standard as enunciated in the United Nations Charter and the Nuremberg Charter. (The latter, in the course of asserting the illegality of certain acts by Nazi Germany, held that all states had recognized Hague rules as recently as 1939.)[46] With such lectures and publications, Laun contributed to his German audience's understanding of "human rights" as concerning Allied wrongs and German victimhood.

In 1949, the Allied military occupation came to an end. From then on, Laun focused his international law work on the expulsions of ethnic Germans, in the hope that one day a case could be brought before an international forum. While his work on the law of war focused on the individual gaining a voice in international law, his work on the expellees turned to the non-state group, here the nationality, as a fuller subject of international law.[47] Laun saw no tension between individual rights and group rights: An individual's cultural rights clearly implied group rights, as cultural rights could not be exercised in isolation. The innovative concept Laun sought to advance here – the other major concept in his postwar arguments for an "international law of human rights" – was the "right to the homeland" (*Recht auf die Heimat*). This concept, which overlapped with the more general concept of national self-determination, has been theorized mainly by Germans and Austrians associated with the expellee lobby.[48] However, the concept certainly reaches beyond that context, as it addresses problems of indigenous and ethnic groups' rights that have arisen all over the world.[49]

Specific aspects of the Sudeten expellee case, along with Laun's progressive international law background, helped to propel him to a radical position on limiting state sovereignty. Like other spokespeople for the expellee cause, Laun tended to lump together two categories of displaced Germans and refer to a total number of about fifteen million "expellees" (*Vertriebene*). While the lived experience of brutalization and trekking westward was similar among persons in this large group, they did have varying legal statuses with corresponding ramifications. At least seven million of them were from the former Prussian provinces and were properly refugees (*Flüchtlinge*), not expellees.[50] German citizens living inside the boundaries of Germany, they fled to escape the advance of the Red Army. A second, legally distinct group was the three and a half million German citizens who found their region of Germany transferred to Poland by the Potsdam Agreement of August

[46] Ibid., 16, 18, 20–21.
[47] Rudolf Laun, "Das Recht der Völker auf die Heimat ihrer Vorfahren," *Internationales Recht und Diplomatie*, 3:2 (1958), 152–153.
[48] Ahonen, *After the Expulsion*, 42–44. The major text is Otto Kimminich, *Das Recht auf die Heimat*, 3rd, rev. and exp. ed. (Bonn, 1989).
[49] Christian Tomuschat, "Das Recht auf die Heimat. Neue rechtliche Aspekte," in Jürgen Jekewitz et al. (eds.), *Des Menschen Recht zwischen Freiheit und Verantwortung. Festschrift für Karl Josef Partsch zum 75. Geburtstag* (Berlin, 1989), 183–212.
[50] Ahonen, *After the Expulsion*, 16.

1945.[51] They were denied the possibility of remaining in the postwar Polish state: The Polish government expelled them. At the same time, postwar Czechoslovakia expelled its three million ethnic German citizens. Unlike the Polish case, almost all of these expellees had been Czechoslovak citizens and, if they were old enough, Habsburg citizens before that.[52] Now they were stripped of their Czechoslovak citizenship; specifically, the Czechoslovak government upheld Nazi-era law that had made ethnic Germans there into citizens of Germany. Finally, postwar Hungary, Romania, and Yugoslavia expelled about 600,000 ethnic Germans from among their own citizens.[53] As many as one and a half million of all these refugees and expellees died in these ordeals.[54] By 1950, about eight million refugees and expellees lived in West Germany, four million in East Germany, and half a million in Austria.[55]

Just as Laun and other expellee spokespeople conflated the refugees and expellees, they also conflated the basis for claims to their homelands. There was a clear legal basis (though little political chance of success) for protesting Poland's annexation of German lands. As West Germany formally asserted until 1990, the Oder-Neisse Line between East Germany and Poland was not to be considered permanent until it was confirmed by a peace treaty between all of Germany, on the one hand, and all four of the Allies, on the other – as had been envisioned before the Cold War. Until such time, West Germany maintained, the legal borders of Germany were those of 1937 (the baseline for determining what was Germany proper, before Nazi Germany's territorial gains). By contrast, ethnic Germans from places outside Germany's 1937 borders had no such legal claim. The largest group in West Germany for whom this was true was the Sudeten Germans.[56] The Sudetenland had never

---

[51] Some Germans fled the area of post–World War II Poland as refugees from the Red Army, then returned, then were expelled by the postwar Polish government. See Stanislaw Jankowiak, "'Cleansing' Poland of Germans: The Province of Pomerania, 1945–1949," in Philipp Ther and Ana Siljak (eds.), *Redrawing Nations. Ethnic Cleansing in East-Central Europe, 1944–1948* (Lanham, Md., 2001), 88.

[52] Eagle Glassheim, "The Mechanics of Ethnic Cleansing: The Expulsion of Germans from Czechoslovakia, 1945–1947," in Ther and Siljak (eds.), *Redrawing Nations*, 209. It is hard to be precise about who held which citizenship in early 1945, because under Nazi occupation some were pressured to take on German citizenship, then changed back after the war. See Chad Bryant, *Prague in Black. Nazi Rule and Czech Nationalism* (Cambridge, 2007), 244–249.

[53] Gerhard Reichling, *Die deutschen Vertriebenen in Zahle. Teil 1. Umsiedler, Verschleppte, Vertriebene, Aussiedler 1940–1985* (Bonn, 1986), 26.

[54] Laun uses the figure of 2 million deaths, which West German scholarship of the 1950s generally did. More recently, Rüdiger Overmans has revised the mortality figures for civilian ethnic Germans downward to half a million. Rüdiger Overmans, *Deutsche militärische Verluste im Zweiten Weltkrieg* (Munich, 1999), 298–299. I am using Ahonen's estimate: Ahonen, *After The Expulsion*, 21.

[55] Ibid., 20–21.

[56] Inside West Germany, the breakdown of refugees and expellees by place of origin was about five and half million from Poland and the Soviet Union, two million from Czechoslovakia, and half a million from southeastern Europe. Ibid., 21.

been part of any German state except for Hitler's, after the 1938 Munich Agreement.[57] Of all the expellee spokespeople, those claiming to represent the Sudeten Germans were the most in need of legal innovations that would help them outmaneuver traditional, state-based international law. The specific legal predicament of the Sudeten German expellees led legal experts such as Laun to commit themselves to concepts and institutions that would place strong limits on state sovereignty. That, in turn, situated them on the radical edge of international law and human rights argument. They became committed to that radical approach because they had no choice: No state would espouse their complaints. Certainly the expelling states and the Allies would not revisit the issue. And while West Germany offered the majority of the expellees a home as well as extensive social legislation and political sympathy, it did not – and could not – bring a case for international deliberation.[58]

No international agreement expressly banned state-ordered mass deportations or expulsions at Laun's time of writing – that happened only in 1963, and then only at the European level.[59] However, the expulsions of ethnic Germans obviously violated numerous basic human rights. It was a simple matter for Laun to establish that individuals had suffered loss of property, liberty, and life without due process.[60] According to Laun, these violations of widely recognized basic human rights showed that a right to the homeland – in its narrowest definition, the right not to be forcibly removed from one's home region – was already practically in existence. To develop the argument for a right to the homeland further, Laun revived his old concept from progressive international law, the *conscience publique*. While mass expulsion was a technique that belonged to traditional international law based on state sovereignty, Laun argued, the new international law of human rights accepted the *conscience publique*'s high valuation of nationality.[61] (Laun never discussed the possibility that expulsions could be truly popular, rather than merely the act of a sovereign state, just as he had not raised the question of whether dictatorship could be popular. To do so would have threatened to dismantle the concept of the *conscience publique*.) Had the *conscience publique* not been drowned out by the hatreds of the First World War and subjected to the coercion of an international law of state sovereignty, Laun continued, it would have offered self-determination for Sudeten and other Habsburg Germans in 1919, permitting

---

[57] That is why the expellee lobby argued for the continued validity of the Munich Agreement. So did Laun: Rudolf Laun, *Das Recht auf die Heimat* (Hanover, 1951), 22–23, 25.

[58] Apart from the political infeasibility of bringing a case, the UN Charter's Article 107 (enemy states clause) precluded it. See Georg Ress, "Article 107," in Bruno Simma (ed.), *The Charter of the United Nations. A Commentary* (Oxford, 1994), 1152–1162. On Adenauer's attitude toward the expellee cause, see Ahonen, *After the Expulsion*, 95–96, 110–115.

[59] The first international document to prohibit it was concluded by the Council of Europe in 1963. See Jean-Marie Henckaerts, *Mass Expulsion in Modern International Law and Practice* (The Hague, 1995), 9–10.

[60] Laun, *Die Menschenrechte*, 17.

[61] Laun, *Das Recht auf die Heimat*, 27, 29–30.

the Sudetenland and Austria to join Germany. Sudeten Germans' rejoicing in 1938 reflected the end of their long-denied national self-determination, Laun insisted, not their admiration for the Nazis: "They would have applauded *any* German regime."[62] Once again, Laun placed nationality on one plane, and politics on another.

Given the ongoing coercion of sovereign states and the ineffectiveness of individual petitions that went unheard, Laun called for extending the right to self-determination to non-state groups: "We stand before the legal question: can a people, in the sense of a natural formation arising from a common descent, sedentary nature and mother tongue, appear in the international law community as an independent legal subject, one that is different in kind from states, but that nevertheless can realize its own rights?"[63] He hoped the answer was yes, and cited two precedents for that. The first was Pasquale Mancini's 1851 argument for the "principle of nationalities," which held that nationality, not domicile, should determine the law under which a person was placed.[64] The second was the Entente's decision during the First World War, in 1917 and early 1918, to deal diplomatically with the Czechoslovak National Council as a valid treaty partner. At that time, Laun pointed out, the Habsburg Empire was still intact, and so the Czechoslovak National Council was a natural, not a political, state-like unit.[65] To treat the nationality as a fuller subject of international law, Laun insisted, would radically democratize international law, which had traditionally been so undemocratic.[66] It certainly would mean a profound transformation of existing international law.

Laun also called for nationalities, newly empowered with his proposed right of self-determination, to link themselves legally to specific territories, through making "homeland" (*Heimat*) a category in international law.[67] The Universal Declaration of Human Rights did state that a person had a right to leave and return to that person's country (Article 13), but here "country" seemed to be defined merely as any state in which a person was normally permitted to live. Laun did not seek a right to just any homeland (after all, the Sudeten Germans did have a legal home in West Germany, where they immediately gained citizenship), but rather to a nationality's supposedly unique and irreplaceable homeland. The Universal Declaration of Human Rights said nothing about what Laun saw as the necessarily collective nature of a homeland, and it did not distinguish between a recent arrival to a given region and a person whose ancestors had lived there for generations.[68] Here Laun was obviously

---

[62] Ibid., 20.
[63] Laun, "Das Recht der Völker auf die Heimat ihrer Vorfahren," 157.
[64] Kurt H. Nadelmann, "Mancini's Nationality Rule and Non-Unified Legal Systems: Nationality versus Domicile," *American Journal of Comparative Law*, 17:3 (1969), 418–451.
[65] Laun, "Das Recht der Völker auf die Heimat ihrer Vorfahren," 159–163. No doubt he relished this part of his argument as a way to trap his Czech nationalist opponents in their own logic.
[66] Ibid., 152–153, 165.
[67] Laun, *Das Recht auf die Heimat*, 24.
[68] Ibid., 35.

thinking of the Czechoslovak government's policy of dispatching settlers to formerly German-speaking areas after the expulsion. Using a phrase redolent of decades of German nationalism and anti-Slav racism, he complained that the excessively individualist Article 13 could not prevent "Slavs and Mongols" from saying tomorrow that the Sudetenland was their land.[69] There had to be a way, Laun insisted, to differentiate among various meanings of the word homeland and various claims of individuals and groups to it. To give priority to a group that could claim greater antiquity for its residence in a given territory, he suggested this refinement to the right to the homeland: a "right to the ancestral homeland" (*Recht auf die angestammte Heimat*).[70]

Laun's idea of international law subject status and self-determination for nationalities and his proposed right to the homeland raised the problem of how to define membership in a group. In the first years after the Second World War, Laun emphasized that nationality was a matter of the individual's choice of affiliation, and not of descent. Like religion, he explained, one's national affiliation was a "spiritual and moral" (*geistig-sittlich*) matter.[71] To determine nationality by descent, which no one could choose, would therefore be absurd, he reasoned, and in any case, inherited traits were often indeterminate. Such arguments fit well with those of his Viennese mentor Edmund Bernatzik, as well as the Austro-Marxists.[72] Yet in 1958, near the end of Laun's scholarly life, he instead emphasized the permanence of inherited traits: "One can no more get rid of one's descent than one can get rid of the history of one's ancestors and one's homeland, or of inherited, physical racial traits and inherited mental qualities of character."[73] He did concede that factors other than descent could affect one's choice of homeland, such as if a child moved with its parents to a different country and learned a new language there. But rather than allowing such real-life ambiguity to stand, he now impatiently asserted that there were limits to it. Contrasting such contingent events with supposedly clearer racial differences, he asserted: "through sudden events and acts of will, a Catholic can become a Protestant, a capitalist can become a proletarian, and vice versa, but an Anglo-Saxon cannot become a Russian or Chinese, for example."[74]

---

[69] Ibid., 35. On Laun's anti-Slav tirades, see Arnold Sywottek, "Kontinuität im Neubeginn: Über die Anfänge der 'Universität Hamburg'," in *Hochschulalltag im "Dritten Reich*," 1399–1400. Karl Renner recounted the legend of the Mongol invasion of the Bohemian lands in his memoirs, *An der Wende zweier Zeiten. Lebenserinnerungen* (Vienna, 1946), 28–29.

[70] Laun, "Das Recht der Völker auf die Heimat ihrer Vorfahren," 149, 151.

[71] Rudolf Laun, *Die Lehren des Westfälischen Friedens* (Hamburg, 1949), 34. In a 1919 article, he was even more relativist, mentioning that it was a "fact that people may change their nationality in the course of time." Rudolf Laun and I. Lange, *Czecho-Slovak Claims on German Territory*, 3rd ed. (The Hague, 1919), 18.

[72] See Tara Zahra, *Kidnapped Souls. National Indifference and the Battle for Children in the Bohemian Lands, 1900–1948* (Ithaca, 2008), 21, 48. She places this ethnic indeterminacy at the centre of her brilliant analysis.

[73] Laun, "Das Recht der Völker auf die Heimat ihrer Vorfahren," 153.

[74] Ibid.

He now insisted that the legal definition of homeland had to take account of these permanent traits.

In addition to calling for the development of a new international law concept of homeland, Laun also proposed to solve the problems of nationality and homeland in Europe by turning back the clock, legally speaking. He cited a precedent for such legal time travel from the Thirty Years' War. To undo the expulsions of Protestant princes, the Peace of Westphalia of 1648 had determined a baseline year of 1624: Princes expelled between that year and 1648 were to be allowed to return home. Laun likened the right to the homeland to religious freedom, and argued that the rights of the Protestant princes "correspond to the right to the homeland of the Poles, Jews, Germans, etc. expelled since 1933 or better since 1914."[75] He proposed turning the clock back to 1914; for Laun, clearly, the First World War and its peace settlement was when everything had begun to go wrong. By declaring a particular date to be the point of departure for the proper or natural arrangement of nationalities, he was implicitly suggesting that all the intervening events, including here the genocide of European Jewry, be simply forgotten. (In fact, Laun mentioned Jews only rarely in any of his work. In his post-1945 work, he mentioned them as an example of a nationality, and Zionism and the Israeli state as evidence of the strength of the right to the homeland.[76] He thereby implied that Jews had never had a proper home in Europe. Meanwhile, he claimed the term "genocide" for the expelled Germans.)[77] Laun's proposal to turn back the legal clock was absurd, but it did show the coherence of his interventions over the previous decades: He had been fighting the Treaty of St. Germain all his life.

Laun and West German International Law after 1945

Laun was no outlier, politically or professionally, in the first postwar years. Yet his standing declined from about 1949 on. His arguments remained the same, but now they began to embarrass his West German colleagues. His polemics had suited the mood of the early occupation era, but as West Germans sought legitimacy for their new state in the new context of the Cold War, his bitter attacks on all four Allies ensured his obsolescence. It is also likely that by the 1950s his opposition to Nazism was no longer so important as a qualification for a public intellectual. While in the late 1940s he was able to lend some respectability and legitimacy to highly compromised colleagues who shared his concern with Germans' ethnic rights but not his liberal principles,[78] by the late 1950s that was probably felt to be unnecessary. Two of his professional

[75] Laun, *Das Recht auf die Heimat*, 31. See also Laun, *Die Lehren des Westfälischen Friedens*, 46.
[76] See, e.g., Laun, *Das Recht auf die Heimat*, 6.
[77] Laun, "Das Recht der Völker auf die Heimat ihrer Vorfahren," 156. He used the term *génocide* as well as *Völkermord* to make that point.
[78] Laun wrote many *Persilscheine*, the letters of reference from opponents and victims of Nazism that supported the postwar careers of colleagues who had been close to Nazism.

endeavors suggest this pattern of early postwar prestige and then rapid obsolescence: his leadership in reconvening the German Society for International Law, and his participation in the massive research project on the expellees, published as the *Documentation of the Expulsion of the Germans from East-Central Europe.*[79]

The German Society for International Law, founded in 1917 as the associational home of Germany's progressive international lawyers, had held its last prewar meeting in 1932.[80] Laun gathered about twenty old members and newcomers for a conference in 1947; in 1948 he hosted a second conference that drew over forty. A third conference in 1949 marked the Society's official refounding, with Laun as chairman. The Society's proceedings in the early years show that not everyone agreed with Laun's criticisms of the Allied occupation – or, if they did agree with them, they did not wish to dwell upon them.[81] Nevertheless, Laun did use the Society as a vehicle for his criticisms of the Allies. In 1947 and 1948 the Society voted unanimously in favor of eight resolutions that summarized Laun's arguments. The first three in 1947 concerned Germany's international law status, holding that the German state had existed continuously before, during, and after Nazism; that Germany was a subject of international law; and that the Hague principles applied to the Allied occupation. Two more resolutions focused on "human rights," stating that "universal human rights" were part of international law and had been violated by both sides in both world wars, and that the human right of

See Paech and Krampe, "Die Rechts- und Staatswissenschaftliche Fakultät," 890–897, and Vogel, "Anpassung und Widerstand," 49.

[79] In addition to his work with the DGVR, Laun also founded and directed the Forschungsstelle für Völkerrecht und ausländisches öffentliches Recht at the University of Hamburg in 1946, and co-founded and co-edited a new journal, the *Jahrbuch für internationales und ausländisches öffentliches Recht*, which today appears under the title *German Yearbook of International Law/Jahrbuch für internationales Recht*.

[80] The DGVR shut itself down in 1934 to avoid *Gleichschaltung;* by 1945 all its pre-1933 board members had died, either in Germany or in exile. This discussion of the DGVR is based on "Die erste Hamburger Tagung der deutschen Völkerrechtslehrer 1947," *Jahrbuch für internationales und ausländisches öffentliches Recht*, 1:1 (1948), 239–242; "Die zweite Hamburger Tagung der deutschen Völkerrechtslehrer 1948," *Jahrbuch für internationales und ausländisches öffentliches Recht*, 1:1 (1948), 243–255; and Hermann Mosler, "Die Deutsche Gesellschaft für Völkerrecht. Ihr Beitrag zum Internationalen Recht seit der Wiedergründung im Jahre 1949," a speech for its fortieth anniversary in 1989, located at www.dgvr.de, accessed 27 August 2007.

[81] While the Hamburg contingent (Hans-Peter Ipsen, Eberhard Menzel, and Rolf Stödter) did hew closely to Laun's arguments, others differed openly (such as Erich Kaufmann), and yet others simply launched into their own topics without referring to Laun (such as Gerhard Leibholz and Hermann Jahrreiss). The strongest dissents from Laun's arguments at these meetings came from Wolfgang Abendroth (apparently the only one present who held that the German state had ceased to exist) and from Adolf Arndt, who eloquently pointed out that the German state was hardly free of deformation before 1945. See "Die zweite Hamburger Tagung der deutschen Völkerrechtslehrer 1948," 251–252. In fact, however, Arndt did agree with Laun's criticisms of the Allied occupation. Dieter Gosewinkel, *Adolf Arndt. Die Wiederbegründung des Rechtsstaats aus dem Geist der Sozialdemokratie (1945–1961)* (Bonn, 1991), 144–147.

individual freedom included the "right to the homeland." The next two resolutions focused on the expulsions: They held that mass deportations violated international law. The final 1947 resolution concerned German prisoners of war, stating that retention of POWs beyond the cessation of hostilities violated international law.[82] In 1948 the group passed one overarching resolution: that the German people had a right to self-determination and could demand protection of their basic rights from the Allies.[83] The fact that all of these resolutions were passed unanimously indicates that Laun was hardly an outlier.

Yet the next year saw a sharp turn. The Society's members voted in 1949 not to issue any more resolutions that took scholarly positions on controversial topics; to do so would "run the risk of lending scientific authority to opinions."[84] In 1953 Laun stepped down as chairman and board member, and the Society's meetings ceased to focus on German issues from that time onward. Instead, they took up topics of general concern among international lawyers everywhere, such as decolonization, economic treaties, and multiple states' use of natural resources. Hermann Mosler, an advocate of this new approach, avoided criticizing Laun directly in an internal history of the Society, but made clear that the Society was only to be taken seriously on the international level after 1953, when it had joined the international consensus regarding which topics were important.[85] Human rights, whether Germans' or anyone else's, were not a major concern in the Society's proceedings.

Laun's last institutional engagement was to join the editorial board of a massive research project on the German refugees and expellees, the *Documentation of the Expulsion of the Germans from East-Central Europe (Dokumentation der Vertreibung der Deutschen aus Ost-Mitteleuropa)*.[86] This project, which lasted from 1951 until the early 1960s, was sponsored by the Federal Ministry for Expellees, Refugees and War-Damaged (Bundesministerium für Vertriebene, Flüchtlinge und Kriegsgeschädigte). Laun, the sole nonhistorian on the board, was to advise regarding the usefulness of the documentation as evidence on behalf of Germans during peace negotiations with the Allies and for a planned

---

[82] "Entschliessungen der Deutschen Völkerrechtslehrer auf der ersten Hamburger Tagung vom 16.–17. April 1947," *Jahrbuch für internationales und ausländisches öffentliches Recht*, 1:1 (1948), 6.

[83] "Entschliessung der Deutschen Völkerrechtslehrer auf der zweiten Hamburger Tagung vom 14.–16. April 1948," *Jahrbuch für internationales und ausländisches öffentliches Recht*, 1:1 (1948), 8.

[84] Mosler, "Die Deutsche Gesellschaft für Völkerrecht," 3. From then on, it passed resolutions only on such unpolitical topics as increasing the prominence of international law in the curriculum. There were two exceptions: a 1970 resolution on the UN Charter's enemy state clauses, and a 1973 resolution on the right of self-determination.

[85] Ibid., 2–4.

[86] Bundesministerium für Vertriebene (ed.), *Dokumentation der Vertreibung der Deutschen aus Ost-Mitteleuropa*, 5 vols. (Munich, 1954–1961). Three supplementary volumes (*Beihefte*) were also published in 1955–1960.

complaint to the United Nations.[87] Yet the unfolding political situation was such that a peace treaty or a United Nations case on behalf of the expellees was hardly feasible. Meanwhile, as the project's team of historians waded through the massive documentary material, their own goals changed. Rather than present the expulsions as unique events, they shifted toward seeing them in the context of Nazi-era forced population movements and the longer history of German nationalism and imperialism in Eastern Europe. This had nothing in common with Laun's analytical or political approach, and he apparently disengaged from the project.[88] Nor did the project's sponsors support such a broad contextualization of the expulsions, fearing that that would seem it would appear to excuse the expulsions. Several volumes were published, but the project remained unfinished.[89] Rudolf Laun did not publish any more scholarly work after 1960.

Laun's usage of human rights points to four elements in the history of human rights thinking in the old Federal Republic. First, his usage of human rights – on behalf of Germans as victims – was one of the earliest major usages among Germans after 1945. It extended from the Social Democrats to the far right. Second, "human rights" came to be associated with a discourse of German victimhood and, by ca. 1960, the right. Soon after Laun concluded his scholarly career, Amnesty International was founded in Britain in 1961, and the first West German local groups formed later that same year. When one of the West German founders, the journalist Carola Stern, was first approached with the idea of Amnesty, however, she noted that some of her colleagues were skeptical, believing that "Then old Nazis will just come and demand that the war criminals imprisoned in the Spandau Citadel be set free."[90] While Laun had sought to attach Germans as victims to the concept of "human rights," Stern and others sought to fuse a critical approach to the Nazi past to that concept – and they thereby developed a third element. Fourth, Laun's call for individuals to have some kind of immediate standing in international law and his defense of group rights and a "right to the homeland" did not disappear, even as the West German political context changed. Indeed, in the context of national liberation movements, decolonization, and indigenous resistance in postcolonial states, these ideas appeared on the left of the German political spectrum. In all cases, the language of human rights served the goals of both universal justice and politics. Both are irreducible – and irreducibly controversial – aspects of using the language of human rights.

[87] Mathias Beer, "Im Spannungsfeld von Politik und Zeitgeschichte. Das Grossforschungsprojekt 'Dokumentation der Vertreibung der Deutschen aus Ost-Mitteleuropa'," *Vierteljahreshefte für Zeitgeschichte*, 46 (1998), 357–358, 368–369.
[88] Personal communication with Mathias Beer, 14 February 2008, confirmed Laun's inactive role.
[89] Beer, "Im Spannungsfeld von Politik und Zeitgeschichte," 378–385.
[90] Cited in Thomas Claudius and Franz Stepan, *Amnesty International. Portrait einer Organisation* (Munich, 1976), 217.

PART III

HUMAN RIGHTS, STATE SOCIALISM, AND DISSENT

7

Embracing and Contesting

The Soviet Union and the Universal Declaration of Human Rights, 1948–1958

Jennifer Amos

According to historians, the 1948 vote on the Universal Declaration on Human Rights was a moment of triumph, an ethical milestone when states reached a consensus on political morality. With this vote the United Nations completed the first step toward a Bill of Human Rights with international agreement on the primary aspects of human rights. Forty-eight states representing Judeo-Christian, Islamic, and Buddhist traditions agreed on twenty-eight rights overcoming historical and philosophical differences.[1]

However, the Declaration was not frozen in 1948 but served, as its authors hoped, as a living document. By focusing on the history of its initial drafting, the Declaration loses its historical, political, and cultural complexity. A narrative of the Declaration after the triumphant vote reveals multiple, conflicting interpretations of human rights that the document's broad language masked. These conflicts reflected neither Cold War nor developed–underdeveloped dichotomies, but were far more fractured. Because of this multiplicity, many powers, including the Soviet Union, were able to compete for moral authority linked to the Declaration. Despite the dominate narrative, the Declaration and human rights diplomacy in general did not freeze during the Cold War but became a battlefield on which many competing ideologies fought.

By including the Soviet Union as an active participant in human rights diplomacy, I hope to challenge the Cold War narrative that has dominated both American and Soviet/Russian histories. Despite its abstention, the Soviet government in ten years managed to become a leading proponent of human rights. After the 1948 vote, Soviet diplomats, scholars, and journalists

I would like to thank the Fulbright-Institute of International Education Program and the International Research and Exchanges Board (IREX), with funds provided by the National Endowment for the Humanities and the United States Department of State, which administers the Russian, Eurasian, and East European Research Program (Title VIII), for supporting research and study leading to this chapter.

[1] Eight states abstained, including Saudi Arabia, South Africa and the communist bloc – the Soviet Union, its two additional representatives Belorussian Soviet Socialist Republic and the Ukrainian Soviet Socialist Republic, Czechoslovakia, Poland, and Yugoslavia.

147

included the Declaration and human rights in multiple frameworks of ideological debate. These ideas served as a complement to Marxist-Leninism, socialist legality, and peaceful coexistences. Issues such as freedom of information,
equal pay for women discrimination, and self-determination were framed,
depending on audience, time, and location, in multiple ways, including human
rights. In many respects, the Soviet government reversed its policy toward
the Declaration as human rights ideas gained traction in the Cold War battle
for ideological legitimacy and supremacy. Although Stalin initially tried to
limit this battle to the international stage, under Khrushchev the Declaration
became part of the domestic politics as well. For the Soviet Union, human
rights interpenetrated domestic politics and international policy.

The Universal Declaration of Human Rights under Stalin

The United Nations drafted the Universal Declaration of Human Rights as a
response to the moral failures of World War II. UN delegates debated which
rights were to be included, often centering on actions that enabled the Nazis
to perpetrate genocide. For example, they included a right to work within the
Declaration after tracing how the German government curtailed the rights of
Jews to employment. Although the Declaration was in many ways a response
to the atrocities associated with Hitler, the Soviet leader at the time, Joseph
Stalin, had committed similar outrages. He had organized a series of concentration camps called gulags to purify the body politic of "class enemies,"
including rich peasants, Orthodox priests, and even stamp collectors. He
ordered the ethnic cleansing of those he deemed unreliable, such as Koreans,
Crimean Tartars, and Chechens. Furthermore, he so mismanaged the Soviet
Union's resources that five million Ukrainians, over 1.6 million Kazakhs, and
thousands of others died in a series of famines.[2]

Given these atrocities it seems obvious that Stalin's representatives
abstained from the UN vote on Universal Declaration of Human Rights.
Despite the Soviet abstention, the Foreign Ministry actively used the
Declaration within the United Nations in order to further its own human
rights agenda. Although initially resisting, the government embraced the
Declaration as yet another weapon in the international ideological struggle
that was part of the Cold War.

It may seem surprising that the Soviet Union remained on the United
Nations Commission on Human Rights after 1948 and became a powerful
voice. After all, it had abstained from the Universal Declaration of Human
Rights, which was to serve as the lodestone for the Commission's subsequent
work. However, many Commission members were relieved that the Soviet
bloc only abstained rather than rejecting the Declaration outright. As one of

---

[2] Martha Brill Olcott, "The Collectivization Drive in Kazakhstan," *Russian Review*, 40:2
(1981), 136; and Ronald Grigor Suny, *The Soviet Experiment: Russia, the USSR, and the
Successor States* (New York, 1998), 228.

the Security Council permanent members, the USSR was represented in all the major UN bodies. Furthermore, the Commission maintained a commitment to geographic and political diversity, which naturally included the communist East. Giving the Soviet Union even more voting power, the USSR had not one representative in the United Nations, but three – one for the Belorussian Soviet Socialist Republic (BSSR), one for the Ukrainian Soviet Socialist Republic (UkSSR), and one for the Union of Soviet Socialist Republics as a whole (USSR) – with two of these three on the Commission for Human Rights. Simultaneously, the Commission typically included one other representative from the East European satellite states.[3] Although the Soviet Union and other Warsaw states voted as one bloc, the West lacked such unity. Even an ally as close as the United Kingdom voted in opposition to the United States, as well as the former U.S. colony of the Philippines. The Soviet Union began negotiating with a conspicuous voting advantage in the Commission before capitalizing on disagreements within the perceived blocs.

After the vote on the Declaration, the Soviets found that in human rights diplomacy even abstaining states were to be measured by this "nonbinding" declaration. The following year, for example, the United Nations General Assembly charged the Soviet Union with failing to let Soviet women married to foreigners emigrate, defying Articles 13 (freedom of movement and exit) and 16 (right to found a family) of the Declaration. In response, the Soviet delegates countered that sovereign states had the right to control who crossed its borders. International law at the time was (and remains) based on positive law, namely, that states had to agree to any treaty before it could be bound to that treaty's terms; nevertheless, the Soviet Union was censured for violating the Declaration.

Many have pictured the human rights debate as divided along Cold War lines with the United States and Western Europe fighting for political and civil rights, while the Soviet Union and its allies pushed for economic rights to the exclusion of political and civil rights. In this interpretation, the Universal Declaration of Human Rights logically was divided into two separate covenants – the International Covenant on Civil and Political Rights and the International Covenant on Economic, Social and Cultural Rights – reflecting international tensions. However, the Cold War blocs did not neatly align during the debates on human rights. For example, capitalist countries such as Australia promoted economic, social, and cultural rights, and the communist countries actively negotiated political and cultural rights. Ignoring its earlier abstention, Soviet diplomats employed the Declaration in their fight to include in the covenant economic, social, and cultural rights. They did not place these

[3] It should be noted that this number does not include the Yugoslav representative as he rarely voted with the Soviet bloc after the Tito-Stalin split. Also, during the drafting of the Declaration, the Soviet representatives occasionally split their votes on an issue to signal a willingness to compromise. They ended this process before the covenant negotiations, perhaps because the votes were often too close.

rights in a hierarchy above the already drafted civil and political rights, but argued that the Declaration constituted a whole and could not be divided into subsequent covenants.

After the 1948 vote, the United Nations began drafting a legally binding human rights covenant based on the Declaration. The initial draft of the covenant contained only a portion of the Declaration – civil rights – with no plans to expand into other areas. In response to this highly contracted draft, the Soviet delegates argued that the future covenant must reflect the entirety of the Universal Declaration because the human rights enumerated therein were indivisible: "[I]f certain of those rights and freedoms [in particular the economic, social, and cultural rights] proclaimed in the Universal Declaration of Human Rights were not restated in the draft covenant, those rights and freedoms would lose all effective value and the meaning of the Universal Declaration would as a result be considerably modified."[4]

As a result, they proposed a series of rights based on the Declaration and omitted from the covenant, including the rights to work, to social security, and to education. During later negotiations one Soviet representative tasked the Secretariat to compare the draft covenant to the Declaration in order to ascertain which rights were missing. The Universal Declaration became a tool with which to push for the rights that the Soviets saw as lost in the early draft of the covenant. They framed the absence of these rights as a deprivation of them and an effort to break what should be indivisible. Furthermore, attempts to form a covenant addressing only parts of the Declaration threatened the strength of the whole.

Although today the Chinese communist government argues for a hierarchy of rights, the Soviet delegation stressed the interdependence of human rights. For them, civil and political rights were meaningless without economic, social, and cultural rights. Soviet Representative Alexei Pavlov began the Soviet lobbying for these rights by highlighting world public demands to guarantee those economic rights "already ... proclaimed in the Declaration." He then proceeded to explain that "[t]he right to work was the most important; without it all the other rights laid down in the covenant would be meaningless. There were no individual freedom for the hungry and unemployed."[5] The Soviet delegation did not discuss the possibility of economic, social, and cultural rights without civil and political rights.

Throughout these debates, the Soviet delegation linked the Declaration and the economic, social, and cultural rights contained therein to the Soviet history of rights. In particular, they cited the Soviet Constitution. For example, the Ukrainian representative highlighted the guarantees in the republic's Constitution of the right to work, education, and medical services and the fulfillment of those rights despite initial economic hardship.[6] Similarly the

[4] UN Human Rights Commission, June 17, 1949, Summary Records E/CN.4/SR 122, 7.
[5] UN Human Rights Commission, June 16, 1949, Summary Records E/CN.4/SR 130, 10.
[6] UN Human Rights Commission, April 16, 1951, Summary Records E/CN.4/SR.203, 23.

representative compared the incomplete draft covenant to the unity of both the Declaration and the Stalin Constitution, which provided for not only economic rights but also the rights to freedom of speech, assembly, and personal liberty.[7]

While the Soviet representatives led the fight for economic, social, and cultural rights, many states agreed with their rationale. Even capitalist Australia supported their inclusion. "In view of the wide publicity given to the Universal Declaration of Human Rights," Representative Harry Frederick Ernest Whitlam "was convinced that the exclusion of those right from the Covenant would cause the latter to be regarded as a mockery."[8] Latin American states originally played the leading role in incorporating these rights into the Declaration and followed the Soviet drive to include them in the draft covenant. The representative of Uruguay rebuked a European proposal to focus on only civil rights because this rights conception ignored "the progress made since the eighteenth century."[9] Similarly, Chilean Representative Carlos Valenzuela lobbied for a covenant that would make clear that economic, social, and cultural rights were equal in importance to civil and political ones.[10] Throughout the debate, economic, social, and cultural rights were transformed, particularly for the newly independent states; they became code for a right to development, "a promise to share in all the benefits of modern civilization."[11] The Pakistani Representative, for example, explained that economic rights "represented the struggle for emancipation and freedom."[12] Although the United States, the United Kingdom, and France accepted certain understandings of economic rights, they justified the exclusion of these rights from the covenant on the status of developing states, who lacked the means to fulfill such legal commitments. For the supporters of economic, social, and cultural rights, the unfulfilled promise was better than silence.

The Soviet government continued its push for unity in human rights based on the Declaration when others began proposing to separate the covenant into two separate but equal covenants. States such as the United States, New Zealand, Lebanon, Belgium, and Nicaragua fought to divide the draft covenant based on what they deemed radically different types of rights – positive and negative rights. In particular, these governments argued that civil and political rights could be implemented almost immediately by changing legal codes, whereas economic, social, and cultural rights could be implemented only incrementally. The British representative stressed both the difference and the novelty of the positive rights: "It was doubtful whether economic and

[7] UN Human Rights Commission, April 19, 1951, Summary Records E/CN.4/SR.207, 17.
[8] UN Human Rights Commission, April 16, 1951, Summary Records E/CN.4/SR.203, 21.
[9] UN Human Rights Commission, April 19, 1951, Summary Records E/CN.4/SR.207, 11.
[10] UN Human Rights Commission, April 16, 1951, Summary Records E/CN.4/SR.207, 21.
[11] John P. Humphrey, A. J. Hobbins, and Louisa Piatti (eds.), *On the Edge of Greatness: The Diaries of John Humphrey, First Director of the United Nations Division of Human Rights: Vol. II, 1950–1951*, 4 vols. (Montreal, 1994), 1:251.
[12] UN Human Rights Commission, April 16, 1951, Summary Records E/CN.4/SR.203, 19.

social rights, which were purely relative conceptions, were legally enforceable; they came within an entirely different category."[13] Furthermore, the parties pushing to divide the Covenant contended that some states were economically underdeveloped and therefore unable to guarantee the latter. As Indian Representative Hansa Mehta explained, the "state of economic development did not permit them to implement the economic and social rights at one stroke of the pen."[14] Foreseeing Soviet and other states' concerns about a perceived rights hierarchy, the advocates of two covenants proposed that both covenants be signed on the same day and take effect simultaneously.

The Soviet delegation not only continued to stress the unity of human rights based on the Declaration but also questioned the motives of those who sought to divide the draft covenant. They insinuated that once the covenant was divided, even developed states such as the United States would choose to sign only one. One Soviet delegate, Planton Dmitrievich Morozov, explained that the capitalist states were not concerned about underdeveloped states and their ability to meet the commitments promised in the Declaration. Instead, the United States, like others, was "not interested in the lives of the workers in its own country," and the U.S. delegate basically warned that "if the Covenant contained provisions calling upon Member States to introduce legislation to relieve their workers of the fear of starvation, to ensure for them the right to health and education, and other economic, social and cultural rights, the United States Government would be unable to ratify it."[15]

In response to concerns about underdeveloped states, the Soviet representatives highlighted their own history of development. They pointed out that after the October Revolution, social security was granted to workers, schools were built, and illiteracy was virtually eliminated. Furthermore, they questioned the division between positive and negative rights. The Belorussian representative explained that while the U.S. delegates argued civil and political rights were easily achieved, "there were in fact many countries – including the United States of America, twenty of whose states had discriminatory legislation against Negroes ... – where political rights were still not enforced." He concluded not only that economic rights would require progressive implementation but also that "time was needed also for the enforcement of political and civil rights, and no valid differentiation could be made between the two sets of rights on that score."[16] Finally, the Soviet delegation questioned the depiction of economic, social, and cultural rights as exclusively positive rights. They highlighted that the rights included trade union rights and equal pay for minorities and women, which were just as legislative in nature as the right to vote.

---

[13] UN Third Committee, January 16, 1952, Summary Records A/C.3/SR.390, 251.
[14] UN Human Rights Commission, May 18, 1951, Summary Records E/CN.4/SR.248, 6.
[15] UN Human Rights Commission, May 18, 1951, Summary Records E/CN.4/SR.248, 14.
[16] UN Third Committee, January 19, 1952, Summary Records A/C.3/SR.394, 280.

As before, the Soviets were not alone pushing for a single covenant. During negotiations, the economic, social, and cultural rights became, to some developing countries, a right to development and, with that, an obligation of the developed countries to provide international aid. The General Assembly initially voted to draft one united covenant, using arguments similar to those of the Soviets. The Human Rights Commission drafted the covenant so that violations of political and civil rights would be investigated by an international body, while economic, social and cultural rights would be promoted through reporting incremental improvements. As a result of these differences in implementation, the General Assembly reversed its decision only a couple of years later.

The unexpected change in the Soviet attitude toward the Declaration did not go unnoticed or unchallenged. A member of the UN Secretariat recorded his incredulity that the Soviets glossed over their abstention: "[I]f one were to judge by their frequent references to it, [then] an uninitiated person might well think that the Soviets had voted for the Declaration."[17] Eleanor Roosevelt at a UN debate "questioned their [Soviet] sincerity in citing for their own purposes the Universal Declaration of Human Rights for which they had not voted."[18] When the Soviet delegation stormed out of the United Nations because of debates over which government legitimately represented China – the Republic of China or the People's Republic of China – the Chilean delegate assured the Human Rights Commission that it certainly would not impact the Commission's work: "Everyone who was aware of the conditions which prevailed in the USSR regarding the guarantee of individual rights knew that the country could never sign a covenant such as that which was to be drafted by the Commission."[19] Although the Soviet bloc rejoined the human rights debates and actively partook in drafting the covenants, doubts remained about Soviet sincerity toward both the covenants and the Declaration.

Although the Stalin-era Foreign Ministry utilized the Declaration in human rights debates at the UN, it tried to defend a boundary between vocal internationalism and internal silence. As part of an effort to educate the public, the General Assembly voted in December 1948 to publish the Universal Declaration of Human Rights globally. To fulfill this goal, the Assembly tasked the Secretariat with making the Declaration available in as many languages as possible, not simply the five working languages of the organization.[20] As a result, the Soviet delegation at the UN received an offer from Secretariat to translate the Declaration, asking in which languages the government had already written the Declaration and which the UN could assist in translating. The delegation forwarded this request to the Foreign Ministry,

---

[17] Humphrey, *On the Edge of Greatness*, 175.
[18] UN Third Committee, December 20, 1951, Summary Records A/C.3/SR.371, 143.
[19] UN Human Rights Commission, March 27, 1950, Summary Records E/CN.4/SR.136, 7.
[20] At that time, the official languages were English, French, Russian, Chinese, and Spanish. Arabic became an official language at the UN in 1973.

where opinions varied on how best to respond. A. A. Sobolev, Head of the
Department of UN Affairs, advocated bluntly reminding the Secretariat that
it abstained from the vote and therefore was "not interested in disseminating
the Declaration." Alternatively, the delegation could inform the Secretariat
that it had translated the Declaration into Belorussian and Ukrainian, as well
as possessed the official UN version in Russian, thereby meeting the needs of
the Soviet delegations.[21] In the end, though, the Soviet representatives received
a directive from Deputy Foreign Minister A. A. Gromyko, who ordered a new
option, namely, that they ignore the Secretariat's offer entirely.[22] In so doing,
the Foreign Ministry both limited UN dissemination within the country and
remained nonconfrontational about its abstention, neither renouncing nor
advertising it.

Despite the initial rebuff on publicizing the Declaration, Secretary General
Trygvie Lie recommended two years later that states convene ceremonies
to promote the anniversary of the Declaration. In response to the Secretary
General's recommendation, the Foreign Ministry's Department for UN
Affairs proposed a series of radio broadcasts and newspaper articles exposing the various ways capitalist countries violated human rights, in spite of
the Declaration. Furthermore, these articles were to contrast these international violations with the "broad democratic rights of USSR citizens which
were guaranteed by the Stalinist Constitution." Although the message was
to be crafted by the Foreign Ministry's own press department, these efforts
would utilize both domestic and international media.[23] In the end, though, the
Foreign Ministry ignored the Department's suggestion, and the anniversary
of Universal Declaration and Human Rights Day passed without notice in
the Soviet press. The lower echelon of the Foreign Ministry believed that the
Declaration could be used in an expanded ideological debate, but the upper
level doubted the efficacy of the Declaration as a tool for public propaganda.

In 1952, the Soviet journal *Trud* (Work) ended four years of silence on the
Declaration. The author of the article, B. Izakov, focused on the Declaration as
an insincere pledge on the part of capitalist countries, beginning with the article's title – "An Empty Declaration." He denounced, as the Foreign Ministry
had debated two years earlier, the failure of capitalist governments to fulfill
the Declaration. For example, he noted the reluctance of other states to include
the right to a free education in the draft of the legally binding human rights
covenant, despite its inclusion in the Declaration: "It is profitable for Wall
Street to keep millions of Americans in darkness and ignorance."[24] Finally,

[21] The first option, reminding the Secretariat about the Soviet abstention, was underlined in
red. Letter to A. A. Gromyko from A. Sobolev 15.III.49 Arkhiv vneshnei politiki Rossiiskoi
Federatsii (AVP RF) f. 047, op. 4, pap. 20, d. 50, l. 14.
[22] Letter to Ia. A. Malik from A. Sobolev April 5, 1949 AVP RF f. 047, op. 4, pap. 20, d. 50, l. 13.
[23] Letter to V. A. Zorin from A. Shubnikov and M. Buev 25.XI.50 AVP RF f. 47, op. 5, pap. 30,
d. 48, l. 58.
[24] B. Izakov, "An Empty Promise" *Trud*, December 10, 1952, in *Current Digest of Soviet Press*
(hereafter *CDSP*) IV:50, 41–42, 41.

Izakov portrayed the Declaration simply as a tool for capitalists, which the Soviet efforts had failed to shape: "The Soviet delegation consistently defended the principle of democracy and progress, peace and the security of peoples. But the Anglo-American bloc attempted to use the declaration for purposes of reaction and aggression. During discussion of the declaration they threw aside all proposals which would have guaranteed the opportunity to enjoy the rights in the declaration."[25] Subsequent articles written after the death of Stalin would stress Soviet influence on the Declaration.

The Soviet Foreign Ministry used human rights as part of its Cold War foreign policy. It highlighted the domestic successes in literacy, social security, scientific progress, workers' rights, freedom of the press, and other rights. The diplomats contrasted these achievements with American discrimination, English unemployment, French imperialism, Lebanese illiteracy, Mexican inequality, and issues in other countries. While actively promoting their under-standing of universal human rights abroad, however, the Ministry actively blocked similar discussion domestically. Instead, it attempted to create a bor-der between the international stage and the domestic arena, where it opposed dissemination of these international efforts and these rights. Despite the Stalin-era silence in 1953, prisoners in a camp in Vorkuta demanded reform, explicitly calling on the government to observe the Universal Declaration.[26]

The Universal Declaration of Human Rights Post-Stalin

After the adoption of the Universal Declaration of Human Rights, the General Assembly of the United Nations called on its member states to promote dissemination and explanation of the Declaration 'chiefly in schools and other educational institu-tions.' I do not know how carefully this Declaration is studied in Soviet schools, or if its studied at all – I know that the contents of the Declaration are generally familiar to people acquainted with *samizdat* publications.

> Valerii Chalidze, written for the Human Rights Committee, December 10, 1970[27]

Historians, political scientists, and human rights activists have focused on the ways that the Declaration acted as an umbrella under which dispa-rate Soviet groups from atheist physicists to Baptist workers to Caucasian nationalists could gather to fight the repressive government. However, the Declaration served as a tool for not only the dissidents but also the very government they opposed. By focusing on the dissidents, scholars have ignored the ways in which the Declaration's contested meanings served not just as a means of protesting a state, but also as a way to buttress the state.

---

[25] Ibid.

[26] Erik Kulavig, *Dissent in the Years of Khrushchev: Nine Stories about Disobedient Russians* (New York, 2002), 108.

[27] Valerii Chalidze, "Important Aspects of Human Rights in the Soviet Union," in Michael Meerson-Aksenov and Boris Shragin (eds.) *The Political, Social and Religious Thought of Russian "Samizdat" – An Anthology* (Belmont, Md., 1977), 214.

The Declaration first crossed the border from international diplomacy to internal politics not through underground dissident movements. In addition to dissidents, the Communist government, the press, and other organizations used the Declaration to reestablish their legitimacy internationally and domestically.

The Soviet leaders faced a unique problem as they dismantled Stalin's policies, namely, the search for legitimacy. Stalin validated his rule by terror by mythologizing his ties to the October Revolution and Vladimir Lenin. Later he elaborated a fictitious history regarding his leadership in World War II.[28] Furthermore, Stalin justified the purges and mass arrests by positing himself as the protector of the Soviet Union against internal perceived enemies. Those hoping to succeed Stalin as head of the Soviet Union were "seeking to be Stalin's successor but not his heir."[29] For example, the new leadership declared the first amnesty within three weeks of Stalin's death. In other words, they sought to eliminate some of Stalin's most repressive policies but maintain the Communist Party's authority.

In their renunciation of Stalin, the new leaders, including but not exclusively Khrushchev, turned to many ideas to bolster their claim to legitimate rule, such as the concept of socialist legality. In contrast to Stalin's reign, socialist legality redefined law away from terror and political whims toward increased adherence to procedural norms and rationalization.[30] The leadership began reforming and stabilizing the legal system soon after Stalin's death, but the idea of socialist legality and the rule of law flourished particularly after Lavrenti Pavlovich Beria, head of the KGB and the Minister of the Interior, was denounced. According to the denouncers, Beria had attempted to usurp leadership by continuing Stalinist terror and the application of law arbitrarily. In place of Beria's cult of personality, the new leadership promised Socialist legality, which entailed "[t]he strict observance of law everywhere and in everything, mandatory for all state agencies, institutions, officials and citizens, provid[ing] a true guarantee for timely suppression of nefarious enemy attempts to harm our people and state."[31] With this renewed focus on legal theory, the government exonerated the communist system of "the trumping up faked criminal cases against innocent persons" or "carrying out terrorism against honest Soviet citizens."[32] Instead, it charged Stalin and Beria

---

[28] See, for example, Nina Tumarkin, *Lenin Lives! The Lenin Cult in Soviet Russia* (Cambridge, Mass., 1983); and Amir Weiner, *Making Sense of War: The Second World War and the Fate of the Bolshevik Revolution* (Princeton, 2001).

[29] Nancy Condee, "Cultural Codes of the Thaw," in William Taubman, Sergei Khrushchev, and Abbott Gleason (eds.), *Nikita Khrushchev* (New Haven, 2000), 168.

[30] Harold J. Berman, "The Dilemma of Soviet Law Reform," *Harvard Law Review* 76:5 (1963), 929–951.

[31] K. Gorshenin, "The Soviet Court and Its Role in Strengthening Socialist Law" *Kommunist*, No. 2, 63–73, in *CDSP* VII:7, 18–22, 18.

[32] R. A. Rudenko, "The Tasks of Further Strengthening Socialist Legality in the Light of the 20th Party Congress Decisions," *Sovetskoe gosudarstvo i pravo*, No. 3, May, 15–25, in *CDSP* VIII:32, 7–10, 7.

with derailing the government through their illegitimate cults of personality. Khrushchev and his supporters promised to revive the Party and to "create an atmosphere of intolerance toward violations of the law ... [and] create confidence that no one may violate the law with impunity."[33]

Attesting to Soviet Socialist Legality: Publicizing the Universal Declaration within the Government

International historians have begun examining the interactions between domestic and foreign politics. However, they have mostly focused on democracies, leaving in question whether such interaction could occur in an authoritarian dictatorship such as the Soviet Union. Examining the diplomacy on the Declaration shows how human rights discourse can flow across borders. Despite Soviet efforts to build a wall between foreign diplomacy and domestic politics under Stalin, this wall eventually collapsed, in part because of the changing nature of human rights diplomacy.

As mentioned earlier, the Foreign Ministry attempted to block UN efforts to publicize the Declaration domestically. However, as the UN began drafting more technical treaties, the Ministry was forced to incorporate other branches of Soviet government into making foreign policy because of their expertise. In so doing, the Ministry not only disseminated the Declaration, along with the draft treaties, within the government, but it tasked other departments to consider their activities in terms of human rights. Initially, the Ministry almost unilaterally evaluated and answered United Nations issues regarding human rights.[34] However, in 1956, the Ministry tasked the Institute of Law at the Soviet Academy of Science to collect information on human rights at home and in capitalist countries "in the event of attacks on us at the General Assembly in connection with alleged human rights violations."[35] One year later, V. Kuznetsov, the Deputy Minister of Foreign Affairs, wrote to the Minister of Higher Education and other officials regarding UN negotiations on the Declaration of Rights of Children, requesting their expertise on draft articles. He also wrote to the Minister of Public Health, the Minister of Social Security, the Chair of the Government Advisors on Work and Pay, and other government agencies. In conjunction with these requests, Kuznetsov circulated the relevant sections of the Universal Declaration of Human Rights and drafts of the covenants and treaties.[36] Through the promulgation of these requests, Kuznetsov revealed the increasing attention and care with which the Foreign Ministry approached these detailed negotiations. While distributing the Declaration, the Foreign Ministry failed to mention the Soviet abstention. Consequently, the Ministry not only expanded other agencies' knowledge of

[33] Ibid., 9.
[34] Beginning in 1951 the Ministry established its one exception to this pattern by asking the Lenin State Public Library for its assistance in compiling lists of publications on human rights. AVP RF f. 54, op. 20, pap 175, d. 6 and f. 54, op. 26, pap. 217, d. 12.
[35] Memo from G. Tunkin November 5, 1956, AVP RF f. 54, op. 26, pap. 217, d. 12, l 31.
[36] AVP RF f. 54, op. 27, pap. 227, d. 11, ll. 60–64.

the Declaration, but also tasked the officials to consider their work in terms of human rights.

By the mid-1950s, the UN Commission on Human Rights had drafted the International Covenants on Human Rights and sought new ways to promote these ideas despite Cold War tensions. The United States along with Egypt, Lebanon, Pakistan, and the Philippines initially proposed a series of in-depth studies on individual rights as a way to publicize domestic practices through international campaigns.[37] The United States, in particular, believed these studies would be circulated to both policy makers and the concerned public around the world in order to enable comparisons between the internal methods of all UN countries and the extent of protecting (or violating) specific human rights. The Soviet and Polish delegates to the Commission repeatedly rejected the proposals, which they portrayed as competition against or, at the very least, a distraction from the draft covenants.[38] Although their objections delayed the U.S. initiative, they were unable to block the research and publication of in-depth studies.

The themes of these studies immediately became part of the Cold War ideological debates. The first study, as advanced by the United States, focused on Article 9 of the Declaration – the right to be free from arbitrary arrest, detention, or exile – as it ostensibly "was the least controversial" and had not been investigated by other UN bodies.[39] That said, the United States and other countries had collected extensive reports from émigrés and others that the USSR and other socialist states violated this right habitually. The Soviet delegation contended that there were more critical human rights violations, namely, the right to be free from discrimination and the right of self-determination, which they asserted threatened large swathes of the world's population. Unstated, these rights were also the Achilles' heel of the United States, which was facing the civil rights movement while its NATO allies were fighting colonial insurrections. Not only did the Soviet delegation fail to block the studies, it lost in its battle over the rights to be examined.

While the Foreign Ministry fought the study, another branch of the government – the Procuracy – interpreted the Commission on Human Rights investigations less hostilely. In 1958, the Foreign Ministry received the UN review of the Soviet laws regarding arrest, detention, and exile based primarily on Soviet entries within the *UN Yearbook on Human Rights*, the published legal codes, and newspapers. After delaying a few months, it forwarded the study to the Procuracy for a review, stipulating both its opposition and its fear that the study was a covert tactic for the United States to attack the USSR

---

[37] UN Human Rights Commission, June 15, 1955 Summary Records E/CN.4/SR.492, 4.
[38] UN Human Rights Commission, March 29, 1956, Summary Records E/CN.4/SR.515, 6 ff., and April 11, 1958, Summary Records E/CN.4/SR.587.
[39] Discrimination was the subject of a human rights subcommission, and a treaty on discrimination in education was being drafted under UNESCO auspices. Self-determination was not yet a formalized human right. UN Human Rights Commission, April 6, 1956, Summary Records E/CN.4/SR.525, 9.

slanderously.[40] In the Soviet system, the Procuracy served as the state prosecutor, supervised preliminary criminal investigations, and was "the organ for the protection of socialist legality."[41] Despite the Foreign Ministry's lack of urgency, the Procuracy responded in less than a month, even with the New Year's holidays, hinting at its enthusiasm for the study. Instead of subversive attacks, the Procuracy commentator P. Kudriavtsev found the Commission's review to be generally an accurate one, which "does not provoke and does not contain factual mistakes."[42] In contrast to Ministry's antagonistic attitude, Kudriavtsev proposed not only consenting to the study, but expanding on it. Since the UN used only published sources, particularly the regularly delayed *Yearbook*, the Procuracy wanted the Soviet response to incorporate the more recent laws. He did not allude to the motives for the modifications in laws, namely, the new policy of socialist legality, nor did he elaborate on the legal situation that existed under Stalin. That said, Kudriavtsev viewed the study as an opportunity to internationally publicize socialist legality: "[T]hese answers to the legal questions will attest to the existence in the Soviet government a regime of legality [*zakonnosti*]."[43] The Procuracy official saw the UN study as a path to gain moral legitimacy not only at the Commission but in the subsequent publication and distribution of the new Soviet laws internationally as well.

Moving beyond the UN: The Declaration in International and Domestic Publics

Given the pervasiveness of government control in the Soviet Union, one might think that human rights diplomacy would remain within the narrow confines of the Foreign Ministry, or, at most, within the government sphere. In fact, various journalists and a voluntary association began promoting Soviet understandings of human rights both abroad and domestically. For these groups, international diplomacy was not distinct from domestic politics. Instead, the promotion of human rights occurred in a sphere where the international and domestic intertwined.

In one of the earliest signs of the change in post-Stalin policy, the journal *Mezhdunarodnaia zhizn'* (*International Affairs*) published the Declaration in its entirety, ending seven years of silence. This journal circulated both within the Soviet Union and internationally, with translations available in English and French. In the article, an anonymous author introduced the Declaration with a brief, two-page history, in which he depicted the Declaration as vindication of Socialist legality and the 1936 Constitution; thus domestic ideology

---

[40] Letter to General Procurator R. A. Rudenko from N. Firiubin, Deputy Minister of Foreign Affairs, December 11, 1958. Gosudarstvennyi arkhiv Rossiiskoi Federatsii (GARF) f 8131, op. 28, d. 4223, l. 41.

[41] George Ginsburgs, "The Soviet Procuracy and Forty Years of Socialist Legality," *American Slavic and East European Review*, 18:1 (1959), 40.

[42] GARF f 8131, op. 28, d. 4223, l. 65.

[43] Ibid.

influenced the rights enumerated globally. The international Declaration was not, despite its more recent origins, a substitute for or improvement on the domestic Socialist legality, as the Soviets compromised with capitalist states. The author explained how the "task of internationally protecting human rights and freedoms" was that of the Soviet Union, the United States, and others of the anti-Hitler coalition. In so doing, he stressed cooperation between the former allies and reflected a reduction of Cold War tensions. The author then inaccurately posited that the Soviet delegation pressed the other great powers to include human rights as one of the goals of the United Nations and instigated subsequent human rights efforts.[44] Subsequent articles would continue to link the Declaration to the Soviet Constitution, but place it in a Cold War context, rather than in that of the World War II alliance.

Not only were journals reaching simultaneously foreign and domestic audiences, but new voluntary organizations began crossing the international–domestic border. At this stage in the Cold War, the Soviet Union began participating in more global organizations, both intergovernmental and nongovernmental organizations (NGOs), in order to gain more influence internationally. Previously the USSR had founded a series of transnational political organizations, such as the Comintern (1919–1943) and the Cominform (1947–1956), but limited interaction to other communist groups. After the death of Stalin, the government reversed earlier positions and began playing an active part in intergovernmental organizations, particularly the International Labor Organization (ILO) and the United Nations Educational, Scientific and Cultural Organization (UNESCO), which were peripheral sites of human rights diplomacy. Additionally, the Soviet Union joined already existing NGOs such as the World Federation of United Nations Associations (WFUNA), which, unlike the Comintern and Cominform, were not communist. The Soviet organization activists justified their projects (and requests for funding) to the government by explaining that their efforts within the larger NGO movement would enable Soviet ideas to reach people outside of governments, who would be more sympathetic to the Bolshevik cause.

The Soviets did not form a branch of the World Federation of United Nations Associations until after Stalin's death, despite sincere international efforts to include the USSR. WFUNA began in 1946, when several NGOs, many developed from the remnants of earlier League of Nations associations, formed a "peoples' United Nations." The Federation pursued two, at times conflicting, goals: (1) to make the United Nations accountable to the international public and (2) to promote the UN and its decisions within the associations' states. At its very beginning, a representative of the nascent organization wrote to Soviet diplomats at the UN inviting them to either recommend an NGO to participate in the founding meeting or attend themselves. The British author of the request, John A. F. Ennols, pointed out that the British and French Communist

---

[44] "K VII godovshchine Vseobshchklaratsii prav cheloveka," *Mezhdunarodnaia zhizn'*, no. 12 (1955).

Parties supported both the UN and the WFUNA initiative. Further, he stressed his regard for communism by revealing that during the war he had worked closely with the communist forces in Yugoslavia.[45] Ten years later, the Soviet government finally formed their own branch of WFUNA, the Association for the Promotion of the United Nations Organization (ASOON), a government-directed organization to participate in this international NGO movement.

In the earliest discussions of establishing a Soviet branch of WFUNA, the Foreign Ministry proposed Anna Mikhailovna Pankratova, a figure who linked the nascent association with de-Stalinization. Pankratova first entered the global arena when she led the Soviet delegation to the Rome International Historians' Conference and was elected to the governing Bureau.[46] While ASOON was being formed, Pankratova served as the editor-in-chief of the journal *Voprosy istorii* (*Questions of History*). She led the journal as it explored the boundaries of de-Stalinization, delving into issues such as the relationship between Lenin and Stalin in 1917, Russian colonialism, and other previously taboo subjects. Furthermore, Pankratova spoke at the Twentieth Party Congress, during which Khrushchev delivered his famous "secret speech" denouncing Stalin's cult of personality.[47] Subsequently she led official discussions concerning the speech at nine different locations throughout Leningrad in a three-day period.[48] In choosing Pankratova to head the ASOON, the Foreign Ministry picked not only someone with international experience, but someone who represented the new spirit of the times.[49]

As part of WFUNA, ASOON was nominally an NGO, by definition independent from the government. In reality, it received direct orders from the Soviet Central Committee and coordinated its policy with representatives of the Foreign Ministry. Despite these government links, ASOON pushed other WFUNA members to stand in opposition to their governments. For example, it urged the American Association for the United Nations to speak out against the U.S. policy of nuclear testing and rearming West Germany. The head of the American Association, Irving Salomon, replied,

I am greatly pleased, to begin with, by your implied recognition of the principle that a United Nations Association ought to be willing and able to oppose the official position of its government on such questions if it so desires. You, of course, know that the AAUN has in fact from time to time spoken out against particular policies of

---

[45] Original letter not in file, but extensively quoted in Vsemirnaia Federatsiia Associatsii druzei Ob"edinennykh Natsii./Spravka/1.IV.46 AVP RF f. 47, op. 1, pap. 1, d. 2, ll. 15–16.

[46] Reginald E. Zelnik, *Perils of Pankratova: Some Stories from the Annals of Soviet Historiography* (Seattle, 2005), 58.

[47] Ibid.

[48] Susanne Schattenberg, "'Democracy' or 'Despotism'? How the Secret Speech was Translated into Everyday Life," in Polly Jones (ed.), *The Dilemmas of De-Stalinization: Negotiating Cultural and Social Change in the Khrushchev Era* (New York, 2006), 65.

[49] The spirit of the times quickly, changed, though. Pankratova was condemned in 1957 for *Voprosy istorii*'s excesses in questioning the past (and thereby the communist regime). That year, she left the journal citing health reasons and died in May.

the United States Government.... It is this independence and our willingness to exert it that qualifies us to deal with your association and others as free agents with no responsibility for upholding the foreign policy of our government.[50]

Although WFUNA was technically composed of organizations independent of their governments, the United States and others assumed, accurately, that ASOON was a tool of the Soviet Foreign Ministry. That said, WFUNA preferred the participation of the Soviet organization, even under false pretences, to its absence.

ASOON received directives from the Foreign Ministry, which focused exclusively on ASOON's international activities, leaving ASOON space for independent initiative domestically.[51] Simultaneously WFUNA tasked the associations, through an annual reporting system, to promote the United Nations domestically. In 1957, WFUNA asked its affiliates to include in their annual report a description of both their activities throughout the year to promote human rights and how the associations observed International Human Rights Day (December 10th).[52] To maintain legitimacy in WFUNA, ASOON had to observe Human Rights Day domestically. Although the Soviet government created ASOON to work internationally, the association needed to work within the Soviet society to achieve its international goals. WFUNA members discussed various associations' domestic activities as part of determining who would be on the global executive board, and highlights of these were disseminated internationally. ASOON conducted domestic human rights programs in order to bolster its claim to leadership during elections to the executive board and with other associations in general. The Soviet Foreign Ministry may have envisioned ASOON as an international instrument when it gave its approval to the group; it certainly drafted the directives to the group only dealing with its international activities. At the same time, WFUNA judged its associations on their domestic activities. One year after its creation, ASOON organized the USSR's first observation of International Human Rights Day, commemorating the vote on the Universal Declaration.

In 1957, ASOON collaborated with the Soviet Committee on UNESCO to celebrate Human Rights Day, focusing on the rights of children, infants, and mothers. It convened discussions with education specialists from the Academy of Sciences, the Soviet Women's Committee, and other domestic volunteer organizations, and the Association concluded the event with a children's concert. According to ASOON's report to the World Federation, it was the organization's "most important" event of the year, and a synopsis of the activities

---

[50] Letter to Golunskii from Irving Salomon, American Association for the United Nations, Inc., June 3, 1958. GARF f. 9569, op. 1, d. 33, l. 110.

[51] See, for example, Reshenie rasshirennogo zasedanie Tsentral'nogo pravleniia assotsiatsii sodeistviia OON v SSSR 27 avgusta 1956 g. o pozitsii sovetskoi delegatsii na XI sessii VFASOON GARF f. 9565, op. 1, d. 6a, ll. 1–6 and Pis'ma v TsK KPSS po voprosam deiatel'nosti Assotsiatsii sodeistviia OON v SSSR GARF f. 9565, op. 1, d. 7a, ll. 13–18.

[52] For example, letter to Robert Smith from V. Poliakov (Secretary General of ASOON) 13.I.58 GARF f. 9565, op. 1, d. 32, ll. 1–4.

were published in the *Izvestiia, Moscow News*, and *Novoe Vremiia* (*New Times*).[53] These newspapers commemorated International Human Rights Day for the first time that year and, building off ASOON's events, wrote particularly about children's rights.

Izvestiia published an editorial, subsequently republished in *Moscow News*, which best explained Soviet attitudes toward the Declaration: "The Soviet Union considers that the implementation of the principles proclaimed in the Universal Declaration of Human Rights is inseparably connected with the struggle of the nations against the danger of a new war, with their fight for peaceful coexistence and friendship."[54] The *Novoe Vremiia* article declared the Declaration "on the whole a progressive document," including some provisions "based on the same principles that underlie the Soviet constitution." The unnamed author echoed earlier writings and condemned the Declaration for its aspirational rather than legal nature. In contrast, as the *Novoe Vremiia* article explained, Soviet laws guaranteed basic human rights, some rights achieved even during the Civil War: "The rights and freedoms proclaimed in the U.N. Declaration are legislatively guaranteed and faithfully exercised in the Soviet Union. The same is true of the People's Republic of China and the other socialist countries."[55]

Meanwhile, the article elaborated, Italy had hungry children, Japan had unemployment, and the United States suffered from not only these problems but also "McCarthyism and the terrible thought-control interrogations that drove scientists and actors to suicide."[56] These articles used the Universal Declaration to legitimize the Soviet rule, as the rights therein were already attained in the Soviet Union, with the Constitution influencing and inspiring the Declaration and shaping international goals. In writing its article, *New Times* continued to bridge the divide between Soviet internal and international press. Like the 1955 article in the monthly *Mezhdunarodnaia zhizn'* (*International Affairs*), this article appeared in a weekly journal that was predominately, but not exclusively, published for an international audience, with six different language editions, including Russian. The article targeted an international audience, but simultaneously reached an internal one.

For the tenth anniversary, ASOON claimed responsibility for the fact that the government had released a commemorative postage stamp – a tangible piece of propaganda for the Declaration it failed to initially support. Additionally, ASOON commissioned Anatolii Petrovich Movchan, a historian and member of the Association, to write a book that provided a brief history of the Declaration and the draft covenants as well as a complete version of

---

[53] Letter to Robert Smith from V. Poliakov (Secretary General AOON), January 13, 1958. GARF f. 9565, op. 1, d. 32, ll. 1–4; "Den' prav cheloveka," *Izvestiia*, December 10, 1957; "In the Soviet Press: Human Rights Day," *Moscow News*, December 11, 1957; "O pravakh cheloveka," *Novoe Vremiia*, no. 50 (1957).

[54] "In the Soviet Press: Human Rights Day."

[55] "O pravakh cheloveka" and "Human Rights," *New Times*, no. 50 (1957).

[56] "Human Rights" and "O pravakh cheloveka."

the Declaration in the annex.[57] Movchan, like previous authors, portrayed the Declaration as the product of a battle between two blocs, the people's democracies against the Anglo-American bourgeois states. The representatives of other states became, in the Soviet version of history, primarily invisible or, on rare occasion, puppets of the Anglo-American cabal. Charles Malik of Lebanon, René Cassin of France, P. C. Chang of China, and Carlos Pena Romulo of the Philippines, who played such influential roles in the drafting of the Declaration, were absent. Similarly, the disagreements between the United Kingdom and the United States over the Declaration (as well as most foreign policy issues) disappeared. In so doing, Movchan glossed over issues on which Soviet and American diplomats agreed.[58]

When the press, journalists, and jurists discussed the Universal Declaration of Human Rights, it was linked to the Soviet 1936 (Stalin) Constitution. The diplomatic corps described the enumerated rights in the Constitution to push for similar rights in the Declaration and the subsequent covenants. Later, articles in both legal journals and general publications used the perceived influence of the Constitution on the Declaration to validate the progressive nature of the Constitution. However, the 1936 Constitution was always depicted as the more progressive of the two documents, as the Declaration was a compromise with the bourgeois powers. What then, if any, was the domestic impact of this diplomatic and internal propaganda? Ben Nathans' work in this volume concludes that the Soviet public did not embrace ideas of universal, inalienable human rights in their proposals to revise the Constitution. Perhaps the domestic discourse failed to foster rights-talk among Soviet citizens, but the diplomatic discourse directly impacted the 1977 Constitution. This Constitution included a greatly expanded section of "The Basic Rights, Freedoms, and Duties of Citizens of the USSR" with forty articles in comparison to the 1936 Constitution's sixteen. Of these, twenty were rights (as opposed to obligations), and they reflected seventeen of the rights enumerated in both the International Covenant on Civil and Political Rights and the International Covenant on Economic, Social and Cultural Rights. The domestic Constitution reflected international diplomacy on human rights.

Conclusion

When Stalin purged his enemies, he directed a cadre of photographers and cinematographers to erase their images from photos. Stalin-era scholars would

---

[57] Perepiska AS OON v SSSR s Vsemirnoi Federatsiei assotsiatsii sodeistviia OON po voprosam sotrudnichestva. GARF f. 9565, op. 1, d. 44, l. 48.

[58] Movchan received a favorable and lengthy review of his book in *Sovetskii ezhegodnik mezhdunarodnogo prava* (*The Soviet Yearbook on International Law*), which should have greatly increased the number of potential readers. V. A. Romanov, "Sovetskii soiuz i mezhdunarodnaia zashchita osnovnykh prav cheloveka" (The Soviet Union and International Protection of the Fundamental Human Rights), *Sovetskii ezhegodnik mezhdunarodnogo prava* (1958).

send revisions to those who purchased the Soviet encyclopedia, replacing entries on the politically excised with elaborate entries on natural science. Although many may think this ended with Stalin's death, Khrushchev's regime similarly erased all mention of the Soviet abstention on the Universal Declaration of Human Rights. Instead, the Declaration became a sign of the progressive nature of Soviet law and morality both domestically and internationally.

Soviet diplomats, journalists, jurists, and others turned to the Universal Declaration in order to further government policies. They succeeded to an extent because the Declaration was elastic, facilitating multiple, even conflicting, interpretations of human rights. In the international sphere, the Soviet Foreign Ministry prevailed on the United Nations to include economic, social, and cultural rights in a legally binding covenant by arguing for a unity of the rights enumerated in the Declaration. As Soviet human rights diplomacy increased, it spread from the confines of the Foreign Ministry and the United Nations to reach international and domestic public audiences through approved publications and volunteer organizations, who used the Declaration to promote socialist ideology, Soviet legality, and their own legitimacy.

The Cold War did not freeze human rights diplomacy; on the contrary, the debates heated up as multiple political ideologies, religious convictions, and historical experiences attempted to move beyond the generalities of the Declaration to the specificities of the covenants. Instead of the silence portrayed by some historians, one prominent delegate – Charles Malik of Lebanon – described this period as "the exciting drama of man seeking to grasp himself."[59] The Declaration did not end this drama, nor did the Cold War. Instead, it provided the vocabulary to define and redefine ideas of human rights, and one of the lexicographers was the Soviet Union. By recognizing the Soviet Union as an active participant in human rights diplomacy, a perceived silence in human rights history – from the Declaration to the 1970s – instead becomes a noisy space of debate.

[59] Charles Habib Malik and Habib C. Malik, *The Challenge of Human Rights: Charles Malik and the Universal Declaration* (Oxford, 2000), 157.

8

Soviet Rights-Talk in the Post-Stalin Era

Benjamin Nathans

Прав тот, у кого больше прав.

Right is he who has more rights.

Russian saying

"The problem with Soviet legal history," my teacher Martin Malia once quipped, "is that there's not enough of it." The remark was meant to register the pervasiveness, among elites and masses alike, of extra-legal ways of doings things, the apparent irrelevance of Soviet law to Soviet practices, and the particular Bolshevik contempt (sanctioned by Marx, Lenin, and others) for the "bourgeois" notion of the rule of law. Soviet law, in this widely shared view, functioned primarily as a façade for domestic and foreign spectators, behind which the real mechanisms of power operated. Implicit in this approach is an assumption of bad faith: that laws, or at least some laws, were not meant to be actionable and instead served a purely ideological function. It is a critique whose pedigree reaches back at least to Max Weber's attack on the "pseudo-constitutionalism" of tsarist Russia following the revolution of 1905.[1]

It should perhaps come as no surprise that the Soviet critique of "bourgeois" legal systems exactly mirrored this view. In capitalist societies, so the argument runs, law serves as an "illusion" behind which economically determined relationships of exploitation freely operate. "Fictions" was one of the favored terms used by Lenin – and therefore by legions of later Soviet scholars – to describe bourgeois constitutions: "A constitution is fictitious when law and reality diverge; it is not fictitious when they coincide."[2] Of course, regardless of time and place, *pays légal* and *pays réel* rarely coincide. It is more productive to think of laws as norms than as descriptions of reality, more fruitful to focus on the tension between law in theory and law in practice. My point is

---

[1] Max Weber, *Russlands Übergang zum Scheinkonstitutionalismus*; Beilage, *Archiv für Sozialwissenschaft und Sozialpolitik*, 23:1 (1906), 165–401.

[2] V. I. Lenin, *Polnoe sobranie sochinenii*, 5th ed. (Moscow, 1974), 17:345.

not to belittle Lenin's (or Malia's) observation, but rather to caution against a dismissive literalism when thinking about the functions and purposes of law under Soviet socialism.

Central to the Soviet critique of the "fictitious" nature of bourgeois constitutionalism were the allegedly inalienable rights they proclaimed – the smokescreen of equality among individuals designed to distract attention from the reality of class domination. Yet even a cursory glance at Soviet legal history reveals that rights claims of various kinds – individual, collective, expressive, material, etc. – quickly assumed a prominent place in the legal lexicon. The rhetoric of rights found expression not only in formal documents such as constitutions and civil codes but in the vernacular of ordinary Soviet citizens. Indeed, it has been argued that, far from functioning as an ideological diversion, officially proclaimed rights may have promoted and/or reflected rights-based thinking among significant portions of the Soviet population.[3] The question, then, is what sort of thinking that was.

If only on a quantitative level, the notion that there is not enough Soviet legal history should be laid to rest by the proliferation of constitutional discourse across the USSR's seventy-four-year history. Four country-wide constitutions were ratified during this period: in 1918, 1924, 1936, and 1977. In this and other respects, the Soviet Union qualifies as an exceptionally "jurisgenerative" state. The 1936 and 1977 Constitutions, moreover (as well as a dress rehearsal for the latter in the early 1960s), were preceded by extensive state-sponsored public discussions that, for all their patently mobilizational purposes, have left us valuable sources for exploring the deployment of rights-talk in a country that understood itself as the laboratory of the future. These sources are doubly useful insofar as they allow us to investigate people's legal consciousness at a moment other than when they were in trouble with the law – the typical way for the voices of ordinary individuals to enter the historical records of legal institutions.

The sometimes spectacular contradictions between Soviet law and Soviet reality, combined with explicit Bolshevik critiques of law as a mode of social control, led more than a few early observers to characterize the USSR as a country of "legal nihilism." Among the proof texts for this viewpoint is the oft-quoted 1927 assertion by the first President of the USSR Supreme Court, Petr Stuchka, that "Communism means not the victory of socialist law, but the victory of socialism over any law, since with the abolition of classes and their antagonistic interests, law will die out altogether."[4] One struggles to find other historical instances of such a radical critique of law as an instrument of public order, particularly in a modern state. Even the early Christians, with their call for the transcendence of (Jewish) law by grace,

---

[3] Sarah Davies, *Popular Opinion in Stalin's Russia: Terror, Propaganda and Dissent, 1934–1941* (Cambridge, 1997), 102–108.
[4] Quoted in Harold Berman, *Justice in the USSR: An Interpretation of Soviet Law* (Cambridge, 1963), 26.

did not repudiate legal frameworks entirely. And yet, however corrosive the early Bolshevik stance may have been for law as a moral or political value, subsequent developments made "legal nihilism" seem less and less useful as a description of either theory or practice in the Soviet Union. Indeed, Stuchka's antinomianism was publicly repudiated in the USSR shortly before his death in 1932. In the decades that followed, observers in the West debated not whether there was law in the Soviet Union, but what *kind* of law it was, and in particular how to classify it vis-à-vis the two regnant paradigms, positivist and natural law. Adherents of each paradigm tended to identify Soviet law with the other. Thus John C. H. Wu, writing in the *Catholic Encyclopedia*, argued that "this is positivism pushed to its logical end. The will of the dominant class becomes the essence of law, and reason becomes the handmaiden of will." By contrast, Hans Kelsen, a leading positivist theorist, insisted that "[Soviet law] is exactly of the same type as the bourgeois theory which the Soviet writers have derided and ridiculed ...: the natural law doctrine [which] works out or pretends to work out principles 'from life,' that is, from nature in general and from the nature of society [or] social relationships in particular."[5]

The present chapter explores rights-talk as a facet of Soviet legal consciousness in the post-Stalin era, a time when Soviet leaders attempted to shift the repertoire of state policies away from terror and coercion in favor of persuasion and cooperation, and the USSR began to enter the orbit of international legal norms. At the heart of my enquiry lies the question how and with what effects the rhetoric of rights – the *lingua franca* of liberalism – was deployed in an avowedly illiberal society. To be sure, the Soviet Union is hardly the only setting in which the flourishing of rights-talk seems to demand explanation. In an influential article, Thomas Haskell has asked how it is that rights-talk, with its implicit moral absolutism, has nonetheless thrived in an era of moral relativism in the United States. His hypothesis – that "rights are the principal means by which duty is smuggled back into cultures dominated by the rhetoric of individualism" – only heightens the distinctiveness of the Soviet case.[6] For the USSR, with its collectivist ethos, had no need to smuggle duty into its culture or its law codes – it was already there, prominently on display. What functions, then, did rights-talk serve in the Soviet setting, and what can one learn by studying its evolving grammar and syntax? If we are to move beyond visions of human rights as an American (or Western) export product, we must grapple with the histories of rights in non-Western environments. The paradigmatic "Other" of liberal rights-talk for much of the twentieth century was the "Second World," an ensemble of socialist states that suppressed private property and the market in a quest to fashion what Bolshevik leader Lev

---

[5] John Wu, "Law," *The Catholic Encyclopedia*, Sixth Section, Supplement II (1955), 13:1; Hans Kelsen, *The Communist Theory of Law* (New York, 1955), 120.

[6] Thomas Haskell, "The Curious Persistence of Rights Talk in the 'Age of Interpretation'," *Journal of American History*, 74 (1987), 984, n.1.

Trotsky famously called an "improved edition of humankind" – the *homo sovieticus.*

What happens to human rights when "the human" is understood as a work in progress?

Rights and Neo-Corporatism

The surprising prominence of rights in Soviet legal discourse is but one facet of the larger about-face regarding the anticipated withering away of law and the state under socialism. Initially, Soviet law harnessed rights to the explicit goal of inverting (rather than abolishing) received patterns of class domination. Thus the 1918 Constitution of Soviet Russia (RSFSR) granted the classic freedoms of conscience, expression, assembly, and association exclusively to "toilers" – a term meant to include urban workers as well as the "rural proletariat" of poor peasants. The Constitution's authors showed less interest in the content of these freedoms than in announcing what the state is obliged to do materially to facilitate their realization by the newly privileged elements of the population:

Article 14: In order to ensure for the toilers real freedom of expression of opinion, the RSFSR abolishes the dependence of the press on capital and turns over to the working class and the poor peasantry all technical and material resources for the publication of newspapers, pamphlets, books, and all other printed matter, and guarantees their free circulation throughout the country.

Article 15: In order to ensure for the toilers real freedom of assembly, the RSFSR, recognizing the rights of the citizens of the Soviet Republic freely to organize assemblies, meetings, processions, etc., shall place at the disposal of the working class and the poor peasantry all premises suitable for public gathering, together with furnishing, lighting, and heating.[7]

From the outset, then, the realization of civil rights ("real freedom") was construed as depending on certain economic preconditions. By promising the necessary material support only to "toilers," the 1918 Constitution in effect redefined the inherited distinction between "active" and "passive" citizenship. It similarly inverted received categories of political rights, which were now granted exclusively to those "who obtain their livelihood from productive and socially useful labor" as well as "soldiers of the Soviet army and navy." The right to vote and to run for office were denied to "persons who employ hired labor in order to extract profit," "persons living on non-labor income," "private traders," "monks and clergymen," and other undesired categories.[8] Furthermore, the 1918 Constitution gave the fledgling Soviet state the authority to deprive any individuals or groups of rights "used to the detriment of the socialist revolution" – thereby sanctioning the use of rights as a weapon

---

[7] English translations of the four Soviet constitutions can be found in Aryeh Unger, *Constitutional Development in the USSR: A Guide to the Soviet Constitutions* (New York, 1981).

[8] Articles 64 and 65.

against political opponents. By the early 1930s, some four million *lishentsy* had been stripped of their civil and political rights (but not of Soviet citizenship). A smaller number of individuals were deprived of their citizenship as well and either expelled from the USSR or rendered stateless within its borders.[9]

The resulting hierarchy of civic belonging and exclusion amounted to a kind of neo-corporatism that put the inherited language of rights to both archaic and modernist purposes.[10] A striking vestige of *ancien régime* estate privilege (inverted, to be sure) can be found in the 1918 Constitution's decree that "the honorable right of bearing arms in defense of the revolution is granted only to toilers; non-toiling elements shall perform other military duties." Toilers thus became a new nobility of the sword – a privilege quickly diluted in the heat of civil war, when the fledgling "Red Army of Workers and Peasants" desperately drafted not only non-toilers but former tsarist army officers. A more forward-looking aspect of Bolshevik rights policies is on display in the extension of "all political rights of Russian citizens to foreigners residing within the territory of the Russian Republic ... and belonging to the working class or the non-labor-exploiting peasantry."[11] This was a neo-corporative citizenship – and therefore a rights regime – of a radically internationalist cast. The Soviet leadership, as one historian put it, "believed that they were leading a transnational social class, not a state."[12]

By the mid-1930s, having extended the state's control from the "commanding heights" to the farthest reaches of the national economy, and having exiled or killed millions of "class enemies," Joseph Stalin officially declared the USSR a socialist society. For Marxists, such a profound transformation in the social and economic base naturally required a parallel adjustment in the superstructure, beginning with the legal system. Accordingly – and in sync with Moscow's courting of Western allies for the emerging popular front against fascism – a new constitutional rights regime was drawn up reflecting the violently altered social landscape.[13] Given the relative longevity of the 1936 "Stalin Constitution" – forty-one years, longer than all other Soviet constitutions combined – and given that it served as the foundational text for virtually

[9] Golfo Alexopoulos, *Stalin's Outcasts: Aliens, Citizens, and the Soviet State, 1926–1936* (Ithaca, 2003), 3; Alexopoulos, "Soviet Citizenship, More or Less: Rights, Emotions, and States of Civic Belonging," *Kritika: Explorations in Russian and Eurasian History*, 7 (2006), 489–490.

[10] On the revival of corporative categories in early Soviet history, see Sheila Fitzpatrick, "Ascribing Class: The Construction of Social Identity in Soviet Russia," *Journal of Modern History*, 65 (1993), 745–770.

[11] Articles 19 and 20.

[12] Alexopoulos, "Soviet Citizenship," 491.

[13] The 1924 Constitution was concerned almost exclusively with regulating the federal structure of the newly formed Union of Soviet Socialist Republics. It left intact the statutes on rights and duties contained in the 1918 Constitution of the Russian republic, which became the model for the constitutions of the ten other union republics.

all post-Stalinist discussions of rights and other constitutional issues – we would do well to spend some time with it.

Stalin's Constitution and the "All-People's Discussion"

Perhaps the most prominent aspect of the new Constitution's discourse on rights was its retreat from neo-corporatism. Gone is the explicit deprivation of rights to entire categories of the population. Article 135 grants the right to vote and be elected to "all citizens of the USSR aged 18 or older, regardless of racial or national membership, faith, educational level, residence, social origin, property status, and past activities." Articles 132 and 133 proclaim the "sacred duty of every citizen" to perform military service – without reference to who may or may not bear arms. Freedom of conscience, expression, assembly, and association (described both as "freedoms" and "rights") are now "guaranteed by law to citizens [rather than to "toilers," as in 1918] of the USSR." And yet traces of the neo-corporative idiom – and more broadly, of the state's use of rights as a political tool – remain. Whereas the various freedoms are granted to "citizens," their exercise must "correspond to the interests of toilers and the strengthening of the socialist system." Moreover, the all-important material guaranties by the state for the realization of civil rights are extended to "toilers" rather than to "citizens." True, "toilers" now meant the troika of officially recognized social groups (working class, peasantry, and intelligentsia), leaving only recalcitrant individuals on the sidelines; but the subtle distinction between "citizens" and "toilers" was not lost – least of all on the toilers themselves, as we will see in a moment.

The Stalin Constitution enumerates most of its rights in Section Ten, "Fundamental Rights and Duties of Citizens," reflecting an implicit quid pro quo whereby the exercise of rights depends not only on material support by the state but on the fulfillment of duties by citizens. Although most duties are listed *after* rights, they – unlike the enumerated rights – are dignified with affective terms such as "sacred" and "a matter of honor." The Stalin Constitution repeatedly distinguishes between "having" a right, something any citizen can do, and being granted (by the state) the material means to exercise it, which depends on one already being a "toiler" – that is, someone engaged in fulfilling the preeminent duty of labor. Labor is the indispensable link between duties and rights, the only activity listed under both categories. Labor is the key by which the fulfillment of duty opens the door to rights.

If there was any truth to the Soviet claim that the 1936 Constitution was "the most democratic in the world," it lay in the opening articles of Section Ten. Here, for the first time, a state legally guaranteed to its citizens a comprehensive program of material welfare and expressed this guarantee in the same language used to grant the more traditional civil and political rights. The economic and social rights pioneered in the Stalin Constitution included the right to employment, to leisure, to material security in old age and in the event of illness or incapacity to work, and to education, up to and including

higher education. Disparities in the distribution of all the aforementioned
rights based on gender, race, and nationality were forbidden.[14]

Here too, however, careful readers could detect a certain neo-corporatism
– updated to reflect the more nuanced hierarchy of the newly proclaimed
socialist order. In the grammar of official Soviet rights-talk, no right could
have practical value without an explicit commitment from the state to ensure
the material prerequisites of its realization. And among the economic and
social rights inaugurated in the 1936 Constitution, those pertaining to leisure
and material security received that commitment only with regard to "workers," leaving the recently collectivized peasantry effectively out in the cold.
Lest we be tempted to regard these terminological distinctions as so much
academic hair-splitting – after all, they could have resulted from the messi-
ness of collective redactions, or perhaps were never meant to inform actual
practices – historians have shown that ordinary Soviet citizens were extraordinarily attuned to such nuances.[15] The Stalin Constitution was made available
for public comment while still in draft form between June and October 1936,
prior to its ratification later that year. This "all-people's discussion" of matters constitutional generated an enormous cache of published and unpublished
comments by Soviet citizens. "In a limited sense," as one historian puts it,
"they are something like the *cahiers de doléances* of the Stalin revolution."[16]
Together with NKVD (secret police) reports on the public mood regarding
constitutional issues, they have made it possible to listen in as Soviet citizens
talk about rights in the 1930s, and therefore can serve as benchmarks for
analogous sources from the post-Stalin era.

Many unpublished comments on the draft 1936 Constitution were critical.
The most widespread complaint came from members of collective farms, who
immediately grasped the import of fine distinctions among the material rights
guaranteed to "citizens," "toilers," and "workers," and who complained bit-
terly about their prospective exclusion from state-financed pensions, sanato-
ria, vacations, and health care. Equally significant, for our purposes, is that
such complaints appear to have been couched in the language not of common citizenship but of a specific form of parity and fairness: If workers get
such-and-such, so should peasants. Theirs was by no means an argument for
general social equality. If anything, the neo-corporative idiom was even more
pronounced in popular comments than in the 1936 Constitution: Apart from
complaints by collective farmers about their exclusion from certain benefits,
the next most common (unpublished) sentiment was hostility toward the
planned Constitution's abandonment of an explicitly class-based regime of
rights. Letter writers protested the granting of equal rights to kulaks, priests,

---

[14] Articles 122 and 123.
[15] J. Arch Getty, "State and Society under Stalin: Constitutions and Elections in the 1930s,"
    Slavic Review, 50 (1991), 18–35; Ellen Wimberg, "Socialism, Democratism, and Criticism: The
    Soviet Press and the National Discussion of the 1936 Draft Constitution," *Soviet Studies*, 44
    (1992), 313–332; Davies, *Popular Opinion in Stalin's Russia*, ch. 6.
[16] Getty, "State and Society under Stalin," 24.

and other "right-less" groups. The Constitution, in their view, seemed to mark a retreat from dictatorship of the proletariat toward a "bourgeois" order. As one worker put it, "I disagree with the policies of the party. We are going toward capitalism, since the new constitution gives the right to vote to all."[17]

The expanded civil rights granted by the 1936 Constitution also elicited substantial opposition. Article 127's guarantee of "inviolability of the person," meaning that "No one may be subject to arrest except by court order or with the sanction of a procurator," struck some as an example of excessive proceduralism. Why wait for official approval before arresting and punishing criminals? Why not hold relatives responsible for the crimes of their kin? One peasant maintained that "using free speech, meetings, and so forth to oppose the Soviet state constitutes a betrayal of the country and should carry heavy punishment."[18] Many peasants indicated that they would gladly relinquish the right (and presumably the duty) to work. One should not exaggerate, however, the weakness of rights consciousness in popular comments on the 1936 Constitution. Substantial numbers of participants advocated the formation of alternative political parties to pursue their collective rights. With textbook accounts of the French Revolution fresh in their minds, pupils at one middle school drafted their own constitution in the form of a "Declaration of the Rights of the Pupil and the Citizen." As this and other examples suggest, the idea of rights found expression in citizens' comments primarily in the idiom of corporative claims (whether as collective farmers, workers, students, etc.) to benefits issued by the state, rather than individual claims of immunity *against* state intrusion, or claims on behalf of the entire citizenry.

Rights-Talk during Khrushchev's "Thaw"

Under Stalin, of course, unpredictable and often violent intrusion by the state in the lives of Soviet citizens reached epic proportions. After the 1956 "Secret Speech" by his successor, Nikita Khrushchev, the official diagnosis of Stalin's crimes emphasized his failure to abide by "socialist legality," rather than the content of socialist law itself. "No matter what distortions of and departures from the constitution of the USSR took place in practice," asserted one Soviet jurist, looking back at the Stalin era, "the constitution's basic principles ... are as solid and stable as the socioeconomic bases of the Soviet state."[19] The first intimations that Khrushchev himself did not share this vision of constitutional stability came in 1959, when Khrushchev proclaimed the goal of "full-scale construction of communism," reflecting "a new and momentous stage" in the USSR's socioeconomic development. Having ceased to be a dictatorship of

---

[17] Quoted in Davies, *Popular Opinion in Stalin's Russia*, 105.
[18] Getty, "State and Society under Stalin," 26.
[19] M. Mikhailov, "Nekotorye voprosy sovetskoi konstitutsionnoi praktiki," *Sovetskoe gosudarstvo i pravo* no. 9 (1956), 3–4, quoted in George Ginsburgs, "A Khrushchev Constitution for the Soviet Union: Projects and Prospects," *Osteuropa – Recht*, 8 (1962), 192.

the proletariat, the Soviet Union, according to Khrushchev, was now an "all-
people's state" in which the "material prerequisites" for communism would
be in place by 1980. The country's international status, too, was changing
dramatically. If one of the justifications for the dictatorship of the proletariat (and the neo-corporative rights regime that went with it) had been the
Soviet Union's encirclement by hostile bourgeois states, then the spread of
socialism to neighboring countries after World War II diminished the need
for such a dictatorship. "Socialism has emerged from the framework of one
country," Khrushchev announced, "to become a mighty world system." These
"sweeping changes" required "expression and legislative consolidation in the
Constitution of the Soviet Union, the Fundamental Law of our land."[20] As
he put it in a proposal to the Supreme Soviet in 1962, "The constitution of a
socialist state must change with the transition of society from one historical
stage to another.... The constitution adopted in 1936 conformed to the period
of the consolidation of socialism.... Naturally, the chief provisions of this constitution are now obsolete."[21]

The key word in this statement is "naturally": in order to avoid becoming
fictions, constitutional laws needed to keep up with the natural laws of change
(*zakonomernosti*, or in the original Marxian formulation, *Gesetzmäßigkeiten*)
in economy and society. Pronounced just twenty-six years – a single generation – after enactment of the Stalin Constitution, this breathtaking verdict
of historical obsolescence faithfully reproduced the logic used to justify the
Stalin Constitution in its own time. Stalin had presided over (and constitution-
alized) the transition from the state capitalism of the New Economic Policy to
socialism; Khrushchev would do the same for the transition from socialism to
communism.

Among the revolutionary "Leninist norms" that fueled Khrushchev's
vision of the communist future were echoes of the "legal nihilism" of the
1920s. In 1961, for example, the party introduced the "Moral Code of the
Builder of Communism," a distillation of twelve supreme ethical values for
the *homo sovieticus*. Beyond its goal of fostering socially productive behav-
iors (e.g., Point 2: "Conscientious labor for the good of society," or Point
6: "Humane relations and mutual respect between individuals"), the Moral
Code was widely understood as preparing the ground for the withering away
of law in the coming communist era.[22] The Twenty-Second Party Congress
in 1961 announced that during the transition to communism, "the role of
moral principles in social life grows, the sphere of activity of moral factors widens, and correspondingly the importance of administrative regulation of relations between people decreases." According to one commentator,
"in developed Communist society, [moral norms] will be the only form

---

[20] Quoted in Unger, *Constitutional Development*, 173.
[21] Quoted in ibid., 174–175.
[22] For the complete text of the Moral Code, see Richard De George, *Soviet Ethics and Morality*
(Ann Arbor, 1969), 83.

of regulation of relations between people."[23] All this was consistent with the long-standing assumption that crime would gradually disappear from socialist society.

What is noteworthy in these formulations is not just the persistence of anti-nomianism in the Soviet moral imagination, but the way the Moral Code performed, in the Soviet context, the function of "regulative ideal" not unlike that of human rights in other parts of the world at the time. As a non–legally binding expression of supreme ethical values with explicitly pedagogical purposes, the Moral Code paralleled the 1948 Universal Declaration of Human Rights (UDHR), a similarly nonbinding "standard of achievement" whose signatories pledged to "strive by teaching and education to promote respect" for the principles it contained.[24] Of course, the contrasts are important too: The Moral Code applied to builders of communism, rather than to all human beings (indeed, Point 11 called for "intolerance towards the enemies of communism"), and its ideals were expressed strictly in terms of duties, without reference to rights or freedoms. Most important, whereas the framers of the UDHR aspired for its norms to be absorbed into the binding legislation of the various signatory countries, the Moral Code of the Builder of Communism was meant eventually to *replace* law, becoming "the only form of regulation of relations between people."

In the near term, however, Khrushchev was determined to put his stamp on a new Soviet constitution. A subcommission established in 1962 began its work by soliciting the views of ordinary Soviet citizens as part of the drafting process. In a review of practices in capitalist countries, it noted that the constitution of the USSR's main geopolitical rival had been composed in 1787 "by a convention in Philadelphia ... consisting of members of the bourgeoisie and slave owners who conducted their sessions behind closed doors."[25] In the Soviet Union, by contrast, the framers planned not only to solicit broad input from the entire Soviet population (public notice of the subcommission's work appeared in *Pravda* in April 1962), but to submit the resulting text to a popular referendum:

This would be something never before seen in the world, an act of genuine *demokratizm*. For in those instances when bourgeois states have conducted referendums for the ratification of constitutions, the people were permitted to vote "for" or "against" a constitution already drafted by the government. But at no time anywhere in the world has there been an instance when the people itself has worked out a draft of the fundamental laws and ratified them itself.[26]

---

[23] Quoted in Deborah Field, "Irreconcilable Differences: Divorce and Conceptions of Private Life in the Khrushchev Era," *Russian Review*, 57:4 (Oct. 1998), 602.

[24] The quoted passages are from the Preamble to the UDHR. Johannes Morsink, *The Universal Declaration of Human Rights: Origins, Drafting, and Intent* (Philadelphia, 1999), 330.

[25] Russian State Archive of Contemporary History (henceforth RGANI), f. 5, op. 30, d. 385, l. 204.

[26] RGANI f. 5, op. 30, d. 441, l. 29.

As in 1936, the people's "work" on the Constitution appears to have had minimal impact on the actual drafting process. Nonetheless, again as in 1936, the attempt to stimulate popular engagement in the constitutional process produced a rich body of sources for the study of Soviet rights-talk, a rare glimpse into vernacular legal consciousness at the height of the Khrushchev's "Thaw."

Before we examine the "talk" itself, a few remarks are in order regarding the textual sources in which that talk is captured. These remarks color not only how we read the sources but how we map the shifts in constitutional rights-talk in the post-Stalin era. Unlike in 1936, no draft of the new Constitution was made available in advance of the solicitation of public input; to the extent that citizen participants invoked an already existing text, it was usually the 1936 Constitution (which remained in force), although in a number of cases letter writers referred to constitutions of foreign countries (e.g., Poland, Yugoslavia, East Germany, France, the United States) – something almost unheard of in the "all-people's discussion" of 1936. In contrast to 1936, citizen comments regarding the planned Khrushchev Constitution appeared exclusively in the form of letters voluntarily sent by individuals (the majority of whom identified themselves by name, occupation, and place of residence) directly to the constitutional subcommission – rather than originating as oral comments at party-organized meetings, then being written down by local officials and sent on to Moscow. The de facto requirement of literacy in the Khrushchev-era discussion may help explain why collectivized peasants, whose voices were strongly present in the 1936 "all-people's discussion," were largely absent in the early 1960s. The Khrushchev-era letters do, however, represent people from a wide variety of occupations – from atomic engineer to factory worker – residing in cities, towns, and villages across much of the Soviet Union.[27]

Few traces of the neo-corporative approach to rights, so characteristic of previous Soviet constitutions and even more so of the public discussion in 1936, appear to have survived into the 1960s. Collectivized peasants (*kolkhozniki*) such as M. A. Parshin of Astakhovo, who was old enough to remember the ratification of the Stalin Constitution, no longer claimed rights via analogy to the privileged category of workers: "During the period of bourgeois ascendancy, they asked, What is the Third Estate? Nothing. What should it be? Everything. With us one could ask, What is the peasantry? It's the *kolkhozniki*. What do they want and what should they be? Citizens with equal rights in all respects."[28] In the "all people's state," citizenship now appeared as the defining criterion for rights-bearing, regardless of what kind of labor one performed. Among letters touching upon

---

[27] The sample size of the 1960s material is significantly smaller: roughly 3,000 letters as opposed to roughly 43,000 in 1936. The Khrushchev-era letters themselves have not (to my knowledge) been preserved; one has to rely on the extensive quotations from them in reports prepared by the constitutional subcommission.

[28] RGANI f. 5, op. 30, d. 384, l. 46.

the different legal rights of various groups of the Soviet population, the majority concerned the nationalities and urged putting an end to "affirmative action"–style policies. "The current structure and division of union republics according to national characteristics," wrote N. Shokhov from Alma-Aty, "has outgrown itself":

Several dozen nationalities reside in Kazakhstan. The Kazakhs here constitute 25 percent of the total. But the republic is Kazakh. One might pose the question, "Why not the Uyghur republic or the Dungan republic?" Should we really create certain privileges for particular nationalities when all these nationalities work in a unified family? Should we really artificially create abnormalities in their relations and [thereby] do great damage to the economy?[29]

Another writer complained that one million Estonians sent the same number of deputies to the Supreme Soviet as 120 million Russians and 43 million Ukrainians.[30] Most letters regarding nationality issues urged the abolition of national categories in official documents.

If rights were no longer to derive from membership in a corporative group (whether defined by class, social origin, or nationality), what was to be their source? One of the most intriguing tensions to be found in the letters sent to the constitutional subcommission (indeed, sometimes within a single letter) was between the notion that rights had to be earned via labor and other duties, and the contrasting idea that they derived automatically from the status of citizen of the USSR or – more rarely – of human being. The assumption that rights needed to be earned came easily in a system that explicitly linked rights with duties. I. M. Abramovich, a history teacher from Murom, submitted his own draft constitution, which included the declaration that "There are no rights without duties and vice versa."[31] Leningrad resident N. F. Boiarskii approvingly quoted the "principle of socialism" from Article 12 of the 1936 Constitution, "From each according to his ability, to each according to his work." If the receipt of food and other life-sustaining goods were conditional upon labor (at least for the able-bodied), argued Boiarskii, why shouldn't the same apply to less vital goods such as civil and political rights?[32] All the more so given that in the Soviet Union rights were typically construed as things the state *bestowed* upon its citizens (or some subset thereof), rather than *recognizing* them as inherent in the latter. Even those rights classified in the Anglo-American tradition as "immunities" or "negative freedoms," claims that in theory merely required the state to refrain from certain activities (censoring speech, barring assemblies, etc.), appeared in letters to the subcommission as requiring positive state action in order to enable their practice on a fair and equal basis. As history teacher Abramovich put it, echoing official sources: "Bourgeois constitutions merely proclaim the

[29] RGANI f. 5, op. 30, d. 385, ll. 11–12.
[30] RGANI f. 5, op. 30, d. 470, l. 245.
[31] RGANI f. 5, op. 30, d. 384, l. 92.
[32] RGANI f. 5, op. 30, d. 444, l. 2.

rights of the citizen, but the Soviet constitution materially guarantees their realization."[33]

As we have seen, Soviet rights-talk was changing over time both in content (adding social and economic claims, for example) and applicability (vis-à-vis an expanding range of citizens). Nonetheless, the ambiguity vis-à-vis rights granted to "citizens" but limited in practice by the interests of "toilers" (i.e., those who fulfilled the duty of working) left ample room to construe the nexus between rights and duties in a variety of ways. Quite a few letters called for tighter and more explicit linkage between the two. Kiev resident A. I. Avgustovskii urged that "prior to receiving rights and using them, citizens of the USSR should know and fulfill their duties." The new constitution should require citizens to complete secondary schooling and engage in at least two years of "socially useful work" before becoming bearers of rights. Even letters strongly in favor of robust civil rights could embrace the rights-duties nexus. "Without freedom of speech and the press," wrote citizen Grigor'ev from Penza, "society cannot develop normally.... The constitution should indicate that in oral and written statements, citizens are *obliged* to express their critical comments."[34]

A substantial number of letters proposed a new right, absent from all prior Soviet constitutions: the right to choose one's place of residence within the USSR and/or to emigrate beyond its borders. The system of residential permits in cities such as Moscow, Leningrad, and Kiev, according to engineer Piman (from Riga), while "justifiable from an administrative-managerial standpoint, is unconstitutional, amounting to a kind of discrimination based on territorial identity."[35] Of those proposing the right to emigrate from the Soviet Union, several noted that constitutions of bourgeois countries routinely grant such a right.[36]

Freedom of expression emerged as a particularly controversial issue. Among the dozens of letters calling for stricter constitutional limits on expression, nearly all targeted religious believers. According to the teacher A. S. Poluektov (from the town of Oktiabr), "the constitution is supposed to defend the rights of the people, to protect them from attacks by religion on citizens' consciousness."[37] For citizen Agapov (from Andizhan), the claim of a "human right to religion" has no place in the Soviet Constitution, since as a "reactionary organization," religion can only impede progress toward communism.[38] Members of religious sects, several people wrote, should be placed "outside the law."[39]

---

[33] RGANI f. 5, op. 30, d. 384, l. 93.
[34] RGANI f. 5, op. 30, d. 385, l. 109. Emphasis added.
[35] RGANI f. 5, op. 30, d. 385, l. 111.
[36] See, for example, RGANI f.5, op. 30, d. 384, l.27 and d. 470, l. 239.
[37] RGANI f. 5, op. 30, d. 471, l. 7.
[38] RGANI f. 5, op. 30, d. 471, l. 29.
[39] RGANI f. 5, op. 30, d. 470, l. 239.

The lion's share of letters regarding freedom of expression, however, advocated stronger constitutional protection of public criticism of official policies. One writer suggested that in order to make the constitutional statute governing freedom of the press more than just a "formality," people should be allowed to publish opposing views – but at their own cost. Prior to publication, moreover, the "sufficient well-foundedness" of the material should be verified.[40] Like a number of letter writers, pensioner D. K. Markov (from Kolpino) was interested in using the (revised) Constitution to prevent a recurrence of Stalin's "cult of personality," but unsure how to do so:

Criticism of our shortcomings, mistakes, defects, and survivals of capitalism is an inalienable, organic characteristic of the Soviet system. Criticism is encouraged in our society and, it must be said, is highly developed. But this criticism is one-sided. It goes mainly from top to bottom.... Along came Stalin. He promoted arbitrariness, made a heap of mistakes, and where was the criticism? Just you try to criticize! Now we have comrade Khrushchev.... I don't even want to compare him with Stalin; it's night and day. But comrade Khrushchev isn't anointed with the holy spirit either. He can make mistakes too.... Down here it's more visible to us when he's mistaken, so why shouldn't we criticize openly and honestly? But how? If you say something – they'll come up with an article especially for you![41]

Still other writers, however, regarded the horrors of the Stalin era as stemming not from insufficient freedom of speech on the part of the population, but from excessive "rights" on the part of Stalin himself. As V. G. Klubov of Cherepovets put it, "Much misfortune was caused by one person, who was in power and who was granted unlimited rights, which are still being eradicated today." Far from representing moral or legal claims, rights in this sense were practically indistinguishable from powers. The way to prevent a recurrence of the "cult of personality," Klubov proposed, was thus not through additional rights of speech and the press but through the institution of a popular referendum every four years, so that Soviet citizens could approve or disapprove of the performance of their leaders.[42]

Klubov's proposal is emblematic of a view widely conveyed (if often only implicitly) in letters to the subcommission, namely, that rights were not the only or even the primary instrument for protecting citizens against abuse of power by state officials. Just as important, if not more so, was the practice of *kontrol'*, public monitoring to ensure official accountability. In this as in other respects, the vernacular rights-talk on display in letters to the subcommission was substantially in sync with official discourse. Both had moved away from the assumption that the selective denial of rights constituted a legitimate political tool. Neither questioned the fundamental rights–duties nexus; on the contrary, rights were uniformly regarded as contingent on the performance of duty, part of an ongoing system of exchange between citizens

---

[40] RGANI f. 5, op. 30, d. 444, l. 11.
[41] RGANI f. 5, op. 30, d. 385, l. 112.
[42] RGANI f. 5, op. 30, d. 444, ll. 7–8.

and the state. A general consensus held that rights emanate from the state and require the state's material resources for their realization. Indeed, the pervasive silence regarding the economic and social rights promulgated by the Stalin Constitution suggests that they had become firmly anchored in popular consciousness as a specifically socialist entitlement. With only one exception, no letters questioned the Constitution's insistence that the exercise of civil rights must "correspond to the interests of toilers and the strengthening of the socialist system." Although rights could legitimately be used to constrain the actions of abusive officials, nowhere does one find the argument that con-stitutional rights can (let alone should) place limits on the authority of the state itself. This is hardly surprising, given letter writers' virtually unanimous rejection (again in sync with official doctrine) of the idea of separation of powers. Even letter writers who passionately defended civil liberties cast rights as emanating from the state, rather than as natural or innately human. In popular as in elite discourse Soviet rights were thus understood as histori-cally specific, made possible only within the context of the breakthrough to a socialist order.

From "Cult of the Person" to "Rights of the Person"

Khrushchev's peaceful removal from power in October 1964 put a temporary halt to the constitutional subcommission's work, but not to the Soviet leader-ship's desire to render in constitutional language what Khrushchev's succes-sor, Leonid Brezhnev, liked to call "developed socialism." Nor did it interrupt the process of selective opening to the outside world that Khrushchev had inaugurated under the slogan of "peaceful coexistence" – the notion that Soviet socialism would outcompete the capitalist countries of the West in the production of material wealth, an educated citizenry, and not least, "real" rights. The claim of outperforming the capitalist West was, of course, hardly new in Soviet rights-talk; as we have seen, the 1918 Constitution already referred confidently to the "real freedom of expression" and the "real freedom of assembly" guaranteed under Bolshevik rule, in contrast to the fictitious freedoms trumpeted by bourgeois states. Casting the Stalin Constitution as "the most democratic in the world" similarly reflected a sense of competition over which system could boast the most progressive rights regime.

In the post-Stalin era, however, the contest of systems had begun to take on a new quality. Tsarist Russia virtually disappeared as the benchmark for Soviet achievements, leaving the contemporary capitalist West (and occasion-ally communist China) to play that role. Khrushchev's "Thaw" significantly expanded the range of information and cultural goods flowing into the USSR, even as an increasingly educated Soviet population became better positioned to put such goods to its own uses. Traces of this process are visible in letters to Khrushchev's constitutional subcommission, which, as we have seen, demon-strate a new awareness of constitutional rights norms in allied socialist as well as capitalist countries. Khrushchev's successors continued, indeed amplified, this trend, selectively moving the Soviet Union into the orbit of international public law and thereby expanding its citizens' chances of gaining knowledge of the rights norms contained therein. In stark contrast to Stalin's decision to abstain from the UDHR in 1948, in 1966 Brezhnev signed the International Covenants on Civil and Political Rights and on Economic, Social and Cultural Rights. Both Covenants were ratified as legally binding instruments by the Supreme Soviet seven years later – well ahead of the United States. Although scholars have focused on the high watermark of this trend in the 1975 Helsinki Accords (and the subsequent founding of unofficial "Helsinki Watch Groups" in various Soviet cities),[43] the entrance of Soviet rights-talk into an increasingly global conversation – including appeals by Soviet citizens to international rights norms vis-à-vis their own government – began nearly a decade earlier.

A combination of domestic and international factors facilitated this development. In the wake of Khrushchev's historic denunciation of his predecessor at the Twentieth Party Congress in 1956, the "cult of personality" (*kul't lichnosti*, also translatable as "cult of the person" or "cult of the individual," thereby emphasizing Stalin's sins against the collective) had become the obligatory explanation for nearly everything that had gone bad during Stalin's reign. And yet in the later years of the Thaw, Soviet jurists began producing a spate of works devoted precisely to articulating the "rights of the person" (*prava lichnosti*) within the socialist collective. The concept of *lichnost'* – the human personality or self – had a long pedigree in the Russian revolutionary lexicon, reaching back to the nineteenth-century intelligentsia and its devotion to "consciousness," the "developed personality," itself a legacy of German Romanticism's ideal of self-perfection and wholeness.[44] *Homo sovieticus*'s subsequent debt to Nietzsche's *Übermensch* found its most extreme expression in Stalin's personality cult and the officially sponsored mini-cults of "spectacular individuals," select Soviet workers celebrated for their heroic overfulfillment of labor norms. The idea that socialism fosters a superior version of the human personality survived Khrushchev's indictment of the Stalin cult fully intact. Indeed, what stands out in the 1961 Moral Code of the Builder of Communism is its emphasis on the elevated *personal* qualities of the individuals who were making and would in turn be made by the communist society of the future.

One way to understand the work of Soviet legal scholars in the 1960s, therefore, is as an attempt to domesticate and democratize the heroic Stalin-era version of the "Soviet person" by attending to his or her status as a duties- and rights-bearing subject within the socialist collective. To be sure, this project was fraught with unresolved tensions stemming from the lingering antinomianism of Soviet social thought – the conviction that morally perfected

43 Daniel Thomas, *The Helsinki Effect: International Norms, Human Rights, and the Demise of Communism* (Princeton, 2001).
44 Oleg Kharkhordin, *The Collective and the Individual in Russia* (Berkeley, 1999), 184–200.

individuals in a society free of exploitation should have no need for a formal
system of rights and duties. But it drew strength from the official insistence
on "socialist legality" as the antidote to Stalin's personality cult, and more
broadly from the Soviet leadership's desire to use law rather than terror as the
preferred instrument of social control.

Along with these indigenous factors, the rise of a Soviet rhetoric of "rights
of the person" owed something to Moscow's evolving role in an increasingly
dense network of international covenants and public law. Whatever its pretensions as the avant-garde of "real" rights, the USSR's participation in that network necessarily exposed it to a language of rights that had already decisively
shifted its attention from the group to the individual.[45] The lines of influence
within the network, of course, were hardly one-way: Even as the Soviet Union
found itself operating within an expanding rhetorical force field of individuated
"human" rights, it successfully secured the inclusion of collective economic
and social rights in major postwar covenants. For our purposes, however, the
key process was the subtle adaptation of international human rights norms to
the Soviet setting in the form of what might be called "Soviet personalism."
The encounter between an indigenous striving for the "developed personality"
and an emerging international human rights regime reached its height in the
early 1970s, a period in which use of the term "human rights" in international
discourse skyrocketed.[46]

Not surprisingly, given the Cold War context, a good deal of that discourse was directed against the Soviet Union and its persecution of dissidents. These were the years of the vilification of Andrei Sakharov by
the Soviet press (1973), the publication of Aleksandr Solzhenitsyn's *Gulag
Archipelago* and his expulsion from the USSR (1973–1974), and the arrest
of numerous activists associated with the *samizdat* journal *Chronicle of
Current Events* (1972–1974), whose masthead reproduced Article 19 of the
UDHR, on the right to freedom of expression and exchange of information.
In 1974, the U.S. Congress passed the Jackson-Vanik Amendment, making
observance of the right to emigrate a requirement for countries with non-
market economies that wished to secure favorable trade agreements with
the United States. Responding to what he called the West's "noisy campaign," Brezhnev assured his countrymen that "there is no reason why we
should walk away from a serious conversation about human rights."[47] A
leading Soviet jurist, Vladimir Kudriavtsev, put it more bluntly: "There are
no human rights in general":

---

[45] Mark Mazower, "The Strange Triumph of Human Rights, 1933–1950," *Historical Journal*,
47 (2004), 379–398.
[46] My thanks to Samuel Moyn for sharing unpublished data on the incidence of the term "human
rights" in the *New York Times* and the *Times* of London from 1785 to 2000.
[47] "Sovetskaia sotsialisticheskaia demokratiia i lichnost'," *Sovetskoe gosudarstvo i pravo*, 6
(1974), 4; G. V. Mal'tsev, "Sotsial'naia spravedlivost' i prava cheloveka v sotsialisticheskom
obshchestve," *Sovetskoe gosudarstvo i pravo*, 11 (1974), 10.

In the ideological struggle against the bourgeois notion of democracy, liberty, and human rights, it is necessary to bear in mind that an anticommunist position is often based on an idealist view of the origin of human rights, which are alleged to be inherent in man by virtue of his biological nature. Denying the social nature of any and all rights and duties, bourgeois ideologists attempt to present human rights as some philosophical substance independent of the social and political essence of a social system and of the state, and attempt to present duties, by contrast, as something foreign to the individual and imposed on him by society. This is the origin ... of anarchist declarations about the universal rights of the individual, allegedly knowing no state boundaries.[48]

The only "scientific approach," insisted Kudriavtsev, is the Marxist one, which recognizes human rights as socially constructed. "Our society," he concluded, "regards human rights not merely as a subjective legal category designed to ensure the personal interests of citizens. They serve the harmonious development of the personality and of society as a whole."

Human rights, in this vision, are to be understood less as guardians of a preexisting, autonomous human dignity than as catalysts of a more perfect, socially embedded human personality in the future. As the Institute of State and Law (part of the Soviet Academy of Sciences) put it in 1974,

Socialism has created conditions and stimuli which have brought to life a new type of person, a new consciousness and human behavior, a new, Soviet way of life. Its essence lies in relations of genuine collectivism.... In the society of developed socialism, ever greater significance is attached to the problem of the formation of the human being in correspondence with the ideals of the personality in a communist society. A characteristic feature [of this process] is the strengthening of the juridical bases of the development of the personality.[49]

Though not unrelated to the project of fashioning a "socialism with a human face" (a face, that is, other than Stalin's), "rights of the person" were not primarily about protecting citizens from neo-Stalinist terror and state lawlessness. In fact, it is difficult to discern precisely what the "juridical bases of the development of the personality" were supposed to be. For insofar as late Soviet personalism drew on the earlier quest for a higher form of moral consciousness, it seems to have remained trapped in the assumption that that consciousness would ultimately render law unnecessary. Soviet personalism's primary *practical* function, therefore, was to serve as a socialist counterweight to what one might call the "cult of the individual" in Western-style human rights.

The Last "All-People's Discussion"

It fell to Leonid Brezhnev to preside over the creation of a constitution for "developed socialism." Published in draft form in June 1977, the "Brezhnev

---

[48] V. Kudriavtsev, "Prava cheloveka i ideologicheskaia bor'ba," *Sotsialisticheskaia zakonnost'*, 3 (1974).
[49] "Sovetskaia sotsialisticheskaia demokratiia i lichnost'," 4.

Constitution" was presented to the Soviet people in the midst of escalating criticism of the USSR's human rights record by newly elected U.S. president Jimmy
Carter. Personalist language figured prominently in the draft text: Section
Two, containing the main articles on rights and duties, bore the title "The
State and the Person [*lichnost'*]." The Constitution repeatedly referred to the
"all-around development of the person" as one of the historic achievements of
socialist society.[50] Only once did the term "human rights" (*prava cheloveka*)
appear, and tellingly, it was in the section on the USSR's relations with foreign
states, which were to be based on (among other things) "noninterference in
internal affairs" and "respect for human rights and fundamental freedoms."
The Soviet Union thus reserved for itself a person-centered lexicon of rights
even as it pledged to fulfill "obligations arising from ... norms of international
law and from international treaties concluded by the USSR."[51]

As regards specific rights and duties, the differences between the Brezhnev
Constitution and its Stalinist predecessor were modest. The 1977 text added
rights to housing and to "the utilization of the achievements of culture." The
right to work expanded to include the freedom to choose one's profession
and employment, provided the choice was consistent with society's needs. The
right to free speech – "in conformity with the aims of communist construction" – now included "freedom of scientific, technical, and artistic creativity."
Even more explicitly than in 1936, the Brezhnev Constitution emphasized the
"inseparability" of the exercise of rights from the performance of duties. And
the list of constitutionally enshrined duties now included a host of personal
qualities reminiscent of the "Moral Code of the Builder of Communism": to
"bear with dignity the lofty title of citizen of the USSR," to perform "conscientious work," to be "intolerant of antisocial acts," "to be concerned about
the upbringing of children."[52]

The "all-people's discussion" of the draft Constitution, held between June
and October of 1977, dwarfed its 1936 predecessor. According to official
sources, some 140 million Soviet citizens – over 80 percent of the adult population – took part, if only in the form of ritual affirmation of the draft text
at obligatory meetings held in workplaces and residential blocs. Newspapers
received millions of letters regarding the new Constitution and filled their
pages with thousands of carefully selected examples.[53] Although the published
discussion consisted overwhelmingly of affirmative statements, letters to
newspapers and to the drafting commission included some 400,000 proposals
for alterations of the draft text. Among the roughly 3,500 published proposals, the single largest category addressed the duty to perform "conscientious
work" (Article 60), urging that it be made more rigorous by specifying the

---

[50] See the Preamble and Article 20.
[51] Article 29.
[52] Articles 44–47 and 59–67.
[53] Eberhard Schneider, "The Discussion of the New All-Union Constitution in the USSR,"
Soviet Studies, 31 (1979), 525; Vladimir Shlapentokh, *Public and Private Life of the Soviet
People: Changing Values in Post-Stalin Russia* (New York, 1989), 100.

need for greater initiative, thrifty use of equipment and materials, and punishment of violations of labor discipline. The second largest group of proposals concerned the upbringing of children (Article 66) and included demands that the Constitution mandate ethical values such as love of work, honesty, patriotism, active participation in the building of communism, and respect for one's elders.[54]

The final text of the 1977 Constitution did indeed incorporate amendments reflecting citizens' proposals on both of the aforementioned topics.[55] Needless to say, neither these nor the other proposals published in the Soviet press constitute a representative sample of the larger corpus of citizens' comments. Scholarly research on the latter has barely begun. The dramatic expansion during the Brezhnev era of alternative technologies for exchanging information and opinions, however, makes it possible to glimpse at least a portion of that larger corpus. Techniques of *samizdat* ("self-publishing" via typewriter, carbon copying, and informal networks of distribution) and *tamizdat* ("over there publishing," smuggling texts for publication abroad and/or transmission back to the USSR via the Voice of America, BBC, and other shortwave radio broadcasts) allowed rights-talk blocked from the Soviet mass media to find substantial numbers of readers and listeners across the Soviet Union. This sampling too cannot be taken to represent public opinion writ large. But it provides evidence for a number of fundamental departures from received ways of talking about rights in the Soviet setting, and for the unanticipated impact of the USSR's participation in an increasingly global human rights conversation.

Dissatisfied with the overwhelmingly celebratory character of the published portion of the "all-people's discussion," a group of Soviet citizens took it upon themselves to make public a selection of letters passed over by the official press. The resulting counter-discussion appeared in a series of *samizdat* bulletins under the title "Around the Draft Constitution of the USSR," edited by the Soviet army general-turned-dissident Petr Grigorenko and the journalist Raisa Lert (both former party members). Appearing in the summer and fall of 1977, parallel to the "all-people's discussion," the bulletins self-consciously abstained from representing a single point of view. "The only thing that brings these texts together," noted the editors, "is the impossibility of publishing genuinely critical viewpoints on the draft constitution in the Soviet press."[56]

[54] Schneider, "The Discussion of the New All-Union Constitution," 528–529.
[55] Unger, *Constitutional Development in the USSR*, 245.
[56] "Vokrug proekta konstitutsii SSSR" (henceforth VPK), no. 1, 1.1; samizdat copy from the archive of the Memorial Society in Moscow (henceforth Memorial-M), f. 101 (L. Alekseeva). VPK was the main but not the only forum in which critical reactions to the draft Constitution appeared. A scathing letter from political prisoners in the Mordovian labor camp reached Radio Free Europe: see "Otkrytoe pis'mo L. I. Brezhnevu. Koe-chto o proekte Konstitutsii SSSR," *Materialy samizdata*, 1/78 (1977), AC#3089. Émigré dissidents, too, published critical reviews; see, for example, *A Chronicle of Human Rights in the USSR*, vols. 26–28 (April–Dec. 1977).

Indeed, within its pages one finds Christians, neo-Leninists, rights activists (*pravozashchitniki*), and others. Taken together, however, their letters demonstrate that certain modes of talking about rights in the Soviet setting – modes hitherto largely shared by state and society – had begun to lose their near-monopoly on legal consciousness.

One of the striking elements of the *samizdat* discussion is the novel uses to which it put the received Soviet concept of the "person" (*lichnost'*). A letter from twelve prominent dissidents, for instance, complained that the draft Constitution "essentially does not even guarantee the *human right to personhood*":

All civil rights are perceived through the prism of the state's functions, while the individual [is perceived] solely as a subject of the state. From this stem the countless limiting clauses whose purpose is to prevent the person, God forbid, from considering himself independent of the state. All those [phrases such as] "should not bring harm to the interests of society and the state" (Article 39), "consistent with the goals of communist construction" (Articles 47 and 51), "consistent with the interests of the toilers and the goals of strengthening the socialist structure," etc. – all this aims at one thing: that someone (the state, the party) standing above the person will resolve all moral, political, social problems on his behalf, will decide what is good and what is bad, what is useful and what is harmful.[57]

Rights and duties, the letter went on to argue, should be completely uncoupled, and responsibility for identifying duties transferred from the Constitution to the conscience of the individual person. Other contributors went further, asserting not just the independence of the "rights of the person" from state interests, but the inescapable tensions between the two.[58] Evgenii Shapoval, a graduate student in mathematical physics, wrote that human rights derived from the consciousness of "the inherent dignity of the person," which required nothing more than "membership in the human race. States can therefore recognize or not recognize them ... but human rights will nonetheless exist as long as humankind exists."[59]

In the *samizdat* discussion, the human personality is no longer a work in progress, to be molded to perfection under the party's guidance. Instead, it appears as a constant, a moral fixture around which rights form a protective fence against incursions by state power. The idea that rights should continually adapt to changes in economy and society was thereby cast in doubt. As one letter noted, during the three centuries since the English Parliament's 1688 Declaration of Rights, "England exited from feudalism, experienced the industrial revolution, was transformed into a global colonial empire which then collapsed before our eyes – and the Declaration of Rights continues to serve as the basis of English political and social life."[60]

[57] VPK no. 1, l. 8. Emphasis in original.
[58] VPK no. 2, l. 6, in Memorial-M f. 175, op. 20.
[59] VPK no. 4, l. 20, in Memorial-M f. 175, op. 20.
[60] VPK no. 1, l. 2.

Appeals to other countries' rights norms, of course, had antecedents in the aborted constitutional discussion under Khrushchev. More frequently, however – and more potently – *samizdat* contributors to the 1977 conversation invoked international human rights agreements such as the UDHR, the conventions of the International Organization of Labor (ILO), the 1966 UN rights covenants, and the Helsinki Accords. Unlike foreign constitutions, these agreements (apart from the UDHR) had been ratified by Moscow. Moreover, contributors cited international human rights covenants not in the context of the USSR's foreign relations (as the Brezhnev Constitution did) but with the goal of transforming Soviet domestic law. The attorney Sofiia Kalistratova, for example, noted that the duty of work enshrined in the Soviet Constitution contradicted the ILO ban on forced labor, while a group of Christians argued that unequal rights of expression for atheists and "believers" in the Soviet Union violated the nondiscrimination clauses in the 1966 UN rights covenants.[61]

As bold as such departures from standard Soviet rights-talk were, they should not obscure the *samizdat* letters' tacit support for the draft Constitution's dense web of economic and social rights, the system of entitlements dating back to the Stalin era. Nor did the *samizdat* debate question the state's duty to provide material prerequisites for the realization of civil and political rights, in the form of state-subsidized use of meeting spaces, the press, radio, and television. What is new, however, is the refusal to regard economic and social rights as necessarily linked to a particular ideological project. In their critiques of the draft Constitution's pronouncement that "the highest goal of the Soviet state is the construction of a classless communist society," *samizdat* letter writers insisted, as one put it, that "this is not a constitutional thesis. To force people to participate in the construction of an ideological structure is inconsistent with democracy." For religious believers, such a goal (including the explicit endorsement of atheism) was incompatible with true freedom of conscience.[62] Secularists, too, insisted that rights be detached from the endorsement of the specific moral values enshrined in the draft Constitution. "[Such] moralizing misses the mark," wrote one; "the law should proceed from firm ethical principles but not busy itself with moral preaching, which rarely leads to the desired results. Only an ethical example can foster the ethical progress of society as a whole and of individual people."[63] Thus whatever their point of departure, participants in the *samizdat* discussion agreed on one thing: The Soviet state should abandon its paternalism while continuing to provide its citizens the full range of material entitlements.

---

[61] VPK no. 1, l. 13; VPK no. 2, ll. 12–13. Article 52 of the draft constitution granted freedom of conscience to all, but the right to "propagandize" to atheists alone. It mandated the separation of church and state, but also church and school, thereby effectively banning religious education for children.

[62] VPK no. 1, ll. 3 and 24.

[63] VPK no. 4, l. 17.

Conclusion

Those who proceed from the liberal notion of rights as moral "trumps," part of a matrix of constraints on state and other forms of power, may be tempted to regard "rights" in the Soviet context simply as an anachronism, a rhetorical "leftover of capitalism."[64] This is roughly the stance taken by figures such as the philosopher Leszek Kołakowski and the legal scholar Georg Brunner: "The existence of fundamental rights cannot be conceptually reconciled with the ideology of Marxism-Leninism in its Soviet form."[65] Unabashed hostility to rights as "bourgeois fictions" was indeed characteristic of early Soviet thought, and as we have seen, the utopian vision of the withering away of the law never entirely vanished from the Soviet horizon. Yet rights became an enduring part of the Soviet legal lexicon, developing their own distinct idioms and patterns of change over time. However persuasive they may be, arguments about the ultimate incompatibility of Marxism-Leninism and human (or other) rights fail to register, let alone account for, this phenomenon. Rather than dismiss Soviet rights-talk as a fiction or public relations exercise or symptom of false consciousness, I have tried to trace its evolving role within the Soviet project of building a new kind of society and a new kind of person, a project that helped define, in ways both intended and unforeseen, the history of human rights in the twentieth century.

Let us review the terrain we have covered. Rights began their career in the USSR as techniques for inverting the pre-revolutionary social hierarchy. Consistent with the neo-corporatist policies of the young Soviet state, the granting and denial of rights to different population groups served as an undisguised political instrument. Just as old regimes had enjoyed the prerogative of selectively bestowing privileges, rights were understood in the Soviet context as originating with the state, whose job it was to determine their form and content as positive law. The most innovative aspects of the Soviet approach to rights were already in place by the 1930s: the commitment to a comprehensive program of material welfare expressed in the same constitutional idiom used to grant the traditional rights of speech, the press, assembly, and conscience, and the reinterpretation of those traditional rights as incomplete unless buttressed by material assistance from the state. Thus the Cold War cliché, according to which the capitalist West championed civil and political rights while the socialist East championed social and economic rights, misses the dialectic between these two "generations" of rights *within* the socialist camp.

Neither of these innovations ever lost its centrality in Soviet rights discourse. What did change was the neo-corporative approach to rights. Already in the 1930s, well ahead of the population it ruled, the Soviet state began to move away from a hierarchical rights regime toward one based on universal duties

---

[64] Ronald Dworkin, *Taking Rights Seriously* (Cambridge, 1978), 184–205.
[65] Georg Brunner, *Die Grundrechte im Sowjetsystem* (Cologne, 1963), 115. See also Kołakowski, "Marxism and Human Rights," *Daedalus*, 112 (1983), 81–92.

of citizenship. To be sure, this process was never completed – unequal urban and rural residential privileges as well as privileges associated with the titular nationalities of the various Soviet republics, for example, remained in force. But by the 1960s, as the analysis of letters to Khrushchev's constitutional sub-commission suggests, the Soviet population had largely caught up with the state's shift away from neo-corporatism. Rights now flowed more from the performance of duties (above all, labor) than from specific social identities. They were in effect part of a system of exchange between citizens and the state. At the risk of being overly schematic, one might say that, whereas in Anglo-American discourse, private property had served as prototype – and sometimes prerequisite – for "rights" as such (including the right to vote), and rights were conceived as a kind of "property" of their bearers, in Soviet rights-talk, labor performed an analogous function. Labor was the gateway to other rights and the linchpin of the rights/duties nexus. On this issue, official and vernacular rights-talk in the post-Stalin USSR were substantially in sync.

With the fading of neo-corporatism in favor of the "all-people's state," the ultimate purpose of rights in the post-Stalinist setting became open to reinterpretation. Even as the "cult of personality" became the ubiquitous explanation for Stalin's misdeeds, cultivation of the person – a Soviet personalism devoted to fashioning the *homo sovieticus* – emerged during Khrushchev's "thaw" as a central theme of rights-talk. The fact that the USSR was simultaneously joining a global contest over the substance and meaning of human rights as the dominant moral language of the postwar era only reinforced this trend. Soviet personalism remained highly distinctive, however, anchored in the conviction that "the human" was still in flux, a work in progress pending the USSR's arrival at the final stage of history. The purpose of rights (and duties) was to foster that progress, rather than to guard some a priori metaphysical dignity allegedly inherent in the current, imperfect version of the human. Socialism itself, having liberated the human personality from the degradation of market forces, was supposed to lead inexorably to a new collective moral sensibility and cognitive style.[66] As the deputy commander of a military construction brigade in Sverdlovsk, A. P. Kopylov, wrote to Khrushchev's constitutional subcommission, a new constitution had to take on three basic tasks: "To create the material-technical basis for communism; to fashion communist social relations; and to raise the new person, combining within himself spiritual

[66] I am indebted here, again, to the work of Thomas Haskell. In a pair of articles on capitalism and the rise of the movement to abolish slavery, Haskell argued that market relations helped shape modern humanitarianism by fostering a shift in the perception of causal connection and hence in the conventions of moral responsibility. See Haskell, "Capitalism and the Origins of the Humanitarian Sensibility," *American Historical Review*, 90 (1985), 339–361, 547–566. My claim is that Soviet rights-talk assumed that the abolition of market relations under socialism would, by itself, foster a genuinely humanitarian sensibility. The difference, of course, is that Haskell's argument represents a retrospective attempt to explain a historical phenomenon, whereas in the Soviet case we are dealing with a theory meant to predict and help bring about a future reality.

richness, moral purity, and physical perfection. The new Constitution of the USSR will be called upon to guarantee juridicially the fulfillment of these three tasks, which are inseparable, mutually constitutive, and to be fulfilled simultaneously."[67]

"Human" rights were thus something for the future – if indeed they would be necessary at all. Rejecting the notion of natural, inalienable rights as surely as it dismissed the idea of natural law, Soviet legal positivism employed rights as manmade means for transforming the human personality and human society in the march to communism. Not rights but the "radiant future" was the card that trumped all else. Yet the "radiant future" itself depended on something like natural law. Not the static law of human moral worth, but a different kind of non-manmade law, the scientific laws of historical change (*zakonomernosti* or *Gesetzmäßigkeiten*) that guaranteed that future. When natural law smuggled its way into Soviet jurisprudence, it did so under the guise not of rights, but of history.

By the 1970s – the most stable, peaceful, and prosperous decade in Soviet history – the reservoir of rights rhetoric shared by state and society began to show signs of leakage as well as contamination from external sources. Although in general the Soviet state, prior to the Second World War, displayed greater dynamism and innovation in its rights-talk than did the Soviet population at large, by the 1970s those roles were reversed – at least as regards the vocal minority of citizens who took part in the production and consumption of *samizdat*. For all that the officially sanctioned "rights of the person" drew on the indigenous tradition of Soviet personalism, by the 1970s they appear to have served primarily as a defense against criticisms from abroad in the name of human rights. By contrast, *samizdat* sources tended to invoke "rights of the person" as immunities, techniques for constraining the Soviet state, and appealed to international rights covenants for similar purposes. "In the last quarter of the twentieth century," wrote one contributor to the unofficial constitutional conversation in 1977, "the problem of human rights has acquired universal significance, not as a consequence of 'political intrigues,' but for profound historical reasons, conditioned by general laws of development of political and economic systems and the evolution of all mankind."[68] Vaguely Marxist in its appeal to the natural laws of history, this pronouncement nonetheless captured the *samizdat* embrace of the globalization of human rights.

---

[67] RGANI f. 5, op. 30, d. 385, l. 102. The entire passage is a pastiche of phrases adapted from the 1961 Communist Party Program.
[68] VPK no. 4, l. 14.

9

Charter 77 and the Roma

Human Rights and Dissent in Socialist Czechoslovakia

Celia Donert

In November 1990 thirty-five heads of state gathered in Paris to sign the "Charter for a New Europe," a declaration that celebrated the triumph of democracy and human rights after forty years of communist rule in Eastern Europe. The Conference on Security and Cooperation in Europe, which produced the Paris Charter, has been credited with supplying a "normative framework conducive to the peaceful demise of Communism."[1] Despite its celebratory tone, the Charter also warned of dangers ahead for the region's most vulnerable groups, condemning "totalitarianism, racial and ethnic hatred, anti-Semitism, xenophobia and discrimination against anyone as well as persecution on religious and ideological grounds," while recognizing the "particular problems of Roma (Gypsies)."[2] References to Roma or anti-Semitism were unprecedented in such an international declaration. Only months after the dramatic revolutions that swept away the Eastern European communist regimes in 1989, the Paris Charter was viewed with immense optimism by observers at the time as a potential constitution for a newly democratic Europe, and the CSCE suddenly became the "sexiest acronym in international diplomacy."[3]

The Paris Charter linked democracy, human rights, and conflict prevention in post-communist Europe to the protection of minorities, devoting more than a dozen paragraphs to minority rights for the first time in an international

I would like to thank Pavel Kolář, Michal Kopeček, Małgorzata Mazurek, Michal Pullmann, and the other members of the research group Sozialistische Diktatur als Sinnwelt (Institute for Contemporary History, Prague/Center for Contemporary History, Potsdam) for their comments on earlier drafts of this chapter.

[1] Andreas Wenger and Vojtech Mastny, "New Perspectives on the Origins of the CSCE Process," in Andreas Wenger et al. (eds.), *Origins of the European Security System: The Helsinki Process Revisited, 1965–75* (London, 2008), 3.

[2] Conference on Security and Cooperation in Europe, *Charter of Paris for a New Europe* (Paris, 1990).

[3] Cited in William Korey, "Minority Rights after Helsinki," *Ethics and International Affairs*, 8 (1994), 119–139, here 119.

statement since the Second World War.[4] The reappearance of minority rights in declarations by international institutions, such as the CSCE, UN, and Council of Europe, at the same time as the "rights revolutions" that saw the fundamental refashioning of rights in post-communist countries, is commonly attributed to the resurgence of ethnic nationalism that followed the collapse of the socialist dictatorships in Eastern Europe. This chapter proposes a different argument and draws on previously inaccessible archives to show how "rights-talk" – including the rights of individuals and minorities – was used by a variety of social actors during the last two decades of socialist rule. The chapter focuses on debates about the human rights of Roma in Czechoslovakia among dissidents, social workers, Romani activists, Communist Party officials, high-level civil servants, and international human rights organizations during the era of "normalization," from the defeat of the Prague Spring to the Velvet Revolution of 1989. By reconstructing these debates, this chapter seeks to understand how the discourse of individual human rights and nondiscrimination, which formed the core of the international human rights regime established after the Second World War, was confronted by a revived emphasis on minority rights and the role of the interventionist state in guaranteeing their implementation. In so doing, it also hopes to challenge triumphalist historical accounts that view the 1989 revolutions as a victory for liberal human rights over the discredited concept of "socialist rights."

Defenders of Rights: Charter 77 and the Roma in Socialist Czechoslovakia

In December 1978, the dissident Charter 77 movement released an essay signed by Václav Havel and the Protestant philosopher Ladislav Hejdánek about violations of the human rights of Roma (Gypsies) in socialist Czechoslovakia, which was circulated to party and state authorities as well as foreign print and broadcast media.[5] Charter 77 appealed to the Universal Declaration of Human Rights, the UN International Covenants, and domestic Czechoslovak law to denounce the widespread discrimination against Roma, whom it described as the most disenfranchised of all citizens of the republic. The essay exemplified the mission of Charter 77 to defend the "civil and human rights" of citizens and the principle of legality against politically motivated abuses by the communist regime.[6] Established in January 1977 by a group of

---

[4] Thomas Buergenthal, "The Copenhagen CSCE Meeting: A New Public Order for Europe," *Human Rights Law Journal*, 11 (1990), 20.

[5] "Dokument o postavení romských spoluobčanů předložený jako podklad veřejné diskusi. Dokument č. 23," in Blanka Císařovská and Vilém Prečan (eds.), *Charta 77: Dokumenty 1977–1989* (Prague, 2007), 198–206.

[6] Markéta Devátá, Jiří Suk, Oldřich Tůma (eds.), *Charta 77. Od obhajoby lidských práv k demokratické revoluci, 1977–1989* (Prague, 2007); Petr Blažek (ed.), *Tentokrát to bouchne: edice dokumentů k organizaci a ohlasům kampaně proti signatářům Charty 77 (leden–únor 1977)* (Prague, 2007); H. Gordon Skilling, *Charter 77 and Human Rights in Czechoslovakia* (London, 1981); Vladimir Kusin, *From Dubcek to Charter 77: A Study of "Normalization" in Czechoslovakia, 1968–1978* (Edinburgh, 1978).

Czechoslovak citizens who defined themselves as a "free, informal, and open" association of people holding various convictions, beliefs, and professions, the Charter was led by prominent political and cultural figures, including the philosopher Jan Patočka, playwright Václav Havel, and former Foreign Minister Jiří Hájek.[7] It was inspired by the criminal prosecution of a rock group called The Plastic People of the Universe, the Czechoslovak regime's signing of the Helsinki Final Act in 1975, and its subsequent ratification of the UN international human rights covenants. Unlike civil disobedience campaigns based on public defiance of official laws or regulations and thus presupposing the existence of a state governed by the rule of law, Benjamin Nathans has remarked, dissidents in socialist states insisted on practices formally guaranteed by law but frequently disregarded for political reasons.[8]

Human rights, the historian Milan Otáhal has written, replaced socialism as a unifying platform for the Czechoslovak opposition after the defeat of the Prague Spring, the most daring attempt by an Eastern bloc communist party to democratize socialism during the Cold War, which had provoked Soviet intervention and a massive invasion of Warsaw Pact troops in August 1968.[9] The invasion had been followed by mass demonstrations, but the new Communist Party leadership acted swiftly to "normalize" political and social life in Czechoslovakia. Most oppositional or dissenting groups disappeared within a couple of years as a result of far-reaching purges of reform communists from the KSČ and public life, as well as a mood of resignation that spread quickly among the general public.[10] In contrast to the relative openness of Kádár's Hungary, or the mass Solidarity movement that emerged in Poland during the late 1970s, Czechoslovakia was ruled by a conservative leadership that maintained its grip on power by political repression, combined with social and economic policies that aimed to raise living standards and depoliticize society by encouraging a retreat into the private sphere of home and family.[11] To a greater extent than in any other socialist state, the defense of human rights became a unifying program for the democratic opposition in Czechoslovakia during the last fifteen years of communist rule in Eastern Europe.[12]

---

7 "Základní (konstitutivní) Prohlášení Charty 77 o příčinách vzniku, smyslu a cílech Charty a metodách jejího působení," in Císařovská and Prečan (eds.), *Charta 77*, 1–5.

8 Benjamin Nathans, "The Dictatorship of Reason: Alexander Vol'pin and the Idea of Rights under 'Developed Socialism,'" *Slavic Review*, 66 (2007), 630–663.

9 Milan Otáhal, "Programová orientace disentu 1969–1989," in Petr Blažek (ed.), *Opozice a odpor proti komunistickému režimu v Československu 1968–1989* (Prague, 2005), 25–40.

10 Milan Otáhal, *Normalizace 1969–1989: Příspěvek ke stavu bádání* (Prague, 2002).

11 Milan Šimečka, *Obnovení pořádku: příspěvek k typologii reálného socialismu* (Cologne, 1979); Oldřich Tůma and Tomáš Vilímek, *Pět studií k dějinám české společnosti po roce 1945* (Prague, 2008).

12 Tomáš Vilímek, "Vnímání helsinského procesu v ČSSR a NDR ze strany moci, opozice a obyvatelstva," in Zdeněk Karník and Michal Kopeček (eds.), *Bolševismus, komunismus a radikální socialismus v Československu* (Prague, 2005), 275–296.

The Charter essay on the Roma was part of a series of documents by dissidents on politically sensitive social problems, including nuclear energy, prison
conditions, censorship, freedom to travel abroad, discrimination in education,
violations of social rights, and freedom of religion. These documents were
meant to provoke public discussion about problems that "normalization" was
failing to solve, despite the regime's success in raising living standards and levels of personal consumption, and thus to rouse society from the state of moral
decay that – the dissidents believed – was deliberately cultivated by the regime
in order to maintain control over the population.[13] Evidence from previously
inaccessible archives suggests, however, that Czechoslovak society was not
necessarily the passive, apolitical monolith depicted in dissident writings.[14]
Research conducted by the government's polling agency showed that a significant proportion of Czechoslovak citizens were listening to Western radio
or watching television from Austria or West Germany. In 1978, one-quarter
of respondents claimed to listen regularly to Western radio, especially for the
news, a figure that rose to over 40 percent of university graduates by 1982.
By the early 1980s, the poll takers concluded from their research that only
one-fifth of the population was untouched by foreign reporting.[15] "In these
reports," writes Kieran Williams, "we encounter a nation outwardly preoccupied with material pursuits and light entertainment, but on closer inspection
we can find the faint pulse of a civic consciousness."[16]

The claims made by the Charter essay were largely based in fact, as the
document was drafted by activists who had been involved with the Roma in
various official and semi-official capacities for many years. The plight of the
Roma was presented as symptomatic of economic deterioration, bureaucratic
centralism, a decline in moral values among the public, and the gap between
official ideology and everyday life. Thus the essay drew a parallel between
anti-Gypsy sentiment among state and society and the older phenomenon
of anti-Semitism, pointing to a whole range of discriminatory measures
ranging from mass sedentarization campaigns aimed at itinerant Roma in
the 1950s, planned resettlement of rural Roma, and denial of their cultural
and linguistic rights, to the forcible removal of Romani children from their
parents and coercive sterilization of Romani women as part of a "planned
administrative policy." The regime's efforts to eradicate the Roma minority through such assimilationist measures, Charter 77 claimed, would soon
render Czechoslovakia vulnerable to charges of genocide (Czech: *genocida*).

---

[13] Charter Document No. 21: "Mission and Activities of Charter 77" (presented by Charter
spokesmen Dr. Ladislav Hejdánek, Marta Kubisová, Dr. Jaroslav Sabata), 19 October 1978.
[14] The classic description is Václav Havel, "The Power of the Powerless," in John Keane (ed.),
The Power of the Powerless: Citizens against the State in Central-Eastern Europe (Armonk,
N.Y., 1985).
[15] Kieran Williams, "The Prague Spring: From Elite Liberalisation to Mass Movement,"
in Kevin McDermott and Matthew Stibbe (eds.), *Revolution and Resistance in Eastern
Europe: Challenges to Communist Rule* (Oxford, 2006), 101–117.
[16] Ibid., 110.

As the Roma were a small but visible minority in all the socialist states, numbering more than several million in total, the Charter essay had a relevance beyond the borders of Czechoslovakia.[17] For this reason the essay was a particular source of irritation for the Czechoslovak regime, which viewed itself as the vanguard of socialism in Eastern Europe and had prided itself on "solving the Gypsy Question" more effectively than either the other socialist states or the capitalist countries.[18] Despite its federal structure and a 1968 law guaranteeing the rights of national minorities, Czechoslovakia firmly refused to grant minority rights to the Gypsies. During the Prague Spring, Romani activists had been given permission to establish Associations of Gypsies-Roma within the National Front, but with the onset of "normalization" these Associations were closed down on the grounds that they were promoting nationalism and embezzling state funds. Until 1989, the Roma were officially defined as an ethnic group living a "backwards" way of life who should be integrated into socialist society by obligatory employment and policies designed to "raise their cultural level."[19] Contemporary ambivalence about whether the Roma constituted an ethnic nation was reflected in the Charter essay, which referred to "Gypsies-Roma" (*Cikáni-Romové*), thus combining the pejorative label "Gypsy" with the ethnonym "Rom" in a term that sounds as awkward in Czech as it does in English. By the 1970s the significance of the term *Roma* was increasing as a result of the emerging Romani nationalist movement, discussed in more detail below, which sought to forge a single political nation from the numerous groups of European Gypsies – including German Sinti, French Manouche, Spanish Cale, Finnish Kale, British Romanichals and Gypsies, Wallachian Lovara and Kalderaš, Slovak Servika, and Hungarian Ungrika Roma.[20]

The Roma did not meet the criteria for recognition as a nation according to Marxist-Leninist nationality policy – originally laid out by Stalin – which stipulated that a common territory, along with a common language, economic life, and culture, were the prerequisites of a national community.[21]

---

[17] Accurate statistics on the size of Roma populations are impossible to find. Because Roma were not given the opportunity to self-identify in censuses, any figures that do exist were collected by government officials or census takers. Nearly 290,000 people were registered as "Gypsies" in the 1980 Czechoslovak census, or 3 percent of the population, although this figure was much higher in Slovakia where two-thirds of all Roma lived. See *Zprávy a rozbory 1983. Cikánské obyvatelstvo a jeho bydlení podle údajů sčítání lidu, domů a bytů 1980 (definitiví výsledky)*, cited in Anna Jurová, *Dokumenty – Rómska problematika 1945–1967* (Prague, 1996), 1015.

[18] Jaroslav Sus, *Cikánská otázka v ČSSR* (Prague, 1961).

[19] National Archives Prague (NA Prague) f. 02/2, sv. 172, a.j. 234, bod. 7. Politické byro Ústředního výboru KSČ, *Usnesení ÚV KSČ o práci mezi cikánským obyvatelstvem v ČSR* (J. Hendrych), 26 March 1958.

[20] For a deconstruction of debates about Gypsy ethnicity, see Wim Willems, *In Search of the True Gypsy: From Enlightenment to Final Solution* (London, 1997); also Alaina Lemon, *Between Two Fires: Gypsy Performance and Romani Memory from Pushkin to Post-Socialism* (Durham, 2000).

[21] Jan Šindelka, *Národnostní politika v ČSSR* (Prague, 1975).

Despite this, some socialist states were more willing than Czechoslovakia to
grant minority rights to the Roma, such as the freedom to establish associations, publish magazines, and support Romani language and culture. The
most expansive in this regard were Hungary and Yugoslavia: A Hungarian
National Gypsy Council was set up in 1974, and Yugoslavia recognized the
Gypsies as a national minority in 1981.[22] Although Hungary's policy toward
its national minorities was largely motivated by concern for the large numbers
of ethnic Hungarians living outside the borders of the Hungarian state, the
federal Yugoslav state used nationality policies to maintain peace, stability,
and legitimacy among its constituent parts. By contrast, strongly nationalizing
states such as Romania and Bulgaria viewed assimilation as the best means
of integrating Roma into socialist society. Previously preoccupied with more
pressing issues of industrialization and modernization, however, Romania did
not launch a specific assimilation policy aimed at Roma until the early 1970s.[23]
In Bulgaria, Roma were often caught up in the violent campaigns directed
against the country's large Muslim minorities.[24] In comparison to these two
countries, however, the Czechoslovak regime had an efficient bureaucracy and
a well-organized political opposition, which goes some way to explaining why
the situation of the Roma could be framed in the language of human rights by
both state and social actors.

How, then, was the Charter 77 essay on the Gypsies-Roma received in
Czechoslovakia and abroad? The vast majority of Czechoslovak Roma were
concentrated in Slovakia, the poorer and less industrialized eastern republic. Many Slovak Roma were living in conditions of dire poverty in remote
rural settlements, and therefore the Slovak state security (ŠtB) immediately
took notice of the Charter essay. Within a few months the ŠtB had inter-
cepted several letters from Slovak Roma addressed to Charter representatives in response to the essay.[25] Other Roma activists approached Charter
signatories Jiří Hájek and Ladislav Hejdánek in person, protesting that the
essay was not critical enough.[26] Radio Free Europe and the BBC broadcast
excerpts from the essay, and it was reported in Western European media such
as *The Observer, Le Monde,* and *Labor Focus on Eastern Europe.*[27] The
U.S. Helsinki Commission, the agency in the U.S. Congress established to
monitor implementation of the Helsinki Accords, included a translation of the

[22] Zoltan Barany, *The East European Gypsies. Regime Change, Marginality and Ethnopolitics*
(Cambridge, 2001).

[23] Viorel Achim, *The Roma in Romanian History* (Budapest, 2004).

[24] R. J. Crampton, *Bulgaria* (Oxford, 2007); on Bulgarian assimilation campaigns see Mary
Neuburger, *The Orient Within: Muslim Minorities and the Negotiation of Nationhood in
Modern Bulgaria* (Ithaca, 2004).

[25] Norbert Kmeť, "Opozícia a hnutie odporu na Slovensku 1968–1989," in Blažek (ed.), *Opozice
a odpor proti komunistickému režimu v Československu 1968–1989,* 41–53.

[26] Císařovská and Prečan (eds.), *Charta 77,* n. 2, 206.

[27] Reports and press cuttings in the Open Society Archives, Budapest, and the Institute of
Contemporary History, Prague (sb. FMV-Ch, sb. RFE). See also *Labour Focus on Eastern
Europe* (March–April 1979).

essay in a collection of Charter 77 documents in 1982, and the first report on the Czechoslovak Roma by Human Rights Watch cited extensively from the Charter 77 document to support its claims about the treatment of the Roma before 1989.[28]

That the Charter essay on the Roma reached a wide international audience itself requires an explanation, given that universal human rights norms and declarations had little to say about the Roma at that time, as a later section of this chapter will show. Foreign interest in human rights violations in Eastern Europe had been aroused after the signing of the Helsinki Final Act in August 1975 launched the Conference on Security and Cooperation in Europe. The CSCE was a multilateral initiative involving thirty-three European states, as well as the United States and Canada, which aimed to facilitate détente by providing a framework for improved international cooperation between East and West, as well as finally reaching a settlement on the political and territorial status quo in Europe after the Second World War.[29] At the instigation of European Community member states participating in the CSCE, an unprecedented reference to human rights was included in the Helsinki Final Act, thus providing dissidents in the socialist bloc with a means of connecting human rights violations – previously viewed in international law as purely internal affairs of state – with the international politics of détente. Numerous commentators have stressed the importance of the human rights dimension of the CSCE in bringing about the demise of communism: "In hindsight," Jack Donnelly has written, "the Helsinki Process can be seen as a chronicle of the gradual demise of the cold war and Soviet-style communism in the face of increasing national and international demands to implement internationally recognized human rights."[30]

The publicity generated by the Charter essay on the Roma was thus related to the burgeoning interest among Western observers in human rights in the Eastern bloc after Helsinki. Western interest in the Charter essay on the Roma, and the revival of "rights-talk" by Eastern European dissidents more generally, was also part of a broader phenomenon of civil society involvement in human rights activism during the late 1960s, that is to say, chiefly

---

[28] "Situation of the Gypsies in Czechoslovakia: Document no. 23," in *Human Rights in Czechoslovakia: The Documents of Charter '77* (Commission on Security and Cooperation in Europe, Washington, D.C., July 1982); Rachel Tritt, *Struggling for Ethnic Identity: Czechoslovakia's Endangered Gypsies* (New York, 1992).

[29] See Daniel C. Thomas, *The Helsinki Effect: International Norms, Human Rights and the Demise of Communism* (Princeton, 2001); William Korey, *The Promises We Keep: Human Rights, the Helsinki Process and American Foreign Policy* (New York, 1993); and most recently, Wenger et al. (eds.), *Origins of the European Security System*.

[30] Jack Donnelly, *International Human Rights*, 2nd ed. (Boulder, 1998); see also Thomas Buergenthal, "The Helsinki Process: Birth of a Human Rights System," in Richard Pierre Claude and Burns H. Weston (eds.), *Human Rights in the World Community: Issues and Action* (Philadelphia, 1992), 256–270; Vojtech Mastny, *Helsinki, Human Rights and European Security: Analysis and Documentation* (Durham, 1986); Arie Bloed and Pieter Van Dijk (eds.), *Essays on Human Rights in the Helsinki Process* (Dordrecht, 1985).

middle-class, Northern, self-mobilized groups that emerged along with the civil rights movement in the United States, student protests, and the women's movement in the West.[31] Human Rights Watch itself was a product of the Helsinki process, having started life as Helsinki Watch before developing into the main rival of Amnesty International in international human rights monitoring.[32] Given the tendency of the Western left at the time to focus on human rights abuses in right-wing and racist regimes, compounded by the disillusionment among Western supporters of reform communism after the failure of the Prague Spring and the shift of interest toward the North-South divide, the language of universal human rights enabled dissidents in the socialist dictatorships in the Eastern bloc once again to gain a hearing in the West.[33]

Dissent and National History: Reviving the Specter of Minority Rights

The Charter essay on the Roma was presented as a contribution to debates about the "minority problem" that had dogged Czechoslovakia since its creation as an independent republic after the First World War. To understand the significance of Czech dissidents' remarks about the Roma, a few words are needed about debates among the democratic opposition about national history and memory and the "minority problem" in socialist Czechoslovakia more generally, as well as in the wider context of international human rights law. East-Central Europe had been the focal point of the first international minority rights regime, established at the 1919 Paris Peace Conference and supervised by the League of Nations, which aimed to safeguard stability and territorial sovereignty in the post-imperial successor states against revisionist and secessionist claims by disgruntled ethnic groups.[34] Czechoslovakia had lain at the heart of the spectacular failure of the minority treaties system, when Nazi Germany managed to instrumentalize alleged violations of the rights of the German minority to justify annexation of the Sudetenland at Munich in 1938. In acknowledgment of the League of Nations debacle, the

[31] On civil society and human rights activism at the UN see Paul Kennedy, *The Parliament of Man: The United Nations and the Quest for World Government* (London, 2006), 158–159, 185–186; Roger Normand and Sarah Zaidi, *Human Rights at the UN. The Political History of Universal Justice* (Bloomington, Ind., 2008), 243–341; Paul Gordon Lauren, *The Evolution of International Human Rights. Visions Seen* (Philadelphia, 1998), 241–280. On the global nature of the 1960s protests that kick-started the explosion of concern for individual rights, see Jeremi Suri, *Power and Protest: Global Revolution and the Rise of Détente* (Cambridge, Mass., 2005).
[32] Morton E. Winston, "Assessing the Effectiveness of International Human Rights NGOs. Amnesty International," and Claude E. Welch, Jr., "Amnesty International and Human Rights Watch. A Comparison," in Claude E. Welch, Jr. (ed.), *NGOs and Human Rights. Promise and Performance* (Philadelphia, 2001), 25–54, 85–118; Stephen Hopgood, *Keepers of the Flame. Understanding Amnesty International* (Ithaca, N.Y., 2006).
[33] Tony Judt, *Postwar: A History of Europe since 1945* (London, 2005), 501–502.
[34] Carole Fink, *Defending the Rights of Others: The Great Powers, the Jews and International Minority Protection, 1878–1938* (Cambridge, 2004).

United Nations rejected the international protection of the collective rights of minorities in favor of the principle of nondiscrimination and the protection of universal human rights.[35]

After the communist regime was established in Czechoslovakia in 1948, Marxist-Leninist nationality policy was formally adopted as the official approach to the minorities question, although in practice Soviet influence coexisted uneasily with pre-socialist traditions and postwar suspicion of minority rights. Demographically, postwar Czechoslovakia looked very different from the multinational first republic: The majority of Czechoslovak Jews were killed during the war, as were most Bohemian and Moravian Roma and Sinti, while nearly 3 million citizens of German nationality were expelled by the postwar Czech government as retribution for Munich and the ensuing Nazi occupation of Czechoslovakia. In comparison to the Czech lands, Slovakia remained ethnically more heterogeneous, with a large Hungarian minority and smaller but substantial Ruthenian and Roma populations, while the "Slovak question" itself was a constant source of political tension between Prague and Bratislava. The evolution of nationalities policy can be traced through successive revisions to the Czechoslovak Constitution, which gradually replaced ethnic with political definitions of the nation. In 1968 a new federal Constitution defined the republic as a "common state of the Czech and Slovak nations, together with the Hungarian, German, Polish and Ukrainian (Ruthenian) nationalities." A separate law guaranteed the nationalities the "possibilities and means of all-round development" in the spirit of socialist democracy and internationalism.[36]

Before Czechoslovakia ratified the International Covenant on Civil and Political Rights in 1976, the Foreign Ministry reassured the Communist Party Presidium that the 1968 nationalities law fully implemented Article 27 of the Covenant on the rights of persons belonging to "ethnic, religious or linguistic minorities ... to enjoy their own culture, to profess and practice their own religion, or to use their own language."[37] The Soviet Union and its allies had long been the champions of minority rights at the United Nations. Despite their efforts, the Universal Declaration of Human Rights contained no minority rights clause, nor did the Genocide Convention make any mention of cultural genocide.[38] Although the Wilsonian principle of national self-determination was recognized in the context of decolonization,

---

[35] Mark Mazower, "The Strange Triumph of Human Rights," *Historical Journal*, 47 (2004), 379–398.

[36] Jan Rychlík, "Normalizační podoba československé federace," in Norbert Kmeť and Juraj Marušiak (eds.), *Slovensko a režim normalizácie* (Prešov, 2003), 8–46.

[37] NA Prague, f. Předsednictvo ÚV KSČ, 1971–1976, f. 02/1, Sv. 133, a.j. 134, 25.10.1974, *Stanovisko oddělení ÚV KSČ k materiálu pro schůzi předsednictva ÚV KSČ k bodu: Návrh na ratifikaci mezinárodních paktů o lidských právech.* See also UN ICCPR Article 27.

[38] For details see Johannes Morsink, *The Universal Declaration of Human Rights: Origins, Drafting and Intent* (Philadelphia, 2000); Normand and Zaidi, *Human Rights at the UN*, 249–260.

newly independent states in Africa and Asia feared the secessionist tendencies of minority groups, and thus supported the Western view at the United
Nations that the rights of minorities should be considered as subordinate to
the interests of states and the imperative of territorial integrity.[39] A similar
logic was at work in international norms dealing with indigenous peoples, as
demonstrated by the highly assimilationist ILO Convention on Indigenous
and Tribal Populations (1957).[40] The minority clause of the International
Covenant on Civil and Political Rights was the first step toward reviving the
principle of minority rights in international human rights law.

Internal Czechoslovak debates about minority rights were revived in the
mid-1970s by the Helsinki Final Act, which referred to the rights of persons
belonging to "national minorities," but not to the collective rights of peoples
or the right to self-determination. Western demands were mainly related to
individual human rights such as family unification and the rights of journalists, which many hoped would lead to the gradual liberalization of authoritarian regimes in Eastern Europe. The minority question was thus approached in
a similar way as the issue of state borders, notes Peter Schlotter, with the aim
of solving practical problems while maintaining the status quo in interstate
relations.[41] Despite the lack of international consensus on the place of minority rights within the UN human rights instruments, the treatment of ethnic
minorities in Eastern Europe was nevertheless often included by contemporary
commentators as an indicator of communist regimes' compliance with the
"spirit of Helsinki."[42] That minority rights were viewed by numerous states
as a threat to state sovereignty, and the inviolability of territorial borders, on
which the postwar international settlement depended, was recognized in the
first major UN report on the implementation of Article 27: "Any international
regime for the protection of members of minority groups arouses distrust and
fear. It is first seen as a pretext for interference in the internal affairs of States
(particularly where the minorities have ethnic or linguistic links with foreign
States). Moreover, certain States regard the preservation of the identity of
minorities as posing a threat to their unity and stability."[43]

Taking advantage of the Helsinki process, Hungarian dissidents in Slovakia
created a Committee for the Protection of the Rights of the Hungarian Minority

[39] Patrick Thornberry, "In the Strong-Room of Vocabulary," in Peter Cumper and Steven
Wheatley (eds.), *Minority Rights in the "New" Europe* (The Hague, 1999), 1–14; on self-
determination and resistance to imperial rule see Erez Manela, *The Wilsonian Moment. Self-
Determination and the International Origins of Anticolonial Nationalism* (Oxford, 2007).
[40] ILO 1988.
[41] Peter Schlotter, *Die KSZE im Ost-West Konflikt. Wirkung einer internationalen Institution*
(Frankfurt, 1999), especially ch. 5.
[42] See, for example, the statement to the U.S. Helsinki Commission (95th Congress) by James
F. Brown, Director of Radio Free Europe, on 9 May 1977 in Vojtech Mastny (ed.), *Helsinki,
Human Rights and European Security. Analysis and Documentation* (Durham, N.C., 1986),
Document 25, 106–114.
[43] Francesco Caportorti, Special Rapporteur on the Rights of Persons Belonging to Ethnic,
Religious and Linguistic Minorities (UN Doc E/CN.4/Sub.2/384/Rev.1).

in 1978 – the year of the Belgrade review conference – which protested against new restrictions on Hungarian-language teaching in Slovak schools and universities.[44] A critical report on the government's failure to implement the 1968 nationalities law appeared the following year.[45] Curtailment of Hungarian linguistic and cultural rights was officially presented as an emancipatory measure to raise the educational level of the Hungarian minority by promoting their knowledge of Slovak, although it was clear that the regime feared that the Hungarian minority would turn into a fifth column as the result of liberalization in neighboring Hungary and Hungarian intellectuals' support for Charter 77.[46] The exile journal *Svědectví* also published in 1978 a study of the expulsion of the Czechoslovak Germans, sparking a debate on the subject among dissident circles and awakening the interest of the StB. In comparison to vocal minority lobbies such as the Hungarian dissidents in Slovakia, however, Charter 77 was generally wary of expressing opinions about the principle of collective rights, preferring to focus on specific cases in which the rights of minorities were violated, or on the moral, philosophical, or historical dimensions of the nationalities question.[47]

Debates about minority rights complicate the claim made by the legal theorist Jiří Přibáň that dissidents used international human rights instruments to reclaim liberal values, civility, and native political traditions.[48] In the Czechoslovak case, the image of the first republic as an "island of democracy" in interwar Central Europe was a central motif for émigré Czech historians during the Cold War. However, this myth was frequently undermined by dissidents' debates about national identity and the "right to history," including taboo subjects such as the Holocaust or the expulsion of the Czechoslovak Germans in 1945.[49] Czech historians such as Miroslav Hroch had begun to investigate the phenomenon of nationalism during the 1960s, although research on the national question in social science remained limited.[50] In response to the communists' appropriation of nationalist discourse to legitimize socialist rule, the founder of the Czech dissident movement, the philosopher Jan Patočka, wrote

---

[44] Norbert Kmeť, "Opozícia a hnutie odporu na Slovensku 1968–1989," in Blažek (ed.), *Opozice a odpor proti komunistickému režimu v Československu 1968–1989*, 47.

[45] Juraj Marušiak, "Maďarská menšina v slovenskej politike v rokoch normalizácie," in Norbert Kmeť and Juraj Marušiak (eds.), *Slovensko a režim normalizácie* (Prešov, 2003), 222–279.

[46] Ibid.

[47] Ibid.

[48] Jiří Přibáň, "Political Dissent, Human Rights and Legal Transformations: Communist and Post-Communist Experiences," *East European Politics and Societies*, 19 (2005), 553–572.

[49] "The Right to History," Charter 77 document 11 in *Listy*, 14:5 (February 1985), 22–23. For an overview see Chad Bryant, "Whose Nation? Czech Dissidents and History Writing from a Post-1989 Perspective," *History and Memory*, 12 (2000), 30–64; Bradley F. Abrams, "Morality, Wisdom and Revision: The Czech Opposition of the Late 1970s and the Expulsion of the Sudeten Germans," *Eastern European Politics and Societies*, 9 (1995), 234–256.

[50] Miroslav Hroch, *Social Preconditions of National Revival in Europe: A Comparative Analysis of the Social Composition of Patriotic Groups among the Smaller European Nations* (Cambridge, 1985).

an influential critical essay about the Czech national character, which was followed some years later by the controversial *Czechs in the Modern Era: An Attempt at Self-Reflection* by the pseudonymous "Podiven."[51] Indeed, recent scholarship on the influence of nationalism in the first Czechoslovak republic suggests that the interwar democracy was not based on liberal concepts of individual human rights, but rather on a communitarian understanding of the political community in which citizens accessed their civil, political, and social rights through membership in a national collective.[52]

The Quest for Romani Rights: A Blank Spot in Czech History?

The Roma minority in Czechoslovakia were, in reality, very far from being the passive victims of totalitarian injustice, although the history of Romani political and social activism remains under-researched. After 1989, the Czech historian Jan Křen observed in a well-known essay that the history of the Roma was one of the "blank spots" in Czech historiography.[53] With the exception of a few studies published in regional journals and publishing houses, notably research on the Nazi persecution of the Gypsies in the Protectorate of Bohemia and Moravia by the historian Ctibor Nečas, there were few attempts to write the Roma into the history of the Czechoslovak state during the socialist era.[54] In fact, domestic and international activism around the so-called Gypsy Question had started some years before Charter 77 took up the Roma cause. As early as 1965, Communist Party ideologists had reported to the Politburo on the creation of an international Gypsy organization, founded by émigré Romanian and Yugoslav Roma in France.[55] During the Prague Spring, leaders of the Czechoslovak "Associations of Gypsies-Roma" established as a result of the political liberalization of 1968 were able to make contact with activists abroad, both in Eastern and Western Europe. A small delegation of Czech Roma was given official permission to attend the first World Romani Congress, held in London in 1971, as the socialist regime was anxious to prove its superiority in "solving the Gypsy Question" to the capitalist world.[56] This

---

[51] Jan Patočka, *Co jsou Češi?* (Prague, 1992); Podiven (Petr Pithart, Petr Příhoda, and Milan Otáhal), *Češi v dějinách nové doby 1848–1939* (Prague, 2003).

[52] Tara Zahra, *Kidnapped Souls: National Indifference and the Battle for Children in the Bohemian Lands, 1900–1948* (Ithaca, N.Y., 2008).

[53] Jan Křen, *Bílá místa v našich dějinách?* (Prague, 1990).

[54] Ctibor Nečas, *Andr oda taboris: Vězňové protektorátních cikánských táborů 1942–1943* (Brno, 1987), and Nečas, *Nad osudem českých a slovenských Cikánů v letech 1939–1945* (Brno, 1981).

[55] NA Prague, Předsednictvo ÚV KSČ 1962–1966, f. 02/1, sv. 110, a.j. 114/4.: *Kontrolní zpráva o plnění usnesení ÚV KSČ o práci mezi cikánskym obyvatelstvem v ČSSR* (s. Jiří Hendrych), 15.6.1965. On the origins of the international Romani movement see Thomas Acton, *Gypsy Politics and Social Change: The Development of Ethnic Ideology and Pressure Politics among British Gypsies from Victorian Reformism to Romany Nationalism* (London, 1974).

[56] NA Prague, f. KSČ ÚV 02/ 4 – Sekretariát 1966–1971, Sv 65, a.j. 117/13: *Vyslání delegace ÚV Svazu Cikánů-Romů ČSR na světový kongres Cikánů do Londýna*, 26.3.1971. On the Congress see Grattan Puxon, "The First World Romani Congress," *Race Today* (June

was indicative of a broader and more significant trend, whereby the nascent international Romani movement was shaped by interactions and conflicts between Roma and Sinti groups from Western and Eastern Europe.[57]

Domestic minority rights law and Marxist-Leninist nationality policy were the most important points of reference for Roma seeking recognition as a national minority in the Eastern bloc during the 1960s and 1970s, given the lack of minority rights provisions in international human rights law at that time. When the Romani activist Anton Facuna petitioned the government and Communist Party for recognition of a Roma nationality during the Prague Spring, he appealed to the rights guaranteed by the 1960 Czechoslovak Constitution rather than the UN human rights covenants. Indeed, Roma were hardly mentioned in debates about self-determination, discrimination, or collective rights until the late 1970s, perhaps because of a widespread lack of consensus as to whether Roma (or Gypsies) constituted an ethnic people or a group defined by social factors. This ambiguity surfaced in the first reference to the European Roma by an international organization: a 1969 Council of Europe recommendation on the situation of "Gypsies and other travellers in Europe," which nonetheless noted that discrimination against the Gypsies as an "ethnic group" was incompatible with the "ideals underlying the European Convention on Human Rights and the United Nations Declaration on Human Rights."[58]

Divisions within the international Romani movement, which remained a rather elite-led affair with limited influence over its intended constituency, also reduced its ability to lobby international human rights institutions. These divisions were influenced by conflicts between national and ethnic factions within the movement, as well as Cold War ideological differences: Many Eastern European Romani activists were members of the *nomenklatura* who identified with the political establishment, whereas Western European activists defended a nonconformist lifestyle against the expectations of state and society.[59] These differences were exemplified in divergent approaches to Gypsy travelling, which Eastern European Roma tended to view as an undesirable indicator of "backwardness" but which was promoted by Western activists as a central aspect of Gypsy identity. A former official of the Slovak Gypsies-Roma Association named Vincent Danihel, writing in an educational textbook about the Gypsies published in 1986, criticized Gypsies and bourgeois governments in the West for representing nomadism (Slovak: *kočovnícvto*) as

1971), 192–199; Donald Kenrick, "The World Romani Congress," *Journal of the Gypsy Lore Society*, 50:3–4 (1971), 101–108.

[57] Thomas Acton and Ilona Klímová, "The International Romani Union: An East European Answer to West European Questions? Shifts in the Focus of World Romani Congresses 1971–2000," in Will Guy (ed.), *Between Past and Future: The Roma of Central and Eastern Europe* (Hatfield, 2001), 157–219.

[58] Council of Europe Parliamentary Assembly, *Recommendation 563 (1969) [1] on the situation of Gypsies and other travellers in Europe*.

[59] Acton and Klímová, "The International Romani Union," 157–219.

the main ethnic marker of the Gypsies, symbolized by the choice of a red
wheel on a blue background as the motif of the international Romani association. For socialists such as Danihel, Gypsy travelling was an indicator of
social development rather than ethnic identity, which was cynically supported
by bourgeois governments as an excuse for "not providing Gypsies with the
material support that they receive in the socialist countries."[60]

International Romani activism briefly boomed in the late 1970s, when
the Caportorti report on minority rights seemed to offer Roma the hope of
gaining United Nations support for their political activities. Romani activists
managed to secure a resolution on Roma from the Subcommission on the
Prevention of Discrimination and Protection of Minorities in August 1977,
which appealed to those countries with a Gypsy population to accord them
all the rights to which they were entitled under the Universal Declaration.[61]
The Caportorti report referred to the existence of the Roma as a minority living within the borders of many states. Activists in the international Romani
movement cooperated with a sympathetic member of the UN Subcommission
to take advantage of this moment. The British delegate to the Subcommission,
Benjamin Whitaker, was a Labour MP who had a special interest in minority rights, having founded an advocacy organization in London called the
Minority Rights Group. This organization had commissioned a study called
The Destiny of Europe's Gypsies from Grattan Puxon, the Secretary-General
of the World Romani Congress, in 1973. Whitaker invited Puxon and other
leading Romani activists, including Jan Cibula, to the Subcommission meeting in August 1977, where the Caportorti report was discussed.[62]

The Romani movement espoused a more radical program of political
nationalism in the late 1970s, claiming recognition as a national minority of
Indian origin. In 1978 activists created a new international organization, the
International Romani Union (IRU), and organized a second World Romani
Congress in Geneva, which called upon the United Nations to "assist us
to combat discrimination and repression" and declared the Roma to be a
"nationality of Indian origin." This strategy was aided by a number of official representatives of India, at both state and federal levels, as well as the
efforts of an energetic Indian diplomat, W. R. Rishi, who set up an Indian
Institute for Romani Studies in his home town of Chandigarh after a visit to
the first World Romani Congress convinced him that the Roma were emigrants from the area of Greater Punjab in the age before the Muslim inva-
sions.[63] A detailed study of Romani lobbying at the United Nations found,

[60] Vincent Danihel, *Manuš znamená človek* (Bratislava, 1986).
[61] Ilona Klimová-Alexander, *The Romani Voice in World Politics: The United Nations and Non-State Actors* (Ashgate, 2005).
[62] Ibid., 40–41, 126–127.
[63] W. R. Rishi, *Roma: The Panjabi Emigrants in Europe, Central and Middle Asia, the USSR and the Americas* (Patiala, 1996), and Chaman Lal, *Gipsies: Forgotten Children of India* (Delhi, 1962). I am grateful to Professor Alok Jha for his help when visiting the archives of the Institute in Chandigarh in December 2007.

however, that although the IRU was granted observer status at ECOSOC, thereafter Roma activists did not cooperate very actively with UN agencies after the Geneva congress.[64]

Dr. Jan Cibula, a Slovak Romani activist who had emigrated to Switzerland during the Prague Spring, was elected as the first President of the IRU. The Slovak Communist Party made a special report on the Congress that highlighted Cibula's identity as a Czechoslovak émigré, and also noted that Anton Facuna, a Czechoslovak citizen who had been the first Chairman of the Slovak Association of Gypsies-Roma, had "done some very useful work" for the new international organization by drafting the statutes of the IRU.[65] Human rights, however, remained a key aspect of the communist regime's interpretation of the Second World Romani Congress. The Communist Party daily *Rudé právo* ran an article about the WRC in May 1978 entitled "Where human rights are absent. The Roma in the capitalist states and the Geneva congress."[66] *Rudé právo* presented the congress in classic ideological terms as a capitalist conspiracy to instrumentalize human rights in the battle to overthrow socialism; the article claimed that "in the capitalist countries the Gypsies are denied all human rights and are oppressed by racism, while the economic crisis condemns them to poverty." Seizing on the fact that a German newspaper, the *Frankfurter Rundschau*, had described Jan Cibula as a refugee from Czechoslovakia, *Rudé právo* sarcastically noted that "the fact that Cibula could study medicine in Czechoslovakia prevented them from presenting him as a victim of socialism."

Official reactions to Czechoslovak Roma participating in events such as the World Romani Congress demonstrate that the internationalization of human rights activism may have constrained the regime in its treatment of dissidents for fear of foreign disapproval, but that such activism was still viewed in ideological terms as a tool of capitalist class warfare against the socialist camp.[67] When the Slovak Communist Party (KSS) discovered that a young Romani journalist, Anna Klempárová, had secretly attended the Geneva World Romani Congress as a private tourist, the young woman was immediately interrogated

---

[64] Klimová-Alexander, *The Romani Voice in World Politics*.

[65] Slovak National Archive (SNA) Bratislava, f. ÚV KSS – Sekretariát, Zasadnutie 26.6.1978 (4.7.1978), kr. 514, fasc. 1112/8, *Kontrolná správa o plnení uznesení stranických orgánov a štátnych orgánov prijatých k riešeniu problémov zaostalej časti cigánskej obyvateľov v SSR – príloha III: Informácia o II. Svetovom kongrese Cigánov.*

[66] Ľudovít Sulč, "Kde chybějí lidská práva: Romové v kapitalistických zemích a ženevský sjezd," *Rudé právo*, 16 May 1978.

[67] Tomáš Vilímek, "Vnímání helsinského procesu v ČSSR a NDR ze strany moci, opozice a obyvatelstva," in Karník and Kopeček (eds.), *Bolševismus, komunismus a radikální socialismus v Československu sv. V*, 275–296; Petr Blažek, "Ale jiná možnost není. Vyšetřování vzniku Charty 77," in Markéta Devátá et al. (eds.), *Charta 77. Od obhajoby lidských práv k demokratické revoluci, 1977–1989. Sborník z konference k 30. výročí Charta 77, Praha 21.–23. března 2007* (Prague, 2007), 225–234; NA Prague, PÚV KSČ, 1971–1976, f. 02/1, sv. 35, a.j. 39, dne 8.4.1977, *Zpráva o plnění úkolů vyplývajících pro resort FMV z usnesení stranických a státních orgánů o realizaci Závěrečného aktu KBSE z roku 1975.*

by the state security police.[68] Before the Third World Romani Congress, held in Göttingen in 1981, the KSS reported that

there are grounds for suspecting that the Third Congress of Gypsies-Roma in the Federal Republic of Germany will be used against the ČSSR by centers of emigration in the capitalist lands as a means of exerting pressure and ideological-diversionary defamation. Therefore increased attention must be paid to the participation of our citizens in order that they do not damage our interests and become the object of enemy manipulation.[69]

Preventive measures, such as refusing passport applications, were taken by the security services to stop the small number of Slovak Roma who received invitations to the Congress from traveling to Germany, even though the people concerned were mainly workers or lower-level managers rather than elites.[70]

The Third World Romani Congress marked the beginning of a split in the international Romani movement that would persist until the early 1990s. Conflicts between West German Sinti and Roma intensified, with the Sinti defending a separate identity and interests against those of the Roma. Moreover, the influence of émigré Yugoslav Roma in West German Romani politics was increasingly resented. For socialist Czechoslovakia, meanwhile, the involvement of the Federal Republic of Germany in the so-called Gypsy Question was intolerable, as was Romani cooperation with the Gesellschaft für bedrohte Völker, a human rights organization campaigning against genocide in post-colonial states that was run by the son of German expellees from the Sudetenland.[71] The secretary of the Slovak government commission for the "Gypsy population," Imrich Farkáš, reported in 1980 that the Gesellschaft für bedrohte Völker had petitioned the Czechoslovak embassy in Bonn against the alleged sterilization of Romani women, claiming that such treatment constituted genocide. For such claims to come from a formerly "fascist" state was unbearable, wrote the Slovak Romani official Vincent Danihel in 1986.[72] However, it was clear that the language of minority rights had again become common currency in transnational debates about minority protection by the early 1980s, although now in the hands of very different actors.

[68] SNA Bratislava, f. ÚV KSS – Sekretariát, kr. 514, fasc. 1112/8, *Kontrolná správa o plnení uznesení stráníckych orgánov a štatných orgánov prijatých k riešeniu problémov zaostalej časti cigánskej obyvateľov v SSR, Informácia o II. Svetovom kongrese Cigánov* (26.6.1978).
[69] SNA Bratislava, f. ÚV KSS – Predsedníctvo – kr. 1597, a.j. 1553/13: *Informácia o príprave III. medzinárodného kongresu Rómov v NSR,* untitled/undated annex.
[70] SNA Bratislava, f. ÚV KSS – Predsedníctvo – kr. 1610, a.j. 128/13: *Informácia o konaní III. svetového kongresu RIJ – Medzinárodnej jednoty Cigánov v NSR* (5.6.1981).
[71] Gilad Margalit, *Germany and Its Gypsies: A Post-Auschwitz Ordeal* (Madison, Wis., 2002).
[72] Vincent Danihel, *Manuš znamená človek* (Bratislava, 1986).

Minority Rights as "Socialist" Rights: The Ambiguity of Rights-Talk in Late Socialism

However natural the Charter 77 allegations about communist violations of Roma rights may seem in retrospect, to contemporaries these claims were far from self-evident, as many of the policies deemed discriminatory by Czech dissidents had been framed as emancipatory by the socialist regime. Communist Party officials and high-level civil servants continued to defend the "socialist" approach to the Gypsy Question during "normalization," arguing that poverty, illiteracy, and anti-Gypsy prejudice would be solved only by assimilating the Roma into socialist society as productive worker-citizens leading a "cultured" way of life. When Imrich Farkáš, the chairman of the Slovak Government Committee for Questions relating to the Gypsy Population, reported to his colleagues that Radio Free Europe had broadcast Charter 77's essay about the Gypsies, he claimed in an internal meeting: "It's not the Gypsies who are protesting or complaining that our socialist order treats them badly or denies their rights, but non-Gypsies … who are living only too well in our country, who have links to internal and external subversives." The only correct response for the Slovak government, continued Imrich Farkáš, was to "continue with the acculturation and social integration of gypsy citizens who live in a backwards way." Special "Gypsy estates" should be built in the massive housing blocks that were then being rapidly constructed across Czechoslovakia, the chairman claimed. Poor housing was one of the main problems facing the Slovak Roma, many of whom lived in isolated settlements in rural areas.

Above all, Farkáš warned his colleagues to act within the law in their dealings with the Roma: "We must take even greater care than before to implement all the resolutions and methodological regulations of the Slovak government, so that we don't make mistakes for which we could be criticized from an international perspective."[73] This emphasis on acting within the law was striking. Eastern European states were displaying a marked interest in the development and implementation of law by the 1970s.[74] A socialist regime such as Czechoslovakia, on the other hand, did not define itself as a *Rechtsstaat*. The orthodox concept of "socialist legality" subordinated law to politics, understood as the will of the ruling party, while law itself was defined as the expression of the interests of the working class.[75] By the 1970s, however, most socialist regimes in Eastern Europe were no longer totalitarian states that relied on the arbitrary use of terror, but instead placed much

---

[73] Ministerstvo práce a sociálních vecí SSR, Sekretariát Komisie vlády SSR pre otázky cigánskych obyvateľov, *Prednášky prednesené na celoslovenskej porade tajomníkov komisií rád KNV pre otázky cigánskych obyvateľov, ktorá sa konala v dňoch 24. a 25. septembra 1980 v Bratislave* (len pre vnútornú potrebu), Bratislava, October 1980.

[74] Inga Markovits, "Law or Order? Constitutionalism and Legality in Eastern Europe," *Stanford Law Review*, 34 (1982), 513–613, here 514.

[75] Jiří Boguszak and Zdeněk Jičínský, *Otázky socialistického práva a zákonnosti* (Prague, 1964).

greater emphasis on the implementation of law in order to achieve political, economic, and social stability, for which a certain degree of legal and administrative predictability and consistency was deemed necessary. Moreover, as Peter Bugge has recently noted, "references to 'law and order' had a central legitimizing function in the social discourse of the Husák regime, and ... the resulting need to translate policies of repression into legal measures inhibited the authorities in their assertion of power and created an ambiguous window of opportunity for independent social activism."[76]

Did the new approach to law in late socialism result in an altered conception of citizens' rights? Socialist constitutions spoke of rights as well as duties. Political rights, as Inga Markovits has noted, were "in most cases limited, conditioned, or dependent upon the fulfillment of duties and in this fashion clearly linked to the interests of the state." Socialist rights were thus not weapons to be wielded by the individual against the state, but were rather more "like railway tickets: they entitle the holder only to travel in the indicated direction."[77] Social rights were considered more important than the traditional political freedoms and were thus given precedence in the constitutions' chapters on citizens' rights and duties. "Despite their constitutional status," notes Markovits, "these social rights do not provide justiciable claims beyond those already provided by ordinary law." Instead, social rights were ensured by so-called material guarantees. For example, the right to work was ensured by the socialist economic system. Moreover, they were collective rather than individual in character, and were understood not as entitlements but as interests and needs, in accordance with a view of well-being that was defined by the Party.

At the global level, the difference between these two concepts of human rights was one of the major ideological fault lines at the United Nations throughout the Cold War. Whereas Western states defended a minimalist concept of civil and political rights as a guarantee of negative freedom in the classical liberal tradition, the Soviet Union and post-colonial states promoted the role of the interventionist state in guaranteeing "progressive" social, economic, and cultural rights. To the extent that minority rights protection implied the need to promote equality as well as prevent discrimination, debates about minority rights were also influenced by this wider problem. One of the most salient aspects of minority rights protection, according to the 1977 UN report on the implementation of Article 27 of the ICPPR, was the role of the state in promoting the equality of minority groups: "Only the effective exercise of the rights set forth in Article 27 can guarantee observance of the principle of real, and not only formal, equality of the persons belonging to minority groups. The implementation of these rights calls for active and sustained interventions

---

[76] Peter Bugge, "Normalization and the Limits of the Law: The Case of the Czech Jazz Section," *East European Politics and Societies*, 22 (2008), 282–318.

[77] Inga Markovits, "Socialist vs. Bourgeois Rights: An East-West German Comparison," *University of Chicago Law Review*, 45 (1978), 612–636, here 615.

by States. A passive attitude on the part of the latter would render such rights inoperative."[78]

By insisting on the socioeconomic roots of Roma poverty and exclusion, the communist regime denied the possibility of a political solution to the so-called Gypsy Question. Problems of cultural integration were coded as social issues. Thus government statistics categorized the entire Gypsy population under three levels of "social adaptability" to presumed wider societal norms. In the early 1970s responsibility for administering state policy on the Gypsy Question was transferred to a unit dealing with "the Gypsy population and other socially unadaptable citizens" in the Federal Ministry of Labor and Social Affairs. Special committees at regional and district levels were supposed to oversee the implementation of policy, aided by a network of social workers who were able to distribute material assistance in cash or in kind to Gypsies deemed both needy and deserving of state support. Unlike the dissidents, who could easily be presented by international human rights organizations such as Amnesty International as the victims of totalitarian injustice, the Roma frequently fell into the broader category of citizens whose constitutional rights were subject to the official criteria of proper civic conduct, as exemplified by the semi-official policy of offering "socially unadaptable" Romani women material incentives to undergo sterilization. In this case, it was precisely the rhetorical emphasis on maintaining "law and order" in Husák's Czechoslovakia that was used to justify breaches of legality.

Both the influence of Soviet *perestroika* and the increasing emphasis on minority protection at the CSCE throughout the 1980s did, however, seem to affect the Czechoslovak regime's approach to the Roma. Minority rights were discussed at the Vienna review conference in 1986, and the Vienna Concluding Document enjoined states to "protect and create conditions for the promotion of ethnic, cultural, linguistic and religious identity of national minorities on their territory." Functionaries in the KSČ Central Committee, aware that the Party's Roma policy was becoming untenable, were now more willing to negotiate directly with Roma representatives. In November 1988 and January 1989, Karel Hoffmann, a secretary in the Central Committee, organized a meeting in the Hotel Prague for some twenty Roma activists who had been nominated by both Government Commissions for the Gypsy Population.[79] After the meeting, Hoffmann submitted a highly critical report to the Party Presidium in February 1989, which strikingly used the term *Romové* rather than *Cigáni* and stated that the "proposals and conclusions contained therein had been discussed with positive results with a group of Roma, selected from

---

[78] Francesco Caportorti, *The Rights of Persons Belonging to Ethnic, Religious and Linguistic Minorities*, ECOSOC document E/CN.4/Sub.2/384, 1977. Cited in Roger Normand and Sarah Zaidi, *Human Rights at the UN: The Political History of Universal Justice* (Bloomington, Ind., 2008), 258.

[79] Petr Víšek, "Program integrace – Řešení problematiky romských obyvatel v období 1970 až 1989," in *Romové v České republice (1945–1998)* (Prague, 1999), 184–218.

all regions of the ČSR," noting that no such discussions had been held since the closure of the Associations of Gypsies-Roma in 1973.[80]

The Central Committee report recommended a reconsideration of the legal status of the Roma and that Roma representatives be included in discussions on the new Constitution.[81] It referred to recent developments in Hungary and Yugoslavia, where Roma had been granted cultural rights as a nationality, and compared these with the assimilation policy still being pursued in Bulgaria. When the Party Presidium discussed the report, Hoffmann told the meeting that "there were commissions for the Roma under the National Committees, but without Roma."[82] The Presidium was, however, reluctant to act on these proposals. Certainly no one agreed with recognizing the Roma as a nationality. The ageing President, Gustáv Husák, demurred that the Roma were a "heterogeneous group in our society" – implicitly referring to the Stalinist dogma that Roma lacked the unifying characteristics of a nation. Miloš Jakeš warned that "their associations cannot have a political or a national character," that "civilized Roma don't want to have any contact with the others," and that "liberalism [toward the Roma] would be seen as our weakness." The only concession was an agreement to publish a Roma cultural magazine. Thus by November 1989 the guiding line on policy toward the Roma – as the Central Committee report itself stated – remained the 1958 resolution on "work among the Gypsy population."

Conclusion

The Velvet Revolution that brought down the communist regime in Czechoslovakia provided the Romani activists discussed in this chapter with an opportunity to engage openly in politics. In November 1989 the Roma Civic Initiative (ROI) was set up along the same lines as the Civic Forum. Its first bulletin, *Romano lav* (Romani Word), was published late in 1989 and contained eighteen points in the Romani language entitled "What the ROI wants." First on the list was recognition as a nationality in the Czechoslovak constitution, followed by a demand for a political party to represent all Roma, Romani language teaching in schools, support for Roma culture, proper housing for all Roma, policies to support the full employment of Roma, the elimination of the social causes of Roma criminality, and the development of international cooperation with Roma organizations abroad, especially the International Romani Union. Point 12 stated: "Immediately stop the sterilization of healthy Romani women."[83] The editors of *Romano lav* attempted to

---

[80] NA Prague, f. N69 – Předsednictvo ÚV KSČ 1989, P 103/89, bod. 8: *Zpráva o stavu řešení problematiky romského obyvatelstva v ČSSR a základní zaměření dalšího postupu.*

[81] NA Prague, f. N69 – PÚV KSČ, 1989, P 103 / 89, bod 8: *Zpráva.*

[82] Ibid., zápis (handwritten notes).

[83] Archive of the Museum of Roma Culture (MRK), Brno: "So kamel Romaňi Občansko Iniciativa," *Romano lav* I, 4, 1990.

explain to their readers the difference between nationality (*národnost*) and state citizenship (*státní příslušnost*) to show what "Roma nationality" would mean in practice: state support for Roma theaters, publishing houses, artists agencies, and education – but not a loss of Czechoslovak citizenship. "WE WILL HAVE RIGHTS, NOT RESPONSIBILITIES! ... For many years to be a member of our nation was a terrible insult.... We Roma do not want to be insulted and humiliated. We want to live with everyone in our country in peace and friendship.... WE ARE CITIZENS OF THE CZECHOSLOVAK REPUBLIC and no one can take this citizenship away from us, even if we have a different nationality."[84]

Although the Roma were recognized as a national minority and allowed to self-identify in the first post-communist census, only 33,000 people opted for Roma nationality. Fears of mass unemployment, racial violence, and a renewed furor over claims about the sterilization of Roma women – sparked by another Charter 77 essay released in 1990 – all serve to illustrate how politically sensitive the link was between Roma cultural identity and the methods used by the state to identify the Gypsy population. Although six Romani parliamentarians were elected in the first post-communist elections – including Anna Klempárová, the journalist who secretly attended the Geneva World Romani Congress in 1978 – their political influence was limited. Non-Romani former social workers in the Prague city administration had a much greater impact on Czech government policy toward the Roma in the immediate post-communist period. Moreover, Romani activists – particularly in Slovakia – were more likely than non-Roma to support social integration policies that, in many ways, were a continuation of socialist practices.[85] Thus the main conflict over Roma rights after 1989 was not between the principle of individual versus collective rights, but rather between the material guarantees of economic and social rights and the liberal vision of "human and civil rights" that eclipsed them in post-communist constitutions.[86] This chapter has tried to explore the historical roots of these conflicts, showing that debates about human rights in socialist Czechoslovakia were not confined to a narrow circle of dissident intellectuals, and suggesting the need for further research on the social history of "rights-talk" in late socialist Eastern Europe.

[84] MRK Brno, *Romano lav*, I, 4, 1990. Emphasis in the original.
[85] Studies that present social integration programs for Roma as "new" policies thus ignore this element of continuity. See, for example, Peter Vermeersch, *The Romani Movement: Minority Politics and Ethnic Mobilization in Contemporary Central Europe* (New York/Oxford, 2006).
[86] István Pogány, "Refashioning Rights in Central and Eastern Europe: Some Implications for the Region's Roma," *European Public Law*, 10 (2004), 85–106, and Pogány, *The Roma Café* (London, 2004).

PART IV

GENOCIDE, HUMANITARIANISM, AND THE LIMITS OF LAW

Toward World Law? Human Rights and the Failure of the Legalist Paradigm of War

Devin O. Pendas

In thinking about the twentieth century, 1945 marks an obvious – in some ways perhaps too obvious – caesura. Certainly much changed after the Second World War, if not always as much as at first it seemed. Among the many apparent changes, one of the most striking was the transformation in the relationship between law, especially international law, and mass violence. For a time, it seemed as if a new era had dawned in international relations, one in which law and international institutions would supplant force and the nation-state as the key determinants of world order. For the optimists, and there were no small number of these in the late 1940s, the catastrophe of the Second World War seemed to have fundamentally altered the global equation, creating an opportunity, even a necessity, for a fundamental transformation in the way global politics worked.

Reason, not power, law, not violence, would henceforth govern world affairs. Organized mass violence, if not abolished outright, would be subject to strict legal regulation. Aggressive wars would be prevented or stopped by united world action operating under the rule of law. Mass atrocities would be dissuaded and penalized by international criminal law. In general, the expectation was that the new United Nations would create an international order that sharply limited global violence and that codified and protected what were coming to be called human rights, even if this meant intervening in the domestic affairs of member states.[1] Although the UN was in many ways simply intended to be a more efficient version of the League of Nations, the new legalism of the post-1945 period was meant to be far more comprehensive than its predecessors.[2] It was intended, as A. H. Feller, General Legal Counsel for the UN, declared in 1949, to mark a gradual move "toward world law." "The trouble with international law is not that it isn't law," Feller maintained,

---

[1] Geoffrey Best, *War and Law since 1945* (Oxford, 1994), 67–79.
[2] Paul Kennedy, *A Parliament of Man: The Past, Present, and Future of the United Nations* (New York, 2006), and Stanley Meisler, *United Nations: The First Fifty Years* (New York, 1997).

but that there isn't enough of it. The rules cover only a small part of the relations between states; many of the rules are only vaguely defined or their meaning is disputed; there are too many loopholes, too many opportunities for quibbling and evasion. If the system is to furnish a secure foundation for the world community it must be developed until its content approximates that of national legal systems.[3]

The legalist paradigm that emerged after World War II thus strove to recapitulate on an international scale the domestication of mass violence that had occurred within the nation-state in the Early Modern period.

Proclaimed in the Moscow Declaration of October 1943 and initially codified in the London Charter of August 1945, a new way of thinking about the relationship between law and organized mass violence emerged in the second half of World War II.[4] As the horrifying scale, if not yet the unique quality, of Nazi atrocities became increasingly clear, the Big Three gradually reached a consensus that it would be both politically expedient and morally justified to prosecute these in courts of law.[5] That this consensus was actually implemented after the war differentiates it sharply from the period after World War I. Borrowing a phrase from Michael Walzer and expanding on its meaning, it is possible to think of this new sensibility as the "legalist paradigm of war."[6] Contrary to Walzer's rather narrow interpretation, this legalist paradigm covered, or came to cover, virtually every category of mass violence, from interstate wars to civil conflicts and insurgencies, conducted by either state or quasi-state actors (e.g., insurgents and guerilla fighters, though "terrorists" have held an ambiguous status within the legalist paradigm throughout the postwar period). Finally, this legalist paradigm combined areas that had traditionally been treated separately as *jus ad bellum* and *jus in bello,* the circumstances in which war may be properly waged and the ways in which it may be legitimately fought. The presumption of the postwar period was that just wars must also be waged justly and that both matters could be subjected to international legal regulation.[7]

The distinguishing feature of this new legalist paradigm was its insistent dualism. Both states and individuals were now held to be subjects under international criminal law, and both could be culpable for criminal acts of mass violence. This dualism – the mutual entanglement of state and individual

[3] A. H. Feller, "We Move, Slowly, toward World Law," *New York Times,* June 5, 1949, SM 10.
[4] Devin O. Pendas, "'The Magical Scent of the Savage': Colonial Violence, the Crisis of Civilization, and the Origins of the Legalist Paradigm of War," *Boston College International and Comparative Law Review,* 30 (Winter 2007), 29–53. See also Mark Mazower's contribution to the present volume, where he makes a substantially similar argument about the role of imperialism and the rhetoric of civilization.
[5] Arieh J. Kochavi, *Prelude to Nuremberg: Allied War Crimes Policy and the Question of Punishment* (Chapel Hill, N.C., 1998).
[6] Michael Walzer, *Just and Unjust Wars: A Moral Argument with Historical Illustrations* (New York, 1977), 61–63.
[7] Chris af Jochnick and Roger Normand, "The Legitimation of Violence: A Critical History of the Laws of War," *Harvard International Law Journal,* 35 (Winter 1994), 50.

criminality – was the source of both the great appeal of the legalist paradigm and, ultimately, its Achilles' heel as well. With the exception of pirates, individuals had traditionally not been subjects of international law.[8] The Hague Conventions, for instance, while criminalizing certain specific actions, held states, not individuals, responsible for these. The state, not the individual perpetrator of war crimes, was the subject at law here. Hence the only sanctions envisioned in the Hague Conventions were reparations, not criminal prosecutions. To be sure, there had been talk of staging international trials of Germans and Turks for atrocities committed in the First World War, but such discussions bore little fruit, all of it spoiled. The trials that did occur, in Leipzig and Istanbul, were conducted under domestic, not international, law. Moreover, both demonstrated the fatal weakness of allowing states to judge atrocities by their own agents.

The legalist paradigm as it emerged after World War II insisted, by contrast, on the mutual entanglement of individual and state culpability. Beginning with the London Charter and continuing in the careful but usually hollow classifications of international crimes that occupied international lawyers off and on for the next sixty years, state sponsorship and responsibility were always coupled with an assertion of individual culpability for mass atrocities. These were crimes of state, carried out by individuals.[9] As *The New York Times* declared in an editorial celebrating the Nuremberg verdict, "aggressive warfare has now been pronounced 'the supreme crime,' and ... in dealing with it national sovereignty has been superseded by the superior sovereignty of international law and international organization, which take jurisdiction not only over states and nations but also over individuals responsible for their governments and policies."[10] It was precisely this that was to cause such problems in future.

The hope was that by criminalizing illegitimate forms of mass violence, aggressive war, crimes against humanity, and genocide, in addition to the more traditional category of war crimes, such acts could be delegitimated. By punishing individuals, precisely in their capacity as state actors, it was hoped that such atrocities could be deterred in the future. More generally, statesmen and jurists hoped in the late 1940s to vastly increase the role of international criminal law, to transform international affairs from an arena of Hobbesian competitive anarchy into a realm governed by consensual norms and the rule of law, what Gerry Simpson has referred to as "the juridification of war."[11] This is made clear in the Americans' April 1945 proposal for an International Military Tribunal to try the Nazi leadership: "Punishment of war criminals should be motivated primarily by its deterrent effect, by the impetus which

---

[8] D. P. O'Connell, *The International Law of the Sea*, vol. 1 (Oxford, 1983).
[9] Pieter N. Drost, *The Crime of State: International Governmental Crime against Individual Human Rights*, 2 vols. (Leyden, 1959).
[10] "This Is the Law," *New York Times*, October 3, 1946, 26.
[11] Gerry Simpson, *Law, War and Crime* (Cambridge, 2007), 156–157.

it gives to improved standards of international conduct and, if the theory of punishment is broad enough, by the implicit condemnation of ruthlessness and unlawful force as instruments of attaining national ends."[12] The Nuremberg and Tokyo trials thus represent the first significant efforts to prosecute individuals for crimes under international law.

The environment of the late 1940s would appear to have been ideal for such endeavors. The Nuremberg Trials were widely lauded internationally.[13] The language of human rights was becoming a political *lingua franca*. International cooperation was to be institutionalized at the new United Nations. Yet with the exception of the Genocide Convention of 1948, almost no headway was made in codifying or institutionalizing the legalist paradigm of mass violence for fifty years after the war. It was not until the 1990s, with the creation first of the ad hoc International Criminal Tribunals for the Former Yugoslavia (1993) and Rwanda (1994) and the drafting of the statute for the permanent International Criminal Court (1998), that the high promises of the 1940s were (seemingly) fulfilled. Why? In other words, why did the optimists of the late 1940s prove to be so spectacularly wrong when they prophesized a new day dawning for international legalism?

The first, and for some the most obvious, answer is that the legalist endeavor was doomed from the start, that Nuremberg was itself an anomaly, an illusion even, created under highly specific circumstances that could not possibly be generalized. International relations "realists" have been the strongest proponents of this hypothesis. As that great skeptic of all international institutions, John Bolton, then Undersecretary of State for Arms Control and International Security, and subsequently a controversial U.S. Ambassador to the United Nations, remarked to the Federalist Society in 2002: "The ICC does not, and cannot, fit into a coherent, international structural 'constitutional' design that delineates clearly how laws are made, adjudicated or enforced, subject to popular accountability and structured to protect liberty. There is no such design, nor should there be. Instead, the Court and the Prosecutor are simply 'out there' in the international system."[14] In a more scholarly vein, Jack L. Goldsmith and Eric A. Posner have argued recently that states accept international jurisdiction only when it is in their interest to do so.[15] The legalist paradigm of war, on this reading, is simply one instrument of state craft among many, used or disregarded as necessary. On this reading, then, the very nature of the international arena renders any efforts to juridify it illusory from

---

[12] "American Memorandum Presented at San Francisco, April 30, 1945," in Robert H. Jackson, *Report of Robert H. Jackson United States Representative to the International Conference on Military Trials* (Washington, D.C., 1949), 34.

[13] See, e.g., the collection of reportage from around the globe in Steffen Radlmaier, *Der Nürnberger Lernprozeß: Von Kriegsverbrechern und Starreportern* (Frankfurt, 2001).

[14] John Bolton, "The United States and the International Criminal Court: Remarks to the Federalist Society" (November 14, 2002). Available at http://www.state.gov/t/us/rm/15158. htm. Accessed on May 19, 2008.

[15] Jack L. Goldsmith and Eric A. Posner, *The Limits of International Law* (Oxford, 2006).

the start. In the absence of both a unified global legislature capable of articulating consensual norms and an executive exercising a monopoly of legitimate force able to enforce them, all efforts to regulate mass violence through international law are really only efforts by some states to impose their will upon others gussied up in legalist terms. International law, in other words, is simply the continuation of politics by other means.

Yet the very revival of international legalism in the 1990s challenges this interpretation. The ICC in particular has attracted very broad support from the international community, including among states with antithetical "real interests." For instance, among the 105 countries that had become state parties to the ICC statute as of October 2007 were almost all of the central African nations (Congo, Democratic Republic of Congo, Central African Republic, and Burundi). These states have been involved in a decade-long, multilateral low-level war involving mass atrocities on all sides.[16] Citizens of each state could plausibly be accused of war crimes and crimes against humanity. One might argue that each of these countries signed the ICC statute in the hope of using it against its opponents. Yet in a situation in which all sides are committing international crimes, it is hard to see how it could be in the interest of any given party to sign a statute that could just as easily be used against them as their enemies. And, indeed, as of May 2008, most of the pending cases at the ICC pertained to the Democratic Republic of Congo, Uganda, or the Central African Republic.[17] So state interest can hardly explain the broad support for the ICC, though it doubtlessly does explain some of the opposition to it.

The timing of the revival of international legalism in the 1990s immediately raises the suspicion that the Cold War offers a necessary and sufficient explanation for the postwar stagnation of the legalist paradigm, and this is indeed the most common account given.[18] Clearly this timing is not coincidental. There is good reason to think that superpower rivalry stymied any significant codification or enforcement of international law. It is telling that the International Law Commission of the United Nations was instructed to stop its work on a Draft Code of International Offenses in 1954, at the height of the Korean War.[19] Nor is it surprising that the breaking point came over attempts to work out a definition of aggression, something of which both sides in the Korean conflict accused the other. Since neither side was willing to allow its

---

[16] Gérard Prunier, *Africa's World War: Congo, the Rwandan Genocide, and the Making of a Continental Catastrophe* (Oxford, 2009).

[17] http://www.icc-cpi.int/cases.html. See also International Criminal Court, "Prosecutor opens investigation in the Central African Republic," May 22, 2007. ICC-OTP-PR-20070522-220_EN. Available at http://www.icc-cpi.int/pressrelease_details&id=248.html.

[18] See, e.g., William A. Schabas, *An Introduction to the International Criminal Court*, 3rd ed. (Cambridge, 2007); Bruce Broomhall, *International Justice and the International Criminal Court: Between Sovereignty and the Rule of Law* (Oxford, 2004); and Phillip Sands (ed.), *From Nuremberg to the Hague: The Future of International Criminal Justice* (Cambridge, 2003).

[19] U.N. Resolution 897 (IX), December 4, 1954. Document A/Resolutions/245.

wars of liberation to be defined by the other as wars of aggression, and given
the prominence of proxy guerilla wars where atrocities were not uncommon,
whether in Vietnam, Angola, or Nicaragua, there can be no doubt that the
Cold War was a particularly hostile environment to the development of international criminal law. The United States' temporary "withdrawal" from the
jurisdiction of the International Court of Justice in anticipation of the suit
brought against it by Nicaragua over U.S. support for the Contras and the
mining of Nicaraguan harbors, as well as the United States' successful efforts
to thwart enforcement of the eventual verdict in that case, further demonstrate
the impotence of international legalism in the face of Cold War proxy wars.[20]
The particular structure of the United Nations, where the General Assembly
was itself heavily divided by Cold War rivalries and where the United States
and the USSR were permanent members of the Security Council, made it all
the easier for superpower rivalries to impose themselves on efforts at international legalism.

   Yet, while there can be no doubt that the Cold War was one major reason
for the stagnation of the legalist paradigm in the postwar period, it would
be overly simplistic to make this the whole story. For one thing, there were
important developments in international criminal law, especially in the early
postwar period, despite the already mounting hostility between the United
States and the USSR. The Genocide Convention is only the most obvious
and important of these. Moreover, the UN General Assembly, which was in
important respects as significant as the Security Council for at least the provisional development of international criminal law, showed itself willing to
buck superpower desires on more than one occasion in the postwar decades,
especially with the growth of the nonaligned movement.[21] Finally, the ongoing, and indeed mounting, hostility of the United States to international legalism over the past fifteen years gives the lie to the notion that it was only the
bipolarity of the Cold War that generated suspicion of international criminal
legal institutions among major powers.[22] There is a degree of complacency in
explaining the postwar stagnation in international legalism solely in terms of
Cold War rivalries. After all, if the Cold War alone was to blame, then the
future should be easy for international legalism. Sadly, this seems unlikely.

   To fully understand the failure of the legalist paradigm to live up to the
high expectations for it, it is useful to examine with some care what exactly
did transpire in the realm of international criminal law between the end of the
Nuremberg Trials and the end of the Cold War. In both the limited successes

[20] See the relevant documents, including the verdict "Military and Paramilitary Activities in and
    against Nicaragua (Nicaragua v. United States), Merits, Judgment, ICJ, 1986. Available at
    http://www.icj-cij.org/docket/index.php?p1=3&p2=3&code=nus&case=70&k=66. Accessed
    on May 28, 2008. For the U.S. response, see William M. LeoGrande, *Our Own Backyard: The
    United States in Central America, 1977–1992,* new ed. (Chapel Hill, N.C., 2000).
[21] A. W. Singham, *The Nonaligned Movement in World Politics* (Westport, Conn., 1977).
[22] Sarah B. Sewall and Carl Kaysen, *The United States and the International Criminal
    Court: National Security and International Law* (New York, 2000).

and the more capacious failings of international legalism in these decades, we can discern both direct and immediate political challenges and deeper, more structural constraints on what international criminal law could hope to achieve. These become clear in particular in the debates surrounding the International Genocide Convention, on the one hand, and the efforts to craft a Code of International Offenses, on the other. The former succeeded in becoming law, albeit with serious limitations on jurisdiction, whereas the later failed to achieve anything of much substance for fifty years. Yet the debates around both international instruments held much in common.

Criminalizing Genocide

Genocide was the term coined by Raphael Lemkin in 1944 to describe efforts to exterminate entire peoples based solely on their identity.[23] The term was mentioned in the International Military Tribunal indictment at Nuremberg and in the indictments of some of the Nuremberg successor trials as well, though it was not codified in the London Charter. Genocide was among the first issues in international criminal law to be taken up by the United Nations and the only one to achieve early success.[24] At the first session of the UN in the fall of 1946, Cuba, India, and Panama put a Genocide Resolution on the agenda.[25] After substantial debate in the Sixth (Legal) Committee, a version of the Cuban Genocide Resolution was passed by the UN General Assembly on December 11, 1946.[26] General Assembly Resolution 96(I) defined genocide loosely, as the destruction, "entirely or in part" of "racial, religious, political and other [!] groups." It affirmed that genocide was a crime under international law, called on states to enact domestic legislation to punish it, and recommended "international co-operation" to prevent and punish instances of genocide. Because this was only a General Assembly Resolution, it did not have the binding force of international law. Consequently, the General Assembly also asked the Economic and Social Council of the UN (ECOSOC) to study the feasibility of a more potent international convention on genocide.

Per Resolution 96(I), ECOSOC requested a draft Convention from the UN Secretariat and took up debate of the draft briefly in August 1947, referring the issue back to the Secretariat for further commentary by member states. In

[23] Raphael Lemkin, *Axis Rule in Occupied Europe: Laws of Occupation, Analysis of Government, Proposals for Redress* (Washington, D.C., 1944). On Lemkin and the genocide convention, see John Cooper, *Raphael Lemkin and the Struggle for the Genocide Convention* (Basingstoke, 2008), and, more generally, Samantha Powers, *A Problem from Hell: America in the Age of Genocide* (New York, 2002). See also Dirk Moses's illuminating comments in A. Dirk Moses, "The Holocaust and Genocide," in Dan Stone (ed.), *The Historiography of the Holocaust* (London, 2006), 533–555.

[24] The best summary of the complex legislative history of the genocide convention can be found in William A. Schabas, *Genocide in International Law: The Crime of Crimes* (Cambridge, 2000), 42–47, 51–81.

[25] UN Doc A/Bur.50.

[26] GA Res. 96(I).

December 1947, the General Assembly referred the draft Convention, together with comments from member states, to the Sixth (Legal) Committee for further discussion. In a bureaucratic back and forth that was beginning to resemble a game of "hot potato," the Sixth Committee referred the whole question of a genocide convention back to the General Assembly, recommending further study by the ECOSOC. The General Assembly then passed a further resolution (Resolution 180(II), November 21, 1948), reaffirming its intention to draft an international convention prohibiting genocide and asking ECOSOC, in consultation with member governments and other UN bodies, to prepare a report by the third session of the General Assembly the following year. In the spring of 1948, an ad hoc committee of the ECOSOC prepared a new draft of the Genocide Convention, which was submitted to the General Assembly in August 1948. Following extensive debate among the General Assembly's Sixth Committee, the Convention on the Prevention and Punishment of the Crime of Genocide was passed on December 9, 1948.

As can be seen from even this rather cursory summary of the legislative history of the Genocide Convention, there was no small degree of bureaucratic dickering and foot-dragging involved. There were good reasons for this having little to do with bureaucratic inertia. It was easy (and cheap) to morally abhor genocide. Doing something about it invariably came with political costs attached. The most obvious and important of these was that formally criminalizing genocide in an international convention would inevitably entail at least nominal restrictions on the behavior of states and potentially provide a pretext for international interference in domestic affairs. There was also the difficult question of jurisdiction. If genocide was a crime of state, who could prosecute it? As many would argue in the subsequent debates, only an international criminal court was likely to have the independence necessary to sit in judgment on such crimes. Yet a permanent court laying claim to a superordinate international jurisdiction proved to be an intolerable threat to national sovereignty for a great many delegates. Finally, there was the simple fact that a convention would require a careful and authoritative definition of genocide. This could either narrow or expand the meaning of what was already becoming a particularly potent term of moral and political opprobrium.

The Cuban delegate, Ernesto Dihigo, in introducing what would become General Assembly Resolution 96(I) sought an expansive definition of genocide. He pointed out that the Nuremberg judgment had restricted its jurisdiction to crimes connected with the waging of aggressive war, raising the possibility that genocide in peacetime might not yet be illegal under international law and thus might "remain unpunished owing to the principle *nullum crimen sine lege*."[27] Dihigo was right to be concerned, given the mounting hostility within Germany to the allegedly ex post facto prosecution of Nazi crimes.[28]

---

[27] UN Doc A/C.6.84.
[28] Devin O. Pendas, "Retroactive Law and Proactive Justice: Debating Crimes against Humanity in Germany, 1945–1950," *Central European History*, 43 (Fall 2010) 428–63.

Yet there were good reasons for strongly linking genocide to more demonstrably international crimes such as aggressive war.

At the London Conference drafting the statute of the International Military Tribunal, Robert Jackson had declared:

It has been a general principle of foreign policy of our Government from time immemorial that the internal affairs of another government are not ordinarily our business; that is to say, the way Germany treats its inhabitants, or any other country treats its inhabitants, is not our affair any more than it is the affair of some other government to interpose itself in our problems. The reason that this program of extermination of Jews and destruction of the rights of minorities becomes an international concern is this: it was a part of a plan for making an illegal war. Unless we have a war connection as a basis for reaching them, I would think we have no basis for dealing with atrocities. They were a part of the preparation for war or for the conduct of war in so far as they occurred inside of Germany and that makes them our concern.[29]

Jackson explicitly wanted to exclude any consideration of Nazi atrocities not linked to the waging of aggressive war. The IMT judgment largely supported him in this.[30] Jackson rejected the notion that international criminal law might impose enforceable obligations on the domestic behavior of states not simply because this might violate the prohibition on ex post facto legislation but more fundamentally because it would undermine the foundational assumption of the international order: the doctrines of sovereignty and noninterference. Indeed, Jackson's sense, shared by most of his colleagues in crafting U.S. policy toward Nazi atrocities, was that it was Nazi war, not Nazi genocide, that had made the Third Reich an unparalleled threat to civilization. Criminalizing domestic state behavior might even legitimate aggressive war, in defense, say, of persecuted minorities in neighboring states. This would have precisely the opposite effect Jackson hoped for from the IMT proceedings. This issue would repeatedly arise in the negotiations surrounding the drafting of the Genocide Convention, where the fear was frequently voiced that international law might cause wars, not deter them.

The initial draft of what became Resolution 96(I), unlike the final resolution, made no reference to "political and other groups" in its definition of the potential victims of genocide.[31] This question as to how broadly to define potential victim groups was to be a recurring source of conflict in the debate. The final draft of the Genocide Resolution noted that such an assault on human groups "results in great losses to humanity in the form of cultural and other contributions represented by these human groups."[32] Here Lemkin's influence on the definition of genocide can be discerned. Lemkin, who had an

[29] Robert H. Jackson, "Minutes of Conference Session of July 23, 1945" in Jackson, *Report*, 331.
[30] Donald Bloxham, *Genocide on Trial: War Crimes Trials and the Formation of Holocaust History and Memory* (Oxford, 2001), 69–75.
[31] UN Doc A/C.6/SR.22.
[32] GA Res. 96(I).

almost Herderian sense of cultural groups as bearers of identity, fought a long and ultimately unsuccessful battle to have cultural genocide included in the final convention.

In the debate on the Cuban/Indian/Panamanian draft Resolution before the Sixth Committee, several interesting positions emerged. The Soviets spoke in favor of the Resolution, but their arguments are telling. The Soviet representative, Alexander Lavrischev, declared, "Racial hate was one of the characteristic features of fascist regimes and many lives had been lost in the fight against fascism; the General Assembly was therefore justified in attaching great importance to racial discrimination."[33] Lavrischev even suggested that the UN "draft [an] international convention concerning the struggle against racial discrimination."[34] The Soviets were thus early supporters of a genocide resolution. This may seem surprising given their subsequent hostility to the Genocide Convention, but in fact it is wholly consistent with the instrumentalism of Soviet attitudes toward international law more generally. It is true that the reference to "other groups" in the definition of genocide might have been a source of some concern to the Soviets, whose own mass murder inclined to the political, rather than racial. Lavrischev redefined "genocide" as a form of fascist racism, linking the two terms inextricably. On Lavrischev's account, it would be impossible for a nonfascist regime to commit genocide. On this approach, genocide becomes a highly specific species of political crime, defined as much by the kind of regime engaged in acts of mass violence as by the nature of the target group or the intent of the killing. On the other hand, Lavrischev's emphasis on racism was not purely retrospective in character. The Soviets had already discerned in the hypocritical policies of racial segregation in the southern United States a useful target for propaganda.[35] Implicitly at least, Lavrischev was linking the past enemy (Germany) to the present one (the United States) and trying to shift the definition of genocide in a direction useful for attacking both. The potential advantage of identifying and condemning racial mass murder as "genocide," and thereby implicitly tarring the United States with the brush of its own racism, outweighed any risk that the Soviets might themselves be accused of the genocidal murder of ill-defined "other groups." Indeed, the Soviets would continually (and unsuccessfully) seek to insert explicit references to Nazi racism into the preamble of the Genocide Convention in its various iterations.[36]

Moreover, the Genocide Resolution was neither binding nor contained enforcement mechanisms, obviating most of the Soviets' concerns about the subsequent Convention. The chief Soviet objection to the Genocide Convention

---

[33] UN Doc A/C.6.84.

[34] Ibid.

[35] Mary L. Dudziak, *Cold War Civil Rights: Race and the Image of American Democracy*, new ed. (Princeton, 2002), and Thomas Borstelmann, *The Cold War and the Color Line: American Race Relations in the Global Arena*, new ed. (Cambridge, 2003).

[36] Schabas, *Genocide in International Law*, 80.

was its potential impingement on the sovereignty of state parties and the atten-
dant risk that it would justify international interference in domestic affairs.
Since the final draft of the Genocide Resolution dropped earlier calls for universal jurisdiction in favor of ill-defined "international co-operation," the
Soviets had little to fear from it and much to gain in their propaganda campaign against the United States.

The second aspect of the debate over the draft text of the Genocide Resolution
worth noting is the uncertainty that prevailed over the relationship between state
and individual culpability for genocide. Hartley Shawcross, former chief British
prosecutor at Nuremberg, now representing the United Kingdom on the Sixth
Committee, proposed an amendment to the Cuban draft, urging the Committee
to declare "that genocide is an international crime for the commission of which
principals and accessories, as well as states, are individually responsible."[37] The
French representative, Charles Chaumont, opposed the British amendment on
the grounds that "French law did not admit criminal responsibility on the part
of states." He suggested instead that the relevant paragraph should simply state
that "genocide is an international crime for which the principal authors and
accomplices, whether responsible statesmen or private individuals, should be
punished."[38] Britain and France worked out an interim compromise a week
later, whereby the paragraph would now read "genocide is an international
crime, entailing the responsibility of guilty individuals, whether principals or
accessories, as well as states on behalf of which they may have acted."[39] In the
final draft, all reference to state responsibility was dropped. The relevant paragraph read simply that "principals and accomplices – whether private individuals, public officials or statesmen ... are punishable."[40]

This issue was of far more than merely technical significance, since it
directly related to the highly political issue of jurisdiction for genocide. At
its core, the issue was whether genocide should be subject to the jurisdiction
of an as yet to be established international criminal court, to the newly created International Court of Justice, to the universal jurisdiction of all states
on the model of piracy, or simply to the jurisdiction of the domestic courts
of the country where genocide was perpetrated and/or where the perpetrators had citizenship. Also possible was some system of mixed jurisdiction (as
both the United States and the United Kingdom were to subsequently suggest).
The British assertion that states as such could be liable for genocide would
mean it needed to be treated under existing norms of international law as an
inter-*state* affair, subject to international sanctions but not, at least as an act
of state, to criminal ones. The British position implied, as they later made
explicit, that there was no need for a new International *Criminal* Court. The
existing International Court of Justice, with its voluntary jurisdiction over

[37] UN Doc A/C.6/84.
[38] Ibid.
[39] UN Doc A/C.6/95.
[40] GA Res. 96(I).

interstate conflicts and its limited range of noncriminal sanctions, would suffice. If states as states could not be held criminally accountable, as the French insisted, then genocide could only be a matter for international criminal law addressed to individuals and would require a reconfiguration of international jurisdiction and institutions accordingly. Ultimately, what was at stake was the nature of international law itself. Would it continue to serve as a referee between independent states whose sovereignty was sustained, not challenged, by international law? Or would it operate more on the model of domestic law, where the law set boundaries on the independence and freedom of action of legal actors?

This issue came up again much more explicitly two years later in the Sixth Committee debates over the secretariat's draft Genocide Convention. Here the debate revolved more openly around the question of whether it was necessary to create a new International Criminal Court with jurisdiction over at least genocide and perhaps over other international crimes as well. (The initial secretariat draft of the Genocide Convention contained, as appendices, two draft statutes for an ICC, one with restricted jurisdiction over genocide alone, another with broader jurisdiction over international crimes to be defined by the International Law Commission.) Here the United States and the United Kingdom both proposed slightly different mixed solutions. Both agreed that national courts ought to have jurisdiction over acts of genocide committed by individuals. The United States favored creating an International Criminal Court to try individuals "where genocide is committed by or with the connivance of the State.... All other cases would involve acts against the laws of the State where they are perpetrated."[41] Because private acts of genocide seem unlikely, the American proposal would have amounted to a de facto grant of jurisdiction for genocide to an as yet to be constructed International Criminal Court.

The United Kingdom, meanwhile, favored a more modest approach whereby the International Court of Justice would have (noncriminal) jurisdiction over government actions, while national courts would exercise territorial jurisdiction over individual criminal acts.[42] This modest approach stemmed from the United Kingdom's general skepticism regarding the whole project of a genocide convention. Hartley Shawcross argued in the course of the debates over the ad hoc Committee's draft Convention that it was important not to artificially inflate expectations for what a genocide convention might achieve: "It was a complete delusion to suppose that the adoption of a convention of the type proposed, even if generally adhered to, would give people a greater sense of security or would diminish existing dangers of persecution on racial, religious or national grounds."[43] Such persecutions, he pointed out, were ongoing even

---

[41] "Communications Received by the Secretary General," Communication from the United States of America, September 30, 1947. UN Doc A/401.
[42] UN Doc A/C.6/SR 95.
[43] UN Doc A/C.6/SR 64, 17.

as the Committee debated. Calling on his moral authority as a Nuremberg prosecutor, Shawcross continued, "nobody believed that the existence of a convention, such as was proposed, would have deterred the Nazis or fascists from committing the atrocious crimes of which they had been guilty." In an obvious dig at the Soviets, he concluded, "Those crimes were largely the crimes of totalitarian states, which would not change their methods because of the existence of a convention to which a number of nations adhered."

France, on the other hand, found the British position disconcerting. Samuel Spanien, the French representative on the Sixth Committee, pointed to the "danger there would be, once the principle of the responsibility of rulers had been admitted, in relying on national courts for the repression of genocide, a crime which was generally committed only by states or with their complicity."[44] He rejected the British proposal of turning over acts of state to the International Court of Justice, on the ground that that court had no jurisdiction in criminal matters. "Genocide was committed only through the criminal intervention of public authorities; that was what distinguished it from murder pure and simple. The purpose of the convention which the Committee was drawing up was not to punish individual murders, but to ensure the prevention and punishment of crimes committed by rulers." Hence, it was imperative, he concluded, to establish an International Criminal Court forthwith.

In the end, of course, no international criminal court was created in conjunction with the Genocide Convention. The British proposal to grant the International Court of Justice a role was upheld in Article IX, which allowed the ICJ to adjudicate interstate disputes regarding the "interpretation, application or fulfillment" of the Convention.[45] Article VI, a U.S. compromise proposal, did leave open the possibility of such an international criminal tribunal being created in future and assuming jurisdiction over genocide.[46] This was an important provision, for otherwise the Convention might have required amendment in the future to allow any international criminal court that came into being to have jurisdiction over genocide. Nonetheless, the very vagueness of this formulation caused considerable consternation among numerous delegates, who were in effect being asked to acquiesce to the jurisdiction of a court whose powers and procedures were as yet unknown. The British, for instance, strongly objected on these grounds.

Other delegates went further, however, objecting to the entire Genocide Convention on the grounds that any mention of an international criminal court was unacceptable. Victor Pérez Perozo representing Venezuela, for example, argued that "the institution of international criminal jurisdiction could only lead to unfortunate results, in view of the existing world situation. Friction might be created which could disturb the peace among nations. The establishment of international penal jurisdiction should be reserved for the future

---

[44] UN Doc. A/C.6/SR 97, 373.
[45] GA Res 260(III).
[46] Ibid. For the U.S. proposal, see UN Doc. A/C.6/SR 130.

when international relations would be more favorable to such an institution."[47] Far from being an instrument for creating world peace, as its more optimistic advocates hoped, Pérez Perozo asserted that an international criminal court could be created only once such peace was already attained. The Polish representative concurred, adding that any future international criminal court, in order to be effective, would have to have compulsory jurisdiction, unlike the ICJ. Such compulsory jurisdiction "might constitute intervention in the domestic affairs of states and a violation of national sovereignty."[48] Despite his general willingness to compromise for the sake of harmony on the Committee, he could not "sacrifice questions of principle," leaving him no choice but to oppose any mention of an international criminal court in the Convention.

If, despite the grave concerns of a number of states, the Genocide Convention nonetheless passed and eventually came into effect, this has to be seen as the high water mark of international legalism in the immediate postwar years. No doubt part of this success was due to the momentum carried forward from Nuremberg. The all too recent memories of Nazi genocide certainly also played a role. At the same time, however, the success of the Genocide Convention was also purchased at the price of watering down its enforcement mechanisms. Despite the controversial inclusion of a reference to a hypothetical international criminal court, jurisdiction over genocide was left to territorial states, making prosecution exceedingly unlikely. The first serious attempt to prosecute genocide in domestic courts came in 1999 when nearly one hundred members of the Argentine military were indicted in domestic courts for genocide, though the only convictions that emerged were for "crimes against humanity within the framework of genocide," a rather hollow and legally meaningless formulation.[49] It is hardly surprising that the first successful prosecution for genocide would not occur until the Akayesu case before the ICTR in 1998. As Samuel Spanien had predicted, without an international court, genocide proved impossible to prosecute.

For all its success in formulating a minimal definition of genocide subject to the vagaries of diplomatic negotiation, the genocide convention could hardly be called a stunning triumph of international law. It is an almost unenforceable law, given that the prosecutors and the perpetrators would have to be the same people. Yet this fatal flaw was the price of its limited success.

Codifying International Criminal Law

If the Genocide Convention succeed by sacrificing most of elements that would have made its success meaningful, additional efforts to codify international

---

[47] UN Doc A/C.6/SR 130.
[48] Ibid.
[49] Daniel Feierstein, "National Security Doctrine in Latin America," in Dirk Moses and Donald Bloxham (eds.), *The Oxford Handbook of the History of Genocide* (Oxford, 2010), 500–501.

criminal law in the postwar decades achieved even less. In November 1947, the General Assembly resolved to have the International Law Commission (ILC) both formulate the so-called Nuremberg principles of international law and "prepare a draft code of offenses against the peace and security of mankind," which would stipulate how this code related to the Nuremberg principles.[50] Since the question of an international criminal court had been left deliberately open in the Genocide Convention, the General Assembly also asked the ILC to "study the desirability and possibility of establishing an international judicial organ."[51] With this, the ILC was put in charge of both codifying the normative principles and legal statutes of the legalist paradigm as well as structuring its (potential) institutional embodiment.[52] That this proved to be a daunting challenge was no surprise, given the controversies that had already manifested themselves in the debates over the Genocide Convention.

At its first annual session in 1949, the fifteen members of the ILC appointed three rapporteurs to consider these issues. Jean Spiropoulos of Greece was charged with drafting a report on both the Nuremberg principles and on the draft code of offenses. Ricardo J. Alfaro of Panama and Emil Sandström of Sweden were asked to draw up reports on an international criminal court. All three were to report back the following year. In April 1950, Spiropoulos presented his report. After considering the nature of his task, he began by restricting the scope of the draft code, insisting that it was clear it ought to refer only to "political" crimes, not other kinds of international criminality. The code "is intended to refer to acts which, if committed or tolerated by a State, would constitute violations of international responsibility.... These are offenses which, on account of their specific character, normally would affect international relations in a way dangerous for the *maintenance of peace.*"[53] Of the nine offenses listed in Spriopoulos's draft code, the first four concerned various forms of aggressive action against other states, while only the last two (genocide and war crimes) concerned crimes against individuals. The remaining three articles (5–7) concerned the observance of international treaties.

Spiropoulos explicitly rejected the notion that states could bear criminal responsibility, noting that although there had been much academic speculation on this matter, there was no precedent for imposing penal sanctions on states as such, only on individuals. He did add, however, that "the limitation of criminal responsibility to individuals, in no way affects the traditional responsibility of states, under international law, for reparations, a topic which is independent of the question of criminal responsibility."[54] This was less a rejection of the mutual entanglement of state and individual criminality

[50] GA Res 177 (II).
[51] GA Res 260 (III) B.
[52] For a general account, see Benjamin B. Ferencz, *An International Criminal Court: A Step Toward World Peace – A Documentary History and Analysis* (London, 1980), 16–90.
[53] UN Doc A/CN.4/25. "Report by J. Spiropoulos, Special Rapporteur," *Yearbook of the International Law Commission*, vol. 2, 1950 (New York, 1957).
[54] Ibid.

characteristic of the legalist paradigm that it was a further specification of it. After all, the IMT had likewise insisted that criminal guilt was personal and that "crimes against international law are committed by men, not by abstract entities."[55] The point had always been that acts of state could be criminal. But it was precisely on this issue that Spiropoulos began to modify and weaken the legalist paradigm. He argued that for reasons of political expediency, it would be wise to drop the Nuremberg Charter's explicit exclusion of the defense of superior orders, "in order to facilitate the adoption of the draft code by governments." Spiropoulos, of course, still noted that state agents could commit crimes (otherwise no code of international law for political crimes would be possible); he did insist, however, that insofar as such agents were acting on superior orders, their official position ought to be considered a mitigating factor in their punishment.

Finally, Spiropoulos briefly considered the potential mechanisms for enforcing the draft code: ad hoc international tribunals, a permanent international court, and enforcement by domestic courts. The first approach would reduce the code to a list of offenses, with no provisions for enforcement. This was hardly the preferred option, but Spiropoulos thought it at least better than nothing, saying it would be "unrealistic" to reject a limited code in favor of a more complete but "unobtainable" one. Spiropoulos was particularly skeptical of the prospects for a permanent international tribunal. In the absence of an international executive with powers of arrest and detention, it was "very unrealistic" to expect states in violation of international criminal law to turn over or extradite their citizens to stand trial for state-sponsored offenses.[56] Spiropoulos's preferred option was to have domestic courts, acting on the basis of domestic legislation incorporating the draft code of international offences, enforce international law. In part, this was because he followed the genocide convention as "a *decisive* precedent," but also because he felt this was the most realistic option, given the current state of international affairs.

Spiropoulos's draft code of international offences thus incorporated all of the weaknesses of the Genocide Convention and added several of its own. A mere five years after the Nuremberg Trials, the legalist paradigm was being actively undermined and diminished by the people most actively involved in its implementation. And even this proved to be more than the international community was willing to swallow, as the ensuing ILC debate concerning a permanent international criminal court quickly revealed. The two rapporteurs assigned to draft reports on a permanent court could hardly have produced more different results. Alfaro came down strongly in favor of establishing a permanent international criminal court, one with broad jurisdiction, though he did suggest limiting the referral of cases to the Security Council. Alfaro rejected sovereignty-based objections to a permanent court, noting that the

[55] International Military Tribunal, *Trial of the Major War Criminals before the International Military Tribunal, 14 November 1945–1 October 1946*, vol. 22 (Nuremberg, 1946), 466.
[56] UN Doc A/CN 4/25, "Report by J. Spiropoulos."

nature of many of the crimes likely to fall under the jurisdiction of such a court (crimes against peace, crimes against humanity, genocide) were such that domestic courts would be incapable of judging them. "A more general but equally direct answer," he added,

is that the principle of absolute sovereignty is incompatible with the present organization of the world.... Against the theory of absolute sovereignty stands the incontrovertible, palpable fact of the interdependence of States.... For States as well as for individuals, the right of everyone is limited by the rights of others. The sovereignty of the State is subordinate to the supremacy of international law.[57]

Sandström, on the other hand, opposed the creation of a permanent court. He pointed out that international law had long existed independently of such a court and obviously therefore did not depend on the existence of a permanent court for its own survival. He feared that "a failure [by such a court] would expose the inefficiency of the international organization and thereby harm its prestige and development."[58] To those who pointed to Nuremberg as a precedent and as an example of the need for a permanent court to avoid the appearance of victor's justice, Sandström replied that this was a false analogy. Nuremberg, he said, "was the result of an extraordinarily complete defeat and a complete agreement between the victors on the questions involved in the trial." This situation was unlikely to repeat itself. "In my opinion," he concluded, "the cons outweigh by far the pros. A permanent judicial criminal organ established in the actual organization of the international community would be impaired by very serious defects and would do more harm than good. The time cannot as yet be considered ripe for the establishment of such an organ."

Although the ILC as a whole sided with Alfaro rather than Sandström, voting eight to one that it would be desirable to establish a permanent court and seven to two that such a court was feasible, it was Sandström who in the long run proved the more astute analyst.[59] In the ensuing debates in the Sixth (Legal) Committee, opinions were sharply divided along the predictable lines of Alfaro/Sandström and, as a result, the Committee recommended further study of both the draft code and the question of international jurisdiction, which the General Assembly approved.[60] This began a pattern that was to continue throughout the 1950s. Reports would be drafted on the code of international offenses and on international jurisdiction, these would be debated by both the ILC and the Sixth (Legal) Committee, then the General Assembly would appoint new committees and ask for further study. Consensus and

---

[57] UN Doc A/CN.4/15. International Law Commission, "Question of International Criminal Jurisdiction: Report by Ricardo J. Alfaro, Special Rapporteur," March 3, 1950.
[58] UN Doc A/CN.4/20. International Law Commission, "Question of International Criminal Jurisdiction: Report by Emil Sandström, Special Rapporteur," March 30, 1950.
[59] UN Doc A/1316. *Report of the International Law Commission Covering its Second Session, 5 June–29 July 1950* (Lake Success, N.Y., 1950).
[60] UN Doc 1/1639; GA Res 488 (V), December 12, 1950; GA Res 489 (V), December 12, 1950.

agreement were nowhere in sight. While much effort was expended, nothing of substance was accomplished.

Adding to these difficulties was the mounting challenge of defining aggression, which, after all, lay at the very heart of the enterprise. In November 1950, in the context of a mounting war of words over aggression in Korea, the Soviet Union had proposed a definition aimed directly at U.S. intervention on the peninsula.[61] In response, the General Assembly asked the ILC to consider a definition of aggression.[62] In other words, although aggression had always been part of the work on the draft code, the General Assembly was now asking the ILC to consider the definition of aggression as an independent matter, part of but more important than the broader work of drafting an international code. As a result, the most politically charged issue of the Cold War became the touchstone for the international code, making the politics of reaching a consensus on the content of international criminal law that much less likely. As Benjamin Ferencz has pointed out, the definition of aggression became inextricably linked to the drafting of a code of international offences, which in turn became coupled to the question of international jurisdiction. In his pointed phrasing, "no code without aggression – no court without a code."[63]

Unsurprisingly, it was precisely on these issues that further work on the draft code of international offences, and with it all substantive work toward creating a permanent international criminal court, faltered. Though the General Assembly appointed special committees to work on the definition of aggression and on the problem of international jurisdiction and the ILC continued to work and rework drafts of the international code, no progress was made for the next four years. In 1954 the General Assembly decided to postpone further work on the draft code until such time as the definition of aggression could be worked out by the special committee appointed for that task.[64] In the context, this meant in effect an indefinite postponement of work on the draft code, a decision formalized in 1957 when all work on the draft code was suspended until the General Assembly decided to resume work on the definition of aggression.[65] Not until the 1980s would this work resume, and then in a fairly desultory manner until the breakthroughs of the 1990s.

Human Rights and the Limits of the Law

What, if anything, does the stagnation of the legalist paradigm of mass political violence in the postwar decades tell us about the history of human

---

[61] UN Doc A/1858.
[62] GA Res 378 B (V), November 17, 1950.
[63] Ferencz, *An International Criminal Court*, 41.
[64] GA Res 897 (IX).
[65] GA Res 898 (IX), December 11, 1957.

rights? Insofar as this stagnation is explicable in terms of Cold War bipolarity, it tells us only that normative politics, including the politics of human rights, are as subject to the vagaries of power as any other form of politics. In the context of superpower confrontation, the ability to claim the moral high ground was only slightly less useful than the ability to claim the strategic high ground. Human rights language could be exceedingly valuable in this regard. Both sides claimed to embody a more perfect human rights regime and frequently criticized their opponents' human rights failings. As Benjamin Nathans has shown, it would be too simplistic to say that the Soviets appealed to social and political rights, while the Western Powers lay claim to civil and political rights.[66] Nonetheless, both the Western and Eastern blocs tended to use human rights-talk as a Cold War weapon. Certainly neither side had any incentive to help create an international legal regime that might slip from their control or be turned against them. But there are broader and less well-known lessons to be drawn from the stagnation of the legalist paradigm as well.

First among these is the broad appeal of national sovereignty arguments in opposition to international legalism. In recent years, it has become popular to explain the United States' opposition to the ICC in terms of a kind of American exceptionalism.[67] As the world's sole remaining superpower, the United States resists constraints on its freedom of action in the international arena and rightly or wrongly fears "abuse" of the ICC to prosecute noncriminal U.S. actions for political reasons. All this is, of course, true. But the United States is less exceptional in this regard than its relatively isolated opposition to the ICC might lead one to suppose. In the postwar period, sovereignty was embraced by a wide range of state actors to oppose international legalism. Two groups in particular made sovereignty arguments central. The Eastern bloc was the first. Poland, Czechoslovakia, and Yugoslavia all abstained in the final vote of the Sixth Committee on the final draft of the Genocide Convention on sovereignty grounds.[68] The second group to oppose international jurisdiction over genocide and indeed over other international crimes were some of the Latin American countries, such as Venezuela and Brazil. As frequent victims of U.S. and European intervention in their domestic affairs, the Latin American states were understandably reluctant to cede their fragile and hard-won sovereignty to international institutions of dubious reliability.

Sovereignty concerns became even more prominent in subsequent decades as the nonaligned movement gained strength and something like a discernable "Third World" bloc emerged in the United Nations. Indeed, in the 1970s, efforts to pass a convention on terrorism and hostage taking repeatedly foundered on the opposition of African and Arab nations, which resisted any attempts to restrict the techniques available to legitimate freedom fighters

---

[66] See Benjamin Nathans's chapter in this volume.
[67] Michael Ignatieff, ed., *American Exceptionalism and Human Rights* (Princeton, 2005).
[68] UN Doc A/C.6/SR 132.

battling colonialism, racism, and foreign domination. Sovereignty could certainly be a cynical shield, useful for sheltering various forms of domestic atrocities and repression. It could also, however, be a rather legitimate concern on the part of nations often only recently independent and still frequently subject to indirect and all-too-direct interference in their domestic affairs.[69] That the ICC appears to have overcome for the time being at least some of these concerns may show the declining significance of sovereignty in a globalizing world. If the world is flat, then perhaps so too is international justice.[70] Yet Columbia's recent rather cynical attempt to bring Venezuela's President Hugo Chavez up on genocide charges before the ICC for his support of the FARC guerilla movement may well test this theory. Though it seems dubious that Chavez will actually be indicted, this represents precisely the kind of politicized proceeding that opponents of the court have long feared. Even if it amounts to nothing in legal terms, in political terms it may demonstrate the risks associated with providing an international sounding board for political grievances disguised as criminal complaints. The irony of the fact that it is the United States' ally Columbia bringing such politicized allegations against the United States' opponent Chavez may also help to spread discontent with the court beyond American shores.

It is also possible that support for the ICC especially among "Third World" states may reflect an expectation that it will be largely non-state actors, separatist rebels, guerilla insurgents, and the like, who will form the chief targets of prosecution. Indeed, the first major case pending before the ICC, against representatives of the Lord's Resistance Army in Uganda, gives reason to think this may prove to be the case.[71] The ongoing trial of former Liberian President Charles Taylor before the Special Court for Sierra Leone may be another example. Frequently touted as an example of the end of impunity for heads of state, Taylor's trial actually demonstrates that it is only failed tyrants who are prosecuted. More significantly, Taylor is charged not with crimes in Liberia but with crimes in neighboring Sierra Leone, that is, with crimes in violation of sovereignty. Far from challenging state sovereignty in the name of universal human rights, the ICC may come to serve as a major supporter of sovereignty, particularly for smaller states incapable of defending it themselves. In this respect, the ICC may ultimately represent less a break with the UN tradition of international support for national sovereignty than its continuation by other means.

On a deeper structural level, though, there is a core tension between international human rights movements as these have developed in the postwar period and the legalist paradigm of war. On some level, the two share certain

[69] Dirk Moses's contribution in this volume highlights several additional challenges facing international prosecutions for mass atrocities in the postcolonial world.
[70] Thomas L. Friedman, *The World Is Flat 3.0: A Brief History of the Twenty-First Century* (New York, 2007).
[71] Tim Allen, *Trial Justice: The International Criminal Court and the Lord's Resistance Army* (London, 2006).

fundamental goals, not least being a shared vision of a world guided by principles of "justice," rather than expediency and *Realpolitik*.[72] At the same time, the logic and tactics of human rights activism, on the one hand, and international legalism, on the other, are not always compatible. The reason for this is that, while human rights claims have often sought legal validation, the success of human rights rhetoric has frequently derived from its plasticity and expansiveness. Human rights can be, and frequently have been, defined quite broadly. This is a crucial source of their political power. Rights-talk is talk of substantive justice. This, however, has often been in marked tension with the precision and strict delimitation required of formal law. This becomes clear if one thinks of the "right to work," for instance. How could such a right be enforced under international law? Who could one sue, for instance, if one became unemployed? One's former employer? One's government? And in what court should such suits be brought? International or domestic? The notion of a right to work, certainly as an international right, is a politically potent expression of a desire for broadly distributed prosperity and the sense that gross poverty is unjust. It is not, however, a right that has, or could have, any actionable meaning under international law. In other words, the factors that enable the political success of human rights rhetoric can make legal codification more difficult, not less.

The same is often true even for civil and political rights that seem more amenable to juridification. For instance, there was considerable debate in the drafting of the Genocide Convention over whether the list of offenses constituting genocide should be, in legal terms, indicative or exhaustive. In the former case, the list would simply indicate some of the kinds of actions constituting genocide, without pretending to list every possible form that genocide could take. The advantage of this approach was that it left open the possibility of prosecuting new forms of genocide and avoided the prospect of genocide perpetrators escaping justice simply by virtue of their inventiveness. After all, no one had envisioned in 1939 that the Nazis would deploy homicidal gas chambers to exterminate millions of human beings. Future perpetrators might be equally creative. This openness and the corresponding commitment to a broad natural law understanding that justice was clearly discernable if not always easily codified was consonant with the logic of much postwar human rights activism. At the same time, these advantages created a corresponding weakness. An indicative list created the risk that future genocide prosecutions would end up in exactly the same boat as the Nuremberg Trials, prosecuting crimes that had not technically been illegal at the time of their commission in violation of the legal principle *nullum crimen sine lege*, there can be no crime without prior law. For this reason, the Genocide Convention in its final draft settled on an exhaustive list, thereby rendering future developments more difficult. Here the requirements of law trumped the politics of justice.

---

[72] Paul Gordon Lauren, *The Evolution of International Human Rights: Visions Seen* (Philadelphia, 2003).

That international law was expanded in the 1990s to include rape as an international crime indicates that such expansions are, of course, possible, but not always easy.[73]

Finally, at a deep structural level, the law itself has very real difficulties coming to terms with collective action. The attempt by the legalist paradigm to circumvent this problem by linking state and individual criminality has never been fully successful. Indeed, the compromise worked out in the Genocide Convention itself between the British and French positions, whereby state leaders but not states as such could be criminally liable for genocide, creates considerable problems in its own right. The frequent success of defendants in genocide or human rights cases in arguing for at least mitigating circumstances for state-sponsored crimes is one indicator of this. The profound challenges confronting the prosecution's efforts to prove genocide against Slobdan Milošević are another. In the end, then, the legalist paradigm failed to develop for fifty years for a combination of circumstantial and structural reasons. The circumstances have changed since the end of the Cold War, but the structural difficulties for the legalist paradigm remain and will likely affect the continued development of international criminal law in the coming decades.

[73] Kelly Dawn Askin, *War Crimes against Women: Prosecution in International War Crimes Tribunals* (The Hague, 1997).

11

"Source of Embarrassment"

Human Rights, State of Emergency, and the Wars of Decolonization

Fabian Klose

> *What Africans are fighting for is nothing revolutionary, it is found in the Charter of the United Nations.*
>
> Tom Mboya, 1958 (Kenyan Politician and Trade Unionist)[1]

By the summer of 1957, Sir Robert Armitage, British Governor of Nyasaland, was so tired of human rights debates that he decided to refuse to introduce the Universal Declaration of Human Rights into the curriculum of his colony's African schools.[2] Considering the anticipated worldwide attention – the coming year would see the tenth anniversary of the Declaration – he felt that the UN document's terminology was too difficult and exotic for an African schoolchild to be able to distinguish ideals from political realities. "We are, of course, doing the exact opposite of that which is set down in a number of the articles [of the Human Rights Declaration], and no doubt will continue to do so for the next generation at least, if not for ever."[3]

Placed in its larger context, Armitage's straightforward description of colonial rule as the "exact opposite" of proclaimed human rights was absolutely correct, corresponding to reality throughout the colonized world. Paradoxically, following the Second World War, colonial powers such as Britain and France had taken part in the creation of a human rights regime under the auspices of international organizations such as the United Nations in New York and the International Committee of the Red Cross in Geneva.

This article was supported by a fellowship within the Postdoc-Program of the German Academic Exchange Service (DAAD) and is based on the research for my Ph.D. dissertation, which is published as *Menschenrechte im Schatten kolonialer Gewalt. Die Dekolonisierungskriege in Kenia und Algerien 1945–1962* (Munich, 2009). For suggestions for this article, I would like to thank Jerome Samuelson, Eric D. Weitz, Martin H. Geyer, and Elena Schneider.

[1] Extract of the opening speech by Tom Mboya at the All African People's Conference at Accra in 1958, quoted in "Africa Talks: Algeria Is a Most Important Topic," *Daily Graphic*, December 10, 1958.

[2] Confidential Paper of the CO, July 1, 1957, TNA CO 1015/1819.

[3] Letter of Armitage to the CO, August 9, 1957, ibid.

From that moment on the Universal Declaration of Human Rights secured for every individual basic rights while Article 3 of the Geneva Conventions of 1949 preserved these rights even in times of armed conflict. At the same time, European colonial powers simultaneously and under all circumstances tried to prevent the extension of fundamental human rights in their colonial possessions. The global spread of such rights did not lie in their interest, because, after all, it delegitimized any claim to colonial rule or foreign domination. In this way a "divided world" with a humanitarian double standard was perpetuated.

This division became most evident in the course of the decolonization struggle after 1945, when various decolonization wars convulsed European colonial empires.[4] In their efforts to put down fierce anti-colonial movements in Indochina, Indonesia, Malaya, Kenya, Algeria, and Cyprus, Europeans did not hesitate to apply radical violence to maintain colonial rule. The result was a specific kind of colonial warfare – characterized by massive internment and resettlement of indigenous populations, systematic torture, and severe war crimes – that violated all norms of the then nascent human rights regime. Britain's Mau Mau war in Kenya (1952–1956) and the French-Algerian war (1954–1962) are two striking examples.

Against the background of these wars, this article treats the interdependence of two parallel and antagonistic developments that have received little attention thus far in scholarly research: the international codification of universal rights and the radicalization of colonial violence. This essay asks how could Britain and France, democratic European states under the rule of law, on the one hand participate actively in international human rights discourse, while on the other hand conduct wars in their overseas possessions that flagrantly violated human rights. It argues that human rights documents that provided a moral basis for the agitation of the anti-colonial movement became at the same time a growing "source of embarrassment" to the colonial powers. Particular attention is given to the colonial state of emergency. By examining two examples of decolonization warfare, Kenya and Algeria, it will be demonstrated that Great Britain and France used emergency laws to abolish elementary rights and provide their security forces with modes of unrestricted repression. This is of crucial importance. By proclaiming a state of emergency, the colonial rulers created the legal preconditions for the radicalization of colonial violence. In short, the article argues that the wars of decolonization became one of the first serious challenges to the newly established regime of human rights. From an international perspective that includes the often forgotten indigenous populations in the African and Asian colonies, the development of universal human rights was not a linear, progressive history, but one accompanied by extreme forms of colonial violence.

---

[4] See especially Robert Holland (ed.), *Emergencies and Disorder in the European Empires after 1945* (London, 1994).

Human Rights as a Moral Basis and Colonial "Source of Embarrassment"

In characterizing the process of decolonization as "the greatest extension and achievement of human rights in the history of the world,"[5] the historian Paul Gordon Lauren underlines the tremendous influence of global human rights discourse on the dissolution of European colonial empires. Especially among anti-colonial movements, universal human rights comprised the moral basis for the struggle for equal rights and national independence.[6] The people in the colonies had already grasped with great enthusiasm[7] the principles pronounced by the Allies during the Second World War in documents such as the 1941 Atlantic Charter.[8] To the young Nelson Mandela, for example, the Charter reaffirmed faith in the dignity of every human being and propagated a host of democratic principles: "Some in the West saw the Charter as empty promises, but not those of us in Africa. Inspired by the Atlantic Charter and the allied struggle against tyranny and oppression, the ANC created its own Charter, called for full citizenship of all Africans, the rights to buy land, and the repeal of all discriminatory legislation."[9] The Filipino general and later President Carlos Romulo spoke of a flame of hope that blazed forth over all Asia when the Atlantic Charter was proclaimed.[10] Africans made stronger claims than ever before on the principles of democracy and self-determination. The Nigerian Nnamdi Azikiwe described the "electrifying impact" of the Atlantic Charter on the indigenous population of West Africa.[11]

In addition, the Allied principles became a concrete reference point for political demands of the national movements in the colonies. On February 1943 the moderate Algerian nationalist leader Ferhat Abbas published his *Manifeste du Peuple Algerien* in which, referring to the Allies' Declaration, he called for an end to colonial oppression, the right to self-determination for all peoples, and an Algerian constitution based on human rights.[12] The central committee of his party, Amis du Manifeste et de la Liberte, commented upon the coming end of the war: "Long live the victory over fascism, Hitlerism,

---

[5] Paul Gordon Lauren, *The Evolution of International Human Rights. Vision Seen* (Philadelphia, 1998), 252.

[6] Bonny Ibhawoh, *Imperialism and Human Rights. Colonial Discourse of Rights and Liberties in African History* (Albany, 2007), 142, 156–160.

[7] See especially Elizabeth Borgwardt, *A New Deal for the World. America's Vision for Human Rights* (Cambridge, Mass., 2005), 34–35, 58; Ibhawoh, *Imperialism and Human Rights*, 152–155.

[8] Text of the Atlantic Charter as a press release of the U.S. State Department, August 14, 1941, NARA, RG 59.3, Records of Harley Notter, 1939–45, Lot File 60-D-224, Box 13.

[9] Nelson Mandela, *Long Walk to Freedom* (Boston, 1994), 83–84.

[10] General Romulo quoted in Lauren, *Vision Seen*, 191.

[11] Nnamdi Azikiwe, *The Atlantic Charter and British West Africa* (Lagos, 1943).

[12] Ferhat Abbas, Manifeste du Peuple Algérien, February 10, 1943, in Jean-Charles Jauffret (ed.), *La guerre d'Algérie par les documents, L'avertissement 10 février 1943–9 mars 1946* (Vincennes, 1990), 31–38.

colonialism and imperialism."[13] For them the Allied victory meant not only the destruction of the totalitarian threat but the end of colonial domination.

Just as the British Colonial Ministry had feared since 1939, the principles of liberty, equality, and independence that the Allies proclaimed during the war started to turn collectively into an "undesired boomerang"[14] for the colonial powers. This trend took on increasing strength after the war's end with the foundation of the United Nations and the creation of an international human rights regime. For instance, in October 1945 the delegates of the Fifth Pan-African Congress in Manchester derived their demands for racial equality, self-determination, and human rights directly from United Nations principles.[15] At the same time, they referred to a readiness to assert their natural rights violently in the case that the Western world would continue to cling to colonial oppression.[16]

The final resolution of the Afro-Asian Conference in Bandung in April 1955 not only placed renewed emphasis on the Universal Declaration of Human Rights but also made national independence the basic prerequisite to the full enjoyment of all other universal rights. By denying fundamental human rights, colonialism represented simultaneously a threat to international security and world peace.[17] Leading intellectuals such as Jean-Paul Sartre adopted this theme and interpreted it thus: "Colonialism denies human rights to people it has subjugated by violence, and whom it keeps in poverty and ignorance by force."[18] Human rights discourse placed colonialism in the pillory of international public opinion. As human rights entered the moral armory of the anti-colonial struggle, African and Asian states invoked human rights themes to attack and expose the colonial powers diplomatically. The codification of a human rights regime and the establishment of human rights discourse in the consciousness of the international public was thus of crucial interest.

For the European powers, however, this development aggravated the dilemma presented by holding themselves out as supporters of human rights while violently defending their colonial ambitions.[19] The British colonial administrations of Gambia, the Gold Coast, and Sierra Leone commented

---

[13] Comité Central des "Amis du Manifest et de la Liberté," Manifestation à l'occasion de l'armistice, May 4, 1945, CAOM 81 F768.

[14] Minute of Dawe, September 22, 1939, TNA CO 323/1660/6281.

[15] See the Resolution "The Challenge to the Colonial Powers," in George Padmore, *Pan-Africanism or Communism* (New York, 1956), 170; and the Resolution "Declaration to the Colonial Workers, Farmers and Intellectuals," in Kwame Nkrumah, *Towards Colonial Freedom. Africa in the Struggle against World Imperialism* (London, 1973), 44–45.

[16] Resolution "The Challenge to the Colonial Powers," in Padmore, *Pan-Africanism*, 170.

[17] Final Resolution of the Bandung Conference, in Ministry of Information and Broadcasting, Government of India Press, *Asian-African Conference* (New Delhi, 1955), 29–33.

[18] Jean-Paul Sartre, *Colonialism and Neocolonialism*, (London, 2001), 50.

[19] See also Mikael Rask Madsen, "France, the UK, and the 'Boomerang' of the Internationalisation of Human Rights (1945–2000)," in Simon Halliday and Patrick Schmidt (eds.), *Human Rights Brought Home: Socio-Legal Perspectives on Human Rights in the National Context* (Oxford, 2004), 60–61.

upon the human rights declaration in a common written statement, saying, "We can hardly expect to win the confidence of Africans by making statements of ultimate ideals while in practice we take steps in precisely the opposite direction."[20] As charter members of the United Nations, the colonial powers Great Britain and France had signed the human rights documents and, in fact, participated actively in the development of the human rights regime. In suggesting its ideas, the British Foreign Office, for example, had tried to mark the content of human rights documents with its own conceits. France, the second largest colonial power, was even called the "motherland of human rights" and affected to maintain the tradition of the French Revolution by drafting its own proposals for the Universal Declaration of Human Rights, the European Convention on Human Rights, and the Geneva Conventions.[21]

However, the colonial powers continued this engagement with growing reluctance as growing anti-colonial movements used the United Nations as an international forum[22] and cited human rights documents as the basis for their demands. Although the states of the Western world dominated the world organization at the time of its foundation, after the Second World War newly independent nations such as India and Pakistan, two former British colonies, became members of the United Nations. Accordingly they utilized their new positions within the organization to achieve their political goals.[23] As early as June 1946 an initiative by India accused South Africa of racial discrimination against its African and Indian population, in response to which the General Assembly, in Resolution 44 (I) of December 8, 1946, called for a dialogue between the two member states with a final report to the General Assembly.[24] This decision of the United Nations truly marked a new beginning. For the first time, an international organization had seriously discussed the racial issue. The Prime Minister of South Africa, Jan Smuts, reacted to this development by saying that the world would now be dominated by the "coloured people."[25] By putting the racial question on the political agenda, the new African and Asian UN member states linked the human rights debate directly to the problem of colonial domination and confirmed their demand for self-determination. The Universal Declaration of

---

[20] Common commentary of the colonial administrations of Gambia, Sierra Leone, and the Gold Coast quoted in Brian A. W. Simpson, *Human Rights and the End of Empire. Britain and the Genesis of the European Convention* (Oxford, 2004), 458.

[21] Stéphan Hessel, "Un rôle essentiel dans la promotion et la protection des droits de l'homme," in André Lewin (ed.), *La France et l'ONU depuis 1945* (Condé-sur-Noireau, 1995), 254.

[22] See statement of Kwame Nkrumah at the UN Headquarters in New York, July 29, 1958, in Dabu Gizenga's Collection on Kwame Nkrumah, Box 128–5, Folder 96, Manuscript Division, Moorland-Spingarn Research Center, Howard University.

[23] See especially Yassin El-Ayouty, *The United Nations and Decolonization: The Role of Afro-Asia* (The Hague, 1971).

[24] UN GAOR Resolution A/RES/44 (I), "Treatment of Indians in the Union of South Africa," December 8, 1946.

[25] General Smuts quoted in Hugh Tinker, *Race, Conflict and the International Order. From Empire to United Nations* (London 1977), 111.

Human Rights served as a defining reference point because in addition to the principle of equality the document expressed the right of self-determination in Article 21. Without explicitly mentioning the term "self-determination," it guaranteed to every human being the right to participate in the public affairs of his or her country while declaring the will of people to be the ultimate public authority.[26]

Thereafter, the African and Asian UN member states attempted time and again to establish the human right of self-determination in common initiatives in various UN documents, which provoked the impetuous resistance of the colonial powers. According to the British Colonial Office, any discussion of self-determination of the dependent territories was to be avoided as much as possible because it could only lead to "disastrous confusion and individual hardship,"[27] especially in territories with mixed populations such as the East African settler colonies. Despite these objections, in February 1952 the General Assembly passed Resolution 545 (VI), which added the right of self-determination to the planned covenants on human rights.[28] The recognition of self-determination as a fundamental human right by the United Nations meant that the debates about decolonization and human rights were inseparably connected to each other. Nevertheless, another fourteen years went by before the world organization passed the International Covenants on Civil and Political Rights on December 16, 1966, Article 1 of which established self-determination as an elementary human right. One of the main reasons for this long delay is to be found in the politics of resistance on the part of the European colonial powers.[29]

The colonial rulers observed the development of the human rights regime with growing anxiety. Great Britain's Secretary of State for the Colonies, Arthur Creech-Jones, in a secret circular to the British colonies on March 28, 1949, characterized the Universal Declaration of Human Rights as a potential "source of embarrassment"[30] that could cause undesirable consequences in the overseas territories. Representing the British colonial administrations' common attitude was the Governor of Kenya, Sir Philip Mitchell, who called the international documents "dangerous to the security of the Colony."[31] His colleague in South Rhodesia, Governor J. N. Kennedy, utterly refused to publish the Declaration of Human Rights in the Official Gazette, arguing that troublemakers would only make use of it in their agitation.[32] Both international

[26] El-Ayouty, *UN and Decolonization*, 56.
[27] Letter of the CO to the FO, January 3, 1951, TNA FO 371/101435.
[28] UN GAOR Resolution A/RES/545 (VI), "Inclusion in the International Covenant or Covenants on Human Rights of an Article Relating to the Right of People to Self-Determination," February 5, 1952.
[29] United Nations Department of Public Information (ed.), *United Nations Work for Human Rights* (New York, 1957), 8, 10–11.
[30] Secret Circular 25102/2/49, March 28, 1949, TNA DO 35/3776.
[31] Secret letter of Mitchell to Creech-Jones, July 29, 1949, TNA CO 537/4581.
[32] Letter of Kennedy to the FO, June 7, 1949, TNA FO 371/78949.

documents, the Declaration and the Covenants on Human Rights, were primarily seen as dangerous threats to colonial interests.

In the opinion of Creech-Jones, Great Britain was nevertheless obliged as a member of the United Nations to work with the UN Human Rights Commission. Under all circumstances the British delegation had to be careful in framing the international treaties in a manner acceptable to the colonies. The Secretary of State for the Colonies therefore outlined future political goals in this way:

> In these circumstances it is the policy of his Majesty's Government to do all it can to ensure that the final texts of international agreements of a political character are framed in such a way as to be acceptable to the majority at least of the territories for which the United Kingdom is responsible.... In fact the requirements and the view of Governors are frequently the decisive factor in determining United Kingdom policy in regard to international agreements of a political character drawn up within the framework of the United Nations, e.g. the draft Covenant on Human Rights or the Freedom of Information Convention.[33]

Thus British human rights policy was guided mainly by colonial requirements; consequently British delegates always intervened when "too much" human rights threatened to upset "colonial security."

A good example in this respect is the refusal of the British Government to accept any mention of internal armed conflicts in international humanitarian law because it feared possible international intervention in colonial disturbances.[34] Some parts of the draft of the Geneva Conventions, such as the prohibition of "collective punishment," were especially embarrassing and unacceptable to them. From the Colonial Office's point of view, burning entire villages in Malaya and using punitive bombing in the Aden protectorate proved the "value" of collective measures in suppressing colonial insurrection. The British authorities resisted attempts to deprive local security forces of these effective methods. Therefore the Colonial Office, fully aware of how complicated the international situation was for the Government, and expecting criticism for being an "imperialist tyranny," justified their attitude by arguing that it would be a very serious thing to deprive colonial administrations of their ability to use these methods.[35]

Not only humanitarian international law but also the planned International Covenants on Human Rights presented a serious problem. If applied to the colonial territories, the binding character of this document could only cause great difficulties and embarrassment to colonial governments.[36] In addition

---

[33] Letter of Creech-Jones to Mitchell, November 26, 1949, TNA CO 537/4581.
[34] Memorandum "Revision of Geneva Conventions" of the FO, January 25, 1949, TNA FO 369/4143; Letter "Civil War Articles" of the United Kingdom Delegation to the Diplomatic Conference for the Protection of War Victims to the FO, July 19, 1949, TNA FO 369/4158.
[35] Letter of the CO to the FO, June 25, 1949, TNA FO 369/4155.
[36] Letter of the CO to the Department of the Lord Chancellor, September 29, 1950, TNA CO 537/5686.

to the legal codification of elementary rights, such as freedom of speech and freedom of assembly, the main problem was the implementation of a right to petition for individuals and nongovernmental organizations, a right that from the British perspective had to be prevented under all circumstances.[37] The Governor in Nairobi, Sir Philip Mitchell, actually regarded such a right among the United Nations as threat to world peace.[38] However, the respected scholar of international law Hersch Lauterpacht repeatedly emphasized the importance of the right to petition. Only by virtue of such a right could the human rights regime be informed of and mobilized against gross human rights violations.[39] From the viewpoint of legal scholars such as Lauterpacht, an international human rights regime without the individual right to petition was a crippled giant lacking eyes and ears, who could neither hear complaints nor react to them.

The UN Human Rights Commission had already vehemently discussed whether the Commission should have the right to receive and respond to petitions. The U.S. Government's anxiety about being accused of racial discrimination, the fear of the colonial powers (Great Britain, France, Belgium, and Portugal) of being held accountable for the situations in their overseas territories, and the vulnerability of the Soviet Union with respect to Stalinist crimes were mainly responsible for the inactivity of the Human Rights Commission.[40] ECOSOC Resolution 75 (V) of August 5, 1947, denied the Commission any direct reaction to complaints of human rights violations,[41] a fact that even the former Director of the UN Division of Human Rights John P. Humphrey described as creating "probably the most elaborate wastepaper basket ever invented."[42]

From the British Colonial Office's point of view, the right to petition in the planned Covenants on Human Rights should suffer the same fate. Because of the worsening situation in their overseas territories in particular, the London Government anticipated a large number of petitions to be sent to the United Nations by individuals and political groups, an eventuality that "may land the United Kingdom in considerable embarrassment internationally."[43] The British officials also feared that the United Nations could possibly intervene in the

---

[37] Secret Circular No. 37 of the CO to all Colonies, March 17, 1948, TNA CO 537/3413; letter of the CO to the FO, June 5, 1950, TNA FO 371/88753.

[38] Response of Mitchell to the Secret Circular No. 37, TNA CO 537/3422.

[39] Hersch Lauterpacht, "State Sovereignty and Human Rights," in Elihu Lauterpacht (ed.), *International Law: Being the Collected Papers of Hersch Lauterpacht* (Cambridge, 1977), 3, 421–423.

[40] Philip Alston, "The Commission on Human Rights," in Philip Alston (ed.), *The United Nations and Human Rights. A Critical Appraisal* (Oxford, 1992), 141.

[41] UN ECOSOCOR Resolution E/RES/75 (V) "Economic and Social Council Resolution on Communication Concerning Human Rights," August 5, 1947.

[42] John P. Humphrey, *Human Rights and the United Nations: A Great Adventure* (Dobbs Ferry, 1984), 28.

[43] Memorandum "Enforcement of the International Covenant of Human Rights" of the CO, 1948, TNA CO 537/3406.

colonies' internal affairs and that colonial populations would come to regard the world organization as the ultimate guarantor of their rights, at the same time disrupting their loyalty to Great Britain.[44] On behalf of the Colonial Office, the British UN delegation adopted the position of strictly rejecting any right to petition.[45] If Great Britain was obliged as a member state of the United Nations to participate in the construction of human rights regimes, it should at least do so as inefficiently as it could, and the final decisions of the Human Rights Commission should be as "harmless as possible."[46]

In order to accomplish this, however, the United Kingdom needed a coalition of like-minded partners in the various UN bodies. With this goal in mind, the Government in London tried to join forces with other colonial powers such as Belgium and France by convincing them to take the same position opposing the right to petition.[47] Already in April 1949, the British Colonial Office addressed a letter to the French and Belgian Ministers for the Colonies in which it emphasized the need for close cooperation in all human rights issues. In the letter, Lord Listowel explained that the right to petition would be a most dangerous weapon in the hands of unsatisfied colonial elements and that the very backwardness of the colonial population would in all probability lead to a distortion of the covenant, as well as its right to petition. To prevent unwanted United Nations interference in the internal affairs of the colonial powers, they should jointly resist the right to individual petition.[48] Thereupon Belgium, with special regard to the situation in the Congo, switched to the British position.[49]

Only Paris remained hesitant. On the one hand, the French state, as a democratic government of laws, conceded the absolute necessity of the right to petition in the implementation of a human rights regime. On the other hand, it feared interference in its colonial affairs.[50] This ambivalent position could also be traced to the fact that the French UN delegation would then be opposing a principle that its own delegate, René Cassin, had proposed in 1948.[51] At that time the French Republic was attempting, through the agencies of Cassin at the United Nations and Henri Teitgen at the Council of Europe, to refurbish its tradition as the "nation of human rights" in order to regain its international reputation and articulate its reclamation of great power status. On

---

[44] Secret Draft Cabinet Paper "Human Rights. Petition to the United Nations," April 1948, TNA CO 537/3413.
[45] Secret Circular "Human Rights" of the CO to the Colonies, July 28, 1948, TNA FO 371/72810.
[46] Confidential Telegram No. 206 of the FO to the British Delegation at the UN Human Rights Commission, January 20, 1947, TNA FO 371/67486.
[47] Letter of the FO, April 22, 1949, TNA CO 537/4579.
[48] Letter of the CO to the French and Belgium Ministers for the Colonies, April 1949, MAE NUOI Carton 385.
[49] Letter of the Belgium Ministry for the Colonies to the CO, May 20, 1949, TNA CO 537/4579.
[50] Memorandum "Droit de Pétition" of the MAE, October 15, 1949, MAE NUOI Carton 385.
[51] Letter of the Ministère de la France d'Outre Mer to the MAE, May 19, 1949, ibid.

the occasion of the French ratification of the Genocide Convention, Raphael
Lemkin himself personally congratulated the French Foreign Minister Robert
Schuman for taking this inspiring step and praised "France as the great leader
of the world, especially in humanitarian affairs."[52]

However, France's leadership role suffered under growing anti-colonial
criticism and military crises in its overseas territories, especially in Indochina.
Even the French Foreign Ministry at Quai d'Orsay then had to recognize that
human rights were becoming a heavy burden and a threat to colonial interests. As a direct consequence, the French Government began shifting toward
Great Britain's position. On March 31, 1952, at a meeting of France's Minister
for the Colonies Pflimlin and his British colleague, Lyttelton, both countries
agreed to closely cooperate in all colonial matters.[53] Besides regular ministe-
rial meetings and consultations, this consisted of taking a common position
against any kind of United Nations interference in the internal affairs of their
overseas territories, opposing especially any foreign investigative missions and
the discussion of political questions, but also the right to individual petition.
The two leading colonial powers thus created an informal alliance (which in
later years also attracted states such as Belgium and Portugal) to coordinate
a common policy at the United Nations.[54] The explicit purpose of this cooperation was diplomatically to prevent the creation of a strong human rights
regime, not only to protect their common colonial ambitions but also to hide
the massive use of violence in their wars of decolonization.

Colonial State of Emergency – The Radicalization of Violence and the Eradication of Human Rights

The major reason why the colonial powers so vehemently opposed the spread
of universal human rights and international protection of them was due to
the nature of colonial domination itself. Leaders and intellectuals of the anti-
colonial movements – such as the Vietnamese revolutionary Ho Chi Minh, the
Tunisian Jew Albert Memmi, and the Martinique-born Frantz Fanon – wrote
of the colonial situation as a divided world,[55] in which elementary rights were
denied on a racial basis to a great part of the world's population. In Memmi's
opinion, racism was the quintessence of the relationship between colonizers
and colonized.[56] Ho Chi Minh agreed with this view of the colonial situation,

[52] Letter of Raphael Lemkin to the French Foreign Minister Robert Schuman, August 25, 1950, MAE NUOI Carton 595.
[53] Secret Circular "Anglo-French Colonial Relations" of the CO, May 15, 1952, TNA DO 35/3842.
[54] For examples see memorandum "Political Discussions with other Colonial Powers" of the FO, March 4, 1957, TNA FO 371/125312; "Confidential Report Quadripartite Talks (with French, Belgians and Portuguese: Paris, July 1st-5th 1957)" of the FO, TNA FO 371/125313.
[55] Frantz Fanon, *The Wretched of the Earth* (New York 1963), 37.
[56] Albert Memmi, *Der Kolonisator und der Kolonisierte, Zwei Porträts* (Frankfurt, 1980), 72, 75.

explaining, "If you have white skin you automatically belong among civilized human beings, and once you belong among civilized human beings you can act as a savage – and still remain a civilized human being."[57] After the end of the Second World War, Allied promises of democracy would be abandoned, and those of liberty and equality, the principles of the French Revolution, would be violated yet again.[58]

In addition to racism, the anti-colonial leaders identified the use of violence as another key element of colonial domination.[59] According to Memmi, the privileged position of Europeans vis-à-vis the indigenous population was solely based on the support of the army and the air force, both of which stood ready at all times to defend with violence the interests of the settlers and colonial powers.[60] Fanon also believed that colonial existence rested on the power of bayonets and cannons: "The colonial regime owes its legitimacy to force and at no time tries to hide this aspect of things."[61] The universal recognition of natural, inalienable rights not only placed this racist, violent mode of domination fundamentally into question, but also led to the inevitable conclusion that the European colonial empires would have to be dissolved.

The violent colonial situation described by Memmi, Ho Chi Minh, and Fanon became radicalized after the Second World War with the outbreak of numerous uprisings and riots in the European colonies. Attempts by anti-colonial nationalist movements to obtain independence collided fiercely with the rulers' strong determination to defend their empires and increased their tendency to employ massive violence in the colonies.[62] In the struggle against the "anti-colonial threat," their position was simply not to be compromised by so-called democratic norms and the rule of law.

For this reason, Great Britain and France resorted to the legal tool of declaring a state of emergency. According to the Italian philosopher Giorgio Agamben, the state of emergency or the state of exception defines "a 'state of the law' in which, on the one hand, the norm is in force but is not applied (it has no 'force') and, on the other, acts that do not have the value of law acquire its 'force.'"[63] For Agamben the state of exception is a space devoid of law, a zone of anomie in which all legal determinations are deactivated, including the elementary rights of the individual.[64] In passing sweeping emergency

---

[57] Extract from Ho Chi Minh's "Accusation against the French Colonial Rule," in Bernard Fall (ed.), *Ho Tschi Minh, Revolution und nationaler Befreiungskampf. Reden und Schriften 1920–1968* (Munich, 1968), 92.

[58] See Ho Chi Minh's speech on the occasion of the beginning of the resistance fight in South Vietnam in November 1945, in ibid., 174–175.

[59] See also Michael Mann, "Das Gewaltdispositiv des modernen Kolonialismus," in Mihran Dabag, Horst Gründer, and Uwe-K. Ketelsen (eds.), *Kolonialismus. Kolonialdiskurs und Genozid* (Munich, 2004), 118.

[60] Memmi, *Kolonisator und Kolonisierte*, 28.

[61] Fanon, *Wretched of the Earth*, 36, 84.

[62] Mann, "Das Gewaltdispositiv," 119.

[63] Giorgio Agamben, *State of Exception* (Chicago, 2005), 38.

[64] Ibid., 50.

laws, the colonial powers abolished universal rights that they had only just approved and codified in documents such as the Universal Declaration of Human Rights and the European Convention on Human Rights. The colonial powers released their security forces from the rule of law and created definitive preconditions for the radicalization of colonial violence.

Striking examples of this are the most viciously violent wars of decolonization of their time, fought by the two leading colonial powers. In Kenya, its East African Crown Colony, Great Britain was confronted with an uprising of the "Land Freedom Army," a resistance movement comprising mainly ethnic Kikuyu. By attacking the farms of white settlers and assassinating African collaborators, this organization, which the British called Mau Mau, managed to entangle Great Britain in a bloody guerrilla war in the Kenyan jungle from 1952 to 1956.[65] Beginning on November 1, 1954, France, in its North African departments, was faced with a violent struggle by the Algerian Front de Libération Nationale (FLN). By using guerrilla tactics to assault French targets, the FLN challenged French colonial power in an eight-year war that ultimately led to Algerian independence in 1962.[66] In both conflicts, the state of exception was the legal precondition for the radicalization of colonial violence.

In a letter of September 1952 to Secretary of State for the Colonies Oliver Lyttelton, the Labour MP Fenner Brockway, deeply concerned about the worsening situation in Kenya, condemned the planned state of emergency as a gross violation of the UN Declaration of Human Rights.[67] The emergency laws reminded him more of totalitarian regimes on the other side of the Iron Curtain than of democratic societies. In his view, the solution to the problems in East Africa was not the extension of colonial repression, but the end of social and political injustice, as well as racial discrimination. Given the concrete danger of violent anti-colonial resistance, Brockway's strong criticism fell upon deaf ears and was never seriously considered.

Instead, the British Government proclaimed a state of emergency in Kenya just a few weeks later.[68] Officially the colonial administration in Nairobi continued to outrank the military and simply provided its security forces with special powers to restore order. The legal basis for this step was the "Emergency Powers Order in Council" of 1939, which empowered Governor Baring to introduce far-reaching emergency laws.[69] Confronted with the threat of political

[65] For the British war of decolonization in Kenya see, for example, David Anderson, *Histories of the Hanged. The Dirty War in Kenya and the End of Empire* (New York, 2005); Caroline Elkins, *Britain's Gulag. The Brutal End of Empire in Kenya* (London, 2005).
[66] For the Algerian war see the exemplary work by Alistair Horne, *A Savage War of Peace. Algeria 1954–1962* (New York, 2006); Mohammed Harbi and Benjamin Stora (eds.), *La Guerre d'Algérie 1954–2004. La fin de l'amnésie* (Paris, 2004).
[67] Letter of Brockway to Lyttelton, September 13, 1952, TNA CO 822/437.
[68] Telegram from Lyttelton to Baring, October 21, 1952, TNA CO 822/438.
[69] The "Emergency Powers Order in Council" of 1939 was also the legal basis for the other colonial states of emergency in the British Empire. See also K. Roberts-Wray, *Commonwealth and Colonial Law* (London, 1966), 642; Simpson, *Human Rights*, 89.

intervention by international organizations, as well as demands to apply standards of humanitarian international law, the Government in London avoided any indication that a war was going on in its East African Crown Colony. The neutral concept of "emergency" helped the British Government conceal the true reality and maintain an appearance of civil normality.[70]

Great Britain had already declared states of emergency during disturbances in Malaya, British-Guyana, and the Gold Coast in 1948, as well as in Nigeria and Uganda in 1949. The state of emergency thus became a repeated phenomenon in the Empire and integral to British colonial politics in the years from 1948 to 1960.[71] An especially significant role was played by the state of emergency in Malaya, which became a paradigm for combating resistance in the colonies.[72] For the British Army, guerrilla war experience in the Malayan jungle evolved into a manual of anti-subversive warfare consequently used during operations in Kenya.[73] The primary and guiding principle of these newly developed military doctrines was "total control" of the indigenous population. Obtaining this control required a significant extension of the secret service and the application of massive internment and resettlement measures.[74] The emergency law provided the security forces with the necessary legal framework to realize this new strategy without any humanitarian restriction.

The "Emergency Regulations"[75] of the colonial government in Nairobi accordingly represented serious intervention into the lives of the African population and led to a tremendous increase in colonial oppression. In addition to prohibiting all African political organizations and restricting freedom of movement, the new regulations officially introduced the principle of "collective responsibility." In a special instruction, Governor Baring ordered the collective punishment of the inhabitants of any territory in which rebels were active in any way.[76] Not only attacks but also such minor offences as holding a Mau Mau initiation ceremony were sufficient for the security forces to confiscate all livestock and crops, close markets, and expel the indigenous population from

---

[70] Frank Füredi, *Colonial Wars and the Politics of Third World Nationalism* (London 1994), 192.

[71] See especially Frank Füredi, "Britain's Colonial Emergencies and the Invisible Nationalists," *Journal of Historical Sociology*, 2 (1989), 240–264.

[72] Ibid., 253.

[73] Thomas Mockaitis, *British Counterinsurgency 1919–1960* (New York, 1990), 192.

[74] See J. M. Forster, Operational Research Unit Far East, A Comparative Study of the Emergencies in Malaya and Kenya, Report No. 1/1957, TNA WO 291/1670.

[75] For the "Emergency Regulations" see Colony and Protectorate of Kenya (ed.), *Official Gazette Extraordinary* (Nairobi, October 30, 1952); Colony and Protectorate of Kenya (ed.), *Emergency Regulations Made under the Emergency Powers Order in Council 1939* (Nairobi 1954); Government Notice "The Emergency Powers Order in Council, 1939. The Emergency Regulations, 1952," TNA CO 822/728.

[76] Emergency Regulation "Collective Punishment," November 23, 1952, in Colony and Protectorate of Kenya, Official Gazette Supplement No. 61 (Nairobi, November 25, 1952), 591–595.

their homes. "Collective responsibility" meant that every person, guilty or innocent, was held accountable for the actions of the insurgents. By employing these brutal measures, especially against the Kikuyu, the colonial government intended to discipline the African population and destroy its support for the rebel movement.[77]

"Detention Orders"[78] also enabled the security forces to arrest and imprison without a formal warrant any person who appeared suspicious and potentially threatening to public order. This arrest and detention authorization by the colonial government in Nairobi created the legal basis for a massive and arbitrary internment of Africans, often based only on a moment's suspicion or an individual's simply belonging to Kikuyu ethnicity. As a result, more than fifty internment camps were created, dispersed over the British Crown Colony. According to the estimates of the historian Caroline Elkins, between 160,000 and 320,000 people were imprisoned during the state of emergency.[79] Forced labor, starvation, epidemic diseases, and systematic torture characterized life in these camps. Between June 1954 and October 1955, the colonial government also ordered the forced resettlement of more than one million widely distributed Kikuyu into 854 so-called new villages.[80] In these new settlements, the indigenous population was not only subject to the strict control of its colonial rulers but also condemned to forced labor and left utterly defenseless against the systematic violence of the security forces.

In the war against the insurgents, Governor Baring also designated special territories deemed dangerous to public order as "prohibited areas."[81] It was strictly forbidden to enter or linger in these zones, mainly located around Mount Kenya and the Aberdare Mountains. Army and police forces were authorized to kill on sight any person found in these "forbidden zones."[82] Furthermore, in adjoining territories called "special areas," security forces were authorized to open fire on anyone who did not halt when ordered to do so. These orders developed into a kind of carte blanche for the killing of Africans, who already were being shot down on the slightest provocation, often without any reason at all.[83] The terminology "shot while resisting arrest" or "shot while attempting to escape" was typically used officially to justify such arbitrary killings.[84] Even the Colonial Office in London became

---

[77] N. F. Harris, "Memorandum for the Operations Committee concerning Economic Sanctions on Kikuyu, Embu and Meru" October, 9, 1953, TNA WO 276/413.

[78] Emergency Regulation "Detention Orders," October 1952, TNA CO 822/728.

[79] Caroline Elkins, "Detention, Rehabilitation and the Destruction of Kikuyu Society," in E. S. Atieno-Adhiambo and John Lonsdale (eds.), *Mau Mau & Nationhood: Arms, Authority & Narration* (Oxford 2003), 205.

[80] Elkins, *Britain's Gulag*, 233–274.

[81] Emergency Regulation "Prohibited Areas," October 29, 1952, in *Official Gazette Extraordinary*, 526–527.

[82] Telegram "Shooting without Challenge in Prohibited Areas" from Baring to the CO, April 11, 1953, TNA CO 822/440.

[83] Peter Evans, *Law and Disorder or Scenes of Life in Kenya* (London, 1956), 183.

[84] D. H. Rawcliffe, *The Struggle for Kenya* (London, 1954), 70; Evans, *Law and Disorder*, 212.

concerned about a certain "trigger-happy attitude" on the part of their security forces.[85]

Despite the already broad sweep of special powers, emergency regulations were subsequently intensified once more. After declaring participation in Mau Mau attacks a capital crime, beginning in April 1953, the colonial authority ordered that all forms of direct or indirect support for the rebels were to be punished by death penalty.[86] The British authorities hanged a total of 1,090 Kikuyu for "Mau Mau crimes," whereof the overwhelming majority were not murder but minor offences such as possession of weapons or conducting initiation ceremonies. The number executed in Kenya exceeded the number sentenced to death in all other emergencies in the British Empire combined and was double the number of French executions during the Algerian war.[87] Even a British veteran such as police officer Peter Hewitt had to admit to the draconian character of the emergency rules in his memoirs, but of course not without justifying them by referring to security reasons.[88] Although the Mau Mau movement's military resistance was completely broken by the end of 1956, the state of emergency officially remained until January 12, 1960.[89] For nearly eight years Great Britain ruled its East African Crown Colony on the legal basis of draconian "Emergency Regulations," which abolished elementary humanitarian norms and principles.

The Algerian case was not much different. It was the French government's official position that there was no war going on in Algeria. Quite like the British in Kenya, the French authorities described the situation in North Africa as merely "events" and played down their fight against the FLN as "police operations," "operations to restore civil peace," and "peace-keeping operations."[90] From the French perspective, they were only "solving" a purely internal problem in their North African departments. The government in Paris deliberately avoided declaring an *état de siege*, which would have invoked martial law.[91] However, the Constitution of the Fourth Republic did not include regulations for civil emergency law. Therefore the Faure Government had to pass a new law in April 1955 creating the *état d'urgence*.[92] Officially this state of emergency only increased the capacity of civil authorities to restore the public order while keeping the Army subject to civilian supervision.[93]

---

[85] Letter of the CO to Crawford, November 24, 1953, TNA CO 822/489.

[86] Telegram from Baring to Lyttelton, April 20, 1953, TNA CO 822/728.

[87] Anderson, *Histories of the Hanged*, 291, 353–354.

[88] Peter Hewitt, *Kenya Cowboy. A Police Officer's Account of the Mau Mau Emergency* (London, 1999), 196–198.

[89] Telegram of Renison to Macleod, January 11, 1960, TNA CO 822/1900.

[90] Not until 1999 did the French National Assembly pass a law in which the Algerian conflict was officially recognized as a war. Guy Perville, "Guerre étrangère et guerre civile en Algérie 1954–1962," *Relations Internationals*, 14 (1978), 171–172.

[91] Arlette Heymann, *Les libertes publiques et la Guerre d'Algérie* (Paris, 1972), 15.

[92] Loi No. 55-385, April 3, 1955, *Journal Officiel, Lois et Décrets*, April 7, 1955, 3479–3480.

[93] Karl-Heinz Gerth, *Der Staatsnotstand im französischen Recht* (Mainz, 1968), 110.

Much like British operations in Kenya, French warfare in Algeria was strongly influenced by new "anti-subversive military doctrines." Leading officers demanded that the Army not be bound to republican principles and the rule of law; on the contrary, the state should adopt the philosophy of anti-subversive warfare. To accomplish its mission, the military needed to utilize all the weapons of modern warfare and had to be governed only by its own laws.[94] In a lecture concerning anti-subversive warfare, Colonel Charles Lacheroy clearly outlined this point of view: "You do not conduct a revolutionary war with a civil code."[95]

In contrast to Great Britain, France could not utilize a "Malayan success model" of anti-guerrilla warfare but had to learn its lesson from the humiliating defeat in Indochina.[96] The result of this learning process was the theory of the *guerre révolutionnaire*, characterized as the enemy's new way of war making.[97] The point of the advocates of this new military doctrine was that the central means to defeating the "subversive danger" was total control of the population. In an interview Colonel Roger Trinquier plainly declared, "Call me a fascist if you like, but we must make the population docile and manageable; everybody's acts must be controlled."[98] Trinquier was fully aware of the radicalism of this new strategy and indeed confirmed the analogy to totalitarian organizations.[99] But he regarded as a fundamental distinction the fact that these measures served only to protect the population from "terrorist danger." With the assistance of tightly meshed intelligence services and sweeping special powers granted to the security forces, this new military imperative would be fully realized.

Declaration of the *état d'urgence*, limited initially to six months, provided the executive power with the dictatorial power to abolish constitutional civil rights. The French Governor in Algiers now had the specific powers to restrict freedom of movement, forbid people from remaining in or entering special security zones, prohibit freedom of assembly, and censor the press.[100] The military and police had the unlimited right to search private houses and carry out round-ups at any time, night or day. The expansion of military jurisdiction to certain criminal acts connected with the emergency situation meant a significant militarization of criminal justice.[101]

---

[94] Roger Trinquier, *La Guerre Moderne* (Paris, 1961), 81.
[95] Lecture of Colonel Lacheroy, May 1958, SHAT 1H 1942.
[96] See Alexander J. Zervoudakis, "From Indochina to Algeria: Counter-Insurgency Lessons," in Martin S. Alexander, Martin Evans, and J. F. V. Keiger (eds.), *The Algerian War and the French Army, 1954–62: Experiences, Images, Testimonies* (Basingstoke, 2002), 43–60.
[97] For the military doctrines of the guerre révolutionnaire see George Armstrong Kelly, *Lost Soldiers. The French Army and Empire in Crisis, 1947–1962* (Cambridge, 1965), 111–119; Pierre Cyrill Pahlavi, *La Guerre Révolutionnaire de l'Armée Française en Algérie 1954–1961. Entre esprit de conquête et conquête des esprits* (Paris, 2004).
[98] Trinquier quoted in Kelly, *Lost Soldiers*, 138.
[99] Trinquier, *Guerre Moderne*, 57.
[100] For the emergency regulations see Loi No. 55–385, 3479–3480.
[101] Hans-Ernst Folz, *Staatsnotstand und Notstandsrecht* (Cologne, 1962), 63.

Article 6 of the emergency law had a particularly massive impact on the situation in Algeria. The designation *assignation à residence* gave security forces and police unlimited authority to proscribe residence in special areas to people deemed to be dangerous to public order and security. The law explicitly prohibited the establishment of internment camps, but Algerian reality made a farce of this. *Assignation à residence* became the legal basis for massive internment and resettlement during the Algerian war.[102] As a news item in the French newspaper *France Observateur* revealed, and the International Committee of the Red Cross (ICRC) stated in an internal report, several hundred people were already imprisoned in May 1955 in four euphemistically identified *centres d'hébergement*.[103] These camps were just an overture to a tight web of internment centers that soon spread over all three Algerian departments. By means of state of emergency laws, the French government enabled their security forces to deprive hundreds of thousands of Algerians of their liberty for years at a time without charge. Emulating the British in Kenya, the French Army also began to concentrate the rural Algerian population into so-called *nouveaux villages*. According to the French sociologist Michel Cornaton, at least 2,350,000 people, or 26.1 percent of the Muslim population of Algeria, were forcibly resettled in this way.[104] People interned or resettled were deprived of elementary rights and exposed to starvation, epidemic diseases, and the systematic violence of their guards.

When the French National Assembly dissolved on December 1, 1955, the *état d'urgence* lost its validity, and the new Government of Guy Mollet refused to renew the state of emergency.[105] In fact, on March 16, 1956, the French Parliament passed a law known as the *pouvoirs spéciaux*,[106] in which Paris announced a program of economic and social development for Algeria. Article 5 of the law, however, empowered the Government to utilize in the North African departments "all extraordinary measures to restore order, protect people and goods, and defend the integrity of state territory." Decrees would clarify "extraordinary measures" to mean restoring *assignation à residence* and subsequently legalizing existing camps.[107] In this way, the *pouvoirs spéciaux* went far beyond the specifications of the *état d'urgence* and became a carte blanche for the French security forces. Although the new emergency law did not legalize torture, the historian Pierre Vidal-Naquet alleged that the

---

[102] For the French internment and resettlement camps, see Michel Cornaton, *Les camps de regroupement de la guerre d'Algérie* (Paris, 1998).

[103] P. Gaillard, Note pour le Comité "Aggravation et extension des troubles intérieurs en Algérie," May 25, 1955, ACICR BAG 200 008-001; "Les Camps de Concentration Algériens," *France Observateur*, June 16, 1955.

[104] Cornaton, *Camps de regroupement*, 120–124.

[105] Gerth, *Staatsnotstand im französischen Recht*, 111.

[106] Loi No. 56-258, March 16, 1956, *Journal Officiel, Lois et Décrets*, March 17, 1956, 2591.

[107] Décret No. 56-274, March 17, 1956, *Journal Officiel, Lois et Décrets*, March 19, 1956, 2665–2666.

legislation created the conditions to do anything at all to protect the public in the name of France.[108]

The Army liberally exercised its new prerogatives and embraced the "extraordinary measures," which from its point of view were sorely needed to combat the FLN. Guided by the military doctrines of the *guerre révolutionnaire*, this meant the systematic use of torture[109] and the introduction of the principle of "collective responsibility."[110] The French security forces no longer distinguished combatant from noncombatant; every Arab was a potential rebel.[111] Starting in the spring of 1956, the French military began to declare rebel areas *zones interdites* in which residence was strictly forbidden, and where – as in "prohibited areas" in Kenya – anyone might be shot on sight.[112]

In addition to this sweeping authorization to use deadly force, French security forces were also provided a "very generous" permission to shoot outside of the prohibited areas. The military manual of conduct toward rebels and prisoners in Algeria included a common order of the French Ministry of the Interior and of Defense of July 1, 1955: "Every rebel using his weapon, holding his weapon, or caught committing a crime is to be shot at once.... Any suspect attempting escape is to be fired upon."[113] With this order the French Government created a legal basis for arbitrary executions. In a theater of war where every Arab was considered a potential enemy, this led to French troops, during clean-up operations called *ratissages*, making use of their weapons randomly against the Arab civilian population. Fleeing civilians were regarded collectively as "suspicious." The term *fuyards abattus*, which came into general wartime use, was employed to justify all kinds of executions and even acquired an air of legality.[114] In March 1960, three Parisian lawyers indicated in a report to the ICRC in Geneva that the total number of those killed in this manner ran into the several thousands, and arbitrary executions were a daily occurrence in Algeria.[115] In the end, even ICRC authorities in Geneva were speaking of a regular "systematization of summary executions of prisoners."[116]

---

[108] Pierre Vidal-Naquet, *La torture dans la république. Essai d'histoire et de politique contemporaines (1954–1962)* (Paris, 1998), 61.

[109] See Raphaelle Branche, *La torture et l'armee pendant la guerre d'Algérie 1954–1962* (Paris, 2001).

[110] Horne, *Savage War*, 114.

[111] Heymann, *Libertes Publiques*, 155, 202.

[112] Letter "Répartition du territoire du point de vue du contrôle des personnes et des biens by Lorillot to the divisional commanders," March 30, 1956, SHAT 1H 2033/D1; Letter "Définition des zones suivant leur règlementation" from the Governor General, April 21, 1956, ibid.

[113] "Mémento sur la conduite à tenir vis-à-vis des Rebelles ou suspects de Rebellion" of the Supreme Command, April 30, 1956, SHAT 1H 1942/D2, 2.

[114] Branche, *La torture*, 74–76.

[115] Report by the lawyers Jacques Vergès, Maurice Courrége, and Michel Zavrian to the President of the ICCR, March 12, 1960, ACICR BAG 225 078–007.

[116] Letter "Exécutions sommaires de prisonniers en Algérie" of the ICRC to its delegate Michel in Paris, June 2, 1960, ACICR BAG 225 008–015.05.

In spite of such far-reaching emergency laws, French Army officers remained strident, especially those who – strongly influenced by the doctrines of the *guerre révolutionnaire* – regarded legality in the struggle against a subversive enemy as inadequate. In a secret study, a military committee came to the conclusion that neither the *état de siege* nor the *état d'urgence* or the *pouvoirs spéciaux* provided security forces with sufficient measures. Although many of these procedures already met military expectations, the committee discovered too many limitations and restrictions in existing law.[117] Since revolutionary war was a matter of total strategy, security forces had to be provided with total power, thus justifying new, radical laws in the anti-subversive defensive struggle. At the same time, the committee recommended that civilian authorities place all their responsibilities in military hands.[118] Only through this concentration of power and complete independence from civilian oversight could the Army effectively fight the subversive threat.

Consequently, the French Army assumed an increasing number of civilian responsibilities and eventually transformed Algeria into a kind of military province.[119] Formally, civil authorities retained the functions which they had actually transferred to the military. This almost complete capitulation of the rule of law became especially obvious in the "Battle of Algiers," in January 1957, when the Town Prefect Serge Baret authorized General Jacques Massu to apply all necessary measures to destroy the urban network of the FLN and restore public order.[120] In a letter of March 27, 1957, Secretary General of the urban administration of Algiers Paul Teitgen, who under great pressure resisted permitting the use of torture, vehemently criticized this gradual erosion of civil authority and blurring of powers. According to him, in such wars one does not become entangled in illegality but in anonymity and irresponsibility, which could only lead to war crimes. He added: "Through such improvised and uncontrolled methods, arbitrariness finds every conceivable justification. Furthermore, France is in serious danger of losing its soul in ambiguity."[121]

Conclusion

As this essay shows, the wars of decolonization presented one of the first serious challenges to the newly established international human rights regime. In order to combat anti-colonial forces, the leading colonial powers Great Britain and France declared states of emergency in their colonies. By enacting

[117] Groupe de Travail, Les insuffisances des textes concernant la lutte antisubversive, SHAT 1H 1943/D1, 20–21.
[118] Ibid., 25.
[119] Raoul Girardet, *La Crise militaire française 1945–1962. Aspects sociologiques et idéologiques* (Paris, 1964), 186.
[120] Heymann, *Libertes Publiques*, 74.
[121] Paul Teitgen quoted in Thankmar von Münchhausen, *Kolonialismus und Demokratie. Die französische Algerienpolitik von 1954–1962* (Munich, 1977), 200.

far-reaching emergency laws they not only abolished recently codified universal human rights, but at the same time also legalized the radicalization of colonial violence. For the colonial powers, their ambition to maintain overseas empires was far more important than their internationally codified obligations to respect and promote universal human rights. A memorandum of the ICRC from October 1962, based on the experiences of various Red Cross missions in the wars of decolonization, underlines this point of view.[122] In this paper officials in Geneva identified torture and violent repression as regular and growing practices in the normal legal system.[123] Especially disturbing was the tendency in the struggle against terrorism to present torture as in the society's interest and consistent with legality. Under the rubric of emergency laws enacted in order to combat terrorism, methods of torture that had been outlawed regained validity and presented a serious threat to humanitarian international law. The ICRC called the strategy of fighting terrorism with its own weapons a "disastrous abdication of humanity."[124] Without explicitly mentioning Great Britain and France, it vigorously criticized the measures implied in colonial states of emergency.

The fear that human rights could become a serious "source of embarrassment"[125] to the colonial powers as expressed by Creech-Jones in March 1949 was never more substantial than during the wars of decolonization. Radicalized violence in the form of massive internment and resettlement, increased state executions and summary killings, and the systematic use of torture gave anti-colonial movements the leverage to attack the colonial powers on an international level and to push them into diplomatic isolation. Even the colonial powers' blockade of important instruments of the human rights regime, such as the right of petition, could not prevent this. Violations of human rights were too gross and obvious to be concealed. By insulting human rights in its suppression of decolonization in Algeria, France found itself subject to permanent indictment by the United Nations' Afro-Asian members for violating the Universal Declaration of Human Rights and the UN Genocide Convention.[126] Referring to the European Convention on Human Rights, Greece accused Great Britain before the Council of Europe in 1956 and 1957 of human rights violations in its war of decolonization on Cyprus,

---

[122] For the various activities of the ICRC in the wars of decolonization in Kenya and Algeria see Rapport sur une mission spéciale du CICR au Kenya, 1957, ACICR BAG 225 108–002; Second Mission of the International Committee of the Red Cross to Kenya, June–July 1959, Report communicated to the United Kingdom Government, ACICR BAG 225 108–001; Raphaelle Branche, "Entre droit humanitaire et intérêts politiques: les missions algériennes du CICR," *Revue Historique*, 123e Année, Tome CCCI/I, (January/March 1999), 101–125.

[123] Memorandum "La Croix-Rouge s'élève contre la torture et l'abus des actes de violence" by the ICRC, October 1962, ACICR BAG 202 000–003.07.

[124] Ibid., 3.

[125] Secret Circular 25102/2/49, March 28, 1949.

[126] See the exemplary UN SCOR Document S/3609, letter of various UN delegations to the President of the UN Security Council, June 13, 1956; "Texte integral du mémoire remis à M. Hammarskjöld, Secrétaire Général de l'ONU par les Delegués permanents des Etats

an unprecedented occurrence.[127] Anti-colonial movements were effectively utilizing human rights documents as a moral basis to force the colonial powers increasingly into the dock of world opinion.

In the end it was the violent attempt to maintain colonial domination and the concomitant worsening of the human rights situation in the overseas territories that ultimately deprived colonialism of any claim to legitimacy. Stirred by the radicalized violence of the wars of decolonization, on December 14, 1960, the UN General Assembly passed Resolution 1514 (XV), called the "Declaration on the Granting of Independence to Colonial Countries and Peoples." Even in its preamble the UN document held the maintenance of colonial domination responsible for the increase in conflicts and called it a serious threat to world peace. Therefore it declared the urgent need to end colonialism in all its manifestations and the immediate prohibition of any use of arms against independent peoples: "The subjection of peoples to alien subjugation, domination, and exploitation constitutes a denial of fundamental human rights, is contrary to the Charter of the United Nations, and is an impediment to the promotion of world peace and co-operation."[128] This declaration was the world community's clear statement against colonialism, branding it a serious human rights violation and thereby decisively depriving colonial ambitions of any foundation to exist. For the development of human rights after 1945 and the establishment of their universal character, this was without doubt a major achievement. However, in the process the indigenous people in the colonies paid an enormous price.

Arabes aux Nations Unies," June 1957, CAOM 81 F1015, 1; "White Paper submitted by the Delegation of the Front of National Liberation to the United Nations Organisation on the Franco-Algerian Conflict," April 12, 1956, MAE NUOI Carton 548. See also Matthew Connelly, *A Diplomatic Revolution. Algeria's Fight for Independence and the Origins of the Post-Cold War Era* (Oxford, 2002).

[127] See especially "The First Cyprus Case," in Simpson, *Human Rights*, 924–989.
[128] UN GAOR Resolution A/RES/1514 (XV), "Declaration on the Granting of Independence to Colonial Countries and Peoples," December 14, 1960.

12

The United Nations, Humanitarianism, and Human Rights

War Crimes/Genocide Trials for Pakistani Soldiers in Bangladesh, 1971–1974

A. Dirk Moses

> [T]he happenings in East Pakistan constitute one of the most tragic episodes in human history. Of course, it is for future historians to gather facts and make their own evaluations, but it has been a very terrible blot on a page of human history.
>
> U Thant, Secretary-General of the United Nations, 3 June 1971.[1]

A significant part of the human rights regime established by the United Nations after the Second World War was the protection of group rights and the further regulation of warfare by prosecuting the violators of these new international laws. Unlike the interwar period when the League of Nations stood by haplessly as Italy invaded Abyssinia, the protection of human rights and international law was supposed to have teeth. Thus the United Nations General Assembly passed the Convention on the Prevention and Punishment of Genocide on 9 December 1948 (it came into force in 1951), one day before it adopted the Universal Declaration of Human Rights. On the heels of the Nuremberg Trials, the Genocide Convention provides explicitly for prosecutions of suspected perpetrators. Article 6 says: "Persons charged with genocide or any other acts enumerated in article III shall be tried by a competent tribunal of the State in the territory of which the act was committed, or by such international penal tribunal as may have jurisdiction with respect to those Contracting Parties which shall have accepted its jurisdiction."[2] What is more, Article 8 stipulates that contracting parties can have recourse to the UN: They "may call upon the competent organs of the United Nations to take such action under the Charter of the United Nations as they consider appropriate for the prevention and suppression of acts of genocide."

[1] UN Press Section, Office of Public Information, Press Release SG/SM1493, 3 June 1971, UN Archives, Series 228, Box 1, File 2, Acc 77/207, 11.
[2] Convention on the Punishment and Prevention of Genocide: http://www.un.org/millennium/law/iv-1.htm.

A year later, in 1949, the Third Geneva Convention was signed by members of the "international community." With respect to "grave breaches" of that Convention, which overlap in part with the Genocide Convention, it requires states "to enact legislation necessary to provide effective penal sanctions" and "to search for the persons alleged to have committed or ordered the commission of grave breaches and to try such persons before their own courts, or alternatively to hand them over to another contracting state that has made out a prima facie case."[3] The Convention also requires that states assist one another in criminal proceedings, such as extraditing suspects, as does the Genocide Convention.

Finally, the General Assembly of the UN authorized the International Law Commission (ILC) to formulate the principles of the Nuremberg Tribunals, which had been affirmed by the Assembly as part of international law. In 1950, the ILC specified the elements of "Crimes against Peace," "War Crimes," as well as "Crimes against Humanity," which, again, overlapped with the Genocide Convention. They are: "Murder, extermination, enslavement, deportation and other inhuman acts done against any civilian population, or persecutions on political, racial or religious grounds, when such acts are done or such persecutions are carried on in execution of or in connexion with any crime against peace or any war crime."[4]

Far from guaranteeing the absence of genocide, war crimes, and crimes against humanity, this legal regime stood by for fifty years as the nation-states of the "international community" consistently violated them. The People's Republic of China was alleged to have committed genocide in Tibet between 1959 and 1960. Dag Hammarskjold called the massacre of Balubas in the State of South Kasai of the Congo in 1960 "a case of incipient genocide."[5] The Hutu killing and expulsion of the Tutsi in the Rwandan revolution of 1963–1964 and the Tutsi massacres of Hutu nine years later in Burundi were also genocidal in character. Then there was the secessionist civil war in Nigeria between 1966 and 1970 in which the Igbos were subject to a famine campaign that took perhaps several million lives. In 1965 the massacre of half a million communists in Indonesia also targeted ethnic Chinese in genocidal attacks.[6]

---

[3] See Antonio Cassese, "On the Current Trends towards Criminal Prosecution and Punishment of Breaches of International Humanitarian Law," *European Journal of International Law*, 9 (1998), 5. "Grave breaches" are defined in Article B as "the wilful killing, torture or maltreatment, including biological experiments, the wilful causing of great suffering or serious injury to body or health, and the extensive destruction of property, not justified by military necessity and carried out unlawfully and wantonly."

[4] http://www.icrc.org/ihl.nsf/INTRO/390? OpenDocument. The ILC was established by the UN in 1948 to develop and codify international law: http://untreaty.un.org/ilc/ilcintro.htm.

[5] Brian Urquhart, *Hammarskjold* (New York, 1994), 435, 438–441. After decolonization of the Congo by Belgium, South Kasais sought independence by seceding from the rest of the territory in August 1960. Four months of hostilities ensued with the Congolese central government in which many thousands of civilians were massacred.

[6] R. W. Edwards, Jr., "Contributions of the Genocide Convention to the Development of International Law," *Ohio NUL Review*, 8 (1981), 300–314.

No trials were mooted by members of the UN. This is a short list of cases until the end of the 1960s. Worse was to follow.

The first successful prosecution for genocide was made by the International Criminal Tribunal for Rwanda (ICTR) only in 1998. Why were so many flagrant breaches of this regime permitted to go unpunished for fifty years? One answer is that only two of the five permanent members of the Security Council had signed the treaty; only in 1988 had all five of them become parties to it. Another answer is that none of these new international treaties set up an international criminal court; national courts were to deal with prosecutions in the first instance, a sure means of preventing justice when it was the state that committed the crimes. The cynical *Realpolitik* of state leaders could rely on Article 2(7) of the UN Charter that guarded state sovereignty.[7] Still others pointed to the stalemate of the Cold War.

All of these factors are relevant, but none go to the heart of the dilemmas that structure the history of human rights prosecutions in the twentieth century. If it is true that nation-states are often the primary perpetrators of genocide and other human rights crimes, it is also the case that they are the context in which such rights can be claimed and redeemed. Just as often, the disintegration of nation-states into civil war leads to gross violations of human rights. Nation-states are not, per se, inimical to human rights. The structure of the international system needs to be factored into the equation. Closer inspection of postwar cases reveals numerous intrinsic dilemmas that are difficult, if impossible to resolve: human rights intervention versus humanitarian aid, striving for human rights versus the imperative of peace and security, the right of nation-states to militarily suppress secessionist/independence movements versus the human rights of its citizens, the interminable debate about the criterion for supreme human rights emergencies that call for humanitarian intervention, the internal tension between the different instruments of international law, and, finally, the agendas of the great powers that protect the regimes committing genocidal crimes.

To illustrate these dilemmas, I focus on the case of the East Pakistani secession and the issue of related war crimes/genocide trials between 1971 and 1974. The reason for this choice is that the West Pakistan Army's brutal, indeed genocidal, suppression of the East Pakistan (now Bangladesh) autonomy/independence movement received more international attention than any other of the above-mentioned cases, yet nothing was done by the UN or nation-states to interdict, let alone condemn, the killing. As I will show, the term "genocide" was used extensively by eyewitnesses, journalists, and politicians throughout 1971 and subsequently. And for the first time since Nuremberg and Tokyo, war crimes trials were seriously considered, in this case by the new

---

[7] "Nothing contained in the present Charter shall authorize the United Nations to intervene in matters which are essentially within the domestic jurisdiction of any state or shall require the Members to submit such matters to settlement under the present Charter": http://wwwo. un.org/aboutun/charter/chapter1.htm.

Bangladeshi state, which wanted to prosecute numerous Pakistani soldiers and officials held in Indian custody. Contemporary legal observers thought that such trials would be as significant as the Nuremberg Trials, although they have received surprisingly little scholarly attention since that time.[8] In the high diplomatic drama between Pakistan, India, and Bangladesh, the trial issue was even listed at the International Court of Justice in 1973, the first time such a notification had occurred. Even though the Bangladeshi state enacted a statute to try Pakistanis for war crimes, crimes against humanity, and genocide, however, the trials never eventuated.

I proceed as follows. The first section highlights the vocabulary that the media used in reporting the events. I show that the genocide concept was used extensively by the media and even diplomats to label the human rights atrocities committed by the Pakistani Army during its "Operation Searchlight" against the East Pakistani nationalists. Then I examine how the various UN agencies responded to the crisis in East Pakistan and to the media reporting. Finally, I briefly reconstruct the domestic and international drama of the proposed war crimes/genocide trials.

The Genocide Debate about the Pakistan Campaign

When Pakistani military violence was unleashed on the evening of 25 March 1971, the press naturally did not call it genocide.[9] Civil war was the vocabulary of the first few days of Western reporting, which noted the existence East Pakistani resistance forces. The *Boston Globe* even spoke about "bloody clashes between staff and students" and the military in what were in truth one-sided massacres.[10] Sydney Schanberg at the *New York Times* was more realistic: "The Pakistani Army is using artillery and heavy machine guns against unarmed East Pakistani civilians to crush the movement for autonomy in this province of 75 million people," he wrote on 27 March.[11] In successive days, he painted a picture of a well-planned military attack on civilian opposition figures and groups, an image captured by the title of his 29 March report, "Sticks and Spears against Tanks."[12] Like the editorial of the *Sydney*

---

[8] John J. Paust and Albert P. Blaustein, "War Crimes Jurisdiction and Due Process: The Bangladesh Experience," *Vanderbilt Journal of Transnational Law*, 11 (1978), 4. There is no mention in Lawrence Howard Ball, *Prosecuting War Crimes and Genocide: The Twentieth-Century Experience* (Lawrence, Kan., 1999). Generally, see Donald Beachler, "The Politics of Genocide Scholarship: The Case of Bangladesh," *Patterns of Prejudice*, 41 (2007), 467–492.

[9] For general background to the crisis, see Richard Sisson and Leo E. Rose, *War and Secession: Pakistan, India and the Creation of Bangladesh* (Berkeley, 1990).

[10] "East Pakistan Secedes, Civil War Breaks Out," *Boston Globe*, 27 March 1971; "Toll Called High: Death Put at 10,000 – Radio Says Army Is in Control," *New York Times*, 28 March 1971; Editorial, *Daily Telegraph*, 27 March 1971.

[11] Sydney H. Schanberg, "Artillery Used: Civilians Fired On – Sections of Dacca Are Set Ablaze," *New York Times*, 28 March 1971. The story was filed on 27 March.

[12] Sydney H. Schanberg, "Sticks and Spears against Tanks," *New York Times*, 29 March 1971; Schanberg, "Heavy Killing Reported," *New York Times*, 30 March 1971.

Morning Herald on 29 March, the civilian casualties were reported as extraordinarily high, between 10,000 and 100,000 – after only three or four days![13] The reporting was the same in England. The *Daily Telegraph*'s Simon Dring, who, unlike other foreign journalists, managed to avoid expulsion from the country, reported 15,000 dead on 30 March, as well as the specific targets of the terror: students and Hindus, whose women and children were burned alive in their homes.[14] The next day, the *Telegraph* reported that "killing was on a mass scale."[15]

Given the general rhetorical caution of the media – no one had mentioned "genocide" – it was all the more remarkable that already on 27 March the American Consul General in Dacca, Archer Blood, sent a telegram to Washington headed with the phrase "Selective Genocide":

1. Here in Decca we are mute and horrified witnesses to a reign of terror by the Pak[istani] Military. Evidence continues to mount that the MLA authorities have list of AWAMI League supporters whom they are systematically eliminating by seeking them out in their homes and shooting them down. 2. Among those marked for extinction in addition to the A.L. hierarchy are student leaders and university faculty.... Moreover, with the support of the Pak[istani] military, non-Bengali Muslims are systematically attacking poor people's quarters and murdering Bengalis and Hindus.... Full horror of Pak. Military atrocities will come to light sooner or later. I, therefore, question continued advisability of present USG posture of pretending to believe GOP [Government of Pakistan] false assertions and denying ... that this office is communicating detailed account of events in East Pakistan. We should be expressing our shock, at least privately, to GOP, at this wave of terror directed against their own countrymen by Pak. military.[16]

Using uncannily similar language, the *New York Times* editorial of 7 April, entitled "Bloodbath in Bengal," condemned Washington's silence on what it called the "indiscriminate slaughter of civilians and the *selective* elimination of leadership groups in the separatist state of East Bengal."[17] Only a day earlier, with the carnage continuing without condemnation from the White House, Blood and twenty-nine diplomatic colleagues sent another telegram from Dacca – the celebrated "Blood Telegram" – to the State Department headed "Dissent from U.S. Policy Toward East Pakistan." This unprecedented cable is also worth quoting at length:

Our government has failed to denounce the suppression of democracy. Our government has failed to denounce atrocities. Our government has failed to take forceful measures to protect its citizens while at the same time bending over backwards to

[13] Editorial, *Sydney Morning Herald*, "Plunge into Chaos," 29 March 1971.
[14] Simon Dring, "Tanks Crush Revolt in Pakistan. 7,000 Slaughtered Homes Burned," *Daily Telegraph*, 30 March 1971.
[15] "'Peace Restored', West Claims," *Daily Telegraph*, 31 March 1971.
[16] Cabal of U.S. Consulate (Dacca) to the Secretary of State, Washington, DC, "Selective Genocide," 27 March 1971. National Security Archive Project: www.gwu.edu/~nsarchiv/NSAEBB/NSAEBB79/BEBB1.pdf.
[17] Editorial, "Bloodbath in Bengal," *New York Times*, 7 April 1971. Emphasis added.

placate the West Pak[istan] dominated government and to lessen any deservedly nega-tive international public relations impact against them. Our government has evidenced what many will consider moral bankruptcy.... But we have chosen not to intervene, even morally, on the grounds that the Awami conflict, in which unfortunately the overworked term genocide is applicable, is purely an internal matter of a sovereign state. Private Americans have expressed disgust. We, as professional civil servants, express our dissent with current policy and fervently hope that our true and lasting interests here can be defined and our policies redirected.[18]

By the time Blood and his colleagues had sent this telegram, the Parliament and Government of India had accused Pakistan of "massacre of defenceless people" that "amounts to genocide."[19] All along, they took the side of the Bangladeshis who, from the first days of the terror, had deployed the word "genocide." Only a few days after the crackdown, the Bangla Desh Students Action Committee in London, for instance, said the murder of innocent civil-ians was "pure and simple genocide" and, conducting a hunger strike outside Downing Street, demanded the British recognition of Bangladesh, pressure on the Pakistani Government, and the raising of the matter in the UN under the Genocide Convention.[20]

As the military campaign unfolded in April and the extent of the vio-lence became more apparent, the general rhetoric increased accordingly. By the middle of the month, India spoke of "savage and medieval butchery" and "preplanned carnage and systematic genocide."[21] Schanberg's reports continued unabated, although they were now filed from India, where he worked after his expulsion. Talking to the refugees who were pouring into the country, he wrote that "[t]here is no way of knowing exactly how many of East Pakistan's 75 million Bengalis the army has killed, but authorita-tive reports from many sources agree that the figure is at least in the tens of thousands; some reports put it much higher." By now the targets of the mil-itary were clear too all, as he reported: students, intellectuals, professionals, "and others of leadership calibre – whether they were directly involved in the nationalist movement or not." Always cautious with his figures, he allowed the victims to speak in their own words, such as a Bengali student, who complained, "This is genocide and people are standing by and looking.... Nobody has spoken out. Has the world no conscience?" If there was reprisal killings against non-Bengalis by Bangladeshi nationalists, Schanberg pointed out that the West Pakistanis' killing was well planned and systematic. This

[18] U.S. Consulate (Dacca) Cable, Dissent from U.S. Policy Toward East Pakistan, April 6, 1971, Confidential, 5 pp. Includes Signatures from the Department of State. Source: RG 59, SN 70–73 Pol and Def. From: Pol Pak-U.S. To: Pol 17–1 Pak-U.S. Box 2535. National Security Archive Project: www.gwu.edu/~nsarchiv/NSAEBB/NSAEBB79/BEBB8.pdf.
[19] Sydney H. Schanberg, "'All Part of a Game' – A Grim and Deadly One," *New York Times*, 4 April 1971. He reported that India regarded the operation as genocide.
[20] Martin Adeney, "Heavy Fighting and Burning in Chittagong," *Guardian*, 31 March 1971.
[21] James P. Sterba, "India Charges Genocide," *New York Times*, 17 April 1971.

was a judgment to which the International Commission of Jurists also came a year later.[22]

In general, so far, there was press acknowledgment that Bengalis and Indians used the term "genocide," while not endorsing it themselves, although Peggy Durdin, in a long piece in the *New York Times* in early May, called the killing the "one of the bloodiest slaughters of modern times."[23] The breakthrough came in mid-June when Anthony Mascarenhas, assistant editor of the *Morning News* in Karachi and an official war correspondent attached to 9th Pakistani Division in East Pakistan, fled to London – he was also a correspondent for the *Sunday Times* – to report what he had seen. The *Sunday Times* devoted two sections plus an editorial to this story, one about him, and a long article in his own words, both under the prominent headlines of "Genocide."[24] Though Bengalis had been responsible for retributive killing of non-Bengalis, the editors wrote, "when all this has been said, there is no escaping the terrible charge of deliberate premeditated extermination leveled by the facts against the present Pakistani Government."[25]

For the first time, the Western public was presented with insider information about Operation Searchlight, replete with incriminating quotations from Pakistani leaders and officers.[26] A skilful writer, Mascarenhas knew what allusion to invoke for a Western audience. Yahya Khan, the Pakistani President, was "pushing through its own 'final solution' of the East Bengal problem." Officers he interviewed told him that they were "determined to cleanse East Pakistan once and for all of the threat of secession, even if it means killing off two million people and ruling the province as a colony for 30 years." "Pogroms" were instituted against recalcitrant villages in "kill and burn" missions. Entire "villages [were] devastated by 'punitive action'," which authorities called a "cleansing process." Hindus were targeted for "annihilation," because they were thought to be a minority of unscrupulous merchants who dominated the economy and siphoned off wealth to India. They "completely undermined the Muslim masses with their money," said one officer. What is more, they were Hinduizing Bengali culture. Like Schanberg, Mascarenhas thought that the terror was not a spontaneous reaction to Bengali violence but was planned by Punjabi political and military elites.

The critical rhetoric now intensified, and visual images of the violence appeared in the press. An editorial in the *Hong Kong Standard* spoke of "Another Genghis!" a few weeks later, playing on the fact that the Pakistani military general was named Tikka Khan. He was worse than Genghis, the paper opined, because at least the Mongol leader had founded an empire. By

[22] Sydney H. Schanberg, "Bengalis Form a Cabinet as the Bloodshed Goes On," *New York Times*, 14 April 1971; Schanberg, "Foreign Evacuees from East Pakistan Tell of Grim Fight," *New York Times*, 7 April 1971.
[23] Perry Durdin, "The Political Tidal Wave That Struck East Pakistan," *New York Times*, 2 May 1971.
[24] "Genocide," *Sunday Times*, 13 June 1971.
[25] Editorial, "Stop the Killing," *Sunday Times*, 13 June 1971.
[26] Anthony Mascarenhas, "Genocide," *Sunday Times*, 13 June 1971.

contrast, "Tikka Khan and his gang of uniformed cut-throats will be remembered for trying to destroy the people of half a nation."[27] A week later, *Time*
magazine, in an article highlighting India's refugee crisis, quoted the Indian
Foreign Minister Swaran Singh's charge that supplying Pakistan with arms
"amounts to condonation [*sic*] of genocide."[28] When Senator Edward Kennedy
visited India in August in his capacity as Chairman of the Senate Judiciary
Subcommittee on Refugees, he condemned the Nixon administration's continued arms aid to Pakistan and for damaging relations with India. He joined
India in denouncing the Pakistani policy as genocidal.[29]

Even as war between Pakistan and India loomed in November and then
broke out in December, the press continued to highlight the scorched earth
tactics of the Pakistani Army.[30] The writer Alvin Toffler, who visited India's
refugee camps, wrote of "West Pakistan's genocidal attack" on refugees and
condemned his government's support of Pakistan.[31] Anthony Lewis, also in the
New York Times, denounced U.S. policy, going so far as to compare Yahya
Kahn's policies with those of Hitler's early days:

in terms of results – in terms of human beings killed, brutalized or made refugees –
Yahya's record compares quite favorably with Hitler's early years. The West Pakistanis
have killed several hundred thousand civilians in the east, and an estimated ten million have fled to India. The victims are Bengali or Hindus, not Czechs or Poles or Jews,
and perhaps therefore less meaningful to us in the West. But to the victims the crime
is the same.[32]

An American witness of the carnage described it as "terror beyond description," and her story was prominently featured in the newspaper.[33]

With the war effectively over by mid-December and the country liberated
by the Indian invasion, journalists could return to the field and report their
findings. Like the Bengali press, which announced the discovery of mass graves
in many stories in late December and January, their American colleagues also
related the scale of the killing, which typically amounted to tens of thousands
for each locality,[34] in total between 500,000 and 1.5 million.[35] Schanberg's

---

[27] Editorial, "Another Genghis!" *Hong Kong Standard*, 25 June 1971.
[28] "Pakistan: The Ravaging of Golden Bengal," *Time*, Monday, 2 August 1971.
[29] Sydney H. Schanberg, "Kennedy, in India, Terms Pakistani Drive Genocide," *New York Times*, 18 August 1971.
[30] Malcolm W. Browne, "East Pakistan Town after Raid by Army: Fire and Destruction," *New York Times*, 6 November 1971.
[31] Alvin Toffler, "The Ravaged People of East Pakistan," *New York Times*, 5 December 1971.
[32] Anthony Lewis, "The Wringing of Hands," *New York Times*, 6 December 1971; Lewis, "Not to Be Forgotten," *New York Times*, 20 December 1971, India's representative to the Security Council, Sen, quoted this article approvingly the same day: 1,608th Meeting, 6 December 1971, 8.
[33] Lewis M. Simons, "Witness Calls E. Pakistan 'Terror beyond Description'," *Washington Post*, 15 December 1971.
[34] Fox Butterfield, "Day of Terror for 50,000 Bengalis: Thousands Were Slain, Homes Razed," *New York Times*, 30 December 1971.
[35] "'Who Knows How Many Millions Have Been Killed' in the East?" *New York Times*, 22 December 1971.

headline of 24 January 1972 reflected this line of reporting: "Bengalis' Land a Vast Cemetery."[36] Particularly notorious was the massacre of hundreds of intellectuals and professionals in Dacca in the last days of the war, an event commemorated today.[37] Although retributive violence against collaborators was widely noted (also in the U.S. television news), the efforts of guerrilla leaders and the Awami League leader, Mujib, to stop it were also reported.[38] At this point, in the first half of 1972, the massive scale of the rapes of East Bengali women received attention, such as in a long piece in *The New York Times* by Aubrey Menen.[39]

By this time, Neil McDermot, the former English Labour cabinet minister, had arrived in Dacca as head of the International Commission of Jurists, which had determined to investigate "The Events of East Pakistan, 1971," as it called its report, delivered in June 1972. It considered the genocide question in its recommendation. With the caution characteristic of lawyers, it dismissed the widespread belief of Bengalis that the repression as a whole constituted genocide:

To prevent a nation from attaining political autonomy does not constitute genocide: the intention must be to destroy in whole or in part the people as such. The Bengali people number some 75 million. It can hardly be suggested that the intention was to destroy the Bengali people. As to the destruction of part of the Bengali people, there can be no doubt that very many Bengalis were killed. We find it quite impossible to assess the total numbers, and we cannot place great confidence in the various estimates which have been made from time to time.[40]

But the selectivity of the Pakistani repression, which was apparent to world opinion from the beginning – that is, to eliminate members of the Awami League, students, and Hindus – was significant, because it evinced an intention to destroy those groups as such. Of these groups,

only Hindus would seem to fall within the definition of a national, ethnical, racial or religious group. There is overwhelming evidence that Hindus were slaughtered and their houses and villages destroyed simply because they were Hindus.... The Nazis regarded the Jews as enemies of the state and killed them as such. In our view there is a strong prima facie case that the crime of genocide was committed against the group comprising the Hindu population of East Bengal.[41]

[36] Sydney H. Schanberg, "Bengalis' Land a Vast Cemetery," *New York Times*, 24 January 1972.
[37] Fox Butterfield, "A Journalist Is Linked to Murder of Bengalis," *New York Times*, 3 January 1972.
[38] James P. Sterba, "In Dacca, Killings amid the Revelry," *New York Times*, 18 December 1971.
[39] Aubrey Menen, "The Rapes of Bangladesh," *New York Times*, 23 July 1972. For analysis, see Nayanika Mookherjee, "'Remembering to Forget': Public Secrecy and Memory of Sexual Violence in the Bangladesh War of 1971," *Journal of the Royal Anthropological Institute*, 12 (2006), 433–450; Susan Brownmiller, *Against Our Will: Men, Women, and Rape* (New York, 1993).
[40] ICJ Report, *The Events of East Pakistan, 1971* (Geneva, 1972).
[41] Ibid.

Here MacDermot was at one with Mujibur, the new Bangladeshi President, who said on 17 April 1971 that Yahya had engaged in "pre-planned genocide"[42] McDermot thought trials were feasible and viable, and he wanted to convince Bangladesh to constitute an international court with a majority of neutral judges and invoke international penal law. But this was not to be, he noted:

In the Western world there seems to be a considerable body of opinion which thinks there ought not to be any trials of those alleged to be responsible.... Unfortunately, there is no one able and willing to set up such a tribunal. The efforts within the U.N. to promote the establishment of such an international criminal court have, for the time being at least, foundered. Even more modest proposals ... have been blocked. There are, it seems, too many governments with too many skeletons for them to agree to any effective enforcement machinery for human rights.[43]

The estimated number of dead varied widely. Between 300,000 and (a greatly exaggerated) 3 million Bengalis (not just Hindus) were killed between late March and December 1971. We now turn to the diplomacy that led to these gloomy observations.

The UN and the Genocide Question

Not once did any body of the United Nations directly consider the crackdown by the Pakistani Army in East Bengal. The Secretary-General wrote to Pakistan's President on 22 April expressing deep concern about the situation and offering Pakistan all possible assistance. President Kahn replied on 3 May welcoming such assistance, which he said would administered by his own agencies but promising full cooperation. At all times, Pakistan gave the impression of being a willing and able member of the international community. In his correspondence, the Secretary-General emphasized the humanitarian and nonpolitical nature of his interest and his respect for Pakistan's sovereignty. After all, he needed Pakistan's consent for UN personnel to be stationed in East Pakistan and for the UN to do its work there generally. Coincidentally, the Indian Government wrote to the Secretary-General on 23 April with a request for assistance with the mounting number of refugees. A three-man UN team visited India from 7 to 19 May, and on 19 May the Secretary-General appealed to governments to support India with humanitarian aid.[44] Henceforth, under the auspices of the UN High Commissioner for Refugees, the UN undertook the largest humanitarian operation of its existence, coordinating a massive, international relief operation to provide food and other necessities to the refugees, above all in India. An inspection of the UN files

[42] Indian representative to the Security Council, Sen, quoting Mujibur. Security Council Official Reports, 1608th Meeting, 6 December 1971, 8.
[43] Neil MacDermot, "Crimes against Humanity in Bangladesh," *International Lawyer*, 7 (1972), 483–484.
[44] "Text of Appeal by SG for Emergency Assistance to Refugees from EP in India," UN Press Section, Office of Public Information, Press Release SG/SM1478, 19 May 1971. UN Archives Series 228, Box 1, File 2, Acc 77/207.

shows that the bulk of its correspondence concerned the logistics of this relief effort: petitioning states for money and equipment, dealing with logjams and delays, attending to the misuse of UN infrastructure, and seeing to the mass transportation of grain and rice. The UN engagement on East Pakistan, then, was driven by humanitarian, not human rights, issues. "United Nations activity in East Pakistan is solely humanitarian in nature," the Secretary-General emphasized to media correspondents. "There is no 'peace-keeping' element in its terms of reference, and it is entirely misleading and erroneous to refer to it as a 'United Nations force' or United Nations observers."[45]

From the outset, the Secretary-General's position was that the refugees should be repatriated as soon as possible, but he was restrained by his office about how that should occur, especially if he and others did not feel licensed to lecture Pakistan about its domestic politics. That was a matter for the Security Council, whose President he addressed with an urgent letter on 20 July. The conflict was complex, and he did not wish to take sides: "It seems to me that the present tragic situation, in which humanitarian, economic and political problems are mixed in such a way as almost to defy any distinction between them, presents a challenge to the UN as a whole which must be met." Accordingly, human rights rhetoric was a distraction:

In the tragic circumstances such as those prevailing in the Sub-Continent, it is all too easy to make moral judgements. It is far more difficult to face up to the political and human realities of the situation and to help the peoples concerned to find a way out of their enormous difficulties. It is this latter course which, in my view, the UN must follow.

He did hint at applying great power pressure to Pakistan:

The political aspects of this matter are of such far-reaching importance that the Secretary-General is not in a position to suggest precise courses of action before the members of the Security Council have taken note of the problem. I believe, however, that the UN, with its long experiences in peace keeping and with its varied resources for conciliation and persuasion, must, and should, now play a more forthright role in attempting both to mitigate the human tragedy which has already taken place and to avert the further deterioration of the situation.[46]

But the Security Council never took the hint and did not explicitly consider the situation on the subcontinent until an outright international conflict was on its hands in December, when India invaded East Pakistan. In fact, the President of the Council did not reply to Thant's letter.

Matters were no different in other areas of the UN. The Committee on the Elimination of Racial Discrimination, which was established under

[45] "Note to Correspondents," UN Press Section, Office of Public Information, Note No. 3675, 2 August 1971. UN Archives Series 228, Box 1, File 2, Acc 77/207. For an insider account of the UN relief effort, see Thomas W. Oliver, *The United Nations in Bangladesh* (Princeton, 1978).
[46] "Statement by the Secretary General," UN Press Section, Office of Public Information, Press Release SG/SM/1516 IHA 32 REF/63, 2 August 1971. UN Archives Series 230, Box 2, File 11, Acc 77/207, "General-Press Reports and Clippings – Feb. 1972-Jan. 1974."

the International Convention on the Elimination of All Forms of Racial Discrimination of 1965 (coming into force in 1969), met in April and September 1971 and did not seriously consider East Pakistan. Although it decided that Pakistan's report was inadequate, the Committee did not specify which aspects needed elaboration or correction. Pakistan did not submit a supplementary paper in September, and the Committee did not complain to the General Assembly about this failure in its report.[47]

India raised the killings and its security problems at the Economic and Social Council in May, and Pakistan predictably objected that "A sovereign State has the right to suppress secession," cleverly mentioning the United States' Civil War. This argument clearly made an impact, because no member questioned Pakistan further. Nor did they at the next meeting in July. The default position of the members was to praise India for dealing with the refugees and to call for their return and for restraint.[48] Also in July, the situation was mentioned in the Social Committee of the Economic and Social Council and at the 51st Plenary Session of the Council, at which the High Commissioner for Refugees made a report on the refugee crisis. The Council referred the report to the General Assembly without debate.[49]

An exasperated Indira Gandhi tried unsuccessfully to rebut the Pakistani position by conceding that "every country has some movement of secession." Consequently, she understood that "every country is afraid of what would happen to themselves if they gave support to Bangla Desh." But the current situation was "quite different," she insisted, "because it is not just a small part of the country that is asking for rights. It happens to be the majority of the country, not a small part wanting to go away." As might be expected, her arguments were ignored, and she was left to complain about the United Nations staff who say "'We will come and see what is happening in India, but we will not prevent genocide, the mass murder, the raping of women that is taking place in East Bengal.'"[50]

Media observers were not reticent to raise the issues, as the exchange between the Secretary-General and the President of the United Nations Correspondents Association (UNCA) in June 1971 demonstrates. The UNCA President asked:

Millions of Pakistani citizens have already crossed Pakistan's international borders to seek refuge in India and each day more are still crossing, thus turning military operations in East Pakistan into a potential threat to India's economic and political stability. At what point do you think that the UN might consider the events as ceasing to be an internal matter of Pakistan's?

---

[47] Ved P. Nanda, "A Critique of the United Nations Inaction in the Bangladesh Crisis," *Denver Law Journal*, 49 (1972/73), 53–68.
[48] Donald F. Keys, "Justice vs. the Sovereign State: The Ordeal of Bangladesh," *New Federalist*, 17:105 (Jan./Feb. 1972), 5–8.
[49] ICJ, *The Events in East Pakistan, 1971*.
[50] Indira Gandhi, *India and Bangla Desh: Selected Speeches and Statements, March to December 1971* (New Delhi, 1972), 31, 98.

Finally, the West Pakistan Army's action in Bangla Desh has already resulted in nearly a million deaths, 4.8 million refugees in India, and many millions more refugees and destitute people inside Bangla Desh. This is a record far more apalling [*sic*] than the Indo-China war, paralleled only by Hitler and Genghis Khan. Yet you and the UN have remained silent, dealing only with peripheral humanitarian problems in a half-hearted way. Does the UN deserve public support with such a record?

The Secretary-General avoided the issues in his reply:

Regarding the happenings in East Pakistan in the last part of March and in April, I am sure that most of you are aware of the action I took on the first two days of those happenings. I offered the Government of Pakistan the international Organization's humanitarian involvement in the area. Of course, the Government of Pakistan complied with my request at last and Mr. Kittani, the Assistant SG for Inter-Agency Affairs, has arrived in Karachi just today, and he is proceeding to Islamabad in the afternoon to discuss with the Pakistani authorities on the modalities of channelling humanitarian aid and materials to afflicted East Pakistan.

In this connexion, I must say that from all information available to me since the beginning of April, the happenings in East Pakistan constitute one of the most tragic episodes in human history. Of course, it is for future historians to gather facts and make their own evaluations, but it has been a very terrible blot on a page of human history. I very much hope that the negotiations now going on between Mr. Kittani and Pakistani authorities will generate appropriate and effective channels of international aid to the afflicted areas.[51]

The tone of the Secretary-General prevailed within the UN throughout the year. There was no joy for human rights advocates in the Sub-Commission on Prevention of Discrimination of Minorities, a body of the Commission on Human Rights charged by the Economic and Social Council with studying "persistent and consistent patterns of Human Rights violations." It met between 2 and 20 August but did not study the East Pakistan case as authorized. Only the representation of twenty-two nongovernmental organizations, led by the delegate of the International Commission of Jurists, put it on the agenda. The delegate spoke before the Sub-Commission on 16 August, quoting eyewitnesses to the terror and highlighting "gross violations of human rights."[52] He requested that the Sub-Commission examine the situation in East Pakistan and make recommendations to the Commission on Human Rights. Again Pakistan said that the UN could not consider human rights in East Pakistan because its role did not extend to internal questions. If it did, separatism would be encouraged, and, besides, no consistent pattern of discriminatory violence was apparent. Both sides had committed violations.[53] Again

[51] "Press Release," UN Press Section, Office of Public Information, Press Release SG/SM1493, 3 June 1971, UN Archives, Series 228, Box 1, File 2, Acc 77/207, 11–13.
[52] Keys, "Justice vs. the Sovereign State."
[53] John Salzberg, "UN Prevention of Human Rights Violations: The Bangladesh Case," *International Organization*, 27:1 (1973), 118.

these arguments were compelling. Members said they should not consider "political" issues, and the matter was laid to rest without any determination. The United States, China, and the Arab and African states trusted Pakistan to deal with its domestic problems. The African states were particularly nervous about secessionist movements after the Biafra and Congo episodes of the 1960s.[54]

By the time that the General Assembly, its Third (Social, Humanitarian, and Cultural) Committee, and the Security Council seriously considered the crisis on the subcontinent, it was too late. They were overtaken by events. Frustrated by the inaction of the international community, indeed by its active and de facto support of Pakistan, India took matters into its own hands, supporting the East Bengali/Mukti Bahini independence forces that were waging a draining insurgency against the Pakistani military all year, and then invading in early December in the name of humanitarian intervention.[55] With more than double the number of Pakistani troops, it won the war in two weeks and occupied Dacca in ten days, on 13 December.[56] During November and December, the General Assembly, the Third Committee, and, belatedly, the Security Council debated stillborn resolutions. But the debates still reveal the international consensus about the relationship between separatist movements, counter-insurgency, human rights, and humanitarian intervention.

With the exception of the Soviet Union and its allies, the nation-states of the world criticized India for its invasion and urged a ceasefire and mutual withdrawal to international borders even though such an outcome would leave Pakistan in control of East Pakistan. India and the USSR also raised the issue of genocide and war crimes in the Security Council, as well as the will of the East Bengali people, which was not acknowledged by other members of the Council:

[S]everal principles have been quoted by various delegations [said the Indian representative Sen]: sovereignty, territorial integrity, non-interference in other people's affairs, and so on. But I wonder why we should be shy about speaking of human rights. What happened to the Convention on genocide? What happened to all the other social rights and conventions which you have so solemnly accepted? Are we therefore to be

[54] Keys, "Justice vs. the Sovereign State," 5–6; ICJ, *The Events in East Pakistan, 1971.*
[55] Nicholas J. Wheeler, *Saving Strangers: Humanitarian Intervention in International Society* (Oxford, 2000), ch. 2; Francis Kofi Abiew, *The Evolution of the Doctrine and Practice of Humanitarian Intervention* (The Hague, 1999), 113–120; Anthony Clark Arend and Robert J. Beck, *International Law and the Use of Force: Beyond the UN Charter Paradigm* (London, 1993), 119; Richard B. Lillich, *Humanitarian Intervention and the United Nations* (Charlottesville, Va., 1973); Thomas M. Franck and Nigel S. Rodley, "After Bangladesh: The Law of Humanitarian Intervention by Military Force," *American Journal of International Law,* 67 (April 1973), 275–305.
[56] Onkar Marwah, "India's Military-Intervention in East Pakistan, 1971–1972," *Modern Asian Studies,* 13 (1979), 549–580; Robert Victor Jackson, *South Asian Crisis: India, Pakistan, and Bangla Desh; A Political and Historical Analysis of the 1971 War* (New York, 1975).

selective in serving what is known as the motto of our era: peace, progress and justice? What happened to the justice part?[57]

Not once were these points addressed by other members of the Council. Most intransigent was China, which, close to Pakistan and mindful of its Tibet question, insisted that East Pakistan was solely an internal matter. There was general sympathy for the refugees (though not by China), but Pakistan's military behavior was never mentioned. The Council, like the General Assembly, was concerned with ending the war and returning to normality as soon as possible. The Saudis complained that Bangladesh had been created by Indian interference rather than by genuine self-determination, by which they presumably meant a successful war of independence without third-party participation.[58]

As might be expected, India objected to the rush for reconciliation, attacking the UN for not responding to the genocide: "So there is no normalcy; there is only butchery." There could be no realistic return of refugees, certainly not with pious calls for political normality, if Pakistan was left in charge of East Bengal, said Sen, the Indian representative to the Council. He was the only one to mention the mass rapes, humiliation, and trauma that Pakistan had occasioned. India, he declared, "shall not be a party to any solution that will mean continuation of oppression of East Pakistan people. ... So long as we have any light of civilized behaviour left in us, we shall protect them."[59]

For its part, Pakistan had already arrogated the UN and the name of civilization to its cause. On 29 November, on the eve of the Indian invasion, Yahya Khan asked that UN observers be stationed in East Pakistan to report on Indian border violations, and earlier he had requested the good offices of the Secretary-General to resolve tensions with India. India had always rejected such entreaties, pointing out in vain that the cause of the refugee crisis needed to be addressed first.[60] In the end, Pakistan angrily accused the Council of not protecting it from Indian aggression and dismemberment.[61] After its defeat later in December 1971, Pakistan suddenly became very vocal about genocide, circulating reports about the mass murder of the Bihari minority in East Pakistan and calling for their protection. With Chinese support, it held India responsible as the occupying power and requested Security Council intervention and action through its special representative. India's naval blockade, Pakistan complained, causes "widespread starvation and famine" and

[57] Security Council Official Reports, 1608th Meeting, 6 December 1971, 27. On 5 December, the USSR representative asked: "What, indeed, has happened to our conventions on genocide, human rights, self-determination, and so on?" Ibid., 32.
[58] UN Yearbook, 1971, 15 December 1971, 155.
[59] Security Council Official Reports, 1604th Meeting, 4 December 1971, 16.
[60] UN Archives, Background – East Pakistan-Pakistan Correspondence, April-December 1971 (1 of 3). Series 228, Box 1, File 3, ACC 77/207. 29 November 1971 from Kahn to SG.
[61] UN Yearbook, 1971, 31 December 1971, 158–159.

"cannot but be considered an outrage to world conscience."[62] This was not the only element of its counter-campaign against India in the UN and international public sphere. The other was the fate of some 90,000 Pakistani soldiers held by Indian forces in Bangladesh after their surrender.

The Pakistani POWs and the War Crimes/Genocide Trials

Upon liberation and with Pakistani soldiers in custody, Mujib, the Bangladeshi leader, declared that war criminals among them would be put on trial for war crimes, crimes against humanity, and genocide. On 31 December 1971, Pakistan complained to the Secretary-General about these proposed trials, which they said would violate the Geneva Convention of 1971 and the Security Council's resolution of 21 December about the exchange of prisoners of war.[63] Indeed, three days before the war had ended, on 13 December, Pakistan complained to the UN about a "serious breach of the Geneva Convention relative to the Treatment of Prisoners of War of 12 August 1949 committed by the Government of India and its armed forces" in relation to an apparent Indian threat to hand over the Pakistani POWs to the Mukti Bahini if they did not surrender.[64] As would soon become apparent, India's and Bangladesh's alleged violations of the Geneva Convention would become the main plank of the Pakistani campaign against these countries in 1972 and 1973. The Pakistani strategy, then, revolved around pressuring the UN for the release of the POWs and preventing their prosecution. In doing so, it sought to take the moral high ground, painting its opponents as violators of international humanitarian law and delinquents of the international community. They largely succeeded, and they were not alone. During 1972 and 1973, the UN was inundated with petitions from expatriate Pakistani groups around the world for the release of the POWs, but also from some NGOs and human rights groups who agreed with the Pakistani case based on the Geneva Convention. Before long, a sign hung at Islamabad Airport reading "90,000 Pakistan prisoners rotting in Indian ghettoes. Is world conscience asleep?"[65]

The tide of public opinion began to turn a little against Bangladesh in 1972 and 1973 as other issues pressed themselves on the agenda. With a ruined economy and oncoming famine, Bangladesh once again faced starvation and a continuing humanitarian crisis.[66] In March 1972, the *Christian Scientist Monitor* was appealing to Indira Gandhi to reconsider her position on the

---

[62] UN Archives, Series 228, Box 1, File 3, ACC 77/207. Letter of 15 December 1971 from Pakistan Mission to UN.

[63] *UN Yearbook, 1971,* 31 December 1971, 159.

[64] General Assembly, 26th session, Agenda item 102. 3 December 1971 A/8587/S10452. UN Archives, Series 228, Box 1, File 3, ACC 77/207.

[65] David Holden, "Why 75,000 Stay Trapped in a Triangle of Bitterness," *Sunday Times,* 3 June 1973.

[66] Sydney H. Schanberg, "With Economy in Ruins, Bangladesh Faces Food Crisis," *New York Times,* 30 March 1972.

POW issue so that it would not prevent peace negotiations.[67] The continuing
plight of the Bihari minority also received press coverage, especially in view
of their status as a sticking point in negotiations between Pakistan, India,
and Bangladesh: Bangladesh wanted many of them to migrate to Pakistan,
but Pakistan did not want them.[68] Then there were the widespread reports of
inefficiency, corruption, and stolen aid that sullied the reputation of the new
government.[69] The mood was summarized by an editorial in the *Guardian* in
November 1972:

On the Indian sub-continent at this moment, almost 12 months since the war that
redrew all its maps, there are still 90,00 Pakistani prisoners of war locked in India
camps ...; at least 700,000 Biharis embattled in Bangladesh compounds, not fully
belonging to the new country, not welcome by other lands; 400,000 Bengalis, a
huge majority of them desperate for repatriation, existing on diminishing incomes
or state encampments within Pakistan; not to mention 30,000 or more alleged
collaborators, held inside Sheikh Mujib's appallingly overcrowded gaols for many
months and now, at least, beginning to race a flood of trials where sheer weight of
numbers drains hope of decent justice. On the most benign calculations ... there
are a million and a quarter people living ... under unlimited detention and in
extreme fear.[70]

The attention of "civilized" opinion, so to speak, was on these people,
not on putting the POWs on trial. A few months later, in March 1973,
officials in the General Secretariat of the United Nations noted "marked
and significant increase in volume of criticism, both in the European and
American press and by influential officials in donor governments, of continued detention of prisoners of war by the Government of Bangladesh
and also of implied threat to expel those Biharis who have not opted for
Bangladesh nationality." This would not augur well for "the ability of the
Secretary-General effectively to generate further support for Bangladesh,"
he noted.[71]

Some members of the Security Council were more direct. While the United
States, which had recognized Bangladesh in April 1972, urged it to return the
POWs in accordance with the Geneva Convention, China said its continuing
violation of that Convention showed that Bangladesh was not fit for membership of the United Nations.[72] Indeed, in August 1972, China was aghast
that India and Bangladesh proposed to conduct trials of war criminals, which
it said showed contempt for the UN Charter. Now, China's representative

---

[67] *Christian Scientist Monitor*, 30 March 1972.
[68] Peter Preston, "Ifs and Bhutto," *Telegraph*, 30 March 1972.
[69] James P. Sterba, "Bangladesh Drifts in Sea of Corruption and Confusion," *New York Times*,
    4 October 1972.
[70] Editorial, "A Time to Be Recognized," *Guardian*, 15 November 1972.
[71] Cable from Jackson/Urquhart to Umbricht, Dacca, 16 March 1973. East Pakistan-Code
    Unnumbered, Outgoing April 1971-March 1973, Series 232, Box 2, File 1, ACC 77/207.
    A/754.
[72] Security Council Official Records, 1660th Meeting, 25 August 1972, 6.

concluded, India was trying to impose Bangladesh on the world community and use the POWs to pressure Pakistan on this matter and Kashmir.[73]

Mujib was undeterred. By all accounts, he had no choice. According to UN observers in Dacca, the line between pogroms against Biharis and collaborators and public order was very thin, and the trials were a necessary sop to public opinion. For all that, the government promised fair trials on the Nuremberg model. During 1972, preparations for the trials unfolded in the form of evidence gathering. Even by March, however, it was no secret that the Indian Government was concerned that such trials might prevent a deal with Pakistan.[74] Perhaps to balance these imperatives, Mujib let it be known to senior UN negotiators in October that he was prepared to settle "90% of claims" with Pakistan if he could do so as an equal with the new Pakistani President, Zulfikar Ali Bhutto. The UN official noted of the planed trials, "Personally I think the soup will not be eaten as hot as it is cooked. Please inform 38th floor."[75] Indeed, a meeting with Mujib a month later revealed that he did not intend to punish any of the Pakistani prisoners. He wanted only international recognition of their crimes, a point he also made in election speeches in early 1973: "not out of vindictiveness but the world should know what the Pakistani army did." The other prisoners could be returned forthwith.[76] By all accounts, Mujib used the word "genocide" in his conversations, prompting the UN official to ask for advice about "the exact implication of [the] expression 'Genocide.'"[77] Even by late 1972, it had not occurred to senior UN staff what this word really meant and entailed.

The same could not be said of the International Commission of Jurists, whose report earlier that year stated that strong prima facie cases could be made out against Pakistani personnel for breaches of the Geneva Convention and the Genocide Convention. The report went into some detail about the points of law, but it had clearly not been registered at the United Nations. The report concluded: "If, as has been reported, the Bangladesh government are to put on trial senior Pakistani officers and civilians, they should set up an international court for the purpose with a majority of judges from neutral countries."[78]

---

[73] Ibid., 8–9.
[74] Sydney H. Schanberg, "India Opens War for Dacca Trials," *New York Times*, 18 March 1972. East Pakistan-Code Unnumbered, Outgoing April 1971-March 1973, Series 232, Box 2, File 1, ACC 77/207. A/754. Cable from Henry, Dacca, to Secretary General, Guyer/Urquhart, 20 December 1971.
[75] East Pakistan-Code Unnumbered, Outgoing April 1971-March 1973, Series 232, Box 2, File 1, ACC 77/207. A/754. Memo from Umbricht to Jackson, 11 October 1972.
[76] Cable to the Secretary Genera from Guyer, Dacca, 15 November 1972; East Pakistan, Cable Unnumbered only, Incoming May 1971 to March 1973, Series 232, Box 2, File 2, ACC 77/207. A/254. Cable to Secretary General from Umbricht, Dacca, 27 February 1973.
[77] East Pakistan, Cable Unnumbered only, Incoming May 1971 to March 1973, Series 232, Box 2, File 2, ACC 77/207. A/254. Geyer to Secretary General, Dacca, 13 November 1972.
[78] ICJ, *The Events in East Pakistan, 1971.*

Pakistan's reaction to the proposed trials was not only to launch legal action in the International Court of Justice and to badger the United Nations. Its leaders made threats of their own. In January 1972, Bhutto threatened to prosecute Bengalis in Pakistan – 400,000 Bengalis were stranded in West Pakistan, which included 30,000 soldiers and 17,000 civil servants – for having opted to emigrate to Bangladesh.[79] The President had his own domestic concerns. If the trials became a "big *tamasha* [carnival], palm tree justice," the President feared, "The story will come to this side and things will become unmanageable." The perception that internal Pakistani stability was at stake was shared by journalists, such as David Holden at the *Sunday Times*, who reported in June 1973 that "it is widely agreed in Islamabad that the Pakistan Army's reaction to any trials in Dacca would be violence. In other words, Bengalis in Pakistan would also go on trial for 'treason' during the war, and the mutual recriminations would probably put any settlement whatever out of reach indefinitely."[80] Pakistan also rejected Bangladesh's authority to hold trials, because "the alleged criminal acts were committed in a part of Pakistan." Instead, Pakistan "would constitute a judicial tribunal of such character and composition as will inspire international confidence."[81] In the event, India did pressure Bangladesh to return all the prisoners and drop the trials; in return Pakistan recognized Bangladesh, whose standing rose in the international community.

Conclusion

Roughly fifty years separate the Nuremberg Trials from the ad hoc tribunals established by the Security Council in 1993 and 1994 to prosecute perpetrators of war crimes, crimes against humanity, and genocide in the former Yugoslavia and Rwanda, respectively. The passing of the Rome Statute to establish the International Criminal Court soon thereafter, in 1998, led some commentators to regard the 1990s as the endpoint of a humanitarian development begun in the later 1940s. "For advocates of peace through justice," wrote one, "the last decade of the twentieth century marks a turning point in international legal history comparable only to the Nuremberg and Tokyo Trials of the 1940s."[82] Now that the Cold War was over and the political will for humanitarian intervention and prosecution had been generated, the international community was moving into a new,

[79] East Pakistan, Cable Unnumbered only, Incoming May 1971 to March 1973, Series 232, Box 2, File 2, ACC 77/207. A/254. DSCO4294, Cable to SG from Umbricht, Dacca, 23 January 1972
[80] Holden, "Why 75,000 Stay Trapped in a Triangle of Bitterness."
[81] S. M. Burke, "The Postwar Diplomacy of the Indo-Pakistani War of 1971," *Asian Survey*, 13 (1973), 1038.
[82] David Wippman, "Atrocities, Deterrence, and the Limits of International Justice," *Fordham International Law Journal*, 23 (1999/2000), 473.

more optimistic phase of its development. Or so these legal scholars would like us to have believed.[83]

The teleological view is too optimistic. After all, Sudan has been a signatory to the Convention since 2004, but that did not prevent it conducting a genocidal counter-insurgency in Darfur with relative impunity. In fact, the Darfur case shows that the pattern of events in East Pakistan between 1971 and 1974 represents the norm rather than the exception in international relations and human rights diplomacy, notwithstanding the indictment of the Sudanese President by the International Criminal Court. Even where such conflicts can be seen as genocidal, as in the East Pakistan case, state leaders find secessionist movements too threatening to be able to link their own suppression of them with the genocide concept. The question raised by M. Maniruzzaman Mia, the former Vice-Chancellor of Dacca University, is salient: "The savagery of the Pakistani army during the nine month period also raised a pertinent question: should a government have the unfettered right to do whatever it likes within its territory and get away with it without being censured by the world community?"[84] The answer is that even if it does not formally possess such a right, it can indeed do so.

The view of legal scholars that national sovereignty is the enemy of humanitarian law only partially captures the different tensions in play in the prosecution of gross human rights violations. Although it is true that the vast majority of states did not want to arm the UN with the capacity to interfere with Pakistan's brutal suppression of East Pakistan, the UN was also overwhelmed by its humanitarian mission. The Bangladeshi case shows that international human rights law, which states consider "political" (relating to gross breaches of human rights), and humanitarian agendas, which are not "political" (such as aiding refugees and famine relief), can clash and lead to the promotion of one at the expense of the other. Of course, in reality, humanitarian relief can also be considered political by a regime, such as Burma's, which was reluctant to admit aid workers in the aftermath of devastating storms in 2007. And, of course, the decision to regard humanitarian aid as nonpolitical is, in fact, highly political. By refusing to pressure Pakistan to negotiate further with the East Pakistani nationalists, who had won an election after all, the international system of states was giving an effective green light to terroristic solutions to internal political problems. And yet, if he had threatened UN censure for "Operation Searchlight," the Secretary-General would likely have been unable to mount the UN humanitarian operation.

[83] Richard Falk, "Humanitarian Intervention: A Forum," *The Nation*, 14 July 2003; Thomas G. Weiss, "The Sunset of Humanitarian Intervention? The Responsibility to Protect in a Unipolar Era," *Security Dialogue*, 35 (2004), 135–153; Michael Barnett, "The New United Nations Politics of Peace: From Juridical Sovereignty to Empirical Sovereignty," *Global Governance*, 1 (1995), 79–97.
[84] M. Maniruzzaman Mia, "Violation of Human Rights and Genocide in Bangladesh," in Kabir Chaudhury et al. (eds.), *A Nation is Born* (Calcutta, 1972), 33.

We also need to consider the proposition that the meaning of human rights is not unequivocal, that human rights rhetoric is open to differing interpretations, and that human rights constituencies can be mobilized in contradictory directions. Thus Pakistan invoked the conscience of the world and "civilized opinion" in relation to its captured prisoners and minorities in Bangladesh while pouring scorn on Indian and Bengali claims of genocide by its military forces. And much of the world were convinced by its case.

It is important to note, too, that smaller, postcolonial states backed Pakistan fully. African and Arab-Muslim countries were sympathetic to Pakistan's self-presentation as a minor country about to be dismembered by an avaricious neighbor (India), and the Muslim countries generally favored Pakistan's occasional Jihadist rhetoric. At the same time, Syria's representative in the Security Council was happy to speak about Israel's "geopolitical murder" of Syrian Arabs but not about East Pakistan.[85] Indeed, the fetishization of state sovereignty was particularly strong in post-colonial states. For them, the rhetoric of human rights and genocide could function as a neo-imperial technology of intervention in their affairs by the UN and great powers that controlled the Security Council. In the period of decolonization, then – including the Bangladesh case – the noninterference principle trumped the interference principle of the human rights/genocide rhetoric. Rather than see the opposition between these principles as the struggle between cynicism and human rights, like many in the "genocide studies" field, it makes more historical sense to see them as rival, constituent principles of the international system.

If consciousness of genocide made a "comeback" in the 1990s, this had less to do with the humanization of the international system than the greater depth of international society. As in the past, the great powers and the UN ignored a genocidal crisis, this time in Rwanda, but the scale and visibility of the killing, the palpable lack of agency of the victims, and the intensity of journalistic and academic attention meant that the "system" could not ignore the case after the fact. But does this subsequent prosecution really represent a breakthrough for human rights? Similar outrage was expressed in Britain, France, and the United States about the fate of Armenians in the Ottoman Empire in the 1890s and during the First World War. Great power politics prevented the effective prosecution of the leaders of the genocide.

The same pattern of events is recurring in Darfur today because prosecutions of war criminals and other violators of humanitarian law are virtually impossible where the guilty parties remain leaders of states. In such cases, war crimes/genocide trials become a diplomatic problem that can hinder the speedy resolution of international conflict. For this reason, human rights justice can conflict with the imperative of the UN to maintain peace and security. For instance, in the Bangladesh case, the UN needed to negotiate and deal with the Pakistani government to administer its aid to refugees as well as to mediate about prisoners of war and massive population exchanges. It could

---

[85] Security Council Official Records, 1580th Meeting, 16 September 1971, 30.

not do so if it was also threatening to put its negotiating partners or their underlings on trial. You cannot have victors' justice without a victory.

This dilemma suggests that the international system of states needs to be distinguished from "international society." Elements in the international public sphere, such as the International Commission of Jurists, spoke openly of war crimes and genocide, recommending trials of suspected criminals. These and other voices were ignored. Has this situation changed dramatically since then? The teleological account of postwar developments in human rights and genocide prosecutions seems implausible in view of the continuing tendency of great powers to flaunt international humanitarian law when it suits them. It makes more sense to conceive of the international system as comprising dilemmas rather than constituted by moral perfidy alone.

PART V

HUMAN RIGHTS, SOVEREIGNTY, AND THE GLOBAL CONDITION

13

African Nationalists and Human Rights, 1940s–1970s

Andreas Eckert

'*Contemplating human rights in the abstract is a luxury that only the most isolated occupants of the ivory tower can afford*'.[1]

I.

It is now something like a truism that the end of the Second World War marked the dawn of a new era of rights. Since the adoption of the United Nations' Universal Declaration of Human Rights in 1948, the subject of rights ranks high among themes of great popular and academic interest. For instance, rights have become the language of choice for making and contesting entitlement claims. Today the language of rights underlies many facets of private and public discourse, from claims within the family unit to national and global political debates.[2] During the process of decolonization, the European colonial powers in Africa made considerable efforts to prevent the extension of fundamental human rights in their African possessions. On the other hand, a human rights discourse is usually regarded as an important tool of

---

[1] Harri Englund, *Prisoners of Freedom: Human Rights and the African Poor* (Berkeley, 2006), 47.

[2] Bonny Ibhawoh, *Imperialism and Human Rights: Colonial Discourses of Rights and Liberties in African History* (Albany, 2007), 1; more generally on this issue, among many others: Michael Ignatieff, *Human Rights as Politics and Idolatry* (Princeton, 2001). For general historical perspectives: Olwen Hufton (ed.), *Historical Change and Human Rights: The Oxford Amnesty Lectures 1994* (New York, 1995); Lynn R. Hunt, *Inventing Human Rights: A History* (New York, 2007). Micheline R. Ishay, *The History of Human Rights: From Ancient Times to the Globalization Era* (Berkeley, 2004), is representative for a good part of the human rights literature because here the commitment to universalism is linked to strong ideas of particularism. The author argues that one of the 'most consequential realities' of the history of human rights is that 'the influence of the West, including the influence of the Western concept of universal rights ... has prevailed' (7). Englund, *Prisoners of Freedom*, 26, rightly criticizes that this assertion builds on exclusion as the cornerstone of a certain kind of universalism. 'Not only does the assertion about origins exclude those scholars of human rights who feel no allegiance to the West; it also fails to explain how a universal notion can be the prerogative of one particular civilization'.

independence movements south of the Sahara. The human rights paradigm of
the Universal Declaration is implicitly state-centred: The nation-state is recognized as both the greatest guarantor as well as the greatest threat to human
rights. Before Africa could fit into this paradigm, modern African states had
to be born. Most of them, under the banner of the right to self-determination,
came into being in the 1960s, and several post-colonial constitutions embodied a bill of rights. In many cases, commitment to human rights remained
rhetorical, however, often sacrificed in the name of ideology, traditions or
institutions. Many of those anti-colonial nationalists who fought against suppression – once in power – suppressed their political opponents. In an article
published in 1980, Dunstan M. Wai gave expression to a widespread disillu-
sion among Africanist scholars and activists: 'Although during the heyday of
anticolonialism and decolonization the founding fathers of African nationalism emphasized their faith in fundamental human rights, freedom, and the
dignity of the human person, their behaviour and policies in their respective
countries after assumption of power shows clear disrespect for human rights.
The record of their successors remains disappointing'.[3]

In most publications on human rights, Africa is in fact one of the problem
children. For the period between independence and the 1990s, many authors
see a 'very poor' human rights record as well as an 'extremely weak' human
rights movement.[4] Without denying or belittling the mistakes of African politicians, it could be seen as a somewhat bitter irony that although European
colonial powers did not respect human rights in their territories and largely
failed to bequeath to the colonized Africans any kind of democratic legacy,
the Western world now tends to lament the absence of democracy and human
rights in Africa. Some African governments have sought to defend what many
observers have judged to be arbitrary or harsh treatment of individuals by
arguing that such actions are occasionally justified in the name of the collective (or national) good, or they have referred to 'African values' different from
Western ones. Two interrelated sets of issues are present in current debates
on human rights in Africa.[5] One is centred around the (essentialist) assumption that 'African' notions of rights are primarily characterized by societal
concern with collective rather than individual rights. The result is said to be
that individualistic conceptions of human rights in Africa are the product of
Western history and derive in part from experiences of European colonial

---

[3] Dunstan M. Wai, 'Human Rights in Sub-Saharan Africa', in Adamantia Pollis and Peter
Schwab (eds.), *Human Rights: Cultural and Ideological Perspectives* (New York, 1980), 115.
[4] Rhoda E. Howard, 'Human Rights', in *Encyclopedia of Africa South of the Sahara*, vol. 2, ed.
John Middleton (New York, 1997), 355–359. For some general accounts along these lines see
Howard, *Human Rights in Commonwealth Africa* (Totowa, N.J., 1986); Ronald Cohen et al.
(eds.), *Human Rights and Governance in Africa* (Gainesville, Fla., 1993); Abdullahi Ahmed
An-Na'im and Francis Deng (eds.), *Human Rights in Africa: Cross-Cultural Perspectives*
(Washington, D.C., 1990).
[5] For the following remarks see Englund, *Prisoners of Freedom*, 27–31.

rule.[6] The other is about the assumption of a hierarchy or generation of rights, an assumption that many of the 'founding fathers' of independent Africa have made and which still is prominent among human rights activists today. According to this assumption, civil and political rights are not realized in full as long as social and economic rights remain rudimentary. Twenty years ago Issa Shivji argued that instead of deciding which set of rights should come first, scholars should replace abstract considerations with empirical investigations into the actual situations of rights and wrongs: 'Human rights-talk should be historically situated and socially specific.... Any debate conducted on the level of moral absolutes or universal humanity is not only fruitless but ideologically subversive of the interests of African masses'.[7]

Harri Englund recently added to this by stating that

cultural relativism has long hampered intellectual and political engagement with human rights discourse. At best a delightfully iconoclastic pursuit, cultural relativism all too often subverts not only its own justification but also the authority of those in whose name it ostensibly speaks. If everything is culturally relative, then the various cultural others have little else to offer than passing instants of bewilderment and thrill, the stuff that the connoisseurs of cultures can build their prowess on.[8]

Finally, Richard Reid warns against the attitude to consider human rights as 'yet another Western invention superimposed upon a wholly different set of cultural and political systems'. He adds that it would be an equally dangerous generalization to construct an essentialist view of 'African cultures' according to which the individualism that underpins human rights in the West is lacking in Africa.[9]

This article, too, argues against the idea that there is a specific African way of conceptualising human rights. It looks at the period of decolonization and early independence in Africa and tries to contextualize debates about human rights in Africa within colonial history and the history of African nationalism. It will show that the intellectuals and activists at the forefront of anti-colonial movements did not excessively draw on human rights as a language of protest. For most African nationalists, human rights were an issue of minor interest compared to matters which seemed to be more pressing for late colonial and early independent states, such as nation building and fighting poverty. The usage of human rights language among African nationalists was largely restricted to the sphere of international diplomacy. In this context, it would be important to think more systematically about the fact that human rights were not only a discourse but a set of conventions as well. Human rights were an international legal instrument, and African newly independent states'

---

[6] Richard Amoako Baah, *Human Rights in Africa. The Conflict of Implementation* (Lanham, Md., 2000).

[7] Issa Shivji, *The Concept of Human Rights in Africa* (Dakar, 1989), 69.

[8] Englund, *Prisoners of Freedom*, 193.

[9] See Richard Reid, *A History of Modern Africa. 1800 to the Present* (Oxford, 2009), 329.

failure to implement them bumped up against the inherent contradiction in the international human rights instrument: the discrepancies between policy and practice. African states apparently found it difficult – or inconvenient – to implement what they signed, and there was a lack of local 'translators' whose task would have been to provide local meanings to abstract concepts.[10] Finally, it should be added that there is to date very little systematic research on human rights in Africa during the period of late colonialism and early independence. Thus this article can provide only a framework for more detailed analyses yet to be written.

II.

The years following World War II in particular have witnessed that some anti-colonial nationalists in Africa employed a human rights discourse to challenge European colonial rule by pointing to its 'double standards': While Britain and France as the main colonial powers in Africa took part in the creation of a human rights regime which emerged in the immediate postwar period, these powers, at the same time, continued to deny 'dignity' and 'equal rights' to many of their colonized subjects and regularly subjected them to 'torture or to cruel, inhuman or degrading treatment or punishment'.[11] However, this ambivalent relationship between an emancipatory discourse and actual colonial policy making characterized by violence, forced labour, racism and violation of rights was characteristic not only for the decolonization period, but also for earlier periods of colonial rule. Alice L. Conklin has shown with the example of French West Africa before 1914 that from the perspective of French policy makers under the Third Republic, the colonial project and practising human rights were no contradiction at all. Ruling elites in France sought

---

[10] For this argument see Sally Engle Merry, *Human Rights and Gender Violence. Translating International Law into Local Justice* (Chicago, 2006). I thank Richard Roberts for directing my attention to this study.

[11] The Universal Declaration of Human Rights states that 'all human beings are ... equal in dignity and rights' (Art. 1) and that 'no one shall be subjected to torture or to cruel, inhuman or degrading treatment or punishment' (Art. 5). There is a tendency in the literature to portray decolonization in Africa as a more or less smooth process (compared to developments in Asia). However, Kenya and Algeria are especially well-known cases of extremely violent ends of colonial rule. See among the recent literature: David Anderson, *Histories of the Hanged: The Dirty War in Kenya and the End of Empire* (London, 2005); Caroline Elkins, *Britain's Gulag: The Brutal End of Empire in Kenya* (London, 2005); Mohammed Harbo and Benjamin Stora (eds.), *La Guerre d'Algérie 1954–2004: La fin de l'amnésie* (Paris, 2004). See also Fabian Klose's contribution to this volume. Cameroon is a less known example of an extremely violent transition to independence. See Achille Mbembe, *La Naissance du Maquis dans le Sud-Cameroun 1920–1960* (Paris, 1996); Marc Michel, 'Une décolonisation confisquée? Perspectives sur la décolonisation du Cameroun sous tutell de la France 1955–1960', *Revue Française d'Histoire d'Outre-Mer*, 86 (1999), 229–258; Richard Joseph, 'Radical Nationalism in French Africa. The Case of Cameroon', in Prosser Gifford and W. Roger Louis (eds.), *Decolonization and African Independence. The Transfer of Power* (New Haven, Conn., 1988), 321–345.

to reconcile themselves and the recently enfranchised masses to intensified overseas conquest by claiming that the newly restored republic, unlike the more conservative European monarchies, would liberate Africans from moral and material want. Conklin writes: 'As France's republican civilizing mission in West Africa makes clear, liberalism, whether at home or in the colonies, did not just produce difference. It also had a universalizing and democratic component as well, which caused many Westerners to see their ideas of freedom as basic human rights, to which all of humankind is entitled'.[12] It was because the French accepted that all humans were born free that they sought to extend – albeit in perverted form – the republican virtues of liberty, equality and fraternity to the colonized. As Conklin argues, it was because French statesmen and public opinion viewed Africans as 'others' who were nevertheless capable of improvement in France's own image, and were constantly taking – or claiming to undertake, as the case may be – inclusionary and reforming measures on their behalf, that democracy and colonialism appeared compatible.[13]

The concept of civilizing mission was not limited to the French colonial empire but was part of the legitimising rhetoric of all European colonial powers in Africa. In short, this rhetoric implied that the colonized Africans were too primitive to rule themselves but were capable of being uplifted. This attitude could still be found in more liberal views in the human rights era after World War II, for example, in the writings of the Fabian Colonial Bureau. As one of their main representatives, Rita Hinden, made clear,

the act of [imperial] withdrawal would not, of itself, open the gateways to prosperity. On the other hand ... if the imperial powers remained, at least for a time, and instead of exploiting these lands, acted as trustees to develop and enrich them for the sake of their own people, then the crushing problems of poverty and backwardness might indeed be overcome.[14]

At this time, some colonial officials were already more sceptical about combining a liberal discourse stressing the importance of human rights and democracy with the defence of colonial rule.[15] In any case, while violence and

---

[12] Alice L. Conklin, 'Colonialism and Human Rights. A Contradiction in Terms? The Case of France and West Africa, 1895–1914', *American Historical Review*, 102:2 (1998), 419–442, quotation at 422.

[13] See ibid. See also Conklin, *A Mission to Civilize: The Republican Idea of Empire in France and West Africa 1895–1930* (Stanford, Calif., 1997).

[14] Rita Hinden, 'Socialism and the Colonial World', in Arthur Creech-Jones (ed.), *New Fabian Colonial Essays* (London, 1959), 13–14. This attitude is also nicely described by the historian John Hargreaves, who taught African history in Fourah Bay College in Sierra Leone in the early 1950s: 'As Labour Party members with Christian beliefs and Fabian tendencies we believed strongly that Africans had the right to govern themselves, but that they would only be enabled to do so after a period of intensive preparatory 'nation-building', during which the architects as well as the master-craftsmen must be foreign'. See John Hargreaves, *The End of Colonial Rule in West Africa: Essays in Contemporary History* (Basingstoke, 1979), 89.

[15] A common statement of colonial administrations of Gambia, Sierra Leone and the Gold Coast on the Universal Declaration of Human Rights said: 'We can hardly expect to win the confidence of Africans by making statements of ultimate ideals while in practice we take steps

a policy of selective terror characterised much of the colonial period and a 'culture of terror' did not disappear, it expressed itself on a shifting terrain in which violence was condemned unless it could be linked to some kind of progressive reform. Cooper and Stoler made the point that the last quarter of the nineteenth century stands out as a moment when colonialisms became part of a pan-European debate on the practices of 'civilized' states that consolidated an imperialist morality. As Cooper and Stoler observe,

on the ground, this 'new' imperialism was no less coercive and brutal than the old. Yet Europe's power elites were now making much efforts to reassure each other that their coercion and brutality were no longer frank attempts at extraction but reasoned efforts to build structures capable of reproducing themselves: stable governments replacing the violent, conflictual tyrannies of indigenous polities; orderly commerce and wage labour replacing the chaos of slaving and raiding; a complex structuring of group boundaries, racial identities, and permissible forms of sexual and social interaction replacing the disconcerting fluidities of an earlier age.[16]

The idea of a civilizing mission implied a competitive and hierarchical imagination of the world. Civilizing discourses also usually pictured the present of the places to civilize as unhappy and therefore in need for reform anyway. The most basic tension of the civilizing mission in colonial Africa lay in the fact that the otherness of those to be civilized was neither inherent nor stable. Their difference had to be defined and maintained. Social boundaries that were at one point clear could shift. The colonial states' project of a civilizing mission designed to make colonized populations into disciplined agriculturalists or workers and obedient subjects of a bureaucratic state led to a discourse on the question of just how much 'civilizing' would promote their subjects and what sorts of political consequences 'too much civilizing' would have in store. Colonial officials usually wanted their African subjects to be 'perfected natives, not imitation Europeans'.[17]

However, the idea of a civilising mission also opened up rooms to move and options for Africans to anchor their grievances and protests and to push through their interests. The realm of rights and law was crucial here. Law was a central aspect of colonialism in Africa. It was conceived and implemented by Europeans and understood, experienced and used by Africans. Laws and courts, police and prisons were crucial for both political and economic purposes – for European efforts to establish and maintain political domination and for attempts to reshape local economies to promote the production of

---

in precisely the opposite direction'. Quoted in Brian A. W. Simpson, *Human Rights and the End of Empire: Britain and the Genesis of the European Convention* (Oxford, 2004), 458.

[16] Ann L. Stoler and Frederick Cooper, 'Between Metropole and Colony: Rethinking a Research Agenda', in Frederick Cooper and Ann L. Stoler (eds.), *Tensions of Empire: Colonial Cultures in a Bourgeois World* (Berkeley, 1997), 31. For the following see ibid. See also Frederick Cooper, 'Conditions Analogous to Slavery: Imperialism and Free Labor Ideology in Africa', in Frederick Cooper et al., *Beyond Slavery: Explorations of Race, Labor, and Citizenship in Postemancipation Societies* (Chapel Hill, N.C., 2000), 107–149, 178–188.

[17] Cooper and Stoler, 'Between Metropole and Colony', 7.

exports for European markets and to mobilize labor for African and European enterprises. As Mann and Roberts observe, 'colonialism sought to impose a new moral as well as political and economic order, founded on loyalty to metropolitan and colonial states and on discipline, order, and regularity in work, leisure, and bodily habits'. Law played a vital role in moral education and discipline, because it was instrumental in regulating such things as health, sanitation, leisure and public conduct. Finally, the idea of rule of law seemed to provide evidence of the fact that Europeans were in Africa for the Africans' own good, and thus law powerfully legitimized colonial rule. Mann and Roberts also refer to the fact that during the colonial period,

> law formed an area in which Africans and Europeans engaged one another – a battle-ground as it were on which they contested access to resources and labor, relationships of power and authority, and interpretations of morality and culture. In the process, Africans encountered the realities of colonialism, and both they and Europeans shaped the laws and institutions, relationships and processes, and meanings and understandings of the colonial period itself.

However, law not only remained a tool of European colonial domination. Africans also used law as a resource in struggles against Europeans (and in struggles among themselves). Legal rules and procedures became instruments of African resistance, adaptation and innovation.[18]

More recently, some authors have argued for employing the concept of human rights within the context of the colonial legal regime. The rhetoric of rights and liberty became imperative for both the colonial regime that employed it to legitimise empire and for the African elites who appropriated it to strengthen their demands for representation and self-rule.[19] It would probably be worthwhile to analyse more closely the effects of the new international order after World War I, represented by institutions such as the League of Nations and the International Labour Office, on a human rights discourse in and about Africa.[20] As Eric Weitz remarks, 'the mandate system provided an opening for reform-minded organizations and individuals in the metropole,

---

[18] Kristin Mann and Richard Roberts, 'Introduction: Law in Colonial Africa', in Kristin Mann and Richard Roberts (eds.), *Law in Colonial Africa* (Portsmouth, 1991), 3–58, quotations at 3. For important case studies see Martin Chanock, *Law, Custom, and Social Order: The Colonial Experience in Malawi and Zambia* (Cambridge, 1985); Richard Roberts, *Litigants and Households: African Disputes and Colonial Courts, 1895–1912* (Portsmouth, N.H., 2005).

[19] Bonny Ibhawoh, 'Stronger than the Maxim Gun. Law, Human Rights and British Colonial Hegemony in Nigeria', *Africa*, 72:1 (2002), 55–83. In this context, some authors argue that concepts of human rights were an integral part of local African traditions and practices. See, for instance, Martin Okey Ejidike, 'Human Rights in the Cultural Traditions and Social Practice of the Igbo of South Western Nigeria', *Journal of African Law*, 43 (1999), 71–98.

[20] For new, albeit rather Eurocentric, perspectives on the history of the League of Nations and especially the Mandates System, see Susan Pedersen, 'The Meaning of the Mandates System: An Argument', *Geschichte und Gesellschaft*, 32 (2006), 560–582, and 'Back to the League of Nations', *American Historical Review*, 112:4 (2007), 1091–1117. For useful accounts of the Mandate System and Africa see Michael D. Callahan, *Mandates and*

and the rhetorical and sometimes the institutional tools for anti-colonial activists in the colonies'.[21] Still, the impact of World War I was much deeper in Asia than in Africa. South of the Sahara, it was the Great Depression and especially World War II that constituted extremely important watersheds for the growth of anti-colonial nationalism.[22]

III.

The war acted as a catalyst for social and economic change. Above all, Africa's major colonial powers were weakened by war, and it could certainly be additionally argued that the war had uncovered many of the frailties of those powers that, with hindsight, had their origins in the final quarter of the nineteenth century. 'If colonial power in Africa had always rested on a mixture of bluff and force, the bluff proved to be a busted flush and the force more questionable than it appeared before 1939'.[23] Colonial governments in Africa were now

anxious to find a new basis of legitimacy and control in an era when social and political movements in the colonies were asserting themselves with new vigor ... as African movements sought to turn the government's need for order and economic growth into claims to entitlements and representation, officials had to rethink their policies in the face of new African challenges.[24]

To what extent did the war stimulate nationalism in Africa?[25] The postwar constitutional reforms of the British and the French represented an attempt to forge new alliances. The educated elite was enlisted as a partner of the

---

Empire: *The League of Nations and Africa, 1914–1931* (Brighton, 1999), and *A Sacred Trust: The League of Nations and Africa, 1929–1946* (Eastbourne/Sussex, 2004).

[21] Eric D. Weitz, 'From the Vienna to the Paris System: International Politics and the Entangled Histories of Human Rights, Forced Deportations, and Civilizing Missions', *American Historical Review*, 113:4 (2008), 1341.

[22] See, for instance, Frederick Cooper, *Decolonization and African Society: The Labor Question in French and British Africa* (Cambridge, 1996).

[23] David Killingray and Richard Rathbone, 'Introduction', in Killingray and Rathbone (eds.), *Africa and the Second World War* (London, 1986), 3.

[24] Frederick Cooper, "Our Strike': Equality, Anticolonial Politics and the 1947–48 Railway Strike in French West Africa', *Journal of African History*, 37 (1996), 83.

[25] There is no space here to discuss in detail the complexities of African nationalism and nationalist movements. It must be emphasized, however, that African nationalism was inspired by numerous aspects, which included examples from outside Africa, Pan-African influences, local and specific grievances against colonial oppression and exploitation, protest against European racial and cultural arrogance, desire to expand the material and social welfare of Africans, but also desire for personal emancipation. Nationalist movements in Africa had many social bases and objectives – ethnic, national, international – and they operated and fought at many levels – political, economic, social and cultural. The growth and force of nationalist movements also varied, since colonies were acquired in different ways and at different times by different colonial powers. Moreover, the number and significance of European settlers, local traditions of resistance and economic conditions affected the nature of nationalist expression. In organizational terms nationalist struggles articulated themselves through

colonial state, although many colonial officials were extremely biased against these elites and opted instead for a co-operation with 'enlightened traditional authorities'.[26] Even modest measures of reform led to further pressure on the cautious reformers. It came from the educated elite, who demanded a greater share of power and who found a measure of popular support from the urban population, many of whom were unemployed or underemployed, from farmers complaining about fixed commodity prices and government policies, and from peasants protesting against the alienation of land by white settlers.

During the war, the British in Africa extensively deployed anti-German propaganda that presented the war as a crusade against fascism in the name of peace and democracy. One of the common formulas in the propaganda efforts was: 'British colonies are loyal and happy under our rule and helping us to the limits of their resources'.[27] In Nigeria, Governor Bernard Bourdillon emphasized that the British Empire was fighting for 'the right of the ordinary man in every part of the world to live out his own life in freedom and peace'.[28] These views were shared within the nationalist movement where there was a consensus that Nigeria should unequivocally identify itself with the Allied nations. The *West African Pilot* stressed the loyalty of Africans to the British Empire and their willingness to make the ultimate sacrifice of 'shedding their blood in order that the ideals of liberty, democracy and peace might thrive in the world'.[29] Still, Nigerian elites continued to push their demands for political reforms and to challenge state policies. Attempting to link their political demands with global issues associated with the war, they used war rhetoric and especially Allied propaganda to press their political agenda by increasingly articulating their demands in terms of universal rights and 'global liberty' rather than merely their rights as citizens of empire.[30]

However, it soon became clear to Nigerian (and other African) nationalists that a contradiction lay between, on the one hand, British wartime rhetoric which ostentatiously claimed that Britain was promoting freedom and

---

different organs as well. There was no straightforward, more or less natural path from cultural nationalism, expressed by elite associations and churches, to modern mass nationalism, but various and complex ways in which nationalism developed over time. See John Parker and Richard Rathbone, *A Very Short History of Africa* (Oxford, 2007).

[26] Killingray and Rathbone, 'Introduction', 4. See for the example of Tanzania, Andreas Eckert, *Herrschen und Verwalten: Afrikanische Bürokraten, staatliche Ordnung und Politik in Tanzania, 1920–1970* (Munich, 2007).

[27] Rosaleen Smyth, 'Britain's African Colonies and British Propaganda during the Second World War', *Journal of Imperial and Commonwealth History*, 14 (1985), 65–82.

[28] Quoted in G. O. Olusanya, *The Second World War and Politics in Nigeria 1939–1953* (Lagos, 1973), 49.

[29] Quoted by Ibhawoh, *Imperialism and Human Rights*, 151. The *West African Pilot*, arguably the most important nationalist newspaper in colonial Nigeria, was established in 1927 in Lagos by Nnamdi Azikiwe, later the first president of Nigeria. He had been educated in the United States and was strongly influenced by black radical journalism there. See his autobiography: *My Odyssey* (London, 1970).

[30] Ibhawoh, *Imperialism and Human Rights*, 151.

democracy and, on the other hand, the fact that the British were determined to maintain colonial rule. The Atlantic Charter of August 1941 was a case in point.[31] What became known as the 'Atlantic Charter' was not originally intended as a formal document; it was a press release on the outcome of a meeting between Prime Minister Winston Churchill and President Franklin D. Roosevelt at Placentia Bay aimed at drawing up a common declaration of purpose concerning World War II.[32] The document declared that both leaders 'respect the right of all peoples to choose the form of government under which they will live' and that they wished to 'see sovereign rights and self-government restored to those who have been forcibly deprived of them'. The Charter immediately became the focus of global discussions about the right to self-determination. The debates centred on the famous third clause of the Charter, which affirmed 'the right of all peoples to choose the form of government under which they will live'. The statement excited the hopes of many African nationalists,[33] while others remained sceptical. The *West African Pilot* stated that the Charter might turn out to be 'just one of those human instruments nobly conceived but poorly executed'.[34] In the British Mandate territory of Tanganyika, Erica Fiah, the editor of the radical newspaper *Kwetu*, published in Dar es Salaam, commented in an editorial: 'The British soap-smoothing policy cannot be tolerated any longer'.[35]

The fears that the ideals formulated in the Atlantic Charter would turn out to be no more than mere platitudes were confirmed in November 1942, when in response to enquiries – eager ones from nationalists and British anti-colonialists, anxious ones from colonial Governors – the War Cabinet in London expressed the view that the restoration of sovereign rights and self-government referred only to the nations under Axis occupation and not to the British Empire.[36] Moreover Churchill stated in the House of Commons that 'we intend to hold what we have. I have not become the King's First Minister to preside over the liquidation of the British Empire'.[37] In an editorial entitled 'The Atlantic Chatter', the *West African Pilot* lamented:

---

[31] The document is reprinted in Andrew N. Porter and A. J. Stockwell (eds.), *British Imperial Policy and Decolonization, 1938–1964*, vol. 1: 1938–51 (London, 1987), Doc. 8, 10–11.

[32] See W. Roger Louis, *Imperialism at Bay. The United States and the Decolonization of the British Empire* (Oxford, 1977), ch. 7; Douglas Brinkley and David R. Facey-Crowther (eds.), *The Atlantic Charter* (New York, 1994).

[33] Azikiwe, for instance, stressed the 'electrifying impact' of the Atlantic Charter on West African populations in *The Atlantic Charter and British West Africa* (Lagos, 1943), 12. Nelson Mandela stated – in retrospect – that the ANC was very much inspired by the Atlantic Charter and by the Allied struggle against tyranny and oppression: 'Some in the West saw the Charter as empty promises, but not those of us in Africa'. Mandela, *Long Walk to Freedom* (Boston, 1994), 83.

[34] Quoted by Ibhawoh, *Imperialism and Human Rights*, 153.

[35] Quoted in Eckert, *Herrschen und Verwalten*, 99.

[36] Stephen Howe, *Anticolonialism in British Politics: The Left and the Ende of Empire 1918–1964* (Oxford, 1993), 141.

[37] Quoted in Ibhawoh, *Imperialism and Human Rights*, 153.

'A charter is a document bestowing certain rights and privileges; chatter on the other hand, means to utter sounds rapidly or to talk idly or carelessly'.[38] However, the language of universal rights underlying discussions about the Atlantic Charter provided a framework for the Nigerian intelligentsia to articulate and legitimate their demands for political reform within the colonial state. Azikiwe, for instance, argued that instead of waiting for others, Africans themselves should prepare their own blueprint of rights. In 1943, he published his 'Political Blueprint for Nigeria' in which he listed the basic rights that should be guaranteed to every 'commonwealth subject'. These included the right to health, education, social equality, material security and even the right to recreation. He recommended that the Virginia Bill of Rights, which served as a model for the American Constitution, should also serve as a model for preparing the Nigerian Constitution, because 'it embodies all the basic rights for which democratic-loving humanity had fought to preserve in the course of history'.[39] In the same year, Azikiwe was part of a delegation of eight West African journalists who visited London. This group submitted to the Secretary of State for the Colonies a memorandum composed principally by Azikiwe and entitled 'The Atlantic Charter and British West Africa'. It made the following proposals based upon 'the declaration of Clause III of the Atlantic Charter': immediate abrogation of the crown colony system of government, immediate Africanization, the award of 400 scholarships annually, and ten years of 'representative' government to be followed by five years of full responsible government. Thus the delegation believed that by 1958 West African territories would be 'independent and sovereign political entities aligned or associated with the British Commonwealth of Nations'. However, the memorandum evoked no response from the Colonial Office.[40]

Azikiwe's *Blueprint* formed the basis for the Freedom Charter of the NCNC, published in April 1948. The document is one of the first comprehensive statements of fundamental human rights in Africa. The Charter affirmed a wide range of political, economic and social rights for all Nigerians. It included a condemnation of slavery, servitude and imperialism; an affirmation of the rights to life and dignity of the human person; the equality of all persons; the right to basic education and health; the right to free expression and association; and the right to recreation and leisure. Apparently alluding to the Atlantic Charter, the document also affirmed the 'right of all peoples to choose the form of government under which they may live'.[41] However, Azikiwe and his political allies in the NCNC made clear that their freedom

---

[38] Quoted in ibid., 154. More generally see Marika Sherwood, "Diplomatic Platitudes'. The Atlantic Charter, the United Nations and Colonial Independence', *Immigrants and Minorities*, 15:2 (1996), 135–150.

[39] Nnamdi Azikiwe, *Political Blueprint of Nigeria* (Lagos, 1943), 40.

[40] James Coleman, *Nigeria: Background to Nationalism* (Berkeley, 1958), 340–341.

[41] See Toyin Falola and Matthew M. Heaton, *A History of Nigeria* (Cambridge, 2008), 145.

charter was mainly founded on African political experience and expressive of
the aspirations of African people.[42]

IV.

At the time of the adoption of the Universal Declaration of Human Rights
by the United Nations in 1948, nearly all Africa was still under colonial rule.
Thus there were no African representatives who could participate in the drafting of the document that would define human rights globally for the next
decades. Although colonialism in Africa entailed a comprehensive catalogue
of human rights violations, Africa was excluded from the process of defining human rights as a part of international law. In fact, the exclusion of the
voices of the colonized in the process of drawing up the UDHR has been
often mentioned as one of the strongest challenges to its claim to universality.[43] The extent to which the UDHR affected the nationalist movements in
Africa is difficult to assess. It was greeted by some nationalist politicians as an
important document helping their cause. In Nigeria, for instance, nationalist
leaders were cautiously optimistic about the impact of the Declaration on their
aspirations for independence and self-rule. The *West African Pilot* hailed the
Declaration as 'a courageous initiative', stating that while its principles would
be difficult to implement by the 'imperialist powers' that subscribed to it, the
fact that they have enunciated these principles and accepted them in theory
was sufficient to provide oppressed and colonial peoples everywhere with a
tribune for their political demands.[44] Eyo Ita, a leading Nigerian nationalist,
stated in 1949 that the UDHR provided a new yardstick with which peoples
of all lands could measure the success or failure of their political system. To
him, the UDHR was a direct condemnation of imperialism in all its forms. Its
universal language ushered a new global era in which Africa was no longer
'an isolated asylum of slavery and oppression'.[45] In the speeches and writings
of most African nationalists there is, however, no explicit reference to the
UDHR.[46] African nationalism in the 1950s was mainly about citizenship, self-
government and development:[47] 'French and British rule in Africa collapsed
not because of an all-out assault from a clearly defined colonized people, but
because the imperial system broke apart at its internal cracks, as Africans

---

[42] Ibhawoh, *Imperialism and Human Rights*, 156.
[43] Claude E. Welch Jr., 'Human Rights in Francophone West Africa', in An-Na'Im and Deng
(eds.), *Human Rights in Africa*, 185.
[44] Ibhawoh, *Imperialism and Human Rights*, 160.
[45] Ibid.
[46] However, the language of human rights played an important role in the critique of colonialism. See, for instance, Ullrich Lohrmann, *Voices from Tanganyika: Great Britain, the United
Nations and the Decolonization of a Trust Territory, 1946–1961* (Berlin, 2007).
[47] See, for the example of the French African colonies, Frederick Cooper, 'Citizenship and the
Politics of Difference in French Africa, 1946–1960', in Harald Fischer-Tiné and Susanne
Gehrmann (eds.), *Empires and Boundaries: Rethinking Race, Class, and Gender in Colonial
Settings* (New York, 2009), 107–128.

selectively incorporated into political structures based on citizenship or self-determination seized the initiative and escalated their demands for power'.[48] Colonial administrators conceptualized the development project as a process during which possessors of knowledge and capital would slowly but generously disperse these critical resources to those less well endowed. To African political parties, however, development meant resources to build constituencies and opportunities to make the nation-state a meaningful part of people's lives. Kwame Nkrumah famously told his followers: 'Seek ye first the political kingdom'. He captured the imagination of a wide range of people, who now saw in the idea of building an African nation a means to combine their personal ambition and idealistic goals, free of the constraints of colonial authority and a stagnant, or even reactionary, traditional elite.[49]

In 1960, the year in which many African colonies gained independence, Nkrumah spoke at the United Nations and referred to the violations of human rights committed by colonial rulers:

One cardinal fact of our time is the momentous impact of Africa's awakening upon the modern world. The flowing tide of African nationalism sweeps everything before it and constitutes a challenge to the colonial powers to make a just restitution for the years of injustice and crime committed against our continent. But Africa does not seek vengeance. It is against her very nature to harbour malice. Over two hundred million of our people cry out with one voice of tremendous power – and what do we say? We do not ask for death of our oppressors, we do not pronounce wishes for ill-fate for our slave masters, we make an assertion of a just and positive demand. Our voice booms across the oceans and mountains, over the hills and valleys, in the desert places and through the vast expanse of mankind's habitation, and it calls out for the freedom of Africa. Africa wants her freedom, Africa must be free. It is a simple call, but it is also a signal lightning, a red warning to those who would tend to ignore it.[50]

Quite typically, Nkrumah spoke of Africa as a group, and he stressed the times of pain and suffer, which would be over now. He called for freedom, not for human rights.

Also, Nkrumah's speech provides a good example of the fact that an explicit human rights discourse was mainly employed in international arenas and, more specifically, in pan-Africanist contexts. For instance, the resolution of the 1945 Pan-African Congress in Manchester echoed United Nations principles: 'We are determined to be free. We want education. We want the right to earn a decent living; the right to express our thoughts and emotions, to adopt and create forms of beauty.... We will fight in every way we can for freedom, democracy, and social betterment'.[51] At the 1955 Asian-African

---

[48] Frederick Cooper, *Africa since the 1940s: The Past of the Present* (New York, 2002), 66.
[49] Ibid., 67.
[50] Kwame Nkrumah, *I Speak for Freedom: A Statement of African Ideology* (London, 1961), 262.
[51] Quoted in J. Ayo Langley, *Ideologies of Liberation in Black Africa 1856–1970: Documents on Modern African Political Thought from Colonial Times to the Present* (London, 1979), 760.

Conference in Bandung, human rights constituted a major dimension in the debates on colonialism. In many ways, this Conference 'marked a highpoint in Third World enthusiasm for human rights'.[52] There were not many delegates from sub-Saharan African present, but among them was the Kenyan national-ist Joseph Murumbi, who would return from Bandung to condemn colonial-ism on the basis of its violations of the UDHR.[53] A few South Africans also attended the Conference, for example, Moses Kotane, who was one of the first anti-apartheid activists in South Africa to be banned under the notorious Suppression of Communism Act. He used the language of rights to condemn apartheid in a statement issued at the Conference.[54]

Kotane was also involved in the drafting of the ANC Freedom Charter. This document was not meant as a draft constitution for a future South Africa, but as a program of human rights. It stressed the freedom of the individual against the authoritarian state. In a period when the apartheid government system-atically expanded its discriminating, racist legislation, the Charter demanded that 'all apartheid laws and practices shall be aside'. Moreover, the Charter underlined the importance of the social rights of individuals and emphasized justice and equality, because 'the rights of the people shall be the same of race, colour or sex'. Finally, the document demanded political rights and participa-tion: 'South Africa belongs to all who live in it ... and no government can justly claim authority unless it is based on the will of the people'.[55]

During the All-African People's Conference, which was held in Accra, the capital of recently independent Ghana, from December 5 to 13, 1958, a Committee on Racialism and Discriminatory Laws and Practices proposed that all independent African states should be advised to give legislative sanc-tion to the Universal Declaration of Human Rights, that African member-states of the United Nations should 'use their good offices to secure that the "Universal Declaration of Human Rights" becomes part and parcel of the fundamental or organic law of all member-states of the United Nations', and that a permanent Commission of Human Rights be set up by the All-African Peoples' Conference 'with powers to receive and to report to it progress made

On the Congress, see Hakim Adi and Marika Sherwood, *The 1945 Pan-African Congress Revisited* (London, 1995).

[52] Roland Burke, 'The Compelling Dialogue of Freedom': Human Rights at the Bandung Conference', *Human Rights Quarterly*, 28 (2006), 961. On Bandung see Christopher J. Lee (ed.), *Making a World after Empire. The Bandung Moment and its Political Afterlives* (Athens, OH, 2010).

[53] See Bethwell A. Ogot, 'Mau Mau and Nationhood: The Untold Story', in E. S. Atieno Odhiambo and John Lonsdale (eds.), *Mau Mau and Nationhood: Arms, Authority and Narration* (Athens, Ohio, 2003), 23f. Murumbi lived in exile in Britain, and beginning in the early 1950s he organized protests against British human rights violations during the Mau Mau war in Kenya. See Caroline Elkins, *Imperial Reckoning: The Untold Story of Britain's Gulag in Kenya* (New York, 2005), 99.

[54] Burke, 'Compelling Dialogue', 963.

[55] The text of the Freedom Charter can be found in Thomas Karls and Gwendolyn M. Carter (eds.), *From Protest to Challenge: A Documentary History of African Politics in South Africa, 1862–1964* (Stanford, Calif., 1987), 205–208. For the context see Deborah Posel, *The Making of Apartheid 1948–1961* (Oxford, 1991).

in the implementation, as well as any denial, of fundamental human rights in any part of the continent of Africa'. These proposals were incorporated partially (with respect to the extension and assurance of fundamental rights to the citizens and inhabitants of independent African states and the creation of a committee of the Conference 'to examine complaints of abuse of human rights in every part of Africa and to take appropriate steps to ensure the enjoyment of the rights by everyone') in the Conference Resolution on Imperialism and Colonialism.[56]

The discussions that followed the All-African Peoples' Conference contributed to the formation of the Organization of African Unity (OAU) in 1963. However, the Organisation soon proved to be of little efficacy, and ideologies and problems of nation building soon superseded pan-African visions and projects. In its founding Charter, the OAU did not give human rights prominence among its concerns. For example, although Article 20 recommended the establishment of five specialized commissions, none of them was devoted to the issue of human rights. The OAU was preoccupied with 'more pressing' issues, such as unity, noninterference and liberation. The first three paragraphs of the Preamble recognized, respectively: 'the inalienable right of all people to control their own destiny', that 'freedom, equality, justice and dignity are essential objectives for the achievement of the legitimate aspirations of the African peoples', and 'the responsibility [of Member states] to harness the natural and human resources' of the continent 'for the total advancement of our peoples in spheres of human endeavour'.[57] African politicians and scholars recognized early on the potency and potential value of a pan-African treaty incorporating international human rights law. But they also insisted on differences between the communitarian and collectivist nature of African societies and the more individualistic societies of the West. According to them, an African human rights treaty would thus have to go beyond the Universal Declaration and reflect individuals as right holders enmeshed in communities, with collective rights and specific duties to others. In 1961, a conference on 'rule of law' was organised in Lagos. In the final document of this conference, known as the Law of Lagos, appeared the first formal reference to a possible African convention on human rights. This convention would follow the model developed in Europe, the Americas and the United Nations, and would include a tribunal and monitor and enforce its provisions.[58]

[56] Quotes from the Committee proposal in Richard Sklar, *Nigerian Political Parties: Power in an Emergent African Nation* (Princeton, 1963), 274. On the Conference, see Immanuel Geiss, *The Pan-African Movement: A History of Pan-Africanism in America, Europe, and Africa* (London, 1974), 420; P. Olisanwuche Esedebe, *Pan-Africanism: The Idea and Movement, 1776–1991* (Washington, D.C., 1994), 250–251.
[57] Keba M'baye and B. Ndiaye, 'The Organization of Arican Unity', in Karel Vasak (ed.), *The International Dimension of Human Rights* (Westport, Conn., 1982), 583; Ahmed El-Obaid and Kwadwo Appiagyei-Atua, 'Human Rights in Africa – A New Perspective on Linking the Past to the Present', *McGill Law Journal*, 41 (1996), 5.
[58] The 'Law of Lagos' is reprinted in M. Hamalengwa et al. (eds.), *The International Law of Human Rights in Africa* (Dordrecht, 1988), 37.

V.

Many of the leaders of African independence movements such as Senghor, Nyerere and Nkrumah regarded themselves as socialists.[59] For them, Western visions of rights were both suspect for their historical coexistence with colonialism and impoverished in their limitation to civil and political guarantees (even the most narrow of which were belied by treatment of blacks in the United States before the Civil Rights movement, a hypocrisy of which African leaders were acutely aware). 'Rights' were an important part of independence rhetoric, but African leaders in the decade after independence generally emphasised 'economic and social' rights, that is, economic development and self-sufficiency, over 'civil and political' rights, to which most of the Universal Declaration is devoted. A Canadian jurist very sympathetic to Julius Nyerere's idea of African socialism expressed a widespread attitude to human rights in early-independent Africa:

For example, the liberal-democratic theory of politics, with its emphasis on the individual and on political freedom, may be of little value in a society where intense poverty and economic inequality are the essential national problems. In fact, in such a society, a state apparatus which dedicated itself to the preservation of the 'individual rights' of liberal democracy would be the opposite of democratic. By putting the needs of individuals above the needs for independence and development of the mass of the people, a government would forfeit the right to be called democratic.[60]

Among the African statesmen of the 'first generation', Julius Nyerere was indeed the one who most frequently referred to 'human rights'. In his opening address to the Pan-African Freedom Movement of East and Central Africa Conference in September 1959, he stressed that human rights for him were more than a rhetorical strategy:

What do some of these people think we are? Here we are, building up the sympathy of the outside world on the theme of Human Rights. We are telling the world that we are fighting for our rights as human beings. We gain the sympathy of friends all over the world – in Asia, in Europe, in America – people who recognize the justice of our demand for human rights. Does anyone really believe that we ourselves will trample on human rights? Why do we get so annoyed when we hear of a Little Rock in America? Because we recognize that the American Negro is human. It doesn't matter whether he is black – we get infuriated when we see that he is not being treated as a true and equal American citizen. Are we going to turn round them, tomorrow after we have achieved Independence and say, 'To hell with all this nonsense about human rights; we are only using that as a tactic to harness the sympathy of the naive?' Human nature is sometimes depraved I know, but I don't believe it is depraved to that extent. I don't believe that the leaders of a people are going to behave as hypocrites to gain their

---

[59] For an excellent introduction to the history of Africa after decolonization see *Paul Nugent, Africa since Independence: A Comparative History* (Basingstoke, 2004).
[60] Robert Martin, *Personal Freedom and the Law in Tanzania: A Study of Socialist State Administration* (Nairobi, 1974), 1.

ends, and then turn around and do exactly the things which they have been fighting against.[61]

In his Independence Message to the Tanganyika National Union (TANU) in 1961, Nyerere once more emphasized the high value of human rights for his struggle for independence: 'All the time that TANU has been campaigning for *Uhuru* we have based our struggle on our belief in the equality and dignity of all mankind and on the Declaration of Human Rights. We have agreed that our nation shall be a nation of free and equal citizens, each person having an equal right and opportunity to develop himself, and contribute to the maximum of his capabilities to the development of our society'.[62]

Immediately after the independence ceremonies, Nyerere gave his Independence Address to the United Nations. Again he stressed that 'what we are in fact saying is that we shall try to use the Universal Declaration of Human Rights as a basis for both our external and our internal policies'. Then, however, followed an important reservation: 'That Declaration confirms that the right of every individual to many things, which we cannot yet provide for the citizens of our country. In that respect this document, the Universal Declaration of Human Rights, represents our goal rather than something we have already achieved'.[63] Human rights remained a goal, but a goal to be subordinated to other goals – to fight poverty, for instance.[64] Not only was this attitude widespread among African politicians, but it became a view shared by most 'Third World' countries. The first UN International Conference on Human Rights in Tehran in 1968, which was dominated by Asian and African countries, could be seen as 'the culmination of a shift from the Western-inflected concept of individual human rights exemplified in the 1948 Universal Declaration to a model that emphasized economic development and the collective rights of the nation'.[65] Article 13 of the Conference proclamation stated that respect for human rights was 'dependent upon sound and effective ... economic and social development'.[66]

At the Tehran Conference, the representatives of the Western states did little to defend the spirit of the Universal Declaration. In any case, the

---

[61] Julius Nyerere, 'Individual Human Rights', in Nyerere, *Freedom and Unity/Uhuru na Umoja: A Selection from Writings and Speeches 1952–65* (Dar es Salaam, 1966), 70.

[62] Nyerere, 'Independence Message to TANU', in Nyerere, *Freedom and Unity*, 139.

[63] Nyerere, 'Independence Address to the United Nations', in Nyerere, *Freedom and Unity*, 146.

[64] 'What freedom has our subsistence farmer? He scratches a bare living from the soil provided the rains to not fail; his children work at his side without schooling, medical care, or even good feeding. Certainly he has freedom to vote, and to speak as he wishes. But these freedoms are much less real to him than his freedom to be exploited. Only as his poverty is reduced will his existing political freedom become properly meaningful and his right to human dignity become a fact of human dignity'. Nyerere, *Stability and Change in Africa* (Dar es Salaam, 1969), 3.

[65] Roland Burke, 'From Individual Rights to National Development: The First UN International Conference on Human Rights, Tehran, 1968', *Journal of World History*, 19:3 (2008), 276.

[66] Quoted in ibid., 288.

arguments of the delegates from Africa and Asia seemed to have confirmed their prejudices. The United States in particular entertained a huge degree of scepticism about the value of individual rights in 'developing countries'. In 1960, the 'Year of Africa', when seventeen African countries gained independence, Maurice Stann, a State Department expert for Africa, announced at a meeting of the National Security Council that 'Africans do not understand Western-style ballot box democracy'. Vice President Richard Nixon was even blunter in his judgement. 'The peoples of Africa', he argued, 'have been out of the trees only for about fifty years'.[67] As a result of this assessment, the State Department opted for supporting dictators or 'strong men' and forgot about rights.[68]

Nyerere and other African statesmen soon became caught by the constraints of the post-colonial era. They often partook of the same arrogance toward peasants and small-scale marketeers than their European predecessors,[69] 'but they were more concerned with the implications of development for patron-client relations, with providing resources to people loyal to them and keeping resources away from potential opponents'.[70] Moreover, the first generation of African leaders had learnt their lesson. From their own experience they were aware of the potential of claims made on the basis of citizenship. The reformist late colonialism of France and Great Britain had been confronted with many demands – for equal wages, equal social services and an equal standard of living – based on a notion (explicit or implicit) of imperial citizenship; their successors now faced such demands from mobilized groups on a national level. The resources available with which to meet them were much smaller now than during the development boom after 1945. Cooper aptly points to the consequences of this: 'Efforts by African states to augment the vertical relationships they could control and to undercut people who could make claims upon them or develop autonomous power bases added a new dimension to the bastion-making, controlling, and gatekeeping qualities of the late colonial states. Subsequent generations of leaders were caught up in competition for control of the gate itself'.[71] Thus in the African gatekeeper states, which emerged out of a peculiar history of decolonization, human rights were not high on the agenda of those who ran the state.

---

[67] Both quotations in ibid., 288–289.
[68] See Walter Leimgruber, *Kalter Krieg um Afrika: Die amerikanische Afrikapolitik unter Präsident Kennedy, 1961–1963* (Stuttgart, 1990); Ebere Nwaubani, *The United States and Decolonization in West Africa, 1950–1960* (Rochester, N.Y., 2001).
[69] For the case of Tanzania see Eckert, *Herrschen und Verwalten*, ch. 5; Leander Schneider, 'Freedom and Unfreedom in Rural Development: Julius Nyerere, Ujamaa Vijijini, and Villagization', *Canadian Journal of African Studies*, 38:2 (2004), 344–392.
[70] Cooper, *Africa since the 1940s*, 197–198.
[71] Ibid. On the development of gatekeeper states in Africa see also Frederick Cooper, 'Africa in a Capitalist World', in Darlene Clark Hine and Jacqueline McLeod (eds.), *Crossing Boundaries: Comparative History of Black People in the Diaspora* (Bloomington, Ind., 1999), 487–488.

14

The International Labour Organization and the Globalization of Human Rights, 1944–1970

Daniel Roger Maul

International Organizations and the History of Human Rights

In the spring of 1944, government, trade union, and employers' delegates from more than forty states convened at Temple University in the heart of Philadelphia. Their objective was to lay the social foundations of a future peacetime order. Host of the gathering was the International Labour Organization (ILO), at that time the only fully functioning part of the League of Nations system. Although today largely faded into oblivion, the meeting nonetheless produced a declaration proclaiming the "right of all human beings, irrespective of race, creed, or sex" to pursue "both their material well-being and their spiritual development in conditions of freedom and dignity, of economic security, and equal opportunity."[1] This document may be regarded as the first official international acknowledgment of the idea of social and economic human rights. The "Declaration of Philadelphia" was an important step in elevating a new subject, universally applicable individual human rights, to the field of international diplomacy.

The prominent role played by the "global community" of international organizations[2] in disseminating the idea of universal human rights during the twentieth century has become a generally accepted fact. Much recent literature on the international history of human rights,[3] as well as

---

[1] ILO, *The Declaration of Philadelphia* (Montreal, 1944).
[2] Akira Iriye uses the term "global community" to describe both intergovernmental and nongovernmental organizations. Akira Iriye, *Global Community. The Role of International Organizations in the Making of the Contemporary World* (Berkeley, 2002).
[3] Paul Gordon Lauren, *Visions Seen. The Evolution of International Human Rights* (Philadelphia, 1998); Micheline Ishay, *The History of Human Rights. From Ancient Times to the Globalization Era* (Berkeley, 2004); Jack Donnelly, *International Human Rights* (Boulder, 1998). For an overview see Kenneth Cmiel, "The Recent History of Human Rights", *American Historical Review*, 109:1 (2004), 117–135.

on the history of the United Nations,[4] points to the significant part exercised by international organizations. Battles surrounding the interpretation of human rights were fought – and a common global linguistic repertoire and moral discourse was forged – within these international organizations. Furthermore, the secretariats of international organizations (UN, UNESCO, etc.) were increasingly perceived as actors and activists in their own right within the spectrum of international human rights policy. This interest almost seems to be a natural consequence of a long-term development, as debates on human rights and their protection have shifted from national to international arenas.

The human rights activities of international organizations represent an important field of historical research. The human rights debate "symbolizes recent global history," as Bruce Mazlish and Akira Iriye have noted.[5] Whether as a Cold War battleground or the object of altercations between developing countries and "the West" about the persistence of colonial structures, the debate surrounding human rights reflects the central divides of the post-1945 period. Important arenas for this debate, international organizations provided unique opportunities to explore the global dimensions of issues central to the human rights discourse, including racism, colonialism, gender relations, and development.

The aim of this chapter is to analyze the human rights activities of the International Labour Organization. I consider these activities both as a part of, and as an exceptional case in, this broader history of international organizations and the "globalization" of the human rights idea after 1945. My primary intention is to place the human rights activities of the ILO – both as a specific forum of human rights discourse and as an independent actor (embodied by the International Labour Office, the Organization's secretariat) – in their wider historical context. The article will explore the motivation behind and the historical-political context in which the ILO became interested in, and committed to, the concept of human rights. It begins with the ILO's decision in Philadelphia to place all its work on a new human rights–based foundation. I then seek to identify the complex factors that caused the Organization to overhaul its program of work during the war years in light of this stronger commitment to human rights issues. The second section demonstrates how the growing emphasis on human rights after the end of World War II was intertwined with developments in the international state system, specifically the Cold War and decolonization.

4 Most recently Roger Normand and Sahra Zaidi (eds.), *Human Rights at the UN. The Political History of Universal Justice* (Bloomington, Ind., 2008). On the example of the UN, see Paul Kennedy, *Parliament of Man. The United Nations and the Quest for World Government* (New York, 2006). For an excellent overview of recent literature on the UN see Sunil Amrith and Glenda Sluga, "New Histories of the United Nations," *Journal of World History*, 19 (2008), 251–274.
5 Bruce Mazlish and Akira Iriye (eds.), *The Global History Reader* (London, 2005), 157.

The ILO and Human Rights

Within the spectrum of UN human rights work, the position of the ILO is unique in at least three ways.[6] Founded at the Paris Peace Conference in 1919 (and integrated into the UN system as a special agency in 1946), the Organization boasts the longest unbroken tradition of all UN agencies: The ILO was already an established institution when the international human rights regime had just begun to take shape. Second, the ILO formed a specific forum for human rights' debates because of its unique tripartite structure, an organizational principle manifest in the fact that the delegations sent by member states to the political bodies of the Organization include (in addition to two government envoys) one representative each of the country's "most representative" employers' and workers' associations, both of whom have full voting rights. Unlike other international agencies the ILO was, and is, not a purely intergovernmental forum. It remains the only international organization that fully involves NGOs in its decision-making processes. The paradox inherent in the human rights activities of all international organizations – that institutions that by their nature embody the principle of a sovereign nation-state should also play an important role in establishing a concept that has the potential to undermine this principle – assumes a different form within the ILO. As a consequence of its tripartite structure, the ILO offers a forum in which the conflicts that characterize the international human rights discourse (between the transnational network of civil society actors and representatives of nation-states bound to defending their claim to sovereignty) are played out *within* the Organization. Third, the ILO is unique in the fact that when the universal human rights regime was beginning to take shape it had already fashioned an extensive collection of international agreements, or "International Labor Standards" (ILSs).[7] These agreements covered a spectrum of issues ranging from minimum age regulations at the workplace to wages, working hours, invalidity insurance, and unemployment provision. In 1945 the ILO was able to turn what was already a working mechanism to a new purpose: to bringing human rights principles into a form binding under international law. When it came to the implementation of its standards, the ILO had at its disposal a wide range of supervisory instruments. Until the adoption of the two UN Human Rights Covenants in the late 1960s, these

---

[6] Most of the literature on the ILO takes some account of the ILO's work for human rights. See Antony Alcock, *History of the ILO* (New York, 1971), 252–284; Victor-Yves Ghebali, *The International Labour Organization* (Dordrecht, 1988), 74–89. On the ILO's human rights work in comparison with that of the United Nations, see in particular Virginia Leary, "Lessons from the Experience of the International Labour Organization," in Philip Alston (ed.), *The United Nations and Human Rights. A Critical Appraisal* (Oxford, 1992), 580–620.

[7] Since 1919 the ILO's annual conferences (International Labour Conferences – ILCs) have adopted a total of roughly 200 conventions and an equal number of (legally nonbinding) recommendations in the field of labor and social policy.

instruments were unique in the field of international human rights protection in terms of their thoroughness.[8]

This is the point, however, at which the problem with portraying the standard-setting activities of the ILO as human rights work *avant la lettre* becomes apparent. The ILO's unique position of strength with regard to the implementation of its standards in the postwar period was a result of the fact that the range of instruments at its disposal had developed within an intellectual framework and for a type of standard in which the concept of universal human rights did not feature at all. Generally speaking, the intellectual and moral pedestal on which the early work of the ILO was built rested less on the concept of "rights" than that of "social justice." Upon its establishment at Versailles, the Organization's founders believed this approach would both contribute to a permanent peace and serve as a means to counter the perceived threat of the Russian Revolution. The ILO's Constitution made the connection clear with its central postulate "that lasting universal peace can only be established if it is based upon social justice."[9]

The group at which International Labor Standards were directed did not consist of individuals armed with rights. Rather, the ILO's clients were workers in a limited number of economically advanced European countries. The non-universal character of the ILSs during the interwar years was even more obvious in those cases in which the ILO tried, via a series of conventions during the 1930s, to tackle the appalling situation of "native" workers living under colonial rule. By their very name these conventions, which focused above all on the widespread practice of forced labor in colonial territories,[10] made clear that they applied exclusively to "native labor." By deeming the colonies a sphere in which different rules applied, these conventions were diametrically opposed to the idea of universal human rights.[11] The work of the ILO showed clear parallels to the League of Nations' minority protection system, which was put into place at the same time and within which rights granted on an internationally binding basis were limited to a clearly defined group. This observation somewhat contradicts Mark Mazower's argument that the "strange triumph of human rights"[12] after 1945 was based primarily on the recognition that the group rights approach of the interwar period had failed. Unlike the minority protection system, the ILO's standards to protect workers had always been regarded as efficient and successful. Whatever its

---

[8] See Leary, "Lessons."

[9] ILO, *Constitution*, 2.

[10] The most important part of the "Native Labor Code" was the Forced Labor Convention (Convention no. 29) from 1930, in ILO (ed.), *Conventions and Recommendations* (Geneva, 1966), 173–182.

[11] On the colonial work of the ILO in the period between the two world wars, see also Luis Rodriguez Piñero, *Indigenous People, Postcolonialism and International Law. The ILO Regime 1919–1989* (Oxford, 2006).

[12] Mark Mazower, "The Strange Triumph of Human Rights, 1933–1950," *Historical Journal*, 47 (2004), 379–398.

merits, however, the fact remains that the ILO's transformation into a human rights agency did not come at all naturally. It was no coincidence that the term "rights" did not appear in any official ILO document until preparations were well underway for the Philadelphia Conference.

"The Second Foundation" – Philadelphia, 1944

Rather than to focus on the *longue durée* of the ILO's human rights work, it makes more sense to trace the concept's origins in the years 1941 to 1944. During this phase, the Organization fled war-torn Europe, finding exile in Montreal, Canada. In this period of uncertainty and fevered attempts to secure itself a place in the future peacetime order, it is possible to discern the multiple concerns that came to bear in the Organization's "second foundation," to use the words of the Chairman of the Philadelphia Conference, New Zealand Prime Minister Walter Nash, under the auspices of human rights.[13]

In this context it is useful to examine closely what ILO officials believed the Organization might gain from redefining its mandate to the cause of human rights. Promoting the human rights concept as a new foundation served the International Labor Office as a way to extend the ILO's own field of activity and influence. It was a widely held view among ILO officials that the organization needed to depart from the narrow labor protection focus of the prewar period. They felt the ILO should enter new fields, such as employment policy and economic planning, in order to ensure their organization's long-term survival. Earlier attempts during the Great Depression to extend the ILO's activities beyond the traditional sphere of labor policy to areas such as employment policy had failed because of the resistance of the member states.[14] ILO officials saw in the legitimizing power of human rights a chance to renew claims on the side of the Allies. In the wake of an ideological confrontation with forces that radically rejected the concept of universal rights to individuals, and with memories of bitter economic and social lessons of the immediate past (in particular the widely accepted failure of laissez faire capitalism in the wake of the Great Depression and the part this failure had played in the eyes of many in the rise of fascism) still fresh, the new focus on human rights served to underscore the long-term moral and political aims of the wartime alliance. From the perspective of the Allied leaders, the ILO provided a forum from within which the promise of a socially just postwar order was transmitted to the home front.[15] The Declaration of Philadelphia's promulgation of social and economic rights deliberately built on earlier wartime proclamations such as Franklin D. Roosevelt's Four Freedoms Speech, the Atlantic Charter, and Ernest Bevin's dictum of a "people's peace." It also mirrored the spirit of

[13] ILC 26 (1944), Record of Proceedings, 295.
[14] Alcock, *History of the ILO*, 35–40.
[15] For the general context of the inclusion of human rights thinking into postwar planning see Mark Mazower, *The Dark Continent. Europe's Twentieth Century* (London, 1998), 267–307; Jay Winter, *Dreams of Peace and Freedom: Utopian Moments in the Twentieth Century* (New Haven, Conn., 2006), 99–121.

national postwar planning programs calling for an expansion of social policy such as the one laid out in the Beveridge Report. The ILO's claim "to examine and consider all international economic and financial policies and measures" in the light of an overriding social objective – politics based on the idea of human rights – confirmed a new understanding of the duties of the liberal democratic state vis-à-vis its citizens and a commitment to active economic and welfare policies.[16]

The prominence of the human rights idea in the Declaration also clearly reflected the growing influence of the United States within the ILO. The ILO was the only subsection of the League of Nations that the United States had joined (during the early years of the Roosevelt administration). New Deal protagonists such as the Secretary of Labor Frances Perkins held the Organization in high esteem. The Americans' support was critical in securing the ILO a place when it came to discussions of postwar reconstruction of the international system.[17] During the drafting of the document, the authors of the ILO's Declaration of Philadelphia[18] were involved in active exchange with various American government agencies and NGOs. Together, they pursued a common goal: to embed the concept of universal human rights in international diplomacy.[19] The ILO drew from its participation in this network both important intellectual impulses and the necessary political and diplomatic support to carry through the project to fashion a declaration based on the concept of human rights. The Declaration could thus be seen in part as a result of the larger project to create a "New Deal for the World."[20] The Organization also received much encouragement in this regard from within its own ranks. Numerous Latin American countries spearheaded by Chile, Mexico, and Panama, and some Asian and Pacific states such as Australia, New Zealand, China, and India (which had its own delegation),[21] were all determined to include the human rights idea in the Declaration.[22]

---

[16] ILO, Constitution, 4.
[17] Edward Lorenz, *Defining Global Justice: The History of U.S. International Labor Standards Policy* (Notre Dame, Ind., 2001).
[18] Wilfrid Jenks, a specialist in international law who at the time was the legal adviser to the ILO and later (1970–1973) would become Director-General of the ILO, was a key figure. He later published widely on the ILO's human rights work. See, for example, C. Wilfrid Jenks, *Human Rights and International Labour Standards* (London, 1960), and *Human Rights, Social Justice and Peace: The Broader Significance of the ILO Experience* (Oslo, 1967).
[19] Normand and Zaidi, *Human Rights at the UN*, 81–107. For an excellent overview of the activities of the American legal community in this period see Hanne Hagtvedt Vik, The United States, the American Legal Community and the Vision of International Human Rights Protection Ph.D. diss., University of Oslo, 2009.
[20] Elizabeth Borgwardt, *A New Deal for the World: America's Vision for Human Rights* (Cambridge, Mass., 2005).
[21] Although part of the British Empire, India sent its own delegations to both the ILO and the League of Nations from the late 1920s onwards.
[22] Alcock, *History of the ILO*, 185.

The adoption of a Declaration with a clear human rights focus was undoubt-edly facilitated further by the fact that the Soviet Union was absent from the proceedings in Philadelphia and observed the Conference from a critical dis-tance.[23] Although this initially looked like a serious setback to the ILO's cam-paign to carve a significant place for itself in the postwar order, the absence of the Soviet Union was possibly the main reason that the issue of human rights in Philadelphia was spared the fate it suffered at the Dumbarton Oaks Conference, at which the basic structures of the future United Nations were worked out just a few months later. At the latter meeting, where negotiations were dominated by the Great Powers, the topic was entirely overshadowed by a clear focus on security matters, to the great disappointment of advocates of an international system of human rights protection.[24] The absence of the Soviet Union in Philadelphia was also mirrored in the fact that many aspects of the Declaration reflected the British and American tendency to emphasize liberal freedoms such as freedom of labor or the principle of freedom of asso-ciation, while a "right to work" did not become part of the Declaration. All in all, then, the beginnings of the ILO's human rights work were characterized only to a limited extent by the "competing universalisms" that Sunil Amrith and Glenda Sluga have accurately described for the early phase of the human rights debates within the United Nations.[25]

Human Rights and Technical Assistance

Although the ILO's human rights work undoubtedly possessed a strong ide-ological point of departure in the Declaration of Philadelphia, it was only when the American Acting Secretary of Labor David Morse became Director-General of the ILO in 1948 that the Declaration's postulates were translated into concrete action. Morse's ideas about the ILO's role in international politics and his attitude toward human rights were the offspring of both his New Deal liberal internationalist convictions and his initial objective to use this interna-tional agency to further American foreign policy goals against the backdrop of the emerging Cold War and the first wave of decolonization in Asia.[26] In this respect the development of the ILO's strong human rights agenda from the late 1940s onward was closely connected to another caesura in the ILO's work also linked to the beginning of the "Morse era" (1948–1970): the advent of technical assistance programs and the redefinition of the ILO as an agency to provide international development aid in areas such as vocational training and to raise productivity more generally.

[23] Ibid., 173.
[24] Normand and Zaidi, *UN and Human Rights*, 107–108.
[25] Amrith and Sluga, "New Histories of the UN," 252–256.
[26] Born in 1907, Morse entered U.S. government service during the early New Deal years and held the office of Assistant Secretary of Labor for International Affairs under President Truman from 1946 to 1948. All information is taken from the author's own research for a biography of David Morse (*New Deal Liberalism Going Abroad: The Life of David A. Morse, 1907–1990*).

In at least three respects one can draw a direct connection between the move away from the establishment of the technical norms and standards of the ILO's past and toward a few basic human rights principles coupled with technical assistance. First, the ILO proposed an integrated approach to development in which human rights standards were promoted not just as a goal but as a *method* of development, claiming that such standards helped to ease the consequences of the development process, paving the way toward the transition to a modern liberal democratic society.[27] This approach was exemplified in the convention on the freedom of association (1948), which expressed the idea that civil liberties were a precondition for the realization of economic and social rights through national social policy. As a means to establish adequate new forms of organization in the transition from traditional to modern societies, freedom of association was seen not only as a human right, but also as a method by which economic progress could be achieved.[28]

Second, against the background of the decolonization process, focusing on the area of human rights had another advantage. The growing number of developing countries within the Organization's ranks wanted and increasingly demanded that the ILO make their problems a priority within its work programs. For countries such as the newly independent India this meant above all *practical* help, in particular with industrialization. In contrast, the significance these countries attached to ILO standards was minor, to say the least. Under these circumstances, concentrating on human rights norms helped the ILO to preserve the fundamentally universalistic aim of ILO standard setting while addressing the criticism leveled at it by permitting flexibility in the application of all the other standards that were technical or specifically oriented toward social or labor policy. The focus on human rights provided effective protection against suggestions that it may be desirable to replace ILS standards altogether, with regional norms better adjusted to the situation on the ground in the less industrialized areas of the world taking their place.[29]

Third and no less important, emphasizing human rights helped to convince some of the most influential and potentially resistant forces within the ILO of the necessity to move toward technical assistance. This was particularly true with regard to European governments and trade union representatives, those groups within the Organization that had profited the most from its standard-setting activities in the past and that therefore initially viewed a change in the

---

[27] This thought was expressed, for example, in Morse's memorandum "The ILO and Economic and Social Development" 7/4/1951, ILO Archives (ILOA) – MF Z 1-1-25. His approach strongly resembled that of the emerging first generation of modernization theorists in the American social sciences, and it shared with modernization theory both its basic premises and its historical origins in early decolonization and the conflict with communism. On the historical origins of modernization theory see Michael Latham, *Modernization as Ideology. American Social Science and "Nation Building" in the Kennedy Era* (Chapel Hill, N.C., 2000).
[28] For a summary of the ILO's attitude toward freedom of association see ILO, *Trade Union Rights and Their Relation to Civil Liberties* (Geneva, 1970).
[29] ILO Asian Regional Conference 1 (1947), Record of Proceedings, 6.

Organization's portfolio with a good deal of skepticism and apprehension.[30] Oft-repeated assurances that the ILO's technical functions would be built on the foundation of the basic and universally applicable values of the Declaration of Philadelphia were also a means to gain the support of groups within the membership that might otherwise have lost interest in the ILO.

Human Rights between Cold War and Decolonization

Against this backdrop, the end of the 1940s marked the beginning of the heyday of the ILO's human rights work, as evidenced by the fact that all but three of what the ILO today regards as its core labor standards[31] were adopted by the Organization's annual conferences between 1948 and 1958. These core standards are the Freedom of Association (1948), the Right to Collective Bargaining (1949), Equal Remuneration (1951), the Abolition of Forced Labor (1957), and Discrimination in Employment and Occupation (1958). Building on these precedents, the ILO also began to include human rights benchmarks in its predominantly technical conventions.[32]

At first glance, the contrast here with the United Nations, where human rights work entered an almost two-decade period of inertia following the 1948 adoption of the Universal Declaration of Human Rights, is striking. Of course, the human rights conventions did provoke some fierce disputes between the power blocs within the ILO as well, especially following the reaccession of the Soviet Union in 1954.[33] In the early days in particular, the West never missed an opportunity during ILO meetings to subject the Soviet Union and its allies to public attack on human rights. Directly after the Soviet Union's accession, for example, a bitter debate erupted with regard to the tripartite character of the Organization, which in some ways boiled down to a fundamental conflict concerning the universal validity of existing ILO standards on freedom of association. Western delegations criticized the fact that the employers' and workers' representatives sent from the Eastern bloc states were not independent from the government, while the socialist states questioned altogether the relevance of this principle to states in which, by their own account, governance was something exercised by and for the workers. The Soviet Union also faced persistent attacks in the area of forced labor, a topic consistently kept on

[30] The strongest reservations came from the workers' group. The workers were also worried that technical assistance would weaken the tripartite structure of the ILO by forcing it to resort to external sources of financing. See Alcock, *History of the ILO*, 219.

[31] Since they mirrored the basic principles of the Declaration of Philadelphia, these standards were treated as core human rights standards even though the term core labor standards was not introduced until the 1990s.

[32] This is illustrated particularly clearly in the case of the Employment Policy Convention (1964), which included references to all the aforementioned documents.

[33] For a short period in the 1930s the Soviet Union had been a (passive) member of the ILO through its membership of the League of Nations. This membership, however, had been suspended as a consequence of the Soviet invasion of Finland in 1939. As a result, the Soviet Union refused offers to return to membership until after Stalin's death.

the postwar international agenda thanks primarily to the joint efforts of the U.S. government and the American trade union movement.

For the West, these human rights debates represented a tightrope walk. The aim was to put the communist states in the dock over issues such as freedom of association or forced labor without exposing the West to accusations of hypocrisy in the light of the policies of the colonial powers, not to mention the United States' own problem of racial discrimination in the American South.[34] The U.S. government found itself in a delicate position. The issue of racial discrimination left it wide open to the attacks of the Soviet Union. By the time the Eisenhower administration had taken office, U.S. delegates found themselves facing impossible dilemmas in all the human rights debates. As the American government began, in the wake of the McCarthy and Bricker era, to refuse on principle to assume international obligations that encroached on national jurisdiction, its representatives found themselves in the paradoxical situation of demanding that the Eastern bloc apply standards that the U.S. government itself was not prepared to ratify. As a result, after playing a leading role during the war in creating a human rights basis for the ILO's work, the United States now found itself trying to slow the process, and as a general rule increasingly lost interest in the ILO's human rights work during the 1950s.

Given this background it is astounding that the ILO managed to set major milestones in its human rights work during the 1950s. To a certain degree each of the human rights documents that the International Labour Conference adopted was a snapshot of a particular moment, reflecting the majorities and balances of power in place at the time of debate. Aside from the issue of power constellations, the very entelechy of the human rights discourse had a significant influence on the final form of each document, including its scope, the strength or weakness of the language it was formulated in, and the implementation mechanisms it was armed with. Despite their very different interpretations of the validity or scope of whatever rights were being discussed, all the participants in the debates in the 1950s were moving within what was in essence a universalistic discourse, thereby placing different emphasis on different groups of rights. The notion of human rights per se was hardly questioned. Apart from a few exceptions (with South Africa being the most extreme), none of the camps wanted to pass up the chance to exploit the moral force of the human rights idea. However, the discourse involved both opportunities and risks that were difficult to control, and depending on the issue under debate, this led participants to decide, on a case-by-case basis, what level of participation, what level of concession, and how much resistance would best serve their own interests.

In addition, the human rights debates within the ILO were made even more idiosyncratic and unpredictable by the Organization's tripartite structure. It is

---

[34] The issue of discrimination was a constant embarrassment for American diplomacy. See Carol Anderson, *Eyes Off the Prize: The United Nations and the African American Struggle for Human Rights 1944–1955* (Cambridge, Mass., 2003).

true that in many cases trade union and employers' representatives respected Cold War loyalties and ultimately voted with their governments, especially when the alternative was a victory for the other side. That said, it was common for specific issues to cause the formation of coalitions that defied the logic of the ideological blocs. This in turn subjected the debates that preceded the adoption of the various human rights standards to their own, very particular dynamics.

The two (complementary) conventions on Freedom of Association (1948) and the Right to Collective Bargaining (1949), for instance, were still clearly informed by the spirit and mood of change that characterized the formative phase of international human rights protection during the immediate post-1945 period, not least the result of a growing recognition by governments that trade unions could be reliable partners and part of a "healthy" democracy. Notwithstanding Britain's and other colonial powers' repeated efforts to prevent the debate from overflowing into the area of overseas policy, with the absence of the Soviet Union, government representatives were generally united in their support for a strong convention. The United States (and David Morse in particular, who at this point was an American government representative and the chairman of the ILO committee charged with preparing the Freedom of Association convention) essentially supported the workers' position. The result was two documents[35] that went a long way toward securing trade union rights. In subsequent years, they were strengthened by particularly effective monitoring mechanisms.[36]

In contrast, the conventions on forced labor and discrimination in employment and occupation became the subject of intense Cold War disputes. The original initiative for a new convention (following colonial documents adopted between the wars) to combat politically or economically (developmental) motivated systems of compulsory labor had been put forward at the end of the 1940s by the American Federation of Labor and was very pointedly targeted at the situation in the Soviet Union and its Eastern European satellites in the late Stalinist era. It was thanks to an initiative by the committee of experts set up jointly by the ILO and the UN to investigate the forced labor situation worldwide as part of preparation of a new convention that the final document also took into account forced labor practices outside the Eastern bloc (such as those seen in South Africa or the Belgian and Portuguese colonies), and this despite the fact that in the discussions the Western camp had largely managed

---

[35] Convention no. 87 (1948): Convention concerning Freedom of Association and Protection of the Right to Organize, in ILO, *Conventions and Recommendations*, 747–751; Convention no. 98 (1949): Convention concerning the Application of the Principles of the Right to Organize and to Bargain Collectively, ibid., 878–881.

[36] The ILO established a Permanent Committee on Freedom of Association in 1950. It received complaints and carried out detailed investigations. In effect, this gave the ILO a permanent tribunal within which any violations of the Freedom of Association Convention could be examined, a mechanism uniquely thorough in the realm of international human rights protection.

to keep the focus on the communist countries, constantly keeping them in the defensive on the issue. As an aside, when it came to the vote in 1957, in a surprise development the Soviet Union actually voted with the majority of the ILO's member states in favor of the new convention, while the U.S. government went so far as to uphold its noncommitment dogma even though it had been the main initiator of the new document.[37]

During the debate preceding the adoption of the anti-discrimination convention in 1958, the context was reversed. Here the countries that resisted a new convention belonged almost exclusively to the Western camp. Opposition to such a document initially came not just from the United States, but also from countries such as Australia, New Zealand, and many Latin American states. These states feared that either their immigration policy or their treatment of minorities and indigenous populations would expose them to criticism by the international public.[38] In this particular case, the international trade union movement resisted the pressure of Western governments, securing the success of a strong convention by building a broad (informal) coalition with Afro-Asian countries and the socialist states.[39]

Another issue that caused the formation of additional new camps and alliances was that of "Equal Remuneration for Men and Women Workers for Work of Equal Value." The matter of "equal pay for equal work" was an essential aspect of the larger human rights issue of gender equality, which, like freedom of association, was discussed before the reaccession of the Soviet Union. On this particular topic the fronts ran through all the constituent groups. In many countries, the idea that women were entitled to the same pay as men for their work had hardly gained any acceptance. The majority of ILSs were clearly based on the male breadwinner model.[40] The decisive factors behind the adoption of a convention that effectively recognized equal treatment as a human right thirty years before the adoption of the UN Convention on the Elimination of All Forms of Discrimination against Women (CEDAW) were recent wartime experience. The unprecedented rise in women's participation in the labor market, coupled with advocacy by the international women movement and a few pioneer states such as Denmark and Sweden, managed to exert pressure in the UN.[41]

---

[37] Convention no. 105 (1957): Convention concerning the Abolition of Forced Labor, in ILO, *Conventions and Recommendations*, 1015 et seq.

[38] For the broader context see Paul Gordon Lauren, *Power and Prejudice. The Politics and Diplomacy of Racial Discrimination* (Boulder, 1996).

[39] Convention no. 111 (1958): Convention concerning Discrimination in Respect of Employment and Occupation in ILO, *Conventions and Recommendations*, 1103–1106.

[40] Convention Concerning Equal Remuneration for Men and Women Workers for Work of Equal Value (Convention no. 100) of 1951, in ILO, *Conventions and Recommendations*, 901–904, For the overall discussion see Sandra Whitworth, "Gender, International Relations, and the Case of the ILO," *Review of International Studies*, 20 (1994), 389–405.

[41] Normand and Zaidi, *UN and Human Rights*, 277–279.

The last point in particular demonstrates that when the ILO's human rights work is examined in the wider UN context, it soon becomes clear that the contrast mentioned above was only a superficial one. The relationship between the human rights work of the UN and that of the ILO was often complementary and always complex. Precisely because the Cold War hindered the UN's work on an internationally binding instrument to extend the UDHR after 1948, the ILO often functioned, within its sphere of competence, as a substitute. Without exception, the ILO's human rights standards came into being either in collaboration with ECOSOC (Forced Labor, Equal Remuneration) or on the initiative of the UN (Discrimination in Employment and Occupation). In turn, advisers from the ILO worked on both the formulation of many passages of the UDHR and preparations for the two International Covenants on Political and Civil Rights and Economic, Social, and Cultural Rights of 1966.[42] If the relationship between the United Nations and the ILO in the field of human rights was nevertheless tense most of the time, this was due to the fact that the ILO's main priority was to keep the "political factor" within its human rights debates as insignificant as possible, the primary reason for the Organization's reluctance to integrate itself fully into the wider UN human rights work.[43] Toward the end of the 1950s, the political and symbolic charge that the human rights discourse possessed against the backdrop of the Cold War and the resentments between the colonial powers and the newly independent states of Asia and Africa was such that ideas were sought as to how the area of standard setting and implementation could be "depoliticized." David Morse and others believed that human rights had to be taken out of the political debates of the Conference and transferred to the Office's practical activities. This was the main consideration behind the new "promotional" or "educational" approach that Morse presented in his 1958 human rights report on the occasion of the UDHR's tenth anniversary.[44] A major step in this direction was, for example, the establishment of the International Institute for Labour Studies (IILS) in 1960, a center of research and training focusing mainly on the sociopolitical challenges faced by the developing world. One of the foundation's aims was to find a new approach to the implementation

---

[42] It is the third section (Articles 22–27) of the Universal Declaration of Human Rights adopted in 1948 that most clearly bears the ILO's signature. This section deals with economic, social, and cultural rights, and includes the right to work, to free choice of employment, to rest and leisure, and to education, all passages directly in line with the Declaration of Philadelphia. The ILO also played a part in setting down political rights/freedoms (Articles 3–19, including freedom of association and the prohibition of forced labor/slavery). See Johannes Morsink, *The Universal Declaration of Human Rights. Origins, Drafting & Intent* (Philadelphia, 1999).

[43] The memoirs of John Humphrey, director of the human rights department of the UN Secretariat in the 1950s, give an idea of the tension between the UN and the ILO that arose as a result of this reluctance. John Humphrey, *Human Rights and the United Nations. A Great Adventure* (New York, 1984), 12, 103.

[44] Note Morse 29/4/1956, David A. Morse papers, Seeley G. Mudd Rare Manuscript and Public Policy Papers Library, Princeton, B 89, F 14: Reflections.

of standards by bringing the world's future social policymakers to Geneva, where they could encounter the methods, principles, and ideals of the ILO, take them back home, and then enact agreed-upon standards in the developing countries.[45]

ILO Human Rights Standards and Decolonization

At the beginning of the 1960s and with decolonization reaching the African continent, the ILO's human rights work entered a new era. From 1945 to 1965, the Organization more than doubled in size. Its growth was accounted for almost exclusively by former colonies. As a result, developing countries soon formed the majority of the ILO's member states.[46]

With regard to human rights, decolonization was a two-edged sword in terms of the process it triggered within the UN system. On the one hand, the new nations began, in some respects, to relax the paralysis of the Cold War and to ensure that human rights returned to the international agenda. This was particularly evident in the Afro-Asian countries' fight against the remnants of colonial rule and the South African apartheid regime, a struggle waged under the human rights banner. On the other hand, the mid-1960s saw international debates on human rights marked by an increasingly clear discursive turn. Against the backdrop of an ever more strongly perceived structural economic North-South divide, disputes about the universality of human rights entered a new phase altogether.[47]

The ILO soon felt the full effects of this dual process, one set in motion by decolonization. First, the ILO became, within the UN system, one of the main venues of the struggle against the South African apartheid regime. In 1963 a group of Afro-Asian countries, supported by the socialist states and large parts of the international trade union movement, managed to force South Africa to leave the ILO and to push the Organization to condemn apartheid in many publications and work programs. These efforts would continue until the end of apartheid during the early 1990s.[48]

These activities were morally underpinned by the fact that virtually all the newly independent states themselves embraced the ILO's human rights standards.[49] In fact, during the 1960s the ILO recorded an unparalleled

---

[45] Morse, memorandum "The International Institute for Labour Studies" 12/6/1961, ILOA-MF Z 11/7/3: IILS 1961–1968.
[46] From 55 countries in 1947 the ILO grew to 115 in 1965. Ghebali, *The International Labour Organization*, 117–118.
[47] Normand and Zaidi, *The UN and Human Rights*, 289–315.
[48] See the memorandum "The ILO and South Africa" 4/26/1966, ILOA-MF Z 6/2/65/2: South Africa. An overview of the measures taken by the ILO to tackle the problem of apartheid is given by Neville Rubin, "From Pressure Principle to Measured Militancy. The ILO in the Campaign against Apartheid" in ILO Century Project (http://www.ilo.org/public/english/century/information_resources/download/rubin.pdf).
[49] ILC 46 (1962) Rep. I: Report of the Director-General, 6.

increase in ratifications of its norms[50] with core human rights standards (anti-discrimination, abolition of forced labor, and freedom of association) at the top of the list.[51] The reasons for widespread adoption are obvious. Within the spectrum of ILO standard setting, the colonies had, until the day of independence, been treated as an area where separate rules applied. In fact, Article 35 of the ILO Constitution, the "colonial clause," had remained in effect right up into the 1960s, permitting the colonial powers to ignore in their overseas territories conventions ratified and enacted at home.

Inasmuch as they represented an end to the colonial double standard, embracing the ILO's human rights standards after independence was imbued with deep political and moral significance. For the governments of the new states, the act of recognizing fundamental human rights symbolized the overcoming of the colonial past and their arrival in the international community of sovereign states. Held in 1960, the first ILO African Regional Conference in Lagos, Nigeria, declared that the strict application of the Organization's human rights conventions was a "question of honor and prestige" for all African countries.[52] Resolutions passed at various Asian Regional Conferences were similar in content and tone.[53]

At the same time it was hard to turn a blind eye to the fact that there were strong currents moving in the opposite direction. These strains within the human rights discourse emerged most clearly when it came to the practical application of the norms once they had been signed. Even as representatives of the newly independent states voiced in international forums support for the universal validity of human rights, a consensus was emerging among the governments of these countries that the wholesale application of certain human rights standards was irreconcilable with the goal to mobilize all possible forces for development. At the ILO's annual conferences after 1960, more and more governments claimed that when push came to shove, economic development must always take priority over compliance with norms.

This trend was particularly apparent with regard to the issue of forced labor.[54] Given the fact that coerced labor, despite the topic's instrumentalization in the Cold War, was regarded by the majority of the post-colonial countries to be a typically "colonial crime," virtually all the new member states had

---

[50] The number of ratification certificates received in Geneva between 1960 and 1964 was about the same as the number of signatures that ILO documents had collected during the entire period between the wars. Ibid., 7.

[51] Two-thirds of the ratification certificates the ILO issued from 1963 to 1983 were to postcolonial countries. Daniel Maul, *Menschenrechte, Sozialpolitik und Dekolonisation. Die Internationale Arbeitsorganisation (IAO) 1940–1970* (Essen, 2007), 451.

[52] Resolution concerning the Work of the International Labour Organization in Africa, ILO African Regional Conference I (1960), RoP, App. III: Resolutions, 256–257.

[53] See, for example, ILO Asian Regional Conference V (1962), RoP, App VII: Resolutions and Observations Adopted by the Conference, 187.

[54] See Daniel Maul, "The International Labour Organization and the Struggle against Forced Labour," *Labor History*, 48 (2007), 477–500.

ratified this convention immediately after independence.[55] In 1962, however, an ILO committee listed by name numerous countries, mostly in West Africa but also in other regions with a colonial past, that had introduced compulsory labor service for young people. These nations were condemned as contravening the spirit of the 1957 forced labor convention, which primarily targeted those forms of forced labor used for development and political purposes.[56] For their part, the states in question defended the practices as a necessary means to mobilize all available forces to promote development.[57]

A similar controversy blighted the freedom of association. On this issue as well, commitment to the principle collided with the situation on the ground. The free growth of trade unions in the developing world, as the debates in the 1950s and 1960s showed quite clearly, was time and again hindered by two main obstacles, one political and a second related to the so-called development first argument. In light of the fact that trade unions had often been on the front line in the independence struggle, governments seemed to fear the oppositional potential of a free trade union movement. The Cold War raging in the background provided another reason to be apprehensive about freedom of association. As time went by, many governments became increasingly doubtful as to whether the concept of freedom of association in the form in which it was anchored in the ILO's conventions could be reconciled with the demands of national development. In their view, this higher aim required the bundling of all the country's social forces under national leadership. As a result, almost everywhere in Asia and Africa states did everything in their power to make sure they had the last word when it came to the organization of industrial relations. Upon his return from a lengthy trip to Southeast Asia in 1959, Deputy Director-General Jef Rens expressed disappointment that the concept of freedom of association had failed to take root even in democratic countries such as India.[58] Western accusations regarding the freedom of association and forced labor provoked great bitterness among the post-colonial countries. In their view, the colonial powers were once again relishing the chance to take on the role of the accuser, turning against them a human rights discourse that had previously been a stock weapon in the long fight against colonialism. So numerous were such voices in developing countries that by the mid-1950s David Morse had begun to speak of a new "intellectual fashion." According to Morse, many in the post-colonial world now held individual freedom and democratic forms of organization to be irreconcilable with the demands of economic growth.[59] Indeed, the leaders of the post-colonial nations tended

---

[55] Maul, *Menschenrechte*, 475.
[56] The report found systems of forced labor for which emergency powers were used as a justification for their existence in all parts of the world, in independent countries such as Kenya and India and the remaining colonial territories alike. ILC 46 (1962), Rep. III: Report of the Committee of Experts on the Application of Conventions and Recommendations, 4.
[57] ILC 36 (1962), RoP,165 et seq.; 358 et seq.
[58] Rens to Morse 9/11/1959, ILOA-MF Z 1/1/1/16: Mission of Mr. Rens to Asia 1959.
[59] ILC 48 (1962), RoP, 446–453.

to describe the under-development of their young national economies as an emergency situation comparable to a state of war. In terms of the struggle for development within the international political and economic order, complying with ILO norms was increasingly seen as tantamount to falling for a type of hidden protectionism that benefited the rich industrial countries.[60] On the internal level, this warlike situation justified, demanded even, the mobilization of all forces for a common goal, and called for a united front. In this new discourse, postcolonial governments were emergency regimes overseeing their new nations' fight for economic emancipation and independence, a struggle that no longer took place on the national level, but instead within the international order.[61]

The ILO's human rights work during this period was much less autonomous than it had been during the 1950s, mainly as a result of the relative decline in the significance of the tripartite principle (itself an indirect result of decolonization). Only a minority of the workers' and employers' delegates could now claim to be independent of their governments. This state of affairs reduced the potential for the international trade union movement (and employers' associations) to act as a counterweight to the claim of inviolability of national sovereignty as they occasionally had during the adoption of ILO human rights standards in the 1950s. Those members of the International Labour Office who regarded the ILO's mission primarily as human rights work did not face an easy task during the 1960s. Moreover, with regard to the question of what actual value human rights standards held in the development process, significant differences of opinion ran through the Office itself. Although a (majority) "labor standards faction" emphasized the normative role of the ILO, a smaller yet increasingly influential "development faction" wanted to see the applicability of ILO standards coupled to economic factors such as productivity.[62] The underlying controversy was about the question of whether, in light of underdevelopment, "development dictatorships" or democratic governments were better prepared to meet the social and economic challenges posed by the process of modernization.

In general, human rights advocates within the ILO saw no other way to respond to decolonization than to redouble promotional and educational methods. Apropos disputed issues such as forced labor and freedom of association, by the end of Morse's time in office in 1970 the ILO had been compelled

---

[60] The Kenyan Secretary of Labor Tom M´boya for example published a text in 1963 in which he quite openly argued for the temporary suspension of ILO human rights standards. Tom M´boya, *Africa: Freedom and After?* (London, 1963), 194.

[61] For an deeper analysis of the discursive turn in human rights issues visible in the UN in the 1960s see Roland Burke, "From Individual Rights to National Development. The First UN International Conference on Human Rights, Tehran, 1968," *Journal of World History*, 19 (2008), 275–296.

[62] Robert W. Cox, "ILO-Limited Monarchy," in Robert W. Cox and Harold K. Jacobson (eds.), *The Anatomy of Influences. Decision Making in International Organizations* (New Haven, Conn., 1973), 102–138.

to find formulas that defused the debates and left both the content of the disputed documents and the fundamental claim to universality of ILO norms intact. What this meant, however, was that further sacrifices had to be made vis-à-vis the practical application of standards and strict compliance to the tripartite principle.[63]

On a rhetorical level the dilemma was resolved in the ILO's approach to the World Employment Program (WEP). Destined to make up a large part of the Organization's activities during the 1970s, this program focused on employment creation in developing countries. In this context the ILO propagated once again its commitment to human rights as part of an over-all strategy to achieve economic and social progress. Under the banner of espousing the "solidarity of human rights," the significance that the ILO placed on the concurrent realization of economic and social rights, on the one hand, and civil and political freedoms, on the other, was emphasized yet again on the occasion of the UDHR's twentieth anniversary. These for-mulas were, of course, primarily designed to paper over conflict. In fact, disputes continued to smolder and differences ran deep. On the surface, however, a rejection of gradualism in human rights was still an important part of the ILO's formal position.[64]

Conclusion

What conclusions can be drawn from this historical study of the ILO, an orga-nization that was both as an example of – and exceptional case within – the global community of international human rights advocacy?

First and foremost, the ILO experience confirms the complexity of inter-national organizations in both reflecting and directing the turns taken by the global human rights discourse in the era following the Second World War. It demonstrates that along with the moral force of the human rights idea per se, the will of various actors, including, not least, the secretariats of international organizations themselves, to instrumentalize human rights in the realization of their own goals exercised a significant influence on the rhythm and dynamics of the debate. In this context, a significant factor informing the human rights postulates of the Declaration of Philadelphia was the ILO's quest to establish an intellectual basis for claims to extend the Organization's sphere of competence. The ILO demonstrated the ability to exploit a historically favorable constellation in the service of this objective, as shown above. During the Cold War, the Organization's tripartite struc-ture, and in particular the international trade union movement, helped to avoid the paralysis that affected the UN's human rights work in the face of the era's deep ideological divisions.

---

[63] ILO, *The ILO and Human Rights* (Geneva, 1968), 44 et seq.
[64] Ibid., 48–58.

Second, this essay traces how a general and increasingly fundamental criticism of human rights – one that grew in strength as decolonization progressed – spilled over into ILO debates. Relatively unchanged, the discussions reflected the two main ruptures in the international human rights discourse that characterized the debates within the UN system during the 1960s. The driver in both instances was the emergence of a new postcolonial community of states. The era witnessed a renewed confirmation and strengthening of the principle of national sovereignty against the universalism of the UDHR (which claimed to transcend the borders of the nation state) and the emergence, closely related to this phenomenon, of a "third generation" human rights discourse in which "solidarity rights" – such as the right to development or the right to freedom from colonialism – moved up the political agenda. What these trends boiled down to was a return to favor of (revamped) group rights of the interwar period versus the individual rights concept of the UDHR. Decolonization changed the coordinates of the discussions surrounding human rights in the ILO. For many postcolonial governments, ILO human rights standards lost the power they had possessed under the conditions of anti-colonial struggle. Rejection of these standards as an expression of a human rights universalism was the new element: In the view of these governments, the Western conception of human rights in fact served Western interests, and thus became subsumed in a larger discourse of decolonization. This argument should, in principle, have hit the ILO harder than other UN human rights agencies, for "competing universalisms" had not played a role in the Philadelphia gathering that marked the start of the ILO's human rights activities (as they had in the genesis of the human rights documents of the UN and UNESCO). Nonetheless, the ILO's human rights standards have survived relatively unchanged, notwithstanding the attacks that the United Nations' human rights work has been exposed to since the 1970s. Growing cultural relativist criticism has not thwarted the human rights work of the ILO. Indeed, of all the ILSs, it is the ILO's human rights standards that remain the most widely ratified.

A partial explanation for this paradox may be derived from the fact that the ILO, more than any other part of the UN, still embodies an integrative concept of human rights. The ILO not only continues to take the position that the realization of political and social rights is mutually dependent processes, but it also places all of its standard-setting work in the service of human rights. Moreover, the ILO has in recent years has demonstrated a growing willingness to include cultural rights and "third generation" rights in its own work, as evidenced by the Indigenous and Tribal Peoples (1989) and Worst Abuses of Child Labor (1999) conventions. During the 1990s, a period marked by renewed emphasis on human rights within the entire UN system, the ILO managed to adopt a Declaration on Fundamental Principles and Rights at Work. Accordingly, all member states committed here to a core inventory of human rights standards. (The Declaration is not, however, legally binding.) Echoing the 1950s, the realization of these rights has once again been defined as an integral part of a "global strategy for economic and social development."[65]

During the past sixty years, the ILO has helped to fashion a global frame of reference for today's international discourse on human rights. International disputes aside, the vast majority of nations today accept this framework as an integral part of international diplomacy. Whether the ILO's efforts have led to practical implementation and the actual realization of human rights are questions historians are just now beginning to address.

---

[65] Apart from the two forced labor documents the Declaration on Fundamental Rights at Work contains the ILO Conventions on Freedom of Association and the Right to Collective Bargaining (Nos. 87 and 98), Equal Remuneration (No. 100), and Discrimination in Employment and Occupation (No. 111) and the two documents dealing with child labor (Nos. 138 and 198). See ILO, *Declaration on Fundamental Principles and Rights at Work* (Geneva, 1998).

15

"Under a Magnifying Glass"

The International Human Rights Campaign against Chile in the Seventies

Jan Eckel

Seldom has it been more appropriate to say that the whole world was watching. The military coup against the democratically elected government of Salvador Allende on September 11, 1973, unfolded as if on a public stage. Since a possible military takeover had been openly discussed in the preceding months, political observers inside and outside the country were hardly taken by surprise. Newspapers in Europe and the United States informed their readers of the "predictable end" to Allende's presidency.[1] TV audiences worldwide could see the images of the burning presidential palace La Moneda and even pictures of obviously ill-treated civilians who had been herded together in Santiago's sport stadium. Estimates of the number of people killed raised notions of a vast human catastrophe. Figures of 25,000–30,000 were considered to be conservative, and some ranged as high as 80,000. The information pouring out of Chile literally shocked human rights activists into action. Within days of the coup, Amnesty International and the International Commission of Jurists sent urgent protests to the military junta, appealing for a stop to the violence.

The worldwide concern of the first months proved to be only a prelude since the eyes of the international community were to be kept on the events in Chile for many years. The bloody establishment and trajectory of the Pinochet dictatorship gave rise to one of the longest and most intense human rights campaigns ever to be waged against a single regime. It stretched over the entire sixteen years of the military junta's existence, from 1973 to 1989, flaring up every time new shocking details reached the media. A broad range of actors supported the efforts, including states from all regions of the world, the various bodies of supranational organizations, and innumerable private groups. These actors applied a wide variety of measures, ranging from public manifestations and humanitarian aid to economic sanctions and on-site investigations.

Exceptional as they may seem for their duration and intensity, the efforts against the Pinochet regime formed part of broader trends in international

---

[1] *The Times*, September 13, 1973.

politics. The late 1960s and early 1970s saw a reinvigoration of political action
against human rights violations that markedly distinguished the era from initiatives that had been taken in previous decades.[2] Only now human rights
turned into the object of widespread popular mobilization, as shown in the
emergence and thriving of countless more or less professional groups working
on human rights generally or organizing around specific countries or persons.[3] Moreover, states in Western Europe and North America in particular
started to pay considerably more heed to what came to be called the "human
rights record" in their relations with foreign governments. Consequently,
international governmental organizations such as the United Nations and the
Organization of American States also became more active in this field. As a
result, numerous widely supported human rights campaigns unfolded in the
1970s – against the apartheid regime in South Africa and the military rule in
Argentina, on behalf of dissidents in Eastern Europe and of Soviet Jews, and
against torture and "disappearances."

Historians of international politics have so far hardly studied these campaigns.[4] On Chile specifically, Thomas C. Wright has given a useful factual
account that covers both the junta's terror against the Chilean population and
the international action taken against it. He does not attempt a detailed analysis of the campaign's dynamics, however.[5] In addition, numerous studies have
dealt with U.S. policy toward Chile both before and after the military coup.[6]

For these reasons, this chapter attempts to analyze the campaign against
Chile as a case study to highlight general mechanisms characteristic of the
human rights politics of the period. More specifically, after a brief overview of
Chile's political history and of the evolution of the campaign, the chapter con-
centrates on two aspects. First, it looks at the factors and motives that precipi-
tated the campaign in the first place. On the surface, the Pinochet junta might
have appeared similar to many other military regimes, especially in Latin
America. Nonetheless, Chile was subjected to unusual political pressures. The
chapter argues that this was the result of a complex interplay of political and
humanitarian dynamics that has to be unraveled in order to account for the
singling out of the regime. Second, the article raises the question of effects.
The avowed aim of human rights advocates was to stop the repressive politics of a regime that had set out to violently reorder society. But even though

---

[2] For the context, see Jan Eckel, "Utopie der Moral, Kalkül der Macht. Menschenrechte in der
globalen Politik seit 1945," *Archiv für Sozialgeschichte*, 49 (2009), 437–484.
[3] On this aspect, see my article, "'To Make the World a Slightly Less Wicked Place': The
International League for the Rights of Man, Amnesty International USA and the Transformation
of Human Rights Activism from the 1940s through the 1970s," forthcoming.
[4] A relatively broad literature can be found on the efforts against the apartheid regime in South
Africa, although historians have usually focused on a single country. For an exception, see
Hakan Thörn, *Anti-Apartheid and the Emergence of a Global Civil Society* (Basingstoke,
2006). For other pertinent studies, see the notes to the conclusion of this article.
[5] Thomas C. Wright, *State Terrorism in Latin America. Chile, Argentina, and International
Human Rights* (Lanham, Md., 2007).
[6] See the titles cited below.

the campaign utilized extraordinary resources, Pinochet managed to stay in power longer than most other Latin American military dictators of the period. By placing the regime's human rights considerations in the context of its larger political project, the chapter shows that the campaign's influence on political change in Chile was relatively weak. For pragmatic reasons, the following analysis is limited to the period from 1973 to the end of the decade. These years can be considered as the most violent of the Chilean dictatorship as well as the most intense of the human rights campaign.

Polarization and Repression – Chile, 1970–1989

After various conservative governments had failed to solve the social and political problems that Chile faced as a consequence of a difficult process of modernization, the Socialist leader Salvador Allende was elected president in 1970.[7] His political project, to bring about a socialist system by constitutional means, attracted worldwide attention because many observers regarded it as a singular case of peaceful change toward socialism. Although the government achieved some of its important aims, such as long-awaited agrarian reform, the chances for its overall goals were slim from the beginning. The governing coalition of Unidad Popular was torn by inner divisions and, despite repeated efforts, could not reach compromise with the Christian Democrat opposition. The political atmosphere in the country was increasingly polarized between the defenders and opponents of Allende, and in the last year of his government, Chile bordered on a state of political chaos.

The perception that "Marxism" was about to disintegrate the traditional order and to spread political anarchy drove military leaders to attempt the coup. From the outset, the generals aimed at reordering society and the political process as a whole. The junta declared a state of siege, ruled by emergency decrees, eliminated political opponents, banned political parties and trade unions, censored the media, and "cleansed" universities and intellectual professions. In this process, the junta resorted to violence as an essential instrument of its rule. Following the coup, a wave of indiscriminate brutality struck the country, including mass arrests, killings, and large-scale application of torture. After this initial phase, state terror became more systematic. It mainly targeted persons associated, in one way or another, with the political left. The doctrine of "national security," however, aimed at protecting the authoritarian order against all perceived forms of subversion, was sufficiently vague as

---

[7] For the following section, see Arturo Valenzuela and Samuel J. Valenzuela, *Military Rule in Chile* (Baltimore, 1986); Lois Hecht Oppenheim, *Politics in Chile: Democracy, Authoritarianism, and the Search for Development* (Boulder, 1993); Mark Ensalaco, *Chile under Pinochet: Recovering the Truth* (Philadelphia, 2000); Detlef Nolte, "Staatsterrorismus in Chile," in Hans Werner Tobler and Peter Waldmann (eds.), *Staatliche und parastaatliche Gewalt in Lateinamerika* (Frankfurt, 1991), 75–103; Verónica Valdivia Ortiz de Zárate, "Terrorism and Political Violence during the Pinochet Years: Chile, 1973–1989," *Radical History Review*, 85 (2003), 182–190.

to include broad categories of people among the presumed enemies – workers, students, members of intellectual professions, and the poor.

At the end of the 1970s, the regime embarked on a course of consolidation and institutional reorganization, which was sustained by a certain economic recovery. In 1977, the head of the junta, Augusto Pinochet, announced a gradual return to civilian leadership, which was to be completed by the end of the 1980s. Two years later, however, with the country stumbling into the next economic crisis, political protest sprang up on a large scale. The regime reacted once again with violent suppression, killing another 470 persons in the next decade. By the middle of the 1980s, civil protest had been thoroughly discouraged. The opposition now concentrated on a legal course, gathering strength for the referendum to be held in 1988, which Pinochet had announced some ten years earlier. Fifty-five percent of the population voted against the military regime. The first free elections after sixteen years of dictatorship, held in December 1989, marked the beginning of the democratic transition.

The exact death toll of the Pinochet regime is difficult to determine. In the 1990s, the Chilean Truth and Reconciliation Commission was able to verify some 3,300 violent deaths.[8] As the fate of many "disappeared" persons could not be ascertained, the number of people killed might be higher but is unlikely to exceed 5,000. Even though the figures are considerably lower than many estimates at the time, this record makes the Pinochet regime one of the most repressive dictatorships ever to emerge in Latin America. In addition to the killings, the regime arrested tens of thousands, tortured thousands, and forced 200,000 people into exile, representing 2 percent of the total population.

Isolating the Regime

The ruthless establishment of the Pinochet dictatorship met with firm and unambiguous opposition by the international community. An important part of the human rights campaign originated with international organizations, above all with the United Nations (UN) and the Organization of American States (OAS). The UN turned its attention to Chile in 1974 and kept it on the agenda until the end of the dictatorship. The relevant organs, especially the General Assembly, the Economic and Social Council, and the Commission on Human Rights, annually adopted resolutions condemning the junta's misdeeds. In 1975, an Ad Hoc Working Group was set up and charged with reporting on current developments. Three years later, after long and intricate negotiations, it was permitted entry into Chile, being the first UN human rights body ever to conduct an on-site visit in a country under scrutiny. In the 1980s, the UN created Special Rapporteurs on Torture, on Disappearances and on Summary Executions, whose mandates were in large part inspired by the methods of the Chilean junta. The OAS took particularly strong action in the initial years of the dictatorship. As early as 1974, the Inter-American

---

[8] See *Informe de la comisión nacional de verdad y reconciliación* (Santiago, 1991).

Human Rights Commission visited Chile and published its findings in a scathing report.[9] Thus, for both organizations, the Chilean case set a series of procedural precedents and marked an important stage in the evolution of their human rights policies.

In addition, numerous NGOs joined the protests against the junta. Amnesty International and the International Commission of Jurists undertook particularly strong efforts. In 1973, both sent missions to Chile, which produced the first detailed evidence of the regime's crimes.[10] In the following years, they made numerous representations to the Chilean government on specific cases of abuse, submitted information to the press, to governments, and to supranational human rights bodies, and provided prisoners and their families with aid and legal support. These efforts were only the tip of the iceberg, however. Gradually, a dense network of private activists evolved that encompassed single-issue groups as well as sophisticated organizations. Virtually all of them were located in the Western world (including Latin America) or in Eastern Europe. They added to the international pressures on the junta by staging public protests, spreading information, and issuing appeals.

Moreover, Chile saw itself confronted with resolute reactions by foreign governments.[11] Socialist states in Eastern Europe immediately broke off diplomatic and economic relations with the military regime. The Soviet Union even went so far as to orchestrate a far-flung campaign, spanning the Eastern bloc and featuring international congresses, mock tribunals, and action weeks full of cultural activities directed against the junta. The reaction of Western European states was no less severe if a little less outraged. Many of them publicly and bilaterally stated deep concern over the violent overthrow. Great Britain, the Federal Republic of Germany, the Netherlands, the Scandinavian countries, and Italy resorted to sanctions, mostly affecting Chile's economic and military sector. They terminated their development aid and supplies of weapons and refused to negotiate the rescheduling of debts.

The great exception to the relatively uniform Western response was the United States. The Nixon administration had viewed Allende's Chile as an enclave of communism in South America that threatened vital U.S. security interests.[12] The U.S. Government had gone so far as to engage in secret

---

[9] See Klaas Dykmann, *Philanthropic Endeavors or the Exploitation of an Ideal? The Human Rights Policy of the Organization of American States in Latin America, 1970–1991* (Frankfurt, 2004), ch. III.1; Cecilia Medina Quiroga, *The Battle of Human Rights. Gross Systematic Violations and the Inter-American System* (Dordrecht, 1988), ch. X.

[10] *Chile. An Amnesty International Report* (London, 1974); International Commission of Jurists, *Final Report of the Mission to Chile, April 1974, to Study the Legal System and the Protection of Human Rights* (Geneva, [1974]).

[11] For overviews, see the reports by the UN Secretary General, UN Documents A/32/234 (October 1977), A/33/293 (October 1978). and A/34/658 (November 1979) and the report of the CHR, UN Document E/CN.4/1268 (January 1978).

[12] On U.S. policy toward Chile here and in the following, see Lars Schoultz, *Human Rights and United States Policy toward Latin America* (Princeton, 1981); Paul E. Sigmund, *The United*

operations to weaken Allende's rule,[13] and it had been informed about the military's plans to topple the Chilean President. After the coup, the Nixon and Ford administrations increased economic assistance to the new regime and supplied it with a continuously high level of military aid. Only when domestic human rights criticism began to swell did the Ford administration softly pressure the military regime for symbolic concessions,[14] but it was not until the election of Jimmy Carter that the United States abandoned its essentially supportive course. The Democratic administration cut off practically all economic and military assistance, fully joined the efforts of the UN, and exerted considerable diplomatic pressure on the Chilean junta to dismantle the apparatus of repression.[15] Having lost its most powerful ally, by 1977 the military regime had become a pariah of the international community.

The Twisted Paths of Emerging Pressures

Why Chile? In much of the historiography, the fact that the Pinochet regime was targeted for international action has not provoked much explanation. Historians have tended to describe the worldwide public concern as a kind of natural reaction to the atrocities committed, which by their horrendous nature forced politicians and private individuals into immediate action.[16] However, even though the 1970s saw unprecedented mobilization against state-sponsored repression, there was not an automatic response by a watchful world community, ready to take action wherever it was needed. Other repressive regimes drew less attention, even though they wreaked more havoc on the civilian population than the destructive rule of the Chilean junta. These cases include the rules of terror under Idi Amin in Uganda between 1971 and 1979 and under Macías Nguema in Equatorial Guinea between 1969 and 1979, the mass murder of Hutu in Burundi in 1972, the repression by the socialist regime in Ethiopia after 1974, the genocide in Cambodia between 1975 and 1979, the large-scale massacres by Indonesian troops in East Timor in the wake of the invasion in 1975, and the crimes of the communist regimes in China and North Korea. If the 1970s were a highpoint of human rights

States and Democracy in Chile (Baltimore, 1993); David F. Schmitz, *The United States and Right-Wing Dictatorships, 1965–1989* (Cambridge, 2006), 143–193.

[13] See Peter Kornbluh (ed.), *The Pinochet File. A Declassified Dossier on Atrocity and Accountability* (New York, 2003). It is still open to debate whether the U.S. Government was involved in the planning of the actual coup.
[14] See National Archives, Record Group 59, Human Rights Abuses in Chile, box "Ford Presidential Library," and boxes 1 through 11 of the State Department's files.
[15] On Carter's policy toward Chile, see Carter Presidential Library, White House Central File, Subject Files, Countries, box CO-15; NSA 3 Brzezinski Material, President's Correspondence with Foreign Leaders File, box 3; NSA 6 Brzezinski Material, Country Files, box 7; NSA 24 Staff Material – North/South, Pastor – Country File, box 9; Vertical File, Chile – Human Rights 6/30/99.
[16] See Wright, *State Terrorism*.

campaigns, they were just as conspicuous for the many non-campaigns in the face of egregious mass murders.

In this perspective, the human rights campaigns of the decade almost appear to be an exception rather than a rule. At the very least, they have to be seen as the result of an intricate combination of factors that had no obvious relation to the scale of violence committed. In the case of Chile, four factors proved to be particularly important: an international political constellation that contributed to isolating the regime, the junta's reaction to the human rights discourse, its information politics, and finally, the strength of private activism directed against the military regime.

Most of this can be inferred from the negotiations within the United Nations, since the world organization provided one of the foremost forums for the criticism of Chile.[17] The international political constellation, the first essential factor for the strength of the campaign, was clearly reflected in the UN negotiations. If on the surface the condemnatory resolutions of the different UN bodies received overwhelming support, this could hardly conceal the strong tensions and contrary strategies that characterized the discussions among member states. Action against Chile was far from transcending the ideological differences and conflict-ridden power relations between the camps. The Soviet camp, forcefully joined by Cuba, primarily aimed to discredit the Pinochet junta politically. In strongly ritualized, repetitive speeches, they heaped fierce accusations on Chile's military leadership, equating its crimes with the worst acts committed by National Socialism. At first, the Eastern European bloc opposed all measures that implied even the least cooperation with the Chilean government and, instead, advocated the insertion of increasingly stronger condemnations in the UN resolutions.

The Western European countries[18] and Canada, in contrast, emphasized the humanitarian aspects of the situation in Chile, invoking the "fate of the people" and refraining from political judgments. Bent on avoiding confrontation with the junta, they pleaded for prolonged dialogue and the force of persuasion. Only when repression continued unabated in spite of numerous appeals did Western delegations become more openly critical. From the beginning, however, most delegations argued in favor of thorough investigations. In this respect, not even the Ford administration could be regarded as a firm ally of the dictatorship. Even though the U.S. delegation attempted to draw attention to positive developments such as the release of prisoners, in 1975 and 1976 it joined the majority of UN members in its vote against Chile.

The least homogeneous bloc was formed by the African and Asian countries. They brought forward a rather wide array of positions, ranging from

---

[17] The following section is largely based on an analysis of the proceedings on Chile of all relevant UN organs, most notably the General Assembly, the Commission on Human Rights, the Sub-Commission on the Prevention of Discrimination and the Protection of Minorities, the ECOSOC, and the Social Committee.

[18] This group included the Netherlands, Great Britain, France, the Federal Republic of Germany, Italy, Norway, Denmark, and Belgium.

Yemen's unswerving support for the Soviet camp to the humanitarian approach
of Senegal, which was reminiscent of the Western European attitude. In the
decisive session of the Commission on Human Rights in 1975 that led to the
establishment of the Ad Hoc Working Group and thereby turned Chile into
a painfully controversial "case" in the first place, an Afro-Asian group consisting of Ghana, India, Egypt, and Senegal acted as a mediator. After long
and delicate negotiations they came up with a compromise resolution that
required all sides – the Western group, the Soviet camp, and Chile – to make
concessions.

The junta's only support came from Latin America. After a wave of military coups had spilled over the continent beginning in the late 1960s, several
dictatorships had emerged that were bound together by astonishingly similar ideological programs as well as by close diplomatic relations.[19] By 1976,
the South American dictatorships in the UN, including Argentina, Brazil,
Uruguay, Paraguay, and Bolivia, were in a position to forge a strong coalition.
The group showed itself to be increasingly outraged by what it claimed was
hypocritical treatment of the "sister country," branding it as undue interference into the internal affairs of a sovereign nation.[20] This was not a purely dictatorial discourse, however. Latin American democracies such as Costa Rica,
Venezuela, and Colombia similarly opposed the "obsession" with Chile in the
world organization.[21] Thus, Latin American solidarity evolved on the Chilean
question that was equally directed against the Western and Communist worlds.
It was not without practical consequences as Latin American delegations occasionally withdrew their support for stronger measures against Chile.

Against this background, the situation in Chile gave rise to intense mutual
recriminations that were an essential feature of the human rights politics in
the United Nations during the Cold War. On human rights questions, Western
democracies routinely attacked the socialist dictatorships of Eastern Europe
and vice versa, developing nations denounced the industrialized countries,
and "small states" spoke out against the Great Powers. When it came to
the junta's crimes, the situation was not very different, as was most clearly
manifested in the question of "selectivity," which played a crucial role in the
debates. All member states were aware of the discrepancy between the United
Nations' stance in this as opposed to similar cases, and, with the exception of

---

[19] See Frederick M. Nunn, *The Time of the Generals. Latin American Professional Militarism
in World Perspective* (Lincoln, Neb., 1992); Alain Rouquie and Stephen Suffern, "The
Military in Latin American Politics since 1930," in Leslie Bethell (ed.), *The Cambridge
History of Latin America*, vol. 6,2, *Latin America since 1930: Economy, Society, and
Politics* (Cambridge, 1994), 233–306; Peter Imbusch, "Die Gewalt von Militärdiktaturen
in Südamerika," in Thomas Fischer and Michael Krennerich (eds.), *Politische Gewalt in
Lateinamerika* (Frankfurt, 2000), 35–60.
[20] See the statement by the delegate of Paraguay in the 1975 General Assembly, UN Document
A/C.3/SR.2151.
[21] Statement by the delegate of Colombia in CHR's session of 1979, UN Document E/CN.4/
SR.1508.

the communist bloc, all delegations openly admitted that a "double standard" applied in the procedures. The conclusions they drew from this fact differed greatly, however. The Latin American states, dictatorships and democracies alike, used it as the prime counterargument against the stigmatization of Chile. The Western states, for their part, used the argument of selectivity against the Eastern bloc, insinuating that human rights problems behind the Iron Curtain were being kept from the agenda "by regimented systems in domestic forums and alliances of silence in international forums."[22] Less powerful Western states such as Australia and Belgium lamented that selectivity impaired a broad humanitarian policy so that the crimes in Cambodia and Uganda, among many others, could not be examined. Finally, some Third World countries seized upon the issue of double standards in order to shame both superpowers for their ideological rivalry, which they waged at the expense of less powerful nations.[23]

Consequently, with the exception of the stance of the Latin American countries, the debate on Chile did not essentially differ from the usual Cold War struggles that bedeviled the UN proceedings. What was astonishing about it was its outcome – the fact that it did not result in a complete stalemate. However deep the fractions, eventually an interplay of political considerations evolved among member states that added up to a common front. The Soviet Union had lost its sole ally in South America and therefore saw the military coup against the Allende government as seriously damaging its foreign policy. Even though the Soviets only reluctantly agreed to support the review process, their concessions were not too costly, as they secured the opportunity to denounce the dictatorship year after year. For the Western bloc, in contrast (with the exception of the United States), little was at stake from a purely diplomatic point of view. They had not been bound to the Allende government by close ties of political friendship, nor did they have a strong interest in Chile as an economic or strategic partner. This made it easy to respond to the outrage in Western public opinion over the junta's crimes. Some of the African and Asian countries took a clearly discernible third position. Since Allende's government had been a prominent member of the Non-Aligned Movement and Allende himself had been an unswerving defender of national independence in the face of international capitalism, many nations had seen Chile as a spearhead of Third World interests. Accordingly, countries such as Tanzania and Iraq attacked the military junta in the name of self-determination and anti-(neo-)colonialism. Therefore, not even the junta's halfhearted appeals to common Third World interests bore fruit.

Thus, a shared, let alone humanitarian, concern was decidedly not the basis for the UN's measures against the regime. Rather, UN action sprang from a

---

[22] Statement by the delegate of the US in CHR's session of 1976, UN Document E/CN.4/SR.1360.

[23] See among others the statement by the Saudi Arabian delegate in the 1976 General Assembly, UN Document A/C.3/SR.2146.

complex mixture of conflicting political and humanitarian interests. Among
member states a kind of negative consensus emerged on how to deal with the
military regime. Irrespective of their varying motives, either most delegations
had a sufficiently strong interest in opposing the junta, or they did not have
sufficient interest in protecting it. Even though the various camps clearly did
not share the attitude toward human rights displayed by their adversaries,
the case of the Chilean junta was not important enough – or not acceptable
enough –to use it against them, up to a point at which the monitoring procedures would have been seriously hampered. As the Chilean dictatorship came
to represent a least common denominator for most of the delegations, the
preconditions for effective action were unusually propitious – or, seen from
the junta's angle, exceptionally unfortunate.

For if there was one thing that the junta had not expected, it was this unlikely
international coalition. Seeing their regime as an integral part of the Western
world, the military was sure that their anti-communist policies would gain
the approval of Western states. In addition, they were obviously surprised by
how fierce and well organized the Soviet bloc's anti-Chilean campaign would
be. Inexperienced and miscalculating, the Pinochet government set out to test
its limits. Initially, it embraced the idea of human rights and entered into discussions. The Chilean delegates at the UN emphasized the long human rights
tradition of the country, given that it had ratified the International Covenants
on Human Rights and assiduously participated in the UN human rights work.
They stressed their willingness to cooperate with the UN bodies, and, more
importantly, they allowed various investigation teams into the country, pointing out that Chile "opened its doors as no other country had ever done."[24] In a
self-justifying historical account, the military claimed to have taken power on
a provisional basis precisely to restore respect for fundamental freedoms and
to overcome the profound "crisis of democracy" that had befallen the country
during the Marxist era. They went on to protest against the distorted public
image of the situation in Chile, which they traced back to the sinister machi-
nations of the Soviet bloc. They appealed to Western countries, in contrast, by
commending their humanitarian concern.

When it became clear that this strategy could not keep member states from
monitoring the regime, the junta saw itself forced to rearrange its discursive
strategies. In 1975–1976, the Chilean representatives in the United Nations
veered to a more resolute defense, strongly protesting against discriminatory procedures "placing Chile under a magnifying glass" while gross human
rights violators such as the Soviet Union and Cuba went unheeded.[25] In addition, the delegation adopted a "small country" discourse, directly appealing
"to the other developing countries" and depicting Chile as the "scapegoat" for
the struggle between the superpowers.[26]

[24] UN Document E/CN.4/Sub.2/SR.754.
[25] UN Document A/C.3/32/SR.72.
[26] Cf. UN Document A/C.3/SR.2153.

The most dramatic shift in Chile's attitude came during the 1977 General Assembly. With an impending resolution that would eclipse all the earlier condemnations, the delegation gave up even the last remnants of its cooperative air. Now for the first time, it rejected the UN investigations as a violation of national sovereignty and as interference into the country's domestic affairs, appealing to two principles that it had explicitly discarded in previous years. The Chilean representatives did not even recoil from harshly blaming the Western countries, accusing them of staging a hypocritical "show of noble, humanitarian sentiments."[27] Consequently, Chile announced that in the future it would cease to cooperate with procedures directed at a single country.

Although this was a considerable change of position, not even at the height of political tensions did Chile entirely rebuke the human rights discourse. Nor did the regime try to develop its own interpretation of the term suited to its political convictions, in the way that various African and Asian countries had done (and would do again). Clinging to a self-conception of Chile as a civilized, Western country, the junta's objections were largely aimed at the specific procedures' lack of balance, the scope of the investigations, and the wording of the resolutions. By contrast, the Chilean representatives could not and did not deny the very norms on which the accusations were founded. This weakened their defense because they were at a loss to give credible reasons for rejecting UN interventions. And it worsened their chances of producing an image of a legitimate government as long as the gap between the proclaimed ideals and the political reality in the country remained very wide.

The "open-door" policy Chile referred to in the discussions was a rhetorical device, designed to persuade the international community of its good faith. But it was also a fact. Especially in the first nine months or so after the military takeover, the doors to Chile were anything but closed. The regime allowed visits by Amnesty International, the International Commission of Jurists, the International Labor Organization, and the Inter-American Commission of Human Rights. Although the authorities kept the investigation teams away from certain persons and places, the observers had the necessary freedom of movement to gather substantial evidence. The decision to admit them into the country surely was a propaganda move in reaction to international pressures. At least in part, however, it was also based on the regime's erroneous assumption that it would be able to convince world public opinion that life in Chile had returned to normal. When the government became aware of the damaging effects of this policy, it closed its doors again in 1974–1975, only to open them once more under renewed pressure, finally allowing the visit by the UN Working Group in July 1978. The back and forth testified to an inexperience in the realm of human rights politics that further worsened the regime's position.

Teams of foreign observers were important sources of information on the situation in Chile, but by far not the only ones. Domestic church and human rights groups, resisting threats and persecution, managed to provide foreign media and international organizations with a vast amount of material.[28] In addition, thousands of refugees brought to their new countries testimonies of their experiences. Even after Chile had ceased to cooperate with international human rights organizations, the country was not shut off against the outside world. Its anti-Marxist ideology did not preclude openness toward friendly countries, and its doctrine of economic internationalism required Chile to be globally connected.

All this had the effect of placing the country under close and prolonged international scrutiny, which produced detailed knowledge about the policies of the military regime. This was a third, important reason for the high intensity and long life of the human rights campaign. It exposed the regime to a degree that would have been inconceivable in earlier decades or in cases such as Cambodia and Equatorial Guinea, where regimes intentionally cut the ties connecting them with the world at large. The topography of the Chilean terror apparatus, for example, was an open secret. Human rights reports gave detailed accounts of the organizational structure of DINA (Dirección de Inteligencia Nacional), the security service responsible for the persecutions. They described the ways in which it conducted arrests, traced the sites of its detention centers, and listed the preferred torture methods and the names of torturers. The human rights campaign turned Chile into a virtual glasshouse where almost nothing could be hidden from the outside gaze. The monitoring by human rights groups created instantaneous knowledge, as it were, which due to the rapidly evolving communication technology could be spread faster and more widely than ever before. Moreover, NGOs such as Amnesty International worked out ways of presenting their material that were well suited to arouse sympathy and pity for the victims.[29] Its reports included victims of all ages and social strata, creating the image of arbitrary state terror that could possibly affect anyone. Information on torture was illustrated by the testimony of persons recounting their ordeals. Photos and short biographies, which gave a human face to the abstract process of political elimination, were also effectively used. All this conveyed a very concrete idea of the repression in Chile and made it easier for potential readers to identify with the people oppressed.

The investigations did not only cast light on the system of repression, however. As a point of reference for its study, the UN Working Group used the Universal Declaration of Human Rights, which consists of a long catalog not only of political and civil rights but also of economic, social, and cultural rights. This enabled the experts to monitor practically all areas of Chile's political and social life. Thus, the human rights standard that had been set

---

[28] See Patricio Orellana and Elizabeth Quay Hutchinson, *El movimiento de derechos humanos en Chile, 1973–1990* (Santiago, 1991); Edward L. Cleary, *The Struggle for Human Rights in Latin America* (Westport, Conn., 1997).

[29] See Amnesty International, *Report on Torture* (London, 1973), and *Disappeared Prisoners in Chile* (London, 1977).

after World War II proved to have a long-term effect, unforeseen at the time, that considerably strengthened the work of advocates in the 1970s. An examination of Chile's "human rights situation" along these lines entailed observations on constitutional provisions and state structures, the economic situation, the state of the educational and health sectors, and the evolution of cultural and intellectual life. In this way, the Working Group's publications became comprehensive country reports, describing the miserable living conditions of the majority of the Chilean people and a daily life marked by unemployment and inflation, bad medical care, poverty, forced prostitution, and hunger.

The vivid picture of the situation in Chile emerging from these reports laid an important foundation for the international campaign. To begin with, it precluded the military regime as well as other states and international organizations from dismissing knowledge about the population's plight. Furthermore, international observers could base their accusations on massive and precise documentation. And finally, for those who cared about events in crisis areas around the world, it was difficult to remain detached from the fate of the innocent Chileans who through the widespread coverage had almost become household figures.

The overwhelming concern among private individuals was a fourth important factor in the campaign. In Western Europe, the military coup led to a huge outcry among adherents of the political left. To many of them, Allende's Chile had symbolized a socialist utopia that the imperialistic forces of fascism – an alliance of the Chilean military, the CIA, and the capital of multinational corporations – had brutally destroyed.[30] Thus, their protest was decidedly political and not primarily framed as a fight for basic rights. In the name of "solidarity with Chile," hundreds, possibly even thousands, of groups and committees were established. A particularly forceful "Chile Solidarity Campaign" was launched in Great Britain, supported by the Labour and Communist parties, trade unions, student and youth organizations, and dozens of local Chile Committees. These groups organized boycotts and mass demonstrations, raised funds, "adopted" Chilean prisoners, assisted refugees, and pressed the British Government to link its economic aid to the political situation in Chile.[31]

At the same time, the military rule in Chile also became a catalyst for the human rights movement and contributed to its rapid expansion in the early 1970s. In the United States, many new groups sprang up, such as the Council for Hemispheric Affairs or the Chile Committee for Human Rights.[32] Moreover, events in Chile were crucial for the increased interest of

[30] See Komitee Solidarität mit Chile, *Konterrevolution in Chile* (1973); W. Eschenhagen, *Revolution und Konterrevolution in Chile* (1974); H.-W. Bartsch, *Chile – ein Schwarzbuch* (n.p., 1974).
[31] See Marguerite Garling, *The Human Rights Handbook. A Guide to British and American International Human Rights Organisations* (London, 1979), ch. I.5.
[32] See Paul Heath Hoeffel and Peter Kornbluh, "The War at Home: Chile's Legacy in the United States," *NACLA Report to the Americas*, 17 (1983), 27–41.

professional organizations and church groups in human rights work. Both
the National Council of Churches and the newly founded Washington Office
on Latin America, for instance, concerned themselves prominently with the
Chilean case.[33] Developments were essentially the same in Western Europe.[34]
This widespread mobilization generated a new and peculiar coalition of transnational actors, consisting of civil rights defenders, lawyers, church activists,
members of the women's movement, academics, artists, and many others.[35]
For most of them, public engagement was an idealistic enterprise and resulted
from moral considerations and a genuine shock at the human misery of the
Chilean population. But many were also driven by the attempt to transform
the domestic political landscape, creating what can paradoxically be termed
politics of the unpolitical. In an attempt to transcend the very boundaries
between "left" and "right," which in their view had produced a political stalemate, they concentrated on human suffering, which they hoped to remedy
by directly assisting individual victims. The human rights movement gained
strong momentum as it enabled activists to infuse politics with new forms of
participation and to intervene at the highest levels of international affairs.

The left-wing political activists and human rights groups did not pursue
identical agendas. The most radical leftist groups, in particular, derided and
discredited nonviolent human rights protests as naïve and counterproduc-
tive. However, both movements merged at least insofar as they maintained
attention to Chile and created a solid basis of public empathy from which the
struggle against the Pinochet regime could draw.

"Disappearances" and Institutional Reform – Impacts on the Junta

The fact that international efforts against Chile were unusually intense did
not necessarily mean that they influenced the dictatorship. The effects of the
campaign cannot be reduced to the military's rhetoric but have to be seen
in the broader context of their political actions. Political scientists studying the Chilean campaign have largely evaluated its effects positively.[36] They
have argued that the combined forces of domestic and international pressure
induced the regime to make a series of political changes, most notably to adopt
human rights discourse and to transform repressive institutions, in order to

[33] See Lowell W. Livezey, *Nongovernmental Organizations and the Ideas of Human Rights* (Princeton, 1988).
[34] See the index of Chile groups in Western Europe in Laurie S. Wiseberg and Hazel Sirett (eds.), Human Rights Internet, *Human Rights Directory: Western Europe* (Washington, D.C., 1982).
[35] A collection of notes and petitions by numerous private groups and organizations can be found in United Nations Office in Geneva, Archives, G/SO 214 (22) and G/SO 215/1.
[36] See Darren Hawkins, *International Human Rights and Authoritarian Rule in Chile* (Lincoln, Neb., 2002); Stephen C. Ropp and Kathryn Sikkink, "International Norms and Domestic Politics in Chile and Guatemala," in Thomas Risse et al. (eds.), *The Power of Human Rights. International Norms and Domestic Change* (Cambridge, 1999), 172–204.

preserve at least some international legitimacy. Moreover, in this perspective international efforts strengthened more liberal fractions within the regime and encouraged domestic opposition. One of the most gruesome features of the junta's techniques of persecution, however, the so-called disappearances, raises questions about this interpretation.

"Disappearances" were a preferred method of the intelligence services, which secretly disposed of their victims' bodies to conceal the crimes and spread uncertainty. Both UN bodies and human rights NGOs were quick to focus on this technique. They confronted the regime with lists of strongly documented cases of missing persons, demanding that it account for what had happened to them. The UN Working Group, for instance, made use of the latest technologies to compile a computerized list of over 1,000 cases on which human rights groups had collected ample material.[37] This gave rise to an eerie confrontation over the whereabouts and often over the very existence of detained persons, with the regime adroitly complicating attempts to clarify the fate of the disappeared persons. In one of the many Kafkaesque episodes, the government replied to a list submitted by the Red Cross by accounting for sixty-three persons, sixty of whom had not been named on the list. When relatives staged hunger strikes in 1977 and 1978, the government tried to appease them by promising comprehensive investigations that subsequently were not conducted or did not yield results. In June 1978, the government published a "final statement" on the problem, which gave a detailed explanation of why so many people were missing: hundreds of false identity cards had been fabricated in the Allende years, or numerous persons had died in confrontations after the coup, had fled the country, or gone into hiding. With a cynicism hardly to be surpassed, the government assured the relatives that it understood "that nothing can lessen the sorrow of those who truly feel that loss."[38]

The conflict over the disappeared persons highlights a central aspect of the human rights campaign against Chile, and many other countries. At its core, it was a battle over facts and how they were to be interpreted. The human rights bodies and groups, not having any means to exert *material* pressure on the regime, had to rely on informational politics – gathering strong evidence, building plausible claims, and making all this public. They certainly succeeded in profoundly discrediting the junta, since the regime's explanations appeared highly unlikely or outright contradictory. But they did not hold the military rulers accountable for the secret killings, let alone force it to uncover the real events. With a combination of denial, evasive replies, and openly farcical investigations, the regime resisted all demands for truth, up to the point that the fates of many missing persons are still unknown. Maybe even more importantly, the campaign was not able to alter the practices of the regime during the high tide of repression. In 1976, while investigations were already in full swing, the number of reported disappearances peaked once again after

[37] UN Document A/32/227, Report of the Working Group, September 1977.
[38] UN Document A/33/331 Report of the Working Group, October 1978, Annex L.

a temporary low in 1975. Despite the fact that world attention had effectively been drawn to the problem of disappearances, the security agencies saw no reason to desist from executing people and hiding all traces of them.

In the course of 1977, however, disappearances stopped, and in the following years no further cases were reported. This was part of a broader change in the politics of the regime that amounted to a notable easing of repression. The junta released some 300 prisoners and closed two detention centers. The event most widely noticed was the dissolution of DINA, which had been the most powerful instrument of state terror. In the same year, Pinochet announced his timetable for the return to democracy in a public speech, repeating his well-known claim that military rule was intended to be transitory.

In the history of the junta, this was undoubtedly the most profound caesura. Even if they were certainly not willing to abandon control, it seems that the military leaders quite abruptly decided to at least end their war against the Chilean population, which previously had been its raison d'être. For a number of reasons, it seems plausible to assume a connection between this political change and the efforts of human rights activists. By 1977, Chile's isolation in the international arena had become obvious, and the human rights campaign had reached its apogee. Pinochet and the military leaders were anything but insensitive to their international stigmatization. They carefully observed international criticism and regularly discussed it in top-level meetings.[39] Considerable energy was put into plans to counter the allegations, among them a $1 million public relations campaign mainly aimed at the public in the United States.[40] Since the political changes in 1977 came well before the outburst of hostilities in the General Assembly of the same year, which led the regime to terminate its supposedly cooperative policy, the regime might still have harbored hopes of rising in the esteem of at least some important member states. The very fact that the institutional transformations, above all the dissolution of DINA, were merely cosmetic points in this direction. The military's tactics clearly were to keep the balance between maintaining domestic control and building an international image of a civilized state. At the same time, moreover, Chile was about to lose its most important ally, as the Carter administration cut aid and demanded that the junta lift the state of siege, release prisoners, and restore due process. It would be rather difficult to argue that these factors did *not* have any influence on the regime's decisions in 1977.

Even if this influence is admitted, however, it cannot be overlooked that domestic conditions for political concessions in 1977 were entirely different from the ones prevailing in previous years. "Marxism" had been eliminated together with all the organizations of the political left. Armed resistance, never impressive in scale anyway, had been overcome and the civil war feared by many had not broken out. The junta held firm control over state

---

[39] See Hawkins, *Rule.*
[40] See Schoultz, *Rights*, 48–108.

and society. Therefore, "national security," one of the two central ideological tenets of the military, had been thoroughly established. The other, economic liberalization, had just begun to yield desired results. The upswing in the economy, in reality a short and low-level recovery, was heralded by the regime as an "economic miracle" confirming that the right course had been taken.[41] By 1977, then, the political project that had driven the military to take power had been carried out successfully – or so at least it seemed to the military leaders. At this time, it hardly weakened the rule of the military when it made superficial changes and announced a long-term liberalization of the regime. This was "not surprising," as Felix Ermacora, Austrian delegate to the UN Commission on Human Rights, put it sarcastically but correctly, "since the regime had had three years in which to kill, torture, exile or otherwise remove their opponents."[42] The international human rights campaign may have contributed to the relative pacification of the junta's rule. However, it did so only at a time when the *domestic* costs seemed acceptable to the junta.

Consequently, to assume that the human rights campaign had substantial effects on the regime's politics seems questionable in many respects. This is further corroborated by the subsequent course of events. As soon as a larger protest movement began to emerge at the beginning of the 1980s and threatened to subvert the junta's project, the regime did not stop short of waging a second war against the Chilean population. This markedly distinguished the Chilean junta from other military dictatorships in Latin America, such as the ones in Brazil and Uruguay, which were not prepared to renew their violent beginnings in the face of new civil protest and instead, if grudgingly, relinquished power.

All this said, however, it should not be forgotten that the campaign against Chile did yield notable results in the humanitarian realm. Victims and their families received vital material as well as legal assistance from states and international organizations. For many, this was even outweighed by the immaterial aid with which they had been provided. The UN Working Group and human rights NGOs received numerous letters from Chileans who expressed profound gratitude for their efforts even though they had been to no avail. All of them emphasized the feeling that they had not been entirely at the mercy of a criminal regime. This suggests that the effects of the Chilean as well as of other human rights campaigns have to be measured in categories different from the traditional analysis of power relations. One of their central effects was to morally support individuals ill-treated by the regimes under which they lived. Thus, they created a different kind of "international community," cutting through the boundaries of nation-states and shaping a transnational alliance of solidarity that linked victims with international organizations and governments worldwide.

---

[41] See Oppenheim, *Politics*.
[42] In the CHR's session of 1977, UN Document E/CN.4/SR.1418.

Conclusion

As far as both the dynamics behind the campaign and its effects are concerned, the Chilean case highlights a number of general factors that may
help to explain some of the patterns undergirding international human rights
action in the 1970s and 1980s. In the action of supranational organizations
and states against Chile, the strong influence of geostrategic considerations
came to the fore precisely because the conflict transcended the binary logic
of the Cold War. Human rights had been a weapon against the communist
countries in Eastern Europe since the end of the Second World War, and once
human rights politics gained strong momentum in the 1970s, they turned
into an even more effective one. In the context of the Conference on Security
and Cooperation in Europe – a process stretching from the early 1970s to
the breakdown of communism in Eastern Europe – the United States and the
states of the European Community used human rights provisions in order
to undermine communist state control.[43] In addition, the U.S. administration under Jimmy Carter initially made the Soviet Union a test case for its
new human rights approach to foreign policy. The same governments were
considerably more hesitant, however, when it came to states that belonged
to their own camp. This was the main reason why international pressure on
the white minority regime in South Africa did not reach a critical point until
the late 1980s.[44] Even though support for action against apartheid had been
strong in the United Nations, where the Afro-Asian majority had made it a
cause celèbre of its anti-colonial struggle, the United States and Great Britain
were careful not to damage a regime that they regarded as an anti-communist
bulwark in a strategically crucial region and as an important trading partner.
The Chilean junta, by contrast, could not offer important goods for trade,
nor did it possess geo-strategic importance. It was its position as a pariah of
the *Western camp* that exposed the regime to almost unbridled worldwide
criticism in the first place.

The junta's conception of Chile as a Western state, for its part, spawned a
concern for the international image that notably distinguished it from other
repressive regimes of the period. As the Chilean military did not manage to
shut itself off from the outside world, it offered human rights advocates important points of leverage, which they lacked against other dictatorships such as
those in Cambodia, North Korea, and even Uganda. These regimes radically

---

[43] See William Korey, *The Promises We Keep. Human Rights, the Helsinki Process and
American Foreign Policy* (New York, 1993); Daniel C. Thomas, *The Helsinki Effect.
International Norms, Human Rights, and the Demise of Communism* (Princeton, 2001);
Andreas Wenger et al. (eds.), *Origins of the European Security System. The Helsinki Process
Revisited* (London, 2008).

[44] See Audie Klotz, *Norms in International Relations. The Struggle against Apartheid* (Ithaca,
N.Y., 1995); Robert Kinloch Massie, *Loosing the Bonds. The United States and South Africa
in the Apartheid Years* (New York, 1997); Roger Fieldhouse, *Anti-Apartheid. A History of
the Movement in Britain. A Study in Pressure Group Politics* (London, 2005).

immunized themselves against international accusations and, partly for this reason, never became prominent targets for international campaigns.

Furthermore, the crimes of the Chilean military energized vast numbers of activists because they allowed differing perceptions to coalesce, the perceptions of those who saw the military rule as only the latest embodiment of fascist imperialism and of those who saw it as a symbol of the oppression of the innocent. An important precondition was the massive flow of information coming out of the country – it turned out that in the age of mass media even the limited degree of openness that the Pinochet regime was prepared to allow had highly damaging consequences.

Similar mechanisms underlay the vigorous protest of private groups against South Africa, where a far smaller number of people were killed than in other African countries such as Uganda or Equatorial Guinea. The media had sufficient access to be able to report extensively on every new round of riots and crackdowns. Moreover, a worldwide movement emerged because apartheid struck a chord with different groups of activists, appealing to human rights advocates, opponents of racial discrimination, anti-colonial groups, and, in the context of the divestment movement, critics of international capitalism. It should also be noted that both Chile and South Africa presented to outside observers fairly clear-cut conflicts in which the oppressors and the oppressed seemed obvious. The situation was different in Uganda, where the nature of ethnic hostilities did not reveal itself easily.[45]

The lack of information was an important factor for the absence of international action against two of the most appalling state crimes of the 1970s. The killing of possibly tens of thousands in tiny Equatorial Guinea, a former Spanish colony with a few hundreds of thousands of inhabitants, was hardly even noticed.[46] The Khmer Rouge in Cambodia arguably sealed off the country from the outside world in a more systematic fashion than any other regime in the second half of the twentieth century.[47] Both Amnesty International and the International Commission of Jurists cited lack of reliable sources as the reason for their inaction. More generally, the non-campaign on Cambodia appears as the virtual mirror image of the worldwide activities against Chile. Left-wing intellectuals, particularly in the United States, not only did not support protests against the mass killings but vindicated the Khmer Rouge's

---

[45] See Wolfgang S. Heinz, *Menschenrechte in der Dritten Welt* (Munich, 1986), 74–103; Samuel Decalo, *Psychoses of Power: African Personal Dictatorships* (Boulder, 1989), 77–128. See also A. Dirk Moses's chapter in this volume.

[46] See Suzanne Cronje, *Equatorial Guinea – The Forgotten Dictatorship. Forced Labour and Political Murder in Central Africa* (London, 1976).

[47] On the following, see Sheldon Neuringer, *The Carter Administration, Human Rights, and the Agony of Cambodia* (Lewiston, 1993); Ben Kiernan, *The Pol Pot Regime. Race, Power, and Genocide in Cambodia under the Khmer Rouge, 1975–1979* (New Haven, Conn., 1996); Jamie Frederic Metzl, *Western Responses to Human Rights Abuses in Cambodia, 1975–1980* (Houndmills, 1996); Kenton Clymer, "Jimmy Carter, Human Rights and Cambodia," *Diplomatic History*, 27 (2003), 245–277.

"revolution." Furthermore, geo-strategic imperatives prevented the Carter administration from making human rights its central concern in this case, as it prioritized normalization of relations with China (which backed the Khmer Rouge) and containment of Vietnam (which was the Khmer Rouge's main adversary).

Finally, the supply of detailed information was also an important precondition for the surge in human rights activism toward Eastern European countries. Whereas the Iron Curtain in the 1950s had been an insurmountable obstacle for the attempts by private groups to collect data,[48] the situation began to change dramatically in the late 1960s. This was facilitated by the activities of dissident groups, which provided Western activists and media with meticulous accounts.[49] In addition, the emergence of a dissident movement was also crucial insofar as it led leftist intellectuals in the West to embrace human rights protest as a common cause against a perverted socialism.[50]

Even when the considerable international efforts against South Africa and the Soviet Union are taken into account, Latin America stands out as the main target of human rights politics in the 1970s and 1980s. Only on this continent did all the factors combine that seemed to be necessary to bring about resolute human rights campaigns. In this respect, the dynamics behind the Chilean case did not essentially differ from the international reactions to the military regimes in Argentina, Uruguay, and Brazil. When international action in the name of human rights came to be a widespread practice in the 1970s, it clearly produced new asymmetries in the international system. They pointed to the dilemma of moral politics that human rights activists were to face continuously in the decades to come: that due to the circumstances, equal standards could not be applied to all equally.

Not even when they were applied did they necessarily succeed. However important their international reputation was for the Chilean junta, its political project of recasting Chilean society along authoritarian lines was given priority. This was the fundamental reason why the campaign failed to stop repression and liberalize the country. It also points to a structural problem of human rights politics. Activists repeatedly emphasized that "the political structure in Chile" was not their "business,"[51] claiming to be politically neutral and motivated by exclusively humanitarian concerns. The concrete demands they put forward, however, were rooted in the ideals of a democratic state and of the rule of law. Activists and politicians called for restoration of

---

[48] See the example of the New York–based International League of the Rights of Man: Minutes of Meeting of Board Members Concerned with Civil Rights in Iron-Curtain Countries, December 16, 1957, International League for Human Rights Records, New York Public Library, box 11.

[49] See the account by Soviet activist Ludmilla Alexeyeva, *Soviet Dissent. Contemporary Movements for National, Religious, and Human Rights* (Middletown, 1985), 267–401.

[50] See Robert Horvath: "'The Solzhenitsyn Effect.' East European Dissidents and the Demise of the Revolutionary Privilege," *Human Rights Quarterly*, 29 (2007), 879–907.

[51] The delegate of Great Britain in the CHR's session of 1975, E/CN.4/SR.1318.

due process, legal control over security agencies, representative elections, and freedom of expression. These, however, were precisely the political values the military regime had set out to fight. What the imposition of human rights norms required from the Chilean regime was no less than self-abolishment. This can be considered an inherent contradiction of human rights politics or a very subtle and subversive form of pressure. Both are true. In any case, it suggests that the most powerful factor limiting the "success" of human rights campaigns was the ability and willingness of the targeted regime to stay in power. The point is corroborated by the examples of South Africa and the Soviet Union. In both cases, human rights protests aimed at the very heart of regime ideology. And until the late 1980s, both regimes could not be forced to relent. The Soviet leadership cracked down on the dissident movement when human rights activism had reached its climax in the late 1970s and early 1980s. And the apartheid regime developed a siege mentality unmatched, it appears, even by the Chilean junta.

Finally, all these events have to be seen as part of a process, and a rapidly evolving one at that. For the protagonists, the Chilean campaign represented a new experience that embroiled them in a politics of trial and error, teaching activists what could be achieved and governments what had to be prevented. Thus, the Chilean campaign must also be seen as transforming the field of human rights politics for years to come.

Index

Abbas, Ferhat 239
Abyssinia 35, 258
Action Française 88, 90
Aden 243
aerial bombing 38
Africa 19–20, 35–36, 38, 119, 147,
    200, 239, 241, 248, 251, 284–291,
    293–298, 300, 311, 313–314, 316,
    322, 338–341
Agamben, Giorgio 247
Algeria 17, 72, 112, 120, 238, 251–256
    état d'urgence 251–253, 255
    Front de Libération National 248
    pouvoirs spéciaux 253
    war of independence 272
Allende, Salvador 321, 323, 325, 329, 335
Alliance Israélite Universelle 111, 117
American Civil War 7, 11
American Federation of Labor 311
Amin, Idi 326
Amnesty International 19, 44, 50, 144,
    198, 209, 321, 325, 331–332, 339
African National Congress (ANC) 239,
    296
anticolonialism 108, 113, 284
anti-Semitism 111, 191, 194
anti-slavery movement 3
apartheid 16, 19, 296, 322, 338–339,
    341
Archambault, Paul 89
area studies 43
Arendt, Hannah 1, 25, 45, 47, 57
Armenians 12, 33, 37, 54, 112, 278

Armitage, Sir Robert 237
Atlantic Charta 305
Austria 15, 46–47, 50, 58, 72–73, 127,
    131–133, 137, 139, 194
Azara, Antonio 70
Azikiwe, Nnamdi 239, 293

Bandung Conference 113
Bangladesh 21, 258, 260, 263, 267, 269,
    272–276, 278
Baring, Evelyn 248–250
Barraclough, Geoffrey 2
Bell, George 103
Beneš, Edvard 49, 53
Beria, Lavrenti Pavlovich 156
Berlin Colonial Conference 34
Beveridge-Report 306
Bevin, Ernest 41, 101, 305
Bhutto, Zulfikar Ali 275–276
Biafra 20–21, 271
bill of rights 55, 113, 284
Blood, Archer 262–263
Bobbio, Norberto 17
Bodet, Jaime Torres 112
Bolton, John 218
Borgwardt, Elizabeth 54
Bourdillon, Bernard 291
Boutmy, Émile 5
Boxer Rebellion 34
Brezhnev, Leonid 180–185, 187
British Anti-Slavery Society 19
British Defence and Aid Fund 19
British-Guyana 249

Bundesverfassungsgericht 103
Burke, Edmund 18, 25, 121

Calas affair 6
Calvin 4
Cambodia 21
Canada 21, 197, 327
Caportorti report 204
Carter, Jimmy 17, 21, 184, 326, 336,
    338, 340
Cassin, René 49, 77, 107–124, 164, 245
Césaire, Aimé 12
Chalidze, Valerii 155
Chang, Peng-Chun 107, 114, 118, 123,
    164
Charter 77 192, 194, 196, 201–202, 207,
    211
Charter for a New Europe 191
Chaumont, Charles 225
Chile 14, 20, 306, 321–340
    church activists 334
    disappearances 322, 335–336
Chile Committee for Human Rights 333
Chile Solidarity Campaign 333
China 13, 34, 36, 43, 50, 114, 153,
    163–164, 180, 259, 271–272, 274,
    306, 326, 340
Christianity 92, 95, 99, 102–103, 105
Churchill, Winston 40, 66, 292
Cibula, Jan 204–205
civil rights movement 158, 198
civil war 170, 259, 269
civilization 1, 10, 13, 19, 29–31, 33–34,
    36–38, 41–43, 120, 151, 223
civilizing mission 7–8, 18, 31, 33,
    287–288
Cmiel, Kenneth 58, 108, 123
coercive sterilization 194
Cold War 14–16, 21–22, 29, 41, 43,
    50, 52, 54, 56, 61, 76, 80, 90, 101,
    113–114, 124, 141, 148–149, 155,
    158, 160, 165, 182, 193, 201,
    203, 208, 219–220, 232–233, 260,
    302, 307, 309, 311, 313–316, 318,
    328–329, 338
Colonial Office 242–245, 250, 293
colonialism 7, 55, 87, 114, 161, 234,
    240, 257, 286–288, 294, 298, 300,
    302, 316, 319, 329

Cominform 160
Comintern 160
Committee on Social Thought 42–43
Committee on the Study of Civilization
    See Committe on Social Thought
Commonwealth 16, 293
communism 14, 16, 42, 44, 88, 90–91,
    101, 105, 161, 173–175, 178,
    189–190, 197–198, 325
compulsory labour 15
Congo 34, 219, 245, 259, 271
Congress of Europe 66, 69, 71
Congress of Vienna 30
conservatism 40, 90, 100, 121
Constant, Benjamin 30
constitution
    Czechoslovakia 199, 203, 210
    France (1946) 108, 251
    Soviet Union 150, 160, 163–164,
        175–176, 178–180
    Weimar Republic 133
Coughlin, Charles 93
Council for Hemispheric Affairs
    333
Council of Europe 67, 69, 72, 192, 203,
    245, 256
Creech-Jones, Arthur 242–243, 256
Crimes against Humanity 259
cultural relativism 107–108, 122, 285
Curzon, George 35
Cyprus 75, 238, 256
Czechoslovakia 17, 40, 126, 133, 137,
    147, 192–196, 198–199, 202,
    205–207, 209–211, 233

Dandieu, Arnaud 87
Darfur 277–278
Dawson, Christopher 95–96
De Gaulle, Charles 111
de Menthon, François 98
de Pradt, Abbe 30–31, 38
de Rougemont, Denis 101
de Visscher, Charles 85, 97–98, 100
*Déclaration des Droits de l'Homme et du
    Citoyen* 5
Declaration on the Granting of
    Independence to Colonial Countries
    and Peoples 18, 257
decolonisation 76, 80

democracy 37, 94–97, 121, 128–132, 155,
  191, 199, 201, 239, 247, 262, 284,
  287, 295, 298, 300, 311, 330, 336
detention 126, 158, 230, 250, 332, 336
Deutsche Gesellschaft für Völkerrecht 132
development *See Right to development*
development aid 307, 325
development dictatorships 317
Dihigo, Ernesto 222
displaced persons 46–47, 50–52, 54, 56,
  59–60
displacement 45, 47, 50–51, 53, 55, 57
dissidents 23, 54, 57, 155, 182, 186,
  192–194, 197–198, 200–201, 205,
  207, 209, 322
*Documentation of the Expulsion of the
  Germans from East-Central Europe*
  142–143
DP *See Displaced Persons*
Dreyfus affair 10
droits de l'homme 9, 73, 107–113, 115,
  118, 121–123
Dumbarton Oaks Conference 307
Dunant, Henri 11
Dürig, Günter 104

East Pakistan *See Bangladesh*
East Timor 326
economic crisis 205, 324
Egypt 30–31, 33, 36, 111, 120, 158, 328
Eppstein, John 97
Equatorial Guinea 326, 332, 339
Ethiopia *See Abyssinia*
European Commission on Human Rights
  15
European Convention on Human Rights
  15, 18, 122, 203, 241, 248, 256
European Court of Human Rights 15,
  108, 122
European integration 62, 80, 100
European Social Charter 71

Fabian Colonial Bureau 287
Fanon, Frantz 18, 246–247
Feller, A.H. 215
feminism 123
Fiah, Erica 292
First World War 7, 29, 109, 127, 131,
  138–139, 141, 217, 278

Fisher, H.A.L. 138
Flanner, Janet 158
forced labor 134, 187, 304, 309–311,
  315–317
forced prostitution 333
France 7–9, 13, 15, 17, 23, 30, 33, 35,
  72, 77, 80, 89, 94, 96–97, 111–113,
  119, 121–122, 124, 151, 164,
  176, 202, 225, 227, 237–238, 241,
  244–248, 252–256, 278, 286, 300
freedom of assembly 169, 180, 244, 252
freedom of association 307–310, 312,
  315–317
freedom of conscience 4, 34, 187
freedom to travel abroad 194
French Revolution 6, 16, 173, 241, 247
Fyfe, Sir David Maxwell 70

Gandhi, Indira 269, 273
Geiger, Willi 103
gender equality 312
Geneva Convention 11, 54–55, 259,
  273–275
genocide 12, 21, 29, 44, 53, 132, 141,
  148, 194, 199, 206, 217, 221–231,
  233–236, 258–267, 269, 271–273,
  275–279, 326
  Convention on the Prevention and
    Punishment of the Crime of
    Genocide 222
  criminal responsibility 225, 229
Germany 12, 14–15, 35, 45–47, 50–53,
  56–58, 72–73, 87, 102, 104, 129,
  131–137, 139, 142, 161, 176, 194,
  198, 206, 222–224, 325
Gesellschaft für bedrohte Völker 206
Ghana 296, 328
Gide, André 91
Gold Coast *See Ghana*
Great Britain 2, 7–8, 13, 17–18, 30–31,
  35–36, 38, 41, 71–72, 95, 101,
  103, 112, 119, 144, 225, 237–238,
  241–249, 251–252, 255–256, 278,
  286, 291, 300, 325, 333, 338
Grigorenko, Petr 185
Gromyko, Andrei 154
Guizot, François Pierre Guillaume
  30–31
Gulag 250

Hague Conventions 217
Hague Peace Conferences 11
Hájek, Jiči 193, 196
Hall, William Edward 31
Hammarskjold, Dag 259
Harrison, George 20, 58
Havel, Václav 192
Hejdánek, Ladilav 192, 196
Helsinki accords 196
    Vienna review conference 209
Helsinki Final Act 193, 197, 200
Hinden, Rita 287
Hindus 262, 264–265
Hitler, Adolf 37, 130, 133, 135, 138, 160,
    265
Ho Chi Minh 246–247
Hobbes, Thomas 22
Holocaust 16, 52, 61, 109, 201
hostage taking 233
Hroch, Miroslav 201
Hull, Cordell 39
human dignity 98, 101–102, 104–105, 183
Human Rights Day 49, 154, 162
Human Rights Watch 197–198
    Helsinki Watch 181, 198
humanism 87–89, 94
humanitarian aid 20, 260, 267, 270, 277,
    321
humanitarian intervention 2, 47, 260,
    271, 276
Humphrey, Jogn P. 151, 244
hunger strike 263
Husák, Gustáv 208–210

Ignatieff, Michael 23
illiteracy 155, 207
ILO *See International Labour
    Organization*
imperialism 11, 33, 35–36, 42, 70, 108,
    144, 240, 288, 293–294, 339
India 14, 31, 43, 50, 119–120, 204, 221,
    241, 261, 263–265, 267–274, 276,
    278, 306, 308, 316, 328
Indochina 111–112, 238, 246, 252
Indonesia 238, 259
industrialization 196, 308
Institut de droit international 128
Inter-American Human Rights
    Commission 325

International Commission of Jurists 264,
    266, 270, 275, 279, 321, 325, 331,
    339
International Committee of the Red
    Cross 237, 253
International Conference on Human
    Rights 121, 299
International Conventions on Human
    Rights 109
    Covenant on Civil and Political Rights
        19, 149, 164, 199–200
    Covenant on Economic, Social and
        Cultural Rights 149, 164
    right to individual petition 65–66, 72,
        245–246
International Court of Justice 85, 220,
    225–227, 261, 276
International Criminal Court 218,
    225–227, 276–277
international criminal law 215–217,
    220–221, 223, 226, 229–230, 232,
    236
    Code of International Offenses 219,
        221
    legalist paradigm of war 20, 216, 218,
        234
*International Federation for the Rights of
    Man* 50
International Labour Organization 160,
    331
    anti-discrimination convention 312
    Declaration of Philadelphia 301,
        305–307, 309, 318
    International Institute for Labour
        Studies 313
    International Labor Standards
        303–304
    World Employment Program 318
International Law 2, 7, 10, 39, 131–132,
    141–142, 219, 226, 229
    Nuremberg Charter 136, 230
*International League for the Rights of
    Man* 50
international organizations 18, 44,
    110, 237, 249, 301–303, 318, 324,
    332–333, 337
International Refugee Organization 47,
    52
International Romani Union 204, 210

Israel 14, 52, 59–60, 278
  Partition Plan 59
Ita, Eyo 294
Italy 15, 46, 72, 98, 163, 258, 325
ius humanum 4

Jackson, Robert H. 98, 223
Japan 13, 163
Jellinek, Georg 4, 6
Jews 6, 12, 46, 51–52, 58, 112, 119, 141,
  148, 199, 223, 265–266, 322
jus ad bellum 216
jus in bello 216
justice 39, 54, 113, 128, 234–235, 252,
  274, 276, 298, 304

Kahn, Roger 19, 264–265, 267
Kant, Immanuel 20, 104–105
Karol Wojtyla *See Paul II*
Kelsen, Hans 168
Kennedy, Edward 242, 265
Kenya 17, 238, 242, 248–254, 316
Khmer Rouge 339
Khrushchev, Nikita 148, 156–157, 161,
  165, 173–175, 180–181, 187
Kingsley, Donald 159
Kissinger, Henry 21, 42, 325
Kołakowski, Leszek 188
Konrád, György 23
Korean War 219
Korey, William 50
Koskenniemi, Reinhart 10, 25, 31
Kotane, Moses 296
Kuznetsov, Vasili 157

Laun, Rudolf 126–144
Lauren, Paul Gordon 60, 64, 126, 239
Lauterpacht, Hersch 40, 49, 53, 67–69,
  244
League of Nations 13, 16, 35, 39,
  41, 54, 100, 108–112, 115,
  160, 198, 215, 258, 289, 301,
  304, 306
Legal positivism 9
Leibholz, Gerhard 103
Lemkin, Raphael 53, 221, 223, 246
liberalism 8, 35–36, 88, 100, 168, 210,
  287
Lieber Code 11

*Ligue pour la Défense des Droits de
  l'homme* 10
Lincoln, Abraham 9, 11
Live Aid 20
London Charter 216–217, 221
Lord's Resistance Army 234
Lorimer, James 32
Luther, Martin 90, 133
Lyttelton, Oliver 246, 248

M'Baye, Kéba 24
Malaya 238, 243, 249
Malik, Charles 99, 107, 164–165
Malraux, André 91
Mancini, Pasquale 139
mandate system 36, 289
Mandela, Nelson 20, 239
Maritain, Jacques 87–88, 90–98, 100,
  102, 106
Marshall, George 81
Marshall, T.H. 32
Martens, Freidrich 35
Marx. Karl 7, 166
Marxist-Leninist nationality policy 195,
  199, 203
materialism 31, 42, 88, 101
Mau Mau war 238
Maulnier, Thierry 88
Mazower, Mark 49, 53, 105, 304
McCarthyism 163
Médecins Sans Frontiéres 19
media 11, 20, 154, 185, 262, 268, 332,
  339–340
Mehta, Hansa 117, 123, 152
Melville, Herman 1, 25
Memmi, Albert 246–247
Menon, Lakshmi 119–120, 123
military jurisdiction 252
Mill, John Stuart 10, 31
Miloševic, Slobodan 236
Minority Rights Group 204
Mitchell, Sir Philip 102, 242, 244
Mitterrand, François 72
modernization 44, 196, 317, 323
Mollet, Guy 253
Monnet, Jean 101
monogamy 116
Morgenthau, Hans 42
Morse, David 307, 311, 313, 316–317

Moscow Declaration 216
Mosler, Hermann 143
Mounier, Emmanuel 89–90, 96–98,
    100–101, 106
Movchan, Abnatolii 163
Muir, Ramsay 36
Mujib, Rahman Sheikh 266, 273–275
Munich Agreement 138
Murray, Gilbert 37–38, 42, 97
Murumbi, Joseph 296

Napoleon Bonaparte 6, 30
Nash, Walter 305
Nathan-Chapotot, Roger 56
National Socialism 12, 98, 327
nationalism 10, 12, 100, 122, 140, 144,
    192, 195, 201, 204, 290, 294–295
natural law 9, 94, 99, 104, 129, 168,
    190, 235
Neff, John 42–43
Netherlands 21, 72–73, 119, 325
new deal 87
Nguema, Macías 326
Nkrumah, Kwame 295, 298
Non-governmental organizations
    (NGOs) 19
North Korea 326, 338
nuclear energy 194
Nyerere, Julius 18, 298–300

October Revolution 152, 156
Ordre Nouveau 87–88
Organization of African Unity 297
Organization of American States 322, 324
Ottoman empire 30, 32–33

Pacelli, Eugenio 92
Pakistan 14, 50, 158, 241, 258, 260–266,
    268–278
Palestine 59, 111
Pan-African Congress 240, 295
Pankratova, Anna Mikhailovna 161
Paris Peace Conference 198, 303
Patočka, Jan 193, 201
Patton, George 58
Paul II 106
Pavlov, Alexei 150
Peace of Westphalia 141
perestroika 209

personalism 86–89, 91–92, 94, 96, 98,
    100–103, 106, 182–183, 189–190
Pflimlin, Pierre 246
Philippines 99, 113, 149, 158, 164
Pinochet, Augusto 321–322, 324,
    326–327, 330, 334, 336, 339
pirates 217
Pius XI 91, 93
Pius XII 92, 97
Poland 13, 52, 59, 106, 126, 133,
    136–137, 147, 176, 193, 233
politics of détente 197
Popper, Karl 53
poverty 196, 205, 207, 209, 235, 240,
    285, 287, 298–299, 333
POW *See Prisoners of War*
Prague Coup 57
prisoners of war 126, 134, 143, 273–274,
    278
protection of motherhood 117
protectionism 317
protectorate 33, 243

racial discrimination 224, 241, 244, 248,
    310, 339
racial equality 36, 240
racism 15–16, 205, 224, 234, 246–247,
    286, 302
rape 236
Red Army 46, 136, 170
Redfield, Robert 43
refugees 45–47, 49–59, 136–137, 143,
    263, 265, 267–270, 272, 277–278,
    332–333
Religious freedom 133
reparations 217, 229
resettlement 52, 59–60, 194, 238,
    249–250, 253, 256
Reut-Nicolossi, Eduard 53
Right
    to development 24, 151, 153, 308
    to divorce 117
    to education 150
    to health 152
    to life 110, 125, 183, 293
    to material security 171
    to national self-determination 12–13,
        18, 112, 127, 130–131, 133
    to recreation 293

to social security 150
to the Homeland 131
to work 17, 99, 148, 150, 162, 168,
    171, 173, 184, 208, 219, 232,
    235, 243, 307
rights
    collective vs. individual rights 51–54,
        59, 89, 110, 112, 122–123, 136,
        200–201, 203, 208–210, 247, 300
    cultural rights 17, 129–132, 150–153
    material rights 171–172
    minority rights 13, 41, 49, 52, 54, 111,
        118, 120, 191, 195–196, 198–201,
        203–204, 206, 208
    natural rights 8–9
    property rights 32, 34–35, 44
    women's rights 116, 120
Ritter, Gerhard 102
Roma 191–192, 194–199, 202–207,
    209–211
    World Romani Congress 202,
        204–206, 211
Roman law 4, 105
Rome Statute 276
Romulo, Carlos 99, 113–114, 123, 164,
    239
Roosevelt, Eleanor 45, 107, 116, 153
Roosevelt, Franklin D. 2, 17, 45, 55, 292,
    305–306
Rousseau, Jean-Jacques 4, 90
rule of law 9, 22, 34, 122, 156, 166, 193,
    215, 217, 238, 247–248, 252, 255,
    289, 297, 340
Russian Civil War 12
Russo-Japanese War 34
Rwanda 29, 218, 260, 276, 278

Sartre, Jean-Paul 240
Scheler, Max 87, 104, 106
Schmale, Wolfgang 4
Schmitt, Carl 15, 40, 95
Schuman, Robert 101, 246
Scramble for Africa 34
Second World War 14, 17, 51, 59, 61,
    118, 122, 135, 239, 247, 291, 318
Security Council 149, 220, 230, 260,
    268, 271–274, 276, 278, 300
Senghor, Léopold 18, 298
Shankar, Ravi 20

Shawcross, Hartley 225–226
Sierra Leone 240
Simpson, A.W. Brian 17, 48, 68, 79, 101,
    217
Singh, Swaran 265
Sinti 195, 199, 203, 206
slavery 7, 112, 118, 189, 294
Smith, H.A. 39
Smuts, Jan 16, 36–37, 241
Socialist legality 23, 156, 159
Society for the Abolition of Slave Trade 7
Solzhenitsyn, Aleksandr 23, 182
    Gulag Archipelago 182
Sørensen, Max 77
South Africa 16, 21, 241, 296, 339
South Kasai 259
sovereignty 10, 12, 14, 34, 44, 48–49, 52,
    69, 78, 80, 92, 104, 119, 128–129,
    131, 134, 136, 138, 198, 217, 223,
    225, 230, 234, 260, 277–278, 303,
    317, 319, 331
Soviet Union 12, 15, 18–22, 68, 70, 89,
    147–149, 156–157, 159–160, 163,
    165, 167–168, 174–178, 181–182,
    184–185, 187, 199, 208, 232, 244,
    271, 307, 309–312, 325, 329–330,
    338, 340–341
Spaak, Paul-Henri 101
Spengler, Oswald 37–38
Stalin, Josef 148, 155–156, 161, 164,
    170, 173, 179, 181, 189, 195
    Stalin Constitution 170
state of emergency 238, 247–251, 253
Stern, Carola 144
Stuchka, Petr 167
Supreme Court 9, 167
Syria 120, 278

Tagore, Rabindranath 38
Taylor, Charles 234
Teitgen, Paul 67, 69–71, 101, 245, 255
terrorism 156, 233, 256
Third World 13, 18, 24, 42, 44, 60, 121,
    206, 233–234, 296, 329
Tibet 259, 272
Tocqueville, Alexis de 7–9, 31, 95
Toffler, Alvin 265
torture 6, 238, 250, 253–256, 286,
    322–323, 332, 337

Toynbee, Arnold 38, 42–43
Treason Trial Defence Fund out of
Christian Action 19
Treaty of Brussels 41
trials 54, 70, 217–218, 221, 235, 258,
    260–261, 267, 273–276, 278–279
Tribute to Nelson Mandela 20
Trotsky, Lev 169
Truman, Henry 41–42, 58
Truman Doctrine 41–42
trusteeship 35
Turkey 12, 35

Uganda 219, 234, 249, 326, 329,
    338–339
United Nations 16, 18, 29, 40, 42, 47,
    49–52, 56, 99, 107–108, 112, 122,
    136, 144, 147–150, 153–155, 157,
    160–162, 165, 199, 203–204, 208,
    215, 218–221, 233, 237, 240–246,
    256–258, 268–269, 274–276, 283,
    294–297, 299, 302, 307, 309, 313,
    319, 322, 324, 327–328, 330, 338
    Commission on Human Rights
        114–115, 135, 148, 158, 270, 324,
        328, 337
    Committee on the Elimination of
        Racial Discrimination 268
    Convention on the Elimination of All
        Forms of Discrimination Against
        Women 312
    Covenants on Human Rights 113, 118,
        243–244, 330
    Economic and Social Council 221,
        269–270, 324
    General Assembly 41, 99, 116, 149,
        153, 155, 157, 220–222, 229,
        231–232, 241–242, 257–259, 269,
        271–272, 324, 331, 336
    High Commissioner for Refugees 267,
        269
    Human Rights Commission 80,
        107–109, 113, 116–117, 119, 121,
        124, 153, 243–245
    International Law Commission (ILC)
        229–232, 259
    Resolution 44, 194, 241, 257
    UN Charter 58, 260, 274
    UNESCO 18, 98, 113, 160, 162, 319

United Nations Relief and
    Rehabilitation Administration 46
    Working Group 324, 328, 331–333,
        335, 337
World Federation of United Nations
    Associations 160
United States 9, 11, 15, 17, 19, 21, 24,
    31, 35, 39–42, 44, 48, 57–60, 149,
    151–152, 158, 160–164, 168, 176,
    181–182, 196–198, 220, 224–227,
    232–234, 265–266, 269, 271, 274,
    278, 298, 300, 306, 310, 312,
    321–322, 325–329, 333, 336,
    338–339
    American Association for the United
        Nations (AAUN) 161
    Universal Declaration of Human Rights
        13–14, 22, 66, 99, 109, 113, 116,
        122, 125, 139, 148–151, 153,
        155, 157, 163–165, 175, 192, 199,
        237–238, 240–242, 248, 256, 258,
        283, 296, 299, 309, 332
    Article 13 50, 139–140, 299
    Article 14 50, 169
    Article 15 50, 52, 169
    Article 16, 117
    Article 3 125, 238
    Article 9, 158
universalism 4, 17, 24, 55, 108, 110, 113,
    117, 122, 319
USSR 38, 44, 54, 58, 149, 153–154, 158,
    160, 162, 164, 167–168, 170–171,
    173, 175, 177–178, 180, 182,
    184–185, 187–190, 271

Vasak, Karel 17
Versailles 12, 35, 39–40, 304
Vichy 94, 97, 111
Vidal-Naquet, Pierre 253
violence 21, 25–26, 34, 38, 211,
    215–219, 224, 232, 238, 247–248,
    250, 256–257, 263–264, 266,
    286–287, 327
Virginia Declaration of Rights 5

Walzer, Michael 216
war crimes 54, 217, 219, 229, 255,
    259–261, 271, 273, 276, 278–279
wars of aggression 220

Warsaw Pact 193
Weber, Max 7–8, 79, 166
Wheaton, Henry 31
Whitehead, Alfred 36
Williams, John Fischer 39, 194
Wilson, Woodrow 12, 36, 58
Wilsonian moment 36, 38
Wintrich, Josef 103
Witte, John 4
women's suffrage 10
Woodward, Ernest 41

world citizenship 112–113
World Jewish Congress 117
Wright, Quincy 40
Wright, Thomas C. 322
Wu, John C.H. 168

Young Right 88, 90
Yugoslavia 29, 137, 147, 161, 176, 196,
    210, 218, 233, 276

Zionism 141

9 780521 142571